ENTERPRISE AND EMPIRE

Enterprise & Empire

MERCHANT AND GENTRY INVESTMENT IN THE EXPANSION OF ENGLAND, 1575–1630

BY THEODORE K. RABB

Harvard University Press: Cambridge, Massachusetts: 1967

TO MY PARENTS

ACKNOWLEDGMENTS

My greatest debt is to my wife, who shared with me the drudgery of alphabetizing and repeatedly checking thousands of names and pieces of information. Her involvement in the most tedious and unrewarding tasks in the preparation of this book was a constant encouragement, and the compiling of the basic material was as much her work as mine. For things less tangible, *quid opus est verbis?*

To various teachers I owe a special gratitude: to Martin Scott, now at Winchester, who first aroused my interest in history; to John and Menna Prestwich at Oxford; to Professor Jerome Blum of Princeton, who first directed me toward statistical enquiries; and above all to the late Professor E. H. Harbison, a mentor of rare wisdom. The one constant influence throughout the last nine years has been Professor W. F. Craven of Princeton, who first suggested Sandys as a subject of research, encouraged me at every stage as my work progressed, and gave me the benefit of his broad familiarity with England's expansion through detailed comments on the manuscript of this book. I have also had profitable discussions with Professor Lawrence Stone of Princeton, whose criticism of the manuscript was most valuable. The most thorough evaluation, made as the book neared completion, was by Professor Barry Supple of the University of Sussex, a critic of unfailing good humor and perception who even took the time to assess the first version of my Introduction during a flying visit to Cambridge, Massachusetts, when he was in the midst of a multitude of official duties. Professor D. B. Quinn of the University of Liverpool has taught me — both in conversation and in his comments on my manuscript — what only he, with his unique knowledge of my subject, could teach.

My gratitude is also due to Professors W. K. Jordan and S. E. Thorne at Harvard for a number of enlightening conversations; to Dr. Louis Wright and the staff and scholars at the Folger Library in the summer of 1960, when this book was first conceived; to the participants in a session at the American Historical Association convention in 1964; to Dr. Gillian Cell of the University of North Carolina and Professor Jack Price of the University of Michigan; to the researchers at the History of Parliament Trust in London, particularly Norah Fuidge; to Roy Schreiber, who provided me with some important references; and to the stimulating critics encountered at a meeting of the Friends of Business History at Harvard. I also profited from comments made at the seminar directed by Professors Joel Hurstfield and J. E. Neale at the University of London; at a gathering of social scientists at the University of Sussex; and at a dinner party at Cambridge where John Elliott, R. W. K. Hinton and J. H. Plumb gave me much food for thought.

I have had countless discussions of method with patient friends and guides at computer centers at Princeton, Stanford, Northwestern, and Harvard. From them I gained my introduction to the intricacies and possibilities of modern data-processing techniques, and three programmers in particular — Betty Benson, Jan Rudy, and John Newell — saw me through many a crisis.

The financial assistance that made the research and the computer work possible came from many sources, because it is still extremely difficult for a historian to obtain sufficient funds to pay the fearsome costs of using a computer. In my own case, total expenses for keypunching, programming, and machine time came to over $10,000. For almost one-tenth of this sum no outside support was forthcoming, and the remainder came from a succession of grants over a period of four years: the provision of free machine time at the Northwestern University Computer Center and a Faculty Research Grant from the Northwestern University Graduate School, both in 1962–1963; grants from the Canaday and

Clark Funds of Harvard University from 1964 to 1966; support from the Department of History at Harvard University in 1965–1966; The National Science Foundation Grant GP–2723 and the assistance of Norman Zachary at the Harvard University Computer Center in 1965–1966; and a Social Science Research Council grant in 1965. The more normal research expenses were covered by a Folger Library fellowship in 1960, by a Dodds fellowship from Princeton University in 1960–1961, and by the grants already mentioned. For all of these grants I am deeply grateful.

The staffs of the Princeton, Stanford, Huntington, Northwestern, Newberry, and various Harvard libraries were most kind, as were the people I encountered at the Institute of Early American History in Williamsburg, the Institute of Historical Research at the University of London, the British Museum, the Public Record Office, the Guildhall Library, the India Office Library, the Bodleian and Cambridge University Libraries, and the Honourable the Irish Society. Their assistance is warmly appreciated. I also wish to thank the officers of the following Livery Companies for permission to use their archives: the Clothworkers, Drapers, Fishmongers, Goldsmiths, Grocers, Haberdashers, Ironmongers, Mercers, Merchant Taylors, Skinners, and Vintners. Working among their papers was one of the more pleasant tasks I had: the graciousness of their librarians and archivists not only resolved all difficulties, but also provided such amenities as a constant stream of tea at one company and photostats of all relevant documents at another.

The editors of the *American Historical Review* and the *Economic History Review* were good enough to allow me to use material that first appeared in their journals (listed in the bibliography). I received invaluable help in the final preparation of the manuscript from the History Department at Harvard University, and from Harvard University Press, which ensured that the list of names would be as self-explanatory as possible without exceeding reasonable limitations of space.

CONTENTS

TABLES

ENTERPRISE AND EMPIRE

INTRODUCTION

By the economic standards of the time, England in the middle of the sixteenth century was an underdeveloped country. The advances that had been made on the Continent during the previous centuries, both in financial techniques and in general commercial expertise, had passed most of her merchants by, with the result that much of her trade was controlled by foreigners. One important port, Southampton, had only recently ceased to be dominated by Italians; London, the chief port of the realm, depended largely on its thriving Hanseatic and Italian communities for whatever status it enjoyed as a European *entrepôt*. Native banking and joint-stock companies were virtually unknown, and cloth was the solitary commodity of any significance produced for export. No other industry operated on a large scale, and none served more than domestic needs. The only major merchant organization was the Company of Merchant Adventurers, which sold the cloth abroad, but those few Englishmen who conducted foreign trade almost always did so close at hand. They rarely ventured beyond their immediate European neighbors, and they penetrated not at all into the major markets of the Mediterranean and the Baltic. Thus the opening of trade with Russia in the early 1550's was a revolutionary enlargement of the country's horizons. In overseas enterprise it had taken a foreigner, Cabot, to arouse any interest at all, and for more than half a century after his first voyage English efforts had remained limited and ineffective.[1]

The changes in this situation that took place between the last years of Edward VI's reign and the first years of Charles I's reign amounted to one of the most striking transformations in economic history. The backwater became the mainstream; or, to use a more Marxian metaphor, the caboose became the engine. Although England could not be considered the leader of European commerce, industrial development, and overseas expansion for another half-century, by 1630 all the foundations for that position had been laid. Control over the country's trade had been wrested from foreign merchants, a reversal symbolized by the expulsion of the Hanse from their huge London headquarters, the Steelyard, in 1598. The export trade's previous reliance on cloth had been substantially undermined by a rapidly growing involvement in the re-export of overseas products; and at home a multitude of new industries, particularly coal mining and ship-building, had begun to flourish. England's merchants were active throughout the world, and already they dominated important routes and markets, notably in the Mediterranean. They had organized dozens of new companies, whose successes in some areas, and persistence everywhere, reflected a growing determination to open new areas of the world to English enterprise. The results of their efforts could be seen in more than a score of separate settlements that stretched from India to North America.

The investors who made this transformation possible are the subject of the present book. Their behavior is one of the few in-

---

[1] Most of the topics discussed in this introduction are treated at greater length in the body of the book and only a minimum of documentation is provided here. For general surveys of the transformation described in these first two paragraphs, see W. R. Scott, *The Constitution and Finance of English, Scottish and Irish Joint-Stock Companies to 1720* (3 vols.; Cambridge, England, 1910–1912); J. A. Williamson, *A Short History of British Expansion*, vol. 1 (3rd ed.; London, 1945); G. D. Ramsay, *English Overseas Trade During the Centuries of Emergence* (London, 1957); and the early chapters of Charles Wilson, *England's Apprenticeship, 1603–1763* (London, 1965). More detailed works are cited in the notes throughout chap. 1, particularly notes 14, 20, 39, 49, 50, and 104. See, too, my introduction to the subject of this book: "Investment in English Overseas Enterprise, 1575–1630," *The Economic History Review* [henceforth *Ec.H.R.*], 2nd ser., 19 (1966), 70–81. It could be argued that the Staplers were still a "major merchant organization" in the mid-sixteenth century, but their great days were clearly over, and the loss of Calais in 1558 was merely the final blow to their fortunes.

gredients of England's expansion that has not been explored down to the smallest detail. By contrast, the other features of the story have long been familiar. Accounts of derring-do on the high seas, of Drake, Grenville, and their fellows, have been among the most popular oft-told tales in history. If Macaulay's "every school-boy knows" applies anywhere, it is to this romance of a nation awakening to her destiny overseas. The lives of the early colonists, too, have been carefully cherished by the generations of descendants for whom they cleared the way.[2] Yet the more glamorous and heroic exploits have not been alone in attracting the attention of historians. Although explorers, adventurers, pioneer traders, and settlers may excite the imagination as they win renown far from home, the forces that set their efforts in motion can be understood only by looking at events at home. There would have been no famous victories abroad without great advances in England herself. New forms of organization, a new breed of merchants and promoters, new sources of capital, a new sense of purpose, and a new vitality in economic enterprise had to appear before the seagoing heroes could embark on their spectacular careers.

This other half of the story — the transformation that preceded the departure of the ships — has also been thoroughly investigated. The tremendous outburst of propaganda for overseas enterprise, spearheaded by Richard Hakluyt; the popular interest in travel literature; and the material and spiritual motives that spurred the pioneers are all well known.[3] And there have been important studies of the more tangible components of the expansion. It was crucial, for example, that the joint-stock company was first widely used in England in this period. Thanks to its distinctive structure, large numbers of investors could pool their resources and finance ventures as expensive as voyages to India on a scale which no single promoter or small group of partners would have been able to support alone. With its shares available to any buyer, whether he was skilled in trade or not, the joint-stock company, from the primitive beginnings of the Muscovy Company in the 1550's to the flowering of the East India Company in the first decades of the seventeenth century, enabled merchants for the first time to attract capital from all sections of society. As a result

[2] See sections B:ii, C:i, and C:ii in the bibliography.
[3] See notes 3, 15, 24, and 25 in chap. 1.

of the labors of W. R. Scott,[4] the early development of this new kind of trading organization — its structure, its various forms, and the experiences of those who first used it — has been familiar for over half a century. In recent years, moreover, a succession of monographs has explored in depth not only the individual companies Scott described, but also the lives of the principal promoters of the period.[5]

From these works, and others of a more general nature, it is now also possible to appreciate the importance of London as the center and catalyst of the expansion. The overwhelming dominance of the metropolis in England's trade, the concentration of money and talent that it contained, and the attraction it held for so many different types of people — from gentry in search of relaxation to paupers in search of a fortune — all ensured that the city would provide the atmosphere in which bold new schemes could take root and grow. And finally, a series of recent studies of general social and economic conditions has illuminated the background to these developments. A considerable body of research has examined the social structure and its tensions, fluctuations in the economy, the rapid growth of industry, economic theories, trading patterns, and the relations of the government to commercial developments.[6] With all this material available, the workings of England's expansion can now be followed in some detail. Thus the general economic growth, the broadening of commercial horizons, and the development of industry can be related to changes in worldwide trading patterns, to the fluidity of England's social structure, to the propaganda and spirit of adventure so noticeable in Elizabeth's reign, to the appearance of joint-stock companies, to the stimulus provided by London, and ultimately to the efforts of individual pioneers, organizers, and seamen. The emphases may change from historian to historian, but by and large these are the features of the expansion which are recognized as vital.

There is still much room for monographs on specific problems, but the basic components of the story, as just outlined, seem firmly established. In fact, although our knowledge of the social

[4] Scott, *Joint-Stock Companies.*
[5] See sections C:ii and C:iii in the bibliography.
[6] See the works cited in note 1, above, and also section C:i in the bibliography.

and economic setting has improved substantially in the last few decades, our view of the central events, the organization and inspiration of overseas efforts, has undergone no fundamental change for 50 years. Details have been sharpened, mistakes corrected, greater depth achieved, and emphases shifted, but the essentials have remained unaltered. The same narratives and explanations have satisfied more than a generation of historians: the picture drawn by such scholars as Corbett, Scott, and Newton before the First World War, though improved, has not been superseded.[7] This is a remarkably long-lived consensus, which is unlikely to undergo important revisions in the future unless new documents are discovered like those which recently prompted a reinterpretation of the importance of Elizabethan privateering.[8]

However, one central subject has received scant treatment in all these studies: the behavior of the ordinary small investor. His very obscurity naturally raises difficult problems of evidence and research that lessen the opportunity for new findings. Nonetheless, a different perspective on the expansion can be gained through his eyes, and parts of the familiar story can achieve a new relevance and precision.

My original interest in the subject of this book, as the reader may well suspect, had little to do with any general concerns about omissions in the historiography of England's expansion. In fact, my intentions at the outset could hardly have been further removed from such ambitions as the wish to fill a gap in scholarly endeavors, or the determination to improve well-known generalizations. The initial impulse came, quite simply, from an attempt to solve a puzzle in the life of Sir Edwin Sandys. I had finished studying Sandys' career through 1603, when he was 42 years old; and I was finding it increasingly difficult to understand why, four years later, this prominent English gentleman, the son of an

[7] Sir Julian Corbett, *Drake and the Tudor Navy* (2 vols.; London, 1898); his *The Successors of Drake* (London, 1900); also others of his works; Scott, *Joint-Stock Companies*; A. P. Newton, *The Colonising Activities of the English Puritans* (New Haven, 1914). The work of this generation of scholars was summed up in the first edition of Williamson's *British Expansion,* which appeared in 1922. Significantly, the most recent edition (1945) required hardly any major revisions, and it is still the best survey of the subject, seriously out of date on very few matters.

[8] See K. R. Andrews, *Elizabethan Privateering* (Cambridge, England, 1964).

5

archbishop of York, should suddenly, at so advanced an age, have plunged energetically into the world of commerce and colonization. The last 20 years of his life were to be devoted as much to company affairs in London as to any other interests. He was to seek and achieve positions of great responsibility in three major trading organizations, and he was to invest as much effort as he could spare, and more money than he could afford, in pursuit of success in the City.

For a distinguished representative of the gentry — he would have been considered an aristocrat in any European country other than England — such behavior seemed surprising, to say the least. It is true that members of the landed classes had occasionally been known to seek adventure overseas, to support a few pioneering ventures, or to take an interest in commercial affairs from positions in the government. So, too, impoverished younger sons had often taken up trade after leaving the family estates, and rich merchants had married and bought their way into the ranks of the gentry. But for a landed gentleman actually to enter the world of finance — not to look for adventure overseas, but to gain control of companies, to become involved in the details of trade and colonization, to wheel and deal and consort with merchants — this certainly seemed unusual in light of the social and economic traditions of western Europe. The barriers between the classes had been breached, and there was little to be learned from Sandys himself to explain his actions.

Not until I began to study the details of his career did it become apparent that his commercial activity, though the most spectacular among the gentry of his day, was by no means unique. Again and again in the company records I would meet his kinsmen and friends: Sir Dudley Digges, the Earl of Southampton, Sir Ferdinando Gorges, and others like them. Sir Edwin was not alone — he was merely a leader in a remarkable process taking place in Jacobean England: the entry of the landed classes into the business world. Soon, too, it became clear that the origins of this unprecedented phenomenon lay in Elizabeth's reign, when the highest level of the aristocracy, the Court, first committed itself deeply to a great new national enterprise, overseas expansion. As propaganda and interest multiplied, the way was prepared for the much more widespread influx of the gentry into trade that was so noticeable under James I. Sandys' activities began to make sense at last, and it seemed that a few references to this background would suffice to explain his involvement in commerce. Unfortunately, however, studies of the expansion have had little to say on this subject.

Historians have long been aware of the overseas efforts of the gentry. Books on the Virginia and Bermuda Companies in particular, and on Raleigh, Gorges, and similar leaders, have dealt with non-merchant participation in commerce.[9] But the topic has been discussed only at the level of individual exploits. There has been no attempt to assess the contribution of the landed classes as a whole, and this is only part of a more general paucity of information. For how is one to judge the gentry's efforts on their own? They make little sense without reference to the role played by other social classes, primarily the merchants, in the organization and promotion of overseas enterprise. The sudden rush of gentlemen into commerce may be of interest on its own, but it gains significance only when seen in the context of the behavior of other classes among the investors.

These considerations inevitably take us far from Sir Edwin Sandys. The major concern of this book, the social composition of the group that invested in England's expansion, holds its own justification. And this subject leads on to matters yet further afield from Sandys himself: how fluctuations in investment reflected general economic or other conditions; why propaganda, London, and joint-stock companies were of particular importance in the history of the expansion; how the gentry differed from merchant investors; and so on. Sir Edwin's life often reflected these larger themes, but for the time being he must remain an interesting example, to be studied further once the setting for his career has been more fully explored.[10]

Given the nature of the data, a study of Elizabethan and Jacobean investors must concern itself with such questions as the

[9] See sections C:ii and C:iii in the bibliography. Of particular relevance here are W. F. Craven, *Dissolution of the Virginia Company* (New York, 1932); H. C. Wilkinson, *The Adventurers of Bermuda* (London, 1958); D. B. Quinn, *Raleigh and the British Empire* (London, 1947); and R. A. Preston, *Gorges of Plymouth Fort* (Toronto, 1953).

[10] Sandys' career is often cited as illustration in the pages that follow, and I hope to complete a full biography shortly. There is much valuable information on his commercial activities in Craven, *Virginia Company*.

differences between the various participating social classes, the size and relative importance of their investments, their motives, and the rise and fall of their interest in overseas ventures. These topics are quite clearly related to a number of problems, including the economic health of the gentry, which historians of this period have been mulling over in recent years. Yet the lack of knowledge about the average investor has been due, not to any shortage of evidence, but to its extreme abundance. The surviving charters and records of the commercial enterprises of the time contain the names of thousands of company members, and the difficulty has been how to use these sources, not how to find them. The raw material embedded in the documents is unfortunately too plentiful and too disorganized to be approached without a great deal of preliminary sifting and sorting. Hence it has lain dormant in the archives, to all intents and purposes unavailable to the historian. With over 6,000 people to be located and disentangled, even the easiest counting procedures would have been far too laborious and inaccurate if attempted by hand; and more complicated calculations, such as multiple company memberships or annual admission totals for each social class, could never have yielded reliable results. Now, however, thanks to the development of the modern computer, mechanical aid can be enlisted that makes it feasible to resurrect this virtually untouched layer of evidence. Systematic evaluation of large masses of information is no longer an excessively unwieldy process, because the computer has the qualities of flexibility, speed, and accuracy which can make an undertaking of this kind both manageable and profitable.

Another advantage of the times is the benefit that this type of investigation can derive from recent advances in the social sciences. Sociologists and economic historians, in particular, have developed techniques of quantification that have led to new insights and higher levels of accuracy in areas which previously seemed too large for anything but intuitive analysis. Among more traditional historical investigations the most important new method has been the one to which is attached the name of Sir Lewis Namier.[11] On all sides, therefore, one finds stimulating precedents and inspiration. Whereas "namierization" uses quan-

[11] See L. B. Namier, *The Structure of Politics at the Accession of George III* (2 vols.; London, 1929). See, too, the discussion at the beginning of chap. 3, below, and the works cited in notes 1 and 4 of chap. 3.

tification to study a small group in minute detail, my approach has been closer to the methods of sociologists or economists in that it uses a limited amount of information about most individuals in a very large group. One might say that this is "namierization" in breadth rather than depth, but the purpose is the same: to bring to the surface a level of documentation which, though long accessible, becomes useful only when categorized and systematically measured.

Fortunately, the number of problems faced by the user of computers has been reduced markedly by the rapid improvement in data-processing machines in the last decade and by the proliferation of standard computer "programs" of wide applicability. I myself have been especially aware of the short cuts and increasing flexibility that have been assured by this progress, because nearly five years elapsed between my first encounter with the machines and my final "runs." Some of the calculations performed with little trouble in the end would have been extremely cumbersome only three or four years earlier. Now, however, there is no doubt that if the historian has an appropriate subject and adequate evidence, he will be capable of answering any question he asks without anxieties about delays which shortcomings of the machine might entail. There is no longer any justification for the hesitance that, till now, has prevented the appearance — so far as I know — of any book on pre-nineteenth century history which uses a computer as an aid to research. Nonetheless, it must be admitted that by undertaking to submit one's material to a computer, one must be prepared to face substantial methodological problems, primarily when one organizes data into the uniform and strictly defined categories which are essential for systematic measurement.[12]

---

[12] These matters are discussed in detail in chap. 3 and the Appendix, below. As will be stressed, the data was copied a number of times during the transition from documents to IBM cards, and typographical errors were especially difficult to spot in the midst of so much information, particularly because it was all reduced to symbols and numbers. Even more important, the material was so extensive that I could never hope to attain so detailed and thorough a familiarity with every single company or investor as could a specialist in one of these subjects. I hope, therefore, that the inaccuracies which may have persisted, despite numerous checks, will be brought to my attention by scholars with greater expertise in particular areas, so that corrections can be made in future revisions. It should not be assumed that the *increased* precision achieved by computer analyses of large masses of evidence is the same as *absolute* precision.

The most crucial step in the whole process of using a computer is the definition of terms. Although the machine functions with absolute accuracy, its output can be no more reliable than the input. Painstaking care must therefore be taken to ensure that the organization of the evidence ("coding"), and the formulation of questions ("programming"), conform exactly to the purposes of the investigation. Unless the definitions that create the final data are strictly relevant and cover all possible variations, the precision of the results will be specious. For this reason, and also because the computer's "output" is merely an automatic tabulation of the symbols, or categories, into which the material has been fitted, it is essential that the original definitions be described at length; without this information the conclusions will have little meaning. Accordingly, a substantial section of this book is devoted to a survey of method. Form is rarely as interesting as content; but because the entire value of a study of this kind depends on the appropriateness of its framework, the results must be accompanied by a detailed exposition of how they were reached. In my own case, it also seemed advisable to publish the data in full, not to justify my figures, but to make this large body of information available to other scholars. All these matters are amplified in Part Two, but a few fundamental decisions must be explained briefly here so that the reader will know what assumptions underlie the figures presented in Chapters 1 and 2.

Chronological boundaries for the study had to be arbitrary, because no single years clearly marked the beginning or the end of the first stage of England's expansion. 1575 seemed a good starting-point because a wave of overseas activity began in the mid-1570's after two desultory decades. Moreover, the 1575–1600 period was quite long enough to provide a setting against which the vital and rapid developments of the early seventeenth century might be measured. 1630 furnished a convenient stopping-point, because by then the major new ventures were well established, and the changing atmosphere of the late 1620's, when new religious and political motives entered the scene, could be included up to the foundation of the Providence Island Company.[13]

Within these terminal points coverage had to be as complete

[13] See further the sections "Coverage" in chap. 3, and "The Rise and Fall of Popular Interest" in chap. 1.

10

as possible if the ordinary investors were to be assessed as a body. Sampling was unfeasible, because the company records were themselves incomplete, and too little was known about general trends to allow even random choices to be made. Furthermore, because fewer than 7,000 names were recoverable, there was no reason why they should not all be gathered together. Some of the more inconspicuous and unimportant undertakings of the time undoubtedly escaped notice; but every major venture, plus all the minor ones that could be tracked down, were included. The larger efforts are listed in Table 11. Investments in industry or in enterprises which seemed too small to deserve a separate category were recorded under "other ventures" — less than 500 additional individual investments. All these groups are described further in Chapter 3, where the reader will also find a detailed justification for my estimate that some three-quarters of the investors of the period appear in my list. In most cases, too, the names are accompanied by dates of admission to the various companies and a record of the company directorships or governorships attained.

This basic material was enlarged in two directions, both related to my original interest in Sandys and the role of the gentry. First, every member of the House of Commons between 1584 and 1630 was included.[14] The parliamentary figures had no direct bearing on the principal subject of the book, and originally they were only an outgrowth of my study of Sandys. But because most of the gentlemen who participated in public affairs during this period were members of the House of Commons, the additional information was not likely to be totally irrelevant. And in fact, as will be seen, it was to shed significant light on the gentry's commercial activities.

The second addition to the basic data was of fundamental importance — the division of the investors into social classes. Here was the crux of the study. Without a valid, consistent, and easily applicable definition of the difference between a gentleman and a merchant, there was no point in trying to evaluate their relative roles in the expansion. Unfortunately, this distinction, on which so much rested, has rarely, if ever, been the subject of much

[14] As is explained in chap. 3, I started with the 1584 session because it witnessed the largest turnover in personnel in Elizabeth's reign, and because it represented the results of the first general election in our period. The M.P.'s of 1576 and 1581 had been elected in 1572.

11

agreement. As soon as one man is considered the social superior of another, a multitude of reasons for the inequality appear, and one must assume that the explanations have diverged since the days of Cain and Abel. In the midst of such a variety of opinions, it would be utopian to hope that any one definition — and a simple one at that — could carry much weight. Nonetheless, it had to be formulated, and for the purposes of this book I regarded as a "gentleman" *anyone whose income originally came from land,* and as a "merchant" *anyone whose income originally came from commerce.* This was a fairly straightforward yardstick, which avoided — as it had to if it were to be "coded" for the computer — the complications and uncertain nuances of more sophisticated criteria. Naturally, there were still shadowy areas, particularly when the younger son of a gentleman took up trade or a merchant's son bought land. These problems are discussed more fully in Chapter 3; but it is worth stressing that strict adherence to my basic test, the *original source* (during his lifetime) of an individual's wealth, left very few cases in which more than one decision was possible. This may be a crude division, but it has been highly effective. Not only did it make most decisions relatively easy, but it used as its touchstone a subject on which evidence was not too hard to find — no small benefit when dealing with obscure people who lived over three centuries ago. As a result, I was able to classify over 75 percent of the people in the list[15] — adding to the gentleman/merchant division the subdivisions of knight and peer, and a very small catchall category consisting of those (such as yeomen) who could not be included elsewhere.

The one essential advantage of this definition was its direct appropriateness to the aims of my study. "Gentleman," after all, is never anything more than a convenient label; and what interested me was not the behavior of those who happened to be considered worthy of this title, for whatever reason, but the behavior of that social grouping which normally did not participate in trade. In western European society the group which traditionally considered commerce beneath its dignity was the landed class, and

[15] It is worth pointing out that the percentage remaining unclassified was much higher among M.P.'s (33 percent) than among company members (18 percent). Thus for those involved in commerce, the prime focus of this book, the information was 82 percent complete.

ownership of land was therefore the criterion best suited to my purposes. Even though other considerations were ignored (with some very small exceptions, discussed in Chapter 3), it was a classification whose results corresponded closely enough to contemporaries' opinions as to who was or was not a gentleman to justify designating my two groups "gentry" and "merchants." (The latter term was of course used in the modern sense of anyone whose career is in trade or commerce, not in the seventeenth-century meaning which excluded retailers and artisans.)

With a clear-cut distinction established between the classes of investors, systematic measurement was possible, and there was now sufficient evidence to throw light on one of the central questions of English social history: Why was it, in this country and at this time, that the gentry broke with the most persistent tradition of their class throughout western Europe? Their involvement in trade set them apart from their peers on the Continent, and as a group they remained unique in this respect for centuries.[16] Moreover, their participation in commerce revealed a cohesiveness and flexibility in the upper levels of England's social structure that was to have a profound effect on the country's history. Particularly in the story whose beginning is investigated here — the rise of England to dominance among European nations overseas — success was in no small measure due to the gentry's close personal and financial support of primarily commercial ventures.

[16] The best introduction to the question of how deeply the landed classes on the Continent became involved in economic activity during early modern times is the series of articles on "The Aristocrat in Business" in *Explorations in Entrepreneurial History*, vol. 6, nos. 2 and 3 (1953 and 1954). Though various examples are given of Swedish, German, and other nobles following "entrepreneurial" pursuits, they reveal nothing like the concentration or breadth of interest that we shall notice among the English gentry. Moreover, agriculture and, to a lesser extent, industry appear to have been the chief commitments of the few continental nobles who pursued such activity openly — foreign trade seems to have been a very rare investment. In contrast, about half of England's peers invested in trade between 1575 and 1630. See also J. U. Nef, *Industry and Government in France and England, 1540–1640* (1940; reprinted Ithaca, 1957), especially pp. 8–11; R. B. Grassby, "Social Status and Commercial Enterprise under Louis XIV," *Ec.H.R.*, 2nd ser., 14 (1961), 19–38; and J. H. Elliott, "The Decline of Spain," in *Crisis in Europe, 1550–1660,* ed. Trevor Aston (London, 1965), pp. 167–193, especially pp. 184–187. As Barthélemy Laffemas bitterly complained in his *Les Tresors et Richesses pour mettre l'Estat en Splendeur* . . . (Paris, 1598), p. 20, the French nobility simply "tient en mespris" all trading activity. See note 43 in chap. 1, below.

This book is not the place to investigate the broader implications or significance of the remarkably widespread participation in the foundation of the British Empire. Nor is there space to enter into the ultimate economic effects of the transformation which took place between the 1550's and the 1630's: the revolutions it brought about in financial organization, industrial activity, trading techniques, and the whole tenor and purpose of English economic activity. It is well that the reader should be aware of the larger context, but the long-term developments can be touched upon only briefly in this study. The principal body of evidence for what follows, though abundant and detailed, is narrowly restricted both in time span and subject matter. These limitations suggest that it might be wise to proceed *nisi caste, saltem caute* before turning the results of a study of investments in England's expansion into substantial conclusions about more far-reaching issues.

Because a considerable part of this book has had to be devoted to such technical matters as definitions, methods, and the detailed minor results of the computer analysis, I have thought it advisable to isolate the principal figures and conclusions. These have been brought together in Chapter 1. Here will be found the discussion of propaganda, of London, and of joint-stock companies — stimuli to the expansion which took on special importance as the subject was approached through the ordinary investor. Here, too, are treated the motives of the investors, the roles of merchants and gentry, the rise and fall of popular interest, and the origin of the funds that were needed to sustain the efforts of the time. Many readers may need to read no more than Chapter 1 (and possibly Sections I and IV of Chapter 3, where general methodological problems are discussed). Chapter 2 contains a series of tables presenting the detailed results of the computer's analysis. These figures were used in Chapter 1, but in their totality they will be of interest only to other scholars working in the field. The remainder of the book, Part Two, is concerned with method. Chapter 3 describes the advantages and difficulties of using quantification and a computer in historical work (Sections I and III) and explains in full the definitions on which my categories were based (Section II). Assembled here is a complete survey of the data: exactly what material was brought together, how the lists of names were handled, which companies were included, what lacunae remained, and where errors might still lurk. Following the bibliography there is the list of investors and Members of Parliament itself, accompanied by a key. Hopefully this will prove to be a useful source of reference for all students of the period.

One final point deserves mention by way of introduction to what follows. It is not hindsight alone that lends significance to the organization of England's expansion. Hakluyt's generation already considered success overseas an objective of major national importance, and the average investor was certainly aware of the larger import of the enterprise he was supporting. For it was not a smug representative of a country long supreme in empire, but Sir Walter Raleigh, living in the early years of England's struggle for dominion in newly discovered lands, who wrote the famous justification for the efforts of his countrymen: "Whosoever commands the sea commands the trade; whosoever commands the trade of the world commands the riches of the world, and consequently the world itself." [17]

[17] Quoted in R. H. Tawney, *Business and Politics under James I: Lionel Cranfield as Merchant and Minister* (Cambridge, England, 1958), p. 3, where the widespread acceptance of this view in the early seventeenth century is further discussed. Pages 3–41 of Tawney's book comprise a most useful introduction to the general economic background of this period, and they deserve to be added to the works cited in note 1 above.

Part One: Patterns of Investment

CHAPTER 1   "THE PATH TO FAME, THE PROOFE OF ZEALE, AND WAY TO PURCHASE GOLDE"

Francis Drake's circumnavigation of the earth between 1577 and 1580 has been regarded since the sixteenth century, and rightly so, as the most striking of the many overseas exploits of Elizabethan Englishmen. But the importance of his achievement, unlike that of most great voyages, does not rest on the discoveries he made. Notwithstanding the inclination of historians to attach the word "first" to his voyage and to compare him with the brilliant explorers of his century,[1] he entered few unknown areas, and he followed the first circumnavigation by nearly 60 years. He was undeniably the first Englishman to complete the journey; but the first Frenchman to do so, two centuries later, made no comparable impression on his contemporaries or the history books. It is elsewhere that one must look for the wider significance of Drake's voyage — to its timing and its effect on his countrymen.

At the most general level the success of the venture symbolized

---

[1] See, for example, A. L. Rowse, *The Elizabethans and America* (London, 1959), p. 24. According to J. A. Froude, *English Seamen in the Sixteenth Century* (New York, 1895), p. 97, Drake "traced the first furrow round the globe"! Sir William Foster, *England's Quest of Eastern Trade* (London, 1933), p. 126, even speaks of Thomas Cavendish's having "the imperishable glory of having been the second Englishman to circumnavigate the globe."

England's emergence as a potential power on the high seas, as a dangerous rival to Spain, and as a possible competitor for the wealth of the East. But Englishmen could draw a more immediate lesson from Drake's successful return. Not only could they rejoice at the startling blow he had struck at the Spanish Empire, but they could marvel at the fabulous riches that accompanied the hero homeward. The display of courage might have been expected, but the booty was unprecedented. Here, revealed as never before, was a double inducement for daring the might of Spain: glory and wealth. It was small wonder that a few days later the Spanish ambassador wrote gloomily to Philip II: "At present there is hardly an Englishman who is not talking of undertaking the voyage, so encouraged are they by Drake's return." The newly dubbed Sir Francis already seemed to be talking of going back to the Pacific and promising a return of £7 for every £1 subscribed. The ambassador could only add that "everybody wants to have a share in the expedition." [2]

Though the Spaniard's dispatch may have been an accurate portrayal of the atmosphere late in 1580, some two decades were still to pass before the aspirations were translated into realities. Nonetheless, Drake's feat was undoubtedly a landmark in the rapidly growing interest of Englishmen in overseas enterprise. After tentative beginnings as early as Henry VII's reign, and an increasing though still sporadic effort starting in the 1550's, the mid-1570's witnessed a remarkable acceleration of activity. A succession of new enterprises was launched, drawing support from a wider group of investors than ever before. And these pioneering entrepreneurs, both at Elizabeth's Court and in the City of London, were to persevere, despite a multitude of failures, while interest throughout the country steadily grew. Not until the turn of the century were major successes achieved or really large numbers of investors drawn into new projects, but the im-

[2] Letter of Bernardino de Mendoza, October 16, 1580, *Calendar of State Papers* [henceforth *CSP*], *Spanish, 1580–1586*, pp. 55–56. In similar vein, the Cologne correspondent of the Fuggers predicted that, with Drake's successful return, "many pirates and adventurers will follow after him." See *The Fugger News-Letters* (*Second Series*), ed. Viktor Von Klarwill, trans. L. S. R. Byrne (London, 1926), p. 46. The rise of anti-Spanish feeling, associated with Drake's exploits, is illustrated in C. F. T. Brooke, "Some Pre-Armada Propagandist Poetry in England (1585–1586)," *Proceedings of the American Philosophical Society*, 85 (1942), 71–83.

portance of those who prepared the ground cannot be overestimated.

As the most spectacular and successful of the ventures of the mid-1570's, Drake's voyage played a vital role in this awakening of the English people to the possibilities for personal and national profit in faraway lands. Nor did he rest content with setting the example. Having raised dramatically the prospect of wealth and glory, he joined the rising chorus of propaganda that was urging his countrymen to turn their eyes abroad. Less than three years after his return he wrote a poem to support an appeal for subscribers to a new venture designed to continue the effort that had been cut short by the tragic loss at sea of Sir Humphrey Gilbert. And here he described succinctly the motives which he felt to be at the root of his contemporaries' taste for adventure:

Who seeks, by worthy deeds, to gain renown for hire:
Whose heart, whose head, whose purse is pressed, to purchase his desire;
If any such there be, that thirsteth after fame:
Lo, here a mean, to win himself an everlasting name.
Who seeks, by gain and wealth, t'advance his house and blood:
Whose care is great, whose toil no less, whose hope is all for good;
If anyone there be, that covets such a trade:
Lo, here the plot for common wealth, and private gain is made.
He, that for ventures sake, will venture far and near:
Whose zeal is strong, whose practice truth, whose faith is void of fear,
If any such there be, inflamed with holy care.
Here may he find, a ready mean, his purpose to declare:
So that, for each degree, this treatise doth unfold:
The path to fame, the proof of zeal, and way to purchase gold.[3]

[3] George Peckham, *A true reporte, Of the late discoveries . . . of the Newfound Landes: By . . . Sir Humfrey Gilbert* (London, 1583), page before fol. 1. (The spelling of quotations has been modernized here and throughout the present book.) The entire tract is reprinted in *The Voyages and Colonising Enterprises of Sir Humphrey Gilbert*, ed. D. B. Quinn (2 vols.; London: The Hakluyt Society, 1940), II, 435–482 (see page 438). On the growth of travel literature and propaganda in this period, see E. G. R. Taylor, *Tudor Geography, 1485–1583* (London, 1930); and her *Late Tudor and Early Stuart Geography, 1583–1650* (London, 1934); G. B. Parks, *Richard Hakluyt and the English Voyages* (2nd ed.; New York, 1961); and John Parker, *Books to Build an Empire* (Amsterdam, 1966). Taylor pinpoints the importance of the Elizabethan revolution in English cosmography in her edition of *The Troublesome Voyage of Captain Edward Fenton, 1582–1583* (Cambridge, England: The Hakluyt Society, 1959), p. lvii. For the effects of the propaganda, and the rising public interest, see J. A. Williamson, "Richard Hakluyt" in *Richard Hakluyt & His Successors* (London: The Hakluyt Society, 1946), pp. 11–46.

Straightforward and down-to-earth, the verse exemplifies the spirit of a movement still in its infancy. For years to come Englishmen were to be inspired by precisely these sentiments, and nobody more fitting than Sir Francis Drake can be found to provide the epigraph for the founding of their empire.

I. LONDON

Any account of the rise and fall of enthusiasm for commercial enterprise in this period must begin with the city of London. Overpopulated, plague-ridden, and "pestered with . . . people, that bear outward show of civil, honest, and gentlemanlike disposition, but in very deed their behaviour is most infamous to be spoken of," [4] the swarming metropolis dominated English life. During the 22 years of James I's reign alone, its population grew by almost one-third, from 250,000 to 320,000.[5] Every element in society was attracted to "the walls, gates, . . . towers and castles, the Schools of learning, and houses of law, the orders and customs, sports and pastimes, watchings and martial exercises" so meticulously described by John Stow.[6] Many doubtless came under the same impulse which, two centuries before, had urged Dick Whittington toward streets paved with gold. And because London was the hub, not only of England's government, law, and culture, but also of her trade, there was much to encourage those who hoped to make their fortunes there. Thus it was that almost every promoter with a new scheme gravitated toward the capital. As might be expected, there were more people in London than anywhere else in the kingdom who were ready to invest their money in these projects.

The efforts of devoted local historians notwithstanding, it is im-

[4] Robert Greene, *The Third and Last Part of Cony-Catching* (London, 1592), reprinted in *The Elizabethan Underworld*, ed. A. V. Judges (London, 1965), pp. 179–205 (see page 179). A good, and brief, depiction of the atmosphere in London can be found in the chapter, "London and the Life of the Town," in H. B. Wheatley, *Shakespeare's England: An Account of the Life and Manners of His Age*, vol. II (Oxford, 1916), pp. 153–181.

[5] N. G. Brett-James, *The Growth of Stuart London* (London, 1935), p. 512.

[6] John Stow, *A Survey of London, by John Stow*, ed. C. L. Kingsford (2 vols.; Oxford, 1908), I, 117. As Stow himself wrote (II, 212), "the Gentlemen of all shires do fly and flock to this City." The best survey of the beginnings of the London "season" can be found in F. J. Fisher, "The Development of London as a Centre of Conspicuous Consumption in the Sixteenth and Seventeenth Centuries," *Transactions of the Royal Historical Society*, 4th ser., 30 (1948), 37–50.

possible to ascribe more than minor importance to the role of other ports in the organization of England's expansion. Despite the belief held by one historian that "it is no exaggeration to say that Hakluyt's opinions found a more ready acceptance in Bristol than in any other part of England," [7] and despite the remarkable contributions of West Countrymen, the pre-eminence of London cannot be doubted. How else is one to interpret the fact that Sir John Hawkins, himself a member of a great Devon family, came to London to raise money whenever he contemplated a voyage, whether in 1562 or 1595? [8] Similarly, the "Plymouth" half of the Virginia Company, granted the right to colonize the northern half of the area described in the 1606 patent, had to turn to Londoners for help even though it was supposed to have been a distinct West Country group. The New England Council, pur-

[7] C. M. MacInnes, A Gateway of Empire (Bristol, 1939), p. 51. Bristol in the early seventeenth century had about 12,000 inhabitants — under five percent of London's size — and only 150 merchants engaged in overseas trade: see Merchants and Merchandise in Seventeenth-Century Bristol, ed. Patrick McGrath (Bristol: Bristol Record Society, vol. XIX, 1955), especially p. ix. The one major undertaking of the period whose inspiration appears to have come from Bristol merchants, the Newfoundland Company, ended up by having "most of the capital and the work of organization . . . [come] from the Londoners." And its charter specified that members of the company's council had to reside in London. See G. M. Cell, "The English in Newfoundland, 1577–1660" (unpub. diss., University of Liverpool, 1964), pp. 122–125, 163–164, 221ff. Some of Cell's findings have been published in her article "The Newfoundland Company: A Study of Subscribers to a Colonizing Venture," William and Mary Quarterly, 3rd ser., 22 (1965), 611–625, but my references (henceforth abbreviated as "Newfoundland") will be to her much more detailed thesis. A similar picture is presented by Miller Christy, "Attempts toward Colonization: The Council for New England and the Merchant Venturers of Bristol, 1621–1623," The American Historical Review, 4 (1899), 678–702. Of course, this is not to deny that the outports had any importance in the organization of England's expansion. That even a fairly small port, Weymouth for example, could play a most useful part in the growth of commerce and colonization is revealed in Maureen Weinstock, Studies in Dorset History (Dorchester, 1953), pp. 1–51. But London's overwhelming importance makes it imperative that a proper perspective be maintained, and the best local studies, like Weinstock's, are careful not to inflate the prominence of their subjects. See, for contrast, Arnold Wright, The Romance of Colonisation: Being the Story of the Economic Development of the British Empire (London and New York, 1923), especially pp. 14–15. He gives chief honors to the Westerners even though his title proclaims that his subject is "economic development." T. S. Willan, "The Foreign Trade of the Provincial Ports," in his Studies in Elizabethan Foreign Trade (Manchester, 1959), pp. 65–91, presents the best balanced introduction to the whole problem of the relative importance of London and the outports.

[8] J. A. Williamson, Sir John Hawkins (Oxford, 1927), pp. 78–79, 92–93, 129, 475–476; and his Hawkins of Plymouth (London, 1949), pp. 48–49.

portedly "an exclusive organization of West Country members of the ruling class," was so apathetic that its one active member, Gorges, soon set himself up in London. Even the Scottish "Canada Company," led by Sir William Alexander, looked for support to the English capital, as did the Plymouth Adventurers of the 1620's, despite their name. And, although the Massachusetts Bay Company originated in the West Country and in Lincolnshire, over 40 percent of its membership eventually came from London.[9] Many of the most fruitful ideas originated in the provinces, but time and again only the financial resources of the Londoners could transform a plan into a reality. The situation was underlined by the stream of complaints about London's overweening pride that came from the outports. In 1617 the men of Plymouth even asserted that the encroachments of the Londoners were more harmful than pirates.[10] But when an expedition was launched against the Barbary pirates in 1620, reputedly for the benefit of all English merchants, only London provided substantial support, eventually subscribing almost the entire cost.[11] If the Crown itself depended so heavily on the City's financiers,[12] the rest of the realm could only follow suit. A few lone ventures, such as John Davis' voyages in 1585 and 1586, obtained backing more readily in other ports — in this case Exeter[13] — but they were rare ex-

[9] R. A. Preston, *Gorges of Plymouth Fort* (Toronto, 1953), pp. 141–167 *passim*, 173, 205–208, 278. On the Plymouth adventurers, see the description by Captain John Smith in his *Works, 1608–1631*, ed. Edward Arber (2 vols.; London, 1895), II, 731–733, 782–783. On the Massachusetts Bay Company, see Frances Rose-Troup, *The Massachusetts Bay Company and Its Predecessors* (New York, 1930), pp. 39–41, 131–162. A similar picture in trade with the Iberian peninsula is presented by V. M. Shillington and A. B. W. Chapman, *The Commercial Relations of England and Portugal* (London, n.d.), p. 155. In industrial ventures, too, entrepreneurs, after exhausting local resources, "inevitably turned to the City; for London was now never without money to lend." See J. U. Nef, *The Rise of the British Coal Industry* (2 vols.; London, 1932), II, 32–33.

[10] Quoted in Preston, *Gorges*, p. 134. See also William Cunningham, *The Growth of English Industry and Commerce in Modern Times* (5th ed.; Cambridge, England, 1912), II, 241–250. Other complaints can be found in British Museum Additional Manuscript 33924, no. 22, fols. 41–43, and Lansdown MS. 86, no. 13, fol. 26.

[11] Preston, *Gorges*, pp. 133–134. The Levant Company alone offered in 1619 to pay £40,000 over a period of two years toward an expedition against the pirates. See their Second Court Book (Public Record Office: S.P. 105/148), fol. 22.

[12] See Robert Ashton, *The Crown and the Money Market, 1603–1640* (Oxford, 1960).

[13] *An Elizabethan Guild of the City of Exeter*, ed. William Cotton (Exeter, 1873), pp. 82–83. But the principal backer was William Saunderson, a Londoner.

ceptions. Every figure that can be calculated — London, for example, accounting for 80 percent of the entire income from customs, and a twentieth of the population living in the capital by 1600 [14] — only reinforces the impression of overwhelming domination conveyed by the descriptions of contemporaries.

With so much wealth and activity concentrated in London, it was natural for the metropolis to become an essential catalyst for the growing interest in overseas enterprises. Not only were nearly all the ventures launched there, but the East India, Virginia, Irish, North-West Passage, Somers Islands, and Guinea and Binney Companies actually had their London origin specified in their official titles, and a number of others, including the Spanish and Newfoundland Companies, were required by their charters to have their headquarters in the capital. Inevitably, too, the great recruitment campaigns were centered in London. So many broadsides and propaganda tracts came from the City's printers, and so many patriotic sermons were delivered in the City's churches,[15] that it could not have taken a visitor long to learn

It might be noted, too, that Davis' two expeditions seem to have exhausted the interest of the Exeter merchants, who had subscribed to Humphrey Gilbert's last voyage only two years before. John Davis in 1587, Carew Raleigh in 1585, Sir Walter Raleigh in 1588, and Drake in 1589 had no success in attempting to raise money there; see *ibid.,* pp. 80–88 *passim.* See, too, W. T. MacCaffrey, *Exeter, 1540–1640: The Growth of an English County Town* (Cambridge, Mass., 1958), pp. 171–72, in which the conservatism of Exeter's merchants is stressed.

[14] See A. M. Millard, "The Imports of London, 1600–1640" (a typescript attached to her "Analyses of Port Books Recording Merchandises Imported into the Port of London . . . between 1588 and 1640," compiled 1950–1959 and deposited in the Harvard College Library), pp. 3–5. See also Charles Wilson, *England's Apprenticeship, 1603–1763* (London, 1965), pp. 36–51; Astrid Friis, *Alderman Cockayne's Project and the Cloth Trade* (Copenhagan and London, 1927), pp. 61–82; E. F. Heckscher, *Mercantilism,* trans. Mendel Shapiro, rev. ed. by E. F. Söderlund (2 vols.; London and New York, 1955), I, 418–31; W. G. Hoskins, *Provincial England: Essays in Social and Economic History* (London, 1963), pp. 86–87; and the succinct description of London's dominance in G. D. Ramsay, *English Overseas Trade during the Centuries of Emergence* (London, 1957), pp. 1–10. For quick reference, some striking figures that reveal the much smaller volume of trade in the outports can be seen in Lansdown MS. 41, fols. 108–168. For the export trade, a similar situation is depicted in F. J. Fisher, "London's Export Trade in the Early Seventeenth Century," *Ec.H.R.,* 2nd ser., 3 (1950), 151–61 (especially p. 152).

[15] Many examples are reprinted in Alexander Brown, *The Genesis of the United States* (2 vols.; Boston, 1890); and *Tracts and Other Papers,* ed. Peter Force (New York, 1947), vols. I, III. See also the works by Taylor cited in note 3; *The Pepys Ballads,* ed. H. E. Rollins (8 vols.; Cambridge, Mass., 1929–1932), I, 24–31; and L. B. Wright, *Religion and Empire: The Alliance between Piety and Commerce in English Expansion, 1558–1625* (Chapel Hill, 1943). For the grow-

about the undertakings that were under way. The merchants already engaged in overseas trade were natural targets for promoters seeking financial backing; courtiers, with their power, wealth, hopes for national glory, and personal ambitions, were another likely source of support, as were the rich, well-organized Livery Companies. Moreover, in addition to the permanent or semipermanent residents of the City, there was a growing stream of visitors: country gentry coming to the Inns of Court, to Parliament, and to the emerging "season" in larger numbers than ever before. Although the consequences of primogeniture had been driving younger sons into trade for centuries, those who remained on the land, like their peers on the Continent, had never engaged in commerce. But now, spurred by the propaganda for a tremendous national enterprise whenever they came to London, and encouraged by the example set by leading courtiers and noblemen, a large section of the landed classes was persuaded to invest — for the first time in European history — in overseas trade. As will be seen, many forces were required to bring about this union between merchants and gentry, but none can have had a more decisive influence than the sheer excitement, magnetism, and commercial expertise to be found in London. The City was the crucible in which an empire was forged.

II. THE JOINT-STOCK COMPANY

The chief consequence of this burst of enthusiasm was the participation of over 6,300 people in the various ventures that were launched between 1575 and 1630. The social classes of the investors are indicated in Table 1. (Percentages in the tables in this book are given to one decimal point. In the text, except for a few detailed figures in Chapter 2, they are given to the nearest whole number.) Almost one-quarter (24 percent) of the *classified* investors were thus non-merchants; and even if the entire total is included, they amounted to almost one-fifth. Following Thomas Wilson's and G. E. Aylmer's estimates,[16] it would appear that the

---

ing numbers of gentry coming to London, discussed below, see note 6 above. By 1617 they had to be *ordered* home to the country in the summer. See *The Letters and the Life of Francis Bacon,* ed. James Spedding (7 vols.; London, 1861–1874), VI, 213.

[16] G. E. Aylmer, *The King's Servants: The Civil Service of Charles I, 1625–42* (London, 1961), pp. 322–330. (Thomas Wilson's estimates at the beginning of the seventeenth century are printed on p. 326.)

Table 1. Investors in companies, according to social class.

Class	Number	Percent of total	Percent of those classified
Unclassified	1,152	18.2	–
Gentlemen	483	7.6	9.3
Knights	515	8.1	9.9
Peers	179	2.8	3.5
Merchants	3,810	60.1	73.5
Merchant knights	123	1.9	2.4
Professionals and yeomen	74	1.2	1.4
Total	6,336		

1,177 gentry and nobility represented approximately one in every 50 of their class who lived in England between 1575 and 1630. And the entire group of investors, 6,336, would represent about one in every 700 men in the nation, taking as the basis for calculation the estimate that England's male population in the two generations was roughly 4,500,000.[17] Such a large proportion, particularly among the landed classes, bespeaks the intensity of the enthusiasm that was generated during these years. But enthusiasm alone never could have achieved such results had means not been at hand to translate the will into the way. On their own, even in small groups, the 6,300 people would have been unable to sustain the costly and intricate undertakings of these years. And it would have been almost impossible to involve the non-merchants in large numbers if all of them had had to manage the details of their investments themselves. The solution for both problems was provided by a new kind of commercial organization, long since created in elementary form by the Italians, but imported to England only in the mid-sixteenth century — the joint-stock company.

[17] Most estimates seem to agree that, by the end of the period under discussion, England's population was 5,000,000 at most. For a recent calculation made for Charles I's reign, see Lawrence Stone, "The Educational Revolution in England, 1540–1640," *Past and Present*, no. 28 (July, 1964), p. 57. Taking into account the rise in population in the late sixteenth and early seventeenth centuries (Wilson, *England's Apprenticeship*, p. 13, suggests that it increased by 30 percent between 1600 and 1640 alone), 9,000,000 would probably be a maximum figure for the total inhabitants of the country during the two generations between 1575 and 1630. However, only males need be included in my figures because very few women — certainly less than 50 — were recorded as investors in commercial ventures.

The traditional organization, the regulated company, was clearly inadequate for the long-distance trades opening up in Elizabeth's reign. Though well suited for groups such as the Merchant Adventurers, it was too much like a guild to be useful for the new enterprises. By its very nature, despite the possession of a monopoly which gave it exclusive rights over the trade in some commodity or foreign country, the regulated company acted as little more than a licensing agency, supervising commerce without actually engaging in business activities itself. Its main purpose was to ensure that all participants in the monopoly were adequately trained for their profession: it admitted them to the fellowship and laid down rules to be observed for the common good. Individual profit and loss was of no concern to the company as a whole. The body acted *in toto* in such matters only when all the members were affected: when their privileges were threatened, when interlopers appeared, or when further benefits might be obtained from the Crown or foreign princes. Thus the regulated company offered little more than protection to its members: they still succeeded or failed on their own merits. In trade with the Continent such a procedure was perfectly adequate. Individual merchants, or small groups of them, could maintain a trade with the Netherlands, Germany, France, or Spain with little difficulty. No great resources were needed, and many of them could even afford to keep an agent in a foreign city. This was their livelihood and they could devote all their efforts to it; they welcomed the protection, yet absence of interference, provided by a regulated company.

The gentry, however, had no interest in organizations of this type. They had neither the time nor the inclination, let alone the skills, to manage their own trade, or to undertake the long apprenticeship that was necessary to qualify for membership. In the rare cases when a gentleman did join a regulated company in anything but an honorary capacity, he left the details in other hands. Thus the Earl of Leicester, though willing to take advantage of the membership in the Barbary Company he had obtained in return for ensuring the creation of a monopoly, evidently took no direct part in the trade. He contributed £3,000 out of the capital of £5,000 in a partnership with three other men, but the commercial dealings themselves were handled by his partners.[18] Such arrangements were possible in regulated companies, but they depended on personal, informal, and undependable connections which were totally inadequate for major undertakings.

The joint-stock company, on the other hand, was designed specifically to bring together larger funds than small groups could supply. Tremendous resources had to be assembled for Englishmen to embark on such costly and complicated ventures as trade with India. Entire fleets were needed, and they had to be supplied for voyages that could be 15 times as long and as dangerous each way as the journey to Spain, the furthest afield that even the most ambitious merchants had traveled hitherto. On the way to Russia or the North-West Passage the ships entered the Arctic circle, and in South America or the Far East they had to be prepared for the tropics. Completely novel circumstances had to be faced, and only by a pooling of effort and money could the enormous difficulties be overcome. Moreover, because each voyage was now a joint undertaking, embracing the investments of a large group of subscribers, the detailed management could no longer be left in the hands of each individual. Thus the company itself, abandoning the role as mere regulator, took over the direction of the trade. The officers, unlike their counterparts in regulated companies, directly controlled all the ventures that were launched. Skills were no longer required of members, and anyone with money to invest could partake of the profits. In this way, not only could the funds be raised for the most difficult enterprises, but non-merchant wealth could be drawn into commerce on an unprecedented scale.

The results of the creation of this new kind of organization speak for themselves. As Table 2 indicates, every organization in which the gentry (including knights and nobles) formed at least one-quarter of the classified membership was a joint-stock undertaking — run, with only a few exceptions, by merchants.

It will be seen that some of the groups with small memberships, and one or two of the larger ones, were composed almost entirely of gentry. There were a few determined nobles and gentlemen, such as the Earl of Warwick and Sir Ferdinando Gorges, who were fully capable of handling overseas or industrial ven-

[18] T. S. Willan, *Studies in Elizabethan Foreign Trade* (Manchester, 1959), pp. 189–190, 240–265.

Table 2. Companies in which gentry totaled at least 25 percent of classified membership.[a]

Company	Total number	Number classified (and percent of total)	Gentry members	Percent gentry among classified members
Africa	38	38 (100.0)	30	78.9
Bermuda	178	151 (84.8)	56	37.1[b]
Cavendish	4	4 (100.0)	4	100.0
Frobisher & Fenton	121	97 (80.2)	47	48.4[b]
Gilbert	146	134 (91.8)	72	53.8[c]
Gosnold	5	5 (100.0)	4	80.0
Guiana	105	92 (87.6)	78	84.8[d]
Hudson	24	24 (100.0)	9	37.5
Irish	762	680 (89.2)	180	26.5
Massachusetts Bay	122	82 (67.2)	26	31.6[e]
Minerals	77	75 (97.4)	36	48.0[e]
Mines	57	56 (98.3)	26	46.4[b]
New England	70	68 (97.1)	57	83.9[e]
Newfoundland	57	50 (87.7)	13	26.0
New River	31	31 (100.0)	11	35.5
North-West Passage	311	307 (98.7)	81	26.4[b]
Providence Island	20	20 (100.0)	17	85.0[d]
Virginia	1,684	1,252 (74.3)	560	44.7[e]
Weymouth	5	5 (100.0)	5	100.0
Other ventures	352	340 (96.6)	143	42.1[b]
Total[f]	4,169	3,511 (84.2)	1,455	41.4

[a] As is explained in Chapter 3, some of these groups, like the Guiana Company, include a succession of separate efforts with a common aim, and the "other ventures" category contains a large number of different small undertakings, mainly in industry. The complete figures for all companies are given in Table 11.

[b] Other non-merchants (professionals or yeomen) constituted a further 0.7 to 2.0 percent of the classified membership.

[c] Non-merchants constituted a further 9.0 percent.

[d] Non-merchants constituted a further 4.3 to 5.0 percent.

[e] Non-merchants constituted a further 2.5 to 3.7 percent.

[f] The totals, of course, represent total *memberships*, not total number of people

tures, and occasionally they organized an enterprise with little or no support from merchants. But such men were a small minority, and as soon as they were joined by other non-merchants they had to rely on a joint-stock company. Thus the Guiana, New England, Africa, and Providence Island Companies, which were almost exclusively gentry, divided their stock into shares and left the management of affairs to a few active entrepreneurs. By and

large, however, the companies listed in Table 2 were either
founded or run mainly by merchants. Their one common attribute (which enabled all of them to attract widespread gentry
support, regardless of the social class of the directors) was a
joint-stock organization. It is significant that when the remaining
companies in my data are included, the gentry's participation
drops from the 41 percent in Table 2 to the 23 percent indicated
in Table 1.

Most of the companies that do not appear in Table 2 were
regulated groups which contained almost no "gentlemen." The
Eastland, French, New Merchant Adventurer, Senegal, Levant,
Muscovy, Spanish, and Venice Companies admitted non-merchants only as honorary members who took no part in the trade.
Naturally, there were also joint-stock companies in which the
gentry did not amount to a substantial proportion. Merchants
were by profession more active in commerce, and it should be
no surprise to find that they constituted 95 percent of the adventurers in Drake's 1587 voyage, or over 85 percent of the East
India Company. What *is* surprising is that gentry should have
appeared in such large numbers in any companies at all. It is
worth noting that their 12 percent[19] of the classified membership
of the East India Company, a figure too small for inclusion in
Table 2, nonetheless represented 145 investors — a group larger
than the total size of all but 13 new companies in this period. Similarly, the 123 gentry who contributed toward privateering voyages amounted to only 17 percent of the classified subscribers.

The purposes for which a company was formed also exercised
a major influence on its composition. While merchants could be
attracted to almost any undertaking that promised a profit, the
gentry were particularly interested in colonization and spectacular explorations, such as the search for the North-West Passage.
Only two of the companies founded in this period with the aim of
colonization or exploration do not appear in Table 2, and they are
minor exceptions. The backers of Baffin amounted to a mere eight
people, the remnants of a large company which had become disil-
lusioned with the prospect of finding a sea route around North
America. Only the most enthusiastic supporters of the scheme

[19] A further 1.9 percent of the classified members were non-merchant professionals and yeomen.

maintained their efforts, and gentlemen were rarely noted for their perseverance in such enterprises. Thus Sir Dudley Digges, an indefatigable investor, was the sole representative of his social class to help set forth Baffin's expedition. The other exception, the Plymouth adventurers, may be the result of the elusiveness of the people involved: 31 of the 49 subscribers proved to be unclassifiable, a proportion (63 percent) almost double that of the next most inadequately documented company. Of the 18 classified members, three were gentry, but the sample is too small to be an accurate indication of the composition of the total group.

The purely trading enterprises interested noticeably fewer gentlemen. This was mainly, but not entirely, due to their usual organization as regulated companies. Had the structure been the only consideration, the landed classes presumably would have joined the Levant and Muscovy Companies during the periods when they traded in a joint stock. But in fact the gentry appeared only when these companies were originally founded, amid great expectations and fanfare, and they paid them little attention thereafter. The relatively low proportion of non-merchants in the East India Company may also have been a consequence of its predominantly commercial aims. Only six gentry subscribed to the first joint stock, and only three more joined the company before 1609. Almost a hundred then became members during the decade between 1609 and 1619, and, as has been mentioned, this was certainly a large number of non-merchants, but it was definitely below the relative level of enthusiasm that colonizing and exploring companies were able to arouse. In the case of the East India Company it may also have been of some importance that shares were very expensive. Though the gentry were happy to buy stocks, most of them were not so ready to pay the £200 or more that became virtually a minimum investment — especially when £12 10s. could entitle a man to 100 acres of land in Virginia.

This last point raises the question of where the money for their investments came from. Some gentlemen were clearly using the surplus that was coming to landowners from rising rents and agricultural profits during our period; others, such as John Chudley, Thomas Cavendish, and Anthony Cook, sold family lands and squandered their estates; still others — such as Sir Percival Willoughby — were making a broad-ranging effort, including investments in industrial enterprises, to better their fortunes; and a great many like Lord Baltimore were using the profits of office for overseas ventures.[20] Of the amounts actually spent — outlined in Table 5 — the large majority undoubtedly came from office-holders and great nobles. The plain country gentleman rarely gave more than small sums; Sir Edwin Sandys was the only notable exception to this rule. The bulk of the gentry's funds were supplied by the lavish investments of a few peers like the Earl of Cumberland, and by such men as Raleigh, who could draw resources from royal favor. Even the Virginia Company's incom-

[20] See Eric Kerridge, "The Movement of Rent, 1540–1640," *Ec.H.R.*, 2nd ser., 6 (1953), 16–34, especially pp. 28–29, 34; R. H. Tawney, *The Agrarian Problem in the Sixteenth Century* (London, 1912), especially pp. 115–121, 139–147, 192–200, 304–310, 403–404; *The Agrarian History of England and Wales*, vol. IV: *1500–1640*, ed. Joan Thirsk (Cambridge, England, 1967), especially pp. 110, 161–162, 196, 199, 204–205, 211, 291–292, 435, 587, 593–685, and 814–865; M. E. Finch, *The Wealth of Five Northamptonshire Families, 1540–1640* (Oxford: Northamptonshire Record Society, 1956), especially pp. xiv, 173, 181, 196; Alan Simpson, *The Wealth of the Gentry, 1540–1640: East Anglian Studies* (Cambridge and Chicago, 1961), pp. 153–156, 179–216; J. U. Nef, *The Rise of the British Coal Industry*, vol. I (London, 1932), pp. 322–326; F. J. Fisher, "The Sixteenth and Seventeenth Centuries: The Dark Ages in English Economic History?" *Economica*, new ser., 24 (1957), 2–18, especially pp. 15–16; the evidence on agricultural profits in note 96 below; K. R. Andrews, *Elizabethan Privateering* (Cambridge, England, 1964), pp. 67–70; and Cell, "Newfoundland," pp. 208–209. Another direction in which extra money was newly spent in this period was in the building and redecorating of homes: see Lawrence Stone, *The Crisis of the Aristocracy, 1558–1641* (Oxford, 1965), pp. 549–55; C. W. Chalklin, *Seventeenth-Century Kent: A Social and Economic History* (London, 1965), pp. 204–205; and Simpson, *Wealth of the Gentry*, pp. 161, 166. Similar evidence of a vastly increased rate of building and house improvements between 1575 and 1625, made possible by agricultural profits, can be found in W. G. Hoskins, "The Rebuilding of Rural England, 1570–1640," in his *Provincial England: Essays in Social and Economic History* (London, 1963), pp. 131–148; in *Agrarian History*, ed. Thirsk, pp. 696–813, especially pp. 711–712, 737–752, 761–766, and 788–789; and in M. W. Barley, *The English Farmhouse and Cottage* (London, 1961), which discusses (pp. 57–179) "The Housing Revolution, 1575–1642," when there was a great deal of new building, particularly before 1615. See also Lawrence Stone, "The Fruits of Office: The Case of Robert Cecil, First Earl of Salisbury, 1596–1612," in *Essays in the Economic and Social History of Tudor and Stuart England in Honour of R. H. Tawney*, ed. F. J. Fisher (Cambridge, England, 1961), pp. 89–116. Finally, it might be noted that there was also a marked acceleration in industrial activity in this period. As Nef, *British Coal Industry*, I, 76, remarks: "From all the coalfields comes overwhelming evidence between 1550 and 1610 of a feverish interest in the discovery and development of mineral resources." He adds that many landed gentry were seeking in this way to bolster their incomes and that "the period of maximum rapidity of growth appears to be the reign of James I" (I, 77). The gentry's activity is illustrated by numerous examples throughout the remainder of Nef's two volumes.

plete lists show that every one of the gentry investors of £50 or more (except for Sandys) came from these two categories. In terms of numbers, one finds every element in the landed classes represented; in terms of capital, the large majority came from those with the readiest supply of money, the peers and the office-holders.

It might be added that, except for the few who invested in the East India Company, just about all of them lost everything they subscribed. Though participating in the growth of England's commerce in this period, the gentry seemed to receive a dispro-portionately small share of the profits. However, until more de-tailed studies on the precise number of officeholders are done, and until the total effects of the losses can be more exactly as-sessed, it is impossible to say whether their contribution to the ex-pansion supports either the "rising" or the "declining" gentry thesis. Nor, with the exception of a few enterprises such as the Providence Island Company, can one make a clear-cut distinction between "in" and "out" groups. My impression is that gentlemen ruining themselves in a tremendous effort to improve their finances were a very small minority; most of the landed investors were obviously subscribing a few extra pounds they happened to have to spare. Although the former provided most of the money, the latter provided most of the numbers; and, since their losses probably meant little to this second group, one suspects that their participation is an indication that, on the whole, the gentry were doing better rather than worse. As for "ins" versus "outs," so many of both groups were involved (and provided such large sums of money) that it would be pointless to argue that commit-ment to the expansion was a reflection of political attitudes, at least before Charles I's reign. Both courtiers and malcontents were liberally represented in nearly every major company until the late 1620's, when, as will be suggested below, a new phase of overseas enterprise began. During the main period of expansion, lasting through the mid-1620's, no meaningful differentiation is possible.

To the merchants, of course, what counted was that they were gaining assistance — and often inspiration — from a group of their countrymen, the gentry, whose interest in commerce pre-viously had been virtually nonexistent.

34

Stimulated by propaganda and tales of fame and fortune whenever they came to London, presented through the joint-stock company with the opportunity to take part in England's expansion simply by paying a few pounds, the upper classes of society began to contribute their wealth to the vast financial resources that were essential for momentous new undertakings at home and overseas. But the alliance between business and land was never easy. For all the long familiarity between the two classes, for all the constant cross-fertilization between them — not only through marriage, but also through the migration of rich merchants to the countryside and younger sons to the towns — and for all their centuries-old association in the House of Commons, the distinctions between them clearly remained. The differences in their respective efforts during these years are significant and revealing.

III. MERCHANTS AND GENTRY

Motives and Activities. There was no doubt in the minds of contemporaries that two quite separate social groups were combining in overseas enterprise. In 1583, writing in support of a project for the colonization of Newfoundland, Sir George Peckham considered it "convenient that I do divide the adventurers into two sorts: the noblemen and gentlemen by themselves, and the merchants by themselves." [21] He said he had heard that in fact two companies were going to be established, one for each class. And he shaped the propaganda accordingly. For the gentry he stressed the fine climate, the conditions favorable to landowners, the crops that could be produced, and the excellent hunting, including a description of a moose. For the merchants he provided a list of over 70 commodities which could bring them profit — with leopards, silkworms, pepper, and rubies quite unabashedly claimed for fair Newfoundland.[22] This was the popular impression of the differences between the aims and interests of the two classes, and it was fairly accurate in gauging the temper of most merchants, whose prime concern was, naturally, for trade. But

[21] *Enterprises of Gilbert,* ed. Quinn, II, 463. As background to the following discussion, which deals with the different concerns of the various classes, the reader is referred to the chapter "The Structure of Class Aspirations" in W. K. Jordan, *The Charities of London, 1480–1660: The Aspirations and the Achievements of the Urban Society* (London, 1960), pp. 47–85.

[22] *Enterprises of Gilbert,* ed. Quinn, II, 463–465. It should be noted, though, that he included the entire area of North America between 30° and 60°N.

the "hunting, planting, and fishing" impression of the gentry reflected a small minority, because few in the landed class invested money (as opposed to service) with any real intention of setting up house overseas. Cheap land was an attractive inducement, and it certainly had more relevance to the gentleman than to the merchant. Yet its direct appeal was to very few of the investors under discussion here. Land hunger was extremely important to the man who adventured in person, but it had less influence on the subscriber of a few pounds who stayed at home. For the latter other ends held greater significance.

The two motives besides profit mentioned by Sir Francis Drake — glory and missionary work — were, to judge by the stress they received in the literature of the time, of major importance. In addition, there were a host of lesser motives. Looking around crowded London, it was no wonder that Sir John Hawkins could bend even poetry to his service to complain about

> . . . England that is pestered now and choked through want of
> ground, . . .
> . . . England, where no room remains, her dwellers to bestow,
> But shuffled in such pinching bonds, that very breath doth lack:
> And for the want of place they crawl one o'er another's back.[23]

The obvious answer seemed to be to send the excess population to colonies. Others argued that overseas enterprise was a nursery of seamen, that it provided raw materials the country needed, that it stimulated shipbuilding, that it lowered prices at home, or that it lessened England's dependence on foreigners. Sir William Alexander, reiterating Peckham's concern, appealed to the love of hunting as a way to raise support,[24] and similar detailed arguments seemed to carry weight in many individual cases. It would be impossible to create a complete picture of the aims of all 6,336 investors. Every man had his own reasons for offering his money, and it is pointless to try to ascribe precise degrees of importance to this multitude of motives. Nonetheless, one basic distinction

[23] *Ibid.*, pp. 438–439: on fol. 1 in the original. The contrary view, that England's population was hardly sufficient to support colonization, is of more recent vintage: see especially pp. 521–527 of E. P. Cheyney, "Some English Conditions Surrounding the Settlement of Virginia," *American Historical Review*, 12 (1907), 507–528.

[24] Cited in K. E. Knorr, *British Colonial Theories, 1570–1850* (Toronto, 1944), p. 27.

can be made: it is clear that the two main classes of subscribers were moved by rather different purposes. In this respect Peckham was undoubtedly right.

Historians usually assess the reasons that these projects were undertaken by detailing the various motives, illustrating each one by examples from tracts, broadsides, and sermons.[25] The result is that, although one gains a clear idea of the arguments that were used and their relative importance, one is not too sure of the different effect these appeals might have had on different people. Since the same exhortations and promises were usually listed — in changing orders — in all the propaganda of the time, one can only assume that most people found something worthwhile in most of the sentiments expressed by the pamphleteers. Thus the benefit to be gained by ridding the commonwealth of unwanted inhabitants probably made sense to just about everyone, as did the increase of shipping, and so on. Few investors can have been impelled to join a company for such reasons alone, though they might well have persuaded a shipbuilder. It is only when one turns to the fundamental ambitions mentioned by Drake that one comes to motives which obviously had a decisive and universal appeal; and here the gentry can be distinguished most noticeably from the merchants.

It was not without significance that Drake, a newly created knight, should have ordered his poem to discuss fame before he turned his attention to gold. As was shown above, the composition of the companies reveals that trade alone, despite its more reliable assurance of profit, could not attract the gentry as easily as could a colony or an exploration. Certainly they were interested in making money — they would not have been concerned with im-

---

[25] See, for examples, *ibid.*, chap. ii, pp. 26–62; Howard Mumford Jones, "The Colonial Impulse: An Analysis of the 'Promotion' Literature of Colonization," *Proceedings of the American Philosophical Society*, 90 (1946), 131–61; and Wright, *Religion and Empire*. The best brief survey of this subject is in C. M. Andrews, *The Colonial Period of American History* (4 vols.; New Haven, 1934–1938), I, 53–77, though the evidence does not support so strong an emphasis on land hunger. The most detailed exposition stressing economic motives is in G. L. Beer, *The Origins of the British Colonial System, 1578–1660* (2nd ed., New York, 1922). A catalogue of some 1,500 surviving books and manuscripts dealing with geography and overseas expansion, all written in our period, can be found in Taylor, *Late Tudor and Early Stuart Geography*, pp. 192–298; the arguments of the most important among these books are summarized and set in context by Parker, *Books to Build an Empire*.

proving their estates, raising their rents, or starting industries if they had not wanted to increase their income.[26] But they rarely if ever came to depend on commerce for their livelihood. There was a glamour in overseas enterprise that inspired motives beyond the desire for profits.

The motivation of the merchant was generally less complicated. He did rely on trade for his living, and the return on his investment had to be his chief concern. There were exceptions, of course, at the very highest levels of the mercantile class. A man as rich as Sir Thomas Smith, for instance, could afford to aspire to lofty ends, with no immediate gain in mind. His attitudes, and those of other leading merchant entrepreneurs, could be as grandiose as any nobleman's. In fact many of the most visionary pioneers did come from the merchant class, and their support was often vital for the survival of a company; but they were the exceptions. It was significant that in 1609, when expectations ran high, merchants outnumbered gentry by more than two to one among those who joined the Virginia Company; but during the next three years, when new investors continued to appear in substantial numbers despite a total absence of profits, the gentry outnumbered the merchants by over two to one. Two-thirds of all merchant subscribers joined the company before the end of 1609; over 60 percent of the gentry were to join after 1609.[27] Although

[26] See Stone, *Crisis of the Aristocracy*, especially chaps. iv, vi, vii. Many gentry undoubtedly hoped to find quick riches in the schemes of the period — as Cell, "Newfoundland," p. 130, stresses with regard to that colony. But on the one hand most of them devoted too little attention to their investments to qualify as people avidly pursuing profit; and on the other hand the more persistent among them, such as Gilbert, Gorges, Sandys, or Baltimore, were usually conspicuous examples of men who were pursuing ideals beyond the financial rewards. Drake's pitiful cry, "We must have gold before we see England," uttered amidst the bleak despair of his disastrous last voyage, was an affirmation of the gentleman-adventurer's crucial need, not for riches, but for glory. See Thomas Maynarde, *Sir Francis Drake His Voyage, 1595*, ed. W. D. Cooley (London: The Hakluyt Society, 1849), p. 19.

[27] This may have been due in part to the fact that in its final six years (1619–1624) the company was controlled by gentry. Even in this last period, however, in terms of total numbers, new merchant members were almost as numerous as new gentry members. The change was in their relative strengths, and there can be little doubt that the commercial classes were far less ready than were gentlemen to subscribe in large numbers to enterprises that promised advantage to the nation but little profit. The gentry fell only too frequently into the pattern, later described by John Pym, of the man who gave money but received no return, who "was accounted a great patriot, but scarce a wise adventurer": quoted in H. C. Wilkinson, *The Adventurers of Bermuda* (London, 1958), p. 227. Much

the early prospect of great riches had faded, the landed classes could still be impelled — more easily than could large numbers of merchants — to invest in a great national enterprise.

An awareness of England's "destiny" was naturally strongest among gentlemen and peers who, by their very position in society, were more attuned to currents of feeling at Court and in the country than were businessmen in towns. The original impulse for gentry participation in commerce came from leading members of the government and great nobles whose principal occupation was the service of the Queen and the realm. The semiofficial atmosphere that surrounded some of their early efforts, particularly the exploits directed against Spain, only served to strengthen the impression that they were acting for the public benefit.

One needs only to turn from the minutes of the staid and solidly merchant East India Company to the records of the exuberantly hopeful and optimistic Virginia Company to appreciate the difference. The great trading corporation pursued its profits singlemindedly. Discussions of national prestige were entirely absent: in fact, it had to be reminded by the government of its

of the propaganda for colonization and exploration, in which most of the gentry's investments were made, stressed that profits would not be immediate and that a long wait might be necessary. See *Nova Britannia* (1609) in *Tracts*, ed. Force, vol. I, no. 6, pp. 12–13; *A True Declaration of the Estate of the Colonie in Virginia* (1610) in *ibid.*, vol. III, no. 1, pp. 21–23; and Richard Eburne, *A Plaine Pathway to Plantations* (London, 1624), pp. 32–38, where the subscriber is warned (p. 37) that "a great store of treasure and wealth must be spent, and many years of time be overpassed" before profits can be expected. As Bacon put it in his essay, *Of Plantations,* "the principal thing that hath been the destruction of most plantations, hath been the base and hasty drawing of profit in the first years." He then went on to draw the distinction between the classes that has been stressed above, for he recommended that the leaders of such enterprises "be rather noblemen and gentlemen, than merchants; for they look ever to the present gain." See *The Works of Francis Bacon,* ed. James Spedding, R. L. Ellis, and D. D. Heath (15 vols.; Cambridge, 1863), XII, 194, 197. George Best, writing in 1578, agreed: merchants, unlike nobles, "never regard virtue without sure, certain, and present gains." (See below, note 30.) The only tract I know that used a detailed financial analysis to persuade potential investors that large profits could be made from a colony was Richard Whitbourne's *A Discourse Containing a Loving Invitation . . . for the advancement of his Majesties most hopefull Plantation in the New-found-land* (London, 1622) — and this piece of propaganda had no success at all in attracting subscribers. F. J. Fisher has shown ("London's Export Trade," pp. 156–60) that merchants did have one major financial reason for backing new overseas ventures: the stimulus given to England's rapidly growing re-export trade by colonies and new markets. In these early years, however, most of the capital used to build up re-exports was concentrated in trade with the Mediterranean. (*Ibid.*, pp. 153–55, 158.) See, too, note 95 below.

national obligations; and even the tracts written in its behalf dealt more with economics than glory.[28] The literature relating to the Virginia Company, on the other hand, was full of the most lofty and ambitious sentiments: Indians were going to be converted, Spain was going to be frustrated, and England's fame was going to be spread abroad.[29]

The ambition to enhance the country's prestige seems to have been particularly strong in the major colonial and anti-Spanish undertakings, where the leading roles were usually played by gentry and such exceptional merchants as Sir Thomas Smith. The one colony that was regarded by its managers as an investment pure and simple was the Londonderry Plantation, which was established comfortably close to home by the careful investors of the London Livery Companies. For the rest, it was clear that the contest with Spain and other great empires was constantly in mind. In 1599, after decades of fruitless effort had passed, Edwin Sandys, who was soon to be a leader of overseas enterprise himself, commented sadly that the southern European countries seemed to have not only a "greater opportunity to traffic to all parts of the world," but also a superiority in "fineness and subtlety of wit" in this endeavor. He laid his feelings bare when he added "Neither have the Northern people ever yet for all their multitude and strength, had the honour of being founders or possessors of any great Empire, so unequal is the combat between force and wit, in all matters of durable and grounded establishment."[30] A

[28] For example, Sir Dudley Digges, *The Defence of Trade* (London, 1615). A major part of his argument rests on the importance of the company's contribution to England's shipping industry. Talk of national enterprise usually had to come from without, as when Elizabeth urged the members to be more vigorous for the sake of the country's honor — see note 108, below.

[29] See the examples reprinted in Brown, *Genesis of the United States.*

[30] Edwin Sandys, *Europae Speculum: Or A View or Survey of the State of Religion* (The Hague, 1629; I cite from this edition of *A Relation of the State of Religion* [London, 1605] because it was the first one paginated), pp. 187–88. Similar views had been expressed 20 years before by George Best, in his *A True Discourse of the Late Voyages of Discoverie, for the Finding of a Passage to Cathaya, by the Northweast, under the Conduct of Martin Frobisher* (London, 1578) — reprinted in *The Three Voyages of Martin Frobisher*, ed. Vilhjalmur Stefansson and Eloise McCaskill (2 vols.; London, 1938), I, 1–129. See especially pp. 7–9, where "lack of liberality in the Nobility" is blamed for England's backwardness — the only other national defect mentioned being the absence of skill in cosmography and navigation. Best piously believed that the failings had now been overcome because the Queen herself and all the nobility had "perfect knowledge in cosmography," and "with their purses do liberally and

decade later a pamphleteer advertising the Virginia colony was still saying enviously that the Spanish monarchs "have extended their dominions, increased their trade, enriched their subjects and their overflowing treasure . . . [and given] strength and reputation to their kingdom." [31] Comparisons could be drawn with Rome and Athens,[32] but ultimately it was always the Spanish Empire that irked Englishmen most, with their memories of San Juan de Ulua and the Armada. And here again the average merchant, conscious of the value of the lucrative trade with Spain in wine and other commodities, tended to part company with the gentleman. The more than 1,000 members of the two short-lived Spanish Companies amounted to more than one-quarter of all the merchants in my list. They comprised a substantial bloc of traders whose sentiments doubtless fell short of the gentry's enthusiasm for schemes that aimed to supplant the Spaniards in America.

Every indication suggests that, in the spectrum of motives that inspired the expansion, the gentry were closer to the vision of national enterprise, whereas the merchants were closer to the concern for profits. Other influences, such as religious aims, seem to have crossed class boundaries; and there were a few individual aims like landowning or personal fame that may well have appealed more to a gentleman than to a merchant. But the basic distinction was clearly in the importance attached to long-range goals. To dismiss references to England's prestige as "hackneyed" clichés, carrying little weight,[33] is to ignore a wave whose force

---

bountifully contribute unto the same." John Dee was also at this time dreaming "of England as mistress of the Northern Empire based on a command of the seas." See W. I. Trattner, "God and Expansion in Elizabethan England: John Dee, 1527–1583," *Journal of the History of Ideas,* 25 (1964), 17–34, especially p. 25. Although the Hakluyts' expectation that England could emulate the Iberian nations by establishing colonies did not appear in print until 1582, when the younger Richard's first book, *Divers Voyages to America,* was published, they had doubtless been promulgating their ideas earlier: see Taylor, *Late Tudor and Early Stuart Geography,* pp. 1–3. Other early examples of English envy of Spain are cited on pp. 509–510 of Cheyney, "Settlement of Virginia."

[31] *New Britain,* reprinted in Brown, *Genesis of the United States,* I, 264.

[32] For example, by John Hawkins in his verse in Peckham's *True Report,* in *Enterprises of Gilbert,* ed. Quinn, II, 438–39. For evidence of the Spanish Company merchants' dislike of England's official hostility toward Spain, mentioned below, see *CSP, Spanish, 1580–1586,* pp. 19, 130, 208–209, 283, 385–386.

[33] Knorr, *Colonial Theories,* pp. 27–28. In contrast, the noticeable difference between the two classes is admirably summed up by K. R. Andrews in his introduction to *English Privateering Voyages to the West Indies 1588–1595* (Cambridge, England: The Hakluyt Society, 1959), p. 22, where he writes that "even

is revealed in every aspect of the differences between gentry and merchant investors.

The wish not to have to manage one's trade oneself was the most obvious mark of a man not overwhelmingly concerned with profits alone. But the attraction of gentlemen to joint-stock companies was not the only sign of this relative indifference. Social class can often be determined by the answer to the question — did a person regard London, or any of the great ports, as his usual residence? Sir Edwin Sandys, for all his deep involvement in trade as a leader of the Virginia, Somers Islands, and East India Companies, still spent most of his time, like a true gentleman, at his country home in Kent. He kept in touch with London by correspondence. But Sir Thomas Smith, for all his love of the estate he had bought in Kent, where he chose to die and be buried, maintained his famous house in Philpot Lane as a center of London's company business to the end of his life. This difference was felt most keenly by the Virginia Company, which attracted by far the largest number of gentry subscribers and officers. In 1623 the General Court even adopted a resolution, recorded in the minutes, which stated quite frankly that "since the nobility and gentry are most of them absent in the vacation when yet diverse weighty and urgent businesses happen, The Council therefore in supply thereof have thought fit that four should be chosen of the Council such as their continual living in town doth promise they will be very careful of the business." [34]

Another significant distinction between the classes was in their

---

when plunder was the main object, . . . fame and honour were also prized. . . . Thus such [gentry] ventures were not strictly business enterprise in the sense that merchants' ventures usually were."

[34] S. M. Kingsbury, *The Records of the Virginia Company of London* (4 vols.; Washington, 1906–1935), II, 447–448. See also I, 555. Note, too, the provision in the charter of the Newfoundland Company, cited in note 7 above. The Bermuda Company dispensed with all meetings of the General Court during long vacations — see J. H. Lefroy, *Memorials of the Discovery and Early Settlement of the Bermudas or Somers Islands, 1515–1685*, vol. I: *1515–1652* (London, 1877), p. 185. R. G. Lang, "The Greater Merchants of London in the Early Seventeenth Century" (unpub. diss., Oxford University, 1963), pp. 302–303 and 344–356, points out that London's aldermen, despite considerable wealth and landholdings, rarely retired to the country. Most of their friends were Londoners, and they preferred to remain in the city until they died. Their buying of land would seem to have been for economic rather than immediate social gain. See, too, T. S. Willan, *The Muscovy Merchants of 1555* (Manchester, 1953), pp. 72–73; and Simpson, *Wealth of the Gentry*, p. 131.

age and continuity of interest. The merchant started his commercial activities very young, frequently no later than his midteens. Either he became a servant, usually to a relative in one of the trading organizations, or he started out as an apprentice in one of the Livery Companies. From then on, because it was his living, his efforts continued unabated. But gentry promoters, even the most determined among them, generally began their activities at a much later age: Chief Justice Popham not until his fifty's, Sandys not until his forty's, Gorges only in his thirty's, and Raleigh and Gilbert when they were over 25. Furthermore, very few of the gentry were as committed to the expansion as the five who have just been mentioned. Most of them were what can be called the passive men, people who were content merely to offer their money and then leave it to others to manage their investment. In Elizabeth's reign the percentage of active gentry participants was undoubtedly higher, because the large companies were not yet founded and individual exploits were more important; but this, in turn, only meant that total numbers of subscribers were much smaller, and that only the leaders of the movement had become involved at this stage. When the great influx of investors began in James I's reign, the passive gentry formed a large majority of their class. Their very lack of concern with the immediate results of their contribution testifies to the influence of aims other than the making of money. Moreover, even when profit and glory coincided, and when the gentry's effort became famous, as it did in privateering, one finds the merchants to have been in control.[35]

For all the impetus provided by Elizabeth's Court and a few notable promoters, gentlemen were never as persistent or consistent in their endeavors as the merchants. Their absences from London might suggest less than complete dedication, and distribution figures confirm the impression. Only 28 percent of the

[35] Andrews, *Elizabethan Privateering*, pp. 61–123. It was characteristic for Raleigh to claim, in support of his Guiana projects, two basic motives: "I have . . . laboured all my life . . . to advance all those attempts, that might either promise return of profit to ourselves, or at least be a let and impeachment to the quiet course and plentiful trades of the Spanish nation." See his *The Discoverie of the large, rich, and beautiful Empire of Guiana*, reprinted in Richard Hakluyt, *The Principal Navigations, Voyages, Traffiques & Discoveries of the English Nation* (12 vols.; Glasgow: The Hakluyt Society, 1903–1905), X, 347–348: fol. 4a in the 1596 ed.

gentry investors joined more than one company; among the merchants, a much larger body of subscribers,[36] the proportion was 35 percent. To illustrate how the activity of non-merchants was dominated by the upper classes, it might be noted that the figure for plain gentlemen was 18 percent, for knights 28 percent, and for nobles 57 percent.

It must be remembered, too, that despite their associations with commerce the landed classes still retained some of the contempt for trade which characterized this stratum of society throughout Europe. The Renaissance ideal of the courtier stressed other pursuits, and the merchant's profession was never held in the highest esteem. Particularly noteworthy in this connection was the attitude in 1604 of Dudley Digges, who soon was to become a prominent member of no less than eight companies and a director of three. Writing in that year in a book which he dedicated to another future leader of commercial enterprise, Theophilus Howard Lord Walden, Digges complained of the "slothful life" of "our decayed gentry." The only remedy he could advocate was war, because "to play the merchants was only for gentlemen of Florence, Venice or the like." [37] Nevertheless, the Italians were dictating the manners of the aristocracy throughout Europe; and

[36] They outnumbered gentry seven to two, as can be seen in Table 1. It is worth pointing out that the merchants' distribution was top-heavy: 80 percent of merchant knights invested in two or more companies. If the figures for average number of companies per investor are calculated, the merchant knights appear as far and away the most active subscribers: they joined 3.7 companies each, whereas even the peers, the most active gentry, joined only 2.6 companies each. On average, therefore, the merchant knights had over 70 percent more investments than the group closest to them, the nobles. Reference to Table 3 will reveal how far ahead of the other members of their classes the merchant knights and nobles were. See also notes 54 and 57 and Table 18.

[37] Dudley Digges, *Four Paradoxes, or Politique Discourses* (London, 1604), pp. 77–79. This conclusion, according to Digges, was the result of 15 years' thought and five years' study! (*Ibid.*, p. 77.) Eleven years later he was to conclude a defense of the East India Company by stressing that he was a friend and kinsman of Sir Thomas Smith, and that he "wisheth well to Trade and Merchants." See his *Defence of Trade*, p. 50.

See, too, the quotations from writers who deplored the rise of merchants at the expense of gentry in A. B. Stonex, "Money Lending and Money-Lenders in England during the 16th and 17th Centuries," *Schelling Anniversary Papers* (New York, 1923), pp. 263–85, especially pp. 270–71. Edward Misselden, in *Free Trade* . . . (London, 1622), pp. 12–13, saw serious economic consequences stemming from the breakdown of social hierarchies, now that "most men live about their callings, and promiscuously step forth *Vice versa* into one anothers *Ranks.*"

soon English gentry were imitating these urban patricians as devotedly in this respect as they did when they admired the sonnet and italic script.

Because merchants were instinctively deeply committed to trade, they also tended to be much more serious and purposeful than the gentry. The contrast between the East India and Virginia Companies has been mentioned, but it is equally clear among individual investors. One does not find businessmen making gestures like the Earl of Southampton's response to his admission to the East India Company: a few weeks after his membership became official, the minutes recorded "a brace of bucks sent by the Earl of Southampton to the Company 'to make merry withal, in regard of their kindness in accepting him of their company.'" The staid merchants at once appointed a committee to organize the merriment. Three months later, determined not to be outdone by Southampton, Lord Monteagle promised the company a brace of bucks once a year in return for his admission.[38]

The merchants, in turn, were fully aware of the advantages of enlisting the support of courtiers and powerful noblemen. In the reigns of the first two Stuarts, when the House of Commons was repeatedly investigating monopolies and the Crown had little compunction about interfering in company affairs,[39] the merchants needed all the protection they could get. The Levant

[38] *CSP, East Indies, 1513–1616*, pp. 185, 196. In strong contrast to this panache was the solemnity of the East India merchants when faced by the peccadillos of one of their most able sailors, an event recorded in the minutes as "Imputations upon Capt. Saris for certain lascivious books and pictures brought home by him, a great scandal to the Company, and unbecoming their gravity to permit." (*Ibid.*, p. 357.)

[39] The experiences of the East India, Levant, and Virginia Companies were typical instances of such interference. See K. N. Chaudhuri, *The English East India Company* (London, 1965), pp. 30–31; S. A. Khan, *The East India Trade in the XVIIth Century in Its Political and Economic Aspects* (London, 1923), pp. 69–76; A. C. Wood, *A History of the Levant Company* (Oxford, 1935), pp. 38–40, 83–89; W. F. Craven, *Dissolution of the Virginia Company* (New York, 1932), pp. 142–144, 261ff. See also J. A. Williamson, *The Caribbee Islands under the Proprietary Patents* (London, 1926), pp. 39–63, for the far more damaging intervention in the colonization of the West Indies; and, for a good brief survey of the entire subject, Robert Ashton, "Charles I and the City," *Essays in Honour of R. H. Tawney*, pp. 135–163. It is customary when discussing England's expansion to give the government little credit for the achievements of this period: e.g., Christopher Hill, *The Century of Revolution, 1603–1714* (Edinburgh, 1961), pp. 40–41. For Elizabeth's reign this clearly would be an unfair conclusion; but even the early Stuarts were not as completely unhelpful as they are often pictured. Craven, *Virginia Company*, pp. 260–261, describes the depend-

Company even appointed a special committee to watch proceedings in Parliament and the Privy Council.[40] But the admission of prominent gentlemen was a far more effective way of influencing events in Westminster and Whitehall. In 1614 Sir James Stonehouse, "one of the King's privy chamber," was admitted gratis by the East India Company which was "willing to have some such their friends about the King that should be tied unto them by some kindness, especially against this time of the Parliament." A few days later Sir Henry Neville received a similar favor, because it was known that he was "a very worthy gentleman, and may do many good offices for the good of the Company." And Dr. Leonard Poe, who had taken care of the Earl of Salisbury, was not even allowed to transfer his "freedom" to a friend. "Knowing how near he is about the noblemen at court," the merchants thought it better to grant a new freedom to the friend, and keep the Court doctor as a member.[41] The admission of a group of

ence of all colonial efforts on some measure of encouragement from the Crown. In terms of cash support, although the royal family made very few investments themselves (they subscribed half the funds of the New River Company and were interested in the East India Company, Prince Henry was interested in Guiana in 1609, and Charles contributed a ship to Fox's expedition in search of the Northwest Passage), their courtiers were just as active as Elizabeth's. The East India Company proudly asserted in 1618 that it included "the greatest part of the Privy Council" (CSP, East Indies, 1617–1621, p. 185); and the Africa, Guiana, and Virginia Companies, and the New England Council, were only the most conspicuous examples of organizations with substantial support from leading courtiers.

[40] Second Court Book (PRO: S.P. 105/148), fol. 50. In the same year, 1621, the East India Company requested Sir Thomas Smith "to give a note of the names of the officers about the King's Majesty, and noblemen whose friendship this Company shall continually stand in need of." See CSP, East Indies, 1617–1621, p. 492. In 1623 Nicholas Ferrar compiled a list of members of the Virginia Company in the House of Commons — see Kingsbury, Records, IV, 157. Even more graphic is the bland entry in the East India Company's minutes, early in December 1619 (CSP, East Indies, 1617–1621, p. 329): "Gratifications and gifts to be offered at Christmas to 'some lords and other officers of whose countenance and favour the Company stand in need; 1,000l. the most that hath been formerly given, although the general opinion for 4,000l. or 5,000l.;' committee to consider thereon." Even in the early seventeenth century people seem to have been aware of the commercial side of the Christmas spirit, but, like everything else, the cost of bribery was always going up.

[41] CSP, East Indies, 1513–1616, pp. 285, 288, 276. These sentiments were echoed by the Levant Company when William Trumbull was admitted free in 1618 because he was clerk to the Privy Council and promised to do service to the company at home and abroad. See the Second Court Book (PRO: S.P. 105/148), fol. 12. A similar motive clearly lay behind the common procedure of granting "freedoms" to prominent lawyers. Sir Edward Coke, for example, was never an active member of the Spanish Company, and his admission was un-

"lords, knights and gentlemen, favorers of the Company" on the same day as the granting of the new charter which extended their monopoly into perpetuity, cannot have been mere coincidence.[42] The Muscovy Company had appreciated the advantages of support in high places over 50 years before, when over a quarter of the members listed in its founding charter had been non-merchant courtiers. And throughout the rest of our period the great trading companies remained only too willing to admit any gentleman who showed an interest in their affairs.

Though primarily interested in political assistance, the merchants were certainly not loath to tap the additional resources that gentlemen could provide. The historian of the Muscovy Company, T. S. Willan, has made the point succinctly. Speaking of the "unprecedented" numbers of courtiers and nobles who undoubtedly helped the company obtain its charter, he adds that it is "difficult to believe that their presence was unconnected with the fact that the company was a joint-stock company in which they could invest their capital without having to play an active part in the management of the trade." As has been mentioned, this was clearly a major factor in bringing the gentry into commerce at all. But in the purely trading organizations like the Muscovy, Levant, and East India Companies, their contribution appears to have been more political than financial. Willan himself has to admit that "there is no evidence . . . that these peers and office holders took any active part in the company's affairs after the charter had been obtained." [43] Similarly, though the Levant Company was sustained during its precarious early years by the

---

doubtedly either in return for services already performed or in hope of services to come. S. E. Thorne has pointed out to me that the Livery Companies had been using such honorary memberships for some time, and that sometimes they served the merely negative but still important purpose of preventing a prominent lawyer from entering a case on the opposing side.

[42] *Ibid.*, p. 185. See also Chaudhuri, *East India Company,* pp. 35–37.

[43] T. S. Willan, *The Muscovy Merchants of 1555* (Manchester, 1953), pp. 10–11. Nonetheless, they continued to have a strong interest, throughout our period, in keeping open their opportunity to participate in all of England's trade. When, for example, the Spanish Company's Charter was being investigated by the House of Commons in 1605, one of the queries raised by the M.P.'s was whether the Company would let "all gentlemen, yeomen, farmers and all others of what quality soever to carry corn into Spain and Portugal, and to make their return in merchandize from thence at their will and pleasure," and also to trade in fish. (See British Museum Additional Manuscript 9365, p. 140.) It is impossible to conceive of French or Spanish gentry asking such a question.

£40,000 the Queen and a few courtiers contributed to its capital of £80,000,[44] thereafter non-merchants took no part in financing the trade. The honorary memberships in other trading organizations, such as Sir Edward Coke's in the Spanish Company, produced no investments as far as can be determined. The one major exception, the East India Company, was more spectacular, profitable, and more consistently a joint-stock organization than the others, and this may account for the gentry investments. But here again it must be remarked, first, that their participation was well below the levels achieved in the companies listed in Table 2, and, second, that the merchants seem to have been interested primarily in political, not financial, support. The City leaders were fully capable of launching the trade on their own — as has been mentioned, there were hardly any gentlemen members until 1609, by which time four joint stocks had already been floated with considerable success. The amounts the gentry subscribed, once they did appear, were substantial — the Earl of Devonshire alone sold £10,000 of stock in May of 1626[45] — but certainly not essential for the survival of a company whose shares were sold without difficulty. Where their financial support *was* essential was in most of the companies listed in Table 2 — the principal colonial and exploring ventures of the period. They formed a majority of the classified membership in eight of the groups, and over 40 percent in five others.

It is clear, therefore, not only that gentry and merchants were generally motivated by different aims, but that their efforts were concentrated in different kinds of enterprises. Nonetheless, conflict was inevitable. The most famous occurred in the Virginia Company where, not surprisingly in view of what has just been outlined, the feeling began to rise around 1617 "that the merchants who then swayed the courts affected nothing but their own immoderate gain."[46] Led by Sir Edwin Sandys and the Earl of

---

[44] W. R. Scott, *The Constitution and Finance of English, Scottish and Irish Joint-Stock Companies to 1720* (3 vols.; Cambridge, 1910–1912), II, 84. See, too, *CSP, Spanish, 1580–86*, p. 432, for the 1583 report of the Court's participation. The only other instance of official royal support for a trading company appears to have been Elizabeth's loan of four ships to the Africa traders in 1561 — for which she obtained £1,000, one-third of their profits. See Scott, *Joint-Stock Companies*, I, 30.

[45] *CSP, East Indies, 1625–1629*, p. 299.

[46] Craven, *Virginia Company*, p. 41.

Southampton, these men, whom W. F. Craven has characterized as "that part of the adventurers with whom the desire to render a public service was especially strong,"[47] ousted the merchants from leadership of the company in 1619. Though Sandys doubtless drew support from merchants in his election (his right-hand man, John Ferrar, was a London businessman), it seems certain that the coalition he formed with the Earls of Southampton and Warwick would have received the backing of virtually all the gentlemen subscribers. And their opponents, Sir Thomas Smith and Alderman Johnson, surely depended primarily on merchant votes. A similar coup was engineered in the Bermuda Company, and another was attempted in the East India Company only two months after the Virginia take-over. In the East India Company, with its much smaller gentry membership, the rising was firmly put down by the merchants, who proceeded to reprimand the troublemakers in no uncertain terms — and not, one suspects, without a sense of smug satisfaction. "Concerning the disturbances and innovations intended at the Court of Election," run the minutes, "it is held an unfit time for any alterations. . . . This 'disturbance' attributed to 'gentlemen who, having been taken into the Company by courtesy, do aim to get all the government into their hands,' which is a business proper only for merchants." Though not the only time the leadership of the East India Company was challenged in the 1610's and 1620's, this was clearly the most serious attack it had to face.[48] Whether Sandys, Southampton, and Ferrar were once again the culprits one cannot tell, but

---

[47] *Ibid.*, p. 42.

[48] *CSP, East Indies, 1617–1621*, p. 282; and *The Letters of John Chamberlain*, ed. N. E. McClure (2 vols.; Philadelphia, 1939), II, 251. This is the only time Chamberlain mentions a disturbance at the elections, though the proceedings were less than smooth for a number of years. See Lang, "Greater Merchants of London," pp. 236–237. James I echoed the merchants' opinion of their own abilities when he said (of the Virginia colony in 1622): "Merchants were fittest for the government of that Plantation." (Kingsbury, *Records*, II, 35.) It might be noted that Sandys continued to be most active in the affairs of the East India Company, the major rebuff to gentlemen notwithstanding. On the same day as that rebuff he was elected a director of the company; in 1627 we find him intervening decisively in a discussion, because he felt that "though he was no merchant, yet seeing the business was to be argued by point of reason and judgment" he could have something of value to say; in 1628 he was proposed as governor of the company; and even a few months before his death he was still a major thorn in the directors' side, stressing, significantly, "the honour of [perpetuating] the trade." (See *CSP, East Indies, 1617–1621*, pp. 383, 524, 635–638.)

49

it is unlikely that they were passive spectators of such a confrontation.

Although two streams of investors can be distinguished quite clearly, and although a number of companies can be categorized as being almost exclusively merchant or gentry, a close union between the classes was the rule rather than the exception. Despite differences in their principal concerns and occasional disagreements, it would be inaccurate to portray their undertakings as two separate efforts. Admittedly, the merchants who restricted their activities to the Eastland, French, Levant, Muscovy, New Merchant Adventurer, Spanish, or a few small trading companies would not have been associated with any gentry — and this was a substantial group: over a third of all the merchants in the list. But this was only to be expected, because so large a part of England's expansion was purely commercial, and of little concern to the landed classes. On their side, however, there were very few gentlemen who invested in the new enterprises without ever combining with a merchant. Even the ventures supported exclusively by gentry were populated primarily by men who also had other interests which brought them into partnership with merchants.

The commercial classes naturally dominated the entire overseas effort, not only because of their larger numbers, their readier access to liquid capital, and their particular skills, but also because of their ubiquity and persistence. With their much heavier investments in the more profitable ventures, such as the East India, Levant and Muscovy trades, and their relatively small contribution to the companies listed in Table 2, they also received the lion's share of the profits. The imports of London alone more than doubled between 1600 and the 1630's; and, from small beginnings, the trade with the East Indies and the Levant accounted for half of those imports by the 1630's.[49]

A tremendous transformation had taken place. Mid-sixteenth-century England, dependent on one product, cloth, much of her trade in foreign hands, and her traffic limited to her continental neighbors, had undergone a spectacular period of growth during the succeeding 70 years. By 1630 native merchants controlled

[49] See Millard, "Analyses of Port Books," Table 28. See also notes 131–136, below.

her commerce, new industries such as coal mining and shipbuilding had grown with amazing speed,[50] and her colonies and trading posts ranged from the Caribbean to the Far East. It was a phenomenal record of economic advance, and it is only natural that the commercial classes should have been at the forefront, not only in organization and investment, but also in profits.

This is not to deny that much of the inspiration for the new schemes of the period came from gentry. The importance of Elizabeth's Court as a center for overseas enterprise can hardly be overestimated. The Queen herself, and many of her leading advisers, gave vital encouragement and financial support to every kind of project, from the infant Levant Company to colonies in Virginia and Guiana. Although merchants contributed the bulk of the funds in the long run, the original impulse frequently came from the court or from the amazingly energetic group of Devon adventurers whose names loom so large in the history of these years — Gilbert, Drake, Davis, Grenville, Raleigh. The Roanoke colony, the first efforts in Newfoundland, the Guiana enterprises, the circumnavigations, the Munster plantation, Fenton's plan to reach the Far East, all these major undertakings were not only conceived but also given their principal support by gentry. And in the next reign Sir Ferdinando Gorges and the Earl of Warwick were only the most famous of an equally active

[50] See Nef, *British Coal Industry*, Vol. I, *passim*, especially pp. 19–21; and Ralph Davis, *The Rise of the English Shipping Industry In the Seventeenth and Eighteenth Centuries* (London, 1962), pp. 2–10, 45–55, 300–305. As is pointed out in Friis, *Cockayne's Project*, p. 47, even England's cloth trade, her most important export, underwent a complete transformation in this period. In the middle of the sixteenth century only half of the trade was in the hands of English merchants, but by the early seventeenth century they controlled over 95 percent. One unsolved question about the collapse of the 1610's and 1620's, and the shrinkage in the number of cloth traders, is whether the decline forced the capital elsewhere (for example, into shipbuilding or the East India Company) or whether the boom in these new areas induced businessmen to switch their investments. I am inclined to support the latter (more adventurous) explanation, because widespread mercantile participation in overseas ventures began well before Cockayne's project, and there was no sudden surge of new interest after 1615–1616. Until the careers of a sizable group of cloth traders have been investigated, however, no firm answer will be possible.
Nonetheless, I think it fair to say that Ramsay, *English Overseas Trade*, p. 245, appropriately characterizes the London merchant of this period as "a jack-of-all-trades, ready to turn his hand to any activity that promised profit." Bacon was not exaggerating when in 1619 he told James I that "your merchants [embrace] the whole compass of the world, east, west, north, and south." See *Letters and Life*, ed. Spedding, VI, 453.

band of gentry pioneers. In new ventures at home, too, notably in industry, the peerage in particular led the way.[51] If, after Elizabeth's death, the Crown was frequently more of a hindrance than a help to the foundation of the empire, this could not detract from the stirring example the Court had already set. The reader need only turn to the entries for Elizabeth Tudor, the Cecils, the Dudleys, the Howards, Walsingham, and Raleigh in the list at the end of this book to appreciate the variety and importance of their efforts.

In the final analysis, however, one must return to the merchants as the chief pillar of the entire undertaking. One can agree with Lawrence Stone's view that the 12 peers he lists as making the widest range of business investments in this period probably surpassed in breadth of interest any equivalent group of City merchants or country gentry.[52] But in totality of effort none of the other classes even approached the merchants. Moreover, the most active of their leaders certainly do not suffer by comparison with Stone's 12 peers. Again, the reader need only turn to the list at the end of this book and look at the variety of projects supported and often *directed* by the Smiths, the Middletons, the Gores, the Cockaynes, the Stapers, the Barnes, the Stiles, the Bonds, the Greenwells, and such men as Sir Christopher Clitheroe, Sir Hugh Hamersley, Robert Bateman, Ralph Freeman, Sir Christopher Hoddesdon, Sir Maurice Abbot, Nicholas Leate, Sir Stephen Soame, and William Harrison to appreciate the versatility of London's outstanding citizens. Membership in nine or more companies was not uncommon among these men, and frequently they acted as *directors* of enterprises as various as commerce with India, the Levant, Spain, the Baltic, and the New World. In addition they engaged in moneylending and other financial activities not recorded here. And their contributions could be just as large as those of the wealthy peers. If the Earl of Devonshire could send Thomas Hobbes to dispose of £10,000 worth of stock in the East India Company in three days, Ralph

[51] Stone, *Crisis of the Aristocracy*, pp. 335–363.

[52] *Ibid.*, pp. 375–377. Though none of the gentry was so wealthy and influential as the peers Stone lists, a number, like Sandys, Gorges, and Digges, played parts no less important (and sometimes more important) in organizing the expansion; and a few, such as Sir Percival Willoughby, had interests as wide-ranging as the Talbots. (See Cell, "Newfoundland," pp. 130–134.)

Freeman could sell £11,000 worth to Hugh Hamersley in one transaction.[53] But it is in terms of total effort that the overwhelming importance of the merchants is most apparent.

In the first place, there were many more merchants, backing many more enterprises, as Table 3 indicates. Thus not only did

Table 3.   Memberships in companies, according to social class.

Number of companies invested in (no more than)	Gentry	Other non-merchants	Merchants	Unclassified	Percent of classified investors who were gentry or non-merchants
1	844	61	2,554	1,105	26.2
2	186	9	709	38	21.6
3	77	3	316	7	20.1
4	27	1	157	2	15.1
5	13	0	82	0	13.7
6	8	0	44	0	15.4
7	4	0	31	0	11.4
8	6	0	15	0	28.6
9	3	0	13	0	18.8
10	3	0	3	0	50.0
11 or more	6	0	9	0	40.0
Total	1,177	74	3,933	1,152	24.2
Total number of investments[a]	1,875	92	6,807	1,210	22.4
Average number of companies per investor	1.58	1.24	1.73	1.05	–

[a] That is, number of people multiplied by number of companies invested in.

merchants outnumber gentry investors seven to two, but on average every 100 merchants invested in 15 more companies than did the same number of gentlemen. Only at the very highest levels, among subscribers to 10 or more companies, were the two classes on anything like equal terms, but there the numbers were much too small to be of any great significance in the overall pic-

[53] CSP, East Indies, 1617–1621, p. 321. See above, note 45. The domination by merchants of those groups which made the widest ranging multiple investments and held the most simultaneous directorships is revealed in Tables 16–18. For other active merchants, see Palmer, the Slanys, Towerson, and Wich in the Appendix.

ture. It is worth noting, incidentally, that the nine gentry in this category consisted of seven peers and two knights — another reiteration of the importance of the upper strata in the landed class. If the figure is extended to five or more companies, one finds 26 peers, 15 knights, and two gentlemen out of a total of 43. Yet in this same "five or more" category one finds 197 merchants, well over four times as many as the gentry.[54] Even if one removes from the figures the French and Spanish Companies, two predominantly merchant groups which could be considered not really central to England's expansion,[55] there would still be over 3,000 merchants in the list, with a little under 6,000 investments credited to them — not a significant reduction of their pre-eminent position.

The disparity is equally pronounced among the directors and governors of the 20 major companies which were substantial enough to have official directorships and governorships,[56] as is indicated in Table 4. Although a higher proportion of the total number of gentry investors became directors (14 percent as opposed to 11 percent of the merchants), they were still outnumbered by over five to two, and their range of influence was considerably less. Only nine percent of their directors held office in more than one company, compared to 27 percent of the merchant directors. Once again, the upper strata of the two classes led the way: the peers provided approximately a third of the gentry figures, and the knights another half; among the merchants, almost 15 percent were knights.[57] Thus, both in ordinary member-

[54] Thirty-eight of these 197 merchants were knights, a proportion six times as high as the ratio of 10 merchant knights to every 308 merchants in the list as a whole. See notes 36, above, and 57, below.

[55] Though these were both newly organized as chartered, monopolistic companies during our period — the reason for their inclusion in the list — the trades they were supposed to control had existed for centuries. In the Levant, Eastland, and Muscovy Companies the direct trades themselves were new.

[56] These were the following companies: Africa, Bermuda, East India, Eastland, French, Irish, Levant, Massachusetts Bay, Merchant Adventurer, Minerals, Mines, Muscovy, New England, Newfoundland, New Merchant Adventurer, New River, North-West Passage, Providence Island, Spanish, and Virginia. Two of them, the Merchant Adventurer and the New Merchant Adventurer, could be considered irrelevant to England's expansion; but their omission would remove only 43 directorships and governorships and 30 merchants — leaving the average number of offices held by merchants at 1.41. See Tables 16 and 17.

[57] This is nearly five times as high as the average ratio of merchant knights to merchants in the list. Among those who were directors of two or more companies, the knights totaled 34, with 2.62 offices each, as opposed to 84 ordinary

Table 4. Directorships and governorships, according to social class.

Number of directorships or governorships held (no more than)	Gentry (number of peers indicated in parentheses)	Other non-merchants	Merchants	Unclassified	Percent of classified directors or governors who were gentry or non-merchants
1	147 (46)	5	317	22	32.4
2	13 (5)	0	86	1	13.0
3	1 (0)	0	21	0	4.6
4 or more	0 (0)	0	11	0	0.0
Total	161 (51)	5	435	23	28.1
Total number of directorships or governorships[a]	176 (56)	5	614	24	22.8
Average number of directorships or governorships each	1.09	1.00	1.41	1.04	–

[a] That is, number of people multiplied by number of directorships or governorships.

ships and in leadership of the companies, the commercial classes held an overwhelming superiority in sheer numbers and breadth of commitment.

Finance. As far as the money actually spent is concerned, it is impossible to be precise about the relative contribution of the two classes. Except in a few of the smaller ventures, notably Frobisher's voyages, no financial records have survived from which calculations can be made. At best, one can only estimate, as W. R. Scott does, the total outlay of the various companies. One can then weight the investments of merchants and gentry according to the percentages they formed of the membership of each company. But the results must not be taken for anything but the crudest approximations. Not only is it impossible to make ac-

merchants with 2.38 offices each. At the highest levels the knights accounted for almost half of the merchants' activity — five out of 11 of those with four or more directorates, holding 26 out of their 54 offices. See notes 36 and 54, above.

curate calculations about total expenditures except in a few cases, but it would be rash to assume that any given percentage of the investors provided the same proportion of the capital as they did of the membership. Outside of the smaller companies, where such percentages are virtually meaningless anyway,[58] the only place where this assumption can even be tested is among the records of the Virginia Company. No other organization has left behind documentation indicating who provided its funds.[59] And the Virginia Company's lists of adventurers are far from complete or entirely accurate. There are variations, and the total capital does not approach the amount we know the company raised. Moreover, in light of the perennial problem of defaulters,[60] it is difficult to know whether people actually paid the sums for which they were credited. Nonetheless, it is the best material we have. Because the purpose of this entire calculation is only to provide very rough figures it is easier to accept a test that is also not too precise.

Given the differences between the various Virginia Company tabulations which have survived, it seems best to regard each individual list of subscribers as a separate entity, consistent within itself and, hopefully, fairly representative of the total investment.[61] No attempt has been made to adjust for the discrepancies between them, or to extrapolate in order to make up for the obvious major lacunae. The results suggest that no great error is introduced by equating percentage of membership with percentage of

[58] When only a relatively small capital had to be raised, one investor could account for a completely disproportionate share — e.g., of the £7,700 donated toward Fenton's voyage by the 22 men whose precise subscriptions are recorded, the Earl of Leicester alone provided £2,200. See Cotton Manuscripts, Otho E VIII, fols. 106–107, in the British Museum; and Taylor, *Edward Fenton*, pp. 10, 14. Fortunately, the proportions in the small companies which have had to be calculated according to percentage of membership represent only a small part of the total figures in Table 5.

[59] The occasional mentions of the size of the adventures held by various investors in the East India Company — usually when stocks were transferred — are too few to serve as a useful sample. See note 63, below.

[60] See Kingsbury, *Records*, III, 34ff. For examples in the East India Company and New England Council see *CSP, East Indies, 1625–1629*, pp. 200, 240; and Preston, *Gorges*, pp. 215–216. The Guiana, Massachusetts Bay, and almost every other company of the period encountered similar problems — see J. A. Williamson, *English Colonies in Guiana and on the Amazon, 1604–1668* (Oxford, 1923), pp. 112, 129; and Scott, *Joint-Stock Companies*, II, 313.

[61] The three principal lists can be found in Kingsbury, *Records*, III, 80–90, 317–40; and *Tracts*, ed. Force, vol. III, no. 4.

capital invested. Just under 75 percent of the Virginia Company members have been classified according to social status — of this number, 52.8 percent were merchants. In the various lists of subscribers, merchants provided between 55 percent and 60 percent of the funds. As more of their money was available for trade, one could expect that merchants would contribute a larger share than their numbers alone would indicate. But the figures are close enough together to suggest that no substantial error is introduced when one uses proportions of membership as indications of proportions of investment.

However, one further test is still possible and relevant. A man could join the Virginia Company with a relatively small investment, and it is by no means certain that the results that emerged here hold good for an organization that called for considerably larger funds, as did the East India Company. Yet even when those subscribers in the Virginia lists who paid £100 or more are isolated, the results remain much the same — around 55 percent of the money came from merchants. These large investments accounted for a third of the company's capital, and it is therefore important that the gentry should have maintained their share in this group. In the East India Company *everyone* had to reach this level. The few indications that survive all suggest that the gentlemen who joined the larger undertakings — and even the outfitting of a fairly small 30-ton privateer cost over £200 [62] — spent about as much per capita as their merchant colleagues. Although nearly all the sums larger than £1,000 mentioned in the sporadic records of transfers of adventures in the East India Company came from merchants, a few did involve gentry[63] and there is no reason to suppose that they did not come close to providing the same proportion of capital as they did of the membership. Even Sir George Calvert, at a time when he was only clerk of the Privy Council (an office that probably brought him

[62] Andrews, *Elizabethan Privateering*, p. 49.
[63] See *CSP, East Indies, 1617–1621*, pp. 99–100, 230–231, 341, 408, 505–506; *1622–1624*, pp. 93, 226, 487–488; and *1625–1629*, pp. 136–137, 298–299, 437–438, 600–601, 698–699. The very large amounts being invested in the East India Company were remarked upon by John Chamberlain in 1617, when the second joint stock was being launched and some people seemed to be willing to subscribe as much as £10,000 to £14,000 each: see *Letters of Chamberlain*, ed. McClure, II, 53.

around £1,000 a year[64]), and not a wealthy nobleman, adventured £1,600 in the East India Company's joint stock. For all the rewards he later gained in office, including his reputed sale of the secretaryship of state for £6,000,[65] it is still remarkable that in the 1620's he probably spent close to £30,000 on his colony in Newfoundland.[66] This was admittedly an exceptional effort, but it indicates that gentry expenditures cannot be slighted merely because most of their investments were made by men with a very limited interest in commerce.

Concerning 13 ventures relatively precise figures can be calculated. By far the largest of them all, the East India Company, raised £2,887,000 in the period under study (including the entire second joint stock, originally floated in 1617, even though it was wound up only in 1632).[67] For the others, given here in chronological order, calculations and estimates have been made from various accounts that have survived: Frobisher's and Fenton's voyages raised about £28,000;[68] the Virginia Company —

[64] Aylmer, *King's Servants*, p. 204. See *CSP, East Indies, 1513–1616*, p. 273.

[65] Aylmer, *King's Servants*, p. 110.

[66] Cell, "Newfoundland," pp. 208–209. It should be noted that this sum is not included in my calculation of the capital invested in the Newfoundland Company (see note 83, below). Baltimore's colony was a separate, private undertaking and was entered under "other ventures," though it is worth stressing that this was probably the largest single amount included among "other ventures."

[67] Chaudhuri, *East India Company*, p. 209. The transfers of stocks (see note 63, above) suggest that Sandys was exaggerating when he said in the House of Commons in 1621 that almost one-third of the East India Company's joint stock was "borne by the Nobility and Gentry." He was trying to show that a joint-stock organization was freer and that it enabled more non-merchants to invest, but there is no evidence that the gentry subscribed any more per man than did merchants. See *Commons Debates 1621*, ed. Wallace Notestein, F. H. Relf, and Hartley Simpson (7 vols.; New Haven, 1935), IV, pp. 216–217.

[68] Scott's calculations for Frobisher's three voyages (*Joint-Stock Companies*, II, 76–82) seem to be perfectly accurate — cf. *The Three Voyages of Martin Frobisher*, ed. Sir Richard Collinson (London: The Hakluyt Society, 1867), p. 358; and *CSP, East Indies, 1513–1616*, pp. 37–66. But for Fenton's voyage Scott made the error (a most unusual one in this very careful work) of entering 11,600 marks as £11,600. Taylor, *Edward Fenton*, p. 13, does not improve matters by claiming that a mark was worth 16s. 18d., when in fact it was 13s. 4d., two-thirds of a pound. This may account for her finding that the detailed account of the investments (*ibid.*, p. 10) adds up to "rather less than 11,600 marks" (*ibid.*, p. 13). However, if one adds the subscriptions of the Earl of Oxford and Customer Smith (*ibid.*, p. 14) which do not appear in the detailed accounts (Taylor mentions only the omission of Smith), one arrives at a total of £7,716 13s. 4d., a mere £16 13s. 4d. (or 25 marks) short of 11,600 marks, which may have been a rounded number. I assumed that a slightly higher amount was raised, since other people interested in the voyage are mentioned; and two of them, Peter Jeffreys and Thomas Baynam, are referred to as "adventurers . . . in good por-

£200,000;[69] the Londonderry Plantation — £70,000;[70] the Bermuda organizations — £90,000;[71] the Africa Company — £7,100;[72] the New River Company — £18,500;[73] the Plymouth adventurers — £7,000;[74] the Guiana Company of 1627 — £5,000;[75] the Massachusetts Bay Company — £5,500;[76] the Providence Island Company — £14,000 through 1630.[77] Finally, the two industrial organizations, the Minerals and Mines Companies, seem to have raised £7,000 and £34,000 respectively,

---

tions in this journey." (*Ibid.*, p. 63.) I have assumed the total investment to have been high enough so that, when added to the £20,160 raised for Frobisher's three voyages, the entire amount came to £28,000. As far as can be determined, gentry and merchants gave just about equal sums to the four voyages, when counted as a whole.

[69] See Scott, *Joint-Stock Companies*, II, 286–287 — an estimate that accords very well with the records.

[70] T. W. Moody, *The Londonderry Plantation, 1609–41* (Belfast, 1939), pp. 254–255, 442–443. See note 82, below.

[71] The first adventurers spent £20,000 between 1612 and 1615 — see Scott, *Joint-Stock Companies*, II, 262; and Wilkinson, *Bermuda*, p. 75. The sum expended after 1615 is difficult to calculate. Technically, 400 shares, at £12 10s. each, were sold (Scott, II, 263; Wilkinson, p. 78) — a sum of £5,000. However, the transportation of colonists was a much more expensive endeavor. It cost approximately £20 to transport a man to Bermuda (Wilkinson, *Bermuda*, pp. 95–96), and by 1623 over 1,000 people had been settled (*ibid.*, p. 192)—an expenditure of £25,000 at least. The estimate of the company in that year of 100,-000 marks spent (Kingsbury, *Records*, II, 48) was undoubtedly an exaggeration; but by the end of our period one can safely assume that this sum had been spent, because by then there were over 2,000 colonists (*CSP, America and West Indies, 1574–1660*, p. 92). Assuming that the cost after 1615 was £70,000, the total investment would amount to £90,000.

[72] Scott, *Joint-Stock Companies*, II, 12.

[73] J. W. Gough, *Sir Hugh Myddelton, Entrepreneur and Engineer* (Oxford, 1964), p. 64. Since the King undertook half the cost, the gentry percentage used in Table 5 represents one-half plus their 28.6 percent of the membership.

[74] See Scott, *Joint-Stock Companies*, II, 306–311; and John Smith's *Works*, ed. Arber, II, 783, 942. S. E. Morison, in a footnote to his edition of William Bradford's *Of Plymouth Plantation, 1620–1647* (New York, 1953), p. 37, suggests that Smith exaggerated wildly, and that no more than £1,500 was subscribed. He offers this opinion without reference to Scott's careful analysis of the venture's finances, cited at the beginning of this note. In the absence of any strong evidence to the contrary (and Morison offers none) I am persuaded by Scott's argument upholding the accuracy of Smith's estimate.

[75] See Scott, *Joint-Stock Companies*, II, 325; and Williamson, *English Colonies in Guiana*, p. 111. Williamson later suggests (p. 129) that no more than £4,000 was raised, but this seems a low estimate in view of the evidence he himself presents on pp. 111–112.

[76] This figure is highly tentative, for it is based on the number of shareholders, the value of a share, and the discussion in Scott, *Joint-Stock Companies*, II, 312–315.

[77] This is again an estimate, probably a generous one, based on *ibid.*, pp. 327–330.

though the first figure is little more than a guess.[78] In addition, the following approximations can be made concerning the remaining ventures in which gentry took part: the early efforts in Virginia (Roanoke) seem to have cost at most £50,000; [79] Gilbert's enterprises raised some £2,000;[80] the various pre-1627 Guiana expeditions probably cost around £75,000;[81] the Munster colonists of Elizabeth's reign may have spent some £30,000;[82]

[78] M. B. Donald, *Elizabethan Copper: The History of the Company of Mines Royal, 1568–1605* (London, 1955), p. 241; and *Elizabethan Monopolies: The History of the Company of Mineral and Battery Works from 1565 to 1604* (Edinburgh and London, 1961), pp. 73–75.

[79] From the material in *The Roanoke Voyages*, ed. D. B. Quinn (2 vols.; London: The Hakluyt Society, 1955), *passim;* in Quinn, "Preparations for the 1585 Virginia Voyage," *William and Mary Quarterly*, 3rd ser., 6 (1949), 208–236; and in J. W. Shirley, "Sir Walter Raleigh's Guiana Finances," *Huntington Library Quarterly*, 13 (1949–1950), 56, it can be estimated that the total investment is unlikely to have exceeded £50,000. Quinn has suggested to me that Raleigh's own investment probably did not exceed £15,000, of which he lost possibly £5,000 in the end. Beyond this, one can only guess at the relative contributions of gentry and merchants. In view of Raleigh's enormous personal involvement, though, it would seem fair to suggest that in this case, despite the preponderance of merchant investors, the gentry probably provided at least half of the amount that was raised. It is worth noting that, as is indicated by Raleigh's return, the adventurers may well have recouped as much as two-thirds of their investment as a result of some successful privateering on the side — a unique level of success among these early colonial efforts. Quinn has also pointed out to me that there were almost certainly at least 100 more investors in the Virginia projects of the 1580's than the 40 or so whom I have tracked down. Unfortunately, however, the records of these early ventures are too sparse to permit the level of precision that can be achieved in the Jacobean companies. The names that reached the list often came from scattered and unlikely sources, and consequently fewer investors survived the application of the standards for inclusion that were used for all companies. Thus it is frequently uncertain whether the adventurers who sailed on the expeditions to Virginia contributed *money* as well as service to the enterprise, and they had to be omitted if nothing beyond their service could be established. Naturally, this meant that harsh limitations were imposed on investors in less well documented undertakings, but no other approach would have allowed me to retain consistency and remove subjective assessments as far as possible.

[80] An estimate based on the figures in *Enterprises of Gilbert*, ed. Quinn, II, 329–333 and 374; and *Elizabethan Guild of Exeter*, ed. Cotton, pp. 85–87.

[81] Shirley, "Raleigh's Guiana Finances," pp. 60–61, indicates that Raleigh spent £50,000 on his expeditions in the 1590's alone. From the sizes of the efforts launched between 1604 and 1625 (Williamson, *English Colonies in Guiana*, pp. 29–106), one can estimate that no more than a further £25,000 was spent before the foundation of the Guiana Company, which has been placed in a separate category: see note 75, above. Since gentry were the heavily preponderant subscribers anyway, there was no need to adjust the proportion used in Table 5 to take account of Raleigh's huge contribution.

[82] This is a pure guess, resting on little more than the knowledge that there were some 80 real "undertakers" (see below, under *Ireland* in the "Companies" section of chapter 3), 20 percent of whom soon gave up the enterprise, but the

and the Newfoundland Company probably spent around £20,000.[83] There remain, then, the exploratory and plundering voyages of the time about which only the roughest guesses can be made. If one begins with privateering, on which recent work has been done, it will be seen that the very approximate magnitudes that can be reached must be treated with the greatest caution.

In calculating total costs of the 18 years of privateering between 1585 and 1603, K. R. Andrews can hazard nothing more precise than two very tentative figures. He suggests that between £100,000 and £200,000 worth of prizes were brought back to England, on average, each year. And he estimates that this represented a profit of about 60 percent on the cost of fitting out the expeditions. He goes on to explain that, because of other considerations, the final profit probably varied widely from this figure.[84] However, for the purposes of working out only the original investments, these figures would seem to furnish enough of a basis to make an approximate calculation, reinforced by the few precise figures available. If one takes the median of Andrews' figures, and accepts a total of £150,000 in prizes per year, the 18 years would have produced £2,700,000. To make a profit of 60 percent, roughly £1,600,000 would have had to be spent in equipping the expeditions. But in fact total costs were probably higher. According to Andrews' tables, the tonnage is known for 40 out of the 86 privateers in 1598 of which any record has survived. Using his calculation of the cost of equipping privateers of various tonnages,[85] it seems that these 40 ships alone probably represented an investment of some £85,000. Even if the remaining 46 ships cost only half this sum to fit out — a most conservative estimate — then the total outlay during the year would have

---

rest of whom appear to have settled about 1,000 Englishmen as colonists. Judging by various estimates of expenses at the time, £30,000 would seem to be a fairly plausible assessment of total investment, although the plan was to raise about £60,000. See CSP, Ireland, 1574–1585, pp. 587ff.; 1586–1588, passim, especially p. 508; 1588–1592, pp. 257–258; and 1592–1596, pp. 14, 58–60. See, too, Robert Dunlop, "The Plantation of Munster, 1584–1589," The English Historical Review, 3 (1888), 250–269. For Table 5, the £30,000 has been added to the £70,000 expended by the Londonderry Plantation. (See note 70, above.)

[83] This is again only a very rough estimate, based on the discussion of the colony's activities in Cell, "Newfoundland," pp. 130–183.

[84] Andrews, Elizabethan Privateering, pp. 127–128.

[85] Ibid., p. 49.

been close to £130,000, and £150,000 is a more likely figure. Nor does this seem to have been an unusual year: in the three-year period 1589–1591, for which Andrews also gives figures, just under 300 ships were sent out, and their sporadically recorded tonnage does not seem significantly different from that of 1598. One can assume, therefore, that annual expenditures came to something over £100,000 at the least. The few larger expenditures alone, as described by Andrews, would have sent total outlay well on its way toward this figure. John Chudley spent over £10,000 on just one expedition, ruining himself in the process;[86] Raleigh borrowed £11,000 to invest in privateering in 1592 alone;[87] and the Earl of Cumberland claimed — with fair accuracy, as far as can be determined — that he spent £100,000 on his expeditions between 1586 and 1597.[88] Assuming, then, that something over £100,000 was subscribed, on average, each year, one can estimate that approximately £2,000,000 was spent in the 18-year period — a figure rather higher than that reached merely by estimating the size of profits, but close enough to suggest that the approximation is fairly correct.

The privateering activity of 1625–1630 is much more fully documented. Using the data in the letters of marque,[89] which indicate that the ships' burden was usually slightly larger than it had been in the 1590's, and adjusting for the rise in prices in James I's reign, one can estimate that on average each of the 1,500 or so vessels cost roughly £1,600 to equip. This would give a total expense of some £2,400,000.

For the North-West Passage Company, the New England Ventures, Drake's 1587 expedition, and the voyages of Hudson, Baffin, Weymouth, and Gosnold, nothing but hazardous guesses can be made. The one voyage of John Davis for which accounts have survived cost about £1,200, and one can only estimate that

[86] *Ibid.*, pp. 243–273, 67–69.

[87] Shirley, "Raleigh's Guiana Finances," p. 57.

[88] G. C. Williamson, *George, Third Earl of Cumberland (1558–1605): His Life and His Voyages* (Cambridge, England, 1920), p. 240.

[89] *CSP, Domestic, 1628–1629,* pp. 285–309, 439–441; *1629–1631,* pp. 151–156, 467–471. Approximately 1,500 letters of marque were granted, roughly one-third of which came from London. The remainder were widely scattered, though principally from the West Country. The most common port of origin after London was Bristol, with a little over one-tenth of the ships. It is noticeable, too, that most of the Bristol ships appeared only in the 1628–1630 period.

the other two probably cost approximately the same.[90] The three expeditions sent out by the North-West Passage Company, rather better equipped, probably cost about £3,000 each. This would make a total outlay by "North-West Passage" investors (in Davis' voyages and the Company) of some £12,600. Hudson's voyage, which required 23 backers, may well have cost £3,000 also, as may the three voyages sent out by the "Baffin" adventurers, a group whose composition is explained in Chapter 3. There is no way of determining the accuracy of these estimates, but £3,000 for Hudson and £9,000 for "Baffin" would seem within the range of plausibility. Similarly, one may assume that the small ships sent out under Gosnold and Weymouth probably cost no more than £1,500 to equip. But Drake's 1587 fleet can be assessed in terms of the privateering expeditions of the day. It is unfortunate that, though we know the cost of his 1585 venture, we do not know the names of the subscribers; and, *per contra,* that we know the investors but not the outlay in the 1587 voyage. The 25 ships in 1585 cost just over £60,000; and, the tonnages being comparable, one can estimate that it cost about £40,000 to send his 16 ships out in 1587.[91] Cavendish's two efforts at circumnavigation appear to have required some £10,000 each.[92] The ventures included under the "New England" category are more difficult to assess. The New England Council appears to have put together less than £2,500, and the expenses for the various voyages and small colonies included in this category can only be guessed at. Sir Ferdinando Gorges is reputed to have spent £20,000 on New England projects, but he was far and away the most active adventurer. In fact, it does not seem likely that more than £30,000 was raised *in toto* by the various undertakings[93] (remembering,

[90] *Elizabethan Guild of Exeter,* ed. Cotton, pp. 82–83.

[91] See Robert Leng, *Sir Francis Drake's Memorable Service Done against the Spaniards in 1587,* ed. Clarence Hopper (London: Camden Society Miscellany, V, 1864), p. 27; *Papers Relating to the Navy during the Spanish War, 1585–1587,* ed. J. S. Corbett (London: Navy Records Society, XI, 1898), pp. xviii, 87, 97–206; and *The Naval Tracts of Sir William Monson,* ed. Michael Oppenheim (London: Navy Records Society, XXII, 1902), I, 121–134, 136–151. The "gentry" contribution listed for Drake's voyage in Table 5 is calculated simply from the fact that Elizabeth provided six out of the 16 ships.

[92] See Andrews, *Elizabethan Privateering,* pp. 69–70, and also p. 67.

[93] Brown, *Genesis of the United States,* II, 903, cites the not implausible estimate of Gorges' expenses. For the much less determined contributions of other venturers to New England, see Preston, *Gorges, passim,* especially pp. 215–

of course, that the Plymouth and Massachusetts Bay Companies appear separately).

In conclusion it might be noted that the "other ventures" category, and all regulated and purely trading companies in the list, were omitted from these calculations. "Other ventures" covers such a wide range, from the tens of thousands of pounds one man could invest in mining projects to the £50 or so given for a share in a minor voyage, and estimates of total expenditures — let alone distribution — would have been so unreliable, that no useful figures could have been calculated. Moreover, it did not seem that the amount 352 people spent on 459 investments could have had a substantial effect on the figures.[94] The regulated trading companies could not be included because there is no way of knowing how much their members spent. As an indication of magnitude, however, the few extant figures for imports are worth mentioning. In four widely scattered and uneven years during our period, over £51,400 worth of commodities were imported into London from Russia, over £660,000 worth were imported from the Levant, and over £239,800 worth were imported in

216. The proportion assigned to the gentry in Table 5 was reached by adding Gorges' £20,000 to the 83.9 percent of the remaining £10,000 to which the gentry were "entitled" by the percentage they formed of the classified membership.

[94] A completely arbitrary guess would suggest that perhaps £1,000,000 was spent on these ventures, well over half of it by the merchants who made up over 56 percent of the investors. The evidence presented by Millard (see "Imports of London," especially pp. 156–161) shows a marked decline in the imports of various manufactured goods in this period — a testimony to the rapid growth of England's new industries, which make up most of the "other ventures" category. How much was spent, though, cannot be determined from the material available at present. No precise figures will be possible until a great deal of work is done to follow up the pioneering researches completed by Donald in *Elizabethan Monopolies* and *Elizabethan Copper;* by Nef in *British Coal Industry* and *Industry and Government in France and England, 1540–1640* (1940; reprinted Ithaca, 1957), especially chap. iii, pp. 58–120; by W. H. Price in *The English Patents of Monopoly* (Boston and New York, 1906); by R. B. Turton in *The Alum Farm* (Whitby, 1938); by H. R. Schubert in *History of the British Iron and Steel Industry from c. 450* B.C. *to* A.D. *1775* (London, 1957), especially Part II; and by Stone in *Crisis of the Aristocracy*, pp. 338–355. In the meantime, a round figure of £1,000,000 has been estimated tentatively on the basis of the information contained in these studies, plus what we know — very roughly — of the cost of the few nonindustrial enterprises included among "other ventures." Even if gentry spent £400,000 of this amount (again, an estimate that is purposely as generous as possible), and it is added to Table 5, their contribution to the total capital would still be only 23 percent — and that, as is indicated in the text, is only in those areas of the expansion where they participated. Their *numerical* proportion of the membership of all these companies (including "other ventures") was 32.4 percent.

five years from the Baltic. Using these figures as a basis, it would seem likely, regardless even of major ups and downs, that London merchants (the dominant group) imported from these three newly opened areas of direct trade at least £10,000,000 worth of goods during our period. The capital that must have been invested to maintain so large a volume was probably double that invested in the East India Company in the same period.[95] It is impossible to be certain about such an estimate, and it would be pointless to include it in total calculations. However, this mammoth contribution, made solely by merchants, is worth bearing in mind as yet further proof of their overwhelmingly dominant role in England's expansion.

The calculations outlined above can now be summarized in a table (Table 5) in which, where the relative amounts invested by the various subscribers are not known, the gentry have been credited with a proportion equal to their percentage of the membership. Figures which have been estimated by using this proportion are indicated by ([b]). No adjustment has been made for the rise in prices, because the ratio between merchants and gentry, the figure being measured, changed very little. Moreover, most of the figures come from the 1600–1630 period, during which, according to the most useful indicators, the rise in prices was under 20 percent.[96]

[95] By 1626 Sir Thomas Roe was estimating that the Levant Company was exporting to Turkey £250,000 worth of goods each year: see Wood, *Levant Company*, p. 42. Wood (pp. 42–43) suggests how rapidly the Levant trade grew in the early seventeenth century, until, in 1638, Lewis Roberts thought it "the most flourishing and beneficial Company to the commonwealth of any in England." See also Richard Stapers' 1607 estimate of the company's annual outlays: *Historical Manuscripts Commission, Salisbury Manuscripts*, vol. XIX (London, 1965), p. 266. Millard, "Imports of London," p. 149, indicates that the average volume of the Baltic trade may have been larger than that indicated by the import figures cited here. See, too, R. W. K. Hinton, *The Eastland Trade and the Common Weal in the Seventeenth Century* (Cambridge, 1959), pp. 1–52, especially pp. 33–50. On the outlay for trade with Russia, see Willan, *The Early History of the Russia Company* (Manchester, 1956), pp. 41–47, 154–156, 180–187, 202–203, 209–216, 251–252, 255, 262–267, 270. There is also a considerable amount of information about the Muscovy Company in E. P. Cheyney, *A History of England from the Defeat of the Armada to the Death of Elizabeth* (2 vols.; London, 1914), I, 311–342. See also Fisher, "London's Export Trade," pp. 152–153. See note 27, above.

[96] Partly as a result of the depression of the 1620's, prices by 1630 had risen much less since 1600 than they had in the previous 30-year period. The 10-year average of the price of wheat rose only 18 percent between the first and third decades of the seventeenth century; in the same time the price of barley, after

Table 5. Relative size of gentry and merchant investments in companies to which both classes contributed (to nearest £100).[a]

Company	Total capital	Provided by gentry and other non-merchants	Percent provided by gentry and other non-merchants
Africa	£ 7,100	£ 5,600[b]	78.9
Baffin	9,000	1,100[b]	12.5
Bermuda	90,000	33,400[b]	37.1
Cavendish	20,000	20,000	100.0
Drake	40,000	16,200	40.6[d]
East India	2,887,000	415,700[b]	14.4
Frobisher & Fenton	28,000	14,000[b]	50.0
Gilbert	2,000	1,100[b]	53.8
Gosnold	1,500	1,200[b]	80.0
Guiana Company (1627–29)	5,000	4,400[b]	88.7
Guiana venturers[c]	75,000	67,100[b]	89.5
Hudson	3,000	1,200[b]	39.1
Irish (Munster and Londonderry)	100,000	26,500[b]	26.5
Massachusetts Bay	5,500	1,700[b]	31.6
Minerals	7,000	3,500[b]	50.7
Mines	34,000	16,400[b]	48.2
New England	30,000	28,700[b]	95.7[e]
Newfoundland	20,000	5,200[b]	26.0
New River	18,500	11,900[b]	64.3[f]
North-West Passage	12,600	9,000[b]	71.7
Plymouth	7,000	1,200[b]	16.7
Privateering	4,400,000[h]	770,000[b]	17.5
Providence Island	14,000	11,900[b]	85.0
Virginia (1606–24)	200,000	94,400[b]	47.2[g]
Virginia venturers[c]	50,000	25,000	50.0
Weymouth	1,500	1,500	100.0
Total	£8,067,700	£1,587,900	19.6

[a] The small variations that can be noticed between the figures in this table and those in Table 2 are caused by the inclusion of all non-merchants among gentry in this table.

[b] See explanation in paragraph before this table.

[c] The venturers who were interested in Guiana and Virginia before the foundation of the principal companies in these areas have been given separate figures. This distinction has been drawn in this table alone because, as is indicated in notes 79 and 81 to this chapter, the relative amounts subscribed by gentry to these ventures must be calculated separately from the larger companies. Had they been combined, different results would have been obtained.

[d] See note 91 to this chapter.

[e] See note 93.

[f] See note 73.

[g] See note 79.

[h] On the importance of privateering see pp. 79–80.

Most of the figures in Table 5 are probably a little generous to the gentry for two reasons. First, their numbers were allowed to determine the percentage of their investment, and one's impression from company records is that merchants tended to pay more, per man, than did gentry. But this discrepancy is unverifiable, as the records are so sparse, and there is no way of deciding how to make any adjustments. Second, the percentage of membership was calculated on the basis of the classified members only, but the percentage of investment was applied to the *entire* capital raised by a company. Some 20 percent of the subscribers remained unclassified, and because they were so obscure the probability is that nearly all of them were petty merchants. The gentry undoubtedly benefit, therefore, from the extrapolation of percentages among classified members to the entire membership. But the figures in Table 5 are so very rough anyway that the few percentage points difference a correction such as this might make would not be worthwhile.

Table 5 indicates that, as might be expected, the gentry pro-

---

rising 7.0 percent in one decade, dropped back, during 1620–1629, to below the 1600–1609 period. See Kerridge, "The Movement of Rent," pp. 28, 34; the more broadly based tables of consumables in E. H. Phelps Brown and Sheila V. Hopkins, "Seven Centuries of the Price of Consumables, Compared with Builders' Wage-Rates," *Economica*, new ser., 23 (1956), 296–314, indicate that the 1600–1630 rise was under 13 percent. The five-year average between 1600 and 1604 was 464; between 1626 and 1630 it was 524, an increase of 12.9 percent. By contrast, the five-year average between 1576 and 1580 was 362: hence in the last quarter-century of Elizabeth's reign the rise was 27.8 percent, and over the full 56 years it was 44.7 percent. The largest jump came between the first and second halves of the 1590's — in fact, the 1595–1599 average was the highest in the entire 1575–1630 period: 552. A similar chronology is presented by J. D. Gould, "Y. S. Brenner on Prices: A Comment," *Ec.H.R.*, 2nd ser., 16 (1963), 351–360. He stresses (p. 356) that the great rise came in the 1570's, 1580's, and 1590's, during which time the mean price of grain almost doubled. In the subsequent three decades the rise was slow. The most recent and complete price tables, published after the above was written, give a more detailed picture: Peter Bowden's contribution to *Agrarian History*, ed. Thirsk, pp. 593–695 and 815–863.

Because over 85 percent of the expenditures in Table 5 were made after 1594, there seemed no point in attempting to adjust for the price rise. Only a small proportion of the investments between 1595 and 1630 can be given a fixed date, and even for the previous 20 years considerable variations would have to be introduced, as exact dates of investment are usually impossible to determine. No consistent adjustment could have been made, and therefore any tampering with the figures as they now stand would have introduced more distortion than it would have removed. It might be noted, too, that even if sufficient data for an adjustment had been available, the gentry/merchant proportion would not have changed significantly.

vided more members than funds. It must be remembered that only those companies to which they contributed have been included (a group slightly larger than the one in Table 2). Although they amounted to almost 25 percent of *all* investors, in the companies listed in Table 5 their numerical proportion was higher — 1,608 out of 5,081 classified memberships, or nearly 32 percent. This makes the discrepancy between their numbers and payments more significant — their numbers were proportionately over 60 percent higher than the size of their investments. If *all* companies, including those which were purely merchant affairs, are taken as the basis for calculations,[97] the results are even more pointed. Assuming, conservatively, that £5,000,000 was spent on these other merchant enterprises, then the total expenditure on the expansion in these years would have been £13,000,-000, of which the gentry and other non-merchants contributed some £1,500,000, or under 12 percent. In this case the discrepancy between numbers and payments (24 percent *versus* under 12 percent) shows that the gentry and non-merchants provided more than twice as large a proportion of the investors as they did of the investments.

The Contribution of the Gentry. The merchants were clearly the vital driving force behind England's expansion. To be more specific, because only a very small percentage of the funds came from provincial ports, it was the London merchant community that dominated the entire effort. Nonetheless, as has been stressed, even commercial growth is not fed by bread alone. The gentry's share of the endeavor cannot be measured solely in terms of their numbers or investments. The fact that they participated at all, and that some 1,200 of them subscribed £1,500,000 (something like $150,000,000 in the mid-1960's) in the course of 56 years was in itself an unprecedented phenomenon in European history. Not only did it testify to a cohesiveness in the social structure that was unique to England among Western nations, but it demonstrated the firm commitment of the country's leaders to overseas enterprise. And there can be no doubt that the whole movement received a tremendous stimulus merely from the par-

[97] Not including "other ventures" — see note 94.

68

ticipation of the landed classes. From the Court and from adventurous gentlemen brimming over with projects and enthusiasm came the momentum that transformed a series of commercial undertakings into a great national enterprise. In ideas and encouragement alone they contributed far more than can be calculated from their numbers or investments. Even in terms of financial support there can be no denying that they helped substantially to amass the enormous funds necessary to surmount the first few hurdles before tangible results could be achieved.

As has been mentioned, a very large part of the money listed in Table 5 was completely lost. Outside of the East India Company and a few windfalls like the 180 pounds of ambergris found in Bermuda,[98] hardly any returns were received on these investments. It could be said that most of the sums simply had to be wasted before the extremely difficult early stages of development were passed. And yet, viewed as a national effort, they were of course not wasted. The individual subscribers may have seen no profits, but when the Virginia Company was dissolved after 18 years of seemingly fruitless effort, the colony it had established remained and eventually waxed profitable on the American mainland. The accomplishments of most of these undertakings cannot be judged by their financial dividends. Certainly at its face value the effort expended in Elizabeth's reign might seem to have been the almost total failure described by Sandys in 1599.[99] But vital experience had been gained, and the interest and determination had been aroused that were to bring spectacular successes in the next decades. During this pioneer stage, when setbacks were frequent, it was essential to marshal as much of the nation's resources as could be found. And here the gentry's role was crucial. It was precisely in the least financially profitable ventures that their money was invested: in the companies listed in Table 5, for which they supplied a fifth of the funds. Perhaps the same capital could have been raised without their help, but it is exceedingly doubtful. In both monetary assistance and inspiration the gentry's participation was vital to the foundation of England's empire.

[98] Wilkinson, *Bermuda*, p. 59: it was worth over £10,000.

[99] See note 30, above. Suppliers of shipping and stores, of course, often profited even from disastrous undertakings. And Bacon, speaking of Virginia and Bermuda, realized that "sometimes a grain of mustardseed proves a great tree." See *Letters and Life*, ed. Spedding, VII, p. 175.

IV. THE RISE AND FALL OF POPULAR INTEREST

Between the incorporation of the Muscovy Company in the 1550's and the launching of Frobisher's expeditions in 1576, interest in new overseas ventures was sporadic. Trade with Russia proceeded steadily; there was a growing interest in Africa; the attempt to enter the Caribbean was cut short at San Juan de Ulua; and the Minerals and Mines Companies were founded. There were a few other voyages, notably Drake's earliest raids, but at most there cannot have been more than 500 investors in these efforts.[100] But in the second half of the 1570's, with the search for the North-West Passage, Drake's circumnavigation, the creation of a Spanish Company, the establishment of the Eastland Company, and Gilbert's first interest in America, a new era opened. Between 1575 and 1579 alone some 500 people were involved in new enterprises or organizations. In the early 1580's, with the foundation of the Levant and Venice Companies, Gilbert's Newfoundland voyage, Fenton's expedition, the first efforts in Virginia, the beginnings of privateering, and colonization in Munster, the momentum increased. Although in the late 1580's and 1590's, faced by repeated failures, an economic recession, and a mounting war with Spain, the pace slackened somewhat — except in privateering — the undercurrent of interest in overseas expansion did not die away completely: there were renewed attempts to colonize Virginia, to find a North-West Passage, and to circumnavigate the earth; there was a growing drive to open a direct trade with the Far East; there were fitful efforts in Munster, and pioneering expeditions to Guiana and the St. Lawrence.[101] The sense of national enterprise was still

[100] See note 12 to chapter 3. On Africa, see J. W. Blake, *European Beginnings in West Africa, 1454–1578* (London, 1937), pp. 138–191. On San Juan de Ulua, see Rayner Unwin, *The Defeat of John Hawkins* (London, 1960).

[101] See above, notes 81 and 82. On the St. Lawrence, see D. B. Quinn, "The English and the St. Lawrence 1577–1602," in *Merchants and Scholars: Essays in the History of Exploration and Trade*, ed. John Parker (Minneapolis, 1965), pp. 117–143, and "The First Pilgrims," *William and Mary Quarterly*, 3rd ser., 23 (1966), 359–390; and Cell, "Newfoundland," pp. 112–117. It should be noted that, although new enterprises were few in the late 1580's and 1590's, interest in overseas affairs was not lacking in stimuli. The impact of Drake's return in 1580 may not have been repeated, but considerable stir was made by such events as the capture of the *Madre de Dios* in 1592 and the return in 1588 of John Eldred, after five years' travel and trade in the Levant, with "the richest ship of English merchants goods that ever was known to come into this realm." See C. L. Kingsford, "The Taking of the Madre de Dios," *Naval Miscellany* (London: Navy Rec-

growing; and when, after the turn of the century, peace with Spain and an economic boom coincided with the foundation of a whole series of new undertakings, investors in unprecedented numbers were drawn into commercial and colonial schemes. The height of the influx came in the first 15 years of James I's reign; then, in the face of a major economic depression and the persistent difficulties encountered by most of the companies, disillusionment set in. The rate of investment declined sharply, though it was to revive briefly again as a result of special circumstances in the late 1620's. Privateering resumed during the war with France and Spain, and a few companies associated with political and religious opponents of the government were founded in this final period; but they were the last manifestation of an effort that had lasted over half a century. Although the great companies were firmly established, and were little affected by the decline of interest, no major new joint-stock ventures were launched after 1630 until the Restoration.[102]

This, in outline, was how the wave of interest rose and fell between 1575 and 1630. The following three tables and figure present the detailed fluctuations. Table 6, which lists the number of people admitted each year, is designed primarily to show differences between the levels of gentry and merchant participation. Because averaging was not possible to compensate for the consolidated figures (marked ^{c}), it is useful as an indication of chronological changes only over a long range. Its prime purpose is to show the relative proportions of the investors supplied by the two classes at different times. Table 7 and the table and figure which follow it (both based on Table 7) incorporate the averaging described in the note. Thus they can be taken as fairly accurate representations of the number of annual admissions to companies. The column in Table 7 showing the number of investments per investor reveals that the basic figure in this table (admissions) is rather different from that used in Table 6 (peo-

ords Society, XL, 1912); and the comment on Eldred in Hakluyt, *Principal Navigations*, VI, 9. Moreover, the Munster Plantation was making considerable progress. Professor Quinn has pointed out to me that some 15,000 colonists may have been settled in Munster by the mid-1590's.

[102] See Figure 1. The next major wave of investment came with the founding of the Hudson's Bay and Royal Africa Companies at the end of the first decade of Charles II's reign. My cut-off point of 1630 is justified in greater detail in the section entitled "Coverage," in chapter 3.

Table 6. Number of people admitted annually to companies, 1575–1630, by class.[a]

Year	Number of people admitted	Percent of 56-year total	Gentry admitted	Percent of 56-year gentry total	Merchants admitted	Percent of 56-year merchant total
1575	42	0.6	17	1.3	24	0.5
1576	10	0.1	2	0.2	5	0.1
1577	383	5.1	31	2.4	336	6.8
1578	42	0.6	29	2.3	9	0.2
1579	59	0.8	–	–	59	1.2
1580[b]	67[c]	0.9	7	0.6	59	1.2
1581[b]	307[c]	4.1	54	4.2	232	4.7
1582	19	0.3	5	0.4	11	0.2
1583	94	1.3	32	2.5	40	0.8
1584	74[d]	1.0	39	3.1	3	0.1
1585	32	0.4	3	0.2	26	0.5
1586	4	0.1	3	0.2	1	0.0
1587	26	0.3	14	1.1	12	0.2
1588	19	0.3	–	–	19	0.4
1589	24	0.3	4	0.3	19	0.4
1590	28	0.4	6	0.5	21	0.4
1591[e]	–	–	–	–	–	–
1592	20	0.3	1	0.1	18	0.4
1593[e]	–	–	–	–	–	–
1594	1	0.0	–	–	1	0.0
1595–97[e]	–	–	–	–	–	–
1598	2	0.0	2	0.2	–	–
1599	94	1.3	2	0.2	91	1.8
1600	154	2.1	2	0.2	152	3.1
1601	19	0.3	–	–	19	0.4
1602	4	0.1	2	0.2	2	0.0
1603	1	0.0	1	0.1	–	–
1604	483	6.5	18	1.4	464	9.4
1605	197	2.6	11	0.9	185	3.7
1606	69	0.9	9	0.7	58	1.2
1607	67	0.9	21	1.7	41	0.8
1608	27	0.4	7	0.6	17	0.3
1609	1,111	14.9	196	15.4	707	14.3
1610[b]	260[c]	3.5	95	7.5	150	3.0
1611	645	8.6	56	4.4	559	11.3
1612	411	5.5	175	13.8	216	4.4
1613	59	0.8	10	0.8	26	0.5
1614	95	1.3	15	1.2	65	1.3
1615	263	3.5	32	2.5	213	4.3
1616	16	0.2	3	0.2	10	0.2
1617	66	0.9	18	1.4	31	0.6
1618	257	3.4	69	5.4	99	2.0
1619	115	1.5	42	3.3	53	1.1

Table 6 (continued)

Year	Number of people admitted	Percent of 56-year total	Gentry admitted	Percent of 56-year gentry total	Merchants admitted	Percent of 56-year merchant total
1620[b]	303[c]	4.1	52	4.1	180	3.6
1621	60	0.8	16	1.3	17	0.3
1622	111	1.5	13	1.0	40	0.8
1623	82	1.1	18	1.4	33	0.7
1624	142	1.9	10	0.8	113	2.3
1625[b]	724[c]	9.7	40	3.1	317	6.4
1626	43	0.6	1	0.1	36	0.7
1627	104	1.4	38	3.0	46	0.9
1628	76	1.0	11	0.9	49	1.0
1629	142	1.9	27	2.1	63	1.3
1630[b]	18[c]	0.2	15	1.2	2	0.0
Total	7,471		1,274 (or 17.0% of 7,471)		4,949 (or 66.3% of 7,471)	

[a] The total for column 1 is greater than the sum of columns 3 and 5 because the breakdowns do not include unclassified or professional/yeomen investors.

[b] See the notes to Tables 6 and 7, following Table 7.

[c] Figures are the results of the special coding adopted for certain companies where precise dates of admission are not known — see chapter 3, especially the sections on the Bermuda, Eastland, Muscovy, and Plymouth Companies and privateering, and pp. 105–106, 154–155 and 166.

[d] See the note on 1584 at the foot of this page.

[e] No admissions were recorded.

ple), but it is just as valid an indicator of fluctuations of interest.

Some of the high points in these figures derive in part from a few specific charters, as is indicated in Figure 1. A few further breakdowns can be given here: *1575* consists mostly of surviving members of the Minerals and Mines Companies, founded a few years earlier; *1579* is made up primarily of founding members of the Eastland Company; *1583* consists very largely of backers of Gilbert; *1584* contains a heavy concentration of the Munster venturers, who were not averaged out because so very little is known about the dates of their interest. (Not until this book was in press, however, did I notice that the date 1584 was the result of a typographical error in the computer program. It should have been 1586, the first year of the undertaking. As will be seen, the long-range annual figures are not significantly affected by the

Table 7.   Total annual admissions to companies, 1575–1630.

Year	Total admissions	After averaging	Percent of all admissions in 56 years	After averaging	Ratio of admissions to people entering companies in this year (column 1 divided by column 1 of Table 6)
1575	65	(69)	0.7	(0.8)	1.55
1576	18	(22)	0.2	(0.2)	1.80
1577	458	(462)	5.0	(5.1)	1.20
1578	51	(55)	0.6	(0.6)	1.22
1579	66	(70)	0.7	(0.8)	1.12
1580[b]	111[a]	(15)	1.2	(0.2)	1.66
1581[b]	399[a]	(108)	4.4	(1.2)	1.30
1582	29	(47)	0.3	(0.5)	1.53
1583	115	(133)	1.3	(1.5)	1.22
1584	82[c]	(100)	0.9	(1.1)	1.11
1585	55	(73)	0.6	(0.8)	1.72
1586	5	(23)	0.1	(0.3)	1.25
1587	35	(53)	0.4	(0.6)	1.35
1588	20	(38)	0.2	(0.4)	1.05
1589	41	(59)	0.5	(0.7)	1.71
1590	37	(55)	0.4	(0.6)	1.32
1591	–	(18)	–	(0.2)	–
1592	29	(47)	0.3	(0.5)	1.45
1593	–	(18)	–	(0.2)	–
1594	5	(23)	0.1	(0.3)	5.00
1595	–	(18)	–	(0.2)	–
1596	–	(18)	–	(0.2)	–
1597	–	(18)	–	(0.2)	–
1598	2	(20)	0.0	(0.2)	1.00
1599	141	(159)	1.6	(1.7)	1.50
1600	197	(215)	2.2	(2.4)	1.28
1601	26	(46)	0.3	(0.5)	1.37
1602	6	(26)	0.1	(0.3)	1.50
1603	1	(21)	0.0	(0.2)	1.00
1604	540	(546)	5.9	(6.0)	1.12
1605	256	(262)	2.8	(2.9)	1.30
1606	85	(108)	0.9	(1.2)	1.23
1607	81	(104)	0.9	(1.2)	1.21
1608	29	(52)	0.3	(0.6)	1.07
1609	1,294	(1,317)	14.2	(14.5)	1.16
1610[b]	301[a]	(239)	3.3	(2.6)	1.16
1611	794	(800)	8.7	(8.8)	1.23
1612	545	(551)	6.0	(6.1)	1.33

Table 7 (continued)

Year	Total admissions	After averaging	Percent of all admissions in 56 years	After averaging	Ratio of admissions to people entering companies in this year (column 1 divided by column 1 of Table 6)
1613	69	(75)	0.8	(0.8)	1.17
1614	107	(113)	1.2	(1.2)	1.13
1615	404	(410)	4.4	(4.5)	1.54
1616	54	(64)	0.6	(0.7)	3.38
1617	71	(81)	0.8	(0.9)	1.08
1618	299	(309)	3.3	(3.4)	1.16
1619	143	(153)	1.6	(1.7)	1.24
1620[b]	375[a]	(154)	4.1	(1.7)	1.24
1621	66	(85)	0.7	(0.9)	1.10
1622	123	(142)	1.4	(1.6)	1.11
1623	99	(118)	1.1	(1.3)	1.21
1624	161	(180)	1.8	(2.0)	1.13
1625[b]	792[a]	(171)	8.7	(1.9)	1.09
1626	46	(165)	0.5	(1.8)	1.07
1627	121	(240)	1.3	(2.6)	1.16
1628	81	(200)	0.9	(2.2)	1.07
1629	155	(270)	1.7	(3.0)	1.09
1630[b]	20[a]	(135)	0.2	(1.5)	1.11
Total	9,104				

[a] Figures are the results of the special coding adopted for certain companies where precise dates of admission are not known — see chapter 3, especially the sections on the Bermuda, Eastland, Muscovy, and Plymouth Companies and privateering, and pp. 105-106, 154-155 and 166.

[b] See the notes to Tables 6 and 7 below.

[c] See the note on 1584 on page 73.

Notes to Tables 6 and 7: Averaging

1580 contains all members of the Muscovy Company during the last quarter of the sixteenth century — 100 people, whose figures have been averaged out in Table 7 over the period 1575–1600. A few known to have been active in 1575 were entered at that year in Table 6.

1581 contains all Elizabethan backers of privateering and raids against the Spaniards: 389 people, whose figures have been averaged out in Table 7 over the period 1581–1603. A few known to have become active at a later date were so entered in Table 6.

1610 contains 85 members of the Levant Company who have been averaged out in Table 7 over the period 1606–1610, from which no records have survived.

1620 contains three consolidations: 111 members of the Russia Company, averaged

Table 8.   Percentages, in successive periods, of total admissions to companies, 1575–1630 (based on the averaged figures in Table 7).

Period	Percentage of all admissions between 1575 and 1630	Average annual percentage, in each period, of all admissions between 1575 and 1630
1575–1598	16.5	0.7
1599–1603	9.9	2.0
1604–1608	11.3	2.3
1609–1615	36.5	5.2
1616–1620	8.0	1.6
1621–1630	17.8	1.8

out in Table 7 over the years 1601–1630; 68 members of the Eastland Company, averaged out in Table 7 over the years 1601–1625; 52 members of the Bermuda Company, averaged out in Table 7 over the years 1616–1628.

1625 also contains three consolidations: 664 backers of privateering during the war with France and Spain, averaged out in Table 7 over the years 1625–1630; 42 members of the Eastland Company, averaged out in Table 7 over the years 1601–1630; 45 Plymouth adventurers, averaged out in Table 7 over the years 1621–1625.

1630 contains no consolidations, but requires special mention. The figure is low because the East India and Levant Company admissions for this year were not included in the list.

Although, for the sake of increased accuracy, these figures were averaged out in Table 7 (the columns in parentheses), the results should not be regarded as precise records of annual admissions. Little more than 60 percent of the company entries in the list can be dated exactly, because the only records that can be relied on for this purpose are founding charters and minutes of meetings. The remainder are entered at the date of first mention, which is hardly better than an approximation of the date of admission. And, though the 1,376 admissions that have been averaged out represent only 15 percent of the entire total, the process of averaging them was uncertain at best. Some of the groups (e.g., the Elizabethan privateers) were doubtless subject to large annual fluctuations, and the terminal dates for the Muscovy and Eastland figures were themselves approximations. Moreover, as is indicated in Table 9, there were some Levant, Virginia, and East India Company lists for which a meaningful chronological distribution could not be devised. Even with averaging, therefore, these figures must be used with caution, and are most useful when taken over a period of years, as is done in Table 8 and Figure 1.

In Table 6 it was impossible to average them out over the years they covered, because the consolidations were of *admissions*, not of *people*, whereas the latter unit was the one used in Table 6. Naturally, the computer could have made the conversion, but such complexities would have been introduced (for example, should a man appear in two separate years if he had two admissions in a "consolidated" year, when a man who had two "nonconsolidated" entries in a year appeared only once?), that the result would not have been very satisfactory. Moreover, Table 7, in which the averaging was relatively simple, was quite sufficient as an indicator of the rise and fall of rates of investment.

It should be noted that investments of no specified date have been omitted from the figures in these tables.

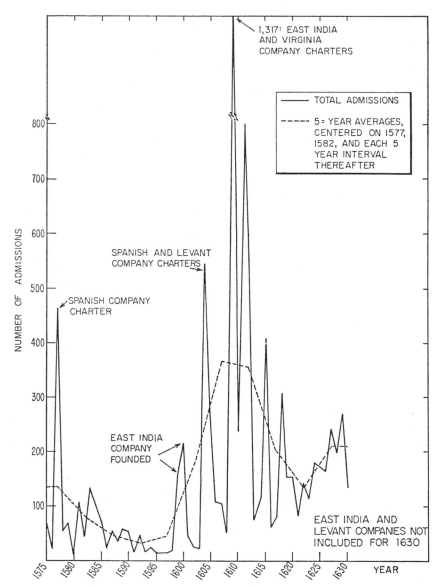

Figure 1. Annual admissions to companies (after averaging), 1575–1630 (based on Table 7)

two-year misplacement of the 76 Munster adventurers.) *1605* consists mainly of Levant and Spanish Company members; *1611* includes the large group of founding members of the French Company; *1612* is made up principally of the founding members

77

of the North-West Passage Company, and the new names in the third Virginia Company charter. *1615* consists primarily of the incorporators of the Bermuda Company, and the founding members of the New Merchant Adventurers; *1618* contains a large number of new names found in a list of Virginia Company investors that Kingsbury ascribed tentatively to this date;[103] *1629* is made up substantially of the charter members of the Massachusetts Bay Company; *1630* consists only of the founders of the Providence Island Company. In addition, consultation of Table 9 will indicate how many admissions each year were recorded by the East India, Virginia, and Levant Companies; and still greater detail can be obtained by reference to the company coding described in the key to the Appendix and the totals given in Chapter 2.

The main interest of Table 6 lies in the differences between the waves of interest among gentry and merchants. Almost 54 percent of the gentry entered a company in just seven years: between 1609 and 1612, and between 1618 and 1620. In the same period, even though it includes consolidations of the Levant, Eastland, and Muscovy Companies — all of which increased the merchant figures substantially and artificially — under 37 percent of the merchants entered a company. These years witnessed a large number of admissions in general (over 41 percent of all people in the list entered a company at this time), but the very much higher gentry level was undoubtedly due to their particular susceptibility to the recruitment campaigns of three companies: the North-West Passage, the Bermuda, and above all, the Virginia. The latter alone accounted for 458 of the 685 gentry admitted in this period. The other major difference comes in the seven years between 1599 and 1605, when just under 19 percent of the merchants joined a company, as opposed to three percent of the gentry. The effects of the peace with Spain (seen in the organization of the Spanish Company and a rapid rise in admissions to the Levant Company) and the opening of trade with the Far East were clearly of greater importance to merchants than to gentry. Since this period also saw the beginning of the tremendous rise in the numbers of annual investors (see Figure 1), it would seem that we have here further evidence of the lead taken by the merchants. The other differences between the two

[103] Kingsbury, *Records,* III, 79–90.

78

classes appear to have little significance. The much higher gentry levels in 1583 and 1584 were caused by the Gilbert and Munster ventures; and the variations in the 1620's were probably due to the consolidations made for 1625. The 10-year total between 1621 and 1630 was almost identical for both classes, and it can only be suggested that perhaps the lower merchant levels in 1621–23 represent the effect of the economic depression.

Tables 7 and 8 and Figure 1 reinforce the pattern described in the opening paragraph of this section. In the first place, it is clear that the period through 1598, though witnessing many more new investments than had ever been made by Englishmen in so short a period, was only a foretaste of what was to come. As can be seen in Table 8, only 16.5 percent of all investments in our 56-year period were made in the 24 years between 1575 and 1598. And three-quarters of the 1575–98 investments were made before 1586. (See Figure 1.) In fact, for most of the 1586–98 period average annual admissions remained below 50, and in five of these years (1591, 1593, 1595, 1596, 1597) none at all was recorded, except for a few small undertakings included under "other ventures," and the continuing interest in the Muscovy Company and privateering which has been averaged out in Table 7. Thus the enthusiasm aroused in the late 1570's and early 1580's by Frobisher, Drake, Gilbert, Raleigh, and the new companies in the Eastland, Spanish, Levant, Venice, and Barbary trades did not continue at the same high pitch. In the end, the failures of Frobisher's, Fenton's, and Gilbert's efforts must have had their effect — doubtless reinforced by the additional failures of Davis and the Roanoke colony. But even more important were the war with Spain — which absorbed so much of the nation's resources in major naval expeditions (and ended the life of the Spanish Company) — and the economic depression that gripped the country, beginning in 1586.[104] There can be no doubt that nearly all the attention devoted to overseas enterprise in this period was concentrated on privateering. Of the 408 admissions entered, after averaging, for these 13 years, 182 were provided, again after averaging, by privateering. And it is arguable that the per-

[104] See B. E. Supple, *Commercial Crisis and Change in England 1600–1642: A Study in the Instability of a Mercantile Economy* (Cambridge, England, 1959), pp. 23–24; and Scott, *Joint-Stock Companies,* I, 88–129.

centage should be even higher, because most of the investments in privateering took place between 1585 and 1603, whereas the averaging in Table 7 starts in 1581. There were some admissions to the Levant and Muscovy Companies, and there were a few voyages such as those by Lancaster and Cavendish. But however well some groups, notably the Levant traders, may have been doing, by 1600 this particular company still had only 87 members[105] — nothing like the breadth of interest concentrated on the privateers. K. R. Andrews' thesis that privateering played a vital role in the formative years of England's expansion is resoundingly confirmed.[106] The "sea dogs" kept alive the maritime activity that was to increase dramatically as soon as more favorable conditions returned.

The period between 1599 and 1603 has been isolated in Table 8 because (although neither the economic depression nor the war with Spain were over) there was new evidence of the growing interest in expansion in the foundation of the East India Company and a new charter for the Levant Company — reflected by the figures for 1599 and 1600, as is indicated in Figure 1. Despite the slump which once again followed this burst of activity, average annual admissions during this half-decade remained over 100. And this was so despite the terrible plague of 1603 which virtually brought London's trade to a standstill.[107] For a while, though, these new exertions certainly did not appear to be producing any lasting results. In late 1601 the Court — as concerned as ever with overseas affairs — was bringing considerable pressure to bear on the East India Company, which, Elizabeth felt, was being rather "slack" in its efforts. The national interest was invoked,

[105] Wood, *Levant Company*, pp. 23–24. This impression of the Levant Company's prosperity is strongly reinforced by the view — accepted by most historians — that the East India Company was founded by Levant merchants as a supplement to, and expansion of, a trade that was already doing very well. See Chaudhuri, *East India Company*, pp. 10–14. For the contrary view, see Scott, *Joint-Stock Companies*, II, 97.

[106] Andrews, *Elizabethan Privateering*, *passim*, especially pp. 159–238. The contrary view, stated in face of all the evidence, is in H. R. Wagner, *Sir Francis Drake's Voyage around the World* (San Francisco, 1926), p. 211: "One of the worst effects produced by the orgy of piracy through which England passed at this period was to engender a profound disdain among the better classes for any legitimate gainful occupation." The only other major overseas enterprise that appears to have flourished throughout the war was the fishing trade centered on Newfoundland (see Cell, "Newfoundland," pp. 67–77).

[107] See Supple, *Commercial Crisis*, pp. 25–26.

and the company was urged to prosecute the trade with more vigor.[108] But then, with the new reign, circumstances changed, and the pressures were no longer needed.

For more than the first decade of James I's rule there was an unmistakable economic boom. On this one point all economic historians, from Scott to Supple, appear to agree.[109] And if the rate of investment can be assumed to reflect the general economic situation, then the figures for the period 1604–15 in Table 7 and Figure 1 strongly confirm the pattern suggested by other indicators, such as volume of exports. The first major wave of admissions followed the conclusion of peace with Spain in 1604. As might be expected, the impact was felt chiefly by the Spanish and Levant Companies. Between them they provided almost 700 of some 900 new admissions (an unprecedented total number) in the three years 1604, 1605, and 1606. Taking the long-range view, however, particular significance must be ascribed to the fact that interest in North America once again began to rise in this period, particularly when it became apparent that peace with Spain would allow Englishmen to turn their energies toward colonies which no longer would be under direct threat of attack from the greatest power in the Western Hemisphere. Following the voyages of Pring, Gosnold, and Weymouth, all between 1602 and 1605, the foundation of the Virginia Company in 1606 marked the beginning of a new era. Although it survived for only 18 years, no other company approached the number of subscribers it attracted. The East India Company in 30 years attained little more than three-quarters the size of membership enjoyed by the Virginia Company. Among the remaining enterprises of the time, none even reached two-thirds of its numbers. Moreover, almost half of all the gentry who contributed to trade during this half-century joined the Virginia Company. The fame and importance of England's first successful colonial venture was unequaled as a means of eliciting commitments to England's expansion.

But the crest of the wave was yet to come. Whichever way one looks at it, and however generously one assesses the efforts of the preceding 30 years or half-century, all of which assuredly pre-

[108] *CSP, East Indies, 1513–1616*, pp. 128–130.
[109] Scott, *Joint-Stock Companies*, I, 129–142; and Supple, *Commercial Crisis*, pp. 26–32. See, too, Fisher, "London's Export Trade," pp. 152–153.

pared the way, one still cannot help but be amazed by the surge of investment between 1609 and 1615. Some 3,500 admissions were recorded in these seven years; and in 1609 alone there were almost as many as in the entire 1575–98 period. Since this was the time when the Virginia Company admitted most of its members, when some 50 gentry joined the East India Company, and when major gentry ventures such as the North-West Passage, Newfoundland, and Bermuda Companies were launched, these years also witnessed the most marked influx of the landed classes into trading and colonial enterprises. Approximately half of all the gentry in the list joined a company in these seven years. As has been mentioned, merchant interest was not, proportionately, as high, but in terms of absolute numbers the merchants still provided over three times as many investors as the gentry (see Table 6). Some 230 of them joined the East India Company in this period — the largest influx since 1599 and 1600 (see Table 9); they easily outnumbered the gentry even in those companies, just mentioned, in which gentlemen had a particular interest; and they founded almost entirely on their own the Londonderry Plantation, the French Company, and the New Merchant Adventurers, all very large organizations. There can be no doubt, therefore, that this was by far the most active period throughout the 56 years.

Why this should have been so can be explained by reference to both long-range and immediate conditions. It was, first, a consequence of interest that had been rising for decades. After 1604, with the coming of peace and economic prosperity, and with joint-stock methods at hand, a major opportunity arose for attracting capital to enterprises that promised great profit in both money and prestige. Merchants were doing well in trade, and gentlemen were doing well from rents and agricultural prices;[110] hence both classes had the capability of supporting large-scale new efforts. The greatest boom did not come immediately after 1604, except in the Mediterranean trade, because a new generation of organizers was only slowly coming to the fore. Drake, Gilbert, Hawkins, Frobisher, the Elizabethan courtiers, and merchants like Sir George Barnes, Sir Rowland Hayward, Sir Lionel Duckett, and Sir Edward Osborne were dead; Raleigh was in the Tower; and Captain John Davis, interested as ever in service

[110] See notes 20, 95, and 96, above.

82

overseas, met an untimely end when, after having worked for the Dutch to gain experience in the Far East and having given his valuable knowledge to the East India Company, he was killed in the Strait of Malacca in 1605. Among the gentry, new faces were slowly emerging — Gorges, Southampton, Calvert, Sandys, and Rich. Many of the old captains like Christopher Newport remained, leading the way in pioneering voyages both to America and India; but their patrons were changing. Among the merchants, a much larger group, there was more continuity than among the gentry: Smith, Watts, the Middletons, Garaway, and the Stapers straddled the two periods. But many new men were coming to prominence in London too — Cockayne, the Crispes, Hamersley, Clitheroe, Wolstenholme, Harrison. It is significant that renewed interest in Virginia appeared as soon as the war with Spain ended, and even before. It just took a period of organization and — more important — the first success before widespread interest could be aroused.

This brings us to the second, more immediate reason for the massive influx of the 1609–1615 period. It was not until 1606, 1607, and 1608 that any real confidence could be commanded by the two principal undertakings of the time, the East India trade and the Virginia colony. After the return of the first voyage to India in 1603, that company's members went through three very difficult years: the profits from the first voyage were badly delayed; there were difficulties in raising money for a second expedition; the King gave Sir Edward Michelborne permission to open a rival trade (in which John Davis was to be killed); and then the second voyage became long overdue. When, in 1606, the second expedition finally returned with a good profit, new life was given the company. As its most recent historian puts it, with the third voyage "the scale of its operation becomes perceptibly more ambitious and the growth of confidence is reflected in the decision to send annual voyages to the Indies even before the result of the previous ones had become known." [111] This was in 1607. In the same year, both halves of the newly organized Virginia Company sent colonists to America. Early in 1608, following the usual pattern of English settlements, the northern colony was abandoned. But the plantation on the banks of the James

[111] Chaudhuri, *East India Company,* p. 40.

River, reinforced by two supply ships, persevered, and the news of its survival, reaching London by midyear, set the stage for a reorganization which was to expand the size of the Company far beyond its founders' expectations. A major propaganda and recruitment campaign was launched, and hundreds of new subscribers were found by the time a new charter was drawn up in May of 1609. A member of the peerage, Lord De La Warr, went out to govern the colony in 1610, and under his leadership the settlement was more firmly established.

The effect of the successes in both these endeavors would be difficult to overestimate, particularly if one recalls that at the same time, in 1608 and 1609, the Londonderry Plantation was also being organized amid much publicity. These activities set the example, and in the next few years many of the same leaders were to be involved in promoting a new search for the North-West Passage, a colony on Bermuda, a fresh effort in Guiana, a renewed attempt to settle Newfoundland, and the other projects which helped to swell the numbers of investors between 1609 and 1615. The interest that Virginia and the East Indies were able to arouse spilled over into a variety of schemes, and thus the great boom was nurtured.

But successes turned out to be few and far between. The East India Company returned a steady profit, and the Irish colony was progressing well, but elsewhere there was little to report except large expenses with little or no return. The Virginia Company became the seat of growing resentment at leaders who seemed to be accomplishing nothing tangible; in Newfoundland and toward the North-West Passage nothing but unrewarding hardship had been endured; and none of the smaller enterprises, in Guiana or elsewhere, were bearing fruit. In 1615, too, the trading community was disrupted by Cockayne's project, the disastrous effect of which on England's vital cloth export would sap the energies of the merchants until they were overtaken by the depression of the early 1620's.[112] Nonetheless, the five years from 1616 to 1620 did witness a continued, albeit smaller, effort to maintain the expansion. A new recruitment drive by the Virginia Company,

[112] Friis, *Cockayne's Project, passim;* Supple, *Commercial Crisis,* pp. 52–72; Kerridge, "The Movement of Rent," p. 28; J. D. Gould, "The Trade Depression of the Early 1620's," *Ec.H.R.,* 2nd ser., 7 (1954), 81–90; and Fisher, "London's Export Trade," pp. 155–158.

launched when the leadership changed hands, brought in some 250 new members between 1618 and 1620. The East India Company organized a new joint stock in 1617, and in its first three years the offering attracted almost 200 new members. (See Table 9, below.) New ventures in Guiana, Africa, and New England were started; and there can be little doubt that the leading entrepreneurs (Smith, Wolstenholme, Sandys, Warwick, Southampton, Gorges) were, if anything, more active in these years than they had ever been before.

In the terrible depression of the early 1620's, however, the momentum built up in James I's reign was clearly lost. Not only trade in general, but even the great companies — in particular the East India and the Virginia — came on very hard times. The East India Company finally and decisively lost its battle with the Dutch for control of the Spice Islands. A reorganization was needed, and the 1620's began what K. N. Chaudhuri has called "the years of crisis." [113] Meanwhile, the Virginia Company was dissolved in an atmosphere of bankruptcy and disillusionment.[114] A terrible plague in London in the following year, 1625, increased the difficulties;[115] and the renewal of war, now with France as well as Spain, bode ill for the future. The crisis was, of course, surmounted, and the 1630's were to be a period of major recovery and consolidation of the new trades which had been established during the expansion.[116] The dependence on cloth had been replaced with a varied and far-ranging commerce that was to be the basis of England's future growth. The East India and Levant Companies were to go from strength to strength; and Virginia and Bermuda, bolstered by a lucrative tobacco crop, were to enjoy growing prosperity. But these were all matters of consolidation: none of these enterprises now attracted large numbers of new investors. Moreover, the undertakings started in the 1620's were very different in character from those of Jacobean times.

True, the war did release a tremendous wave of privateering,

---

[113] Chaudhuri, *East India Company*, pp. 56–73. See also *Letters of Chamberlain,* ed. McClure, II, 440, 509, 524.

[114] Craven, *Virginia Company*, pp. 148–336.

[115] Supple, *Commercial Crisis*, pp. 25–26.

[116] See Millard, "Imports of London," pp. 115–149; Fisher, "London's Export Trade," pp. 153–154, 159–160; Hinton, *Eastland Trade*, p. 49; Wood, *Levant Company*, pp. 42–52; and Supple, *Commercial Crisis*, pp. 118–119.

which in six years involved more people than it had in 18 years of Elizabeth's reign.[117] But this was a lone phenomenon, and even this enterprise lacked the aura of crusade and pioneering adventure that had surrounded the "sea dogs" of the sixteenth century. The sense of national effort, of opening new areas for England's profit and glory, was noticeably subdued. Hakluyt was dead, Purchas died in the mid-1620's, and thereafter the propaganda was at a much lower pitch. Understandably, none of the ventures attracted large numbers of people; and the annual admissions, even including the huge spurt of privateering, were only about 60 people more per year than in the 1575–1585 decade, when far fewer organizations had existed. The principal new exploits of the time succeeded only when they depended on a very small group of subscribers, or when they turned to aims totally unlike those which the earlier promoters had pursued. Gorges and Mason in New England, and the Courteens and the Herberts in the West Indies, were the lone survivors of the tradition of Raleigh and Gilbert. Significantly, they had to finance their schemes virtually on their own. The only sizeable undertaking along old lines was the Guiana Company, a joint-stock organization that hoped to establish a colony where others had failed since the 1590's. But it fared dismally, for it attracted less than 70 members and proved to be incapable of raising adequate funds. Meanwhile, those larger companies which did succeed turned out to be very different from the companies of previous decades.

With the high hopes of earlier years crumbling away; with merchants either hampered by economic difficulties or content to follow the new trades that were now well established; and with the "passive" gentry withdrawing in disillusionment from commerce, leaving behind only their most determined representatives, such as Gorges or Sandys; a motive other than profit — so conspicuously absent hitherto — was needed. It was provided by the rising religious and political difficulties which, though for

[117] The respective figures are 664 and 389, but the size of the Elizabethan group is undoubtedly too small, because the records are nowhere near so complete as they are for Charles I's reign. The more businesslike atmosphere of the Caroline efforts is indicated by the presence of East India Company privateers. In 1628 and 1629 the Company obtained letters of marque for the largest privateers of the period under discussion: a 500-ton ship in 1628, and ships of 400, 500, 600, and 700 tons in 1629. See *CSP, Domestic, 1628–1629*, p. 308; and *1629–1631*, p. 153.

many people an added distraction that lessened concern for overseas expansion, for others proved to be a stimulus to interests outside of England. Thus the adventurers in Plymouth Plantation supported emigrants who wished to leave their homeland because "religion hath been disgraced, [and] the godly grieved, afflicted, [and] persecuted." [118] Within a few years after leaving, the new colonists bought out the subscribers who stayed in England, making themselves completely independent of the home country.

Much the same was true of the largest new foundation of the 1620's, the Massachusetts Bay Company. Its parent organization, the Dorchester Company, had been set up to give religious instruction to fishermen in America, "and to provide a refuge to which Churchmen could flee when no longer able to comply with Laud's demands." [119] When the Massachusetts Bay Company was first organized in 1628, at least 25 of its 41 founding members had taken part in other Puritan ventures.[120] Their aim was quite clear, and the most detailed historian of the company has stated categorically that "their main object was religious; at the first opportunity they recorded that their enterprise was 'for the propagation of the Gospel of Jesus Christ.'" [121] In the following year, when the company could count 121 members, the aim was still "the planting of the Gospel" in New England,[122] a motive which received exclusive stress, unlike any colonizing effort between 1580 and 1620. Following the Plymouth adventurers, the company soon decided to transfer its government to America,[123] cutting off its dependence on England. Trade was not entirely neglected, but it was left in the hands of subscribers who remained in London, and within a few years their joint stock was wound up[124] and the last transatlantic bonds removed. Even the settlers themselves noticed the difference from previous English undertakings. One of them wrote in 1633 that whereas Virginia had

[118] William Bradford, *Of Plymouth Plantation 1620–1647*, ed. S. E. Morison (New York, 1953), p. 7.
[119] Frances Rose-Troup, *The Massachusetts Bay Company*, p. 13. The reference to Laud is obviously premature, but the general point retains its validity.
[120] *Ibid.*, pp. 19–21.
[121] *Ibid.*, p. 19.
[122] *Ibid.*, pp. 40–41.
[123] *Ibid.*, p. 72.
[124] *Ibid.*, pp. 82, 84, 97–98, 103–106.

been settled for profit, emigrants went to Massachusetts "some to satisfy their own curiosity in point of conscience, others, which was more general, to transport the Gospel to those heathen that never heard thereof." [125] The colonists did try to recompense the London investors, and they even took along a man "skilful & experienced in the discovery and finding out of . . . mines." [126] For a while, too, the adventurers in London, who represented three-quarters of the pre-embarkation members of the company, did pursue commercial possibilities. But as the immigrants poured into New England in the 1630's it became clear that the company was primarily concerned with the establishment of a colony "where the Church of God [was] being seated in sincerity." [127] A light was being set on a hill; but the Jacobeans would have made it shine at home. This was the crux of the difference. The earlier speculative merchant and gentry venturers were interested as much in profit and glory as they were in religion, if not more so. In the late 1620's the concerns were completely reversed.

The Providence Island Company, as A. P. Newton has shown,[128] was similarly a political and religious grouping as much as a venture aiming for prestige or profit. And the numbers involved in all these enterprises could not compare with those in the Virginia, Bermuda, or North-West Passage Companies. Only the Massachusetts Bay Company exceeded 100 members, almost a

[125] Quoted in *ibid.*, p. 96. Not surprisingly, one of the Puritans' most important organizations, the feoffees for the purchase of impropriations, consisted almost entirely of investors or colonists in Massachusetts Bay. See I. M. Calder, "A Seventeenth Century Attempt to Purify the Anglican Church," *The American Historical Review*, 53 (1948), 760–775, especially pp. 761–762.

[126] N. B. Shurtleff, ed., *Records of the Governor and Company of the Massachusetts Bay in New England*, vol. I (Boston, 1853), p. 32. According to Williamson, *Caribbee Islands*, p. 7, the New England colonies relied mainly on the profits to be gained from timber and fishing as attractions for London investors.

[127] Edward Winslow, *Good Newes from New England* (London, 1634), reprinted in *Collections of the Massachusetts Historical Society*, vol. II (1832), p. 75. Good general discussions of the motives of the New England emigrants can be found in N. M. Crouse, "Causes of the Great Migration, 1630–1640," *The New England Quarterly*, 5 (1932), 3–36; in Alan Simpson, *Puritanism in Old and New England* (Chicago, 1955), pp. 19–60; and especially in Perry Miller, *Orthodoxy in Massachusetts, 1630–1650: A Genetic Study* (Cambridge, Mass., 1933), pp. 3–147. See pp. 104–105 for the transformation of John White's more general aims into the congregational undertaking that the Massachusetts colony became.

[128] A. P. Newton, *The Colonising Activities of the English Puritans* (New Haven, 1914).

third of whom were gentry; but no other organization of comparable size was founded again until the Restoration.

The 1620's, therefore, represent the tail end, and the transformation, of the Elizabethan and Jacobean expansion. George Calvert Lord Baltimore himself mirrored the change. In the early years of James I's reign he had been swept along into the East India, Virginia, and Irish Companies, but in the 1620's he turned to the idea of a colony as a religious refuge — first in Newfoundland, and then, in the 1630's, in Maryland. Significantly, too, he made no attempt to enlist support from other people through a joint-stock company. Like the Herberts, he obtained a proprietary patent and acted on his own. One suspects that he would not have gained many investors even if he had tried to find them. The older ventures certainly were not doing very well. The New England Council accomplished little on its own; the Africa Company disappeared, though a few merchants resumed the trade in the late 1620's; the Bermuda Company obtained few new members; and the rate of new investment in the East India and Levant Companies fell appreciably. The Ulster Plantation obtained no fresh subscribers; and elsewhere, in Newfoundland, Virginia, and Guiana, there were only failures and disbandments.

In only three organizations — the Virginia, the East India, and the Levant Companies — can relatively precise year-to-year figures be calculated, and they confirm the general trends. The figures are given in the following table, together with the gentry's representation in the Virginia and East India Companies.

As the figures marked (°) indicate, this table does not purport to give an absolutely precise record of admissions to these three companies. The gaps are noticeable, and low numbers (as in the Levant Company between 1606 and 1609, or the East India Company in 1612–13 and 1620–21) frequently represent little more than inadequate evidence. Since these low figures are usually followed shortly thereafter by one of the large numbers based on a list of members, they should not be taken as evidence of severe ups and downs.

The Virginia Company contains the most unmistakable parallel to the figures for all admissions (Table 7): a small show of interest in the 1580's, a slow rise early in James I's reign, a tremendous influx between 1609 and 1612, a smaller one in the late

Table 9. Annual admissions to the Levant, Virginia, and East India Companies, 1575–1629.

Year[a]	Levant Company Number admitted	Levant Company Percent of all members	Virginia Company Number admitted	Virginia Company Percent of all members	Virginia Company Gentry (and percent of all gentry members)		East India Company Number admitted	East India Company Percent of all members	East India Company Gentry (and percent of all gentry members)	
1581	10	1.7	–	–	–		–	–	–	
1584	–	–	4[b]	0.2	3	(0.5)	–	–	–	
1585	–	–	3[b]	0.2	3	(0.5)	–	–	–	
1586	–	–	1[b]	0.1	–		–	–	–	
1587	–	–	14[b]	0.8	14	(2.5)	–	–	–	
1589	–	–	19[b]	1.1	1	(0.2)	–	–	–	
1590	31[c]	5.4	–	–	–		–	–	–	
1592	29[c]	5.1	–	–	–		–	–	–	
1599	4[c]	0.7	–	–	–		137	10.4	2	(1.4)
1600	59[c]	10.3	–	–	–		138	10.5	4	(2.8)
1601	–	–	–	–	–		26	2.0	–	
1602	–	–	–	–	–		1	0.1	–	
1603	–	–	–	–	–		1	0.1	1	(0.7)
1605	75[c]	13.1	–	–	–		–	–	–	
1606	29	5.1	21	1.2	13	(2.3)	–	–	–	
1607	10	1.7	17	1.0	14	(2.5)	40	3.0	1	(0.7)
1608	–	–	1	0.1	1	(0.2)	21	1.6	1	(0.7)
1609	2	0.3	812	48.2	196	(35.0)	78[c]	5.9	12	(8.3)
1610	85[c]	14.9	123	7.4	77	(13.8)	12	0.9	2	(1.4)
1611	10	1.7	4	0.2	1	(0.2)	93[c]	7.1	14	(9.7)
1612	19	3.3	213[c]	12.6	137	(24.5)	3	0.2	1	(0.7)
1613	12	2.1	1	0.1	1	(0.2)	–	–	–	
1614	9	1.6	–	–	–		98[c]	7.4	15	(10.3)
1615	14	2.4	1	0.1	–		52	3.9	5	(3.4)
1616	12	2.1	6	0.4	3	(0.5)	4	0.3	–	
1617	7	1.2	17	1.0	4	(0.7)	47	3.6	16	(11.0)
1618	23	4.0	125[c]	7.4	17	(3.0)	88	6.7	20	(13.3)
1619	13	2.3	31	1.8	8	(1.4)	46	3.5	9	(6.2)
1620	9	1.6	91	5.4	22	(3.9)	8	0.6	–	
1621	9	1.6	50	3.0	16	(2.9)	7	0.5	–	
1622	10	1.7	76	4.5	13	(2.3)	37	2.8	1	(0.7)
1623	16	2.8	31	1.8	8	(1.4)	36	2.7	4	(2.8)
1624	12	2.1	6	0.4	1	(0.2)	145[c]	11.0	10	(6.9)
1625	6	1.0	–	–	–		34	2.6	7	(4.8)
1626	19	3.3	–	–	–		27	2.0	–	
1627	21	3.7	–	–	–		50	3.8	6	(4.1)
1628	5	0.9	–	–	–		36	2.7	5	(3.4)
1629	7	1.2	–	–	–		49	3.7	8	(5.5)
Unknown	5	0.9	17	1.0	7	(1.2)	4	0.3	1	(0.7)
Total	572		1,684		560		1,318		145	

[a] In the years that are omitted (1582–83, 1588, 1591, etc.) no admissions were recorded.

[b] The Virginia adventurers in the 1580,s have been included for completeness. See note 79.

[c] These figures were obtained from lists of current members. All of them undoubtedly include members who entered in earlier years but whose names had not appeared in previous records. Since it is impossible to know how many were new, and how much earlier the others may have been admitted, these figures were not averaged out in Table 7 — with the exception of the Levant Company figure for 1610. Since most of these larger figures usually follow years with considerably lower levels of admissions, one can make a few rough adjustments, but their accuracy is questionable and they do not affect the figures substantially. The one exception is the 1624 figure for the East India Company (see note 130 to this chapter), which is completely out of joint as a result of a list which contains names of people who may have been admitted as long as 15 years previously. But again, too little is known about these investors to suggest that an averaging out would produce greater long-term accuracy than leaving matters as they stand. Finally, it should be noted that the 1590 Levant figure consists, not of members taken from a specific list, but of all those who are known to have been in the company in the 1580's but whose dates of admission are unknown.

1610's and early 1620's, and then the collapse. Because a large number of gentry joined the company, one finds their numbers closely following the overall figures. The one significant difference came in 1609 and 1612. In the former year, the proportion of gentry admitted was much smaller than the overall figure, and in the latter year it was much larger. This was undoubtedly due in part to the land offering of 1612, but this explanation alone cannot account for the fact that total numbers were smaller in 1612 than in 1609. The great change appears to have been in merchant interest, which declined sharply as profits failed to materialize.

The Levant and East India Companies, less reliant on gentry support, maintained less dramatic growth. The chief rises in the Levant Company came at the time the East India Company was being founded (though these figures should probably be averaged over the 1590–1600 period), and after the peace with Spain. Only 233 admissions were recorded in the 19 years from 1611 through 1629 — well under half the membership, although the period was no shorter than the length of time that elapsed between the merging of the Levant and Venice Companies, in 1592, and 1610. Trade with the Levant does not seem to have suffered badly from the depression of the 1620's;[129] but after the first flush of interest the company's membership apparently grew at the slow but steady rate that its profits merited and that the London merchants were inclined to support.

The East India Company, as one of the more spectacular undertakings of the time, and with a fair proportion of gentry members, reflected the general expansion more directly. After the widespread interest expressed at its foundation, and following the early difficulties, it expanded rapidly between 1609 and 1615, and again between 1617 and 1619. Apart from the very large figure for 1624, caused by a petition which contains many otherwise unmentioned names,[130] the company seems to have settled down to a stable pattern of growth following the depression years of 1620 and 1621. Most interesting here is the contrast between the gentry and the other members. There were enough gentry for

[129] Millard, "Imports of London," pp. 85–89; Fisher, "London's Export Trade," pp. 153–155; Ralph Davis, "England and the Mediterranean, 1570–1670," in *Essays in Honour of R. H. Tawney*, ed. Fisher, pp. 117–137.
[130] *CSP, East Indies, 1622–1624*, pp. 491–493.

fluctuations to be noticeable, and yet they were relatively few so that their interests did not — as in the Virginia Company — materially affect the total figures. Whereas almost 65 percent of the gentry joined between 1609 and 1619, only 39 percent of all members were admitted in these years. It is quite a startling contrast showing once again that, although the years of maximum enthusiasm affected all investments, the gentry were particularly susceptible to the pressures at work in James I's reign.

The difference between the solid commercial undertakings and the glamorous exploits, between merchant and gentry investors, is only too apparent from Table 9, and it is a difference that runs through all the companies of the period (see Table 6). The great surges of interest by non-merchants were concentrated in a few years and on those efforts in which a small contribution could lead — or so it was hoped — to fame and fortune. But in the background, building up the achievements that transformed England's commercial position in this period, were the major merchant organizations, none of which were so directly affected by the ebb and flow of interest that ran through London in the early seventeenth century.

V. MEMBERS OF PARLIAMENT

This survey of the expansion can most fittingly conclude, as it began, by reference to the dominance of London. One set of figures is particularly revealing in this connection — the record of parliamentary membership. Election to the House of Commons was by no means the only, or even the most common, reason a gentleman came to the City, and many of the M.P.'s had come long before their first session. Nonetheless, attendance at Parliament did require a visit to London; and if it can be shown that investments by gentry tended to follow their sitting in the House, then the importance of the capital will be reinforced. This is particularly true in light of the fact that there were so many other reasons for coming to the City — the Inns of Court, the royal Court, and so on. Thus the chances are that even those recorded as entering a company before entering Parliament had probably been to London previously. In addition, it might be pointed out that the parliamentary figures are particularly appropriate to the story of investments, because membership in the House of Commons was coming to be an attribute of the most active gentry. If gentlemen were to be found in the companies, many of them would surely be among those who were also M.P.'s. These were the leaders of their class, and they were to be expected at the head of the influx into trade. On average, every investor who was also in Parliament joined 1.96 companies; those who never sat in the House joined, on average, 1.53 companies each. These figures have not been broken down by class, but the discrepancy would undoubtedly be greater if only gentry were tabulated. As it is, each M.P. investor joined over 28 percent more enterprises than did his nonparliamentary fellow-adventurer.

Taking the landed classes as a whole, and including only those peers who sat in the House of Commons, 502 out of the 1,177 gentry who contributed to companies were also Members of Parliament — nearly 43 percent. If all peers are included, the proportion rises to 53 percent — a clear indication of the correlation between political and commercial activity. Among those for whom sufficient information about dates is known, over 56 percent joined a company *after* sitting in the House. If by using this indicator alone it becomes apparent that more than half had been to London before making an investment, one must suspect that a large majority — if not virtually all — of the gentry became aware of the expansion during a visit to the City.

The following, more detailed figures, which cover the parliamentary data session by session, show that here, too, the wave of interest in the first half of James I's reign is the most distinctive feature of the investments in the expansion.

This is not the place to enter into the figures that have relevance only to parliamentary history, such as the dramatic drop in the turnover of M.P.'s in the 1620's. These matters will be discussed in the biography of Sandys on which I am working. For our purposes the chief significance lies in the very high level of interest maintained by M.P.'s who served between 1604 and 1621, and in the complete dominance of investments made during the 1609–15 period. Enthusiasm for the expansion among the M.P.'s was clearly at its height during the very period when the

Table 10. Parliamentary data.[a]

Session starting	1584	1586	1589	1593	1597	1601	1604	1614	1621	1624	1625	1626	1628
Members	467	465	468	462	459	466	563	464	514	510	485	492	518
New M.P.'s	467	219	238	237	251	234	261	258	274	203	127	124	139
Percent new	100.0	47.1	50.9	51.3	54.7	50.2	46.4	55.6	53.3	39.8	26.1	25.2	26.8
Investors	91	99	103	103	103	135	216	181	188	169	145	153	144
Percent of M.P.'s in session	19.4	21.3	22.0	22.3	22.4	29.0	38.4	39.0	36.6	33.1	30.0	31.2	27.8
Percent supplied by non-merchants	16.5	17.2	17.1	17.5	18.1	24.5	31.8	32.5	28.6	26.1	24.7	23.3	20.7
Percent of all M.P. investors at any time	13.2	14.3	14.9	14.9	14.9	19.5	31.2	26.2	27.2	24.4	21.0	22.1	20.8
First investment													
Before 1600	52	50	54	42	29	23	35	20	18	10	9	10	7
1600–08	8	11	17	20	17	28	38	28	23	17	14	15	11
1609–15	22	29	23	29	43	57	108	90	87	57	56	60	55
1616–20	1	2	3	5	7	16	17	27	31	34	27	21	22
1621–30	1	–	2	1	–	5	7	8	21	35	26	30	35
Investors who were new M.P.'s	91	39	44	43	55	62	92	71	72	43	24	25	31
Percent of new M.P.'s	19.4	17.8	18.5	18.1	21.9	26.5	35.2	27.5	26.3	21.2	18.9	20.2	22.3

[a] The year-by-year breakdown does not add up to the same total as the number of investors because unknown dates of admission have not been included. It should be noted that the percent supplied by non-merchants is a percentage of *all* Members of Parliament, not of M.P. investors or gentry M.P.'s alone. The latter figure, substantially higher, is given in the second paragraph after the table — it was not included in the table because its meaning could be conveyed equally well without graphic representation.

Because no sessions before 1584 have been included, the figures for new M.P.'s are obviously high during the first few Parliaments. However, as can be seen from the "percent new" figures, the discrepancy does not seem to be serious. Already by 1593 there can have been no more than one or two M.P.'s who, though listed here as new, had in fact sat in the House before 1584 but not after.

See also Tables 20 and 21.

propaganda and the new projects were being trumpeted most loudly in London. The figures for the sessions of 1604 and 1614 are particularly noteworthy, straddling as they do the most active years of the expansion. In both sessions almost 40 percent of the M.P.'s in the House invested in trade. This level of interest tapered off only slowly in the 1620's; but the sudden increase between 1601 and 1604, emphasized by the fact that over a third of the new M.P.'s in 1604 were investors — a proportion far higher than in any other assembly — is a remarkable indication of the sudden surge of interest in commerce. Over 31 percent of all M.P.'s who were interested in trade sat in the House that met between 1604 and 1611; and, although this is not shown in the table, there were 179 gentry investors in that particular House — over 15 percent of all the gentry who invested in companies in this entire period.

The figures for the percentage of gentry M.P.'s who joined a company are equally decisive. Between 1584 and 1597 the proportion remained between 31 percent and 34 percent. In 1601 it was 40 percent; in 1604, 46 percent; in 1614, 45 percent; in 1621, 40 percent; in 1624, 38 percent; and thereafter between 31 percent and 33 percent. Such a very large percentage, particularly in 1604 and 1614, testifies to the tremendous impact that a stay in London must have made on the average gentleman. Nor can it have been without significance that some of the leaders of the House, notably Sandys and Digges, were also at the forefront of the gentry's participation in commerce. Members of Parliament were so deeply concerned with discussions of public welfare that they may well have been particularly vulnerable to propaganda which shrewdly stressed that the national interest was at stake in overseas ventures.

Looking at the figures from the point of view of dates of first investment, the preponderance of the 1609–1615 period fits the pattern already outlined. In every session except the first four, the largest number of M.P.'s first joined a company (where this date can be determined) in these seven years. In the two assemblies that met during the peak period, 1604 and 1614, a clear majority of all first investments was made between 1609 and 1615.

The figures for the numbers of M.P.'s in the various companies are given in the next chapter (see Table 20). Here, however, they have relevance insofar as the date of admission is concerned. Leaving out all companies founded before 1584, and treating only gentry, the following statistics emerge regarding the percentage of gentry M.P.'s in various companies who joined the company at the same time as, or after, they sat in Parliament:

Africa:	79%	New England:	83%
Bermuda:	76%	Newfoundland:	86%
East India:	71%	New River:	89%
Guiana:	87%	North-West Passage	74%
Hudson:	100%	Plymouth:	100%
Irish:	65%	Providence Island:	100%
Massachusetts Bay:	100%	Virginia:	69%

These figures leave little doubt that attendance at Parliament paved the way for investments in commerce among the gentry. To some extent this was a matter of status. Thus, of those in the list who were knighted, and whose date of knighthood and date of first investment are both known, 62 percent entered a company *after* having received the title. Certainly a man was not likely to put his money in a risky new venture until he had achieved some standing, quite apart from the probability that he would have had no access to his family's wealth before reaching the station in life that entitled him to a seat in Parliament. Nonetheless, status alone cannot have impelled a gentleman to contribute to overseas enterprise. The unmistakable conclusion suggested by the parliamentary figures is that the visit to London provided the spark for his interest.

VI. THE SMALL INVESTOR: CONCLUSION

The death of a great man is often taken to mark the passing of an era. For the Elizabethan and Jacobean expansion the symbol is particularly appropriate in that an entire galaxy of leaders died between 1624 and 1631 — Sir Thomas Smith, Sandys, Southampton, Cockayne, Garaway, Hugh and Thomas Middleton, Captain John Smith, two Earls of Devon, the Earls of Pembroke and Shrewsbury, the two most active members of the Howard family (the Earls of Nottingham and Suffolk), and Samuel Purchas. Nonetheless, prominent as these men were, it must be remembered that the investors who made the successes possible came from almost every walk of life, and that the sheer number of subscribers was possibly the most important feature of the entire movement. Just as the merchants could not have accomplished everything on their own, so too the leaders alone, whatever their class and influence, could not have kept the momentum alive without the support of the masses of obscure people who contributed to the expansion. And there was a remarkable aura of common purpose surrounding the entire group, fed as it was by propaganda that repeatedly stressed general rather than specific goals. Hakluyt was the prophet for all the ventures, regardless of differing immediate aims.

Furthermore, personal relations among the investors were so close that it would be safe to estimate that at most 10 percent of the people in the list had no close relative elsewhere among company members. Although the precise figures have not been calculated, I would suspect that there was hardly a single investor who had no relatives in the list at all. Sandys was joined by four brothers and three sons in trading enterprises, and Sir Thomas Smith's relatives among the adventurers of the time would have been numerous enough to found a good-sized company on their own. Not only was the leadership a honeycomb of intermarriage and kinship (Smith linked to Warwick, Sandys to Southampton, and nearly all the great merchant families to one another), but the small investors were frequently connected with one of the more important promoters. This situation has been outlined in detail for the Bermuda Company,[131] but it could be extended, in ever denser concentrations, throughout all the enterprises of the time.

The large numbers of subscribers were clearly essential for the support of this multitude of projects which no small group could have sustained. The more wealthy contributors rarely provided

[131] Wilkinson, *Bermuda*, p. 88. In gathering the data, I made a preliminary attempt to assemble information on family relationships. But the web of marriages and kinship was so tangled that it would have taken as long to unravel as it took to compile the entire list. Consequently, this information has not been entered on the cards. Nonetheless, the short survey I did complete provided something of a basis for the estimates made in this paragraph.

The other type of information which I did no more than begin to assemble was data on geographic origins. Once again it did not seem worth postponing publication for the sake of a long and difficult undertaking whose outcome may have been of minor significance in view of the admirable discussion of the origins of London's merchants in Jordan, *Charities of London*, pp. 308–318. There is also a discussion of this subject, based on a much smaller sample, in Lang, "Greater Merchants of London," pp. 1–6, 69–79. A brief survey of easily accessible data on gentry investors suggested that there was no particularly heavy concentration in any one area, with the well-known exception of Devon and much of the West Country.

even half of the capital of a major company.[132] Hence it was crucial to the success of Elizabethan and Jacobean efforts that the promoters were able to generate the thousands of small payments which supplied the bulk of their funds. The Virginia Company's need for additional colonists, as described in a broadside of 1616–1617, was very similar to the perennial need for new investors: "[We] have been thoroughly informed and assured of the good estate of the Colony, and how by the blessing of God and good government, there is great plenty . . . ; and that there wants nothing for the settling of that Christian Plantation, but more hands to gather and return those commodities which may bring profit to the Adventurers, and encouragement to others. . . . Whereby in short time (by the favor and assistance of Almighty God) that good work may be brought to good perfection, . . . to the contentment and satisfaction of all well affected subjects, which either love the advancement of religion, or the honor and welfare of this kingdom." [133] Fortunately, many hands did gather and return commodities from all over the world, and the energies of these "well affected subjects" produced results which justified considerable contentment and satisfaction.

Judging from the growth of imports alone, one economic his-

[132] There are not many places where this assertion can be tested, but it is based on calculations made from the Virginia and East India Company lists cited in notes 61 and 63, above. From the data in Andrews, *Elizabethan Privateering*, and the lists of letters of marque, cited in note 89, above, it would seem that this form of maritime enterprise was also predominantly supported by large numbers of small investors — often joined together in groups so as to amass sufficient capital — rather than a few conspicuous contributors. No man had the resources to subscribe a significant amount of money when millions of pounds were being raised (see Table 5 and notes 67–95, above). Not even a few hundred of the richest subscribers could have put together even half of the sums expended in this period. The records suggest that there were, at most, 100 to 200 East India Company members who invested more than £1,000 in the voyages of this period. Sir Thomas Smith himself, who did more than anyone else to set the undertaking on its feet, and who acted as its first governor and led it for some 20 years, claimed to have ventured less than £20,000 (*CSP, East Indies, 1617–1621*, p. 435); no other member approached this amount, as far as can be determined. It would seem, therefore, that no more than a third of the capital for the East India trade came from the leading promoters. In less expensive enterprises, a few leaders may have played a greater role; but when the expansion is viewed in its entirety such individual efforts lose their prominence. One needs only to go through the records of the London Livery Companies, and see the masses of tiny contributions for Virginia and Ireland — some as small as 2s. — to get a sense of the breadth of support that overseas enterprise depended on and, luckily, inspired.

[133] Brown, *Genesis of the United States,* II, 797–798.

torian has recently written that "the foundations of something like a world trade were laid between 1615 and 1630."[134] A similar conclusion can be drawn from London's export figures.[135] Only 80 years before England had been virtually a commercial backwater of Europe, with little of her trade in native hands, entirely dependent for exports on her wool and cloth, and in contact only with her western European neighbors. But by 1630 the foundations of her later economic strength had been laid. Her merchants had supplanted the foreigners who had controlled her commerce; they were coming to dominate the Levant;[136] they had established a substantial trade with Russia, the Baltic, the Far East, and the New World; new industries were booming; and already the dependence on cloth had been outgrown by a versatile and diverse carrying trade. Only 25 years before, despite her naval victory over Spain, England had had no overseas possessions. By 1630 she had settlements strung along the coast of North America whose population was to grow to some 50,000 within another decade. In Newfoundland, the West Indies, the Mediterranean, and India, colonies and trading posts heralded the beginning of a far-flung empire.

As we have seen, most of these enterprises rested primarily on merchant capital and adventurers, but they also drew vital support from the gentry. The efforts of the non-merchants broadened the scope of overseas activity, made new funds available (particularly for the more risky ventures), and gave the entire undertaking an assurance that it would have lacked without the encouragement and assistance of the leaders of English society. Nevertheless, the enthusiasm of a few notable gentlemen promoters (Gorges, Sandys, or Baltimore, for example) should not obscure the fact that considerable pressure was required to bring the landed classes into commerce. They did not take lightly this crucial and unprecedented step away from their traditional contempt for the world of business.

Conditions were certainly favorable to investment, because late sixteenth- and early seventeenth-century England was enjoying remarkable and widespread economic prosperity. Landed income

[134] Millard, "Imports of London," p. 115.
[135] Fisher, "London's Export Trade," *passim*.
[136] Davis, "England and the Mediterranean," pp. 126–132. See also notes 49 and 50, above.

was increasing, trade and industry were flourishing, the population was growing, and a manifestation of the rising wealth could be seen in a tremendous burst of new building. But these advances alone were not sufficient to induce the gentry to participate in trade in significant numbers. Not until the last 20 years of the boom did they invest en masse. It is true that when they did finally offer their support they helped to sustain the most spectacular period of the expansion — 1604–20, when 57 percent of all admissions to companies in the years 1575–1630 were recorded. But this was rather late in the day. In the last decades of Elizabeth's reign 26 percent of the admissions had already been registered, and the gentry had been poorly represented.[137] The merchants had begun the process largely on their own. The landed classes, though interested in industry and in agricultural improvements, were not yet prepared to take a conspicuous part in trade merely because incomes and prosperity were rising. Even the creation of a practical channel for their investments, the joint-stock company, could not attract their attention until other stimuli had taken effect.

It was of prime importance that overseas activity began to take on the character of a national undertaking. Colonies, explorations, and new markets brought more than profits; they also enhanced England's prestige, particularly vis-à-vis Spain. This was the argument, combined in some cases with the promise of adventure or the spread of God's word, which first induced Elizabeth's courtiers and a few daring West-countrymen to join the merchants. And this display of interest by the nobles and gentlemen closest to the Queen confirmed the impression that investments could help one's country as well as one's pocket. If the leaders of the nation thought it appropriate to become involved in commerce, then gentlemen everywhere could follow suit without any qualms about status. When the war with Spain focused attention on exploits on the high seas, it was only a matter of time before they succumbed to the enthusiasms inspired by Drake and the other pioneers.[138]

[137] See Tables 6 and 8.

[138] Even the first description of a major privateering voyage, Walter Bigges's *Expeditio Francisci Draki in Indias Occidentales A.M.D. LXXXV* . . . (Leyden, 1588), published in Latin so that all of Europe could read about England's glory, emphasized that Drake had sailed "augere studens nomen Principis patriaeque

But the change in attitude did not take place overnight. The significance of these new enterprises still had to be communicated to the gentry. Had they not found London so attractive, and had they not come to town so often, they might never have concerned themselves with commercial affairs. Once in the capital, however, they were bound to become aware, through the people they met and above all through the promoters' ceaseless propaganda, of what was happening overseas. They could hardly avoid encountering demands for contributions to all kinds of worthy projects. In 1612 the invitation to buy a ticket in the Virginia lottery even took the form of a popular ballad, in which the fund raiser sang: "Come Knights and gallant Gentlemen,/ put in your ventures all." [139] And when successes were finally reported from India and Virginia, their last hesitation was overcome.

Although the gentry's enthusiasm, once aroused, did not last long, and remained sporadic at best, its importance was considerable. The establishment of the British empire, the revolution in the forms and aims of English economic activity, and the coalescence of England's social structure — epitomized by the close relationship between merchant and gentleman — all can be perceived before 1600, and even before 1575. But in each of these developments the crucial period was from 1600 to 1630, when thousands of adventurers from the landed and mercantile classes combined to seek success overseas. In the process they helped to create a sense of national identity and mission to which, in turn, they pledged their wealth and their lives. By trying to convey why these efforts deserved support, Hakluyt and his followers defined and invoked a national spirit. Thanks largely to their activities, the country achieved a unity of purpose that it had never had before. And it came to be perfectly natural for Shakespeare to have Henry V claim even "God for Harry, England, and Saint George!"

---

suae," and had returned "non sine Principis nostrae ac patriae & nostrum omnium honore," plus, of course, £6,000 worth of booty (see pp. 3, 20).

[139] *Pepys Ballads*, ed. Rollins, I, 127. On the lotteries, see R. C. Johnson, "The Lotteries of the Virginia Company, 1612–1621," *The Virginia Magazine of History and Biography*, 74 (1966), 259–292. See pp. 273–292 on the ballad. Johnson demonstrates that the lottery sustained the company in its last years; however, the names of the thousands who bought tickets have not survived.

CHAPTER 2   SOME DETAILED FIGURES

In this chapter the remaining results of the computer analysis will be described. These figures were the basis for some of the calculations discussed in Chapter 1, and they provide some interesting additional information which scholars concerned with this subject might care to have. I have not been able to pursue all the possible implications of every individual result,[1] but future students of particular companies or Parliaments should be able to make use of my findings. The computer also supplied me with a host of other calculations which did not warrant publication

[1] For instance, the fact that members with at least four other investments formed a much higher proportion of the Muscovy and French Companies than they did of the Levant and Spanish Companies — see Table 13, and the discussion which follows it. A similar small but intractable problem is the steady decline of the number of men interested in Irish ventures in successive Houses of Commons — see Table 21. The only further work that I intend to do on the company figures is the publication in appropriate journals of a few full lists of members of the larger companies, including data on their dates of admission, directorships, and other investments.

One striking connection uncovered in the course of my researches that merits further attention is the close attachment of members of the Middle Temple to overseas enterprise. Among the leaders of the movement who were linked with this particular Inn were: the Courteens, Cranfield, Digges, Drake, the Ferrars, Frobisher, the Gerrards, Adrian Gilbert, the Gores, Gorges, Gosnold, the Hakluyts, John Hawkins, Sir Robert Lee, the Locks, Mansell, the Offleys, the Pophams, Raleigh, the St. Johns, Sandys, the Slanys, the brother of Sir Thomas Smith, the Welds, the Winters, Wolstenholme, and the Zouches. This was a remarkable concentration of the leading pioneers, and was presumably the result of the presence of the Hakluyts.

here; but I would be glad to pass them along to anyone who is interested in a specific trading organization or assembly of the House of Commons.

Table 11 gives an exact breakdown, class by class, of all the companies.

These are the more detailed figures on which the tables in Chapter 1 are based. The percentage of people left unclassified can be seen more precisely, and the breakdowns within each class can be determined. It might be pointed out that the merchants accounted for nearly 69 percent of all *investments*, a higher proportion than their percentage of *investors* because on average they each contributed to more companies than did gentry. As for concentrations of interest, 10 percent or more of all gentry in the list were members of the following organizations: East India (12 percent), Irish (15 percent), privateering (10 percent), Virginia (48 percent), and "other ventures" (12 percent). Among the nobility the interests were broader: over 10 percent were in each of the East India (19 percent), Frobisher & Fenton (11 percent), Guiana (18 percent), Irish (13 percent), North-West Passage (18 percent), privateering (15 percent), Virginia (49 percent), and "other ventures" (31 percent) groups. Over 10 percent of the merchants were in the following organizations: East India (26 percent), French (14 percent), Irish (13 percent), Levant (15 percent), privateering (15 percent), Spanish (28 percent), and Virginia (17 percent). This only emphasizes the differences already noticed. Of the five largest enterprises, four, the East India, Irish, and Virginia Companies and privateering, attracted large numbers from both classes; the fifth, the Spanish Company, was a purely merchant interest. Otherwise, the merchants had major interests only in the French and Levant Companies — the Muscovy and Eastland Companies never reached sufficient size to attract 10 percent of the merchant investors. The gentry, on the other hand, were more deeply committed to colonies, voyages of exploration and "other ventures" — minor expeditions and industrial enterprises.

The 18 companies whose dates of admission came from more than one source (see Appendix) can be broken down into groups according to the year members' names were first recorded. Be-

Table 11. Company memberships, by class.

Company	Membership	Unclassified (and percent of total)	Class, with percent of those classified					
			Gentlemen	Knights	Peers	Merchants	Merchant knights	Yeomen/ professionals
Africa	38	—	10 (26.3)	17 (44.7)	3 (7.9)	7 (18.4)	1 (2.6)	—
Baffin	8	—	—	1 (12.5)	—	2 (25.0)	5 (62.5)	—
Barbary	47	1 (2.1)	1 (2.1)	—	2 (4.2)	40 (87.4)	3 (6.3)	—
Bermuda	178	27 (15.2)	17 (11.3)	24 (15.9)	15 (9.9)	82 (54.3)	12 (7.9)	1 (0.7)
Cavendish	4	—	1 (25.0)	2 (50.0)	1 (25.0)	—	—	—
Drake	21	—	—	1 (4.8)	1 (4.8)	14 (66.7)	5 (23.8)	—
East India	1,318	156 (11.8)	54 (4.6)	57 (4.9)	34 (2.9)	937 (80.6)	58 (5.0)	22 (1.9)
Eastland	197	—	—	1 (0.5)	—	184 (93.4)	12 (6.1)	—
French	548	2 (0.4)	4 (0.7)	8 (1.5)	4 (0.7)	512 (93.8)	18 (3.3)	—
Frobisher & Fenton	121	24 (19.8)	8 (8.2)	19 (19.6)	20 (20.6)	39 (40.2)	10 (10.3)	1 (1.0)
Gilbert	146	12 (8.2)	45 (33.6)	21 (15.7)	6 (4.5)	49 (36.6)	1 (0.7)	12 (9.0)
Gosnold	5	—	2 (40.0)	—	2 (40.0)	1 (20.0)	—	—
Guiana	105	13 (12.4)	12 (13.0)	33 (35.9)	33 (35.9)	7 (7.6)	3 (3.3)	4 (4.3)
Hudson	24	—	—	3 (12.5)	6 (25.0)	6 (25.0)	9 (37.5)	—
Irish	762	82 (10.8)	82 (12.1)	75 (11.0)	23 (3.4)	477 (70.1)	23 (3.4)	—
Levant	572	7 (1.2)	3 (0.5)	4 (0.7)	2 (0.4)	520 (92.1)	35 (6.2)	1 (0.2)
Massachusetts Bay	122	40 (32.8)	20 (24.4)	5 (6.1)	1 (1.2)	52 (63.4)	1 (1.2)	3 (3.7)
Merchant Adventurer	269	—	—	—	1 (0.4)	245 (91.0)	23 (8.6)	—
Minerals	77	2 (2.6)	20 (26.7)	5 (6.7)	11 (14.7)	29 (38.7)	8 (10.7)	2 (2.7)
Mines	57	1 (1.8)	11 (19.6)	6 (10.7)	9 (16.1)	25 (44.6)	4 (7.1)	1 (1.8)
Muscovy	211	—	—	9 (4.3)	4 (1.9)	166 (78.7)	30 (14.2)	2 (0.9)
New England	70	2 (2.9)	7 (10.3)	35 (51.5)	15 (22.1)	7 (10.3)	2 (2.9)	2 (2.9)
Newfoundland	57	7 (12.3)	6 (12.0)	5 (10.0)	2 (4.0)	35 (70.0)	2 (4.0)	—
New Merchant Adventurer	257	1 (0.4)	—	1 (0.4)	2 (0.4)	249 (97.3)	5 (2.0)	—
New River	31	—	1 (3.2)	7 (22.6)	3 (9.7)	17 (54.8)	3 (9.7)	—
North-West Passage	311	4 (1.3)	16 (5.2)	32 (10.4)	33 (10.7)	202 (65.8)	21 (6.8)	3 (1.0)
Plymouth	49	31 (63.3)	1 (5.6)	1 (5.6)	1 (5.6)	15 (83.3)	—	—
Privateering	1,051	349 (33.3)	43 (6.1)	52 (7.4)	28 (3.7)	549 (78.4)	29 (4.1)	1 (0.1)
Providence Island	20	—	6 (30.0)	6 (30.0)	5 (25.0)	2 (10.0)	—	1 (5.0)
Senegal	22	—	—	—	2 (9.1)	20 (90.9)	—	—
Spanish	1,096	—	2 (0.2)	9 (0.8)	6 (0.6)	1033 (94.2)	46 (4.2)	—
Staple Merchants	18	—	—	—	—	14 (77.8)	4 (22.2)	—
Venice	14	1 (7.1)	—	—	—	11 (84.6)	2 (15.4)	—
Virginia	1,684	432 (25.7)	209 (16.7)	263 (21.0)	88 (7.0)	609 (48.6)	52 (4.2)	31 (2.5)
Weymouth	5	—	—	3 (60.0)	2 (40.0)	—	—	—
Other ventures	352	12 (3.4)	15 (4.4)	73 (21.5)	55 (16.2)	165 (48.5)	27 (7.9)	5 (1.5)
Total	9,867[a]	1,209 (12.3)	596 (6.0)	779 (7.9)	419 (4.2)	6,319 (64.0)	454 (4.6)	91 (0.9)

[a] To the total of 9,867 should be added the 191 "other ventures" investments made by people who are entered only once in the "other ventures" category but who were interested in more than one of these undertakings. See *Companies* in the key to the List in the Appendix for further explanation.

cause the evidence is so limited these figures cannot be used as indications of fluctuations of interest within a company, as was done in Table 9. Their importance lies in their contribution to the overall figures presented in Tables 6 and 7.

In the *Bermuda* Company, 21 (11.8 percent) joined in 1612; 104 (58.4 percent) in 1615; and 52 (29.2 percent) subsequently.

In the *Eastland* Company, 66 (33.5 percent) joined in 1579; 42 (21.3 percent) between 1601 (?) and 1625; 68 (34.5 percent) between 1601 (?) and 1630; and 21 (10.7 percent) at an unknown date.

In the *French* Company, 539 (98.4 percent) joined in 1611; and nine (1.6 percent) at an unknown date.

Of the backers of *Frobisher and Fenton,* one (0.8 percent) subscribed only to Frobisher's first voyage; 36 (29.8 percent) only to the second voyage; six (five percent) only to the third voyage; and 24 (19.8 percent) only to Fenton's expedition. The remainder were interested in more than one of the voyages: 24 (19.8 percent) in Frobisher's second and third ventures; 12 (9.9 percent) in all three of Frobisher's ventures; seven (5.8 percent) in his last two ventures and also Fenton's; five (4.1 percent) in all four voyages; and six (five percent) in Frobisher's second voyage and Fenton's expedition.

Of the backers of *Gilbert,* 45 (30.8 percent) became interested in 1578, and 101 (69.2 percent) in 1583.

Among the *Guiana* venturers, five (4.8 percent) became interested in the 1590's, three (2.9 percent) in 1604, five (4.8 percent) in 1609, two (1.9 percent) in 1613, two (1.9 percent) in 1618, 22 (21 percent) in 1619, 50 (47.5 percent) with the foundation of the Guiana Company in 1627, and 16 (15.2 percent) more by 1629.

Among the *Irish* venturers, there were 78 (10.2 percent) undertakers in the Munster Plantation of the 1580's; when the Ulster Plantation was organized, a further seven (0.9 percent) became interested in 1608, 395 (51.8 percent) in 1609, 148 (19.4 percent) in 1611, 54 (7.1 percent) in 1613, 23 (three percent) by 1618, and 57 (7.5 percent) at an unknown date.

In the *Massachusetts Bay* Company, 39 (32 percent) were interested by 1628, and 83 more (68 percent) joined in 1629.

In the *Minerals* Company, 41 (53.3 percent) joined by 1575, five (6.5 percent) by 1582, five (6.5 percent) by 1585, six (7.8 percent) by 1590, and 20 (26 percent) by 1604.

In the *Mines* Company, 24 (42.1 percent) joined by 1575, 11 (19.3 percent) by 1580, and 22 (38.6 percent) by 1605.

In the *Muscovy* Company, 100 (47.4 percent) were members in 1575 or had joined by about 1600, and 111 joined between 1601 (?) and 1630.

Of the venturers in *New England* through the Northern Virginia Company or the New England Council, six (8.6 percent) became interested in 1606, 14 (20 percent) in 1607, two (2.9 percent) in 1609, 32 (45.7 percent) in 1620, and 16 (22.9 percent) by 1623.

The *New Merchant Adventurers* Company was joined by 225 (87.6 percent) in 1615, and 32 (12.4 percent) in 1616.

Of the *North-West Passage* seekers, 22 (7.1 percent) invested in Davis's efforts in the mid-1580's, and 289 (92.9 percent) joined the 1612 joint-stock company.

Of the *Plymouth* adventurers, four (8.2 percent) were involved in 1620, and 45 (91.8 percent) by 1625.

Among backers of *privateering*, 389 (37 percent) invested during Elizabeth's last years, and 664 (63 percent) during Charles I's reign — including two (one of them Sir John Watts, the son of the famous Sir John who was one of the leading organizers of Elizabethan privateering and later governor of the East India Company) who seem to have been the only men active in both periods.

In the *Spanish* Company, 385 (35.1 percent) joined in 1577, 517 (47.2 percent) in 1604, 154 (14.1 percent) in 1605, 29 (2.7 percent) in 1606, and 11 (one percent) at an unknown date.

Of the investors in *other ventures*, 278 (79 percent) contributed to only one of these, 47 (13.4 percent) to two, 16 (4.6 percent) to three, eight (2.3 percent) to four, two (0.6 percent) to five, and one (0.3 percent) — the Earl of Shrewsbury — to seven.

The distribution figures and cross-memberships reveal the extent to which East India and Virginia Company memberships dominated the figures. Of the 6,336 investors, 2,689 (42 percent) invested in one or the other or both. Among non-merchants the concentration is particularly noticeable — of 1,251 investors, 699

(56 percent) were in the two companies, 591 of them in the Virginia. The merchant proportion, 1,410 out of 3,933, was only 36 percent. The difference is due to the fact that the other large companies — the French, Irish, Levant, and Spanish, and privateering (all over 500 members) — were primarily merchant undertakings, whereas the heavily gentry organizations were considerably smaller. However, when the figures are restricted to people with multiple investments, the pre-eminent position of the two great companies becomes even more apparent. Among the 1,772 investors in two or more ventures, 1,124 (63 percent) joined the East India or Virginia Companies; of the 830 in three or more, 637 (76 percent) joined one of these two companies; and of the 427 in four or more, 348 (82 percent) joined one of the two companies.

The cross-tabulation figures reinforce this conclusion. The principal figures for each company are given in Table 12, whose main use is as a source of reference, and as confirmation of some of the statements in Chapter 1. It will be seen that the East India Company, though not as large, was almost as popular as the Virginia Company for second investments. If one calculates, company by company, the percentage of all investments in other organizations that went to the East India and Virginia Companies, and the total is then averaged out, one finds that 37 percent of all people in at least one other company chose the East India Company, and 38 percent chose the Virginia. If these figures are broken down by class, for the East India Company the totals are 41 percent of the merchants and 28 percent of the gentry; for the Virginia they are 33 percent of the merchants and 52 percent of the gentry. Once again, the dominance of these two great enterprises is manifest and the differences between merchants and gentry clearly revealed.

As might be expected, the East India Company percentage is particularly high in heavily merchant companies, while the Virginia percentage rises noticeably whenever gentlemen make a substantial showing. The figures for the Drake, Eastland, French, and New Merchant Adventurer organizations point up the former trend, while the latter is revealed in totals for the Bermuda, Guiana, Hudson, New England, Newfoundland, North-West Passage, and Providence Island enterprises. The French, Levant,

107

Table 12. Memberships in other companies, by company.[a]

Company	In other companies (and percent of all members)	Average number of other companies	Gentry in other companies (and percent of column 1)	Of those who joined at least one other company, the following percent joined these companies or groups (the eight largest)							
				East India	French	Irish	Levant	North-West Passage	Privateer	Spanish	Virginia
Africa	25 (65.8)	2.88	19 (76.0)	32.0	4.0	8.0	8.0	8.0	20.0	24.0	56.0
Baffin	8 (100.0)	6.00	1 (12.5)	75.0	37.5	12.5	12.5	87.5	50.0	25.0	75.0
Barbary	41 (87.2)	3.39	2 (4.9)	36.6	14.6	9.8	22.0	4.9	43.9	19.5	14.6
Bermuda	158 (88.8)	3.07	53 (33.5)	49.4	8.9	5.2	15.8	31.0	12.0	13.3	94.3
Cavendish	4 (100.0)	2.50	4 (100.0)	25.0	25.0	0.0	0.0	25.0	50.0	0.0	25.0
Drake	21 (100.0)	4.15	2 (9.5)	52.3	0.0	9.5	38.1	14.2	90.5	47.8	23.8
East India	757 (57.4)	2.60	88 (11.6)	-	19.7	16.5	32.2	23.9	16.8	22.7	41.4
Eastland	96 (48.7)	3.20	1 (1.0)	40.6	33.3	14.6	21.9	14.6	20.8	48.9	17.7
French	307 (56.0)	2.87	15 (4.9)	48.5	-	16.0	22.5	19.2	17.6	56.0	28.7
Frobisher & Fenton	76 (62.8)	3.12	34 (44.7)	11.8	5.3	9.2	13.2	10.5	39.5	40.8	10.5
Gilbert	58 (39.7)	2.40	29 (50.0)	3.5	6.9	8.6	1.7	13.8	34.5	39.7	15.5
Gosnold	5 (100.0)	3.20	4 (80.0)	20.0	0.0	0.0	0.0	20.0	60.0	0.0	100.0
Guiana	56 (53.3)	2.80	44 (78.6)	33.9	5.4	5.4	3.6	17.9	21.4	7.1	67.9
Hudson	24 (100.0)	6.86	9 (37.5)	83.3	37.5	25.0	33.3	91.7	40.0	41.7	75.0
Irish	267 (35.0)	2.78	40 (15.0)	47.2	18.4	-	19.9	21.0	0.8	21.4	55.4
Levant	367 (64.2)	2.88	6 (1.6)	66.5	18.8	14.4	-	15.8	21.5	32.4	25.9
Massachusetts Bay	43 (35.2)	2.28	7 (16.3)	41.9	11.6	9.3	30.2	7.0	30.2	7.0	16.3
Merchant Adventurer	245 (91.1)	2.92	1 (0.4)	42.9	18.0	15.9	19.6	16.3	18.4	29.8	24.5
Minerals	42 (54.5)	3.26	20 (47.6)	11.9	9.5	11.9	16.7	9.5	16.7	28.6	16.7
Mines	35 (61.4)	3.29	18 (51.4)	8.6	5.7	8.6	8.6	8.6	22.9	28.6	22.9
Muscovy	147 (69.7)	3.49	12 (8.2)	47.6	18.4	12.2	37.4	20.4	19.7	37.4	27.9
New England	52 (74.3)	2.73	41 (78.8)	21.2	0.0	7.7	1.9	13.5	26.9	36.6	63.5
Newfoundland	41 (71.9)	3.49	7 (17.1)	48.8	17.1	22.0	19.5	22.0	26.8	23.4	56.1
New Merchant Adventurer	201 (78.2)	2.78	1 (0.5)	50.8	21.9	13.4	20.4	15.4	10.5	12.5	26.4
New River	24 (77.4)	2.79	9 (37.5)	50.0	20.8	20.8	16.7	4.2	29.2	20.7	41.7
North-West Passage	266 (85.5)	3.43	67 (25.2)	68.1	22.2	20.7	21.8	-	16.6	0.0	59.0
Plymouth	20 (40.8)	1.80	2 (10.0)	35.0	5.0	10.0	5.0	5.0	25.0	34.2	15.0
Privateers	393 (37.4)	2.66	76 (19.4)	32.6	13.8	9.7	20.1	11.2	-	0.0	30.9
Providence Island	10 (50.0)	3.20	8 (80.0)	30.0	10.0	0.0	10.0	15.4	20.0	69.2	80.0
Senegal	13 (59.1)	2.15	2 (15.4)	7.7	15.4	0.0	0.0	10.7	38.5	0.0	7.7
Spanish	516 (47.1)	2.54	14 (2.7)	33.3	33.1	11.1	23.1	0.0	26.0	-	21.5
Staple Merchants	8 (44.4)	3.13	- (0.0)	25.0	25.0	12.5	25.0	0.0	0.0	50.0	25.0
Venice	12 (85.7)	4.17	0 (0.0)	41.7	12.8	8.3	91.7	16.7	58.3	33.3	16.7
Virginia	681 (40.4)	2.43	211 (31.0)	46.0	0.0	21.6	14.0	23.1	17.8	16.3	-
Weymouth	5 (100.0)	4.40	5 (100.0)	20.0	0.0	20.0	0.0	40.0	60.0	0.0	40.0
Other ventures	278 (79.0)	2.95	97 (34.9)	29.5	8.6	11.5	21.6	15.8	38.9	26.6	33.1

[a] The gentry percentage is calculated on the basis of all members in other companies; their percentage of classified members alone would be higher.

The Merchant Adventurer and Staple Merchant figures serve primarily to indicate their distribution among the companies in the list. As is explained in chapter 3, no attempt was made to include all Merchant Adventurers or Staple Merchants, and the percentages of their total numbers would be very much lower. As can be seen, those who did appear in the list were very active, but they formed only a tiny percentage of the members of their organizations.

Each "other venture" was counted as a separate investment in the Average number of other companies column.

and Spanish Companies fared much the same as the East India, with the largest of the three, the Spanish, accounting for substantial numbers of cross-investments in merchant companies. This was so even though the leading regulated companies had strict rules about their exclusiveness. The Spanish Company at one point refused a man his freedom for no better reason than that his wife owned a retail shop, and thus he was no "mere merchant." [2] Similarly, a man was supposed to concentrate all his efforts on one overseas trade. Thus, after solemn deliberation, the General Court of the Spanish Company decided in September of 1605 that membership in the East India Company would not in future prevent the granting of freedom in their own organization, but only because the East India Company "is dissolved, and not to be any longer accounted for a Company." [3] Yet exceptions were in fact freely made. In 1605 Sir Stephen Soame asked to be admitted to the Spanish Company, though he was also a Staple and Eastland merchant. He offered, in exchange, to have one of the Spanish traders admitted to one of the other organizations in which he was a member. Thomas Boothby promptly offered the company £20 for the privilege of becoming a Stapler, and the trade was arranged.[4] Later in the same year William Greenwell made a similar proposal, this time promising membership in the Eastland Company.[5] It was this fluidity (in spite of the regulations) that made possible the remarkable level of cross-membership among the major trading companies.

[2] Minutes of the meetings of the General Court: British Museum: Additional Manuscript 9365, p. 81. The most famous clash between retailers and merchants was in Chester in Elizabeth's reign: see *CSP, Domestic, 1547–1580*, p. 619.

[3] Additional Manuscript 9365, p. 100 — meeting of September 6, 1605. Presumably the merchants had in mind the winding-up of the joint stock for the East India Company's first voyage, and not some rumor concerning the collapse of the entire enterprise.

[4] *Ibid.*, p. 82.

[5] *Ibid.*, p. 133. Although the regulations concerning "mere merchants" and multiple memberships often appeared to be little more than technicalities, they could become serious matters when scapegoats were needed in times of crisis. Thus it was not surprising that Parliament was called upon to reconfirm the regulations in the early 1620's — see W. R. Scott, *The Constitution and Finance of English, Scottish and Irish Joint-Stock Companies to 1720* (3 vols.; Cambridge, England, 1910–1912), I, 172–173, 182. The Levant Company appears to have been consistently much stricter, and to have relaxed its requirements only with the greatest reluctance. See their First Court Book (PRO: S.P. 105/147), fol. 82, and their Second Court Book (PRO: S.P. 105/148), fols. 84, 87, 134, 137, 155, 167.

The most surprising of these connections was between the Eastland and Spanish Companies. Although two very different trades were involved, covering widely separated areas, almost half of the Eastland merchants also engaged in trade with Spain. And a similar high proportion (nearly 40 percent) of the Muscovy merchants traded with the Iberian peninsula. The flexibility of London's mercantile community can have no better illustration. The Muscovy merchants in particular had wide interests: not only their substantial membership in the East India, Levant, Spanish, and Virginia Companies, indicated in Table 12, but also major contributions to other, very different undertakings. With their natural interest in a North-East Passage to the Pacific, they could be counted on to be concerned with explorations to the North-west, too. Thus 28 percent of the backers of Frobisher and Fenton, 38 percent of the backers of Hudson, and two out of eight backers of Baffin were Muscovy merchants. The Russia traders also comprised 36 percent of those members of the Minerals Company who made other investments, and 34 percent of the same group in the Mines Company.

Some of the other figures also bear stressing. The very high level of interest in other companies among subscribers to the four North-West Passage organizations (Baffin, Frobisher, Hudson, and the 1612 company) can be ascribed in part to the fact that the four were separated and not entered as a single undertaking. The main effect of the separation can be seen in the smaller Baffin and Hudson groups; but it can have had little effect on the much more substantial organization founded in 1612, and this venture proved to be the only one of the eight largest companies to have its members investing on average in more than three other companies apiece. They joined 55 more companies per 100 members than their nearest rivals, the Levant merchants. Moreover, the percentage of the membership (86) involved in other enterprises was much higher than that attained by the members of other major undertakings. In the absence of a detailed history of the organization of the search for a North-West Passage in these years,[6] one cannot explain this phenomenon because too little is

[6] The best account of the origin of these efforts is still Sir William Foster's *England's Quest of Eastern Trade* (London, 1933), especially pp. 227–233. But this is a very brief survey which comes in the midst of a book primarily concerned with other matters. The fullest account is in *The Voyages of Captain Luke*

known about the background of the effort. The one thing that is clear from the figures is that the company was an offshoot of the East India Company, much as the Bermuda Company was sired by the Virginia Company. With their natural interest in the Far East, the merchants in the India trade were, obviously, particularly interested in new routes to the Pacific.

The smaller companies tended to be supported by people with a number of other commitments — not surprising in view of the fact that such voyages as those of Gosnold and Weymouth were part of the growth of interest in North America, and hence unlikely to be the last investment made by their promoters. It is noticeable, too, that subscribers to Drake's 1587 expedition were very active people, nearly all of whom also took part in the privateering of the time. One can guess that *all* of them were interested in privateering, but the records are not sufficiently complete to confirm the hypothesis.

One of the most interesting smaller groups was the Venice Company. Though numerically never the equal of its competitor, the Levant Company, with which it was eventually merged in 1592, its members during its brief life in the 1580's included some of the most prominent of the merchants who led the way toward new ventures in the second half of Elizabeth's reign — Henry Anderson, probably the Newcastle merchant knighted in 1603, a Member of Parliament, an alderman of his home city, a Levant and Muscovy merchant, and a privateer; Andrew and Paul Banning, both London aldermen, directors of the Spanish Company, privateers, backers of Drake, and members of the East India and Levant Companies — in each of which one of them acted as a director, Paul becoming treasurer of the East India Company at its foundation; Thomas Cordell, an alderman and Master of the Mercers, a director of the Spanish, East India, and Levant Companies, an investor in privateering, Ireland and Virginia, a backer of Drake and Fenton, and a pioneer of sugar refining in England; William Garaway, knighted in 1615, a director of the East India and Levant Companies, a backer of Drake and privateering, and an investor in Virginia, Bermuda, and the search

Fox of Hull, and Captain Thomas James of Bristol, in Search of a North-West Passage, in 1631–32, ed. Miller Christy (2 vols.; London: The Hakluyt Society, 1894), but this needs considerable revision. See pp. cxxxii–cxxxiii for the connection between the East India and North-West Passage Companies.

111

for the North-West Passage; Edward Holmeden, knighted in 1603, alderman and Master of the Grocers, a founding director of the East India Company, a Barbary and Levant merchant, and a backer of Drake and privateering; and Robert Sadler, a member of the Levant Company, and a backer of Drake, Fenton, and privateering. No other organization of similar size could boast a comparable concentration of the leaders of the mercantile community.

A few other cross-memberships not listed in Table 12 are worth noting. The Bermuda Company, an offspring of the Virginia Company, also included 15 percent of the New England Venturers and 33 percent of the backers of Hudson who were interested in other companies. The close connection between the four major organizations with substantial gentry support in Jacobean times — the Virginia, North-West Passage, Bermuda, and New England enterprises — is a marked feature of the figures. As a result of their recruitment campaigns among the Livery Companies, there was also a large cross-membership between the Irish and Virginia Companies. It might be mentioned, though, that the Livery Companies as such contributed little of importance to the expansion. They can be equated in this respect with the Merchant Adventurers who, as is outlined in Chapter 3, were being left behind by events. The centers of activity were in the new organizations, and the older groupings were rarely directly involved. This is not to say that the leaders of the expansion were not also active in London's life. The careers of the outstanding Venice Company members, described in the last paragraph, are sufficient testimony to the possibilities for prominence both in the craft guilds and overseas. But the two pursuits were coming to seem like different worlds. As the Livery Companies increasingly became social and welfare organizations, the centers of commercial enterprise moved elsewhere. Their prosperity was growing,[7] but as entities they became only minimally involved in the new projects of the time.

[7] See, as examples of this rising prosperity, the discussions in A. H. Johnson, *The History of the Worshipful Company of the Drapers in London*, vol. II (Oxford, 1915), pp. 239–241; C. M. Clode, *The Early History of the Guild of Merchant Taylors*, vol. I (London, 1888), p. 261, where James I's reign is seen as a time of "advancing commercial prosperity" for the company; J. S. Watson, *A History of the Salters' Company* (London, 1963), p. 54, where the seventeenth

The Africa, New England and Guiana Companies, all heavily gentry, enjoyed a close interconnection — 36 percent of the members of the Africa Company who joined other ventures contributed to the New England ventures, and the Guiana and New England enterprises had approximately a fifth of their members in common. Possibly because of the large group of Virginia Company subscribers in the Providence Island Company, 80 percent of the latter who joined other companies were also in the Bermuda Company.

It is also interesting to see the extent of interlocking memberships in the efforts of the 1570's and 1580's. Among the backers of Frobisher and Fenton, for example, over 27 percent of those who were in other companies participated in the new trade with Russia,[8] nearly 40 percent backed privateers, over 21 percent were in the Minerals Company, and almost 28 percent supported Gilbert. Fully 24 percent of the backers of Drake and two of Cavendish's four supporters invested in the voyages of Frobisher or Fenton; among Gilbert's backers who joined other companies, over 36 percent supported Frobisher or Fenton, and over 10 percent were in both the Minerals and Mines Companies. In the Minerals and Mines Companies themselves, half of whose membership invested in *both* of these industrial projects, over 30 per cent contributed to Frobisher or Fenton, and to the trade with Russia, while some 15 percent backed Gilbert.

---

century is considered "the heyday of its prosperity"; Cyprian Blagden, *The Stationers' Company: A History, 1403–1959* (Cambridge, Mass., 1960), pp. 110–117; and Frances Consitt, *The London Weavers' Company* (Oxford, 1933), p. 172. A good general discussion of the history of the Livery Companies in this period can be found in George Unwin, *Industrial Organization in the Sixteenth and Seventeenth Centuries* (Oxford, 1904). Apart from their financing of the Ulster colonies, the only overseas venture to which the Livery Companies made corporate subscriptions was the Virginia Company. Their contributions were relatively small — a few thousand pounds — and were often regarded as a form of charity. See Alexander Brown, *The Genesis of the United States* (2 vols.; Boston and New York, 1890), and T. H. O'Brien, "The London Livery Companies and the Virginia Company," *The Virginia Magazine of History and Biography*, 68 (1960), 137–155, especially p. 148. In terms of numbers, Livery Company records provided me with the names of approximately 400 merchant investors who otherwise would not have appeared in the list.

[8] This is not surprising in view of the Muscovy Company's close links with Far Eastern trade, its effort to penetrate Persia, its search for a North-East Passage, and its later support of Hudson and other explorers of the far North. At one point it even cooperated with the Levant Company in seeking to trade in Italy. See the Levant Company: First Court Book (PRO: S.P. 105/147), fol. 82.

Figures for triple and quadruple memberships have also been calculated, but they only confirm the importance of the largest companies, particularly the East India and the Virginia. Virtually everyone with three or more memberships invested in one of the eight principal undertakings of the period. The largest single bloc of triple memberships consisted of the 107 members of the East India, Virginia, and North-West Passage Companies. They were clearly the hard core of the wave of interest in the first half of James I's reign, but they were not conspicuously committed to any other undertakings. The next largest bloc, on the other hand, consisting of 74 investors in the East India, Virginia, and Levant Companies, joined, on average, *another* 3.35 companies each. These 74 men were easily the most active definable group in the list, and they were almost exclusively mercantile: 33 were Spanish merchants, 28 French merchants, and 34 joined the North-West Passage Company.

Certain companies were also quite clearly the most popular among multiple investors. It will be seen in Table 12 that a number of ventures had a large proportion of members who joined no other organization: in particular, the East India, Eastland, French, Gilbert, Guiana, Irish, Massachusetts Bay, Minerals, Plymouth, privateering, Providence Island, Spanish, and Virginia enterprises. But some of these were so large that they also included many of the most active promoters. Thus, of the 427 men who joined four or more companies, a substantial number joined the organizations listed in Table 13.

Not surprisingly, because it was the most famous profitable venture of the period, the East India Company attracted by far the largest number of multiple investors. Most of the other large figures were the result only of the size of the respective companies. However, seen from the point of view of the proportions within the individual companies, a rather different picture emerges. Once again the North-West Passage Company proves to have the greatest relative concentration of large-scale investors. It was clearly a favorite investment for leading promoters. The Bermuda Company, too, another outgrowth of a major organization, included many of the most determined entrepreneurs of the day. However, why the Muscovy and French Companies should

Table 13. Members of four or more companies.

In these Companies		Percent of all members of this company
Bermuda	72	41.4
East India	288	21.9
Eastland	46	23.4
French	133	38.2
Frobisher & Fenton	37	30.6
Irish	116	15.2
Levant	157	27.4
Muscovy	80	37.9
New Merchant Adventurers	86	33.5
North-West Passage	147	47.3
Privateers	149	14.2
Spanish	185	16.9
Virginia	228	13.5

have had so many more active investors than did the Levant and, particularly, the Spanish Companies, is difficult to understand. I can only suggest that the much lower Spanish figure may have been due to the fact that a substantial percentage of its membership came from the outports, where multiple investments were much less common; but this explanation would not hold good for the Levant Company. The particularly low percentage in the Irish and Virginia Companies and among the privateers shows that, for all their size, they depended to a great extent on the contributions of less spectacular adventurers. The Irish and Virginia undertakings especially, with their widespread support at all levels in the City and (in the latter case) the nation, drew much of their support from obscure investors. To a lesser extent this was also true of the East India Company. The privateers' figures were this low primarily because of the second group, active in Charles I's reign, in which prominent City investors, with a few exceptions, were conspicuously missing. The much more important Elizabethan promoters, who played so large a role in sustaining overseas efforts in the 1590's, included slightly over 20 percent of "four or more companies" investors in their ranks.[9]

[9] In a few cases, contributors to a number of "other ventures" helped to swell the ranks of those members of a company who had four or more different investments. Because these were rather special interests, it might be mentioned that in the companies listed in Table 13 the following number of investors in four or more companies had investments in "other ventures." (The figure in parentheses

Some of the smaller enterprises were completely dominated by these very active promoters. The Venice Company, six of whose 14 members invested in six or more companies, has already been mentioned. Equally remarkable were the eight backers of Baffin, six of whom joined six or more companies; the Barbary Company, 26 of whose 47 members were in four or more companies; the 21 backers of Drake, 10 of whom joined six or more companies; the 24 energetic men who backed Hudson and were to form the nucleus of the North-West Passage Company, 20 of whom joined six or more companies; and the 57 dedicated but unsuccessful planters of Newfoundland, 25 of whom joined four or more companies and 15 of whom joined six or more companies.

One final set of figures sheds additional light on the relative importance of the various companies. Isolating those people who joined two or more companies, and all of whose dates of admission are known, the numbers that follow in Table 14 made their first investments in the expansion in the indicated companies (where two companies were joined in the first year, both have been counted).

This group represents over three-quarters of all the people in the list who made more than one investment (the remainder were omitted because a date of admission was unknown). The importance of the East India, Virginia, and Spanish Companies, in

is the number among these people who invested in three or more "other ventures.")

Bermuda	18	(16)
East India	67	(11)
Eastland	9	(0)
French	23	(2)
Frobisher/Fenton	25	(4)
Irish	26	(4)
Levant	43	(3)
Muscovy	31	(3)
New Merchant Adventurers	11	(1)
North-West Passage	39	(9)
Privateers	77	(17)
Spanish	55	(4)
Virginia	63	(16)

Because most investments in "other ventures" were in industry, they were a good test of the breadth of interest of those people recorded as entering a large number of companies. Of the people listed in Table 13, a high proportion (over one-half) of the privateering and Fenton and Frobisher groups joined "other ventures," and this may be an indication that these organizations attracted people with particularly wide interests. But considerably more research would be needed before such a tentative suggestion could be expanded.

Table 14. Companies first joined by members who joined two or more companies.

Company	First admissions	Percent of all first admissions	Percent of members of this company who joined two or more companies
Africa	5	0.4	20.0
Baffin	1	0.1	12.5
Barbary	14	1.0	34.1
Bermuda	14	1.0	8.9
Drake	5	0.4	23.8
East India	268	19.6	35.4
Eastland	29	2.1	30.2
French	71	5.2	23.1
Frobisher & Fenton	35	2.6	46.1
Gilbert	9	0.7	15.5
Gosnold	1	0.1	20.0
Guiana	3	0.2	5.4
Hudson	1	0.1	4.3
Irish	95	6.9	35.6
Levant	133	9.7	36.2
Massachusetts Bay	9	0.7	20.9
Minerals	8	0.6	19.0
Mines	13	0.9	37.1
Muscovy	16	1.2	10.9
New England	10	0.7	19.2
Newfoundland	10	0.7	24.4
New Merchant Adventurer	15	1.1	7.5
New River	2	0.1	8.3
North-West Passage	35	2.6	13.2
Plymouth	4	0.3	20.0
Privateers	59	4.3	15.0
Senegal	6	0.4	46.2
Spanish	213	15.5	41.3
Venice	4	0.3	33.3
Virginia	281	20.5	41.3
Total	1,369		

which over half these people made their first investments, is emphasized yet again. These companies also led the way proportionately, since well over a third of their members who joined more than one organization came to them first. If to these figures are added those who invested only once, but did so in these three companies (an additional 2,149), it will be seen that nearly half (2,911 out of 6,336) of all the investors first became interested in the expansion through one of these companies. Removing the 403 people who were omitted because a date could not be determined, one finds a proportion of 2,911 out of 5,934, a shade over 49 percent. Narrowing the focus slightly, the importance of the East India and Virginia Companies alone was even more dramatic. They provided over 40 percent of the figures in the above table, and between them they brought 2,113 people into commerce, 36 percent of all the investors for whom dates are available. In other words, one in every three of the men who contributed to England's expansion made his first commitment by joining either the East India or the Virginia Company.

The early ventures, particularly the Barbary, Levant, and Senegal Companies, and the backers of Frobisher and Fenton, are naturally well represented in this table, because so little preceded them. This is also a prime reason for the prominence of the Spanish Company, whose first charter, in 1577, appeared at the very beginning of our period. Among the privateers, the Elizabethan group accounted for 50 of the 59 first admissions, which would make the figure in the last column in Table 14 slightly under 25 percent for the first body of these investors. A large portion of the Irish Company's figures also come from the Elizabethan planters. In both these cases, particularly the high proportion (36 percent) in the Irish Company, there is confirmation of the views recently put forward that Ireland and privateering were the battlefields on which Englishmen won their spurs as colonizers and seamen.[10]

The strikingly low figures for the Hudson, Baffin, and North-

[10] See D. B. Quinn, *Raleigh and the British Empire* (London, 1947; 2nd ed., 1962), pp. 129–161; his "Sir Thomas Smith (1513–1577) and the Beginnings of English Colonial Theory," *Proceedings of the American Philosophical Society*, 89 (1945), 543–560; and *The Elizabethans and the Irish* (Ithaca, 1966), chap. ix, pp. 106–122; Howard Mumford Jones, "Origins of the Colonial Idea in England," *Proceedings of the American Philosophical Society*, 85 (1942), 448–465; and K. R. Andrews, *Elizabethan Privateering* (Cambridge, England, 1964), *passim*. The importance of Irish colonization for other overseas ventures was first suggested, though, by E. P. Cheyney, "Some English conditions surrounding the settlement of Virginia," *American Historical Review*, 12 (1907), 507–528, particularly pp. 514–521. It is also worth recalling Sir Arthur Chichester's not inappropriate comment: "I had rather labour with my hands in the plantation of Ulster than dance or play in that of Virginia." Quoted in Richard Bagwell, *Ireland under the Stuarts*, vol. I (London, 1909), p. 67. Bacon felt that Virginia differed from Ireland "as Amadis de Gaul differs from Caesar's Commentaries." See *The Letters and the Life of Francis Bacon*, ed. James Spedding (7 vols.; London, 1861–1874), IV, 123.

West Passage Companies contrast strongly with their showing in Tables 12 and 13. This would seem to confirm the impression that, although these ventures were strongly supported by the more active promoters, they were usually a second interest. However exciting the search for the North-West Passage may have been, and however stirring a chapter in the history of exploration was written in the icy seas to the north of Canada, the effort to reach the Pacific by sailing westward soon lost its central importance in the history of the expansion.

To set these first-time memberships in perspective, the table on page 120 gives the number of initial admissions — whenever all dates in a man's entry are known — year by year. As will be seen, the figures closely parallel those in Tables 6 and 7.

Table 15 is not so accurate an indicator of waves of interest as Tables 6 or 7, because here the consolidations are particularly distortive; nevertheless, it does exhibit the same basic trends as were discussed in Chapter 1. For our purposes it is useful as further testimony to the importance of a handful of companies in attracting investments. This can best be seen by comparing the merchant and gentry percentages in the 11 years when admissions to the East India, Spanish, and Virginia Companies were most frequent: 1577, 1599–1600, 1604–1605, 1609–1612, 1618, and 1624. Nearly half of all first admissions were recorded in these years (49 percent). But the gentry alone made the largest proportion of their first investments (50 percent) in the five years 1609–1612 and 1618 when Virginia Company activity was at its height. In the 1609–1612 period, 45 percent of their initial admissions were recorded, as opposed to 31 percent of the merchants'. In 1618 the gentry and merchant figures were five percent and two percent respectively — another large discrepancy, mainly due to Virginia Company memberships. On the other hand, in 1577, 1599–1600, and 1604–1605, when the Spanish and East India Companies were founded (with the addition of the smaller numbers in the Levant Company) nearly a third (30 percent) of the merchants made their first investments, in contrast to six percent of the gentry. The two years at which privateering was entered on the cards, 1581 and 1625, also showed a very high proportion of first investments, especially among the merchants — further reiteration of the importance of these ventures.

Table 15. Annual first-time memberships in companies, 1575–1630.[a]

Year[b]	First-time member-ships	Percent of all first-time member-ships	Gentry first-time member-ships	Percent of all gentry first-time member-ships	Merchant first-time member-ships	Percent of all merchant first-time member-ships
1575	42	0.7	17	1.7	24	0.7
1576	8	0.1	1	0.1	4	0.1
1577	374	5.9	29	3.0	329	9.5
1578	36	0.6	25	2.6	7	0.2
1579	47	0.7	–	–	47	1.4
1580	47	0.7	5	0.5	41	1.2
1581	273	4.3	47	4.8	205	5.9
1582	13	0.2	3	0.3	7	0.2
1583	69	1.1	22	2.3	25	0.7
1584	67	1.1	35	3.6	1	0.0
1585	19	0.3	2	0.2	15	0.4
1587	13	0.2	13	1.3	–	–
1588	16	0.3	–	–	16	0.5
1589	19	0.3	1	0.1	17	0.5
1590	19	0.3	5	0.5	14	0.4
1592	13	0.2	1	0.1	11	0.3
1598	1	0.0	1	0.1	–	–
1599	75	1.2	2	0.2	72	2.1
1600	133	2.1	2	0.2	131	3.8
1601	15	0.2	–	–	15	0.4
1602	2	0.0	–	–	2	0.1
1603	1	0.0	1	0.1	–	–
1604	380	6.0	13	1.3	366	10.6
1605	145	2.3	8	0.8	136	3.9
1606	44	0.7	5	0.5	37	1.1
1607	57	0.9	21	2.2	31	0.9
1608	21	0.3	6	0.6	12	0.4
1609	946	14.9	180	18.4	561	16.2
1610	179	2.8	82	8.3	82	2.4
1611	427	6.8	41	4.3	359	10.3
1612	234	3.7	136	13.9	80	2.3
1613	45	0.7	8	0.8	14	0.4
1614	73	1.2	5	0.5	53	1.5
1615	131	2.1	13	1.3	104	3.0
1616	10	0.2	2	0.2	5	0.1
1617	55	0.9	13	1.3	25	0.7
1618	203	3.2	52	5.3	63	1.8
1619	73	1.2	23	2.4	31	0.9
1620	170	2.7	26	2.7	79	2.3
1621	52	0.8	14	1.4	11	0.3
1622	91	1.4	12	1.2	25	0.7
1623	59	0.9	14	1.4	16	0.5
1624	86	1.4	4	0.4	66	1.9
1625	583	9.2	23	2.4	203	5.9
1626	31	0.5	1	0.1	24	0.7
1627	77	1.2	25	2.6	35	1.0
1628	55	0.9	8	0.8	32	0.9
1629	96	1.5	23	2.4	28	0.8
1630	10	0.2	9	0.9	–	–
Total	5,635		979		3,461	

[a] In the class breakdowns, unclassified and professionals/yeomen account for the difference between the total memberships and the sum of gentry and merchant figures.

[b] In the years that are omitted (1586, 1591, and 1593–97), no first-time memberships were recorded.

120

The figures for directorships and governorships show in detail the dominance of the merchants discussed in Chapter 1. The following 20 companies were the only ones with official directors or governors, though it might be remembered that all members of smaller ventures could also be regarded as directors because they organized and directed their individual projects. Though this latter consideration might have some effect on the "number of directorships held" table (Table 17), it is of no great significance in relation to Table 16, where the leaders of the great commercial and colonial efforts appear.

Table 16. Directors and governors of companies, by company and class.[a]

Company	Directorships	Number and percent held by gentry	Number and percent held by merchants	Governorships	Number and percent held by gentry	Number and percent held by merchants
Africa	–	–	–	1	1 (100.0)	–
Bermuda	6	1 (16.7)	5 (85.3)	7	5 (71.1)	2 (28.9)
East India	128	6 (5.5)	121 (94.5)	7	–	7 (100.0)
Eastland	2	–	2 (100.0)	5	–	5 (100.0)
French	16	–	16 (100.0)	3	–	3 (100.0)
Irish	68	19 (27.9)	37 (44.4)	1	–	1 (100.0)
Levant	85	–	85 (100.0)	6	–	6 (100.0)
Massachusetts Bay	18	1 (5.6)	14 (77.8)	1	–	1 (100.0)
Merchant Adventurer	10	–	10 (100.0)	6	–	6 (100.0)
Minerals	13	3 (23.1)	10 (76.9)	4	2 (50.0)	2 (50.0)
Mines	7	2 (28.6)	5 (71.4)	4	1 (25.0)	3 (75.0)
Muscovy	47	–	47 (100.0)	11	–	11 (100.0)
New England	12	11 (91.7)	–	1	1 (100.0)	–
Newfoundland	11	2 (18.2)	9 (81.8)	1	–	1 (100.0)
New Merchant Adventurer	26	–	26 (100.0)	1	–	1 (100.0)
New River	1	–	1 (100.0)	1	–	1 (100.0)
North-West Passage	24	2 (8.3)	22 (91.7)	1	–	1 (100.0)
Providence Island	2	1 (50.0)	1 (50.0)	1	1 (100.0)	–
Spanish	107	–	107 (100.0)	2	–	2 (100.0)
Virginia	161	115 (71.5)	35 (21.7)	3	2 (66.7)	1 (33.3)

[a] The few unclassified and professionals/yeomen directors and governors have not been included in the breakdowns.

The proportion of directors and governors to total memberships was higher than five percent in the following organizations: Bermuda, seven percent (over half were governorships); East India, 10 percent; Irish, nine percent; Levant, 16 percent, Massachusetts Bay, 16 percent; Minerals, 22 percent; Mines, 19 percent; Muscovy, 28 percent; New England, 19 percent; Newfoundland, 21 percent; New Merchant Adventurers, 11 percent; New River, six percent; North-West Passage, eight percent; Providence Island, 15 percent; Spanish, 10 percent; and Virginia, 10 percent.

The Merchant Adventurers' six percent is this high only because a very small percentage of the company appears in the list. The Muscovy figure may also be relatively high because a number of members are missing, but the company was not seriously under-represented, and it is clear that the directorate formed a larger proportion than was usual. The other high percentages are due mainly to the smaller size of the companies. Among the largest organizations, the figure remains remarkably close to 10 percent — except for the French Company, whose three percent probably reflects the short life of the organization. The much higher figure for the Levant Company, which proportionately had some 50 percent more directors than most of the other major enterprises, may reflect only the fact that it enjoyed the longest life of these organizations. As time went by the number of directors presumably increased faster than did the number of members.

The following table reveals the merchants' predominance among directors and governors, and the relative importance, within their classes, of peers and merchant knights.

Table 17. Number of directorships and governorships, by class.

Class	Number of directorships and governorships						
	1	2	3	4	5	6	7
Unclassified	22	1	–	–	–	–	–
Gentleman	21	3	–	–	–	–	–
Knight	80	5	1	–	–	–	–
Peer	46	5	–	–	–	–	–
Merchant	288	62	16	4	–	2	–
Merchant knight	29	24	5	2	1	1	1
Professionals/yeomen	5	–	–	–	–	–	–

The significance of these figures is discussed in Chapter 1, but it is worth stressing once again the concentration of officers in the upper strata of the two classes, considering how small a proportion of the total numbers they represented. It is particularly noteworthy that over half the merchant knights in the list were directors, and that over half of these held office in more than one company.

The same situation is depicted, though not quite so dramatically, in Table 18, which shows the number of companies the

Table 18. Number and percent of company memberships, by class.[a]

Number of companies	Unclassified	Gentleman	Knight	Peer	Merchant	Merchant knight	Professionals and yeomen	Totals
1	1,105	396	372	76	2,529	25	61	4,564
	95.9	82.0	72.2	42.5	66.4	20.3	82.4	72.0
2	38	66	72	48	687	22	9	942
	3.3	13.7	14.0	26.8	18.0	17.9	12.2	14.9
3	7	16	38	23	293	23	3	403
	0.6	3.3	7.4	12.9	7.7	18.7	4.1	6.4
4	2	3	18	6	142	15	1	187
	0.2	0.6	3.5	3.4	3.7	12.2	1.4	3.0
5	–	2	3	8	73	9	–	95
		0.4	0.6	4.5	1.9	7.3		1.5
6	–	–	4	4	35	9	–	52
			0.8	2.2	0.9	7.3		0.8
7	–	–	2	2	23	8	–	35
			0.4	1.1	0.6	6.5		0.6
8	–	–	2	4	11	4	–	21
			0.4	2.2	0.3	3.3		0.3
9	–	–	2	1	9	4	–	16
			0.4	0.6	0.2	3.3		0.3
10	–	–	1	2	–	3	–	6
			0.2	1.1		2.4		0.1
11	–	–	1	1	7	1	–	10
			0.2	0.6	0.2	0.8		0.2
12	–	–	–	2	–	–	–	2
				1.1				0.1
13	–	–	–	1	1	–	–	2
				0.6	0.0			0.1
14	–	–	–	–	–	–	–	–
15	–	–	–	1	–	–	–	1
				0.6				0.0
Total	1,152	483	515	179	3,810	123	74	6,336

[a] The percentage below each figure is of the total at the foot of the column.

investors in the various classes joined. The percentage entered beneath each figure is the proportion of all investors in this class who joined this number of companies (that is, percent of the total at the foot of each column).

The significance of these figures is discussed in Chapter 1, notes 36 and 54. One can see only too clearly how much more active than any other group the merchant knights were. A mere fifth of their number invested in only one company, half the proportion of the next most active group, the peers. Almost half the merchant knights invested in four or more companies — compared to eight percent of the merchants, the virtual absence of gentlemen, under seven percent of the knights, and 18 percent of the peers. The nobility were also highly active, but at a much lower level.

One other table of correlations (19) provides further detail on the connection between widespread investments and directorships. No enormously important conclusions emerge from these figures, but they are provided for the sake of completeness and as a source of reference.

Multiple directorships appear to have been of such small significance, and the result only of the widespread interests of a

Table 19. Correlation of number of company memberships with number of directorships and governorships.

Number of company memberships	Number of offices held[a]							Total
	1	2	3	4	5	6	7	
1	157 (31.9) 100.0	–	–	–	–	–	–	157
2	116 (23.6) 89.9	13 (13) 10.1	–	–	–	–	–	129
3	94 (19.1) 83.9	17 (17) 15.2	1 (4.6) 0.9	–	–	–	–	112
4	51 (10.6) 68.0	22 (22) 29.3	2 (9.1) 2.7	–	–	–	–	75
5	31 (6.3) 68.9	12 (12) 26.6	2 (9.1) 4.5	–	–	–	–	45
6	22 (4.5) 62.9	12 (12) 34.3	1 (4.6) 2.8	–	–	–	–	35
7	10 (2.0) 40.0	5 (5) 20.0	7 (31.8) 28.0	3 (50) 12.0	–	–	–	25
8	4 (0.8) 25.5	11 (11) 64.7	2 (9.1) 9.8	–	–	–	–	17
9	3 (0.6) 25.0	4 (4) 33.3	3 (13.6) 25.0	–	1 (100) 8.3	1 (33.3) 8.3	–	12
10	1 (0.2) 25.0	–	1 (4.6) 25.0	1 (16.7) 25.0	–	–	1 (100) 25.0	4
11	1 (0.2) 11.1	2 (2) 22.2	3 (13.6) 33.3	1 (16.7) 11.1	–	2 (66.7) 22.2	–	9
12	1 (0.2) 50.0	1 (1) 50.0	–	–	–	–	–	2
13	–	1 (1) 50.0	–	1 (16.7) 50.0	–	–	–	2
Total	491	100	22	6	1	3	1	624

[a] The percentages in parentheses are of the total at the foot of each column; the percentages below each figure are of the total at the end of each row.

few major investors, that no "hunting in packs" phenomenon can be discerned. Only where there was a close parent-child relationship between companies was there a noteworthy correlation on the boards of directors.[11] Thus 85 percent of the directors in the Bermuda Company were also directors of the Virginia Company; 35 merchants were directors of both the Levant and East India Companies (39 percent of the officers of the former and 26 percent of the latter); and 36 percent of the directors of the North-West Passage Company held the same position in the East India Company. In addition, seven (12 percent) of the Muscovy directors were East India Company directors; 10 (nine percent) of the Spanish Company directors were East India Company directors; and 13 men were directors of both the East India (10 percent) and the Virginia (eight percent) Companies. And six (nine percent) of the Irish Company directors were also officers of the East India Company.

Triple and quadruple directorships were so uncommon as to have little meaning. Only two groups shared four common directors: the Levant, East India, and Irish Companies; and the Levant, East India, and Muscovy Companies. The one group which had three directors in common consisted of the Virginia, East India, and Levant Companies. No other groups of three had more than two directors in common. A few great merchants did dominate the boards of directors in quite spectacular fashion, the most famous being Sir Thomas Smith with his six governorships and one directorship, and William Cockayne, governor of three companies and a director of another three. Far less well known is William Harrison, who was a director of six companies; because he was never prominent in City or Livery Company affairs — with the one appropriate exception of his interest in Ulster — he has received none of the fame surrounding Smith or Cockayne, but his activity was hardly less remarkable. Nonetheless, the multiple directorships of these few people were no more than a reflection of their wide interests in new ventures: no particular pattern can be detected. Similarly, though the East India directors were the ones most frequently to be found on other boards of directors,

---

[11] The three notable instances of such outgrowths were the East India from the Levant Company; the Bermuda from the Virginia Company; and the North-West Passage from the East India Company.

this was simply the result of the central place held by their company in the overseas efforts of the time — a position already revealed in Table 12. In conclusion it might be mentioned that, as Table 17 indicates, gentry investors figured minimally among the multiple directorships.

A few additional parliamentary figures will serve as further evidence for the correlations made in Chapter 1. The group of investors who also sat in Parliament were noticeably the most active M.P.'s: 65 percent of them sat in more than one session, whereas the figure for all M.P.'s was 50 percent; 40 percent sat in more than two sessions, as opposed to 24 percent of all M.P.'s; and 27 percent were in more than three sessions, as opposed to 16 percent of all M.P.'s. On average, the investors sat in 2.65 Parliaments each, whereas for the M.P.'s as a whole the average was 2.09. Conversely, M.P.'s were also more active than the average investor: 39 percent of M.P. investors joined more than one company, as compared with 28 percent of *all* investors, 28 percent of *gentry* investors, and 35 percent of *merchant* investors. Those who joined more than two companies were 21 percent of M.P. investors, 13 percent of all investors, 13 percent of gentry investors, and 17 percent of merchant investors. Though not very much more active than the merchants, the M.P.'s, consisting mainly of gentlemen, had considerably wider interests than the average investors of their own class: they joined, on average, 1.97 companies each, as opposed to the 1.58 companies of all investors, and the 1.58 and 1.73 companies of the gentry and merchants respectively.

Two final tables add further detail to the parliamentary figures in Chapter 1. The first, Table 20, shows the proportion of the members of various companies who also sat in Parliament. Only those organizations with at least five percent M.P.'s have been included.

This table reveals an exact correlation between gentry and M.P. members of companies. All the companies with over 11 percent parliamentary membership drew at least 25 percent of their subscribers from the gentry. Conversely, all those below 11 percent were over three-quarters merchant. The cut-off point between the Irish Company and the privateers is precisely the

Table 20. Percentage of company members who sat in the House of Commons (totals are given for the six companies that included more than 50 M.P.'s).

Africa	39.5
Baffin	37.5
Bermuda	24.7
Cavendish	25.0
Drake	9.5
East India	9.3 (123)
Eastland	5.1
French	8.6
Frobisher & Fenton	15.7
Gilbert	17.1
Guiana	39.1
Hudson	33.3
Irish	11.0
Merchant Adventurers	8.9[a]
Minerals	19.5
Mines	24.6
Muscovy	8.1
New England	45.7
Newfoundland	21.1
New Merchant Adventurers	5.8
New River	48.4
North-West Passage	19.0 (59)
Plymouth	6.1
Privateering	10.6 (111)
Providence Island	55.0
Spanish	7.3 (80)
Staplers	5.6[a]
Venice	7.1
Virginia	19.8 (333)
Weymouth	40.0

[a] The figures for these companies are excessively high because they refer only to that small proportion of the membership which appears in the list.

dividing line between those organizations included in Table 2 because of their substantial gentry membership, and those which were omitted. Some of the high proportions were, of course, caused by small total numbers (in particular, the Baffin, Cavendish, Hudson, New River, Providence Island, and Weymouth figures). But a small heavily merchant organization, the backers of Drake for example, still fell below 10 percent. The most notable absence in Table 20 is that of the Levant Company, which included only 24 M.P.'s in its membership: less than the number of M.P.'s among the supporters of Gilbert, a body of investors little more than a fifth the size of the Levant Company. On the other hand, the number of M.P.'s in the one major company that included a substantial proportion of gentry, the Virginia, is quite remarkable. They were almost three times as numerous as the next largest group, and they comprised almost half of all the M.P.'s who contributed to companies in this period. From these figures alone one can appreciate the overwhelming importance of the Virginia Company as a lure to gentry investors, the impact of the expansion on Members of Parliament, and the remarkable breadth of activity of the leaders of the landed class.

With the exception of the Virginia Company, the members of individual organizations did not reach noteworthy proportions of the membership of any of the Parliaments of the time, as is indicated by the table which follows.

Table 21.   Members of selected companies in each Parliament.

Session starting	Total number of investors	East India	Irish	North-West Passage	Priva-teers	Spanish	Virginia
1584	91	6	11	4	14	10	19
1586	99	8	12	7	12	10	23
1589	103	8	10	8	13	15	26
1593	103	11	11	6	13	9	33
1597	103	17	15	8	12	7	45
1601	135	19	11	10	9	10	58
1604	216	29	16	21	15	18	96
1614	181	24	16	17	9	10	78
1621	188	25	12	12	12	12	79
1624	169	25	8	12	18	11	64
1625	145	24	7	11	13	7	53
1626	153	27	7	12	17	8	54
1628	144	20	5	5	11	7	44

The remarkable concentration of Virginia Company members in the House of Commons is strikingly apparent. They amounted to some 40 percent of the investors sitting in the House between 1597 and 1624. In those six sessions they totaled, successively, 10 percent, 13 percent, 17 percent, 17 percent, 15 percent, and 13 percent of all M.P.'s.[12] This was more than double the

[12] It would seem to be as a result of the concentration of Virginia Company members in Parliament in this period that between 1604 and 1626 there were

proportion in the company with the next largest representation. The corollary, too, is plain: M.P.'s, like the gentry as a whole, were attracted most strongly by England's first permanent colony. The East India Company members, though a substantial and steady group, never amounted to more than 5 percent of the M.P.'s. The remainder were all below five percent.

The dates at which the people in the list received their knighthoods followed closely the rise and fall of the rate of new creations in this period.[13] Thirteen percent were knighted between 1590 and 1602, whereas 29 percent were knighted in 1603 and 1604, during the spree with which James opened his reign. Approximately half of all knights created between 1575 and 1630 appear in the list, though it is interesting that in the period of greatest "debasement" of this honor, 1603 and 1604, only some 35 percent of the new knights made an investment or sat in Parliament. In Elizabeth's last years, too, the proportion (44 percent) was below the average. It would seem, therefore, that one can speak quite appropriately of a debasement: when the title was cheaply bestowed, its recipients were people who were significantly less involved in the commercial and political activity of the day — in other words, they were not quite as conspicuously the leaders of society.

---

also between 11 and 13 Bermuda investors in the House. Before 1601 their numbers were three or less.

[13] See Lawrence Stone, "The Inflation of Honours, 1558–1641," *Past and Present*, no. 14 (1958), pp. 45–70.

Part Two: The Data

CHAPTER 3   METHODS AND DEFINITIONS

I. QUANTIFICATION

Despite the recent growth of such disciplines as economics, statistics, and sociology, the benefits of quantification still find scant appreciation among historians. Even the widely discussed techniques developed by Namier, who uncovered new levels of evidence through multiple biographies and elementary quantification, remain confined to relatively few fields of inquiry.[1] The use

[1] L. B. Namier, *The Structure of Politics at the Accession of George III* (2 vols.; London, 1929). Eighteenth-century English parliamentary history is still, nearly 40 years later, easily ahead of all other fields in the number of studies using techniques similar to Namier's. In fact, much of the quantification that has been done by historians in recent years has been influenced more by sociologists and economists than by Namier and his followers — see Bernard and Lotte Bailyn, *Massachusetts Shipping, 1697–1714: A Statistical Study* (Cambridge, Mass., 1959); Stephan Thernstrom, *Poverty and Progress: Social Mobility in a Nineteenth Century City* (Cambridge, Mass., 1964), and Charles Tilly, *The Vendée* (Cambridge, Mass., 1964), none of which, however, used a computer. This is not the place to attempt to survey all recent uses of quantification by historians, but it is clear that only a few subjects (mainly the French revolution, demographic history, and scattered topics in economic and social history) have benefited from the techniques developed in other disciplines. It is easy to speak about the "current fashion" of "a taste for counting (preferably by computer)," as did an anonymous reviewer in the *Times Literary Supplement* (December 9, 1965), p. 1118; but it is more difficult to demonstrate that this has become anything like a fashion in history — as opposed to sociology, economics, demography, or other social sciences. Historians using quantification extensively and for a variety of purposes, as has Lawrence Stone for sixteenth- and seventeenth-century England (see note 5, below), are few and far between, and those using a computer are almost nonexistent. The prevalent attitude is probably still much

133

of numbers is certainly beset by hazardous pitfalls, not the least of which is the temptation to regard method alone as a panacea for all intractable problems — "set it up so that you can count, and the rest will follow." But the fear that statistics may provide an escape from careful reasoning should not be allowed to impugn their undoubted ability to clarify, simplify, and make new information available through organization. The dangers of improper usage are no greater than those encountered whenever evidence is transformed into history.

The material that made possible the findings described in Chapters 1 and 2 was assembled, as has been pointed out in the Introduction, in the belief that "namierization" could be extended fruitfully by research in breadth rather than depth. Instead of studying exhaustively each member of a small group, I gathered a few specific pieces of information about a very large number of people. There was no change in the underlying aim of splitting some well-defined entity into the individuals who formed its components. But there was a difference in the scope of coverage: although a new level of evidence was unearthed, it was thinly spread, not deeply concentrated. Inevitably this shift of emphasis led to a heavier reliance on quantification because the data were too extensive and unwieldy for anything but statistical analysis. The information itself might be reduced to a few categories, and the varieties of possible findings might be severely restricted, but the sheer bulk required rigid systematization. In fact, hardly any conclusions about the evidence would have been possible without the assistance of modern computers. Calculations undertaken by hand or by primitive counting devices were far too inaccurate to be useful,[2] whereas machine processing was dependable, flexible, and fast.

In effect, the computer has created opportunities for a new kind of historical study. Not only can the historian take advantage

closer to the sentiment expressed by Arthur Schlesinger, Jr., in "The Humanist Looks at Empirical Social Research," *American Sociological Review,* 27 (1962), 770: "Almost all important questions are important precisely because they are not susceptible to quantitative answers." (Cited on p. 820 of a superb survey of this entire subject, William O. Aydelotte's "Quantification in History," *American Historical Review,* 71 [1966], 808–825.) See further note 4 to this chapter.

[2] At an early stage of the research, when I had only 4,500 names, I encountered variations of as much as 15 percent in successive attempts to make simple tabulations by hand.

of methods evolved by other social scientists — as has been done in various fields, notably social, economic, and demographic history[3] — but he can also gain access to a new dimension of evidence. Now that vast bodies of material can be handled accurately and swiftly, he no longer has to limit his focus to subjects whose documentation is small enough to be managed by one person; nor does he need to muster a team of researchers. The most ambitious projects, like the tabulation of all American election returns currently in progress at the University of Michigan, will still require many hands, but only because new horizons have opened at every level. Studies that a few years ago could have been attempted only by a team can now be covered by one man. The teams can devote themselves to tasks that might once have been considered completely impossible.

The combination of quantification and modern data processing is so flexible in making evidence amenable to study that it can be applied to many different kinds of investigation. It would be relatively simple, for instance, to collect certain types of information about every man who has been elevated to the College of Cardinals. Long-term changes in the composition of the Sacred College (for example, in the social or geographic origins of the cardinals) could be documented with an accuracy not previously possible, and the results could have considerable significance for the history of the Catholic Church. Under present conditions an expert on the subject might be able to estimate degrees of change or continuity in a given period, but with the help of the computer one could give precise answers to a multitude of questions over the entire history of the institution. Similar studies could be pursued with any large group of people, from scientists to painters, or with any well-documented subject, from the building of new houses to decisions in a court of law. An example of work already in progress which could put these methods to excellent use is the comprehensive collection of biographies being prepared by the History of Parliament Trust. Instead of having to rely on the fallible impressions gained from reading thousands of brief lives, the historian could obtain precise information on many topics by resorting to numerical analysis.[4] Naturally, the trans-

[3] See the works mentioned in note 1, above.
[4] Despite the one volume of analysis, there is obviously still a great deal of

formation of biographical details into symbols on a card must be very carefully planned. The definitions and the coding ("encoding" to computer people) are the crucial steps in the whole procedure, but they are no more demanding of a historian's skills, and no more susceptible to distortion, than any other process involving an assessment of evidence.

The approach taken in this book rests on the important advances in method that have been made possible by computers and quantification: accessibility to hitherto unmanageable material, speed and accuracy of analysis, and increased precision in generalization. But enthusiasm for these benefits needs to be tempered by some general cautions and limitations.

By abandoning depth and seeking breadth the historian must accept losses as well as gains. Although he may uncover a new level of evidence, it is likely to be so thin that he will not be able to achieve the richness of detail and exposition that other types of quantification have allowed. The contrast between the wide-ranging familiarity with the lives of 382 noblemen displayed by Stone's recent study of the English aristocracy,[5] and the three restricted types of information on which my statistics rest (social class, election to Parliament, and membership of companies), is an obvious example of the differences between the two kinds of research.

---

material lying undigested (and, without machine help, undigestible) in the first work issued by the Trust: Sir L. B. Namier and John Brooke, *The House of Commons, 1754–1790* (3 vols.; London, 1964). It is a sign of the growing appreciation of recent advances in data processing that Basil Henning, the editor of the volumes dealing with late Stuart Parliaments, is coding his material for a computer. The Trust's attempt to gather together all the data it can find about every member of the House of Commons is the kind of undertaking which obviously will become more frequent in the future, and historical scholarship cannot help but benefit from such comprehensive assemblages of information. The "gentry" controversy, for example, is only the most obvious recent demonstration of the truism that far-reaching issues cannot be settled until at least a majority of the evidence is available. I need hardly add that the historian's reliance on quantification is bound to grow as these thorough and detailed surveys of the archives become more common. Apart from the article by Aydelotte cited in note 1, above, the most sensible general comments on quantification and computers in history, stressing both prospects and limitations, can be found in "New Ways in History: 3," an issue of the *Times Literary Supplement* (September 8, 1966), pp. 790–848. See in particular the articles by Ladurie, Chevalier, and Kahk, and the leader, "10000101010 and All That."
    [5] Lawrence Stone, *The Crisis of the Aristocracy, 1558–1641* (Oxford, 1965).

More important, because a few features are isolated and no sustained effort is devoted to any one individual, the likelihood of mistakes is much greater. It is a temptation to react against this danger by stressing that one's numbers are so large that errors are statistically insignificant. To some extent this is true — when one is dealing with the group as a whole; but many calculations concern only a fraction of the total. Frequently some special category is under consideration, which may be very small by the time various qualifications are met and successive groups eliminated. For example, a substantial difference in the composition, and hence the evaluation, of one of the smaller companies I studied would have been caused by the mistaken classification of a handful of merchants as gentlemen. In the Africa Company, by no means the smallest, a wrong appraisal of just seven merchants would have changed relative strengths from 79 percent gentry, 21 percent merchant, to 60 percent gentry, 40 percent merchant, a doubling of the mercantile percentage. One may agree that so many errors in so small a group should never occur, regardless of the scope of the research; but the possibility exists, and it must not be ignored simply because overall numbers are so large. On the contrary, greater vigilance must be exercised in studies of this kind precisely because the individuals remain relatively unfamiliar; and because the reduction of information to symbols and numbers is particularly vulnerable to inconspicuous yet damaging typographical mistakes when the data is repeatedly copied, as it must be during the transfer from documents to IBM cards. It may be comforting to find elementary slips even in studies which stress depth rather than breadth,[6] but the need for accuracy is no less when the range of generalizations supported by the research widens, and the excuse of statistical insignificance becomes an easy escape.

[6] Examples that I have noticed — primarily because they made me think I was wrong — are Stone's description of Viscount Banning as an alderman (*ibid.*, p. 535) when the office was in fact held by Paul Banning, *Senior*, before the future Viscount reached the age of 15 (A. B. Beaven, *The Aldermen of the City of London*, vol. II [London, 1913], pp. 44, 48); and K. R. Andrews' mistaking George Talbot, who did not succeed to the title until 1590, for the Gilbert Talbot who was Earl of Shrewsbury in 1582 (*Elizabethan Privateering* [Cambridge, England, 1964], p. 295). Such errors in identification in books so painstakingly researched make me shudder to think of what has probably escaped my attention among nearly 8,700 names.

My own experience might provide a salutary warning in this connection. Although constant checks eventually gained diminishing returns, and had to end sometime, their effect was little short of startling in the early stages. The rates of typographical error discovered during the first few major tests were alarming and intolerable. Despite the strictest caution during research and codification, the first exhaustive comparison with the original sources uncovered a mistake in roughly one out of every 50 entries. This figure of two percent was soon lowered, and the final inspection brought to light only five lapses among almost 9,000 people — but those five had survived repeated checks over a period of four years!

The lesson to be learned from this exposure of human fallibility is that quantification and machine processing provide no simple or final solution for the problems to which they can be applied. The job of assembling sufficient data to make the method worthwhile is enormous and tedious. And the entire endeavor can be undermined if categories or definitions are imprecise or fallacious. Furthermore, flexibility must be maintained until the task is nearly complete. Even as one is compiling the evidence unforeseen patterns become discernible, and until the very last stages one should be prepared to add or subtract information. The plain drudgery is inescapable, for only by wading through it all himself can the historian keep in close touch with his material and discover — as I did a number of times — unsuspected correlations and promising new lines of inquiry. In my own case, for example, the hypothesis about the importance of a visit to London as a catalyst for gentry investments emerged slowly as the research progressed. The connection may seem perfectly logical in retrospect, but I did not realize that there was any way of testing it until I kept noticing that gentlemen seemed to start investing in companies only *after* serving as Members of Parliament. Arranging this particular calculation was then a simple matter, but it would never have occurred to me had the monotony of marshaling the evidence been delegated to others. This is not to deny that aims and methods must be formulated on the basis of clear hypotheses and expectations long before final organization of the data begins. But so much information is being amassed that it is impossible always to know what is going to be significant. Some connections will become apparent as one proceeds, but others may have to be sought quite consciously.

To this end, I made a preliminary run with the computer when the list was approximately two-thirds complete. The purpose was not only to see what kinds of results the obvious calculations were producing, but also to carry out a broad search which might bring to light unexpected findings. It was far too complicated to work out every possible correlation in the data, and in the final tabulations figures were computed only if the preliminary run indicated that they were likely to be significant. For example, a table showing how many members of certain companies sat in each Parliament became necessary when it appeared that a large percentage of M.P.'s invested in trade, and that a few companies included substantial numbers of M.P.'s. The more detailed table revealed which companies were represented — and in what strengths — at each session. Such random computer surveys can be valuable in many fields of research. Nonetheless, like the retention of close contact with the evidence at all times, this technique accords especially well with the needs of the historian, for whom the computer is particularly useful as an organizer and elucidator of intractable archival material.

Nevertheless, when all the effort is over, the new material uncovered, the right categories chosen, and the right questions asked, the results may contribute no more than increased precision to impressions long since familiar. Conclusions of absolute exactness cannot be reached because slips are elusive, and because every subject will encounter particular difficulties — in my case, the problems of documentation and identification discussed below. But even if one is content merely with an improvement in accuracy — the substitution of figures for metaphors like "floods of gentry" investing in trade — one must also accept the possibility of an advance only in degree, not in kind. The phenomenon of gentry investments, for example, is nothing new to historians of the English expansion. My more detailed findings, too, concerning the effect of peace with Spain or the importance of privateering and Irish colonies, have been apparent in outline for some time. But it does not lessen the importance of quantifying large bodies of material to admit that the entire endeavor may serve only to increase precision, or provide a more solid and

139

reliable basis for generalizations already proposed. Just as it would be a mistake to regard quantification as unnecessary or misleading per se, so it is unfair to expect too much. As it happens, this type of investigation will always stand a very good chance of unearthing information that is new in kind as well as degree, simply because it reduces otherwise excessively cumbersome problems to manageable proportions.[7] But such results should not be *expected*, for it is all too easy to create grandiose theories from figures which promise to be revolutionary only because previously they have been inaccessible.

Finally, and most important, it can be argued that the subjects of greatest interest to the historian, particularly analyses of causation, are the very topics which cannot be approached through numbers. Figures may explain how something happened, but rarely why: although the tables in this book display patterns of investment, they cannot expose the motives of the investors. To a degree this is true, but it is equally true that the attainment of more exact knowledge (about the rise and fall of rates of investment, for example) may indicate where answers to qualitative questions are likely to be found. The plausibility of those answers may not depend on the researcher's arithmetic, but statistical series can certainly suggest new hypotheses and also allow them to be tested. By pinpointing a dramatic increase in the number of English investments after 1603, the figures have provided the basis for an explanation of that increase. The statistics, therefore, are no less important than any other evidence the historian uses when he devises questions and answers about the documents of the past.

In the following pages, where my own methods and definitions are described in detail, the general virtues and vices of quantification will become more sharply etched. Many of the problems may seem peculiar to the subject and period under consideration, but in one form or another they are probably typical of the sea of troubles that must be opposed whenever large quantities of historical data are gathered and systematized for machine analysis. If the emphasis seems to be on cautions, qualifications, difficulties,

[7] A typical windfall of this kind was my discovery of widespread interest in trade among the members of the 1604–1611 Parliament — see my article, "Sir Edwin Sandys and the Parliament of 1604," *American Historical Review*, 69 (1964), 661–669.

and lacunae, that may well be only because I consider the advantages of the method self-evident, whereas the limitations may not be obvious unless carefully delineated.

II. ASSEMBLING THE DATA

Coverage. The early years of England's expansion overseas provide a subject well fitted in one crucial respect for computers and quantification: a huge amount of dormant information can be brought to light from the charters and minutes of company meetings where it has survived, unused and unapproachable, for centuries. Although there are gaps, it is possible to reconstruct a large part of the membership of most of the undertakings set in motion during the vital period between 1550 and 1630, when an empire was founded and the beginnings of a great commercial hegemony were established.

As is indicated in the bibliography, the story of the accomplishments of these years has enjoyed an enduring popularity out of proportion to its relatively small scope and time span. Partly this is due to its fame as one of the most stirring of history's tales of adventure: a David overcoming a Goliath. But much interest has also been turned toward the techniques and the administration that made this spectacular growth possible. Beginning with Scott's monumental study of joint-stock companies, many scholars in the last half-century have probed the developments in England that were essential to the entire enterprise.[8] Instead of relat-

---

[8] W. R. Scott, *The Constitution and Finance of English, Scottish and Irish Joint-Stock Companies to 1720* (3 vols.; Cambridge, England, 1910–1912). See Sources and Annotated Bibliography, below, for subsequent studies of the commercial organizations of this period. For obvious reasons, historians of this subject have not been so numerous as those who concentrate on the more exciting developments overseas. As A. F. Pollard put it in his lecture, "The Elizabethans and the Empire," *Proceedings of the British Academy*, 10 (1921–1923), 139–156, behind the glamour lies the "duller background in the prosaic details of joint-stock companies" (p. 153). The rather different view of this material, which has inspired a whole new approach to the expansion, was heralded over 50 years ago, before Scott's work appeared, by Walter Raleigh, the Oxford don who closed his essay in the great MacLehose edition of Hakluyt with the words: "The record is one of failure. But on the other side of the account there is an item which cannot be neglected. It is to be found in those long and dull lists of unknown names, of merchant promoters, gentlemen adventurers, intending colonists, and ship's companies, which give so business-like an air to Hakluyt's pages. It may be true . . . that these detailed summaries 'leave as little impression of excitement . . . upon our minds as so many almanacks.' But they held in them the promise of Empire. The ideas of colonial expansion and of the command of

ing deeds of derring-do on the high seas, they have concentrated on what happened before the ships left harbor: How was the money raised? How was the effort organized? What economic and social changes prepared the way? However, although Scott's three volumes opened the field and many advances in general economic and social history have been made in the intervening half-century, Scott's own subject, the actual organization, has advanced mainly in detail. A number of individual companies have been investigated exhaustively, and Scott's conclusions have been revised and broadened. So, too, a few leading merchants and gentleman adventurers are much better known than they were 50 years ago, and important work has been done on travel literature, propaganda, technology, and the political and cultural context of the expansion. But seen *in toto*, despite a considerably clearer understanding of the background, our picture of the launching of this mammoth enterprise has not changed significantly since Scott. Documentation has improved but slightly, and descriptions of the mechanics of this national undertaking have gained little in added precision. It is a testament to the enduring value of Scott's labors as a pioneer that only the invention of the computer could permit the exposure of a new level of evidence from which to explore his subject.

As mentioned in the Introduction, the original impetus for the present book was provided by the wish to understand the wider setting of Sir Edwin Sandys' tumultuous career in commerce. Naturally, therefore, my chief interest has been the gentry's role in trade, and this will explain some of the decisions described below. The most substantial consequence was the inclusion of parliamentary membership in the data, an addition that had only tangential importance for the analysis of investments. On the whole, however, categories, definitions, and questions were chosen primarily for their relevance to the organization of the English expansion.

The first task was to assemble the names of all the people who invested in, or became members of, a new commercial venture

the sea had captured the nation; the seeds had been scattered, and were germinating in tens of thousands of minds." See "The English Voyages of the Sixteenth Century," in Richard Hakluyt, *The Principal Navigations Voyages Traffiques & Discoveries of the English Nation* (12 vols.; Glasgow, 1903–1905), XII, 120. Cf. note 39, below.

during the period that was isolated for study. Fortunately, an unusually large accumulation of evidence concerning the expansion has survived. The publications of the Hakluyt Society alone suggest the wealth of primary materials dealing with voyages and discoveries. The many charters and company records are an equally rich source for the names of those whose expenditures made the voyages possible. As will be seen in the pages that follow, there are certainly important gaps, and often there is no way of telling what is missing. Nonetheless, the 6,336 investors in new enterprises who have reached the list clearly represent a very large proportion of the entire total during these years. The more notable lacunae are outlined in the descriptions of each company, below, but the few checks that can be applied indicate that the omissions are not serious enough to render the sample unrepresentative.

Almost every company, short-lived or long-lived, was survived by a charter, in the patent rolls if not elsewhere. These charters invariably included a meticulous list of all founding or current members. If the company did not last long, the odds are that the original members comprised a substantial majority of all who were interested in its affairs. This assumption is borne out whenever subsequent records can be found. For instance, although G. M. Cell has used previously unknown documents relating to the Newfoundland Company, she has been able to add only eight members to the 48 named in the charter.[9] On the other hand, when a company had a longer, more active life, and was more likely to attract new investors, it also tended to preserve many of its records. Thus the Virginia, East India, Levant, Spanish, and other major new companies of the period have left behind minutes of meetings and sundry documents which include considerable information about membership. Even if admissions themselves are not recorded, one can usually track down most of the names from lists and outside sources.

To give an illustration, Levant Company records between the charter of December 14, 1605, and the first minutes of the General Court in 1611 are a complete blank, except for a short list from 1606 and a few references to members in 1607 and 1609. But a careful combing of the subsequent minutes brings to light

[9] G. M. Cell, "The English in Newfoundland, 1577–1660," (unpub. diss., University of Liverpool, 1964).

various people who seem to be members even though there is no record of their official admission: they obviously entered the company between 1606 and 1610, and they have been assigned to the latter date. The reassuring result of this piecing together of information is that the total number of entries for the 1606–10 interval accords well with the pattern of higher than usual admissions in this period in most companies.

Another useful test can be derived from outside sources, and here one example in particular has been most heartening. The two major enterprises of the early seventeenth century which have left behind the least documentation, and which have had to be reconstructed almost entirely from other sources, are the Eastland and Muscovy Companies. For the Eastland Company recent studies have been of some help, but for the Muscovy Company after 1603 there has been no such research. Nonetheless, the names of 111 of the latter's members during the 1620's were recoverable. I suspected at first that this must still be one of the most poorly represented companies. It was most reassuring, therefore, to find that in 1604 the company's size had been estimated at about 160 members by someone wishing to inflate total membership as much as possible in order to draw a contrast with the few leaders who managed the trade.[10] Because the company's fortunes declined markedly during the next 20 years,[11] it would appear that the 111 names in the 1620's may well have constituted a good three-quarters of the current membership. The 211 Muscovy merchants in the list from the full 56-year period I have covered probably amount to at least half of the entire membership. A proportion this high for an organization with such inadequate records augurs well for the other companies — all of whom are as well, if not better, documented.

As a result of such checks as those just outlined, it can be assumed that sufficient investors have reached the list to serve as a safe statistical sample, and in many cases also as a good indication of absolute figures. Because the research has had to be limited to relatively accessible sources, however, no claim of having recov-

[10] *The Journals of the House of Commons*, vol. I (London, 1803), p. 220.

[11] See Scott, *Joint-Stock Companies*, II, 52–65; and M. S. Anderson, *Britain's Discovery of Russia, 1553–1815* (London, 1958), pp. 33–34. It is almost certain, too, though there have been no studies to prove it, that the Russian trade suffered from the depression of the 1620's.

ered every surviving name can be made. The likelihood of major discoveries in the port books and the endless local and private records of sixteenth- and seventeenth-century England seemed too small to render such an undertaking worthwhile. It cannot be said, therefore, that the list is as complete as the records will permit; nor can a precise estimate be made as to the percentage that is missing. A very rough guess, based on little more than plausibility and the few checks that were possible, would suggest that some three-quarters of all the investments of the time appear in my figures.

The terminal dates were set at 1575 and 1630 because, for a variety of reasons, they encompassed most clearly and concisely the crucial decades when the great rise of interest and the first major successes became apparent. 1553, when the first significant new trade of the sixteenth century was opened by the Muscovy Company, might have been a more obvious beginning. But activity between 1553 and 1575 was sporadic, and it involved relatively few people.[12] No real purpose was served by adding an extra generation when the 25 years before 1600 were sufficient to reveal the contrast between Elizabethan investment and the sudden surge during the reign of James I. The succession of new and important overseas projects which began in the mid and late 1570's provided a natural starting-point, particularly because the main reason for including this material was to establish background for the dramatic change after 1600.

The closing date was again somewhat arbitrary, since the dis-

---

[12] Moreover, a virtually complete biographical dictionary of these people can be found in T. S. Willan, *The Muscovy Merchants of 1555* (Manchester, 1953), pp. 75–132. There are few investors in the new ventures of the 1553–1575 period who do not appear in his list. For example, 22 of the 34 Guinea venturers of 1558 were also in the Muscovy Company (*ibid.*, p. 27). It is doubtful that even the most generous estimate could allow a total of more than 300 to 400 people interested in new enterprises during these years. If only one-quarter remained active after 1575 (the lowest possible proportion because a quarter of the Muscovy merchants of 1553 lived that long) then the addition of this 22-year span would enlarge my list by 300 new names at the very outside. When such small numbers are involved, no computer is needed: the activities of the period can be reconstructed from the pages of Hakluyt and Willan. The contrast between this quarter-century and the one that followed should be sufficient to indicate why my cut-off point of 1575 was chosen. As for the amount of money invested, Scott, *Joint-Stock Companies*, I, 41–42, estimates that £100,000 was raised for new overseas ventures through 1570. Table 5, above, indicates how vastly the outlay increased during the next 60 years.

solution of the Virginia Company in the mid-1620's marked the end of widespread interest in the expansion. Thereafter new commercial enterprises were never again to be so popular until the eighteenth century. The decline of enthusiasm can be noticed, as we have seen, in the early 1620's if not before, and soon there remained only a scattering of the most determined promoters, such as Sir Ferdinando Gorges and Lord Baltimore. But a few major schemes were still to be launched in the late 1620's, and they deserved to be included, even though the aims of the Massachusetts Bay and Providence Island Companies were very different from those which guided Jacobean organizations. The Providence Island Company proved to be the last prominent joint-stock overseas venture for 32 years, and its incorporation in 1630 furnished a convenient closing date, even though Gorges, Baltimore, and a few lone promoters did continue their efforts in the 1630's. The one slight exception in this respect can be noticed in the East India and Levant Company figures. My original intention was to regard 1629 as the terminal date — the year of Sandys' death. Not until the first computer results appeared did I realize that when 1630 was added so as to bring the Providence Island Company and a few other small ventures within my scope, the memberships in the East India and Levant Companies were not extended for one more year. It makes no important difference, but the figures for those two organizations end in 1629.

The optimistic aim at the outset was to make the list as comprehensive as possible, and to include every company or venture of note founded between 1575 and 1630. Though the complete membership might be unobtainable, at least all the various organizations would be represented. In the end, 36 separate groups appeared in the list. The sources that were used for the names of their members are given in detail in the next chapter, but at this point the procedure that was followed in each case must be described.

Most of the time there was no major difficulty in deciding how an entry was to appear. But the evidence was too sporadic to allow absolutely straightforward and uniform treatment of more than a few companies. A multitude of individual problems, both of definition and of documentation, had to be surmounted: each organization will therefore be discussed in turn. The one general consideration that bears stressing at the outset, because it affected my categories in a number of places, was the limitation of the symbols available on a keypunch (and hence on an IBM card) to 33 nonnumeric punches. Thus only 33 separate companies could be distinguished,[13] and occasionally it became necessary to unite under one heading groups that did not overlap and that might otherwise have been kept apart. My general aims in the coding of the investment data should become apparent from the detailed descriptions which follow, but they will be explained further when the individual examples have been covered.

The Companies. 1) The *Africa* (or Gynney and Bynney) Company, incorporated in 1618, was a short-lived enterprise whose membership was listed in its charter. Because its activities lasted little more than two years it can be assumed that the founders were the only investors, though one later subscriber, Humphrey Slany, is known.

2) The backers of *Baffin* in 1615 were separated from the North-West Passage Company to emphasize the continued activity of the few members of that company who sustained its efforts after the failures of the first three voyages between 1612 and 1614. This group came to be a virtually new, much smaller assembly of men determined to find a route past America long after the nearly 300 charter members of the parent company lost interest.[14]

3) The *Barbary* Company, incorporated in 1585, can be reconstructed with relative ease thanks to the detailed study by T. S. Willan.[15] Because it is not known when the handful of members

[13] Plus the East India, Virginia, and Levant Companies, which were coded in a special way — described in the Appendix. They did not need a symbol, and consequently 36 groupings could appear in the list. One possible symbol, $, was available but not used. I had it included in the program, and kept it in readiness in case a new category became essential, but the need did not arise.

[14] The further voyages sent out by this group were led by Baffin and Bylot in 1616, and Hawkridge in 1619. The sense that by 1614 the old group had become defunct is confirmed by Bacon, who said in that year that there *had been* "not long ago, some Undertakers for the north-west passage." See *The Letters and The Life of Francis Bacon,* ed. James Spedding (7 vols.; London, 1861–1874), V, 43.

The italicized words in the title of each company in this listing (e.g., *Africa* and *Baffin*) indicate the name by which the company is usually referred to in the rest of this book.

[15] T. S. Willan, "English Trade with Morocco," *Studies in Elizabethan Foreign Trade* (Manchester, 1959), especially pp. 163–312.

who were first mentioned in the 1590's joined the company, they have also been counted as having joined in 1585.

4) The *Bermuda* (or Somers Islands) Company, first organized in 1612, and incorporated in 1615, has been given considerable attention by recent historians, and the subscribers at various dates are fairly well known. But the dates of admission of the 52 adventurers who were not mentioned until after 1615 have not survived. As most of them first appeared in the early 1620's, it seemed reasonable to assign them all to 1620 — a date that cannot be more than a year or two wrong in most cases, and one that comes at a sufficient interval after the charter for new members to have been recruited.

5) The backers of *Cavendish's* attempts at circumnavigation in 1586 and 1591 may have been a tiny group (4 members, as far as can be discovered), but they were clearly supporting more than a mere privateering exploit and deserved to be entered as a separate organization.

6) The joint-stock company formed to back *Drake* in 1587 was also a venture rather different from the average privateering expedition. As Andrews has noted, Drake's raids of 1585, 1587, 1589, and 1595 were "semiofficial," carrying out "a strategic purpose apart from mere prize-hunting" in which Sir Francis acted as the Queen's admiral with official instructions.[16] Although the activities of a navy under royal direction clearly do not come within the scope of the present study, it is very difficult in this period to distinguish between private and government enterprise on the high seas. The defense against the Armada, the 1589 attempt to capture Lisbon, Essex' attack on Cadiz, the abortive relief of La Rochelle, and the expedition against the Barbary pirates in the early 1620's were obviously matters of national policy; but the line is much harder to draw among the privateers of the late sixteenth century. The blurring of this distinction is particularly noticeable in Drake's fleets, to which Elizabeth contributed substantial amounts (in 1585 she owned a third of the stock, and in 1587 she provided six out of 16 ships). All such combined ventures should, by rights, be entered under a special category —

---

[16] Andrews, *Elizabethan Privateering*, p. 5. See, too, p. 94. In 1587 the "official" half of the voyage was the singeing of Philip II's beard in Cadiz and elsewhere; the "private" half was the capture of the *San Felipe*, worth over £100,000.

separated, like Cavendish's circumnavigation, from mere privateering. Unfortunately, however, only the 1587 voyage has left behind records which are better than fragmentary. Our information about the subscribers is sufficiently complete to permit its inclusion as a distinct company, but it is alone in this respect. All the other part-official, part-piratical expeditions, including the 1577–80 circumnavigation, have been treated solely as privateering because the evidence is so scanty.[17]

7) The *East India* Company, despite occasional gaps in the minutes of the General Court, is about as fully represented as could be hoped for so large and successful an organization and one which attracted so much interest. Nearly all the official members and investors, whose names the company scrupulously preserved, have reached the list. The minutes that are missing for a total of just over four years have undoubtedly had some effect,[18] but more important may be the "hidden" investors who bought part of a stock through a member of the company. Sometimes these transactions were openly admitted, but it is hard to believe that so profitable an enterprise did not attract many that are not recorded. This problem is encountered in a number of companies, where subscribers are often described, for example, as "Giles Elbridge and others" privateering in 1626.[19] But no other company enjoyed profits comparable to those of the East India trade, and the temptation to avoid entrance qualifications and fees must have inspired many secret subscriptions. It is astonishing, for instance, that Robert Delean, a merchant of no apparent great wealth, should suddenly have made a spectacular appearance in the East India records, purchasing in less than three months, in the autumn of 1617, £5,400 worth of stock in the company.[20] One can only guess that he was buying for other, unknown investors. This is a frustrating admission to have to make, but it should be

[17] The Azores expeditions of 1591 and 1597 are the principal semiofficial ventures, in addition to Drake's, which are entered as privateering. The distinction between public and private activity seemed to be clear to Drake himself when he said in 1586 that he would demonstrate "how great was the difference between a buccaneer and the supreme commander of so weighty a sovereign," but the Spaniards of course rejected vehemently such claims to legality. See *CSP, Venice, 1581–1591*, p. 180.

[18] For example, the names of some of the members listed in a petition of 1624 (*CSP, East Indies, 1622–1624*, pp. 491–493) do not appear in any other records.

[19] *CSP, Domestic, 1628–1629*, p. 288.

[20] *CSP, East Indies, 1617–1621*, pp. 99–100.

added that the 1,318 names that have been gathered cannot be regarded as anything less than a very large majority of the entire total. This number is exceeded only by the 1,684 subscribers to the Virginia Company, whose shares were much cheaper and much more wildly popular for many years. It might be remembered, too, that even the "hidden" investors may later have entered the company legitimately. When the date of actual admission is unknown, the year a name first appeared in the records has been used with a question added to the man's data. Four members have been entered with no date at all because only the fact of their membership has survived.

8) The *Eastland* Company, incorporated in 1579, provides the historian with uneven documentation. After the founding charter, in which 66 names are recorded, there is a long gap until the 1620's. Then, thanks to the researches of R. W. K. Hinton in the port books[21] and the survival of some official papers, 110 members can be added. Because their dates of admission are unknown, they have been divided into two groups (those whose names first appeared either before or after 1625) and entered as having joined in 1620 or 1625. The likelihood of error here is of course much greater than in the similar assignment of dates in the Bermuda Company. Some of these merchants may in fact have started their trade with the Baltic as much as 30 or even 40 years before the 1620's, a possibility that is noted whenever these figures are used. Finally, 21 other names have been gleaned from various sources, but about these merchants so little is known that they have been entered as members without any year of admission. The gaps in the records are so large that possibly only half of the venturers — if that many — are listed, assuming (as seems likely) that the company was roughly the same size as the Muscovy Company, whose membership is discussed in detail above.

9) For the Company of Merchants trading to *France* we have the names recorded in the charter of 1611, plus nine others of unknown date. Unlike the Spanish Company, which was a similar brief attempt to create a regulated monopoly in a long-standing trade, this organization left behind no minutes. It is possible that

---

[21] R. W. K. Hinton, *The Eastland Trade and the Common Weal in the Seventeenth Century* (Cambridge, England, 1959), especially pp. 219–220.

additional members might be discovered in port books, but they are unlikely to reach significant numbers in view of the short life of the company.

10) Investors in the well-documented voyages of *Frobisher and Fenton* between 1576 and 1582 were gathered together under one heading. Scott considered the adventurers in all four expeditions to have been members of a clearly defined "Kathai" company, but it has since been shown that Fenton's supporters were a separate group, led by the Earl of Leicester, and uninterested in a North-West Passage.[22] However, at this point the restrictions dictated by the limited number of company symbols available on a keypunch came into play: a few distinct enterprises would have to be consolidated, and the subscribers to Fenton's "troublesome voyage" seemed among those least likely to be seriously affected by taking this liberty. In the first place, almost half of them (18 out of 42) had already been associated in the Frobisher ventures. Furthermore, all four voyages came in a short time span, and they did have a common aim of legitimate trade with the Far East which was unique among the expeditions of this six-year period. Nonetheless, this shaky justification was not left to stand on its own merits.

To ensure that each entry would still reflect accurately the original source, this company (signified by a "W" in the list) was divided into nine subcategories. W1 indicated Frobisher's first voyage, W2 the second, W3 the third, and W4 Fenton's voyage. Five further subcategories were then set up for investors in more than one of these expeditions: W5 represented a combination of W2 and W3; W6 a combination of W1, W2 and W3; W7 a combination of W2, W3, and W4; W8 a combination of all four; and W9 a combination of W2 and W4. No other categories were necessary. In this way it was simple to reconstruct the membership of each undertaking. For example, everyone with a W4, W7, W8, or W9 entry was involved in Fenton's expedition. The meaning of these symbols was unraveled for the computer, and the appropriate adjustments were made for all tables. As a result, the only compensation that needs to be made when assessing the figures is to

---

[22] Scott, *Joint-Stock Companies*, II, 76–82; *The Troublesome Voyage of Captain Edward Fenton, 1582–1583*, ed. E. G. R. Taylor (Cambridge, England: The Hakluyt Society, 1959).

151

recall that "Frobisher and Fenton," when treated *in toto,* represent two different companies. What this comes down to is that 18 people who are entered as joining only one organization in fact joined two. Although I have stressed the danger of allowing statistical insignificance to serve as a convenient excuse for carelessness, in this case an inconsistency of such minor proportions did seem tolerable. But since this decision is at best questionable, the names of the 18 people who might be credited with an extra company are given below, so that the appropriate adjustment can be made if deemed necessary:

Richard Bowland
William Burd
Sir Julius Caesar
Henry Carey, Lord Hunsdon
John Castelin
William Cecil, Lord Burghley
Ambrose Dudley, Earl of Warwick
Robert Dudley, Earl of Leicester
Edward Fiennes, Earl of Lincoln
Martin Frobisher
Sir Thomas Heneage
Henry Herbert, Earl of Pembroke
Sir Edward Horsey
Charles Howard, Earl of Nottingham
Henry Ughtred
Edward Vere, Earl of Oxford
Sir Francis Walsingham
Richard Young

11) The subscribers to *Gilbert's* enterprises in 1578 and 1583 have been resurrected by D. B. Quinn,[23] and it is safe to estimate that most of them have reached the list.

12) The backers of *Gosnold* in 1602 proved to be one of the smallest entries, with only five members; but they probably constituted the entire company.

13) The various subscribers to the many *Guiana* and Amazon ventures from Raleigh onward were united in one group, and

[23] *The Voyages and Colonising Enterprises of Sir Humphrey Gilbert,* ed. D. B. Quinn (2 vols.; London: The Hakluyt Society, 1940).

in this instance there was no distortion as in the case of "Frobisher and Fenton" because there was clearly a unity of purpose to these separate ventures. In fact, it would have been inconsistent to list each organization as a new enterprise, because the investors in other long-lived undertakings were credited with only one company. They appeared only once, for example, as members of the East India Company or as privateers despite successive investments over a period of years. For this reason it would have been unfair to assign two companies to Sir Walter Raleigh simply because he revived in 1618 a venture to which he had already devoted considerable money and effort in the 1590's. The following groups were included: Raleigh's expeditions in the 1590's and 1618, Leigh's in 1604, Roe's and Harcourt's in 1609, the grantees of 1613, and the Guiana and Amazon Companies of 1619 and 1627 (plus those who joined the latter in 1629). Eight subcategories were created, corresponding to the eight different dates at which people became involved in Guiana, and thus I could indicate when a man's interest was first manifested.

14) The backers of *Hudson* in 1610 obviously formed the original nucleus of the North-West Passage Company that was incorporated in 1612. Nevertheless, they clearly constituted a distinct group, because two of the 23 members did not join the large organization formed two years later. It could be argued that, as in the case of the Guiana, Irish, and New England ventures, all investors in "North-West Passage" voyages, including Hudson's and Baffin's, should have been incorporated into one large "North-West Passage" category, particularly since the grantees of 1584 were given the same symbol in the list as the patentees of 1612. But in this case it seemed that a greater distortion would be introduced by adopting this procedure than would be avoided by giving only one entry to the 24 people who are now given two because they supported Hudson or Baffin *and* the 1612 company, or the five people now given three entries because they backed all three.

To have assigned one category to all these groups would have removed the objection that prompted the consolidation of Guiana, Irish, and New England investors — namely, that the consistency of their aims transformed these separate organizations into parts of one long-lived enterprise similar to the various joint stocks of the East India Company. But here the problem was not quite so simple. Within the Guiana group no single component had more than 50 members, and there was little cross-membership; among the Irish subscribers there was *no* cross-membership; and in the case of the New England investors no component was larger than 32. But the North-West Passage Company attracted almost 300 investors to the voyages it set forth in 1612–14. To have allowed this mammoth to absorb the small groups which subscribed to Hudson's and Baffin's voyages would have been to force their virtual disappearance. In fact, only three out of the 32 people who adventured in the smaller undertakings would have been entered as anything but members of the large company founded in 1612. The problem of cross-membership, and the disappearance of the smaller subdivisions into the largest, was minimal in the Guiana, Irish, and New England groupings. But in the North-West Passage category the lesser undertakings could have been recorded only by complicated codification (and instructions for the computer), as was done with the Frobisher and Fenton voyages. It did not seem worth the trouble in view of the very small inconsistency introduced by keeping Hudson and Baffin separate.

For the grantees of 1584 and the backers of Davis, this consideration did not arise because there was no cross-membership between these venturers and their successors nearly three decades later. Incidentally, as must be obvious by now, it would have been most complicated to have added the investors in Frobisher's voyages to this category, though as seekers of a North-West Passage they could have qualified. Without attempting to lessen the difficulties posed by the problems just discussed, I might add that the figures for total number of company memberships would have had to be changed for only 37 people even if *all* North-West ventures, from Frobisher to Baffin, had been counted as one continuing enterprise instead of four, as at present.

15) The various investors in *Irish* colonization were also brought together under one heading. In this case only two groups were involved, with no overlap between them. The investors interested primarily in Munster in the 1580's, and the subscribers to London's colony in Ulster from 1608 onward, were two quite separate groups, but they were united by a common purpose. Since precise dates of first interest in the former cannot be ascer-

tained, they have all been entered at 1586 (possibly a little early for some of them, because this was the year in which investments began, following the drawing up of final plans in December 1585, but well within a small margin of error). None can have been active in the undertaking earlier, and none appeared later than 1592. (As is indicated in Tables 6 and 7, above, and in the paragraph immediately following those tables, a typographical error in the computer program caused the Munster investments to be entered as 1584, not 1586, but this made no appreciable difference in the long-term year-by-year calculations.) It must be remembered, incidentally, that "undertakers" alone were included, and those who were solely colonists or venturers in service rather than money were omitted. The second group was culled from various records of the Londonderry plantation, and was divided according to the date of first mention of a name. Again, only "undertakers" were admitted — a distinction that is discussed more fully below. Both the Munster and Londonderry groups are relatively complete, thanks to the survival of extensive documentation among the State Papers and the London Livery Company archives.

Of course, these two ventures by no means comprised the entirety of English colonization in Ireland in this period. The Munster group of the 1580's and 1590's was crucially important as the first such enterprise to have any major success, but there were further efforts in Munster in James I's reign, and elsewhere there was even more activity. The Londonderry plantation, also included in my data, was probably the largest single undertaking of the time; but the proportion it represented even of Ulster colonization is difficult to calculate at the present stage of research, and D. B. Quinn has suggested to me that it may have amounted to no more than one-sixth of efforts in Ulster. There were also English plantations in Westmeath, Longford, Leix, and Offaly. However, to have tracked down the investors in these other colonies would have required a huge and totally disproportionate special project. The venturers in Munster and Londonderry were fairly accessible in the State Papers, Livery Company records, a charter, and various secondary sources. But virtually no detailed work has been done on the other plantations, and it would have taken at least two to three years to have assembled the names of the investors. Seen in perspective, there seemed little point in embarking on so large a task because, as is indicated below, the main purposes of gathering material on Ireland seemed sufficiently well fulfilled by the data available on Munster and Londonderry.

The remaining Irish projects might have yielded a few hundred additional names, but they could not have had an importance in relation to the 8,700 already uncovered which would have justified the endeavor required to find them. The list of names would have been more complete, to be sure, and had they been more accessible these investors would certainly have been included; but in view of their inaccessibility it seemed appropriate to invoke the law of diminishing returns. The omission was reluctantly decided upon, but it drew added justification from two considerations. In the first place, the principal focus of this book is on enterprises which took Englishmen across wider bodies of water than the Irish Sea. And all investors in more distant projects, however elusive, *have* been sought to the full extent of the available documentation. But Ireland, though undeniably of major importance in the expansion, was significantly unlike the other areas which drew England's attention overseas. The differences are obvious, and need no elaboration: the proximity, the long familiarity, the inhabitants, and the trading relationship are only the most conspicuous ways in which Ireland differed sharply from colonial sites in America and elsewhere.

In the second place, as was mentioned above, the main objectives in including any Irish data at all were reasonably well served by the Munster and Londonderry material alone. Despite the lack of completeness, the figures did make some assessment of Irish investments possible. Seven hundred and sixty-two, or 12 percent of all the investors in the list, were involved in Munster and Londonderry. Thus there was already enough evidence at hand to derive from analyses of cross-memberships strong confirmation of the thesis advanced by E. P. Cheyney, Howard Mumford Jones, and D. B. Quinn that Ireland frequently provided Englishmen with their first introduction to colonial enterprise. (See above, especially Chapter 2, at note 10.) Data from the remaining ventures might have further strengthened the confirmation of the Cheyney-Jones-Quinn hypothesis, and would obviously have increased the completeness of the figures, but neither of these aims seemed likely to be advanced so substantially as to merit the considerable further research that the unearthing of the additional names would have required.

16) The *Levant* Company, founded by patent in 1581 and growing steadily, with the help of various new charters, throughout the rest of the period under study, left behind uneven but relatively full records of membership. For the early years there are a series of grants, petitions, and other documents from which one can discover the names of most of those interested in the trade. And from 1611 on, the minutes of the meetings of the General Court provide a complete account of all admissions. As in the East India Company, when a date of admission is not known the year of first mention in the records is entered, together with a question indicating that there is doubt about the entry. Five members appear without any date.

17) The *Massachusetts Bay* Company, survived by numerous documents which have been carefully edited by N. B. Shurtleff,[24] can be reconstructed with little difficulty, and the gaps among names of investors are probably minimal.

18) *Merchant Adventurers* were entered only if they qualified for the list in some other way: this was no new trade, and therefore it had no relevance to the present study. But the activities of the people in the list would have been only partially presented if this important interest had been omitted. To have listed Sir Rowland Hayward's investments, for example, and to have ignored this major concern, would have distorted his entry. Unfortunately, it would have been impossible to discover every Merchant Adventurer in the list, even by scouring the port books; but 269 were fairly easy to identify and were included. Of these, 24 subsequently turned out not to be the same as people already in the list, but, though listed only as Merchant Adventurers, they did not seem worth removing.

It is difficult to know how many Merchant Adventurers there were in England in this period, but the ones in the list possibly represent five percent of the total. Sir Edwin Sandys, in 1604, after long discussions about trade with leading merchants and wishing to stress how large the total group was in contrast to the few

---

[24] *Records of the Governor and Company of the Massachusetts Bay in New England*, vol. I: *1628–41*, ed. N. B. Shurtleff (Boston, 1853).

who controlled it, suggested that there were 5,000 to 6,000 people free of the various companies in England.[25] If one takes the lower figure, to compensate for Sandys' prejudices, and subtracts the nearly 2,000 people in the Spanish, East India, Levant, Muscovy, and other companies such as the Staplers at this time, one is left with approximately 3,000 Merchant Adventurers, *if* the overlap between Merchant Adventurers and the other companies was as small as the figures in my list suggest. This total would tally well with the Merchant Adventurers' own estimate two years later when they, too, were trying to emphasize their size (in this case because they felt it was too large), and gave a figure of 3,000.[26] Accepting 3,000 members at the beginning of James I's reign, and doubling this number to account for the two generations between 1575 and 1630 (a generous adjustment in light of the decline of the company during and after Cockayne's project),[27] we arrive at a total membership of 6,000 for the full 56-year period. The 269 in the list therefore amounted to some 4.5 percent of the entire body.

If one agrees that Sandys' figure can be made to accord with the Merchant Adventurers' own assessment only if the overlap between the older and the new companies was about as small as it is in the list, then we have here remarkable evidence that the men in this traditional trade were being left behind by England's tremendous expansion. London's dominance of the new enterprises may be partially responsible for this, because many Merchant Adventurers were in the outports; but the minimal involvement of these overseas traders of long standing in the risky but tempting trades now starting suggests that England's growing commercial vigor was due to a new kind of merchant as well as a new kind of venture.

19) The Company of *Mineral* and Battery Works was included

[25] *Journals of the House of Commons,* I, 218.

[26] Lansdown MS. 487, fols. 146–148. The estimate of 3,500 made by John Wheeler in 1601 would seem to be excessively high. As secretary to the company, he was writing a partisan account of its usefulness, and the figure is given at the point where he is trying to show that the society is large enough to sell all English cloth abroad — see his *A Treatise of Commerce,* ed. G. B. Hotchkiss (New York, 1931), p. 377.

[27] Astrid Friis, *Alderman Cockayne's Project and the Cloth Trade* (Copenhagen and London, 1927), *passim,* especially p. 98, where it is noted that only 132 Merchant Adventurers were actively trading in 1618, only 115 in 1620, and 126 in 1622.

as a new joint-stock enterprise of the period. Its purpose may have been industrial, and not commercial or colonial, but the growth of new industries was symptomatic of England's expansion, and investors in these efforts have been included so as to give a more complete picture of their interests. M. B. Donald's researches, moreover, have provided extensive information about the members.[28]

20) The Company of *Mines* appears for the same reason as its sister organization, the Mineral Company. And once again information is readily available as a result of the researches of M. B. Donald.[29]

21) The *Muscovy* (or Russia) Company is most thoroughly documented during the first two decades of its existence. But three-quarters of the charter members had died by 1575, and thereafter the membership must be gleaned from other sources. Some 100 members in the late sixteenth century can be traced, probably a little over half of the total. Because dates of admission cannot be established, all have been entered at 1580 — sufficiently early to be within five years of the opening of the list, and under 15 years before the last date at which a member is first mentioned. Where this figure is of some importance, however, the arbitrary uniformity of 1580 has been taken into account. Thereafter comes a long gap until the 1620's, when the interest of the House of Lords in the company's affairs created a few records which have survived. These, together with passing references elsewhere, have brought 111 members to light. As with the earlier group, a single date had to be devised that would be within a fairly limited margin of error for most of the members, and 1620 was chosen as being in the middle of the 20-year span during which almost all of these people probably joined the company.

22) The *New England* ventures, including the Northern Virginia Company of 1606 and the activities of the New England Council of 1620, were placed in one category, as the second group was clearly taking over the same undertaking that the first had failed to bring to fruition. The members were entered according to the year when they showed their first interest in New England

[28] M. B. Donald, *Elizabethan Monopolies: The History of the Company of Mineral and Battery Works from 1565 to 1604* (Edinburgh and London, 1961).
[29] M. B. Donald, *Elizabethan Copper: The History of the Company of Mines Royal, 1568–1605* (London, 1955).

159

— in the Northern Virginia Company in 1606, 1607, or 1609, or in the New England Council in 1620 or 1623. All other New England voyages and colonies appear separately: the backers of these expeditions are credited with a separate undertaking either under a special symbol (Gosnold, Weymouth) or under "other ventures" (Pring, Smith, Harlow, Cooper). The patentees of the New England Council who attempted to establish small colonies also received "other ventures" entries (Mariana, Maine, Wessagusset, Messachustac, Casco Bay, New Hampshire, Laconia, Saco, Muscongus, and the "divisions" of the Council). The two major colonies, Plymouth and Massachusetts Bay, were regarded as entirely separate groups. The documentation for all these ventures is excellent, and there are few noticeable omissions.

23) The *Newfoundland* Company, incorporated in 1610, is rare in being relatively simple to enter. As a result of G. M. Cell's researches,[30] our information about the members is remarkably complete, and as far as is known they all joined in 1610. The later colonizers of Newfoundland, William Vaughan, Henry Carey, Viscount Falkland, Sir William Alexander, and George Calvert Lord Baltimore, have been given entries under "other ventures."

24) The *New Merchant Adventurers* were also easy to assemble, thanks to their short existence, their charter, and the exhaustive study by Astrid Friis.[31] They appear according to the year in which they joined: most in 1615, but a few in 1616.

25) The *New River* Company has been added for the same reason that governs an investment in industry — it was a major new profit-seeking enterprise. And this one, like the Mineral and Mines Companies, was also formally incorporated as a joint-stock undertaking. The names have been taken from the charter of 1619, with two additional names obtained from J. W. Gough's book on Sir Hugh Middleton.[32]

26) The *North-West Passage* Company has already been discussed in relation to the backers of Baffin and Hudson. I need only add that this category includes the charter members of 1612, plus the quite distinct group that received a patent in 1584 and then subscribed to the voyages of John Davis. Since the 1612

[30] See note 9, above.
[31] See note 27, above.
[32] J. W. Gough, *Sir Hugh Myddelton, Entrepreneur and Engineer* (Oxford, 1964).

company all but disappeared after three unsuccessful voyages in two years, leaving only the hardy entrepreneurs who supported Baffin and his successors, it is unlikely that there were many additions to the charter members during its short life. The information about Davis is less certain, and there is no way of knowing what percentage is represented by the 22 who are listed. Though we have good records from the Exeter and other west-country merchants who subscribed in 1585,[33] the remainder are fragmentary at best.

27) The adventurers in the *Plymouth* colony were divided into two subcategories: the recipients of the original grant from the Virginia Company in 1620, and those with whom the composition of 1626 was signed. The latter had obviously ventured their money before 1626, but because there is no evidence of when they became interested in the colony they were all entered as 1625. These records appear to be complete.

28) *Privateers* during Elizabeth's reign and the first years of Charles I's reign have been entered under one heading but divided into two groups. Those whose names have survived from the earlier period (taken primarily from the various works by K. R. Andrews on this subject[34]) cannot be given any one year to mark the beginning of their interest, because the records are so sparse. All have therefore been assigned to 1581 — certainly a few years early for most of them due to the fact that privateering officially began only in 1585, but at least closer to such exploits as Drake's early raids, which have also been counted as privateering. The entire issue is somewhat academic, as the precise year of first involvement cannot be discovered, and this figure is important only in the tables showing the year-by-year rate of investment where a simple averaging adjustment can be made to account for the large figure for 1581. The second group, during the war starting in 1625, is somewhat better served by the sources, but it is still by no means complete because many subscribers are

[33] *An Elizabethan Guild of the City of Exeter*, ed. William Cotton (Exeter, 1873), pp. 82–84.

[34] In addition to Andrews, *Elizabethan Privateering*, already cited, there is his more detailed dissertation, on deposit at the Institute of Historical Research in London, "The Economic Aspects of Elizabethan Privateering" (unpub. diss., London University, 1951), and the volume of documents he edited, *English Privateering Voyages to the West Indies 1588–1595* (Cambridge, England: The Hakluyt Society, 1959).

listed as "and company" or "and others," following the chief promoter.[35] Again, therefore, the date of first interest cannot be specified, and the five-year period of activity has been reduced to one, with all the entries counted as 1625 but averaged out for year-by-year calculations. With 389 people in the first category and 664 in the second (including two in both) it seems that a good majority of the investors has been included.

29) Only the founders of the *Providence Island* Company qualified chronologically for the list, and they were easily assembled — straight out of the pages of A. P. Newton.[36]

30) All the members of the *Senegal* Company, incorporated in 1588, were entered as of this date. The year of admission of the 12 traders who are not mentioned in the charter, but who appear in company petitions in the 1590's, cannot be traced. However, an adjustment in the chronological tables has been made for the two grantees of the 1598 patent — their first appearance in the records.

31) The *Spanish* Company is survived by excellent records easy to codify. The charter of 1577, with its long list of members, is probably close to a complete record of the participants in this first monopoly, since the company was overtaken within eight years by Philip II's confiscation of all English ships in Spanish ports. The charter of 1604, though lasting only two years, is again a voluminous source of names, and this time the minutes of the company's meetings during its short life have survived. From these sources a very high percentage of the membership can be recovered.

32) *Staple* Merchants have been entered for the same reason, and under the same conditions, as Merchant Adventurers. Only very few (18) were identified.

33) The *Venice* Company, founded in 1583 and merged into the Levant Company in 1592, has been reconstructed from the version of Elizabeth's charter with the longest list of members. Even so, only 14 names have been forthcoming, which is probably a small percentage in light of the 58 people (not including

---

[35] See note 19, above. The much better documentation on the 1625–1630 privateers is due to the survival of the warrants for issuing letters of marque, printed in *CSP, Domestic, 1628–1629* and *1629–1631, passim.*

[36] A. P. Newton, *The Colonising Activities of the English Puritans* (New Haven, 1914), pp. 59–79.

Venice Company members) who joined the rival Levant Company between 1581 and 1592.

34) The *Virginia* Company, thanks to the voluminous publications of Alexander Brown and S. M. Kingsbury,[37] is the most thoroughly researched of all the major enterprises of this period. Nevertheless, there are major gaps, and the date of admission of many of the investors is unknown. The same procedure as in the East India and Levant Companies has therefore been followed: in doubtful cases I have entered the first year the name is mentioned, adding a question about the data on the card. Seventeen people appear without a date because only the fact of their membership is certain. The various venturers of the 1580's have been included with their appropriate dates. (See Chapter 1, note 79.)

35) The backers of *Weymouth* in 1605, a tiny group of five people, were probably the only subscribers to this voyage.

36) The final category, *"other ventures,"* is the most difficult of all to describe because it became a catchall for investments which deserved to be recorded but did not seem worth a category of their own. A number of these undertakings have already been mentioned. The following were also included: a few individual voyages to Africa and Brazil; the West Indies colonies of the 1620's; the Ramea voyages; ventures in Canada; the attempt to found an East India Company in 1584; the voyages of John Walker, John Oxenham, Henry Challons, Sir James Lancaster, Christopher Carleill, William Hawkridge, Edward Harlow, Thomas Bailey and Edward Elliott; and the slave trade.

However, almost 300 of the 352 people with "other ventures" entries were assigned to this group because of their interest in new industrial enterprises: mainly coal, iron, alum, copper, sugar refining, glass, tin, lead, gold, silver, and cotton. These investments were so important a part of England's expansion in this period that fairness demanded their inclusion. But because they were not organized by formal companies and were not central to the concerns of the present study, I decided to include them only if a man had already qualified for the list by some other means, or if he was particularly important as an industrial entrepreneur

[37] Alexander Brown, *The Genesis of the United States* (2 vols.; Boston and New York, 1890); and *The Records of the Virginia Company of London*, ed. S. M. Kingsbury (4 vols.; Washington, 1906–1935).

alone, as was Sir Bevis Bulmer in the mining for coal, silver, and gold. By its very nature, this procedure determined that no extensive research would be undertaken to discover such investments. The specific "other venture" is not even recorded, because the entry serves only to indicate that the man in question had other relevant interests besides the 35 major groups already described. It would have been ludicrous, for example, to leave Sir Percival Willoughby as a member of only two undertakings, the Newfoundland and Virginia Companies, when he invested much more heavily in four different types of industry: coal, iron, and silver mining and glassmaking.

The "other venture" category, therefore, does no more than round up a few loose ends and provide a more accurate total number of separate investments for each individual. It is not intended to supply information about the investments themselves. Moreover, three very important new enterprises of this period have been left out almost completely because they would have taken me too far afield: fen draining, shipbuilding and fisheries. It must also be stressed that, outside of the 35 main categories, information was included only when it was easily accessible. Hundreds of small ventures were launched in this period, but unless they came to the attention of Hakluyt or Purchas they usually remained obscure and forgotten. It was clearly not worth tracking down these ephemeral projects. A line had to be drawn somewhere, and even a solemn assurance from an informant that the Essex records are full of Barnaby Gooche's plans to send a ship to Ireland could not draw me to Chelmsford for the sake of one further entry.

There was a final purpose served by the "other ventures" category. One man, Nicholas Leate, had more investments than the IBM card could accommodate. For the sake of this solitary exception it did not seem necessary to revise my entire coding, and his participation in Hudson's voyage was therefore entered under "other ventures." The appropriate adjustment has been made in the tables.

The basic principles followed in the collection and systematization of this material should now be apparent. There was no insistence that each one of the 35 groups should be a distinct, formal company. My concern was rather to group together all the people with a common interest in some definable enterprise, be it Irish colonization, the organization of settlements in New England, or the exploitation of Guiana. Only in this way could some semblance of consistency be maintained between large, long-lasting undertakings that dominated their particular field of endeavor for decades, as did the East India Company, and the multitude of small, short-lived efforts, pursuing virtually identical aims, which succeeded one another in some areas, such as Guiana. The value of the fundamental unit in my figures, an investment, would have been irretrievably distorted if a man who subscribed to, say, three separate Guiana projects (as did Robert Harcourt) were given three entries, whereas a contributor to at least 12 East India voyages (such as Sir Thomas Smith) were credited with only one. As has been noted, serious exceptions and difficulties were by no means eliminated, but at least this approach gave some consistency to the meaning of "an investment." The adjustment was essential to compensate for the impossibility of devising anything but crude estimates of the amounts actually ventured.

Individual payments can be calculated precisely in so few cases that no purpose could have been served by trying to enter this information on the cards. Few companies kept a tabulation of the sums each member invested; in the regulated, as opposed to joint-stock, organizations this was a matter of no concern to the body as a whole. Even when lists of subscribers were kept, as they were by the Virginia Company, it is often difficult to know whether a man really paid for the share he offered to buy. Nor can one be sure that every person officially admitted actually contributed the amount needed to qualify for membership. Some of the people who appeared in a company's lists may have donated no more than a willingness to show an interest in its affairs. Even tangible promises were far from binding. Annoyance at defaulters was often expressed; and the conflicting sums recorded by different bookkeepers are a further indication that precision is impossible. The added problem of "hidden" payments has already been described in connection with the East India Company. Thus although I clearly had to include every "member" or "adventurer" mentioned in my sources, I could never depend on the records to provide exact information on how much each investor spent. The only genuinely reliable documents would have been the personal accounts of the people in the list, but these were beyond reach. Apart from a few conspicuous examples, therefore, discussion of the money that was expended has had to remain at a very general level.

The year a man first showed interest in a group has also been indicated, when possible. Outside of the various charters with which companies were founded, dates of admission of new members can be traced only in the few cases where minutes of meetings have survived. And even in the East India, Virginia, and Levant Companies, whose minutes are the most complete, I have often had to resort to listing the date when a name is first mentioned. There was one additional problem here. Sometimes an actual admission, or the granting of a freedom, might come considerably later than a man's first investment in an enterprise. Often this discrepancy arose because a man had to come to a meeting to be admitted officially, and the decision to accept him might have been taken long before. Thus, on October 11, 1609, the East India Company records noted the "admission of Richard Osmotherley, named in the charter of May 31, 1609." In such cases, the earlier date has of course been entered. But what is one to do with the fact that over two years earlier, on February 23, 1607, this statement appeared in the company's minutes: "Richard Osmotherley admitted an adventurer for 100*l.* for this voyage only"? [38] Here was a man investing in 1607, but technically a member only in 1609. I decided, again, that the year of first interest should appear in the list. Similarly, anyone who is named as a subscriber is entered as of that date, even if there is no record of his formal admission. In the many organizations where such detailed information has not survived the dates are much less precise and, as has been indicated, occasionally I have had to resort to the roughest of approximations. All such arbitrary entries have been noted in the tables.

The other criteria for inclusion in the list were simple to apply. Because I was interested in "undertakers," not colonists, only subscribers of *money* to colonial enterprises were recorded. Peo-

[38] *CSP, East Indies, 1513–1616,* pp. 194, 149. In the Spanish Company the prominent London merchant Lawrence Green was even elected an "assistant" (equivalent to a director) before he became officially free of the company: see the Court Book in the British Museum, Additional Manuscript 9365, p. 15.

ple who contributed their labor or service or (as in Ireland) rent certainly donated more than most investors, and they were just as essential for success; but this is not a study of emigration or the fortunes of the companies overseas. I have been concerned solely with the organization of the expansion at home — once the ships weigh anchor, as far as I am concerned, a different chapter begins. Without wishing in any way to detract from the amazing achievements of those who actually set sail, my basic premise has been that they only reaped the harvest sown by the thousands of adventurers who never left England. The colonists, captains, and traders provide the more dramatic and exciting story, and it has often been told. Here, however, the attention has been focused strictly on those whose subscriptions made it possible.[39] Settlers qualified for inclusion only if they were investors in the home company, as were the early members of the Massachusetts Bay Company. The one major problem of identification was created by the Munster ventures of the 1580's and 1590's, because no formal company was established whereby membership (as opposed to mere settlement) could be determined. I decided, therefore, that someone who merely became a tenant or gave service to the company would not qualify. Thus Sir Walter Raleigh is recorded as an investor in Ireland, but Thomas Hariot and John White are omitted. This seemed exactly parallel to the decision whereby Lord De La Warr appears as an investor in Virginia but John Rolfe does not.

This distinction naturally applied only to colonial ventures. In commercial enterprises a similar decision had to be made with regard to sailors on ships and other employees of a company. Most of these people were entitled to partake of the activities and profits of their employer in one way or another. Agents abroad could trade for themselves, as could the mariners who brought

[39] As a balance to the concerns of the present book, it might be worth recalling Sir William Foster's pointed assessment of the relative importance of the individual contributions of those involved in England's expansion: "No one will deny that the directing minds in London deserve full credit for their vision and their perseverance in the face of many discouragements. But the place of honour must be given to the sailors who endured so manfully the dangers and difficulties of the sea voyage, and to the bold merchants who took without complaint the risks of residing or making long journeys in countries where life was unsafe and disease rampant." See his *England's Quest of Eastern Trade* (London, 1933), p. 335. Cf. note 8, above.

the cargoes home; and the crews of privateers were entitled to a third of the booty. In all such cases it was deemed that labor alone had been contributed, and that therefore, in the absence of an investment or membership at home, these names should not appear in the list.

Finally, only subscribers to English enterprises were entered. The few Welsh undertakings, led by William Vaughan and the Middletons, were included because they originated in England. But the exclusively Scottish ventures, such as Nova Scotia, were left out except in the cases of people who were active in England, like Sir William Alexander.

Company memberships conclude with a listing of all officers and governors. The titles varied, but all assistants, directors, councillors, deputies, and committeemen are recorded. Governors and heads of organizations are also distinguished. The dates of election to office were assembled, and it might have been interesting to investigate such questions as how long it took, on average, to become a director. But to have coded this information for the 624 people who qualified would have been so complicated, requiring the addition of a second IBM card for each entry, that I decided to postpone this inquiry for the time being. As will be mentioned below, there were not only additional data, but also further questions about my present data that I would very much have liked to investigate. But a halt had to be called at some point, particularly as the funds for the present research were fast disappearing. The more detailed analysis of the directorships, therefore, will have to await a future study.

Parliaments. The members of the House of Commons between 1584 and 1629 form the second basic component of the list. The original decision to add this information was made with only the vaguest expectations. A duty regarded increasingly as an important public and social responsibility, attendance at Parliament was likely to be a good indicator of particularly active gentry. For a start, the man whose career led me to this study, Sir Edwin Sandys, devoted nearly all his energies during 25 years of public life to these two interests — the Commons and overseas enterprise. Because a striking number of his friends — Sir Dudley Digges and Sir Richard (later Lord) Lovelace, for example —

had similar interests, there seemed a good chance that the inclusion of parliamentary data might improve our understanding either of debates on trade or of gentry participation in commercial ventures. For it did not seem without significance that the companies of the period were often quite specific on this subject. It was certainly no isolated event when, on March 31, 1614, the East India Company admitted a member of that year's Parliament, William Fanshawe, "conceiving they shall have need of such person's assistance against the Parliament." [40] The eventual fruitful results of this shot in the dark were unforeseeable at the outset. I certainly did not anticipate that over 42 percent of the gentry and nobles who invested in new enterprises would turn out to have sat in the House of Commons. One could only hope that something useful would emerge either while the figures were being assembled or during wide-ranging computer searches. There were many potentially revealing types of information like this which could have been added — holders of Crown office come to mind at once. But the names of the M.P.'s were the most easily accessible, and at least a start has now been made toward broadening the data. New material for future work can, of course, be put on the cards at any time.

Assembling the M.P.'s was relatively easy, because the *Return of the Members of Parliament,* supplementary returns, and the researches of the History of Parliament Trust were all readily available. The decision to begin with the session of 1584, rather than 1576 (which was the first in the 1575–1630 period), was made for reasons similar to the choice of 1575, not 1553, for companies. Just as in the mid-1570's a new era had opened with a succession of enterprises that sent Englishmen to the Arctic, the Baltic, and the Levant as never before, so in 1584 a new generation appeared in Parliament. Its historian has called it "an unusually young House, an unusually new House," and he has pointed out that over 70 percent of its members were newcomers, nearly double the usual proportion.[41] This appeared to be reason

[40] *CSP, East Indies, 1513–1616,* p. 288. In this book the parliamentary figures have been used primarily for their relevance to investments. An analysis of their significance with regard to developments in the House of Commons will be a part of my forthcoming biography of Sir Edwin Sandys.

[41] J. E. Neale, *Elizabeth I and Her Parliaments, 1584–1601* (London, 1957), pp. 25, 23.

enough to omit the two sessions between 1575 and 1584, and there was the added justification that the last general election before 1584 had been in 1572, before the start of the period I was covering. The decision to begin in 1584 was reinforced when it became apparent that the significance of connections between trade and Parliament increased markedly at the turn of the century. The earlier assemblies would have added only to the background that was already sufficiently full to provide the context for developments after 1600 — an argument identical to the justification for omitting pre-1575 investments.

The parliamentary entries created few problems of definition or systematization, because each session to which a man was elected appeared on the card. No distinction was made between general elections and by-elections, even though the latter might mean somewhat later admission to the House. In this case statistical insignificance had to be allowed to override complications that would have added little by way of precision. Also, every man entitled to sit in the House was included even if his election was later disputed or overturned: both Goodwin and Fortescue appear for 1604.

The Members of Parliament totaled 3,032, including 692 already eligible because they had joined a company. In other words, 2,340 people (slightly over one-quarter of the entire list) were added so as to achieve completeness for the House of Commons data.

The final qualification for inclusion, which brought in only six extra people, was membership in one of the two Royal Commissions for trade set up in the 1620's. This was originally the beginning of an attempt to enter all Crown office holders, an effort that was soon abandoned, at least for the present book. Little information of any value was obtained about the composition of the commissions.

Social Classes and Identifications. The fundamental data having been collected, the most precarious stage in the creation of the list now began — the final consolidation. What was required was the integration into a single, unified grouping of 38 separate components (the 36 companies, the M.P.'s, and the trade commissioners). Each individual had to be identified and given all the memberships that belonged to him. The raw material consisted of 16,250 entries (9,867 in companies, 6,333 in Parliament, and 50 commissioners); when the consolidation was finished there would be 8,683 men and women with, on average, just under two memberships each. At the same time, as part of the process of identification, each person had to be classified according to social status if possible — information that was clearly vital to any analysis.

These aims were easy to formulate: they were virtually self-evident. But their implementation was by far the most laborious, complex, and elusive undertaking in the whole process of producing the finished list. The uncertainties and difficulties of earlier stages of the research, as described above, were minor by comparison. However complicated the previous decisions may have been, they were at least few in number — and they covered large blocks of evidence. Now there was an individual situation to be faced and assessed in every single entry, and I could feel relatively confident only when dealing with the very famous, like Sir Francis Bacon. But even prominent people had namesakes (for instance, there were three men named Sir Edwin Sandys in the early seventeenth century), and absolute assurance — let alone easy handling of an entry — was an impossible luxury. An unusual name appearing only once might save me the trouble of deciding how many memberships to assign, but the problem of social classification remained. On the other hand, it might be perfectly clear that the William Green who represented Portsmouth in the 1597 Parliament was a merchant, and that the William Greens in the French Company, the New Merchant Adventurers, and the East India and Virginia Companies (in 1609) were also merchants. But were they all the same man, or two, three, four, or five men? And what about the William Green, merchant, who ventured in the Plymouth colony in 1620, and the other namesake, again a merchant, who joined the East India Company in 1619? This was a particularly intractable situation, but some such difficulty was encountered in almost every single entry. To describe every decision that had to be made would, of course, take more space than is feasible. The results can be examined in the list itself, and here I can indicate only the general procedures and problems of this final stage in the compilation of the list.

171

As has been mentioned in the Introduction, the one distinction in the social classification that was crucial to my purposes was the difference between a merchant and a gentleman. None of my results was going to be of much value unless these two could be separated. And yet the nature of my inquiry, covering so large a body of material, required that a fairly simple, easily applicable yardstick be devised to bring order and consistency to a subject full of the subtlest and most devious nuances. The more abstract or indefinable characteristics that might have had a bearing on a man's status, such as breeding, the opinion of his fellows, or the manner in which he rode a horse, could have no place in my assessment. Nor could such outward manifestations as the granting of arms be considered essential, because my chief interest was in types of investment, which depended on the origins of the money, not the current standing of the investor.[42] My distinction therefore came to rest on the answer to the question: *Where did the money originally come from?* For my purposes, the judgment "once a merchant, always a merchant" remained true in all cases save elevation to the nobility. And a gentleman was he whose entry into commerce was financed by landed wealth. In both cases, moreover, the classification was always restricted to one generation. A merchant who bought an estate was still backing

[42] There is a good discussion of the problems of defining a "gentleman," particularly during the sixteenth and the seventeenth centuries, in A. R. Wagner, *English Genealogy* (Oxford, 1960), pp. 102–121. For a contemporary discussion of the characteristics of a gentleman, see Henry Peacham, *The Compleat Gentleman* (London, 1622). The final version (1634) is available in a modern edition by G. S. Gordon (Oxford, 1906), in which the general assessment is on pp. 1–17. See pp. 11–12 for a highly ambiguous answer to the question of whether a merchant can be a noble. Other contemporary definitions are quoted in H. C. Wilkinson, *The Adventurers of Bermuda* (London, 1958), pp. 108–109. See, too, Ruth Kelso, *The Doctrine of the English Gentleman in the Sixteenth Century* (Urbana, 1929); and the various articles in the "gentry" controversy — conveniently listed in *The Origins of the English Civil War: Conspiracy, Crusade, or Class Conflict?* ed. P. A. M. Taylor (Boston, 1960), p. 104. It is worth noting, however, that on the whole the storm over the gentry has contributed little to social history. The disputants have been concerned mainly with the political opinions and economic well-being of England's upper classes, and they have given almost no attention to such problems as whether one can define a gentleman, what class characteristics can be established, and so on. Two recent studies *have* been concerned with questions of this kind, but unfortunately only in connection with the strata of society above and below the gentry: Stone's *Crisis of the Aristocracy*, and Mildred Campbell's *The English Yeoman under Elizabeth and the Early Stuarts* (New Haven, 1942). As for the term "merchant," though it is used in its modern sense throughout the present book, its earlier meanings can be found outlined in Charles Gross, *The Gild Merchant* (Oxford, 1890), p. 157.

companies with money made primarily in business. Despite his lands, his fortune was mercantile, regardless of his aspirations for the position of country squire. But his son might qualify as a gentleman by my terms, if he lived off rents and was uninterested in trade as a primary occupation. On the other hand, younger sons of gentry who came to the City without an income, hoping to make their way in commerce, were also regarded as merchants, even if they brought a few pounds from home.

This division seemed to correspond reasonably well with the feelings of the gentry themselves when they decided whom to regard as a social equal. It is hardly likely, for instance, that Shakespeare would have been considered a true gentleman merely because he obtained a coat of arms. And Sir Thomas Smith, for all his magnificent lands in Kent, remained to the end of his life a "great merchant" rather than a country gentleman. But his son Sir John, uninterested in trade, was equally surely a gentleman. In fact, one reason for the strained relations between father and son when John married into the family of the Earls of Warwick may well have been the change in status that was becoming apparent in the course of one generation. Within another generation a marriage with the Sydneys, Earls of Leicester, placed the Smiths incontrovertibly among the gentry. Only for merchants who reached the peerage was an exception made in the classifications, because here there could be no doubt as to status. Very few of the nobles in the list rose that rapidly through society, and it is illustrative of the anomaly that only at the very last minute before the computer began its work did I remember that Sir Lionel Cranfield and Sir Baptist Hickes were still depicted as merchant knights, and not as the Earl of Middlesex and Viscount Campden. (In all fairness, it should be added that I remembered at the same time that Sir Francis Bacon was also still listed as a knight, and not as Viscount St. Albans.)

On the other hand, perhaps because of the many close contacts between English gentlemen and merchants for centuries, particularly in the House of Commons, a younger son of a landed family could make the transition quite easily, and become a merchant as soon as he began to earn his living in trade — usually in London. A typical example was the transition in three generations of the Wolstenholme family from gentleman to merchant and back to gentleman. The grandfather, John, a younger son in an old Derbyshire family, came to London and worked in the customhouse. His son, Sir John, became one of the City's greatest merchants, a leading investor in Jacobean enterprises, and eventually the purchaser of a country estate in Yorkshire. The grandson, another Sir John, a fervent royalist in the Civil War, married into the Vere family, obtained a baronetcy after the Restoration, and established the line back on the land. Despite their background, therefore, the first two were clearly "merchants" by my definition, and probably also in the eyes of contemporaries, whereas the third re-entered the ranks of the gentry.[43]

I have no wish to argue that the distinction I drew is the only, or even the most accurate way of determining who was considered a gentleman in Elizabethan or Stuart England. I merely suggest that it is a plausible distinction, according sufficiently well with the feelings and attitudes of the time to serve as a basis for my figures. And for my purposes it has the great advantage of resting on a determinant, origin of wealth, which is closely related to the aims of the present study. It is particularly appropriate to my use of "gentleman" as someone who is not skilled in trading, and therefore likely to appreciate the advantages of a joint-stock company. The very fact that he is investing money that comes primarily from land, and not from business exploits, argues for his being in the gentry, not the merchant class. And the gentleman is also likely to be someone who does not depend on trade for his income, just as the merchant, regardless of the size of the estates he buys, will continue to rely on trade to provide a living.

Finally, in addition to its relatively accurate reflection of the social stratification of the period, and its appropriateness to a study of investments, the definition has the great advantage of being fairly easy to apply. In the first place, it was possible to assign a class to a substantial group immediately simply because they were referred to as merchants at some time in their careers. As far as I was concerned, anyone who was called a merchant was categorized as such *ipso facto*. No gentleman would ever have allowed this designation. Company records, as might be expected, frequently used the term, saving me a great deal of

[43] Other leading merchants of our period who were younger sons of gentry were Sir Edward Osborne, Sir Lionel Duckett, and Sir William Herrick.

trouble. The title "gentleman" or "esquire," however, was accepted only after careful scrutiny, as it was freely adopted, particularly by merchants with social pretensions. One example was the rise of John Hazard, a leading citizen of Lyme Regis who represented his borough in the 1586 Parliament as "merchant," but by 1604 was called "gentleman" in the *Return*.

The one exception to the "landed-origins" rule occurred with knighthood. I felt that any man who rose — not directly through trade, but by some other means — to prominence and knighthood deserved to be considered a gentleman regardless of his origins. Sir Francis Drake, for example, despite nonlanded background, was placed among the gentry knights. To this decision a sixteenth-century gentleman might well have demurred. The Grenvilles are hardly likely to have agreed that Drake became their equal, his purchase of Buckland Abbey notwithstanding.[44] There were very few cases like this, where a decision could have gone either way, but when they did arise I usually sought further assistance from some of the differences between merchants and gentry described in Chapters 1 and 2. Drake, for example, was clearly associated with the Court rather than London commercial circles in the financing of the ventures of the late sixteenth century. This seemed a more useful determinant than the opinion of long-established Devon families.

Knighthood, being well documented, was most useful as a determinant of status. Though merchant knights were kept separate, they were prominent enough to be recognized immediately. These two categories accounted for 1,236 people in the list, 134 of them merchants.[45] Another 241 were easily classifiable because they held titles of nobility (including bishoprics). A further 4,009 could be identified as merchants with the help of company records, Livery Company memberships, and such recent studies as those by W. K. Jordan and T. S. Willan.[46] Out of the remaining 3,197 individuals in the list, 987 could be classified as gentry.

---

[44] If anything, Drake's acquisition of Buckland is likely to have increased Sir Richard Grenville's resentment of the upstart. See A. L. Rowse, *Sir Richard Grenville of the Revenge* (London, 1940), pp. 155–156; and Ernle Bradford, *The Wind Commands Me* (New York, 1965), pp. 151ff.

[45] The date of first knighthood or baronetcy was included in the data.

[46] In particular, W. K. Jordan, *Philanthropy in England, 1480–1660* (London, 1959); his *The Charities of London, 1480–1660* (London, 1960); and T. S. Willan, *Muscovy Merchants;* and his *Elizabethan Foreign Trade.*

Finally, a small catchall category was used for any man who, though not unclassifiable for want of information, did not belong in any other pigeonhole. Most of these entries were professional men, particularly minor clergymen or lawyers, whose income came neither from land of their own nor from trade. Also included in this category were the few yeomen who reached the list without having become merchants. Only 74 people appeared in this special class, ranging from John Selden, the lawyer, to Captain John Smith, the yeoman-turned-explorer. In the end, only 25 percent of all entries had to be left without any social classification — clearly a small enough proportion to permit meaningful analysis of the social divisions among investors and M.P.'s.

It would be pointless to pretend that this sevenfold division (unclassified, gentleman, gentleman knight, noble, merchant, merchant-knight, and professional/yeoman) presents a well-rounded picture of English society. The most obvious defect is that it allows only one small distinction (between knights and the rest) among the huge blocks of merchants and gentry. Admittedly, this distinction did enable me to isolate the most prominent members of these classes, but considerable diversity still remained, particularly within the "merchant" category. William Harrison, one of London's most active promoters and a director of six different companies, was treated no differently than was one Richard Sabin, a mercer who gave £1 5s. toward his Livery Company's plantation in Ireland. And yet the small tradesman or shopkeeper, no less than the great entrepreneur, earned his living in commerce, not from land. True, the humbler members of the Livery Companies would never have received from their contemporaries any title so illustrious as "merchant," but for my purposes they had to be placed in the same category. To have tried to devise distinctions between the various levels would have created more problems than it would have solved. The same was true for the gentry, for the knights, and even for the nobles, because every class had its "greater" and "lesser."

By and large, if any information at all could be found, it was usually quite straightforward to assign the social classification. The different attitudes and styles of life of merchants and gentry that are discussed in the previous chapters were used only rarely, as in the case of Drake, to help distinguish between the classes.

176

Retirement to the country during the summer may be a habit worth mentioning, because it increases one's understanding of the outlook of a gentleman; but as a test of status it has obvious drawbacks. Such qualities may be more interesting than the source of a man's money, but they are much less precise, they do not have the same breadth of application, and they are useful only when position in society has already been established by some other means. For this first step the origin of wealth was perfectly adequate. The greatest difficulty was caused, not by doubt as to how to treat the available information, but by the problem of identification.[47] This one remaining task proved more persistent and insidious than all the others combined.

The difficulties of sorting out a plethora of William Greens have already been mentioned. Fortunately, situations of such nightmarish proportions arose only rarely, for the simple reason that there were not that many very common names. Certainly, the problems of the Henry Lees, the John Moores, and the John Smiths, particularly when complicated by variant spellings (Leigh, More, and Smythe, to name but three), usually outweighed all the lesser difficulties that surrounded them.[48] But here one was obviously on treacherous ground, and compensations could be made, if only by leaving an issue in doubt through the device of a question about the data. Much more dangerous were the unsuspected traps: unusual names which, though seemingly unique, were in fact held jointly by a father and son, or by any number of relatives.

Families had great attachments to traditional first names. When one thinks oneself safest (when, for instance, it seems inconceivable that there could actually have been *two* people named Bassingbourn Gawdy) — lo and behold, that is precisely when the improbability becomes the reality. In four of the Parliaments of the period one of the two Bassingbourns is to be

[47] The one borderline activity between landed and commercial wealth, speculation in land, was considered the mark of a merchant — as in the case of Sir Arthur Ingram.

[48] In the case of the Lees and the Smiths one is in fact helped by a number of genealogical studies, notably the pedigree in E. K. Chambers, *Sir Henry Lee: An Elizabethan Portrait* (Oxford, 1936), pp. 244–263; the section on the Smiths in Brown, *Genesis of the United States*, II, 1004–1018, and the Smith pedigree in *Archaeologia Cantiana*, 20 (1893), 76–81.

177

found, carrying his highly appropriate surname (other members of the family were adorned by the names Clipesby and Framlingham). And the confusion was not restricted to fathers, sons, and cousins: even brothers could be indistinguishable — for example, the William Gilbert of *De Magnete* fame and his brother, William. Nor was the mere discovery of a namesake the end of the problem. It was all very well to know that there were two Hugh Hamersleys, father and son, in Jacobean London, but which did what? The father was not knighted until 1628, by which time two of the companies in question, the French and the North-West Passage, had become defunct. Was it the father or the son who joined them? In the absence of personal papers, all one can do in such a case is to make the most logical assignment. The father was a much more prominent and active man, a known member of the Spanish, Virginia, East India, Muscovy, and Levant Companies, a director of the last three, and governor of the last two; the son is known definitely to have joined only the Spanish Company. The likelihood, therefore, is that the father was the natural candidate for inclusion in the French and North-West Passage Companies.

The disentangling of the Hamersleys is fairly typical of the problems that were encountered whenever a name was mentioned more than once in the records. For the parliamentary entries I was fortunate to have available the researches of the History of Parliament Trust. These at least helped me to make sure that the different M.P.'s appeared with the correct information.[49] But as soon as I had to deal with more than one company — or a company plus a parliamentary entry — the difficulties appeared. Eventually there turned out to be 2,194 people with multiple memberships (not including attendance at more than one Parliament). There were also, I would estimate, some two or three hundred namesakes of these people who were finally given only one company entry or only parliamentary data. All in all, there-

---

[49] But the lack of detailed material on the sessions after 1601 was an unfortunate drawback: almost half the people in the list who have been given no social class were solely M.P.'s; yet people who were M.P.'s alone amounted to little more than a quarter of all entries. The proportion of unclassified among this category was thus nearly double the overall average (42 percent as opposed to just under 25 percent). In contrast, slightly less than 20 percent of the people in companies alone, and only 4.0 percent of those in both companies and Parliament, remained unclassified.

178

fore, some 2,500 individuals (just under 29 percent of the total) required disentanglement.

As it happened, most of the problems could be solved either because the investors were sufficiently prominent to be carefully identified at the time (courtiers, aldermen, etc.), or because a strong logical case could be made for one particular solution (as in the case of the Hamersleys). Helpful in this respect were certain clear patterns of multiple memberships. For example, an interest in both the Virginia and Somers Islands Companies, or both the Spanish and the French Companies, was so common that namesakes in these pairs of enterprises were always likely to have been the same man. By the same token, an adventurer known to have been active in the 1570's or 1580's was not likely to have disappeared from the records, and suddenly become active again in the late 1620's: in all probability the latter was a second person. But if, finally, the uncertainties could not be resolved, a doubt about the data was entered on the card. Thus a single asterisk before the name in the list at the end of this book denotes someone who received a separate entry, but who might in fact be identical with a namesake elsewhere in the list. Similarly, a double asterisk indicates that the data assigned to one man might belong to two, or more, separate individuals. Eventually 276 people received such questions — over 10 percent of the 2,500 "problem" entries, but only slightly over three percent of the list. The figure is reassuringly small, but I must add the warning that mistakes undoubtedly still remain. If such detailed and precise studies as those mentioned in note 6, above, could contain small lapses in identification, my own are likely to be much larger. At this point one must take refuge in statistical insignificance and hope that the errors have not seriously affected the figures. I trust that scholars who are more familiar with the careers of particular individuals in the list will let me know of any mistakes they notice so that revisions can be made.

The problems of identification were of course not lessened by the bewildering spelling habits of the sixteenth and seventeenth centuries. Even the commonest names lacked uniformity, and the slightest hint of singularity gave the clerks of the time no end of trouble. The letters "I" and "Y" were generally interchangeable, and the addition of an "E" was entirely at the mercy of passing whims. Far more difficult to deal with was the laxness with which vowels were handled. They could be changed without warning, disrupting completely all attempts at alphabetization. Eldred became Aldredd, Revett appeared as Rivet, Rudyard as Ridiard, and so on. The letter "H" was readily dispensable (as in Baynham or Baynam), and doubled letters vanished with disconcerting ease (as in Bedell or Beedel). Occasionally even a man's first name might be confused. In most cases, it was not too difficult to resolve the diversities, but real havoc was wrought as soon as a name became at all unusual. Christopher Clitheroe, for example, notwithstanding his prominence in London commercial circles, or the fact that he bore the name of a Yorkshire parliamentary borough, suffered quite startling metamorphoses at the hands of copyists or clerks. One vaguely alphabetical list placed the elusive Mr. Clitheroe among the "L"s, as Mr. C. Lethro. One can imagine the difficulties of *self*-identification that must have plagued Richard Kenneridgburg, who appeared occasionally as Richard Knaresborough.

Once identification, and thus compilation of the list, was complete, the final entries on the card — the questions — were made. The various kinds of doubts which they recorded are described in the Appendix. All in all, 549 people were assigned a total of 572 different questions.

III. USING THE COMPUTER

The organization and analysis of my card would probably not be of any great value to readers. Most, I expect, are unfamiliar with the mechanics of coding, establishing fields, and numeric and nonnumeric punches. To start from the very beginning would require too much space; instead, I shall use my card as the main example in a pamphlet I am preparing, designed to introduce laymen-historians to the few skills required for work with a computer. Those who are familiar with the techniques will be able to understand my approach from various details provided in the Appendix.

Before concluding this review of method, however, it might be appropriate to mention some of the more personal reactions of a "humanist" historian as he came into contact with the world of the computer, inhabited as it is primarily by scientists and by those among the social scientists who put as much emphasis on the science as on the society. If one is tempted to say, with Miranda, "O brave new world, that has such people in 't," then "brave" will mean "courageous" rather than "splendid." The impression of difference and newness is certainly striking, and it is all too easy to be swept up by an atmosphere in which time, measured in milliseconds and less, has come to be used so efficiently that it nearly loses its meaning. The computer works almost incessantly, and one's life can become geared to it, particularly if it is necessary to hurry. "Turn-around time" (the waiting period for one's turn at the computer) assumes vast significance and — as in my case for a while — one may have to stay awake during the eight P.M. to four A.M. shift because that is when one's programmer works. In such surroundings, urged by statisticians and mathematicians to adopt more elegant and "scientific" methods, considerable courage and determination are needed to persevere in a particular task. The temptations offered by the universality of the computer and the strictly systematic ways of thought developed and encouraged by its users must be resisted unless strictly relevant to one's own purposes. And at the end of the ordeal, one must be able to say, with Prospero, "Now my charms are all o'erthrown,/ And what strength I have 's mine own."

The one constant blandishment I encountered was the suggestion that there really were much simpler and more efficient ways of handling my data, if only I would use the computer's capabilities to the full. "You compiled and alphabetized that list *by hand?*" I was asked incredulously. "Why, it would have been so much simpler to have the computer do it for you. Just have it scan the material and assemble the list mechanically." And such critics could not be deterred by problems of variant spellings and seventeenth-century handwriting, let alone the fearsome difficulties of identification — all of which would have required the most incredibly complicated programs. Quite apart from the inaccessibility of some of the documents — how, for instance, could one get any kind of machine into a large, iron-barred room, securely padlocked even while I did my work, in the basement of a Livery Company which permitted no reproduction of its documents? — it was clear that no program to do this work could have been written in less than the time it took me to finish the research. Even then it was likely to be far less reliable because all problems would have had to be specified in advance. By the time I found out what all the problems were, my work was over.

More subtle suggestions came with regard to handling of the data once it was assembled. I should stress from the start that, as far as I could tell, it was not necessary for someone like myself to become proficient in the details of programming, as long as one could convey to a programmer the exact nature of the data and the analyses that were required. The intricacies of the various Fortran and other languages, and their relative merits, are technicalities. Gaining sufficient mastery over them to be able to write decent programs would have taken considerable time, because in this field experience is essential. And what would have been the purpose? Such major questions as whether to make use of a computer language called Cobol, which was well suited to my investigation but not widely familiar, would still have had to be settled by the advice of experts. And I never could have become as efficient as the professionals, whose experience enables them to spot difficulties quickly and accurately. Nor was there any point to my being able to check on the programmer: the results spoke for themselves. Just as one leaves the making of microfilms in the hands of technicians — they do it much better, and they save time and effort — so one can leave the mechanics of programming to programmers.

This becomes increasingly true with the growing use of "packages" — ready-made programs of wide applicability available in various "libraries." It takes experience to know which package can be useful in a particular project, and how the data should be prepared accordingly. In my own case, a great deal of time and trouble was saved by a package designed to correlate two groups of variables. By including, at the end of each card, three figures which represented the total number of Parliaments, companies, and directorships entered on that card, I could take advantage of this program to produce tables in which one total formed the column and the other the row. These figures could also be used in conjunction with the social classifications, which appeared as numbers from one to six. Thus I could distinguish how many people were in one, two, three, or more Parliaments or companies, and how many directorships they held. These tabulations could then be broken down further by social class, or by comparison with one another. Percentages were automatically calculated. All this information would have been exceedingly laborious and complicated to extract without the use of this ready-made program.

It is usually a straightforward matter to communicate to the programmer the questions one wants answered; but it is less easy in a computer center to retain the conviction that a vast sorting and cross-tabulating process can provide, without further and more sophisticated mathematical analyses, enough answers to satisfy one's interest in one's data. "Why not," I was asked, "construct a model of the typical East India Company investor, and then assess the membership in terms of deviations from the ideal-type?" This approach would doubtless have offered opportunities for expositions of great elegance; and, had the information been available, a fascinating comparison might have been made between this model and, say, the typical mid-eighteenth-century East India investor. Performed without any comparative intentions, however, this kind of complex statistical exercise does not necessarily provide the historian with a better understanding of the problem he is studying. Unless he is quite sure, therefore, that the techniques devised by other social scientists are relevant to his concerns and provide information both necessary and otherwise unavailable, he must resist the temptation to employ recent analytic advances, particularly in the realm of systematic measurement, simply because they are easily accessible in the form of ready-made computer programs. Tables 11–13 and 15–19 in this book contained the figures most frequently singled out by those who urged me to use my findings to make econometric projections, create typical portfolios, and so on. Nevertheless, however valid these suggestions often seemed from a statistical or other methodological point of view, I was far from certain that they had a bearing on the situation of the sixteenth- and seventeenth-century investor, and it was at this point that Prospero's boast came most readily to mind.

The one inevitable restriction on the historian's freedom of action when he adopts new techniques of social analysis is the realization that projections which may be appropriate to twentieth-century conditions are not necessarily helpful when one attempts to assess the very different society that existed more than 300 years ago. For example, the missing data (which are substantial) may be significantly different from those we possess. The very fact that a specific piece of evidence has survived so long may set it apart from the evidence that is lost. Thus it would be misleading to assume that the one-quarter of the investors and M.P.'s who remained unclassifiable were made up of the same proportion of gentry and merchants as the remaining three-quarters. If the analysis were of present-day investors and politicians, the extrapolation could be made with little hesitation. But my data may well be missing because of the very obscurity of the people involved, and this suggests that they may have been *all* merchants, not 75 percent merchants.

Like the evidence itself, the norms and assumptions of sixteenth- and seventeenth-century life were so different from our own that we cannot simply transfer our attitudes and concerns to this distant age. The analysis of "portfolios" is a case in point. To the twentieth-century investor, a portfolio of holdings is a perfectly natural concept. Because a stockholder self-consciously pursues certain specific goals, his investments can be subjected to the most sophisticated analyses. So, too, the shareholders in a company can be assessed in terms of their interests, speculative ambitions, and so on. But in Elizabethan and Jacobean times the historian is faced by completely different attitudes and conditions. Apart from anything else, companies open to all comers were an entirely new creation. Never before had there been a choice of this nature for an investor. Even the notion that the price of a share could fluctuate was a novelty, and not as yet a determinant in the mind of the ordinary adventurer. Discussion of a self-conscious investment *policy* would have been totally alien to his mentality. Some broad basic aims and attitudes can be discerned, as is shown in Chapter 1. But to attribute any degree of sophistication to the process of joining a company would be to misunderstand the very simple motives that led to participation in commerce. Subscriptions were, on the whole, so haphazardly made and so easily explicable in terms of recruitment campaigns or conspicuous successes, that the deeper meanings that could be extracted by the application of elegant statistical techniques would contribute little or nothing that is relevant to our understanding of Elizabethan and Jacobean investments.

These considerations should not be taken to imply that mathematical analyses cannot help historians. Although I do believe that there are certain questions with more intrinsic interest to historians than to other students of human society — and vice versa — this entire book is predicated on the assumption that there is much to be learned from advances in related disciplines. I have emphasized limitations only because it is so easy to be overwhelmed by the obvious benefits that these new techniques can bestow.

By way of compensation for this cautionary attitude, it is worth stressing that the historian should not succumb to the self-deprecating attitude that I, at least, found natural when engaged in seemingly crude and elementary operations with the computer. Physicists, econometrists, statisticians, and most of its other users rely on the advanced mathematical functions and intricate problem-solving capabilities of the machine. What I was doing could have been done by a desk calculator: it would have taken far longer and been more inaccurate, but it would not have been impossible. At times it seems almost impertinent to have the computer give such mundane assistance, and yet it is a mistake to believe that the absence of difficult mathematics removes all complexities. Programming can still be tortuous if, as in my case, a very long succession of functions has to be performed. The process of perfecting the program, known as "de-bugging," can be most wearisome, and because most programmers are not used to this kind of inquiry, it may take even longer than usual.

From my own experience the one technical suggestion I would make (for those who may be interested) is that considerable use be made of sub-routines, a series of small functions attached to a "main" program, each of which solves just one problem. In this way difficulties can be isolated more easily and corrected. A long, continuous program is too susceptible to slight errors that are difficult to track down and — in computer center language — "clobber" the data. And if, as I suggested at the beginning of this chapter, the historian makes a preliminary survey of his material, after which he revises the program to make more detailed explora-

185

tions,[50] the subroutine becomes essential, because even the slightest change can cause a multitude of logical errors. Some general rules of procedure for this kind of historical investigation can probably be devised, with the help of some fairly simple set theory. It should also be possible to work out a standard "main" program that could be applied to all similar problems. Made available as a "library package," it could save other historians a great deal of trouble; and my hope is that we will be able to write such a program as soon as a few more projects like my own get under way.[51]

At some future time, too, there might be an opportunity to add the material that could not be included in the present study. Calculations based on family relationships, geographic origins, Crown office holding, size of estates, and various other characteristics had to be postponed for reasons of time and money. There was no point in holding up all the results that I could already tabulate and publish merely because more information was accessible. Two of the great advantages of the cards are their permanence and their adaptability: the entries that have been made will always be there, and new ones can be added at any time. Moreover, the possibilities of the present data are certainly not exhausted. Investigations that have not occurred to me can still be pursued, not to speak of those of my own inquiries which had to remain unsatisfied. A number of detailed breakdowns that

[50] My preliminary "run" was made at the Northwestern University Computer Center in the summer of 1963. There were 7,460 people in the list at that time, and the 1,400 or so entries added since were all company members. The principal additions were the Spanish merchants of 1577, the Munster venturers of the 1580's and 1590's, the Guiana Company of the late 1620's, some extra members of the East India, Virginia, and Levant Companies, and the investors in industry. Most of the final job of identification also lay ahead, and many changes were still required among entries already recorded. The fundamental features of my data, published in two articles using the results of the preliminary run, have remained basically the same; but the details need to be revised, as should be apparent from the first two chapters of this book — compare my "Sir Edwin Sandys and the Parliament of 1604," pp. 661–669, and "Investment in English Overseas Enterprise, 1575–1630," *Ec.H.R.*, 2nd ser., 19 (1966), 70–81. (The final "runs," incidentally, were made at the Aiken Computation Laboratory of Harvard University in December 1965 and January 1966.)

[51] A program of great flexibility and wide application which is especially well suited to the needs of historians is described in the forthcoming article by Judith E. Selvidge and Theodore K. Rabb, "DATA-TEXT: A simple and flexible programming system for historians, linguists, and other social scientists," which will appear in *Computer Studies in the Humanities,* a new journal.

would have been interesting, but of slight importance, were foregone because results of such minor significance did not merit so complex a task of programming. Although one's precise limits cannot always be foreseen, one should remember that computers open up infinite possibilities. It is vain to expect to explore them all, and as mentioned earlier, a degree of restraint must be maintained. As a last resort, one knows that the data can be expanded or the work resumed whenever one wants.[52]

The warnings about computer work expressed at various places in this chapter are the product of experience laboriously gained. They reflect the most serious difficulties I encountered, and naturally they could not — and cannot — always be heeded. I have no doubt that some of the problems I faced might be resolved differently were I to start the research all over again. But that is only to offer the truism that lessons are often learned too late. There is some compensation in the knowledge that the trials and errors of the present study should never have to be repeated.

[52] To this end, my data tape and programs (a few of them still capable of slight improvements) have been deposited in the Harvard College Library. Another copy of the tape is available at Princeton. This material may be used by any scholars who wish either to use my data for other investigations or to add further information and extend my inquiries.

SOURCES AND ANNOTATED BIBLIOGRAPHY

Since the appearance of Volumes I and IV of *The Cambridge History of the British Empire*, nearly 40 years ago, no substantial bibliography of England's expansion in this period has been published. What follows, therefore, is not only a listing of the sources of the present book, but an introduction to the literature on the subject. The emphasis is on the scholarship of the last 40 years, and only the more important or representative works from the preceding decades have been included. Even for more recent publications, though, there has been no attempt to achieve completeness. Any selection is bound to be highly personal, but my aim has been to assemble those books and articles which present the basic materials and the current state of research on most of the topics connected with the expansion. Although such studies of the general background as histories of Elizabeth's reign have been omitted, works on the general economic or social history of England have been included (with the exception of the "gentry" controversy, admirably and briefly surveyed recently by D. C. Coleman in *History*, 51 [1966], 165–178). As a further guide, I have added short explanatory or descriptive comments wherever they seemed appropriate. Finally, to indicate where more detailed bibliographical information may be found, books with useful bibliographies are preceded by an "x." Most editions of primary materials (the publications of the Hakluyt Society, for example), have introductions that describe the existing documentation of their subjects, but only those with bibliographies of the secondary literature have been marked with an "x."

The entries have been classified according to three basic categories: primary sources, published documents and sources for the data in the list, and secondary works. The first category consists of documents that are not available in published form or that must be consulted in the original because published versions (for example, of the 1577 Spanish Company charter) are inaccurate. They are listed by place of deposit, and the nature of the material is described.

191

The second main category (published documents and sources for the data in the list) is in three sections. The first two sections contain those books that, together with the primary sources, provided the information for the list of names. They are divided between works of a general nature, encompassing a large number of enterprises, investors, or M.P.'s; and works concerned only with specific ventures. The relevant Hakluyt Society publications are listed en masse in the first section. The last section in this category contains other significant published materials, mainly sixteenth- and seventeenth-century tracts dealing with such subjects as economic theory or the motives of the promoters (often clearly exhibited in dedications).

The third main category, secondary works, is again divided into three parts: general works on the expansion and its background, studies of individual enterprises, and biographies of people prominently involved in the expansion. These should be self-explanatory.

Cross references to books of particular importance are provided in the two sections arranged not alphabetically, but by ventures: B(ii) and C(ii). In addition, all place names, proper names, and principal subjects have been included in the index, where an italicized page reference indicates an entry in the bibliography.

A: *PRIMARY SOURCES*

British Museum

Additional Manuscripts:
  3767 (fols. 61–64 and 88–89: industry)
  5496 (fols. 48–50: industry)
  9365 (Court Register Book of the Spanish Company, 1604–1606)
  12496 (fol. 165: industry; fols. 448–449: Virginia Company)
  14027 (fol. 94: privateering)
  18849 (fol. 1: East India Company)
  30567 (fol. 194: Barbary Company)
  30671 (fols. 51–60: French Company; fols. 234–237 and 254–261: Muscovy Company)

Cotton Manuscripts:
Nero B XI (no. 16, fols. 116–117: Levant Company)
Otho E VIII (fols. 6–7: Newfoundland; fols. 41–189, *passim:* Fenton, Frobisher, and other late-Elizabethan voyages)
Sloane 1453 (fols. 2–46: Merchant Adventurers)
Titus B V (*passim:* industry)
Vespasian C XIII (no. 14, fol. 47: Spanish Company)
Vespasian F XI (fols. 259–260: Venice Company; no. 57, fol. 287: Levant Company)

Harleian Manuscripts:
  306 (fol. 18: East India Company)
  1327 (no. 6, fol. 8: industry)
  1855 (nos. 1–5, fols. 1–36: Spanish Company)

Lansdown Manuscripts:
  24 (no. 44, fols. 108–122: industry)

31 (no. 63, fol. 166: industry)
41 (fols. 108–168: import and export figures and Spanish merchants)
48 (no. 67, fols. 160–163: industry)
55 (no. 14, fols. 53–54: industry; no. 23, fols. 73–74: Guinea trade)
58 (no. 77, fols. 176 and 178: industry)
60 (no. 3, fol. 8: Levant Company)
67 (no. 25, fols. 68–69: industry)
73 (no. 25: Levant Company; fols. 155–156: industry)
74 (no. 20, fol. 42: privateering)
81 (fols. 12–13: industry; no. 48: import and export figures)
86 (no. 13, fol. 26: Bristol Levant merchants; no. 69, fol. 176: industry)
142 (fol. 30, and no. 69, fols. 404–411: Muscovy Company)
150 (no. 10, fol. 18: Merchant Adventurers)
152 (no. 36, fols. 201–202: merchants' names; fols. 316–342: industry)
487 (fols. 187–89: Spanish Company)

Public Record Office

State Papers:
     14/10 (no. 8: Levant Company)
     14/121 (no. 125: industry: patent holders)
     14/141 (p. 126: Guiana — Grant Book, Domestic, James I)
     39/8 (no. 77: New Merchant Adventurers — Sign Manual, James I)
     91/2 (fols. 139, 183–184, and 221: Muscovy Company)
     105/109 (fol. 6: industry)
     105/110 (Levant Company Letter Book)
     105/143 (Levant Company Register Book)
     105/147–148 (Levant Company Court Books, 1611–1629)
     105/157 (Levant Company Ledger Book)

Patent Rolls:
19 Elizabeth, VIII (Spanish Company — C66/1158, no. 49)
21 Elizabeth, II (Eastland Company — C66/1185, m. 21–6)
25 Elizabeth, II (Venice Company — C66/1224, no. 17)
 3 James I, VI (Spanish Company — SP 14/14, no. 21)
 4 James I, XXII (industry — C66/1722: alum)
11 James I, XV (Muscovy Company — C66/1992, no. 5)
13 James I, XIII (Londonderry Plantation — C66/2068, no. 18)
15 James I, VI (Staplers — C66/2135, no. 4)
20 James I, XVI (Royal Committee for Trade — m. 10)
21 James I, XIX (Newfoundland — C66/2313, no. 7)

Colonial Entry Book:
XVII, 1–46 (Bermuda Company — CO 38/1)
LIX, 1–28 (New England Council — CO 5/902)

House of Lords
House of Lords Papers, 2 June 1628 — 20 June 1628, especially fol. 175: Muscovy Company)

India Office Library
East India Company Records:

Court Books, vols. 1–11 (1599–1629)
Original Correspondence, vols. 1–12 (1602–1630)
Parchment Records, no. 5
Home Miscellaneous Series, no. 764

Guildhall Library
Manuscript book of names of all inhabitants of London and its suburbs, 1572

London Livery Companies
Various records were used in tracking down individual merchants, but the following were of major importance in identifying subscribers to the Virginia and Londonderry colonies:
Clothworkers: Company Court Orders, April 1609
Drapers: Minutes and Records of the Court of Assistants, 1603–1640, especially fol. 101; also manuscript survey of Irish lands
Fishmongers: Court Ledger, Vols. I and II, 1592–1631, especially I, 549–550 and 561–562, and II, 5, 15, 105, and 129
Goldsmiths: Minutes of the Court of Assistants, especially 1618; Records, No. 1645, especially pp. 113–114, 121, and 475–484; Documents, boxes 2, 4–7, 11, and 12
Grocers: Orders of the Court of Assistants, 1591–1616, 527–528 and 545–546; and 1616–1639, 82
Haberdashers: Documents 24 and 26; Minutes of the Court of Assistants, 1583–1652, fol. 179.
Ironmongers: Company Court Book, vol. 2, 1602–1611, fols. 58–88, *passim*, and vol. 3, 1616–1629, fols. 31–32
Mercers: Acts of Court, 1595–1629, fol. 115; Names of all Freemen of the Company, 1347–1643, *passim*
Merchant Taylors: Ancient Records, vol. 5, 369–399, *passim*
Skinners: Court Book no. 2, 1577–1617, *passim* in 1609–1611; no. 3, 1617–1651, May 1618; and Receipts and Payments Book, 1596–1617, see 1609 and 1615–1616
Vintners: Court Books, nos. 1–2, 1608–1629, *passim*, especially 1, 166–172, and 2, 274–275

Nottingham University
Middleton Manuscripts: Mi X 1/1, fol. 2 (Newfoundland — I owe this reference to Dr. G. M. Cell)

Huntington Library
Ellesmere Manuscripts:
EL 2294: Muscovy Company
El 2306–2307: Guinea traders
EL 2362: Levant Company
EL 2378: Merchant Adventurers
EL 2423: industry

Folger Library
Folger Manuscripts: Z. e. l., items 12–14: industry

Institute of Early American History, Williamsburg
Microfilms of documents in English archives relating to Virginia and other early American enterprises, especially the following:

194

Survey no.   700, p. 4, fols. 155–156
         701, p. 3, fols. 157–160 and 175–178
            p. 4, fols. 200 and 210
    1106, p. 19, item 288
           p. 20, item 291
           p. 26, item 327

B: *PUBLISHED DOCUMENTS AND SOURCES FOR THE DATA IN THE LIST*

(i) *General Sources*

Beaven, A. B. *The Aldermen of the City of London.* 2 vols. London, 1908–1913.

Brown, Alexander. *The Genesis of the United States.* 2 vols. Boston, 1890. The biographies in vol. II are only rarely inaccurate.

Calendar of State Papers. Various volumes but especially the following:

    Colonial America and the West Indies, 1574–1660. All African, Caribbean, and North American ventures.

    Colonial, East Indies, 1513–1629. 4 vols. Frobisher, Fenton, East India Company, Levant Company, North-West Passage Company.

    Domestic, passim, from the *1547–1580* volume through the *1629–1631* volume. Particularly useful are *1547–1594* (3 vols.) on privateering and the Levant Company, and *1628–1631* (2 vols.) on privateering.

    Ireland, 1574–1596. 4 vols. Munster.

Carr, C. T., ed. *Select Charters of Trading Companies, A.D. 1530–1707.* London: The Selden Society, 1913.

Chamberlain, John. *The Letters of John Chamberlain.* Ed. N. E. McClure. 2 vols. Philadelphia, 1939.

Cokayne, G. E. *Some Account of the Lord Mayors and Sheriffs of the City of London . . . 1601–1625.* London, 1897.

——. *The Complete Baronetage.* 5 vols. Exeter, 1900–1909. Volume I.

——, H. A. Doubleday, G. H. White, and Lord Howard de Walden, eds. *The Complete Peerage.* 13 vols. London, 1910–1959.

Hakluyt, Richard. *The Principall Navigations Voiages Traffiques and Discoveries of the English Nation.* 3 vols. London, 1598–1600. (Standard modern ed. in 12 vols.; Glasgow, 1903–1905). It should be noted that the recent edition (2 vols.; Cambridge, 1965) by D. B. Quinn and R. A. Skelton of the shorter first version of this work (London, 1589) contains an excellent introduction and a superb 140-page modern index, compiled by Mrs. Quinn.

Hakluyt Society Publications. First Series, Volumes

    I: Bethune, C. R. D., ed. *The Observations of Sir Richard Hawkins, K^{nt} in his Voyage to the South Sea in the year 1593.* London, 1847.

    III: Raleigh, Sir Walter. *The Discovery of the Large, Rich, and Beautiful Empire of Guiana.* Ed. Sir Robert H. Schomburgk. London, 1848.

IV: Maynarde, Thomas. *Sir Francis Drake His Voyage, 1595.* Ed. W. D. Cooley. London, 1849.

V: Rundall, Thomas, ed. *Narratives of Voyages towards the North-West, in Search of a Passage to Cathay and India, 1496–1631.* London, 1849.

VII: Hakluyt, Richard, ed. *Divers Voyages touching the Discovery of America and the Islands Adjacent.* Ed. J. W. Jones. London, 1850.

XVI: Vaux, W. S. W., ed. *The World Encompassed by Sir Francis Drake.* London, 1854.

XX: Bond, E. A., ed. *Russia at the Close of the Sixteenth Century.* London, 1856.

XXVII: Asher, G. M., ed. *Henry Hudson the Navigator.* London, 1860.

XXXVIII: Collinson, Sir Richard, ed. *The Three Voyages of Martin Frobisher.* London, 1867.

LVI: Markham, C. R., ed. *The Voyages of Sir James Lancaster, K^t., to the East Indies.* London, 1877.

LVII: Markham, C. R., ed. *The Hawkins' Voyages.* London, 1878.

LIX: Markham, A. H., ed. *The Voyages and Works of John Davis.* London, 1880.

LXIII: Markham, C. R., ed. *The Voyages of William Baffin, 1612–1622.* London, 1881.

LXV: Lefroy, Sir J. H., ed. *The Historye of the Bermudaes or Summer Islands.* London, 1882.

LXXII and Morgan, E. D., and C. H. Coote, eds. *Early Voyages and*
LXXIII: *Travels to Russia and Persia by Anthony Jenkinson and other Englishmen.* 2 vols. London, 1886.

LXXXVII: Bent, J. T., ed. *Early Voyages and Travels in the Levant.* London, 1893.

LXXXVIII Christy, Miller, ed. *The Voyages of Captain Luke Fox of*
and *Hull, and Captain Thomas James of Bristol, in Search of a*
LXXXIX: *North-West Passage, in 1631–1632.* 2 vols. London, 1894.

Second Series, Volumes

III: Warner, G. F., ed. *The Voyage of Robert Dudley . . . to the West Indies, 1594–1595.* London, 1899.

V: Satow, Sir Ernest M., ed. *The Voyage of Captain John Saris to Japan, 1613.* London, 1900.

VI: Ravenstein, E. G., ed. *The Strange Adventures of Andrew Battell. . . .* London, 1901. South American venture, 1589.

XXXIV: Nuttall, Zelia, ed. *New Light on Drake.* London, 1914.

LVI: Harlow, V. T., ed. *Colonising Expeditions to the West Indies and Guiana, 1623–1667.* London, 1925.

LX: Harris, Sir C. Alexander, ed. *A Relation of a Voyage to Guiana by Robert Harcourt, 1613.* London, 1928.

LXVII: Foster, Sir William, ed. *The Travels of John Sanderson in the Levant, 1584–1602.* London, 1931.

LXXI: Wright, I. A., ed. *Documents Concerning English Voyages to the Spanish Main.* London, 1932.

LXXV: Foster, Sir William, ed. *The Voyage of Thomas Best to the East Indies, 1612–1614.* London, 1934.

LXXXII: Foster, Sir William, ed. *The Voyage of Nicholas Downton to the East Indies, 1614–1615.* London, 1939.

LXXXIII Quinn, D. B., ed. *The Voyages and Colonising Enterprises of*
and *Sir Humphrey Gilbert.* 2 vols. London, 1940. (See also
LXXXIV: Cotton, *Exeter* . . . , under North-West Passage Ventures in the next section of the bibliography.)

LXXXV: Foster, Sir William, ed. *The Voyages of Sir James Lancaster to Brazil and the East Indies, 1591–1603.* London, 1940.

LXXXVI
and Blake, J. W., ed. *Europeans in West Africa, 1450–1650.* 2 vols.
LXXXVII: London, 1942.

LXXXVIII: Foster, Sir William, ed. *The Voyage of Sir Henry Middleton to the Moluccas, 1604–1606.* London, 1943.

XCIX: Wright, I. A., ed. *Further English Voyages to Spanish America, 1583–1594.* London, 1951.

CIII: Wright, L. B., and Virginia Freund, eds. *The Historie of Travell into Virginia Britania (1612) by William Strachey, gent.* London, 1953. Supersedes the edition of this work by R. H. Major in the *Hakluyt Society Publications,* 1st ser. (Vol. VI; London, 1849).

x CIV and Quinn, D. B., ed. *The Roanoke Voyages, 1584–1590.* 2 vols.
CV: London, 1955.

CXI: Andrews, K. R., ed. *English Privateering Voyages to the West Indies, 1588–1595.* Cambridge, England, 1959.

CXIII: Taylor, E. G. R., ed. *The Troublesome Voyage of Captain Edward Fenton, 1582–1583.* Cambridge, England, 1959.

Heralds' visitations of various counties of England in the sixteenth and seventeenth centuries, published in Vols. 73–75, 85–87, 89, 92, and 93 of the *Publications* of the Harleian Society; in Vols. 4–5 of the *Publications* of the Norfolk Record Society; in Vol. 8 of the *Publications* of the Lincoln Record Society; in Vols. 122, 133, 144, and 146 of the *Publications* of the Surtees Society; and in J. L. Vivian, ed. *The Visitation of the County of Devon* (Exeter, 1895).

Hopwood, C. H., ed. *Middle Temple Records.* 4 vols. London, 1904–1905.

House of Commons Records:

Return. Members of Parliament . . . *1213–1702.* 2 vols. Parliamentary Papers, 62 (London, 1878), together with the "Supplementary Returns" and corrections compiled by the researchers at the History of Parliament Trust in Tavistock Square, London.

The Journals of the House of Commons. Vol. I, London, 1803.

Notestein, Wallace, F. H. Relf, and Hartley Simpson, eds. *Commons Debates 1621.* 7 vols. New Haven, 1935.

Also the following unpublished theses and dissertations, available at the Institute of Historical Research, University of London:

Davy, C. M. "The Personnel of Parliament, 1597." University of Manchester (1927?).

Gabriel, R. C. "Members of the House of Commons, 1586–1587." University of London, 1954.

Matthews, H. "Personnel of the Parliament of 1584–1585." University of London, 1948.

Mort, M. K. "The Personnel of the House of Commons in 1601." University of London, 1952.

Robert, J. C. "The Parliamentary Representation of Devon and Dorset, 1559–1601." University of London, 1958.

Thomas, J. D., "A General Survey of the Parliamentary Elections of 1625–1628." University of London, 1952.

Trafford, E. E., "Personnel of the Parliament of 1593." University of London, 1948.

Lee, Sir Sidney, and Sir Leslie Stephen, eds. *The Dictionary of National Biography.* London, 1885–1901. See, too, *Corrections and Additions to the Dictionary of National Biography,* collected by the Institute of Historical Research, University of London (Boston, 1966).

Purchas, Samuel, *Hakluytus Posthumus or Purchas His Pilgrimes.* 4 vols. London, 1625. Standard modern ed. in 20 vols., Glasgow, 1905–1907.

Shaw, W. A., compiler. *The Knights of England.* 2 vols. London, 1906.

Stow, John, *A Survey of London, by John Stow,* ed. C. L. Kingsford. 2 vols. Oxford, 1908.

The Victoria History of the Counties of England, various volumes (London, 1900 and thereafter). There is no space here to enumerate all the local studies used to identify the individuals in the list. The Livery Company Records, the Heralds' Visitations, the Parliamentary Returns, and the Victoria County History were the four most abundant sources of information. Among other sources some of the more useful (Alexander Brown's *Genesis, The Complete Baronetage,* and *The Complete Peerage,* for example) have already been mentioned, and the most important local studies will be listed below. However, the multitude of genealogical articles, pious family histories, and local studies — consulted primarily in the Library of the Institute of Historical Research at the University of London, which is superbly designed, notably in its "London" room, to serve those with interests in specific localities or families — cannot all be listed here.

(ii) *Sources for Particular Groups* (see also *Hakluyt Society Publications,* above)

African Ventures

De Castries, Le Comte Henri, ed. *Les Sources Inédites de l'Histoire du Maroc: Archives et Bibliothèques d'Angleterre.* 2 vols. Paris, 1918 and 1925.

Donnan, Elizabeth, ed., *Documents Illustrative of the History of the Slave Trade to America.* 4 vols. Washington, 1930–1935. Volume I.

Bermuda and Virginia Companies

Hazard, Ebenezer, ed. *Historical Collections.* Vol. I. Philadelphia, 1792. Virginia Company.

Jester, A. L. *Adventurers of Purse and Person, Virginia, 1607–1625.* Princeton, 1965.

Johnson, A. H. *The History of the Worshipful Company of the Drapers of London.* Vol. IV. Oxford, 1922. Pages 85–90. Bermuda, Virginia, and North-West Passage Companies.

Kingsbury, S. M., ed. *The Records of the Virginia Company of London*. 4 vols. Washington, 1906–1935. Bermuda and Virginia Companies: documents from the Ferrar Papers in the Cambridge University Library.

Lefroy, J. H., ed. *Memorials of the Discovery and Early Settlement of the Bermudas or Somers Islands, 1515–1685*. Vol. I: *1515–1652*. London, 1877. Bermuda Company.

Smith, John. *The Generall Historie of Virginia*. London, 1624. Pages 130–138: Virginia Company.

(See also Arber, *Smith . . .* , under *New England Ventures*, and Cotton, *Exeter . . .* , under *North-West Passage Ventures*, below.)

Canadian Ventures

Acts of the Privy Council, Colonial. Volume I, pp. 136–144.

Historical Manuscripts Commission. 12th Report. Cowper, pp. 375–377.

Drake's Voyages

Bigges, Walter, *Expeditio Francisci Draki in Indias Occidentales A.M.D. LXXXV. . . .* Leyden, 1588.

Corbett, Sir Julian S., ed. *Papers Relating to the Navy during the Spanish War, 1585–1587*. London: Navy Records Society, vol. XI, 1898.

Leng, Robert, *Sir Francis Drake's Memorable Service Done against the Spaniards in 1587*. Ed. Clarence Hopper. *The Camden Miscellany*. Vol. V. London: The Camden Society, 1864.

Oppenheim, Michael, ed. *The Naval Tracts of Sir William Monson*. Vol. I. London: Navy Records Society, vol. XXII, 1902. Pages 121–134.

Taylor, E. G. R., "The Missing Draft Project of Drake's Voyage of 1577–1580," *The Geographic Journal*, 75 (1930), 46–47.

Temple, Sir Richard C., ed. *The World Encompassed and Analogous Contemporary Documents Concerning Sir Francis Drake's Circumnavigation of the World*. London, 1926.

East India Company

Foster, William, ed. *Early Travels in India 1583–1619*. London, 1921.

Rymer, Thomas, ed. *Foedera*. Vol. XVI. London, 1715. Page 582.

Stevens, Henry, ed. *The Dawn of British Trade to the East Indies as Recorded in the Court Minutes of the East India Company, 1599–1603*. London, 1886.

Eastland Company

Sellers, Maud, ed. *The Acts and Ordinances of the Eastland Company*. London: The Camden Society, 1906.

Frobisher and Gilbert

See Cotton, *Exeter . . .* , under *North-West Passage Ventures*, below.

Guiana

Acts of the Privy Council, Colonial. Vol. I: *1613–1680*. Pages 25 and 37.

Domestic Correspondence, Charles I. XXIV. Page 302.

Harlow, V. T., ed. *Raleigh's Last Voyage.* London, 1932.

Irish (Londonderry)

Hill, George, ed. *An Historical Account of the Plantation in Ulster at the Commencement of the Seventeenth Century 1608–1620.* Belfast, 1877.

Historical Manuscripts Commission. Carew MSS. Vol. VI: *1603–1624.* Pages 321–332.

Phillips, Sir Thomas. *Londonderry and the London Companies, 1609–1629.* Belfast, 1928.

Levant Company

Historical Manuscripts Commission. Salisbury MSS. Volume X, pp. 214–217 and vol. XIX, p. 266.

Massachusetts Bay Company

Shurtleff, N. B., ed. *Records of the Governor and Company of the Massachusetts Bay in New England.* Vol. I: *1628–1641.* Boston, 1853.

Merchant Adventurers (and merchants' names in general)

Cawston, G., and A. H. Keane. *The Early Chartered Companies.* London and New York, 1896. Pages 254–277.

Clode, C. M., ed. *Memorials of the Guild of Merchant Taylors.* . . . London, 1875.

McGrath, Patrick, ed. *Merchants and Merchandise in Seventeenth-Century Bristol.* Bristol: Bristol Record Society, 1955.

————. *Records Relating to the Society of Merchant Venturers of the City of Bristol in the Seventeenth Century.* Bristol: Bristol Record Society, 1952.

Millican, Percy, ed. *The Register of the Freemen of Norwich, 1548–1713.* Norwich, 1934.

See also Cotton, *Exeter* . . . , under *North-West Passage Ventures,* below, and note 7 to Chapter 2, above.

Muscovy Company

Historical Manuscripts Commission. Salisbury MSS. Volume V, pp. 462–463.

New England Ventures

Adams, C. F., ed. *The New English Canaan of Thomas Morton.* Boston: The Prince Society, 1883. Page 6.

Arber, Edward, ed. *Travels and Works of Captain John Smith.* (New ed. by A. G. Bradley, 2 vols.; Edinburgh, 1910.) Virginia, Plymouth, and New England ventures.

Baxter, J. P., ed. *Sir Ferdinando Gorges and His Province of Maine.* 3 vols. Boston: The Prince Society, 1890.

Dean, J. W., ed. *Captain John Mason, the Founder of New Hampshire.* Boston: The Prince Society, 1887.

Deane, Charles. "Records of the Council for New England," *Proceedings of the American Antiquarian Society* (1875), pp. 49–63. See, too, "Records of the Council for New England," *ibid.* (1867), pp. 56–131.

Farnham, Mary, ed. *Documentary History of the State of Maine.* Collections and Proceedings of the Maine Historical Society. 2 vols. Portland, 1901. Volume I, pages 20–128.

———. *Documents Relating to the Territorial History of Maine, 1603–1871.* Portland: Collections and Proceedings of the Maine Historical Society, 1900. Pages 1–136.

Slafter, E. F., ed. *Sir William Alexander and American Colonization.* Boston: The Prince Society, 1873.

Thayer, H. O., ed. *The Sagahadoc Colony.* Portland: Gorges Society, 1892.

North-West Passage Ventures

Cotton, William, ed. *An Elizabethan Guild of the City of Exeter.* Exeter, 1873. Pages 82–87, *passim:* Davis, Virginia (Raleigh), and Gilbert.

Stefansson, Vilhjalmur, and Eloise McCaskill, eds. *The Three Voyages of Martin Frobisher.* 2 vols. London, 1938. Fuller information than in *Hakluyt Society Publications,* 1st ser., Vol. XXXVIII.

See, too, Johnson, *Drapers* . . . , under *Bermuda and Virginia Companies,* above.

Plymouth

Bradford, William. *Of Plymouth Plantation, 1620–1647.* Ed. S. E. Morison. New York, 1953.

See also Arber, *Smith* . . . , under *New England Ventures,* above.

Privateering

Drake, W. R. "Notes upon the Capture of 'The Great Carrack' in 1592," *Archaeologia,* 33 (1849), 209–240.

Kingsford, C. L. "The Taking of the Madre de Dios." *Naval Miscellany.* London: Navy Records Society, vol. XL, 1912. Pages 85–121.

Mainwaring, G. E., ed. *The Life and Works of Sir Henry Mainwaring.* 2 vols. London: Navy Records Society, vols. LIV, LVI, 1920, 1922.

See, too *Drake's Voyages,* above.

Royal Commission for Trade

Rymer, Thomas, ed. *Foedera.* London, 1717. Volume XVII, page 410.

Spanish Company

Shillington, V. M., and A. B. W. Chapman, eds. *The Commercial Relations of England and Portugal.* London, n.d. The excerpts from the 1577 charter printed on pp. 313–326 must be used with extreme caution, as there are numerous errors: for example, five of the totals are incorrect, and "Stavely" appears both as "Sladeby" and as "Stavely."

Virginia Company

See *Bermuda and Virginia Companies,* above; and also Arber, *Smith* . . . , under *New England Ventures;* and Cotton, *Exeter* . . . , under *North-West Passage Ventures,* above.

(iii) *Other Contemporary Works or Published Documents of Particular Importance*
Only those writings which, in addition to the ones already listed, proved to be of major interest are included here. Complete bibliographies of Elizabethan and early Stuart literature dealing with overseas exploits and related matters can be found in the books by E. G. R.

Taylor, John Parker, and D. C. Collins, under *General Works on the Expansion,* below.

Collections of the Massachusetts Historical Society. 3rd ser. Vol. III. Boston, 1843. Treatises by John Brereton, Edward Hayes, and the elder Richard Hakluyt concerning Elizabethan voyages to Virginia and New England.

Craven, W. F. "Lewis Hughes' 'Plaine and True Relation of the Goodness of God Towards the Sommer Islands,'" *William and Mary Quarterly,* 17 (1937), 56–89.

Digby, Sir Kenelm. *Journal of a Voyage into the Mediterranean by Sir Kenelm Digby.* Ed. J. Bruce. London: The Camden Society, 1868.

Digges, Sir Dudley, *The Defence of Trade. In a Letter to Sir Thomas Smith Knight, Governor of the East-India Companie, &c. From one of that Societie.* London, 1615.

Digges, Dudley and Thomas Digges. *Four Paradoxes, or Politique Discourses.* London, 1604.

Eburne, Richard. *A Plaine Pathway to Plantations.* London, 1624. Propaganda for Newfoundland.

Eden, Richard, ed. and trans. *The History of Travayle in the West and East Indies.* . . . New ed. by Richard Willes. London, 1577. A translation of Peter Martyr's collections of Spanish and Portuguese voyages, with an interesting dedication by Eden to the Countess of Bedford.

Force, Peter, ed. *Tracts and Other Papers.* . . . Vols. I and III. New York, 1947. Reprint of the original, 1836–1846. Pamphlets about Virginia and Bermuda.

Foster, Sir William, ed. *Early Travels in India 1583–1619.* London, 1921.

Gentleman, Tobias. *Englands Way to Win Wealth, and to Employ Ships and Marriners.* London, 1614. Propaganda for the fisheries, showing bitter jealousy of the Dutch. Pages 5–19.

Greepe, Thomas. *The True and Perfecte Newes of . . . Syr Frauncis Drake . . . 1587.* Ed. D. W. Water. Hartford, 1955.

Hacket, Thomas, trans. *The Newfound World, or Antarctike . . . ,* by André Thevet. London, 1568. With an interesting dedication by Hacket to Sir Henry Sidney.

Hamor, Ralph. *A True Discourse of the Present State of Virginia.* London, 1615. Modern ed. by A. L. Rowse, Richmond, Virginia, 1957.

Herbert, Thomas. *Travels in Persia, 1627–1629.* Ed. Sir William Foster. London, 1928.

Jenner, G. F. B. "A Spanish Account of Drake's Voyages," *English Historical Review* [henceforward E.H.R.], 16 (1901), 46–66.

Levett, Christopher. *A Voyage into New England.* London, 1628. Reprinted in J. P. Baxter, ed., *Christopher Levett of York.* Portland: Gorges Society, 1893.

Locke, J. C., ed. *The First Englishmen in India.* London, 1930.

M———, R———. *Newes of Sr Walter Rauleigh. With the true Description of Guiana.* London, 1618.

Malynes, Gerard. *The Center of the Circle of Commerce. Or, a Refutation of a Treatise, Intituled the Circle of Commerce.* . . . London, 1623.

――――. *Consuetudo, Vel Lex Mercatoria, Or the Ancient Law-Merchant.* . . . London, 1622.

――――. *England's View, in the Unmasking of Two Paradoxes.* London, 1603.

――――. *The Maintenance of Free Trade.* . . . London, 1622.

――――. *A Treatise of the Canker of Englands Common Wealth.* London, 1601.

Misselden, Edward. *The Circle of Commerce, Or the Ballance of Trade, in Defence of Free Trade: Opposed to Malynes.* . . . London, 1623.

――――. *Free Trade, Or, The Meanes to Make Trade Flourish.* . . . London, 1622.

Mun, Thomas. *A Discourse of Trade, From England unto the East-Indies.* . . . London, 1621.

――――. *England's Treasure by Forreign Trade.* London, 1664. Modern ed. by the Economic History Society, Oxford, 1933.

Nicholas, Thomas, trans. *The Pleasant Historie of the Conquest of the Weast India, Now Called New Spayne.* London, 1578. A translation of the second part of Francisco López de Gómara's *La Istoria de las Indias y Conquista de Mexico,* with an interesting dedication by Nicholas to Walsingham.

Nicholl, John. *An Houre Glasse of Indian Newes.* London, 1607. On the 1605 Guiana colony.

Peacham, Henry. *The Compleat Gentleman.* London, 1622. The London edition of 1634 was reprinted in a modern ed. by G. S. Gordon, Oxford, 1906.

R――――, I――――. *The Trades Increase.* London, 1615. Propaganda for the fisheries, with attacks on the East India, French, Muscovy, and Virginia Companies for hampering fishermen. Pages 52–53.

Rosier, James. *A True Relation of the Most Prosperous Voyage made . . . by Captaine George Waymouth.* . . . London, 1605. Modern ed. by H. S. Burrage in *Rosier's Relation of Waymouth's Voyage to the Coast of Maine, 1605,* published by the Gorges Society, Portland, 1887.

Sandys, Sir Edwin. *Europae Speculum. Or A View or Survey of the State of Religion in the Westerne Parts of the World.* . . . The Hague, 1629. First published as *A Relation of the State of Religion* . . . , London, 1605.

Slafter, E. F., ed. *Sir William Alexander and American Colonization.* Boston, 1873. Includes Alexander's *An Encouragement to Colonies* (1624).

Stow, John. *A Survey of London.* London, 1603. Modern ed. by C. L. Kingsford; 2 vols., Oxford, 1908.

Strachey, William. *For the Colony in Virginea Britannia. Lawes Divine, Morall and Martiall, &c.* London, 1612.

Tawney, R. H., and E. E. Power, eds. *Tudor Economic Documents.* 3 vols. London: University of London Historical Series, 1924.

Wheeler, John. *A Treatise of Commerce.* . . . Middleburgh, 1601. Propaganda for the Merchant Adventurers.

Whitbourne, Richard. *A Discourse Containing a Loving Invitation . . . to all such as shall be Adventurers . . . for the Advancement of His Maiesties . . . Plantation in the New-found-land.* London, 1622.

Wilson, Thomas. *A Discourse Upon Usury.* London, 1572. Modern ed., with a brilliant 170-page introduction on sixteenth-century credit, by R. H. Tawney, London, 1925.

Wolfe, John, trans. *John Huighen van Linschoten his Discours of Voyages into ye Easte & West Indies.* . . . London, 1598. A translation of Linschoten's *Itinerario* . . . with an interesting dedication by Wolfe to Julius Caesar.

C: THE PRINCIPAL SECONDARY LITERATURE

(i) *General Works on the Expansion and Its Background*
Including the main general social and economic studies of the period, surveys of the expansion or of such major related subjects as shipping, and important specialized works that have a bearing on the expansion or the investors.

Andrews, C. M. *British Committees, Commissions, and Councils of Trade and Plantations, 1622–1675.* Johns Hopkins University Studies in History and Political Science. Baltimore, 1908.

———. *The Colonial Period of American History.* Vol. I. New Haven, 1934. The most solid and useful survey of the voyages and settlements in North America in the period under study.

Ashton, Robert. *The Crown and the Money Market, 1603–1640.* Oxford, 1960. A great deal of information on the credit system and customs farming.

Aylmer, G. E. *The King's Servants: The Civil Service of Charles I, 1625–1642.* London, 1961. Information about many of the investors.

Barley, M. W. *The English Farmhouse and Cottage.* London, 1961.

———. "Farmhouses and Cottages, 1550–1725," *Economic History Review* [henceforward *Ec.H.R.*], 2nd ser., 7 (1955), 291–306. Evidence in both of Barley's works of a considerable building boom in the countryside during the period of the overseas expansion.

Barnes, T. G. *Somerset 1625–1640: A County's Government during the "Personal Rule."* Cambridge, Mass., 1961. Very useful for the background of a number of investors.

Bates, E. S. *Touring in 1600.* Boston and New York, 1911. Travel conditions, mainly in Europe.

Beer, G. L. *The Commercial Policy of England toward the American Colonies.* Columbia Studies in History, Economics and Public Laws. New York, 1893.

———. *The Origins of the British Colonial System, 1578–1660.* New York, 1922. First ed., 1908. A good general survey.

Bell, Douglas. *Elizabethan Seamen.* London, New York, and Toronto, 1936. A good blood-and-thunder account.

Beveridge, Lord William, and others. *Prices and Wages in England from the Twelfth to the Nineteenth Century.* London, 1939.

Bowden, P. J. *The Wool Trade in Tudor and Stuart England.* London, 1962.

Brebner, J. B. *The Explorers of North America, 1492–1806.* London, 1933.

Brenner, Y. S. "The Inflation of Prices in England, 1551–1650," *Ec.H.R.*, 2nd ser., 15 (1962), 266–284.

Brett-James, N. G. *The Growth of Stuart London.* London, 1935.

Brooke, C. F. T. "Some Pre-Armada Propagandist Poetry in England (1585–1586)," *Proceedings of the American Philosophical Society* [henceforth *A.P.S.*], 85 (1942), 71–83. Evidence of growing anti-Spanish feeling and admiration for Drake.

x Campbell, Mildred. *The English Yeoman under Elizabeth and the Early Stuarts.* New Haven, 1942. An invaluable analysis.

Chalklin, C. W. *Seventeenth-Century Kent: A Social and Economic History.* London, 1965. See pp. 191–217 for a general account of the gentry of the county.

Chatterton, E. K. *English Seamen and the Colonization of America.* London, 1930. A solid survey.

Cheyney, E. P. *A History of England from the Defeat of the Armada to the Death of Elizabeth.* Vol. I. London, 1914. Pages 311–459 contain an excellent detailed account of the expansion during Elizabeth's reign.

———. "Some English Conditions Surrounding the Settlement of Virginia," *The American Historical Review* [henceforward *A.H.R.*], 12 (1907), 507–528. A suggestive essay.

Clapham, Sir John. *A Concise Economic History of Britain from the Earliest Times to 1750.* Cambridge, England, 1949. Especially Book III.

Clark, G. N. *The Wealth of England from 1496 to 1760.* Oxford, 1947.

Clifton-Taylor, Alec. *The Pattern of English Building.* London, 1962. Evidence of increased building in Elizabethan and Jacobean times.

Clowes, Sir William L., Sir Clements Markham, A. T. Mahan, H. W. Wilson, Theodore Roosevelt, Edward Fraser, and L. C. Laughton, *The Royal Navy, A History from the Earliest Times to the Present.* 7 vols. London, 1897–1903. Vols. I and II.

Coleman, D. C. "Labour in the English Economy of the Seventeenth Century," *Ec.H.R.*, 2nd ser., 8 (1956), 280–295.

Collier, J. P., and W. H. Smyth, "Communications," *Archaeologia*, 33 (1849), 191–208. On the cost of Elizabeth's navy.

Collins, D. C. *A Handlist of News Pamphlets 1590–1610.* London, 1943.

Connell-Smith, Gordon. *Forerunners of Drake: A Study of English Trade with Spain in the Early Tudor Period.* London, 1954.

Corbett, Sir Julian S. *Drake and the Tudor Navy, with a History of the Rise of England as a Maritime Power.* 2 vols. London, New York, and Bombay, 1888.

———. *England in the Mediterranean: A Study of the Rise and Influence of British Power within the Straits, 1603–1713.* Vol. I. London, New York, and Bombay, 1904.

————. *The Successors of Drake*. London, 1900. The exploits of the 1595–1603 period.

Crouse, N. M. *In Quest of the Western Ocean*. New York, 1928. The search for a route to the Pacific.

Darby, H. C. *The Draining of the Fens*. 2nd ed. Cambridge, England, 1956.

Davis, Ralph. "England and the Mediterranean, 1570–1670." *Essays in the Economic and Social History of Tudor and Stuart England in Honour of R. H. Tawney*. Ed. F. J. Fisher. Cambridge, 1961. Pages 117–137.

x ————. *The Rise of the English Shipping Industry in the Seventeenth and Eighteenth Centuries*. London, 1962.

Dietz, F. C. *English Public Finance 1558–1641*. New York, 1932.

Dodd, A. H. *Studies in Stuart Wales*. Cardiff, 1952. Especially pp. 14–38.

Edmundson, George. *Anglo-Dutch Rivalry during the First Half of the Seventeenth Century*. Oxford, 1911.

Finch, M. E. *The Wealth of Five Northamptonshire Families, 1540–1640*. Oxford: Northamptonshire Record Society, 1956. Important case studies of gentry.

Fisher, F. J. "Commercial Trends and Policy in Sixteenth-Century England," *Ec.H.R.*, 10 (1939–1940), 95–117.

————. "The Development of London as a Centre of Conspicuous Consumption in the Sixteenth and Seventeenth Centuries," *Transactions of the Royal Historical Society*, 4th ser., 30 (1948), 37–50. The beginnings of the "season."

————. "London's Export Trade in the Early Seventeenth Century," *Ec.H.R.*, 2nd ser., 3 (1950), 151–161.

————. "The Sixteenth and Seventeenth Centuries: The Dark Ages in English Economic History?" *Economica*, new ser., 24 (1957), 2–18.

Foster, Sir William. *England's Quest of Eastern Trade*. London, 1933. The search for a direct route to the Far East in Tudor and early Stuart times.

Fox Bourne, H. R. *English Seamen under the Tudors*. 2 vols. London, 1868.

François, M. E. "The Social and Economic Development of Halifax, 1558–1640," *Proceedings of the Leeds Philosophical and Literary Society*, 11 (1964–1966), 217–280.

x Friis, Astrid. *Alderman Cockayne's Project and the Cloth Trade*. Copenhagen and London, 1927. Much more than a mere study of the New Merchant Adventurers, this massive work is virtually an economic history of James I's reign, with a great deal of valuable information about many of the individual investors in my list.

Froude, J. A. *English Seamen in the Sixteenth Century*. New York, 1895.

Gay, E. F. "The Temples of Stowe and Their Debts," *The Huntington Library Quarterly*, 1 (1937–1938), 367–390, and 2 (1938–1939), 399–438.

Gill, Crispin. *Plymouth: A New History*. Newton Abbot, 1966.

Gillespie, J. E. *The Influence of Overseas Expansion on England to 1700*. Columbia University Studies in History, Economics and Public Law. New York, 1920.

Gould, J. D. "The Trade Depression of the Early 1620's," *Ec.H.R.*, 2nd ser., 7 (1954), 81–90.

―――. "Y. S. Brenner on Prices: A Comment," *Ec.H.R.*, 2nd ser., 16 (1963), 351–360.

Gras, N. S. B. *Business and Capitalism*. New York, 1939.

Gross, Charles. *The Gild Merchant*. 2 vols. Oxford, 1890.

Richard Hakluyt & His Successors. The Hakluyt Society, 2nd ser., vol. XCIII. London, 1946. Essays on Elizabethan and Jacobean geographers and propagandizers of overseas ventures.

Hannay, David. *The Great Chartered Companies*. London, 1926. A brisk survey.

x Harper, L. A. *The English Navigation Laws: A Seventeenth-Century Experiment in Social Engineering*. New York, 1939.

Heckscher, E. F. *Mercantilism*. Trans. Mendel Shapiro. Rev. ed. by E. F. Söderlund, 2 vols. London and New York, 1955. This second edition discusses and takes into account the large body of criticism that followed the appearance of the first edition (1934–1935 in English). Despite some oversimplification, it remains the best general treatment of the subject.

Hill, J. W. F. *Tudor and Stuart Lincoln*. Cambridge, 1956. Especially pp. 128–144.

Hinton, R. W. K. "The Mercantile System in the Time of Thomas Mun," *Ec.H.R.*, 2nd ser., 7 (1955), 277–290.

Hoskins, W. G. "The Elizabethan Merchants of Exeter," in *Elizabethan Government and Society: Essays Presented to Sir John Neale*. Ed. S. T. Bindoff, Joel Hurstfield, and C. H. Williams. London, 1961. Pages 163–187.

―――. *Provincial England: Essays in Social and Economic History*. London, 1963. Revealing studies of local history; see especially chaps. v, vii, and viii on Leicester, rural building, and Leicestershire farmers in our period of study.

Howard, C. M. *English Travellers of the Renaissance*. New York, 1913. Especially chaps. i–iv.

Innes, A. D. *The Maritime and Colonial Expansion of England under the Stuarts (1603–1714)*. London, 1932. A very simple narrative.

Insh, G. P. *Scottish Colonial Schemes, 1620–1686*. Glasgow, 1922. The first part of the book contains good accounts of the projects of Alexander, Gorges, and Mason.

Jones, Howard Mumford, "The Colonial Impulse: An Analysis of the 'Promotion' Literature of Colonization," *A.P.S.*, 90 (1946), 131–161.

―――. "Origins of the Colonial Idea in England," *A.P.S.*, 85 (1942), 448–465.

Jordan, W. K. *The Charities of London 1480–1660: The Aspirations and the Achievements of the Urban Society*. London, 1960. Considerable information about many of the investors and on the London background.

―――. *Philanthropy in England, 1480–1660: A Study of the Changing Pattern of English Social Aspirations*. London, 1959.

Keith, Theodora. *Commercial Relations of England and Scotland, 1603–1707.* Cambridge, 1910.

Kellogg, L. P. "The American Colonial Charter. A Study of English Administration in Relation Thereto, Chiefly after 1688," *Annual Report of the American Historical Association for the Year 1903,* 1 (1904), 185–341. See pp. 191–198 for the pre-Civil War period.

x Kelso, Ruth. *The Doctrine of the English Gentleman in the Sixteenth Century.* University of Illinois Studies in Language and Literature. Urbana, 1929.

Knorr, K. E. *British Colonial Theories, 1570–1850.* Toronto, 1944. A good introduction, though the analysis of the colonists' motives is rather too simple.

x Lach, D. F. *Asia in the Making of Europe.* Vol. I. Chicago, 1965.

Lang, R. G. "The Greater Merchants of London in the Early Seventeenth Century." Unpub. diss. Oxford University, 1963. A wealth of detailed information.

Latimer, John. *The History of the Society of Merchant Venturers of the City of Bristol.* Bristol, 1903.

———. *Sixteenth-Century Bristol.* Bristol, 1908.

x Lipson, Ephraim. *The Economic History of England.* Vol. III: *The Age of Mercantilism.* 3rd ed. London, 1943. The standard general history.

Loomie, A. J. "Religion and Elizabethan Commerce with Spain," *The Catholic Historical Review,* 50 (1964), 27–51.

Lucas, Sir C. P. *The Beginnings of English Overseas Enterprise: A Prelude to the Empire.* Oxford, 1917. A good introduction to the Staplers, the Merchant Adventurers, and the Eastland Company.

———. *Introduction to a Historical Geography of the British Colonies.* Oxford, 1887.

———. *Religion, Colonising & Trade: The Driving Forces of the Old Empire.* London, 1930.

Lucas, Sir C. P., H. E. Egerton, J. D. Rogers, and P. E. Roberts, eds. *A Historical Geography of the British Colonies.* 9 vols. Oxford, 1888–1920.

Lythe, S. G. E. *The Economy of Scotland in its European Setting, 1550–1625.* Edinburgh, 1960.

MacCaffrey, W. T. *Exeter, 1540–1640: The Growth of an English County Town.* Cambridge, Mass., 1958. Especially pp. 171–173 and 246–283.

MacInnes, C. M. *England and Slavery.* Bristol, 1934.

———. *A Gateway of Empire.* Bristol, 1939. Bristol's role in the expansion.

Mathew, David. *The Social Structure in Caroline England.* Oxford, 1948.

McCann, F. T. *English Discovery of America to 1585.* New York, 1952. Changing attitudes toward overseas ventures.

McIntyre, R. A. "The Role of the English Merchant in the Promotion of Discovery and Colonial Enterprise, 1496–1616." Unpub. diss. University of Minnesota, 1947. Much useful information on the financing of Elizabethan voyages.

Mercer, Eric. "The Houses of the Gentry." *Past and Present,* no. 5 (1954), pp. 11–32. Despite some curious interpretations of England's social and economic structure, a great deal of interesting material about the boom in house building in the period under consideration.

Millard, A. M. "Analyses of Port Books Recording Merchandises Imported into the Port of London . . . 1588–1640" Manuscript 1959. Photocopy, Widener Library, Harvard University.

———. "The Imports of London, 1600–1640." Typescript. Photocopy, Widener Library, Harvard University.

Miller, L. R. "New Evidence on the Shipping and Imports of London, 1601–1602," *Quarterly Journal of Economics,* 41 (1927), 740–760.

Mousley, J. E., "The Fortunes of Some Gentry Families of Elizabethan Sussex," *Ec.H.R.,* 2nd ser., 11 (1959), 467–483.

Neill, E. D. *The English Colonization of America during the Seventeenth Century.* London and Edinburgh, 1871. Mainly on Virginia, but one of the most solid of the nineteenth-century accounts.

x Notestein, Wallace. *The English People on the Eve of Colonization 1603–1630.* New York, 1954. The best general survey of English society in this period.

Oakeshott, Walter. *Founded upon the Seas.* Cambridge, England, 1942. A good narrative of the chief exploits of Tudor and Jacobean seamen.

Oppenheim, Michael. *A History of the Administration of the Royal Navy and Merchant Shipping in Relation to the Navy.* Vol. I: *1509–1660.* London, 1896.

x Parker, John. *Books to Build an Empire.* Amsterdam, 1966. A survey of the overseas propaganda and travel literature of the period.

Parks, G. B. "The Forerunners of Hakluyt," *Washington University Studies,* 13 (1926), 335–370.

x Parry, J. H. *The Age of Reconnaissance.* Cleveland and New York, 1963. The best general account of the Europe-wide movement of which the English expansion was a part.

Pearl, Valerie. *London and the Outbreak of the Puritan Revolution: City Government and National Politics, 1625–1643.* Oxford, 1961. An important analysis of the City's problems and leaders, with an excellent biographical appendix on the aldermen.

x Penrose, Boies. *Travel and Discovery in the Renaissance, 1420–1620.* Cambridge, Mass., 1952.

———. *Tudor and Early Stuart Voyaging.* Washington, 1962.

———. *Urbane Travellers, 1591–1635.* Philadelphia, 1942. Accounts of the travels of seven Englishmen, mainly in the Middle and Far East.

Phelps Brown, E. H., and S. V. Hopkins. "Wage-Rates and Prices: Evidence for Population Pressure in the Sixteenth Century," *Economica,* new ser., 24 (1957), 289–306. See also the articles by the same authors in the same journal, 22 (1955), 195–206, and 26 (1959), 18–38.

Pollard, A. F., "The Elizabethans and the Empire," *Proceedings of the British Academy,* 10 (1921–1923), 139–156.

Quinn, D. B. *The New Found Land: The English Contribution to the Discovery of North America.* Providence, Rhode Island, 1965.

————. "Sir Thomas Smith (1513–1577) and the Beginnings of English Colonial Theory." *A.P.S.*, 89 (1945), 543–560.

Rabb, T. K. "Investment in English Overseas Enterprise, 1575–1630," *Ec.H.R.*, 2nd ser., 19 (1966), 70–81.

————. "Sir Edwin Sandys and the Parliament of 1604," *A.H.R,* 69 (1964), 646–670, especially pp. 661–669.

Ramsay, G. D. *English Overseas Trade during the Centuries of Emergence.* London, 1957. An excellent general introduction.

Rich, E. E. "The Population of Elizabethan England," *Ec.H.R.*, 2nd ser., 2 (1949–1950), 247–265.

Rich, E. E. and C. H. Wilson, eds. *The Cambridge Economic History of Europe.* Vol. IV: *The Economy of Expanding Europe in the Sixteenth and Seventeenth Centuries.* Cambridge, England, 1967. An excellent survey.

Richmond, Sir Herbert W., and E. A. Hughes. *The Navy as an Instrument of Policy, 1558–1727.* Cambridge, England, 1953.

Rogers, J. E. T. *A History of Agriculture and Prices in England.* Vol. VI. Oxford, 1887.

x Rose, J. H., A. P. Newton, and E. A. Benians, eds. *The Cambridge History of the British Empire.* Vol. I: *The Old Empire.* Cambridge, England, 1929. The standard detailed survey of the ventures of the period under consideration. See, too, vol. IV (1929).

Rowse, A. L. *The Expansion of Elizabethan England.* New York, 1955. A good narrative of the more spectacular exploits, but no mention of the East India, Eastland, or Levant Companies.

————. *The Elizabethans and America.* London, 1959. A good introduction.

————. *Tudor Cornwall: Portrait of a Society.* London, 1941.

Ruddock, A. A. *Italian Merchants and Shipping in Southampton, 1270–1600.* Southampton, 1951.

Russell, Percy. *Dartmouth: A History of the Port and Town.* New York, 1950.

————. *The Good Town of Totnes.* Exeter: The Devonshire Association, n.d. [1964?].

Scott, W. R. *The Constitution and Finance of English, Scottish and Irish Joint-Stock Companies to 1720.* 3 vols. Cambridge, 1910–1912. The great work on the organization of the expansion. Although (as can be seen in this bibliography) much has been done since 1912 on England's social and economic history and on individual companies and adventurers, it will also be seen that no major efforts of research have been devoted to the organization of the expansion, in contrast to the constant attention devoted to exploits at sea and overseas.

Seeley, J. R. *The Expansion of England.* London, 1883. On p. 8 is the famous "fit of absence of mind" remark about England's empire, an interpretation that is hardly supported by recent work in the field.

Simpson, Alan. *The Wealth of the Gentry, 1540–1660: East Anglian Studies.* Cambridge, England and Chicago, 1961. See in particular the chapter on the rise of Thomas Cullum, the London merchant.

Stephens, W. B. "Merchant Companies and Commercial Policy in Exeter, 1625–88," *Report and Transactions of the Devonshire Association*, 86 (1954), 137–160.

―――. *Seventeenth-Century Exeter*. Exeter, 1958.

Stone, Lawrence. *The Crisis of the Aristocracy 1558–1641*. Oxford, 1965. A study in depth of the economic and social situation of the English peerage.

―――, "Elizabethan Overseas Trade," *Ec.H.R.*, 2nd ser., 2 (1949–1950), 30–58.

Stonex, A. B. "Money Lending and Money-Lenders in England during the 16th and 17th Centuries." In *Schelling Anniversary Papers*. New York, 1923. Pages 263–285.

Stoye, J. W. *English Travellers Abroad, 1604–1667: Their Influence in English Society and Politics*. London, 1952.

x Supple, B. E. *Commercial Crisis and Change in England 1600–1642: A Study in the Instability of a Mercantile Economy*. Cambridge, England, 1959. The most important recent study of the economic history of this period.

―――. "Currency and Commerce in the Early Seventeenth Century," *Ec.H.R.*, 2nd ser., 10 (1957), 239–255.

Tawney, R. H. *The Agrarian Problem in the Sixteenth Century*. London, 1912. Still the most valuable general study of the economic situation of those who derived an income from agriculture or rents.

x Taylor, E. G. R. *Tudor Geography 1485–1583*. London, 1930.

x ―――. *Late Tudor and Early Stuart Geography, 1583–1650*. London, 1934.

x Thirsk, Joan, ed. *The Agrarian History of England and Wales*. Vol. IV: *1500–1640*. Cambridge, England, 1967. A superb survey of a neglected subject.

Waters, D. W. *The Art of Navigation in England in Elizabethan and Early Stuart Times*. London, 1958.

Weinstock, Maureen. *Studies in Dorset History*. Dorchester, 1953. See especially pp. 13–51, on Weymouth.

Wernham, R. B. *Before the Armada: The Emergence of the English Nation 1485–1588*. New York, 1966. An excellent account of England's foreign policy.

Wheatley, H. B. "London and the Life of the Town." *Shakespeare's England: An Account of the Life and Manners of His Age*. Vol. II. Oxford, 1916. Pages 153–181 provide a good brief depiction of life in London in this period.

Whitty, R. G. H. "The History of Taunton under the Tudors and Stuarts." Unpub. diss. University of London, 1938.

Willan, T. S. *The English Coasting Trade, 1600–1750*. Manchester, 1938.

―――. *Studies in Elizabethan Foreign Trade*. Manchester, 1959. A collection of important studies, particularly a long section (pp. 92–312) on the Morocco trade and the Barbary Company.

Williamson, J. A. *The Age of Drake*. London, 1938. The best of the many surveys of overseas exploits in Elizabeth's reign.

―――. *Maritime Enterprise 1485–1558*. Oxford, 1913.

x ―――. *A Short History of British Expansion*. Vol. I: *The Old Colonial Empire*, 3rd ed. London, 1945. The best general survey.

x Wilson, Charles. *England's Apprenticeship 1603–1763.* London, 1965. An excellent general economic history.

Wood, A. C. *A History of Nottinghamshire.* Nottingham, 1947. Especially pp. 146–154.

Woodrooffe, Thomas. *The Enterprise of England: An Account of Her Emergence as an Oceanic Power.* London, 1958. A solid and well-written narrative of overseas activity through the Armada.

Wright, Arnold. *The Romance of Colonisation: Being the Story of the Economic Development of the British Empire.* London and New York, 1923. The romantic glow and the inaccuracies obscure some interesting, albeit unsubstantiated, interpretations.

Wright, L. B. *The Dream of Prosperity in Colonial America.* New York, 1965. Essays on the subjects stressed in the propaganda of the period.

x ———. *Middle-Class Culture in Elizabethan England.* Chapel Hill, 1935. See especially chap. xiv, "The Wonders of Travel."

x ———. *Religion and Empire: The Alliance between Piety and Commerce in English Expansion, 1558–1625.* Chapel Hill, 1943.

(ii) *Studies of Particular Enterprises*

African Ventures (including Barbary)

Blake, J. W. "The English Guinea Company, 1618–1660," *Proceedings and Reports of the Belfast Natural History and Philosophical Society,* 2nd ser., 3 (1945–1950), 14–27.

x ———. *European Beginnings in West Africa, 1454–1578.* London, 1937.

See also Willan, *Studies . . .* , listed above.

Bermuda Company

Craven, W. F. "An Introduction to the History of Bermuda," *William and Mary Quarterly,* 2nd ser., 17 (1937), 176–215, 317–362, and 437–465; 18 (1938), 13–63.

x Wilkinson, Henry C. *The Adventurers of Bermuda.* Oxford, 1933. See also the works listed under *Virginia Ventures,* below.

Canadian Ventures

Kirke, Henry. *The First English Conquest of Canada.* London, 1908.

Lanctôt, Gustave. *A History of Canada.* Trans. J. Hambleton. Vol. I. Toronto and Vancouver, 1963. Especially pp. 76–147 and 306–308.

Quinn, D. B. "The English and the St. Lawrence 1577–1602." In *Merchants and Scholars: Essays in the History of Exploration and Trade,* ed. John Parker. Minneapolis, 1965. Pages 117–143.

———. "The First Pilgrims," *William and Mary Quarterly,* 3rd ser., 23 (1966), 359–390.

See, too, the works under *New England Ventures, Newfoundland,* and *North-West Passage Ventures,* below, and the works on Alexander and Gorges in the Biographies section, below.

East India Company

Chaudhuri, K. N. "The East India Company and the Export of Treasure in the Early Seventeenth Century," *Ec.H.R.,* 2nd ser., 16 (1963), 23–38.

x ————. *The English East India Company: The Study of an Early Joint-Stock Company 1600–1640*. London, 1965. Very valuable.

Foster, Sir William. "Charles I and the East India Company." *E.H.R.*, 12 (1904), 456–463. Mainly on the Civil War period.

Grey, Charles. *The Merchant Venturers of London: A Record of Far Eastern Trade and Piracy during the Seventeenth Century*. London, 1932. An imprecise and romantic account, though there are narrative details not to be found in Chaudhuri, Foster, or Khan.

Khan, S. A. *The East India Trade in the XVIIth Century in Its Political and Economic Aspects*. London, 1923.

Wright, Arnold. *Early English Adventurers in the East*. London, 1917. A narrative similar to Grey's, but with a somewhat different focus.

See, too, Foster, *Quest* . . . , listed above.

Eastland Company

Deardorff, N. R. "English Trade in the Baltic during the Reign of Elizabeth." In *Studies in the History of English Commerce in the Tudor Period* (The University of Pennsylvania). New York, 1912.

Hinton, R. W. K. *The Eastland Trade and the Common Weal in the Seventeenth Century*. Cambridge, England, 1959.

Frobisher and Fenton

See *North-West Passage Ventures*, and the Biographies section, below.

Guiana and West Indian Colonial Ventures

x Burns, Sir Alan. *History of the British West Indies*. London, 1954. 2nd ed., 1965. Especially pp. 138–295, *passim*.

Harlow, V. T. *A History of Barbados, 1625–1685*. Oxford, 1926.

Newton, A. P. *The European Nations in the West Indies, 1493–1688*. London, 1933. Especially pp. 49–176.

Williamson, J. A. *The Caribbee Islands under the Proprietary Patents*. London, 1926.

————. *English Colonies in Guiana and on the Amazon, 1604–1688*. Oxford, 1923.

See, too, the works under *Providence Island Company* and on Raleigh in the Biographies section, below.

Industry

In addition to the works listed in chap. 1, note 94, and under *Newfoundland* (Fishing), below, the following are useful studies of early industrial development and the related topic of patents and monopolies:

Archer, J. "The Industrial History of London 1603–1640." Unpub. diss. University of London, 1934.

Clarkson, L. A. "English Economic Policy in the Sixteenth and Seventeenth Centuries: The Case of the Leather Industry," *Bulletin of the Institute of Historical Research*, 38 (1965), 149–162.

Coleman, D. C. *The British Paper Industry, 1495–1860: A Study in Industrial Growth*. Oxford, 1958.

Court, W. H. B. *The Rise of the Midland Industries, 1600–1838*. London, 1938.

Cunningham William. *The Growth of English Industry and Commerce in Modern Times.* Vol. II. 5th ed. Cambridge, 1912.

x Fox, Harold G. *Monopolies and Patents: A Study of the History and Future of the Patent Monopoly.* Toronto, 1949.

Gardiner, S. R. "On Four Letters from Lord Bacon to Christian IV, King of Denmark," *Archaeologia,* 41 (1867), 219–269.

Gough, J. W. *The Mines of Mendip.* Oxford, 1930.

Hughes, Edward. "The English Monopoly of Salt in the Years 1563–71," *E.H.R.,* 40 (1925), 334–350.

Hulme, E. W. "English Glass-Making in the Sixteenth and Seventeenth Centuries," *The Antiquary,* 30 (1894), 210–214 and 259–263; and 31 (1895), 68–72 and 102–106.

———. "The History of the Patent System under the Prerogative and at Common Law," *The Law Quarterly Review,* 12 (1896), 141–154.

Letwin, W. L. "The English Common Law Concerning Monopolies," *The University of Chicago Law Review,* 21 (1953–1954), 355–385.

x Mund, V. A. *Monopoly: A History and Theory.* Princeton, 1933.

Nef, J. U. "Prices and Industrial Capitalism in France and England, 1540–1640," *Ec.H.R.,* 7 (1937), 155–185.

———. "The Progress of Technology and the Growth of Large-Scale Industry in Great Britain, 1540–1640," *Ec.H.R.,* 5 (1934), 3–24.

Sanderson, W. A. *Restraint of Trade in English Law.* London, 1926.

Unwin, George. *Industrial Organization in the Sixteenth and Seventeenth Centuries.* Oxford, 1904.

See, too, Scott, *Joint-Stock Companies* . . . , listed above, and the works on Bulmer, Beaumont, and Middleton in the Biographies section, below.

Ireland

Bagwell, R. *Ireland under the Tudors.* 3 vols. London, 1885–1890.

———. *Ireland under the Stuarts.* 2 vols. London, 1909–1916. Volume I: to 1642.

Bonn, M. J. *Die Englische Kolonisation in Irland.* Vol. I. Stuttgart and Berlin, 1906. Especially pp. 169–397: a solid survey of all the ventures of the period.

Dunlop, Robert. "The Plantation of Munster 1584–1589." *E.H.R.,* 3 (1888), 250–269.

———. "Sixteenth Century Schemes for the Plantation of Ulster," *Scottish Historical Review,* 22 (1924–1925), *passim.*

x Moody, T. W. *The Londonderry Plantation, 1609–41: The City of London and the Plantation in Ulster.* Belfast, 1939.

Quinn, D. B. *The Elizabethans and the Irish.* Ithaca, 1966.

———. "Ireland and Sixteenth Century European Expansion." *Historical Studies.* Ed. T. D. Williams. London, 1958. Pages 20–32.

See, too, the works by Cheyney, H. M. Jones, and Quinn listed above, and the works on Gilbert, Grenville, and Raleigh in the Biographies section, below.

Levant Company

Epstein, Mordecai. *The Early History of the Levant Company.* London, 1908.

Horniker, A. L. "William Harborne and the Beginning of Anglo-Turkish Diplomatic and Commercial Relations," *Journal of Modern History,* 14 (1942), 289–316.

Kurat, Akdes N. *Türk-Ingiliz Münasabetlerinin Baslangici ve Gelismesi (1553–1610)* [The Beginning and Development of Turkish-English Relations]. Ankara, 1953. I owe this reference to my student Mr. Ronald Jennings. This seems to be the most thorough book on the subject that uses both Turkish and English sources.

Rainey, T. B. "Sir Thomas Roe and the Barbary Pirates, 1621–1624," *The Historian,* 27 (1965), 382–403.

Rawlinson, H. G. "The Embassy of William Harborne to Constantinople, 1583–1588," *Transactions of the Royal Historical Society,* 4th ser., 5 (1922), 1–27.

Rosedale, H. A. *Queen Elizabeth and the Levant Company.* London, 1904.

Willan, T. S. "Some Aspects of English Trade with the Levant in the Sixteenth Century," *E.H.R.,* 70 (1955), 399–410.

x Wood, A. C. *A History of the Levant Company.* Oxford, 1935. The standard work.

See, too, Corbett, *Mediterranean* . . . , Davis, "Mediterranean . . . ," and Foster, *Quest* . . . , listed above, and the works on Jenkinson and Shirley in the Biographies section, below. (The dissertation on the Levant merchants now being written by Mr. David Fischer [under the direction of Dr. Chaudhuri] at the University of London promises to add considerably to our knowledge of the organization of the trade.)

Massachusetts Bay Company (including Puritan colonization)

Bellord, J. E. M. "Puritan Ideas on Colonisation, 1620–1660." Unpub. thesis, University of London, 1950.

Crouse, N. M. "Causes of the Great Migration, 1630–1640," *The New England Quarterly,* 5 (1932), 3–36.

French, Allen. *Charles I and the Puritan Upheaval: A Study of the Causes of the Great Migration.* London, 1955. A not very well-documented study.

Miller, Perry. *Orthodoxy in Massachusetts, 1630–1650: A Genetic Study.* Cambridge, Mass., 1933. A superb study of the Puritans' background.

Moody, R. E. "A Re-Examination of the Antecedents of the Massachusetts Bay Company's Charter of 1629," *Proceedings of the Massachusetts Historical Society,* 69 (1947–1950), 56–80.

x Morison, S. E. *Builders of the Bay Colony.* Boston and New York, 1930.

x Rose-Troup, Frances. *The Massachusetts Bay Company and Its Predecessors.* New York, 1930.

Simpson, Alan. *Puritanism in Old and New England.* Chicago, 1955.

See, too, the works listed under *New England Ventures,* and on White in the Biographies section, below.

Merchant Adventurers (and New Merchant Adventurers)

Rees, J. Aubrey. *The English Tradition, The Heritage of the Venturers: A Survey of Six Centuries.* London, 1934. A very general survey.

See Friis, *Cockayne* . . . , Lucas, *Beginnings* . . . , and Supple, *Crisis* . . . , listed above.

See, too, the works on livery companies in note 7 of chap. 2, above, to which can be added J. Nichols, *Some Account of the Worshipful Company of Ironmongers.* London, 1851.

Muscovy Company

Anderson, M. S. *Britain's Discovery of Russia, 1553–1815.* London, 1958. Pages 1–34.

x Liubimenko, I. *Les Relations Commerciales et Politiques de l'Angleterre avec la Russie avant Pierre le Grand.* Paris, 1933.

Willan, T. S. *The Early History of the Russia Company 1553–1603.* Manchester, 1956.

————. *The Muscovy Merchants of 1555.* Manchester, 1953. The biographical appendix (pp. 75–132) is a mine of information about the leading early-Elizabethan merchants.

Wrett-Smith, M. "The Policy and Activities of the Muscovy Company in the Late Sixteenth and Early Seventeenth Centuries." Unpub. thesis, University of London, 1959.

New England Ventures

x Bolton, C. K. *The Real Founders of New England: Stories of Their Life Along the Coast, 1602–1628.* Boston, 1929.

Burrage, H. S. *The Beginnings of Colonial Maine, 1602–1658.* Portland, 1914.

————. *The Plymouth Colonists in Maine.* Portland: Maine Historical Society [1904?]. Read before the Society, 1899.

Christy, Miller. "Attempts toward Colonization: The Council for New England and the Merchant Venturers of Bristol, 1621–1623," *A.H.R.,* 4 (1899), 678–702.

de Costa, B. F. "Ancient Norumbega, or the Voyages of Simon Ferdinando and John Walker to the Penobscot River, 1579–1580," *New England Historical and Genealogical Register* (April 1890), pp. 3–12.

x Howe, H. F. *Prologue to New England.* New York and Toronto, 1943.

Preston, R. A. "The Laconia Company of 1629: An English Attempt to Intercept the Fur Trade," *Canadian Historical Review,* 31 (1950), 125–144.

See also the works listed under *Canadian Ventures* and *Massachusetts Bay Company,* above; under *Newfoundland,* below; and the works on Gorges, Gosnold, Hayes, Pring, and Captain John Smith in the Biographies section, below.

Newfoundland (including fishing)

Cell, G. M. "The English in Newfoundland, 1577–1660." Unpub. diss. University of Liverpool, 1964.

————. "The Newfoundland Company: A Study of Subscribers to a Colonizing Venture." *William and Mary Quarterly,* 3rd ser., 22 (1965), 611–625. This is the first of a number of publications based on the research for her detailed doctoral dissertation in which Dr. Cell will undoubtedly provide us with a definitive account of the English in Newfoundland.

Elder, J. R. *The Royal Fishery Companies of the Seventeenth Century.* Aberdeen University Studies. Aberdeen, 1912.

Innis, H. A. *The Cod Fisheries. The History of an International Economy.* 2nd ed. Toronto, 1954.

x Judah, C. B. *The North American Fisheries and British Policy to 1713.* University of Illinois Studies in the Social Sciences. Urbana, 1933.

x Lounsbury. R. G. *The British Fishery at Newfoundland, 1634–1763.* New Haven, 1934.

Moore Smith, G. C. "Robert Hayman and the Plantation of Newfoundland," *E.H.R.,* 33 (1918), 21–36.

Powell, J. W. D. "John Guy: Founder of Newfoundland," *United Empire,* new ser., 24 (1933), 323–337.

————. "John Guy's Voyage in the 'Endeavour,'" *ibid.,* 28 (1937), 16–17.

Preston, R. A. "Fishing and Plantation: New England in the Parliament of 1621," *A.H.R.,* 45 (1939), 29–43.

Prowse, D. W. *A History of Newfoundland, from the English, Colonial, and Foreign Records.* 2nd ed. London, 1896.

Stephens, W. B. "The West-Country Ports and the Struggle for the Newfoundland Fisheries in the Seventeenth Century," *Report & Transactions of the Devonshire Association,* 88 (1956), 90–101.

Williams, E. R. "Cambriol: The Story of a Forgotten Colony," *Welsh Outlook,* 8 (1921), 230–233.

See, too, *Canadian Ventures* and *New England Ventures,* above.

North-West Passage Ventures

Markham, Sir Clemens R. *The Lands of Silence: A History of Arctic and Antarctic Exploration.* Cambridge, 1921.

Neatby, L. H. *In Quest of the Northwest Passage.* New York, 1958.

Stefansson, Vilhjalmur. *North West to Fortune: The Search of Western Man for a Commercially Practical Route to the Far East.* London, 1960.

None of these is a really satisfactory account — all three books touch on the 1575–1630 period only briefly, as part of a more general survey. Because the books on Button, Davis, Frobisher, and Hudson, listed in the Biographies section below, are sorely out of date, this is a subject that could benefit greatly from modern research. At present, the most useful material is in the documentary collections published by the Hakluyt Society, the documents on Frobisher edited by Stefansson, and the Brebner and Foster books, all listed above.

Plymouth

See the works listed under *Massachusetts Bay Company* and *New England Ventures,* above.

Privateering

Andrews, K. R. "The Economic Aspects of Elizabethan Privateering." Unpub. diss. University of London, 1951. Considerably more detail than in the book listed next.

x ————. *Elizabethan Privateering: English Privateering during the Spanish War 1585–1603.* Cambridge, England, 1964. An important pioneering work, based on hitherto unused documents.

Clark, G. N. "The Barbary Corsairs in the Seventeenth Century," *The Cambridge Historical Journal*, 8 (1944–1946), 22–35.

Haring, C. H. *The Buccaneers in the West Indies in the XVII Century.* New York, 1910.

Powell, J. W. D. *Bristol Privateers and Ships of War.* Bristol, 1930. A very useful local study.

See, too, the general books on seamen listed under General Works, above, and the works on such leading privateers as Chudley, Digby, Drake, Hawkins, Newport, Rich, and Ward, listed in the Biographies section, below.

Providence Island Company

Newton, A. P. *The Colonising Activities of the English Puritans: The Last Phase of the Elizabethan Struggle with Spain.* New Haven, 1914.

Virginia Ventures

Basset, J. S. "The Relation between the Virginia Planter and the London Merchant," *Annual Report of the American Historical Association for the year 1901*, 1 (1902), 553–575.

x Craven, W. F. *Dissolution of the Virginia Company: The Failure of a Colonial Experiment.* New York, 1932. The standard work.

Gayley, G. M. *Shakespeare and the Founders of Liberty in America.* New York, 1917. Pages 1–114 are a perfect example of the traditional, simple portrayal of the Virginia Company as a center of political liberalism.

Johnson, R. C. "The Lotteries of the Virginia Company, 1612–1621," *The Virginia Magazine of History and Biography*, 74 (1966), 259–292.

Kingsbury, S. M. "A Comparison of the Virginia Company with the Other English Trading Companies of the Sixteenth and Seventeenth Centuries," *Annual Report of the American Historical Association for the year 1906*, 1 (1908), 161–176.

Neill, E. D. *History of the Virginia Company of London.* Albany, 1869. The standard older account, superseded by Craven's work.

O'Brien, T. H. "The London Livery Companies and the Virginia Company," *The Virginia Magazine of History and Biography*, 68 (1960), 137–155.

Quinn, D. B. "Preparations for the 1585 Virginia Voyage," *William and Mary Quarterly*, 3rd ser., 6 (1949), 208–236.

See, too, the works listed under *Bermuda Company*, above, and the works on Gosnold, Raleigh, Rich, and Smith in the Biographies section, below.

(iii) *Biographies and Studies of Families Prominent in the Expansion*

Alexander: T. H. McGrail. *Sir William Alexander, First Earl of Stirling: A Biographical Study.* Edinburgh and London, 1940.

Aucher: See *Lovelace*, below.

Barne: See *Lovelace*, below.

Beaumont: R. S. Smith. "Huntingdon Beaumont: Adventurer in Coal Mines," *Renaissance and Modern Studies*, 1 (1957), 115–153.

Bulmer: H. M. Robertson, "Sir Bevis Bulmer, a Large-Scale Speculator of Elizabethan and Jacobean Times," *Journal of Economic and Business History*, 4 (1931) 99–120.

Button: See *Mansell,* below.

Cecil: P. M. Handover, *The Second Cecil: The Rise to Power, 1563–1604, of Sir Robert Cecil, Later Earl of Salisbury.* London, 1959. See especially pp. 85–90, 124–145, and 276–283.

Conyers Read. *Lord Burghley and Queen Elizabeth.* London, 1960.

Lawrence Stone. "The Fruits of Office: The Case of Robert Cecil, First Earl of Salisbury, 1596–1612," in *Essays in the Economic and Social History of Tudor and Stuart England in Honour of R. H. Tawney.* Ed. F. J. Fisher. Cambridge, England, 1961. Pages 89–116, especially 91–94.

Chudley: R. W. Cotton. "An Elizabethan Adventurer," *Macmillan's Magazine,* vol. 71, no. 423 (January 1895), pp. 190–194. On John Chudley, Devon privateer and friend of Davis and Raleigh.

Clifford: G. C. Williamson. *George, Third Earl of Cumberland (1558–1605): His Life and His Voyages.* Cambridge, 1920.

Cornwallis: See *Lovelace,* below.

Courtenay: John Roberts. "A Notable Devon Knight (Sir William Courtenay, 1553–1630)," *Report and Transactions of the Devonshire Association,* 88 (1956), 174–188, especially pp. 178–181.

Cranfield: Menna Prestwich. *Cranfield: Politics and Profits under the Early Stuarts: The Career of Lionel Cranfield Earl of Middlesex.* Oxford, 1966.

x R. H. Tawney. *Business and Politics under James I: Lionel Cranfield as Merchant and Minister.* Cambridge, England, 1958.

Davis: C. R. Markham. *Life of John Davis, the Navigator, 1550–1605.* London, 1889.

Dee: W. I. Trattner. "God and Expansion in Elizabethan England: John Dee, 1527–1583," *Journal of the History of Ideas,* 25 (1964), 17–34.

Devereux: G. B. Harrison. *The Life and Death of Robert Devereux, Earl of Essex.* New York, 1937. Especially pp. 36–44, 108–124, 140–167, and 211–247.

Digby: R. T. Petersson. *Sir Kenelm Digby, the Ornament of England, 1603–1665.* Cambridge, Mass., 1956. Especially pp. 76–82.

Drake: E. F. Benson. *Sir Francis Drake.* London and New York, 1927. Takes account of research done through the mid-1920's, but is often inaccurate.

Ernle Bradford. *The Wind Commands Me.* New York, 1965. The most recent biography, splendidly written, but far from being the full-scale, modern reinterpretation that is now possible.

Julian S. Corbett. *For God and Gold.* London, 1887. A fascinating novel by the great Drake scholar, who imaginatively fills the gaps in Drake's life that have been left by missing evidence. His major work, *Drake and the Tudor Navy,* is listed under General Works, above.

A. E. W. Mason. *The Life of Francis Drake.* London, 1941. The best full-scale biography, but still somewhat uncritical.

H. R. Wagner. *Sir Francis Drake's Voyage around the World.* San Francisco, 1926. A highly individual but always interesting interpretation.

J. A. Williamson. "Books on Drake," *History*, 12 (1927–1928), 310–321. A good review article.

———. *Sir Francis Drake*. London, 1951. The best brief introduction, though it should be noted that there is a fine assessment of Drake in Garrett Mattingly, *The Armada* (New York, 1959), *passim*.

Dudley: A. G. Lee. *The Son of Leicester: The Story of Sir Robert Dudley*. London, 1964.

Ferrar: A. L. Maycock. *Nicholas Ferrar of Little Gidding*. London, 1938. Especially pp. 65–104.

Frobisher: K. M. Eliot. "The First Voyages of Martin Frobisher," *E.H.R.*, 32 (1917), 89–92.

R. G. Marsden, "The Early Career of Sir Martin Frobisher," *ibid.*, 21 (1906), 538–544.

William McFee. *The Life of Sir Martin Frobisher*. New York, 1928. An unsatisfactory account, but no modern replacement has appeared.

G. B. Parks. "Frobisher's Third Voyage, 1578," *The Huntington Library Bulletin*, no. 7 (1935), 181–190.

Gilbert: W. G. Gosling. *The Life of Sir Humphrey Gilbert*. London, 1911. A fairly solid account, but mostly superseded by Quinn's introduction to his edition of Gilbert documents for *Hakluyt Society Publications* (2nd ser., vols. LXXXIII and LXXXIV).

Gorges: x R. A. Preston. *Gorges of Plymouth Fort*. Toronto, 1953. An excellent study.

Gosnold: x W. F. Gookin and P. L. Barbour. *Bartholomew Gosnold, Discoverer and Planter*. Hamden, Connecticut, 1963.

Grenville: A. L. Rowse. *Sir Richard Grenville of the Revenge, an Elizabethan Hero*. London, 1937.

———. "Sir Richard Grenville's Place in English History," *Proceedings of the British Academy*, 43 (1957), 79–95.

Greville: R. E. L. Strider. *Robert Greville Lord Brooke*. Cambridge, Mass., 1958. Especially pp. 17–27.

Hakluyt: J. P. Collier. "On Richard Hakluyt and American Discoveries," *Archaeologia*, 33 (1849), 283–292. A pioneering assessment.

x G. B. Parks. *Richard Hakluyt and the English Voyages*. 2nd ed. New York, 1961. The standard work. But see, too, the introduction to Quinn's edition of the 1589 *Principal Navigations* . . . , and vol. XCIII of the *Hakluyt Society Publications*, second series, listed under General Secondary Works, above.

Hatton: E. St. John Brooks. *Sir Christopher Hatton, Queen Elizabeth's Favourite*. London, 1946. Especially pp. 182–196.

Hawkins: Rayner Unwin. *The Defeat of John Hawkins: A Biography of His Third Slaving Voyage*. London, 1960.

J. A. Williamson. *Sir John Hawkins: The Times and the Man*. Oxford, 1927.

———. *Hawkins of Plymouth*. London, 1949. An excellent account of the family's activities.

Hayes: D. B. Quinn. "Edward Hayes, Liverpool Colonial Pioneer," *Transactions of the Historic Society of Lancashire and Cheshire*, 111 (1960), 25–45.

Hudson: E. M. Bacon. *Henry Hudson: His Times and His Voyages.* New York, 1907. An uncritical account.

Ingram: A. F. Upton. *Sir Arthur Ingram, c. 1564–1642.* Oxford, 1961.

Isham: G. D. Ramsay, ed. *John Isham, Mercer and Merchant Adventurer.* Durham: Northamptonshire Record Society, 1962.

Jenkinson: M. B. G. Morton. *The Jenkinson Story.* Glasgow, 1962. A pleasant account, much concerned with Shakespeare, but lacking even an index.

Lee: E. K. Chambers. *Sir Henry Lee: An Elizabethan Portrait.* Oxford, 1936. Pages 244–263 contain a most useful genealogical appendix.

Levett: J. P. Baxter. "Christopher Levett," in his *Historical Addresses.* Portland, n.d.

Lovelace: A. J. Pearman. "The Kentish Family of Lovelace," *Archaeologia Cantiana,* 10 (1883), 184–220; and 20 (1893), 54–63.

J. H. Pleasants. "The Lovelace Family and Its Connections." *The Virginia Magazine of History and Biography,* 28 (1920), 83–90, 176–187, 285–295, and 375–392; and 29 (1921), 110–128 and 227–243. A very useful genealogical account, not only of the Lovelace but also of the Aucher, Barne, Cornwallis, Rich, Sandys, and Wroth families.

Mansell: G. T. Clark. *Some Account of Sir Robert Mansel K^t^, . . . and of Admiral Sir Thomas Button K^t^. . . .* Dowlais, 1883.

Middleton: A. H. Dodd. "Mr. Myddelton the Merchant of Tower Street." In *Elizabethan Government and Society: Essays Presented to Sir John Neale,* ed. S. T. Bindoff, Joel Hurstfield, and C. H. Williams. London, 1961. Pages 249–281.

J. W. Gough. *Sir Hugh Myddelton: Entrepreneur and Engineer.* Oxford, 1964.

Newport: K. R. Andrews. "Christopher Newport of Limehouse, Mariner," *William and Mary Quarterly,* 3rd ser., 11 (1954), 28–41.

D. B. Quinn. "Christopher Newport in 1590," *North Carolina Historical Review,* 29 (1952), 305–316.

Palavicino: Lawrence Stone. *An Elizabethan: Sir Horatio Palavicino.* Oxford, 1956.

Pring: J. H. Pring. *Captaine Martin Pringe, the Last of the Elizabethan Seamen.* London, 1888. A reverent biography.

Tercentenary of Martin Pring's First Voyage to the Coast of Maine, 1603–1903. Portland: Maine Historical Society (1905?).

Raleigh: T. N. Brushfield. *The Bibliography of Sir Walter Raleigh.* 2nd ed. Exeter, 1908. This work already filled 181 pages and included writers as diverse as Martin Hume and Henry Thoreau. Listed below are only the works most relevant to the subject of this book, and two biographies selected from the many available. See also the introduction and excellent bibliography in Quinn's edition of Roanoke documents for the Hakluyt Society (2nd ser., vols. CIV and CV).

D. B. Quinn. *Raleigh and the British Empire.* London, 1947. 2nd ed., 1962. The best account of his overseas activities.

221

J. W. Shirley. "Sir Walter Raleigh's Guiana Finances," *Huntington Library Quarterly*, 13 (1949–1950), 55–69. An important article, based on hitherto unused documents.

E. A. Strathmann. *Sir Walter Raleigh: A Study in Elizabethan Skepticism*. New York, 1951. The best analysis of the man's mind.

W. M. Wallace. *Sir Walter Raleigh*. Princeton and London, 1959. The best recent straightforward biography.

Rich: W. F. Craven. "The Earl of Warwick, A Speculator in Piracy," *Hispanic American Historical Review*, 10 (1930), 457–479.

————. "The Life of Robert Rich, Second Earl of Warwick, to 1642." Unpub. diss. Cornell University, 1928.

See also *Lovelace*, above.

Sandys: T. K. Rabb. "The Early Life of Sir Edwin Sandys and Jacobean London." Unpub. diss. Princeton University, 1961.

E. S. Sandys. *History of the Family of Sandys*. Barrow-in-Furness, 1930.

Shirley: A. D. Aldersen. "Sir Thomas Sherley's Piratical Expedition to the Aegean and his Imprisonment in Constantinople," *Oriens*, 9 (1956), 1–40.

Boies Penrose. *The Sherleian Odyssey*. Taunton, 1938.

Sidney: M. W. Wallace. *The Life of Sir Philip Sidney*. Cambridge, England, 1915.

Mona Wilson. *Sir Philip Sidney*. New York, 1932. Especially pp. 63–79, 211–213, and 226–235.

Smith (Captain John): x P. L. Barbour. *The Three Worlds of Captain John Smith*. Boston, 1964. Though it does not entirely solve all the fearsome problems of Smith's life, this is by far the best biography, with an excellent bibliography.

Smith (Sir Thomas the Elizabethan Courtier): Mary Dewar. *Sir Thomas Smith: A Tudor Intellectual in Office*. London, 1964. Especially pp. 149–209.

See also the article by Quinn listed under General Works, above.

Smith (Sir Thomas the London Merchant): Sir Stanley Spurling. *Sir Thomas Smythe, Knt. (1558?–1625)*. New York: The Newcomen Society, 1955. A brief survey of his career. No full biography has yet appeared.

J. J. Stocker. "Pedigree of Smythe . . . ," *Archaeologia Cantiana*, 20 (1893), 76–81.

J. F. Wadmore. "Sir Thomas Smythe, Knt. (A.D. 1558–1625)," *ibid.*, 82–103.

Vere: B. M. Ward. *The Seventeenth Earl of Oxford, 1550–1604*. London, 1928. Especially pp. 236–243.

Walsingham: Conyers Read. *Secretary Walsingham and the Policy of Queen Elizabeth*. 3 vols. Oxford, 1925.

Ward: C. L'Estrange Ewen. *Captain John Ward, "Arch-Pirate."* Paignton, 1939.

White: x Frances Rose-Troup. *John White, the Patriarch of Dorchester and the Founder of Massachusetts, 1575–1648*. London and New York, 1930.

Wriothesley: C. C. Stopes. *The Life of Henry, Third Earl of Southampton, Shakespeare's Patron.* Cambridge, England, 1922. Especially pp. 314–333 and 416–446.

A. L. Rowse. *Shakespeare's Southampton, Patron of Virginia.* New York, 1965. Especially pp. 234–262.

Wroth: See *Lovelace,* above.

APPENDIX   THE LIST OF NAMES

The main reason for publishing the list of names *in toto* is to provide a useful source of reference for students of the late Elizabethan and early Stuart periods. The availability of the list early in 1964, for example, might have saved A. L. Rowse from a pitfall in his attempt to prove the identity of Shakespeare's "W. H." He suggested that the phrase "wisheth the well-wishing adventurer in setting forth" in the dedication of the sonnets "refers to the immense enthusiasm in London in this year 1609 for the plantation of Virginia. Almost everybody who was anybody was subscribing to the Virginia Company." [1] That there was a flood of new subscribers in 1609 cannot be denied, but Rowse's selection of William Harvey as "W. H." is unfortunate, because nobody of that name joined the Virginia or any other company in 1609. Sir William Harvey's only investments appear to have been in the East India Company in 1618 and the Amazon Company in 1619. If "adventurer" does in fact mean what Rowse suggests, then "W. H." will have to be picked from among the following:

William Hampson, about whom nothing is known apart from his inclusion in the 1609 Virginia charter.
William Hancock, a Spanish merchant.
William Harebrowne (or Harborowe), a Spanish and Levant merchant and fishmonger, who subscribed to both the Virginia and the Irish enterprises in 1609.
Sir Warwick Hele, a prominent Devonshire gentleman.
William Herbert, Earl of Pembroke, surely the most likely candidate, particularly as he was appointed to the Council of the Virginia Company in the same year: a good reason to stress his "adventure." Moreover, although the first record of his membership in the East India Com-

---

[1] A. L. Rowse, "Dr. Rowse & Mr W. H.," *Sunday Times* (London, May 3, 1964), p. 35. He makes the same case, with even greater confidence, in *Shakespeare's Southampton, Patron of Virginia* (New York, 1965), pp. 198–200.

224

pany dates from 1611, this is only a list of current members, and he may well have been among the "other lords, knights, and gentlemen, favourers of the Company, and no mere merchants" [2] who were admitted, together with the Earls of Salisbury, Nottingham, Worcester, and Southampton in 1609. If so, he would be a "W. H." who joined *two* companies in 1609, a step that might certainly merit comment.

If companies other than the Virginia are included, one must add as candidates for "W. H." William Hawkins, of the famous Plymouth family, who subscribed to the East India Company in 1609; William Harrison, a prominent London merchant appointed to the Council for Ireland in 1609; and William Hickman (a London merchant), William Hide (a grocer), and William Hobson (a vintner), each of whom gave money to the Irish venture in 1609.

Perhaps in view of the above Rowse might modify his interpretation of the phrase in the dedication, or he might now throw his support behind the Earl of Pembroke. Lest it be assumed that I wish to enter the treacherous arena of sonnet scholarship, let me hasten to add that I make this point only to indicate the potential uses of the list (if only to prevent error) in many types of historical investigations of this period. Whether the above findings give comfort to the advocates of the Earl of Pembroke, promote new candidates for "W. H.," or merely disprove a hypothesis about the term "adventurer," is for others to decide.

The appendix which follows lists the contents of my 8,683 cards. Before using it, however, the reader should recall the cautions raised in Chapter 3. The entries cannot claim to be exhaustive, because many of the essential records have disappeared. Even more important, problems of identification are so troublesome that complete confidence about the data should be reserved only for the most prominent people. Where serious doubts remain, they have been indicated by asterisks, question marks, and daggers, as is explained in the key. But the absence of these symbols often denotes only a fair degree of assurance. Despite repeated checks over a period of six years, I found errors even after the cards had been transferred onto computer tape, and the changes that were made *after* the analysis of the data are indicated immediately before the key.

The haphazard spelling habits of Jacobean times caused further difficulties, which could not always be overcome. Identification, for example, became far more difficult in the absence of standardization. What concerns us here, however, is that it was impossible to reduce every similar name to a single, uniform version. Thus there is an Allen, an Alleyne, and an Allyn. Clearly no rigorous system for dealing with such variations could be imposed, but I did try to follow a few simple principles. In the first place, spelling was modernized for convenience whenever justified by contemporary usage. The great merchant Sir Thomas Smith, for example, though often spelled 'Smythe' in historical literature, was frequently spelled 'Smith' in his own day, and it seemed far less confusing to have the 62 Smiths, Smithes, Smyths, Smythes, and so forth all in one place. But if there were only a few people of a similar name, and the spelling for each individual remained con-

---

[2] *CSP, East Indies, 1513–1616*, p. 185.

sistent, I left them as I found them. The result is that there are the different Allens; and also a Graves and a Greves; a Hiccocke, a Hickockes, and a Hitchcocke; a Honywood and a Hunniwood; a Mainstay and a Manesty; a Michell and a Mitchell; a Monck and a Munks; a Revett and a Rivett; a Saman and a Samon; and a Sayer and a Seyer, to mention but a few.[3]

When the groups were large, and would have been widely scattered if left in their original form, I consolidated them into the version that came first in the alphabet. Hence there are Barkeleys rather than Berkeleys, Beamounts not Beaumonts, Grays instead of Greys, and Smiths not Smythes. This sometimes resulted in the adoption of the spelling which — though still recognizable to modern eyes — is less common in present-day usage. The usual form now is Lord *Grey* of Groby, for example. But it was much more convenient to begin a grouping at the earliest possible place in the alphabet.

In most instances this system was easy to apply. But the dangers of distorting a name by changing it, and the very large numbers involved, soon convinced me that strict uniformity could not be maintained. Putting Hyll, Hylle, and Hille under Hill is relatively simple, but should one add the Wights to the Whites? Should Parry remain separate from Perry, or Barrington from Berrington, when even contemporaries had difficulty distinguishing them? Such problems led me to decide that differences would have to remain, except in the most clear-cut cases (like Hill and Smith), or where one of the variations in the documents allowed me to add an individual to a large grouping (e.g., where a Wight also appeared as White).

This decision, however, raised further anomalies when it split families because of idiosyncrasies in spelling. As long as a man was on his own, his exact position did not matter too much. Thus Sir Henry Lello, though often spelled Lillo nowadays, could be left as Lello — as he was in the first document in which I found him — because this had no effect on other entries. The reader will simply have to be prepared to search for names that were susceptible to wayward spellings, because there was no room for the multitude of cross-references that would have been needed to relieve him of this task. When two relatives were separated by the spelling of their names, however, standardization had to be imposed.

So far as I know, all families have been brought together, with three exceptions, which have been indicated by cross-references in the list itself: Thomas Bonist and Thomas Bownest; John Hassard and John Hazard; John Oughtred and Henry Ughtred. Other separations of relatives may have escaped my notice, and readers are strongly advised to look for all possible

---

[3] A few further examples of conspicuous variations in spelling should give the reader an idea of what he is likely to encounter: Arundell and Erundell; Caldwell and Coldwell; Coke and Cooke; Crashaw and Croshaw; Daubney and Dawbeney; Ellawood and Elliwood; Facet and Fawcet; Fairweather and Fawether; Fleet and Flete; Foulkes, Fowkes, and Fulkes; Grame and Greame; Honyngs and Huninges; Parkins and Perkins; Paulsteed and Polsteed; Pearce and Peirse; Peirson and Pierson; Pelham and Pulham; Prentice and Printis; Radford and Rodford; Saule and Sawle; Tirhitt and Tyrwhite; Tooker and Towker; Trelawney and Trilany; Walden and Welden; Whaphlet and Wipplet; Willeston, Wooleston, and Woolverston; Wooten and Wotton.

versions of a name. In some cases they will find only one variant (Knevit, Knowles, Powlett), and in others they will find more than one (both Parrett and Perott). It should be remembered that vowels (including 'y') were interchangeable at whim, that an 'h' or double letter could come or go as one pleased, and that similar sounds were constant temptations to clerks in search of originality. In the absence of a host of cross-references, readers are urged to consider all possible spellings. The discovery that the only Levinge is a Timothy should not bring to an end the search for Edward Leaveinge.[4]

More important than the problems of alphabetization are the errors that must have remained in the data themselves. So many steps had to be taken between the discovery of a name in a document and its appearance on a computer tape that slips were inevitable. A series of careful checks back to the original sources from the final list revealed very few such lapses, but some have undoubtedly remained undetected. I am more concerned with the probability that a number of entries are inaccurate, not because of typographical mistakes, but because of the basic difficulty of identification (described in Chapter 3). There must be many scholars who are much more familiar with a particular family, individual, or company than I could ever hope to become, and I would be most grateful to any reader who discovers an error and communicates his findings to the publisher.

To give an example, Mrs. Marjorie McIntosh, who has been studying the Cookes of Gidea Hall, Essex, in this period, informed me *after* my computer "runs" that the Francis Cook who invested in Ireland was the same man as the Francis Cook (whom I had thought to be someone else) later knighted, far from home, in Staffordshire. This correction has been made in the list that follows, but the figures in Chapters 1 and 2 do not reflect the change (that is, one of the "gentlemen" investing in Ireland [and no other company] should be a "knight"). Francis was evidently given the middle name Hercules, but since he appears never to have used it, it was not entered in the list. The following 30 changes and additions were also discovered and incorporated into the list *after* the tables in Chapters 1 and

---

[4] It should be noted that first names have been standardized. There seemed no point in adding to the difficulties of checking so many names by retaining the picturesque spellings of the seventeenth century. A man might appear as Brian in one document and Bryan in the next. All Brians, Bryans, Brianes, etc. have been reduced to Brian. Similarly, the following versions were picked for names that commonly appeared in more than one form: Abell not Able, Adolph not Adolphus, Anne not Anna, Barnabas not Barnaby, Barnard not Bernard, Bevill not Bevell, Clement not Clements, Blase not Blaise, Cadwell not Caldwell, Chidiac not Chidiock, Digory not Degory, Edmund not Edmond, Eleazar not Eliezer, Fulke not Fouke, Gerard not Gerrard or Garrard, Gerson not Gershon, Grevile not Grenvile, Hamman not Hamon or Hammond, Harris not Harrison, Horatio not Horace, Huntington not Huntingdon, Jarvis not Jervys, Jasper not Jaisper, Jessy not Jessua, Katherine not Catherine, Lancelot not Launcelot, Lawrence not Laurence, Luke not Lucas, Maurice not Morris, Mildmay not Mylemy, Moses not Moyses, Othowell not Ottwell, Piers not Pearce, Randall not Randle, Raphe not Rafe or Raufe, Roland not Rowland, Sidrake not Sidrack, Simon not Simion, Toby not Tobias, Tedder not Tudor, Tristiam not Tristram, Urie not Urian, Zachariah not Zachary. The choices were, of course, arbitrary.

2 were compiled.[5] (The number in parentheses indicates the man's position in the list if there is more than one person with the same name.)

Anderson, Henry (first): knighthood and date; question whether two people
Anderson, Henry (second): date of knighthood
Baker, Thomas (first): Virginia Company 1618?
Benson, Peter: Irish Company
Blissard, Francis: "other ventures"
Boothby, Thomas: "other ventures"
Bowdler, Richard: "other ventures"
Burlamachi, Philip: "other ventures"
Cambell, James: governor, not merely director, of French Company
Carter, William: Ireland in 1586, not 1609
Crispe, Ellis: Merchant Adventurer
Crispe, Nicholas (second): Merchant Adventurer
Daubney, Clement: Gentleman; "other ventures"
Delean, Robert: Merchant
Dike, John (first): "other ventures"
Eldred, John (first): "other ventures"
Freeman, Martin: "other ventures"
Gilbert, Adrian: "other ventures"
Halliday, William: question whether two people
Houghton, Richard: "other ventures"
Hynde, William: Merchant Adventurer
Jones, Thomas (third): "other ventures"
Kellett, William: "other ventures"
Lowe, George (second): "other ventures"
Pinder, Paul: "other ventures"
Russell, Thomas (third): "other ventures"; question whether same as another Thomas Russell
Somerset, Edward Earl of Worcester: "other ventures"
Staper, Hewett: *two* "other ventures"
Tudor, Queen Elizabeth: Drake
Villiers, Edward: "other ventures"
Walsingham, Francis: Virginia 1585

KEY TO THE LIST

The entry for William Cavendish, second Earl of Devonshire, can serve as an appropriate example; it contains almost every kind of information that appears in the list. It reads as follows:

Name & title	Class; date of knighthood	Parliaments (starting dates)	E. Ind. Co.	Va. Co.	Levant Co.	Other Companies
Cavendish, William, Lord, Earl Devonshire	Nob.09	04–26		12c		Q/T3/GG3

Name & title is almost self-explanatory. If the entry is preceded by one or two asterisks, this means that there is doubt about the man's identity.

[5] In addition, six people who were in my original data were removed from the list that follows because they were members of the Royal Commissions for Trade and in no companies or Parliaments: Clement and Gabriel Harvey, Ralph Madison, Emanuel Scrope Earl of Sunderland, Alexander Stafford, and John Tracy.

One asterisk (°) indicates that his data may belong to someone else with the same name (usually next to him in the list, or occasionally under a slightly different spelling — e.g., John Butcher may be the same as John Bucher[6]). *Two asterisks* (°°) indicate that the data given to this one man may in fact belong to two people with identical names.

Names are given in full unless, as sometimes happens, a first name is represented by an initial or abbreviation in the documents (e.g., M. Thompson and Jo Kirrell). If the first name is missing (e.g., Mr. Banggam), a *question mark* is used, and it also follows a few first names that are not entirely certain (e.g., Edward Clarke). Major variants are indicated in parentheses — e.g., D(J)olliffe. Titles appear as normal except that "of" has been omitted, and each separate title is followed by a comma. Thus William Cavendish was Lord Cavendish and Earl of Devonshire. He took his surname for his first title, and therefore only "Lord" appears. Had he taken a different title, as did Thomas Cecil, Lord Burghley (eight entries later in the list), it would have been given in full. When a man retained the same nomenclature for successive titles, they are linked by an "&". Thus William Cavendish's cousin, the next entry in the list, appears as Cavendish, William, Visc. Mansfield, Earl & Marq. & Duke Newcastle, meaning that he was Viscount Mansfield, Earl of Newcastle, Marquis of Newcastle, and Duke of Newcastle. Once or twice, for reasons of space, titles have been slightly abbreviated, but they should be very simple to recognize (e.g., Visc. for Viscount and Marq. for Marquis).

Class: date of knighthood, though again abbreviated, should be easy to decipher. The abbreviations are as follows:

> Unkn. = Unknown (not classified)
> Gent. = Gentleman
> Kt. = Knight
> Nob. = Noble
> Merc. = Merchant
> M.Kt. = Merchant Knight
> Pfl/y = Professional or Yeoman

Should the classification be doubtful, it is followed by a *question mark.* If a date of first knighthood is known, the last two digits of the date appear after the class. Thus William Cavendish was a Noble knighted in 1609. Where the date is unknown, or doubtful, a *dagger* (†) is entered after the class, or after the doubtful date (e.g., Richard Aldeburgh or William Barnes). The only "knights" for whom neither a date nor a dagger is given are the knights' wives (Lady Elianor Carr, for example), who obviously shared their husbands' status, but hardly the date of knighthood.

Parliaments (starting dates) are listed again by the last two digits of the

---

[6] The following are other "same as" names which are separated by variations in spelling: Cowper and Cooper; Duke and Duche; Gasset and Garsett; Greves and Graves; Horsley and Horsey; Leechland and Lackland; Stonnard and Stannard; Wooleston and Willeston. One whose first name is unknown may, of course, be the same as someone with the same surname. Occasionally it is the first name which is in doubt. Thus *Richard* Hyde may be the result of a clerk's error, and he may really be either Robert or Nicholas Hyde. Similarly, it is not certain that Samuel Leonard is a separate person; he may be the same as Sampson Leonard.

date (from 1584 to 1628, thirteen Parliaments in all). Only the *opening* date of the assemblies to which a man was elected is entered. Thus 04 refers to the Parliament of 1604–1611, and appears even if a man became an M. P. at a by-election in 1606. If he attended consecutive sessions, only the first and last, joined by a hyphen, are listed. Nonconsecutive sessions are separated by commas. William Cavendish's 04–26, therefore, means that he sat from the 1604–1611 through the 1626 Parliament. Edward Cecil, Viscount Wimbledon, five entries later in the list, attended the assemblies of 1601, 1604–1611, 1621, and 1624, as is indicated by his 01–04, 21–24. If there is doubt about a man's election, this is indicated by a *double dagger* (‡) at the end of the parliamentary entry (e.g., Edward Alford).

E.Ind.Co., Va.Co., Levant Co. indicate memberships in the East India, Virginia, and Levant Companies. Each has a separate column, in which the date of admission (or first appearance in the records as a member) is entered — again the last two digits of the date. If the man was a director of the company, a lower case "c" appears after the date; if a governor, it is a lower case "g." William Cavendish entered the Virginia Company in 1612 and was a director of the company. Dates of election to directorships or governorships have not been included. If there is doubt about the date of admission to the company, a question mark follows the date; or, if only the fact of membership is known, there is a question mark alone in the column. If the man was a director or governor, the question mark precedes the "c" or "g." See, as examples, Richard Ashcroft, Henry Brooke Lord Cobham, and William Bourchier Earl of Bath.

Other companies is the only column for which the key will be needed at all times. Entered here are 33 different companies, each represented by a different symbol: the 26 letters of the alphabet, plus the first seven letters doubled. They all appear as italicized capitals (e.g., *A* or *AA*). As with the East India, Virginia, and Levant Companies, the symbol followed by a "c" or "g" denotes a director or governor. The companies are separated by slashes, and the only other feature to note is that some symbols are followed by a number, from 1 to 9. These indicate the date of the document from which the evidence for membership was drawn. The investors in some companies (e.g., *A*, the Africa Company) were taken from only one source (in this case a charter), and in the absence of other records no chronological differentiation was possible. The symbol on its own, therefore, indicates both the company and the date of admission (the latter is given in the key). For most of the companies, however, there was more than one source — and hence more than one date — for members' admissions. These are distinguished by the addition of a number after the symbol. The dates these numbers represent (and they differ from company to company) are given in the key. Thus *I* (Irish Company) is always followed by a number, each with its own meaning (*I*1 = a member in 1613; *I*9 = a member in 1586). The numbers following *GG*, however, indicate the total *number* of "other ventures," not their dates. It will be noticed in the key that two numbers sometimes represent the same date (e.g., both *J*2 and *J*3 = 1629). This means that there were two sources of names dating from that year. The "*W*" entries are a special case discussed in detail in Chapter 3. When a man's membership in a company is in doubt, the entry is followed by a question mark (e.g., John Backhouse). Doubts about the *date* of membership were not recorded, because this information — dependent on very few sources — was often tentative at best. Moreover, as is explained in Chapter 3, some of the groups (for example, the privateers) were consolidated and entered at one date. Although averaged out in the tables, there seemed no point in adding a question mark to all these entries.

Those interested in computer techniques may wish to have a brief description of the design of my IBM card. Columns 1–5 were the identifying number: four digits plus "A," "B," etc. for insertions. Column 6 represented social class, reduced to single-digit numbers: a blank for unknown, 1 for gentleman, 2 for knight, 3 for noble, 4 for merchant, 5 for merchant-knight, and 6 for professional/yeoman. In columns 7 and 8 the last two digits of the date of knighthood, if known, were punched. The sessions of Parliament were numbered, from 01 for 1584 to 13 for 1628, and were punched in successive two-column fields between columns 9 and 32. Because no man was in more than 12 sessions, only 24 columns were needed. Between columns 33 and 59 were entered the companies represented by symbols in the list that follows. Each company was given a three-column field, and as nobody was in more than nine of these companies, only 27 columns were needed. In the first column of the field appeared the company symbol — a letter identical to those used here, except that the seven double letters were represented by symbols such as asterisks and parentheses signs. The second column either contained the number indicating the source and date of membership, or else was left blank; and the third column had a "C" or "G" for director or governor, if applicable. Columns 60–68 contained the East India, Virginia, and Levant Company memberships exactly as they appear in the list that follows. In column 69 membership in the royal commissions for trade was entered — data not used here. Columns 70–73 were reserved for the various kinds of doubts and questions, all reduced to single-digit numbers. No man had more than three questions, and therefore only three columns were needed. A "1" meant he might be the same as another man; a "2" that the data might belong to two people; a "3" that there was doubt about his class; a "4" doubt about the date of knighthood; a "5" doubt about a parliamentary entry; a "6" doubt about one of the companies in columns 33–59; and a "7" doubt about one of the companies in columns 60–68. Finally, in columns 73–78 there was room for three two-digit numbers, representing the total companies, parliaments, and directorships entered on the card. By including these totals a great deal of computer time was saved, because they could be correlated simply with each other and with the numbers representing social class.

231

A = Africa Company (1618).
B = Barbary Company (1585).
C = Senegal Company (1588).
D = Drake venturers (1587).
E = Eastland Company: $E1 = 1579$; $E2 = 1625$; $E3 = 1620$; $E4 =$ date unknown.
F = French Company: $F1 = 1611$; $F2 =$ date unknown.
G = Guiana Companies: $G1 = 1594$; $G2 = 1604$; $G3 = 1609$; $G4 = 1613$; $G5 = 1618$; $G6 = 1619$; $G7 = 1627$; $G8 = 1629$.
H = Staple Merchant (no date).
I = Irish Companies: $I1 = 1613$; $I2 = 1611$; $I3$ and $I4 =$ unknown; $I5 = 1608$; $I6$ and $I7 = 1609$; $I8 = 1618$; $I9 = 1586$.
J = Massachusetts Bay Company: $J1 = 1628$; $J2$ and $J3 = 1629$.
K = New England venturers: $K1 = 1606$; $K2 = 1607$; $K3 = 1609$; $K4 = 1620$; $K5 = 1623$.
L = New Merchant Adventurers: $L1 = 1615$; $L2 = 1616$.
M = Merchant Adventurer (no date).
N = Newfoundland Company (1610).
O = New River Company (1619).
P = Plymouth venturers: $P1 = 1620$; $P2 = 1625$.
Q = North-West Passage Companies: $Q = 1612$; $Q1 = 1584$.
R = Muscovy Company: $R1 = 1580$; $R2 = 1620$.
S = Spanish Company: $S1 = 1604$; $S2 =$ unknown; $S3 = 1604$; $S4 = 1605$; $S5 = 1606$; $S6 = 1577$.
T = Bermuda Company: $T1 = 1612$; $T2 = 1615$; $T3 = 1620$.
U = Baffin venturers (1615).
V = Cavendish venturers (1586).
W = Frobisher and Fenton venturers: $W1 = 1576$; $W2 = 1577$; $W3 = 1578$; $W4 = 1582$; $W5 = 1577$; $W6 = 1576$; $W7 = 1577$; $W8 = 1576$; $W9 = 1577$.
X = Privateers: $X1 = 1581$; $X2 = 1625$.
Y = Gosnold venturers (1602).
Z = Hudson venturers (1610).
AA = Company of Mines: $AA1 = 1575$; $AA2 = 1580$; $AA3 = 1605$.
BB = Company of Mineral and Battery Works: $BB1 = 1575$; $BB2 = 1604$; $BB3 = 1582$; $BB4 = 1585$; $BB5 = 1590$.
CC = Gilbert venturers: $CC1 = 1578$; $CC2 = 1583$.
DD = Venice Company (1583).
EE = Weymouth venturers (1605).
FF = Providence Island Company (1630).
GG = "Other ventures": $GG =$ one other venture; $GG1 =$ two other ventures; $GG2 =$ three other ventures; and so on.
 * = Doubt as to whether same as namesake.
 ** = Doubt as to whether data should belong to two people.
 † = Doubt about date of knighthood.
 ‡ = Doubt about parliamentary entry.
 ? = Doubt about name, social class, about date of membership in East India, Virginia, or Levant Companies, or about entry in one of the other companies, depending where the "?" appears.

Name & title	Class; date of knight-hood	Parlia-ments (starting dates)	E. Ind. Co.	Va. Co.	Levant Co.	Other companies
Abbot, Bartholomew	Merc.				23	
Abbot, Edward	Merc.				26	
Abbot, Edward	Merc.				00c	
Abbot, George						
Archbishop Canterbury	Nob.		12			Q
Abbot, George	Merc.				10	
Abbot, Jacob	Merc.		24			
Abbot, Maurice	M. Kt. 25	21–26	00g	10c	00c	F1/I1c/Qc/ T2/X2/GG
Abbot, Richard	Merc.		23			
Abbot, Toby	Merc.					E3
Abbot, William	Merc.					I7
Abdy, Anthony	Merc.		09c	18	06c	T2
Abraham, Thomas	Merc.					F1
Ackworth, Edward	Merc.					X2
Acland, John	Kt. 03	86, 04		10		
Acton, John	Kt. 03	97				
Acton, William	Merc.		29			L1
Acyll, Richard	Unkn.	04				
Adams, Barnabas	Merc.					F1
Adams, Lawrence	Merc.	14				F1
Adams, Nicholas	Unkn.	89				
Adams, Nicholas	Merc.			09		
Adams, Richard	Unkn.					X1
Adams, Robert	Unkn.					X2
Adams, Thomas	Merc.					J1c
Adams, William	Merc.					F1
Adderley, John	Merc.					Q
Adderley, William	Merc.		99			S3/T2
Adderton, Henry	Unkn.					I4
Addington, William	Merc.					S3
Addison, John	Merc.					S6
Addison, Thomas	Unkn.			22		
Adland, John	Merc.					F1
Agarde, Francis	Merc.					BB1
Aglionby, Edward	Merc.	84, 93				
Aglionby, Edward	Unkn.	24–25				
Agmondesham, John	Unkn.	86, 93–97				
Ailmer, Joshua	Unkn.	89				
Ailworth, Humphrey	Pfl/y.					G8
Aimonere, Thomas	Unkn.					X2
Alabaster, Thomas	Merc.		00c			S1c/X1
Alban, James	Merc.					F1
Albany, William	Merc.		01			I7
Alcocke, Thomas	Unkn.			09		
Alden, Robert	Unkn.			23		N/P2
Aldeburgh, Richard	Kt.†	25–26				
Aldersey, Fulke	Merc.					S1c
Aldersey, Lawrence	Merc.				81	
Aldersey, Samuel	Merc.					J1c/L2/M
Aldersey, Thomas	Merc.	84–89				S6c/GG

Name & title	Class; date of knight- hood	Parlia- ments (starting dates)	E. Ind. Co.	Va. Co.	Levant Co.	Other companies
Aldersey, William	Merc.		00			S1c/W4
Aldrich, Edward	Merc.					I7
Aldridge, Nicholas	Merc.			09		
Aldridge, William	Merc.				00	
Aldworth, John	Merc.					S1
Aldworth, Richard	Merc.		99		99	F1/M/S4/ X1/GG
Aldworth, Robert	Merc.					N/S1/X1/GG1
Aldworth, Thomas	Merc.	86–89, 04	14			N/S6/W2/X1/ CC2/GG2
Alesbury, William	Merc.			09		
Alexander, Walter	Unkn.		27			
Alexander, William Earl Stirling	Nob. 27					X2/GG3
Alford, Edward	Gent.	93–97, 04–25, 28‡				
Alford, Edward	Gent.	28				
Alford, Edward	Merc.					I7
Alford, Francis	Gent.	84–89				
Alford, John	Gent.	89				
Alford, John	Gent.	26–28				
Alford, Lancelot	Kt. 03	89				
Alford, Richard	Gent.					X2
Alford, Samuel	Merc.					S1
Alford, William	Kt. 03	25–28				
Allanson, Richard	Merc.					I7
Allen, Edward	Merc.		07c	09		I7/N/Q/GG
Allen, Gregory	Merc.		00			Q
Allen, John	Merc.			09		S6/CC2
Allen, Peter	Unkn.					X2
Allen, Raphe	Merc.		00			Q
Allen, Richard	Merc.				05	M
Allen, Robert	Merc.					S6
Allen, Thomas	Merc.			09		E1/R1c/W5
Allen, Thomas	Gent.					N
Allen, William	Merc.		99			I7/Q
Allen, William	M. Kt. 71					M/R1c/S6
Allenson, Christopher	Merc.		11			Q
Allet, Richard	Unkn.					X1
Alleyne, Edmund	Gent.			10		
Allington, Giles	Kt. 03			12		
Allyn, Thomas	Merc.		19		25	
Alport, Thomas	Merc.					N
Altham, Emanuel	Unkn.					P2
Altham, James	Gent.	89, 04				
Altham, Thomas	Merc.					S6/GG
Altroppe, John	Merc.					S6
Alured, Thomas	Unkn.	28				
Amadas, Francis	Merc.					X2
Ambler, Humphrey	Merc.		14			
Ambrose, Nicholas	Unkn.					I1

Name & title	Class; date of knight-hood	Parlia-ments (starting dates)	E. Ind. Co.	Va. Co.	Levant Co.	Other companies
Amerideth, Edward	Gent.					*X2*
Amerideth, John	Gent.					*CC1*
Amhurst, Richard	Unkn.	14–21				
Ampleford, William	Merc.			09		
Amy, Edward	Merc.					*S1*
Amy, Thomas	Merc.					*S1*
Anderson, Edward	Gent.	01				*GG*
**Anderson, Henry	M. Kt. 03	84–93			90	*R1/X1/DD/GG*
Anderson, Henry	M. Kt. 08	14–28				
Andrew, Arnold	Unkn.					*J1*
Andrews, Christopher	Unkn.					*W6*
Andrews, Edward	Merc.			09		*I7*
Andrews, George	Merc.					*X2*
Andrews, Henry	Merc.		14c		16	*M/X2/GG*
Andrews, John	Pfl./y.			09		
Andrews, John	Pfl./y.			09		
Andrews, John	Merc.					*S4*
Andrews, Jonathan	Merc.					*R2c*
Andrews, Nicholas	Merc.		17	09		
Andrews, Peter	Merc.					*X2*
Andrews, Richard	Merc.		14			*F1/J3/P2/X2*
Andrews, Thomas	Merc.					*J3/P2*
Angell, John	Merc.	21–24				*S1*
Angell, Robert	Merc.				05	*F1/L1c/M/ S3/GG*
Angell, Thomas	Merc.					*I7*
Angell, William	Merc.		00		05	*I7/Q/S1/GG*
Anketill, John	Unkn.	21				
Annesley, Francis Viscount Valentia	Nob. 16	25, 28				*I8*
Ansell, Edmund	Merc.				90	*R1/S6/X1*
Ansell, Edmund	Merc.					*S6*
Anthony, Charles	Merc.			09		*Q/T2*
Anthony, Francis	Pfl./y.			17c		
Anthony, Lawrence	Unkn.					*P2*
Anthony, Thomas	Unkn.					*F1/S1*
Anton, George	Unkn.	89–93, 01				
Antrobus, Thomas	Unkn.	04				
Anwick, John	Unkn.					*BB4*
Anys, Dunstan	Merc.					*S1*
Anys, William	Merc.				05	*S4*
Applyn, John	Merc.					*M/Q1/S6*
Apshawe, John	Merc.					*S3*
Apshawe, John	Merc.					*S1*
Apsley, Allen	Kt. 05					*A/G7/K4*
Apsley, Henry	Unkn.	89–93				
Archbut, Robert	Unkn.					*X2*
Archdale, John	Gent.					*I2*
Archdale, Richard	Merc.		11			*F1c/S4/X2*
Archer, Gabriel	Gent.			09		*Y*
Archer, Henry	Merc.		00			

Name & title	Class; date of knight-hood	Parlia-ments (starting dates)	E. Ind. Co.	Va. Co.	Levant Co.	Other companies
Archer, Henry	Gent.					*J3*
Archer, John	Unkn.			20		
Archer, John	Merc.					*Q1*
Argall, James	Kt.†					*K5*
Argall, John	Gent.			17		*K4*
Argall, Samuel	M. Kt. 22		27	17		*K5*
Arkenshall, Giles	Unkn.					*CC2*
Armitage, Samuel	Merc.		00c		05	*Q*
Armyne, Everard	Gent.	26				
Armyne, William	Kt. 03	89, 21–28				
Arnewood, William	Gent.					*X1*
Arnold, John	Gent.	97				
Arnold, Nicholas	Gent.	26–28				
Arthors, Owen	Unkn.					*T3*
Arundel, Charles	Gent.					*CC1*
Arundell, John	Gent.	97–01, 21–24, 28		10		
Arundell, Matthew	Kt. 74					*CC1*
Arundell, Thomas Lord Arundell & Wardour	Nob.					*Q/EE*
Ascock, Bartholomew	Kt.†	04				
Ashbornham, Adam	Unkn.	93				
Ashbornham, John	Kt. 03					*I2/GG*
Ashbornham, John	Unkn.	28				
Ashby, William	Unkn.	86, 93				
Ashcroft, Dorothy	Merc.		29			
Ashcroft, Richard	Merc.		14	18?		
Ashe, Abraham	Merc.					*R2*
Ashe, Francis	Merc.					*R2c*
Ashe, John	Merc.	89				*S6*
Ashe, Thomas	Kt. 03					*I4*
Ashe, Thomas	Merc.	84–86				
Ashley, Anthony	Kt. 96	89–93		09		
Ashley, Francis	Kt. 18	14–21, 25				
Ashley, Henry	Kt. 03	86–89				
Ashley, Henry	Merc.			09		
Ashley, James	Merc.			09		
Ashley, John	Kt. 03	14				
Ashley, John	Merc.		19	09		
Ashley, John	Unkn.	86–89				
Ashley, Margaret	Merc.			00		
Ashley, Ralph	Merc.			92		
Ashley, Robert	Unkn.	97				
Ashtell, John	Unkn.	01–04				
Ashton, Edmund	Merc.					*M*
Ashton, Ralph	Gent.	25–26				*GG*
Ashton, Richard	M. Kt. 03	01				
Ashton, Roger	Kt. 03	04		09		
Ashton, William	Gent.	14, 24–28				*GG*
Ashwell, William	Merc.		23		22	

236

Name & title	Class; date of knight-hood	Parlia-ments (starting dates)	E. Ind. Co.	Va. Co.	Levant Co.	Other companies
Aske, John	Gent.	93				
Askew, Elizabeth	Merc.		27			
Askew, James	Merc.		09	09		
Askwith, Nicholas	Merc.		15			*I*2
Askwith, Robert	M. Kt. 17	89, 04–21		10		
Aspinall, Edmund	Merc.		14	.		
Assetyne, Jacques	Merc.					*X*2
Asteley, William	Merc.					*S*6
Asten, Ambrose	Unkn.			18?		
Asten, Anthony	Pfl/y.			20		
Aston, Walter, Lord	Nob. 03			12		
Atherton, John	Gent.	86–89				
Atkins, Aden	Pfl/y.		15			
Atkins, Henry	Merc.		15			*I*7
Atkins, Humphrey	Unkn.		26			
Atkins, Richard	Merc.					*S*0
Atkins, Robert	Merc.					*L*1/*S*2
Atkins, Thomas	Merc.	84–93				
Atkins, William	Merc.					*I*1/*S*4
*Atkins, William	Merc.					*S*6
Atkinson, Anthony	Unkn.					*I*4
Atkinson, Clinton	Merc.					*X*1
Atkinson, Edward	Merc.			09		*I*7
Atkinson, Richard	Merc.		11		15	*Q*
Atkinson, Roger	Unkn.					*I*4
Atkinson, William	Unkn.			09		
Atye, Arthur	Kt. 03	89–97, 04				*B*
Aucher, Anthony	Kt. 03		15	09c		*T*2
Aucher, Anthony	Gent.			09		
Aucher, William	Gent.					*CC*2
Aucher, William	Gent.					*CC*2
Audley, Fernando	Kt.†					*I*2
Audley, Henry	Unkn.	84–89				
Audley, John	Unkn.	84, 93				
Audley, John	Merc.					*S*6
Audley, John	Merc.					*S*6
Audley, John	Unkn.	93				
Audley, Marvin	Kt.†	14				*I*2
Audley, Nicholas	Merc.					*I*7
Audley, Thomas	Merc.				06	*I*2/*S*6
Audley, William	Merc.					*A*/*I*7/*S*1
Audney, Nicholas	Merc.					*X*2
Aungier, Francis, Lord	Nob. 09	89, 97				*I*8
Aunway, Richard	Merc.					*I*7
Austin, Benjamin	Merc.				26	
Austin, George	Unkn.	97, 04				
Austin, Henry	Merc.		11		10	*F*1
Avenant, Cornelius	Pfl/y.					*BB*3
Avenon, Alexander	Merc.					*B*/*S*6
Awbrey, John	Merc.		24			
Awbrey, Robert	Merc.					*L*2/*M*

Name & title	Class; date of knighthood	Parliaments (starting dates)	E. Ind. Co.	Va. Co.	Levant Co.	Other companies
Awbrey, William	Gent.	93				
Ayleworth, Edward	Unkn.	86				
Ayloffe, William	Kt. 03	21		12		
Ayskough, Edward	Kt. 03	21, 28				
Ayskough, Edward	Gent.	24				
Ayskough, Vincent	Merc.		17			
Babb, Thomas	Unkn.					X2
Babbington, John	Merc.		24			
Babbington, Urie	Merc.		99			
Baber, John	Unkn.	28				
Bace, Robert	Merc.				00	
Bache, George	Merc.			09		
Backer, George	Merc.					F1
Backhouse, John	Kt. 26	25–28	29			O?
Backhouse, Nicholas	Merc.					S1
Backhouse, Roland	Merc.		99			I2c/M/Og/S4
Backhouse, Samuel	Gent.	04–14	00			O
Backhouse, William	Gent.					J3
Bacon, Anthony	Gent.	93–97				
Bacon, Edmund	Gent.	89–93				
Bacon, Edmund	Kt. 03	25				
Bacon, Edward	Unkn.	84–86				
Bacon, Francis, Ld. Verulam, Viscount St. Albans	Nob. 03	84–14	18	09c		N/Q
Bacon, Nathaniel	Gent.	84, 93–97, 04				
Bacon, Nicholas	Kt. 58					R1/W2/BB1
**Bacon, Robert	Unkn.	21	29			
Badger, John	Unkn.			09		
Badger, Thomas	Kt.†	25–28				
Badger, William	Merc.	97				
Badram, George	Merc.					S6
Bagge, James	Merc.	01–04		06c		S1c/X1
Bagge, James	Kt. 25	21–28		20?		X2
Bagge, Thomas	Merc.					X1
Bagnall, Henry	Kt. 78	86				
Bagnell, ?	Unkn.					T3
Bagnoll, William	Unkn.	97				
Bagott, Harvey	Kt. 27	28				
Bagott, Walter	Unkn.	86				
Bagshawe, Robert	Merc.		14			
Bagshawe, Thomas	Merc.			09		I7/GG
Bagwell, William	Unkn.			22		
Baildon, Francis	Kt. 03	14				
Bailiffe, Henry	Gent.	86–89				
Bailiffe, John	Unkn.	21				
Bailis, Thomas	Unkn.	97				
Baily, John	Unkn.	89				
Baily, Robert	Merc.		00			
Baily, Stephen	Merc.					L1
Baker, Alexander	Merc.					L1

Name & title	Class; date of knight- hood	Parlia- ments (starting dates)	E. Ind. Co.	Va. Co.	Levant Co.	Other companies
Baker, Christopher	Merc.					*X1*
Baker, Daniel	Merc.					*F1/S1*
Baker, George	Merc.					*S1*
Baker, John	Gent.		14	09		*I1*
Baker, Jonas	Merc.					*S1*
Baker, Richard	Unkn.	93–97				*GG*
Baker, Richard	Merc.					*S5*
Baker, Thomas	Merc.			18?	23	*S4*
Baker, Thomas	Unkn.	01				*GG*
Baker, Walter	Merc.					*L1*
Baker, William	Merc.					*L1*
Bakett, Ansellnus	Merc.					*S6*
Baldocke, Richard	Merc.					*F1*
Baldwin, Francis	Merc.			12		
Baldwin, William	Merc.					*L1*
Bale, Edward	Unkn.		26			
Bale, Francis	Unkn.		14			
Balgey, Thomas	Unkn.	97				
Ball, Baily	Merc.		14			
Ball, Henry	Merc.					*S4*
Ball, John	Merc.		18		11	*R2/T3/GG*
Ball, Nicholas	Merc.	84				*S1*
Ball, Peter	Unkn.	26–28				
Ball, Richard	Merc.		00	21c		*E4/F1/L1c/ Q/U*
Ball, Thomas	Merc.		01			*F1/S4*
Ballard, Daniel	Unkn.					*J1*
Ballowe, John	Merc.					*X2*
Balmford, ?	Unkn.			22		
Balser, Ralph	Merc.			09		
Bamfield, Amias	Kt. 03	97, 04		12		*I9*
Bamfield, John	Gent.	21, 28				
Bamfield, William	Kt.†	14				
Banaster, Henry	Unkn.	14, 25				
Bancroft, Thomas	Unkn.	24–28				
Bande, John	Unkn.	01				
Banger, John	Unkn.		23			
Banggam, ?	Merc.		15			
Banister, Alexander	Merc.					*GG*
Banister, Daniel	Unkn.					*X2*
Banister, Henry	Merc.					*F1*
Banister, Richard	Merc.			09		
Banister, William	Merc.			09		
Bank, Martin van	Merc.					*X1*
Banks, John	Merc.	24, 26–28	07	09	05	*I2/L1/Q/T2*
Banks, Miles	Merc.			09		
Banning, Andrew	Merc.		00		90c	*D/S1c/X1/DD*
Banning, Paul	Merc.		99c		90	*D/Q/S6c/X1/ DD/GG*
Barber, Anthony	Merc.		24			
Barber, Edward	Merc.			12		

Name & title	Class; date of knight-hood	Parlia-ments (starting dates)	E. Ind. Co.	Va. Co.	Levant Co.	Other companies
Barber, Gabriel	Merc.		22	16c		T2c/FF
Barber, Jeremy	Merc.					F1/S1
Barber, John	Unkn.					X1
Barber, Thomas	Merc.		09	09		Q
Bardon, John	Merc.					X2
Bardwell, William	Unkn.			09		
Barefoote, Henry	Merc.				05	
Barefoote, John	Merc.					I2
Barefoote, Thomas	Merc.	04				
Bargrave, George	Unkn.			17		
Bargrave, John	Unkn.			17		
Barkeham, Edward	M. Kt. 22	25–26	00	10c	05	
Barkeham, Thomas	Merc.					R2
Barkeley, ?	Kt. †			21		
Barkeley, Charles	Kt. 23	21–28				
**Barkeley, Edward	Gent.	86		09		
Barkeley, Edward	Merc.				15	
Barkeley, Elizabeth	Unkn.			22		
**Barkeley, Francis	Unkn.	14–24				I9
Barkeley, George	Merc.			09	10	T1
Barkeley, Henry	Kt. 84	84–86				
Barkeley, Henry	Kt. 09	26–28				GG
Barkeley, John	Merc.		25			M
Barkeley, Maurice	Kt. 96	97–14	11	07c		I2
Barkeley, Maurice	Kt. 21	21–26		23		
Barkeley, Ninian	Unkn.					X2
Barkeley, Richard	Kt. 74	04				
Barkeley, Richard	Gent.	14		19		
Barkeley, Robert	Gent.	01, 21–24		12		
Barkeley, Roland	Merc.	93–04				
Barkeley, Thomas	Kt. 03	04				
Barkeley, William	Merc.		18	09		X2/GG
Barker, Andrew	Merc.					X1
Barker, Anthony	Kt. 08	21				
Barker, Charles	Merc.					M
Barker, Christopher	Merc.					E2
Barker, Edmund	Unkn.			23		
**Barker, Edward	Merc.	84–86, 93–01	00			
Barker, Edward	Unkn.					X2
Barker, Francis	Merc.		00			
Barker, John	Merc.	84–89		09	10	F1/S6c
Barker, John	Merc.	24, 28	24			R2/S6/X2
Barker, John	Gent.	01				I1
Barker, John	Merc.					S1
**Barker, Matthew	Merc.			09		X2
Barker, Michael	Merc.					S6
Barker, Reginald	Merc.					S6
Barker, Richard	Merc.	84, 04				S1/X1
Barker, Robert	Merc.	97–14		09		S4
Barker, Robert	Merc.	93				
Barker, Thomas	Merc.		14		16	X2

240

Name & title	Class; date of knight-hood	Parlia-ments (starting dates)	E. Ind. Co.	Va. Co.	Levant Co.	Other companies
Barker, William	Merc.					$E1/S6$
Barkham, Lawrence	Merc.					$CC1$
Barley, Edward	Merc.					$S1$
Barley, George	Merc.					$F1$
Barley, Robert	Merc.		99			Q
Barlow, Edward	Merc.					$F1$
Barlow, John	Merc.					$F1$
Barlow, William	Pfl/y.					Q
Barnaby, Alexander	Merc.					$F1/I7$
Barnaby, John	Merc.					$F1/S4$
Barnaby, William	Merc.					$F1/X2$
Barnard, Edward	Merc.				06	
Barnard, John	Gent.			21c		$T2g$
Barnard, William	Merc.		09			$F1$
Barnardiston, Elizabeth	Merc.		27			
Barnardiston, George	Merc.		27			
Barnardiston, John	Merc.		24		15	
Barnardiston, Nathaniel	Kt. 18	25–28				$J3$
Barnardiston, Thomas	Merc.		19		27	
Barnars, Anthony	Gent.			09		
Barnes, Bartholomew	Merc.		99			M
Barnes, Edward	Merc.		99	09		$I2/R2/AA1$
Barnes, Francis	Merc.					$S1c$
Barnes, George	M. Kt. 87	89			81	$D/E1/I2/R1g/$ $S6c/W4/X1/$ $BB1g/GG$
Barnes, Henry	Merc.					$X2/AA3$
Barnes, John	Merc.					$S6/GG$
Barnes, John	Merc.					$S1/X2$
Barnes, Richard	Merc.				00	$M/R1/S1/AA1$
Barnes, Richard	Merc.					$R1$
Barnes, Robert	Merc.					$S1$
Barnes, Thomas	Merc.					$M/X1$
Barnes, William	Kt. 03	93				$I2$
Barnes, William	M. Kt. 18†			09		$S1$
Barnesly, Nicholas	Merc.		99			
Barnestrawe, George	Merc.					$X1$
Barnham, Benedict	Unkn.	89, 97				
Barnham, Francis	Kt. 03	04–24, 26–28		12		
Barnham, Francis	Merc.					$R1c$
Barnham, Stephen	Unkn.	01				
Barnhowse, Richard	Merc.					$X2$
Baron, Benjamin	Merc.		18		10c	
Baron, Christopher	Merc.			09		$T2$
Baron, Peter	Merc.					$F1$
Barr, John de la	Merc.		20			$X2$
Barr, Robert de la	Merc.		19			
Barrell, William	Merc.		99			
Barrer, John	Unkn.					$I8$
Barrett, Edward	Kt. 08	14–21				
Barrett, James	Unkn.	97				

Name & title	Class; date of knighthood	Parliaments (starting dates)	E. Ind. Co.	Va. Co.	Levant Co.	Other companies
Barrett, Richard	Merc.		99			D/S6
Barrett, Richard	Merc.		00			
Barrett, Robard	Merc.					D/X1
Barrett, Thomas	Merc.				19	
Barrett, William	Merc.		00	10	00	
Barringer, Peter	Merc.		18			
Barrington, Francis	Kt. 03	01–04, 21–28		10		
Barrington, Henry	Unkn.	89				
Barrington, Robert	Gent.	28				
Barrington, Thomas	Kt. 21	21–28				FF
Barrowes, Richard	Merc.					I7
Barry, Richard	Unkn.	84–86				
Bart, John	Merc.					I7
Bartey, Francis	Merc.					BB1c/GG
Bartey, Francis	Merc.					BB2
Bartey, Stephen	Merc.					S6
Barthe, William	Merc.					F1/X2
Bartlett, Walter	Unkn.	25–26				
Bartlett, ?	Unkn.	04, 24				
Bartley, Edward	Gent.					CC1
Bartley, Peter	Merc.			10		
Barton, Edward	Gent.?				92	
Barton, John	Merc.					I7c
Barton, Michael	Merc.					S6
Barton, Thomas	Gent.					I2
Barwick, Henry	Merc.					S6
Barwick, Thomas	Unkn.			22		
Barwick, William	Unkn.	04				
*Barwick, William	Merc.					CC2
Barwis, Richard	Unkn.	28				
Bash, Edward	Kt. 16	14, 28				
Baskerville, Humphrey	Kt. 09	14				
Baskerville, Thomas	Kt. 88	93–97				
Bass, Edward	Unkn.					P2
Bass, Humphrey,	Merc.		00c	12		F1c/M/Q
Bass, Nathaniel	Merc.		17			
Bass, Richard	Merc.		17			
Bassett, Arnold	Merc.					X2
Bassett, Arthur	Merc.	25–26				
Bassett, George	Merc.			09		X1
Bassett, Robert	Merc.	93				
Bassett, Robert	Merc.					X2
Bassett, Thomas	Merc.					F1
Bassett, William	Gent.	86				
*Bassett, William	Merc.					X1
Bastard, William	Unkn.	01				
Bastwick, Edmund	Unkn.					X2
Bate, Anthony	Merc.				90	
Bate, Henry	Merc.		24			
Bate, John	Merc.		99c		90c	S1c/GG
Bate, Robert	Merc.				90	

Name & title	Class; date of knighthood	Parliaments (starting dates)	E. Ind. Co.	Va. Co.	Levant Co.	Other companies
Bateman, John	Unkn.	84				
Bateman, Raphe	Merc.			22	10	
Bateman, Richard	Merc.		26		26	
Bateman, Robert	Merc.	14–26	99c	09	05c	F1/J3/M/Oc/ Q/S5/X1/GG
Bateman, William	Merc.				28	F1/J3/O/X2
Bates, William	Merc.					I7
Bathurst, Thomas	Merc.?			09		
Bathurst, Timothy	Merc.			09		
Batteshell, Henry	Merc.					X2
Batty, Richard	Merc.		14			
Bavand, Richard	Merc.	84				
Bavidge, Gregory	Unkn.					X2
Bawle, Robert	Unkn.	93				
Bawtrey, Leonard	Unkn.	14				
Baxter, John	Merc.	01–04				
Baycock, William	Merc.					F1
Bayert, William	Unkn.		22			
Bayert, William	Unkn.		22			
Bayley, Thomas	Merc.			09		I7
Baylie, Raphe	Merc.					I7
Baylie, Richard	Merc.					I7
Bayly, Roger	Gent.			87		
Bayly, Walter	Merc.			89		
Baynam, Benedict	Unkn.	89				
Baynam, Edmund	Unkn.	97				
Baynam, John	Unkn.	93				
Baynam, Richard	Unkn.			20		
Baynam, Thomas	Merc.					W4
Baynam, William	Unkn.	84–97				
Baynard, Robert	Unkn.	84–86				
Baynbrigg, Robert	Unkn.	86				
Baynes, Richard	Merc.					E2/F1
Baynton, Edward	Kt. 74	89				
Baynton, Edward	Kt. 13	21–26				
Baynton, Edward	Gent.	14				
Baynton, Henry	Kt.†	84–97, 04				
Beadle, Matthew	Merc.		24			L1
Beadle, Michael	Merc.					I7
Beale, Anthony	Merc.					F1
Beale, Edward	Merc.		07	09		
Beale, Francis	Gent.	14				AA3
Beale, Henry	Unkn.					X2
Beale, James	Merc.					E3
Beale, John	Merc.		24			
Beale, Richard	Merc.		00			
Beale, Robert	Gent.	84–93				AA2c/BB3
Beale, Thomas	Gent.					BB5g
Beamishe, Julius	Merc.				00	
Beamount, Farnaby	Merc.				12	
Beamount, Henry	Kt. 03	84, 89, 04				GG

243

Name & title	Class; date of knight-hood	Parlia-ments (starting dates)	E. Ind. Co.	Va. Co.	Levant Co.	Other companies
Beamount, John	Merc.			12		
Beamount, Nicholas	Unkn.	84				
Beamount, Richard	Kt. 03	24–25				
Beamount, Thomas	Kt. 03	04, 21		10		GG
Beane, Edmund	Unkn.					X2
Beane, Peter	Unkn.					X2
Beane, Richard	Merc.					L1
Beanley, John	Merc.					F1
Beanley, Thomas	Merc.					F1
Beaple, Elthreed	Unkn.					X2
Beaple, James	Merc.					S1c
Beaple, Richard	Merc.					S1
Beard, George	Merc.			09		
Beareblock, James	Merc.		14			O
Beareblock, William	Merc.		01			
Beareblock, William	Merc.		09	17c		T3?
Beauchamp, John	Unkn.					P2/X2/GG
Beauvoir, Abraham	Merc.					S4
Beauvoir, Peter	Merc.					F1/S1
Becher, Henry	Merc.					X1/GG
Becher, Vane	Unkn.					I9
Becher, William	Kt. 22	01, 14–28	29			
Beck, Abraham	Unkn.		24			
Beck, Charles	Unkn.			18?		
Beck, William	Gent.			12		
Beckingham, Thomas	Kt. 03	04				
Beddingfield, Henry	Kt. 03	14		12		
Beddingfield, Thomas	Gent.	86				
Beddingfield, Thomas	Gent.	21, 26				
Bedell, Capel	Kt. 22	26–28				
Bedell, Gabriel	Unkn.			09		
Bedell, John	Unkn.		24	09		
Bedford, Henry	Merc.					X1
Bedford, Richard	Merc.					S1/X1
Bedford, Thomas	Merc.					F1/S1
Bedham, Thomas	Merc.					L1
Beedoe, John	Merc.					S1
Beere, William	Merc.				28	
Beeston, George	Kt. 88	89				
Beeston, Hugh	Kt. 03	89–14				I9
Beeston, William	Gent.	24				
Bele, Jerome	Merc.					E1
Belfield, Ralph	Merc.					S4
Belfield, Richard	Merc.					S1
Belford, James	Kt.†					I8
Belfrey, Richard	Merc.					F1
Belgrave, George	Unkn.	01				
Belke, Thomas	Merc.				90	
Bell, Edmund	Gent.	86				
Bell, Robert	M. Kt. 11	26	99c			F1c/S1
Bell, Robert	Merc.		19c	12		Qc/T3

Name & title	Class; date of knighthood	Parliaments (starting dates)	E. Ind. Co.	Va. Co.	Levant Co.	Other companies
Bell, William	Merc.				10	
Bellamy, John	Merc.					F1
Bellasis, Henry	Kt. 03	86–01				
Bellasis, Henry	Gent.	25–28				
Bellasis, Thomas Viscount Fauconberg	Nob. 03	97, 14–24				
Bellasis, William	Kt. 17					K5
Bellingham, Henry	Kt. 20	25–26				
Bellingham, Henry	Unkn.	28				
Bellingham, Richard	Unkn.	04				
Bellingham, Richard	Gent.	28				J1
Benbowe, Francis	Merc.					L1/M
Benbowe, William	Merc.			09		
Benbowe, ?	Unkn.	24				
Bence, Alexander	Merc.					X2
Bence, John	Merc.	24				X2
Bence, Squire	Merc.					X2
Bence, William	Merc.	89–93				
Bendishe, Thomas	Unkn.		11			
Benham, William	Unkn.			18?		
Benley, John	Merc.					L1
Bennett, Anthony	Unkn.	93				
Bennett, David	Unkn.			20		
Bennett, Edward	Merc.			21c	23	X2
Bennett, George	Merc.		01c	09		Q/S5
Bennett, Henry	Merc.					F1
Bennett, John	Kt. 03	97–21	10			
Bennett, John	Unkn.	86–89				
Bennett, John	Merc.					X2
Bennett, Nicholas	Unkn.	24				
*Bennett, Nicholas	Unkn.					X2
Bennett, Richard	Merc.		25			L1/M
*Bennett, Richard	Merc.					S6
Bennett, Robert	Kt. 19	21, 25				
Bennett, Sampson	Merc.		09			F1
Bennett, Thomas	M. Kt. 03					I7c
Bennett, Thomas	Merc.					I2
Bennett, William	Gent.	93				
Bennett, William	Merc.			09		I7
Benskin, John	Merc.					I7
Benson, George	Merc.		11		21	F1/L1c/S3
Benson, Henry	Unkn.	26–28				
Benson, John	Merc.					I7
Benson, Nicholas	Unkn.			09		T2
Benson, Peter	Unkn.			09		I8
Benson, Richard	Unkn.	04				
Benthall, John	Merc.					R2c
Bents, Alexander	Unkn.			09		
Beresford, George	Merc.					S4
Beresford, Richard	Merc.		22		17c	
Beresford, Robert	Merc.			07		

Name & title	Class; date of knight-hood	Parlia-ments (starting dates)	E. Ind. Co.	Va. Co.	Levant Co.	Other companies
Beresford, Roland	Merc.					L1
Berple, Henry	Merc.					F1
Berple, James	Merc.					F1
Berple, Richard	Merc.					F1
Berrington, Humphrey	Merc.		24			L1/M
Berry, Christopher	Unkn.					X2
Berry, John	Pfl/y.		29			
Berry, ?	Pfl/y.		29			
Berry, Robert	Merc.	84–04				
Bertie, Montague						
Earl Lindsey	Nob. 16	24–26				
Bertie, Peregrine						
Lord Willoughby	Nob.					X1
Bertie, Peregrine	Kt. 10	14			12	G6
Bertie, Robert						
Earl Lindsey	Nob.					X1/X2
Besart, William	Unkn.		22			
Besse, William	Merc.					I7
Bessell, Martin	Merc.	93				
Best, John	Merc.					S5
Best, Michael	Merc.					A
Best, Phineas	Merc.					S6
Best, Thomas	Kt.†	26				X2
Best, ?	Unkn.					T3
Bethell, David	Unkn.					X2
Bethell, Zachariah	Unkn.	93				
Beton, David	Unkn.					X2
Betton, John	Unkn.			18?		
Bevan, Andrew	Merc.					X2
Bevans, Francis	Unkn.	93				
Bevill, Robert	Gent.	84				
Bevill, Robert	Kt. 03	21				
Bevill, William	Kt. 89	93				
Bewick, Robert	Merc.					M
Bewie, Nicholas	Merc.					S1
Bewley, John	Merc.					L1
Bickley, Francis	Unkn.			23		
Biddulph, Anthony	Merc.		24	20		L1/M
Biddulph, William	Merc.		14			
Bigge, Thomas	Kt. 03	04, 21				
Bigge, Thomas	Gent.	14				
Bigget, John	Merc.					F1
Biggs, Richard	Unkn.			23		
Billett, Ambrose	Unkn.	97				
Billett, Thomas	Unkn.	01				
Billingsley, Henry	Kt. 03	04				I9
Billson, Thomas	Kt. 13	14				
Bilson, ?	Unkn.					J3
Bindlose, Francis	Kt. 24	28				
Bindon, John	Merc.					S1
Bing, George	Unkn.	84, 04				

Name & title	Class; date of knight-hood	Parlia-ments (starting dates)	E. Ind. Co.	Va. Co.	Levant Co.	Other companies
Bing, Henry	Unkn.	14				
Bing, Isabel	Merc.		27			
Bing, Thomas	Unkn.	14				
Bing, William	Unkn.	04–14		22c		
Bingham, John	Unkn.		09			
Bingham, Richard	Gent.					CC2
Bingley, John	Kt. 18	04–14		09c		A
Bingley, Ralph	Kt. 03					I4
Bingley, Richard	Kt. 11			12		A/I4
Birch, William	Unkn.					X2
Bird, Henry	Unkn.	97				
Bird, John	Merc.					S6/X1/GG1
Bird, Richard	Merc.	93				
Bird, Robert	Merc.					S6
Bird, William	Kt. 17	04, 21				
Bird, William	Unkn.					X2
Birkby, James	Merc.	93–97				
Birkheved, Richard	Merc.	84–93				
Bish, Edward	Unkn.	24–28				
Bishop, Edward	M. Kt. 25	26		09		T2
Bishop, George	Merc.?			09		
Bishop, Nathaniel	Merc.					I2
Bishop, Richard	Merc.		18		22	
Bishop, Thomas	Kt. 03	84–86, 04				
Bisse, James	Unkn.	84				
Blachford, John	Unkn.					X2
Black, Humphrey	Merc.					S1
Blacker, William	Unkn.	97				
Blackerby, William	Merc.					I7
Blackford, Richard	Merc.					F1
Blackford, Thomas	Merc.					F1
Blackhall, George	Unkn.					X2
Blackhall, John	Unkn.		17			
Blackhall, Leonard	Merc.					F1/S1
Blackhall, William	Merc.					X1
Blackiler, Thomas	Merc.					S1
Blackley, Richard	Merc.					I1c
Blackman, Jeremy	Unkn.					X2
Blackmore, Arthur	Merc.					I7
Blackmore, Richard	Unkn.			18?		
Bladwell, John	Merc.		29			L2/M
Bladwell, Richard	Merc.		11c			I2/L2/M/R2c
Bladwell, William	Merc.		29			R2c
Blagge, Henry	Unkn.	84–86				
Blagge, William	Merc.					S6
Blagrave, Anthony	Unkn.	01				
Blake, Alexander	Unkn.					X2
Blake, Humphrey	Merc.					F1
Blake, John	Merc.				10	X2
Blake, Nicholas	Merc.					F1/X2
Blake, Patrick	Merc.			09		

Name & title	Class; date of knighthood	Parliaments (starting dates)	E. Ind. Co.	Va. Co.	Levant Co.	Other companies
Blake, Peter	Unkn.					X2
Blake, Richard	Merc.				19	
Blake, Robert	Unkn.	84–89				
Blake, William	Unkn.	26				
Blake, William	Merc.				15	I7/X2
Blancher, John	Merc.					L1
Blanck, Thomas	M. Kt. 83					Mc/S6
Bland, Benjamin	Unkn.			18?		
Bland, Gregory	Merc.			09		S4
Bland, John	Merc.		15	18c	23	M/R2c/GG
Blandy, Henry	Merc.					L1
Blenerhassett, Edward	Kt. 03					I2
Blenerhassett, Edward	Gent.					G8
Blenerhassett, Francis	Gent.					I2
Blenerhassett, Henry	Gent.					G8
Blenerhassett, Mason	Gent.					G8
Blenerhassett, Thomas	Merc.	84–86, 04				
Blenerhassett, Thomas	Gent.					I2
Blincowe, George	Unkn.	04				
Blissard, Francis	Merc.		11		?	L1c/M/X2/GG
Blithe, John	Merc.					E3
Blithe, William	Merc.					X2
Blowse, William	Merc.					F1
Bloy, Sampson	Unkn.					X2
Bludder, Thomas	M. Kt. 03	21–28		09		GG
Bludworth, John	Merc.		24			I7
Bluett, John	Unkn.	28				
Blundell, Francis	Kt. 18	21	23			A
Blundell, John	Unkn.			09		
Blunden, William	Unkn.	25–26				
Blunt, Charles Earl Devonshire	Nob. 87	84–86, 93				S1/X1
Blunt, Charles	Kt. 96	97				
Blunt, Christopher	Kt. 88	93–97				
Blunt, Edward	M. Kt. 99			20		I2
Blunt, James Lord Mountjoy	Nob.					AA1/GG
Blunt, John	Merc.		11	09		S1
Blunt, Richard	Unkn.	93, 01		18?		
Blunt, Walter	Unkn.	24				
Boast, John	Merc.					I7
Boddenham, Francis	Kt. 16	26				
Boddins, Adam	Unkn.		22			
Bodham, George	Unkn.					X2
Bodleigh, John	Merc.					E1
Bodleigh, John	Merc.					E1
Bodleigh, Thomas	Unkn.	84–86				
Bodname, Roger	Merc.					S6
Bogan, William	Merc.					F1
Bogans, Christopher	Merc.	97				
Bogans, John	Merc.	04				

Name & title	Class; date of knighthood	Parlia-ments (starting dates)	E. Ind. Co.	Va. Co.	Levant Co.	Other companies
Boggas, Robert	Gent.					*I2*
Bohun, Lawrence	Pfl/y.			12		
Bointon, Matthew	Kt. 18	21				
Bois, Peter de	Merc.					*X2*
Bold, Henry	Unkn.					*I9*
Bold, Richard	Unkn.	84				
Boldro, Edmund	Merc.					*E1*
Boldro, John	Merc.					*B*
Bolls, George	M. Kt. 18		99	09		*I7/Q/R2*
Bolt, Robert	Merc.					*F1*
Bolton, John	Merc.					*F1/S1*
Bolton, Thomas	Unkn.					*I1*
Bolton, William	Unkn.			18		
Bonall, John	Unkn.			21		
Bonamy, Jacob	Merc.					*I7*
Bond, George	Merc.				92	*S1*
Bond, George	M. Kt. 87					*E1/R1/S6/ BB1c*
Bond, John	Merc.					*X1*
Bond, Margaret	Merc.					*E1/S1*
Bond, Martin	Merc.	24–25		09		*I7c/S1c/T3*
Bond, Nicholas	Merc.					*S1*
Bond, Thomas	Gent.	04, 21–24		20		
Bond, William	M. Kt. 03		99			*B/E1/S1/W1/ X1/BB2c*
*Bond, William	Merc.			09	00	*F1/I7/M/R1/ S1/W5/BB2*
Bonham, William	Merc.		00c	09		*I7/Q*
Bonist, Thomas (see Bownest)	Merc.				29	*R2/GG*
Bonitham, John	Unkn.	86				
Bonner, Humphrey	Merc.	93–97				
Bonner, John	Merc.					*F1*
Bonner, Michael	Merc.					*I7*
Bonnyvale, Samuel	Merc.			09		
Booker, William	Unkn.					*I1*
Booth, James	Merc.	97				*X1*
Booth, Robert	Merc.	01				
Booth, William	Gent.	24				
Boothby, Henry	Merc.		10		10	
Boothby, Richard	Merc.		23	19		*F2/G8/L1/S2*
Boothby, Thomas	Merc.		00	09	05	*F1/H/L1c/ S1/GG*
Boothby, William	Merc.				26	
Boreman, Simon	Merc.					*D/S1/X1*
Bornford, William	Merc.					*M/S4*
Borough, John	Kt. 24	24–26				
Borough, Stephen	Merc.					*R1*
Borro, Walter	Merc.					*S1c*
Borrough, William	Merc.				92	*R1/S6/W5/GG*
Borrough, William	Merc.					*M/S1*

Name & title	Class; date of knight-hood	Parlia-ments (starting dates)	E. Ind. Co.	Va. Co.	Levant Co.	Other companies
B(W)orsley, Bowyer	Kt. 07			21		
Bostock, Charles	Unkn.		22			
Bostock, George	Merc.		24			
Bostock, Philip	Merc.					S5
Bostock, Richard	Unkn.	84, 89				
Bostock, Thomas	Merc.		99		00	F1/Q/S1c
Bostock, Thomas	Merc.				11	
Boston, Thomas	Merc.	89				
Bosvile, Nicholas	Merc.			09		
Boswell, David	Kt. 25					X2
Boswell, William	Unkn.	24–25				
Botham, William	Merc.	84–93				
Boughton, Edward	Unkn.	84				
Bourage, William	Merc.					S1
Bourchier, Elizabeth Countess Bath	Nob.					X1
Bourchier, George	Kt. 79					I9
Bourchier, Henry	Gent.	89–97				K4
Bourchier, John	Kt. 11	14		10		I4/K4
Bourchier, Ralph	Kt. 84	84–89				
Bourchier, William Earl Bath	Nob.			12?c		K4
Bourke, Richard Earl Clanricard	Nob.			12		
Bourman, Hugh	Merc.					S4
Bourne, David	Merc.		09	09	05c	F1/R2/S5
Bourne, John	Merc.					S6
Bourne, Richard	Merc.		09c			Q
Bourne, Robert	Merc.					I7
Bourne, Ruben	Merc.			12		
Bourne, William	Merc.					I7
Bowater, Edward	Merc.					L1
Bowater, John	Merc.			22		L1
Bowcher, John	Merc.?					BB3
**Bowde, Simon	Merc.	84				
Bowden, Martin	Merc.			09		
Bowdler, Paul	Merc.					M
Bowdler, Richard	Merc.		01			M/N/GG
Bowdler, William	Unkn.		09			
Bowdocke, Henry	Merc.					F1
Bowe, John	Merc.					I7
Bowen, John	Merc.					I7
Bower, Robert	Unkn.	93				
Bowes, Henry	Merc.					M
Bowes, Jerome	Kt. 70	01–04				GG
Bowes, Ralph	Gent.	89				X1
Bowes, Robert	Gent.	84–89				
Bowes, Robert	Gent.	84–86				GG
Bowes, Talbot	Kt. 17	93, 01–21, 25, 28				
Bowes, William	Kt. 86	93				

Name & title	Class; date of knight- hood	Parlia- ments (starting dates)	E. Ind. Co.	Va. Co.	Levant Co.	Other companies
Bowes, William	Gent.	21				
Bowland, Richard	Unkn.					W7
Bowle, Henry	Merc.					F1
Bowle, Richard	Unkn.	93				
Bowles, John	Unkn.					J3
Bowles, Michael	Unkn.					CC2
Bowles, Philip	Merc.					M
Bowman, Roger	Merc.					S1/X1
Bowmer, Thomas	Merc.					S1
Bowne, Edmund	Merc.					S6
Bownest, Thomas (see Bonist)	Merc.		14c			L1/M/GG
Bowser, John	Merc.					F1/I7
Bowyer, Edmund	Kt. 03	93–97, 04–14, 24		10		
Bowyer, Francis	Merc.					S6c
Bowyer, Henry	Kt. 03	01				Q
Bowyer, John	Kt. 07	97, 04				
Bowyer, Robert	Merc.		09		05c	B/I7/M/S1c/ GG1
Bowyer, Robert	Merc.				27	
Bowyer, Robert	Unkn.	01–04				
Bowyer, Roger	Merc.					X1
Bowyer, Thomas	Kt. 28†	14–28				
Bowyer, Thomas	Merc.		28		26	
Bowyer, William	Kt. 03	04, 21–24, 26				
Bowyer, William	Merc.					I7
Box, Henry	Unkn.			20		
Boyer, Bartholomew	Merc.					I7
Boyer, Simon	Gent.					W5/CC1
Boyle, James	Merc.	84				
Boyle, James	Merc.					S4
Boyle, Michael	Merc.					S6
Boylesonn, Thomas	Unkn.		24			
Boys, Edward	Kt. 03	25–26				
Boys, George	Merc.					S1
Boys, John	Kt. 04	93–04				
Boys, William	Unkn.	89				
Braborne, Henry	Merc.					I7
Brace, Francis	Unkn.	86–89				
Brace, John	Unkn.	04				
Brace, Thomas	Merc.		19			
Bracken, Edmund	Merc.					L1
Bradford, Thomas	Merc.			09		
Bradford, William	Merc.					L1/GG
Bradley, Francis	Pfl/y.			09		
Bradley, John	Merc.					H
Bradley, Thomas	Merc.		26			
Bradshaw, Job	Merc.					J3
Bradshaw, John	Merc.					S6
Bradshaw, Joseph	Merc.	28				J1

Name & title	Class; date of knight-hood	Parlia-ments (starting dates)	E. Ind. Co.	Va. Co.	Levant Co.	Other companies
Bradshaw, William	Merc.	04				
Bragdon, John	Merc.		26			
Bragg, Matthew	Merc.					*S1*
Bragg, Richard	Merc.					*X2*
Bragg, Robert	Merc.					*S1/X1*
Bragg, William	Merc.					*X1*
Braines, Daniel	Merc.					*L1*
Brakin, Francis	Unkn.	14, 24				
Bramble, John	Merc.					*F1*
Brames, Arnold	Unkn.					*X2*
Bramley, Thomas	Merc.		01c			*B/E1/S6c/ X1/GG*
Branch, John	M. Kt. 80					*R1*
Brand, Benjamin	Gent.			12		
Brand, Cuthbert	Merc.					*S6*
Brand, John	Unkn.					*I8*
Brand, Josias	Merc.					*S1*
Brandling, Francis	Kt. 17	24–25				
Brandling, Robert	Gent.	21				
Braunche, William	Merc.	93				
Brawne, Hugh	M. Kt. 03					*I7*
Brayley, William	Merc.					*C*
Brearey, Christopher	Merc.					*E2*
Brearey, Samuel	Merc.					*E2*
Brearey, William	Merc.					*E2*
Bree, John	Gent.			09		
Breet, Dionise	Unkn.					*CC2*
Breres, Edmund	Unkn.	24				
Breres, Henry	Merc.	86–89, 01–04				
Brereton, Roger	Gent.	04				
Brereton, Theophilus	Merc.		23			*L1c/M*
Brereton, Thomas	Unkn.	21–25				
Brereton, William	Kt. 88	97, 14–21				
Brereton, William	Kt. 26†	24, 28				*J3/GG*
Brethers, Thomas	Merc.		24			
Brett, John	Unkn.	01				
Brett, Robert	Kt. 03	04–14				
Brett, Thomas	Merc.		19	09		
Brett, Thomas	Unkn.	21, 26–28				
Bretton, Edward	Merc.					*L1/M*
Bretton, Henry	Kt. 17	14–21				
Bretton, John	Unkn.	84				
Bretton, Thomas	Unkn.	01				
Brewen, George	Merc.					*L1/M*
Brewer, John	Merc.				00	
Brewer, Thomas	Unkn.					*P2*
Brewer, William	Merc.					*Q*
Brewsey, Ambrose	Unkn.			18?		
Brewster, Edward	Unkn.			09		
Brewster, John	Merc.					*F1*
Brewster, Mark	Merc.					*R2*

Name & title	Class; date of knight-hood	Parlia-ments (starting dates)	E. Ind. Co.	Va. Co.	Levant Co.	Other companies
Brewster, William	Unkn.			09		
Briarly, James	Merc.		29	09		I7
Briarly, John	Merc.		29			
Briary, Matthew	Merc.					F1
Briary, William	Merc.					F1
Bridgeman, Edward	Unkn.	25–28				
Bridgeman, George	Unkn.	28				
Bridgeman, Henry	Merc.		99		05	S5
Bridgeman, Susan	Merc.		14			
Bridger, Richard	Merc.					I7
Bridges, Anthony	Merc.		14		11	L1
Bridges, Giles	Kt. 26†	21, 25, 28				
Bridges, Grey Lord Chandos	Nob.	97		09c		
Bridges, John	Merc.					F1
Bridges, John Bishop Oxford	Nob.			12		
Bridges, Samuel	Merc.				17	
Bridges, William Lord Chandos	Nob.	84–86				
Briggs, David	Unkn.		14			
Briggs, Henry	Unkn.			22		Q/T3
Briggs, Richard	Merc.				10	
Briggs, Robert	Unkn.			20		
Briggs, Robert	Unkn.	86				
Bright, Richard	Merc.					I7
Bright, William	Merc.			10		
Bringborne, Robert	Merc.					S6
Brinsley, ?	Unkn.			09		
Briscoe, Raphe	Merc.					I7
Britton, John	Merc.			12		T2/Y
Britton, Thomas	Unkn.			09		
Brittridge, Francis	Merc.			09	10	
Brittridge, Richard	Merc.				10	
Brittridge, Roger	Merc.				11	
Broad, John	Merc.					I7
Broadbent, William	Merc.					X1
Broadgat, Martin	Unkn.					X2
Broadribb, Stephen	Unkn.					X2
Broadstreate, Simon	Merc.				00c	J1
Brocas, Pexel	Unkn.	84				
Brock, William	Unkn.	97, 04				
Brocken, Richard	Merc.					E2
Brocket, John	Kt. 77					W5
Brocket, Thomas	Gent.			09		
Brockhouse, John	Merc.				10	
Broderidge, Christopher	Merc.					M/Q1/S1
Brograve, John	Unkn.	86–01				
Brome, Bartholomew	Merc.	89				
Brome, Simon	Merc.	84–89				
Bromesgrave, Thomas	Merc.			09		I7

Name & title	Class; date of knight- hood	Parlia- ments (starting dates)	E. Ind. Co.	Va. Co.	Levant Co.	Other companies
Bromfield, Arthur	Gent.	04–21		18		T2
Bromfield, Robert	Unkn.	21–24				
Bromley, Edward	Gent.	86–04				
Bromley, Francis	Gent.	84				
Bromley, Henry	Kt. 92	84–86, 93–97, 04				
Bromley, Robert	Merc.					S4
Bromley, Thomas	Kt. 79					CC2
Bromley, Thomas	Kt. 03	14, 28				
Bromrick, Matthew	Merc.		08?	12		Q
Brooke, Arthur	Merc.					F1
Brooke, Basil	Kt. 03	04				GG
Brooke, Basil	Kt. 17					I4
Brooke, Calisthenes	Kt. 97			09		
Brooke, Christopher	Gent.	04–26		09c		
Brooke, George	Unkn.	84				
Brooke, Giles	Merc.	04				F1
Brooke, Henry	Kt. 75	86–89				S6
Brooke, Henry	Kt. 98	93				
Brooke, Henry	Merc.					S6
Brooke, Henry	Merc.		29		10	F1/L1
Brooke, Henry Lord Cobham	Nob.			?		X1/Y
Brooke, John	Kt.†	14–21, 25		09c		K4/GG
Brooke, John	Merc.	97	00	09	12	S1/X1
Brooke, John	Merc.					R1
Brooke, Percival	Merc.					F1/S1
Brooke, Richard	Unkn.			09		
Brooke, Robert	Kt. 15	24–25, 28				
Brooke, Robert	Merc.	84–86	99			L1/M/S6
Brooke, Simon	Merc.					S6
Brooke, William Lord Cobham	Nob.					BB1
Brooke, William	Kt. 91	84–86, 97				
Brooke, William	Kt. 26	28				
Brooke, William	Merc.					F1
Brooker, Hugh	Gent.			09		
Brookes, George	Unkn.			22		
Brookes, Thomas	Unkn.	04				
Brookinge, Allen	Merc.					F1/S1
Brookinge, Christopher	Merc.	04				F1/S1
Brookinge, William	Merc.					S1
Brookshaw, John	Unkn.					X2
Brough, John	Unkn.			18?		
Broughton, Richard	Unkn.	86–93				
Brouncker, Henry	Kt. 97	84–89, 01				R1
Brouncker, William	Kt. 92	84–93				
Browker, Hugh	Unkn.	93				
Brown, Ambrose	Kt. 27	28				
Brown, Anthony	Unkn.			20		
Brown, Brutus	Unkn.	86				

254

Name & title	Class; date of knighthood	Parliaments (starting dates)	E. Ind. Co.	Va. Co.	Levant Co.	Other companies
Brown, David	Merc.					X2
Brown, Edward	Gent.	84–86				
Brown, Edward	Merc.					F1/S1
Brown, George	Merc.					BB2
Brown, George	Unkn.	14, 26–28				
Brown, Ham.	Merc.					X2
Brown, Humphrey	Merc.		11c		22c	F1/M/Q/X2
Brown, John	Unkn.	14–28				
Brown, John	Unkn.	21, 28				
Brown, John	Unkn.	01				
**Brown, John	Merc.		24	09	10	F1/J2c/N/ S1/X2
*Brown, John	Merc.					F1
Brown, John	Merc.					S6
Brown, Kellam	Unkn.					J3
Brown, Matthew	Kt. 96	01				
Brown, Matthew	Unkn.			09		
Brown, Nicholas	Unkn.					I9
Brown, Richard	Kt. 03	84–93, 01–04				
Brown, Richard	Gent.	01				
Brown, Richard	Unkn.	84				
Brown, Richard	Merc.		99			
Brown, Robert	Unkn.	01				
*Brown, Robert	Unkn.	24				
*Brown, Robert	Merc.		14	19		
Brown, S.	Merc.	84				
Brown, Samuel	Unkn.					J2c
Brown, Strange	Merc.					X1
Brown, Thomas	Kt. 76	86				
**Brown, Thomas	Merc.		28		14	L2/M
Brown, Thomas	Gent.					I2
Brown, Valentine	Kt. 70	86				I9
Brown, Valentine	Kt. 03	04				
**Brown, William	Kt. 03	14–21		09		
Brown, William	M. Kt. 23†			09		F1/M
Brown, William	Merc.		27			X2
Browning, Henry	Unkn.					P2
Brownlowe, John	Unkn.					I2
Brownlowe, William	Gent.?		07			I2
Brownrigg, ?	Merc.					E3
Bruce, Edward, Lord	Nob.			23c		
Bruce, John	Kt. 28					GG
Brudenell, Edmund	Unkn.			09		
Brudenell, Francis	Unkn.			22		
Bruen, William	Merc.					B/M
Bruerton, Thomas	Merc.	84				
Bryant, Thomas	Merc.					X2
Bryard, John	Unkn.					X2
Bryard, William	Unkn.					X2
Bucher, John	Unkn.			18?		
Buck, George	Unkn.	93–97				

Name & title	Class; date of knighthood	Parliaments (starting dates)	E. Ind. Co.	Va. Co.	Levant Co.	Other companies
Buck, John	Unkn.	01				
Buck, Richard	Pfl/y.			12		
Buck, Robert	Merc.		00			
Buckeridge, Nicholas	Merc		24	19		L1/M/S3
Buckfold, Richard	Merc.					S4
Buckford, William	Merc.					F1
Buckine, Emanuel	Merc.					S1
Bucking, Robert	Merc.	93, 04				S1
Buckley, Lawrence	Merc.				00	
Bucknam, William	Merc.					I7
Buckner, Thomas	Merc.					I2
Bucock, Nathaniel	Merc.					I7
Budden, John	Unkn.	01–04				
Budge, John	Unkn.			20		
Budley, John	Unkn.					X2
Buffkyn, Leven	Unkn.	93				
Bugganne, William	Unkn.					X2
Bugges, Anthony	Kt. 18		24			A
Buggin, Walter	Merc.					Q1
Buggin, William	Unkn.	89				
Bulbecke, Thomas	Unkn.	93				
Bulkeley, Richard	Kt. 04	89, 04		21		
Bulkeley, Richard	Gent.	24, 26–28				
Bulkeley, Thomas	Gent.	84–93				
Bulkeley, Thomas	Gent.?			21		
Bull, John	Merc.					I7
Bull, Thomas	Unkn.		11			
Buller, Francis	Gent.	24–25, 28				
Buller, Richard	Kt. 08	04, 21, 25–28				
Bullingham, Francis	Unkn.	01–04				
Bullock, John	Gent.			09		
Bully, John	Merc.					GG1
Bullycard, John	Merc.					S6
Bulmer, Bevis	Kt.†					GG3
Bulmer, Thomas	Merc.					F1
Bulstrode, Henry	Gent.	14, 25				
Bulstrode, William	Kt. 99	04, 21–28		10		
Bunbury, Richard	Merc.			09		
Bunce, James	Merc.	28				
Bundocke, William	Merc.					X2
Bunnington, Humphrey	Merc.				06	
Burd, William	Merc.					W8/AA1c/BB1
Burdett, Robert	Unkn.	01				
Burfield, George	Unkn.					X2
Burge, Thomas	Merc.					S4
Burgh, John	Unkn.			23		
Burgh, Thomas	Merc.					S3
Burgins, Matthew	Merc.					X2
Burgis, John	Pfl/y.		14			
**Burgis, Richard	Merc.					F1/S1
Burgis, Richard	Unkn.	14				

Name & title	Class; date of knighthood	Parliaments (starting dates)	E. Ind. Co.	Va. Co.	Levant Co.	Other companies
Burgis, Thomas	Unkn.	04–14, 24				
Burgoyne, Peter	Unkn.			09		
Burgoyne, Robert	Unkn.			09		
**Burgoyne, Thomas	Unkn.	93		09		
Burie, William	Merc.					H
Burke, Adam	Merc.					F1
Burke, ?	Unkn.					W4
Burkett, Christopher	Merc.					X2
Burlacy, Edmund	Merc.					E1
Burlacy, Henry	Gent.	21				
Burlacy, John	Kt. 06	86		09		
Burlacy, William	Kt. 03	04–14				O
Burlacy, William	Kt. 17	14, 28				O
Burlamachi, Olanus	Merc.					S6
Burlamachi, Philip	Merc.		29			Qc/Z/GG
Burley, Francis	Unkn.					X1
Burley, Rice	Unkn.					X1
Burman, Simon	Merc.					S6
Burnell, Edward	Merc.					S6
Burnell, Francis	Unkn.					G7
Burnell, John	Merc.		09			E3/F1/L1c/Q
Burnell, John	Merc.					E1
Burnell, Thomas	Merc.					E3/J3/L1/Q
Burnett, William	Merc.				10	
Burnham, Samuel	Unkn.			09		
Burnham, William	Unkn.			23		
Burningham, John	Merc.					E3
Burray, ?	Unkn.			09		
Burre, Humphrey	Unkn.		11			
Burre, Olyffe	Unkn.					W2
Burrell, Daniel	Unkn.		14			
Burrell, Mineon	Unkn.			18?		
Burrell, Richard	Merc.		99			I7
Burrell, William	Merc.		01c	10		Qc
Burton, Edmund	Merc.					Mc/S3/X1
Burton, Edward	Unkn.	97				
Burton, George	Gent.			09		
Burton, John	Merc.					F1/I7
Burton, Stephen	Merc.		14			L1/M
Burton, Thomas	Unkn.	19				
Burton, William	Merc.					F1
Burwell, Edward	Unkn.			09		
Busbridge, John	Merc.		99c	09	05	Q
Busby, Michael	Merc.					F1
Busby, Ralph	Merc		99	09		I7/Q
Busfield, John	Merc.					S4
Bushell, William	Unkn					X2
Bushrode, Richard	Merc.	24, 26				K5/P1/GG
Busse, Nicholas	Merc.					L1
Bust, William	Unkn.					X2
*Butcher, John	Merc.					X2

Name & title	Class; date of knighthood	Parliaments (starting dates)	E. Ind. Co.	Va. Co.	Levant Co.	Other companies
Butcher, Nathaniel	Merc.					X2
Butler, Edward	Unkn.			22		
Butler, George	Gent.	14–21		09		
Butler, Gregory	Merc.		24			
Butler, Henry	Merc.		01			M
Butler, John	Unkn.	86–89				
Butler, John	Merc.					M/X2
Butler, John, Lord	Nob. 03	25–26				
Butler, Nathaniel	Unkn.			19?c		
Butler, Philip	Kt. 84†	89				
Butler, Stephen	Kt. 16					I2
Butler, Thomas Earl Ormond	Nob.					I9
Butler, William	Unkn.	86				
Butt, Giles de	Unkn.		25			
Button, Francis	Unkn.	84				
Button, James	Unkn.	14				
Button, John	Unkn.	25				
Button, Thomas	Kt. 16			09		Q/X2/GG
Button, William	Kt. 05	14, 28				
Buxton, Benjamin	Unkn.		26			
Buxton, Robert	Unkn.	84				
Bygate, William	Merc.					X1
Bygrave, Matthew	Merc.		24			
Bylott, Robert	Merc.					Q
Byron, John	Kt. 26	24, 26–28				GG
Byron, John	Kt. 03	97				GG
Bysonne, Richard	Merc.					S6
Bysse, John	Merc.					S6
Cable, Joseph	Merc.				10	
Cable, Robert	Merc.					S6
Caddock, Thomas	Unkn.					T3
Caesar, Charles	Kt. 13	14				
Caesar, Julius	Kt. 03	89–21	18			F1/Q/V/W9/ BB3g
Caesar, Robert	Gent.	25–26				
Caesar, Thomas	Gent.	01				W2/BB2c
Cage, Edward	Merc.			09		
Cage, John	Merc.					S6
Cage, John	Merc.		27	19		S4
Cage, Nicholas	Unkn.		07			
Cage, Toby	Kt. 27		27			
Cage, William	Unkn.	21–28				
Cakott, John	Unkn.		27			
Caldicott, Matthias	Gent.	24		23		
Caldwell, Lawrence	Merc.					I7
Caldwell, William	Merc.					F1
Calefield, Toby	Kt. 03					I4
Calfeilde, George	Merc.	84–01				
Calley, William	Merc.					M
Calmady, John	Merc.					X2

Name & title	Class; date of knight-hood	Parlia-ments (starting dates)	E. Ind. Co.	Va. Co.	Levant Co.	Other companies
Calthorpe, Richard	Unkn.		24			
Calthrope, Martin	Merc.					W4
Calverley, Hugh	Unkn.	01				
Calvert, George Lord Baltimore	Nob. 17	04, 21–24	09	09		I3/GG1
Calvert, John	Pfl/y.					CC2
Calvert, Leonard	Gent.					X2
Calvert, Nicholas	Merc.					F1
Calvert, Robert	Gent.					I2
Calvert, Samuel	Kt.†					I1
Calway, William	Merc.					X2
Cambell, James	M. Kt. 30		02g	09		F1g/S1
Cambell, Robert	Merc.		22		12	F1/I7/S1
Cambell, Thomas	M. Kt. 03		99		10	E1/F1g/I7/S6c
Cambell, Thomas	Merc.				13	S1
Cambry, Calcott	Unkn.					X2
Camden, Edmund	Merc.		14			
Camden, Richard	Merc.		15			
Came, Matthew	Merc.					F1/S1
Came, William	Merc.					S1
Cammock, John	Merc.					F1
Cammock, Leonard	Merc.					F1
Campe, Lawrence	Merc.			09		
Campion, Henry	Unkn.	21				
Campion, William	Unkn.	86				
Candler, Richard	Merc.					I2
Canland, Thomas	Merc.	86–01				
Canning, George	Merc.		99			
Canning, Paul	Unkn.			09		
Canning, William	Merc.			09c		S5/T2c
Canning, William	Merc.					S5
Cannon, John	Gent.	01				
Cannon, Thomas	Kt. 23	25–28		09		
Cantrel, William	Gent.			09		
Cape, Christopher	Merc.					F1
Capell, Arthur, Lord	Nob. 17	24				
Capell, Christopher	Unkn.	25–26				
Capell, Gamaliel	Kt. 03	04				
Capell, Henry	Unkn.	01				
Capelyn, Edmund	Gent.					CC2
Capelyn, Nicholas	Merc.					CC2
Capelyn, Peter	Merc.					S1
Caper, Paul de	Merc.		14			
Caplyn, John	Merc.					S4
Capp, William	Merc.			09		I7
Capper, Philip	Merc.					R2
Capper, Richard	Merc.		18			
Cardinall, Christopher	Merc.					F1/S1
Careles, Robert	Unkn.			22		
Careles, Thomas	Merc.			09		GG
Carew, Edward	Unkn.			09		

Name & title	Class; date of knight-hood	Parlia-ments (starting dates)	E. Ind. Co.	Va. Co.	Levant Co.	Other companies
Carew, Francis	Kt. 26	24–28				
Carew, George, Lord, Earl Totnes	Nob. 86	97, 04	14	07c		
Carew, George	Kt. 03	84–04				
Carew, John	Merc.					*F*1/*X*2
Carew, John	Merc.					*S*6
Carew, Nicholas	Kt. 03	21				
Carew, Ralph	Kt. 14	97, 14				
Carew, Richard	Gent.	84, 97				
Carew, Richard	Gent.	14–21				
Carew, William	Merc.					*F*1
Carey, Adolph	Kt. 03	01–04				
Carey, Allen	Merc.		12			*Q*
Carey, Christopher	Merc.					*S*1
Carey, Edmund	Kt. 87†	84, 89–14				
Carey, George Lord Hunsdon	Nob. 70	84–93			87	*X*1/*GG*
Carey, George	Kt. 98	86–89			10	*F*1/*CC*1/*GG*
Carey, Henry Lord Hunsdon	Nob.					*V*/*W*7/*X*1
Carey, Henry Viscount Falkland	Nob. 99	21		09c		*I*3/*Q*/*GG*
Carey, Henry, Lord Hunsdon, Earl Dover	Nob. 10	01–14		18?		*G*7/*GG*
Carey, Henry Earl Monmouth	Nob. 16	21–28				
Carey, Henry	Gent.	04				
Carey, John Lord Hunsdon	Nob.	84, 89–93				
Carey, Philip	Kt. 05	14–25		20c		
Carey, Richard	Merc.					*F*1
Carey, Robert Earl Monmouth	Nob. 91	86–01, 21		09		
Carey, Thomas	Gent.	21–28				
Carey, William	Gent.	84, 89, 04				
Carey, William	Unkn.					*X*2
Carey, ?	Nob.?			18?		
Carleton, Bingley	Merc.		24			
Carleton, Dudley	Kt. 10	04, 25–26				
Carleton, Erasmus	Merc.		24			
Carleton, John	Kt. 27	28				
Carleton, Thomas	Unkn.	97				
Carlile, Christopher	Unkn.					*W*4/*GG*
Carlill, Lawrence	Merc.					*S*4
Carmarden, Brian	Merc.					*E*1
Carmerden, Richard	Gent.	97‡		12		
Carmynoe, Oliver	Unkn.	86				
Carnaby, William	Kt. 19	24, 28				
Carne, Edward	Gent.			12		
Carne, Thomas	Gent.	86–89				
Carnesew, William	Unkn.	97–01				

Name & title	Class; date of knighthood	Parliaments (starting dates)	E. Ind. Co.	Va. Co.	Levant Co.	Other companies
Caron, Joseph	Merc.		24			J1
Carpenter, Abraham	Unkn.			18?		
Carpenter, George	Merc.					I7
Carpenter, Henry	Merc.					X1
Carpenter, John	Merc.					L1/M
Carpenter, John	Merc.					L1
Carpenter, Robert	Merc.	84–93				
Carpenter, Thomas	Unkn.		09	09		
Carpenter, William	Merc.			09		
Carr, Edward	Kt. 03			12		
Carr, Edward	Unkn.	21–24	11			
Carr, Elianor	Kt.			10		
Carr, John	Merc.					S6
Carr, Robert	Merc.					F1
Carr, Robert	Kt. 07†	24–25, 28				
Carr, Robert, Viscount Rochester, Earl Somerset	Nob.					Q/GG
Carr, William	Unkn.	26				
Carrell, Robert	Merc.		00			
Carrowe, Thomas	Merc.					S4
Carter, Francis	Merc.			12c		
Carter, Henry	Gent.	14				
Carter, James	Unkn.			23		
Carter, John	Merc.					I7
Carter, Randall	Merc.			09		
Carter, Richard	Merc.		99			
Carter, Thomas	Merc.					I7
Carter, William	Merc.					I9/S3
Cartwright, Abraham	Merc.		08c	09	20c	T2
Cartwright, James	Merc.			16		
Cartwright, John	Merc.					B/R2c/S5
Cartwright, Magdalena	Merc.		09			
Carvill, John	Gent.?	21–26		09		
Cason, Edward	Merc.		25			F1
Cason, Honora	Merc.		25			
Cason, John	Merc.		00	09		Q
Cassemarte, Matthew	Unkn.					X2
Cassen, Allen	Unkn.			09		
Casson, James	Merc.					F1
Casson, Richard	Merc.					I7
Casson, William	Merc.					F1
Castelin, Edward	Merc.					M/R1/BB1c
Castelin, John	Merc.					I2/M/Q/R1/ S6c/W9/GG
Castelin, Thomas	Merc.					S6
Castilion, Francis	Unkn.	97				
Castle, Nicholas	Merc.		27			
Castle, Roger	Unkn.			21		
Castle, William	Merc.					S4
Castleman, John	Merc.				10	

261

Name & title	Class; date of knight-hood	Parlia-ments (starting dates)	E. Ind. Co.	Va. Co.	Levant Co.	Other companies
Castleman, Richard	Merc.		24		20	
Caswell, Richard	Merc.		25	09c		T2
Caswell, William	Merc.					T3
Catcher, John	Kt. 19	21				
Catchmay, Richard	Kt. 08					K4
Cater, George	Merc.		00			
Cater, William	Merc.		00c	09		F1c/L1c/Q/R2
Catesby, Thomas	Unkn.	84				
Catlyn, ?	Unkn.	21				
Cavady, John	Unkn.			09		
Cave, Daniel Galliard	Merc.					X2
Cave, John	Unkn.	89				
Cavendish, Charles	Kt. 82	93, 01				
Cavendish, Charles	Kt. 19	24, 28				G7
Cavendish, Henry	Gent.	84–93				
Cavendish, Richard	Unkn.	84				
Cavendish, Thomas	Unkn.	84–86				
Cavendish, Thomas	Gent.			85		V
Cavendish, Thomas	Unkn.			16c		
Cavendish, William, Lord, Earl Devonshire	Nob.	86–89	00	12c		Q/T1g/GG3
Cavendish, William, Lord, Earl Devonshire	Nob. 09	04–26		12c		Q/T3/GG3
Cavendish, William, Visc. Mansfield, Earl & Marq. & Duke Newcastle	Nob.					G6/GG1
Cavendish, William	Gent.					I9
Cavill, Matthew	Unkn.			19		
Cawley, William	Unkn.	28				
Cecil, Edward Viscount Wimbledon	Nob. 01	01–04, 21–24		09c		G6/Q
Cecil, Richard	Kt. 16	93–97, 04–21				
Cecil, Robert Earl Salisbury	Nob. 91	84–01	09	09		F1/G1/I2/S1/ X1/Z/AA3/ BB2/GG4
Cecil, Thomas, Lord Burghley, Earl Exeter	Nob. 75	84–86, 93		09c		AA3/BB1
Cecil, William, Lord Cranbourne, Earl Salisbury	Nob.	04		12		K4/Q
Cecil, William Earl Exeter	Nob. 03	86–89, 97, 04				
Cecil, William Lord Rosse	Nob.					Q
Cecil, William Lord Burghley	Nob.					R1/W8/X1/ AA1/BB1/ CC2/GG1
Cervington, William	Merc.	84–89				

Name & title	Class; date of knighthood	Parliaments (starting dates)	E. Ind. Co.	Va. Co.	Levant Co.	Other companies
Chace, Thomas	Merc.		11			F1/Q/R2/S1
Chaffin, Bampfield	Unkn.	28				
Challenger, John	Merc.					S1
Challoner, Francis	Unkn.			20		
Challoner, Thomas	Kt. 91	86, 04		07c		G4/Q/R2?/GG
Chalmer, William	Kt. 91					GG
Chamber, Calcott	Unkn.	26				
Chamber, George	Merc.			09		E3/F1
Chamber, John	Merc.		08			Q
Chamber, Richard	Merc.				10c	
Chamber, Robert	Merc.					F1/I2/S1c
Chamber, Thomas	Merc.					I7
Chamber, William	Merc.		99c			F1/S1
Chamberlain, Abraham	Merc.		11	09		M/Qc/S1/Z
Chamberlain, Abraham	Merc.		24			
Chamberlain, Andrew	Merc.		00			
Chamberlain, David	Merc.		16			
Chamberlain, George	Merc.		00	10		I7/Q/S1
Chamberlain, John	Kt.†	21				
Chamberlain, John	Merc.		09			T3
Chamberlain, John	Gent.	93–97				
Chamberlain, Peter	Merc.		11			Q
Chamberlain, Richard	Merc.		00	09c		I7/M/Q/T1
Chamberlain, Richard	Unkn.			12		
Chamberlain, Robert	Merc.		00c	18?		R1g/S6c/T3
Chamond, Emanuel	Unkn.	84–93				
Champernon, Arthur	Merc.	24, 26				X2
Champernon, Charles	Gent.					CC1
Champernon, Francis	Merc.					X2
Champernon, Richard	Unkn.	86				I9
Champion, Richard	Merc.		22	09	05c	M/Q/S5/X2
Champion, Richard	Merc.				05	
Champnoies, Justinian	Unkn.	89				
Chancellor, Nicholas	Merc.					R1
Chandler, George	Merc.		00	09		M/Q
Chapell, John	Merc.					S6
Chapell, John	Merc.					S6
Chapell, Thomas	Merc.					S6
Chapell, William	Merc.					S6
Chapley, William	Merc.					F1
Chaplin, Richard	Merc.					S6
Chaplin, Thomas	Unkn.					X2
Chapman, Francis	Merc.		24			
Chapman, Henry	Merc.	97				
Chapman, John	Merc.		14			E4/F1/L1c
Chapman, Libby	Merc.				06c	
Chapman, Robert	Merc.					F1
Chapman, Thomas	Merc.		11			E4/L1/Q/X2
Chapman, Thomas	Merc.					CC2
Chapman, William	Merc.	26				F1/X2
Chapman, ?	Unkn.	04				

263

Name & title	Class; date of knighthood	Parliaments (starting dates)	E. Ind. Co.	Va. Co.	Levant Co.	Other companies
Charke, Benjamin	Merc.		24			
Charles, John	Merc.					GG
Charleston, Robert	Merc.		18			
Charnock, Roger	Unkn.	14				
Charnock, Thomas	Unkn.	24				
*Chase, Thomas	Unkn.					X2
Chatfield, James	Unkn.			09		
Chatterton, Lawrence	Pfl/y.			17		
Chatterton, Thomas	Unkn.					I9
Chauncy, Thomas	Merc.		24			
Chauntrey, James	Unkn.					X2
Chawe, Francis	Merc.					S6
Chawe, Robert	Merc.					I7
Chaworth, George	Kt. 06†	21–24				
Chaworth, George	Gent.	89				
Check, Henry	Unkn.	84				
Cheeke, Hatton	Kt. 03			09		
Cheeke, Thomas	Kt. 03	14–28		12c		G6/T3
Cheeke, Thomas	Gent.	04–14				
Chening, Robert	Unkn.			09		
Cherie, Francis	M. Kt. 03		99c		00	R1
Cherry, John	Merc.					X1
Chester, Edward	Merc.					S6
Chester, Thomas	Merc.					S6c/W2
Chester, William	Unkn.			18?		
Chetle, Richard	Gent.			21		
Chetonly, Robert	Gent.			21		
Chettle, Thomas	Unkn.	14				
Chetwynd, Walter	Kt. 03	84–86, 04–14‡				
Chewe, Thomas	Unkn.					X2
Cheyne, Francis	Unkn.	84–86				
Cheyney, Oliver	Kt.†					G7
Chibourne, Charles	Unkn.	14				
Chichely, Clement	Unkn.			09		
Chichely, Thomas	Kt. 07	01, 14				
Chichester, Arthur	Kt. 96					I6c
Chichester, John	Unkn.	24				
Chichester, John	Gent.					X1
Chichester, Thomas	Kt. 07					I4
Chidley, William	Merc.					S6
Chidley, ?	Unkn.					I9
Chilcott, John	Unkn.		14			
Chilcott, Robert	Merc.		09			
Childe, Alexander	Merc.			12		
Childe, George	Kt.†			12		
Childe, Robert	Merc.					I7
Childe, Robert	Merc.					F1
Chilton, Leonard	Merc.					S6
Chippingdale, John	Unkn.	89				
Chitting, George	Unkn.	89–93				
Chokke, Alexander	Unkn.	04, 21				

Name & title	Class; date of knight- hood	Parlia- ments (starting dates)	E. Ind. Co.	Va. Co.	Levant Co.	Other companies
Cholmley, Henry	Gent.	97				
Cholmley, Henry	Merc.					*I7*
Cholmley, Hugh	Kt. 26†	24–26				
Cholmley, Hugh	Gent.	84				
Cholmley, Jasper	Unkn.	84–86				
Cholmley, Richard	Kt. 03	21				
Cholmley, Robert	Kt. 11	25				
Cholmley, William	Gent.	24–26				
Cholmley, William	Unkn.	01				
Chowne, George	Unkn.	93				
Christmas, Robert	Gent.					*BB1*
Christmas, William	Merc.					*L1/M*
Chubb, Matthew	Merc.	01–04				
Chudley, George	Kt. 22	01, 14–24				*K4*
Chudley, John	Kt. 25	26–28				*G5*
Chudley, John	Gent.	86				*Q1/X1*
Church, Thomas	Merc.			09		*F1c/Q/S3/T2*
Churchar, Thomas	Unkn.	84–93				
Chute, Charles	Gent.	93				*BB2*
Chute, Christopher	Gent.					*BB1c*
Chute, George	Kt. 08		12			
Chute, Walter	Kt. 03	14	10			
Clapham, John	Gent.	97	09			
Clare, Henry	Kt. 03					*I2*
Clare, Ralph	Kt.†	14–28				
Clarke, Abraham	Unkn.					*X2*
Clarke, Alexander	Unkn.					*I9*
Clarke, Christopher	Merc.					*I7*
Clarke, Edward	Gent.?	25	25			
*Clarke, Edward?	Unkn.			09		
Clarke, Ferdinand	Unkn.	89				
Clarke, Francis	Merc.		09			*E1/GG*
Clarke, George	Unkn.		24	20		*M*
Clarke, Henry	Unkn.	21, 25–26				
Clarke, Humphrey	Merc.					*R2/GG*
Clarke, James	Unkn.	89				
Clarke, James	Unkn.	93				
Clarke, James	Unkn.	14				
*Clarke, James	Unkn.	24, 26				
Clarke, John	Unkn.	01				
Clarke, John	Merc.					*S6*
Clarke, John	Unkn.			22		
Clarke, John	Merc.				10	
Clarke, Katherine	Unkn.			19		
Clarke, Matthew	Unkn.	14–21				
Clarke, Peter	Unkn.		15			
Clarke, Richard	Merc.	84–89	00			
Clarke, Richard	Unkn.					*X2*
Clarke, Robert	Unkn.		09			
Clarke, Robert	Merc.		29			
*Clarke, Robert	Merc.					*S6*

Name & title	Class; date of knighthood	Parliaments (starting dates)	E. Ind. Co.	Va. Co.	Levant Co.	Other companies
Clarke, Roger	Merc.				90	
Clarke, Thomas	Merc.					*S6/CC2*
Clarke, William	Unkn.	84				
**Clarke, William	Gent.?	26	25	22		
Clarke, William	Merc.		24c		05c	
*Clarke, ?	Unkn.					*J3*
Clarkesonne, Jacob	Merc.					*S6*
Clatlory, John	Merc.					*S1*
Claudey, William	Unkn.			09		
Clavell, John	Unkn.	84				
Claxton, Hamon	Unkn.		23			
Claxton, Thomas	Merc.			09		
Clay, Hugh	Merc.					*I7*
Cleave, Christopher	Kt. 05			09		
Cleave, Thomas	Merc.		18			*M*
Clevinger, Nicholas	Merc.					*X1*
Cley, ?	Unkn.					*T3*
Cleyborne, Henry	Unkn.					*X2*
Cleygates, Nicholas	Merc.					*I7*
Clifford, Coniers	Kt. 91	93				
Clifford, Francis Earl Cumberland	Nob.	84–86, 04	08			*GG2*
Clifford, George Earl Cumberland	Nob.		00			*Q/W5/X1/GG*
Clifford, Henry, Lord, Earl Cumberland	Nob.	14–21				
Clifford, Margaret Countess Cumberland	Nob.			12		
Clifford, Nicholas	Kt. 91	93				
Clifton, Gervase, Lord	Nob. 96†	97–01				
Clifton, Gervase	Kt. 03	14–28				
Clifton, John	Kt. 74					*I9*
Clifton, John	Unkn.		29			
Clifton, Richard	Merc.					*I7*
Clifton, Thomas	Merc.					*I7*
Clinch, John	Merc.		01			*E3/F1/S1c*
Clinch, Thomas	Gent.	21				
Cline, Richard	Unkn.			09		
Clitheroe, Christopher	M. Kt. 36	28	01c	09	10c	*E2g/F1/L1c/ Q/S3/T2/X1 S1/X1*
Clitheroe, Henry	Merc.					*S1*
Clitheroe, Henry	Merc.		29			
Clitheroe, Robert	Merc.		24			
Clitheroe, Thomas	Merc.		28			
Clobery, William	Merc.					*X2/GG*
Clough, George	Merc.					*S6*
Clovell, Humphrey	Merc.					*X1*
Clovell, Samuel	Merc.					*X1*
Cluninge, Peter	Unkn.					*X2*
Clutterbuck, John	Merc.		24			
Coach, Thomas	Kt. †					*I2*

Name & title	Class; date of knighthood	Parliaments (starting dates)	E. Ind. Co.	Va. Co.	Levant Co.	Other companies
Coachman, John	Merc.		00			*R2*
Cobb, Nathaniel	Merc.					*S4*
Cobb, Richard	Merc.					*AA3*
Cobb, Robert	Merc.		00			*S6c/X1/GG*
Cobelton, Peter	Merc.					*S1*
Cobham, Henry Lord Windsor	Nob.					*AA2*
Cobham, John	Gent.	84, 93				
Cockayne, Charles	Unkn.	28				
Cockayne, Francis	Merc.					*E4/L1/S1*
Cockayne, John	Merc.					*S1*
Cockayne, Richard	Merc.		99			*S1*
Cockayne, Roger	Merc.					*S1*
Cockayne, Thomas	Merc.					*E1/S1*
Cockayne, William	Merc.					*E1g*
Cockayne, William	M. Kt. 16		07c	20		*E4g/F1/I1g/ L1g/Qc/S6c/ U/X1/GG*
Cockayne, William	Merc.		24c		23	*E3/F1/L1/Q/ S4/X2/GG*
Cocke, Edward	Unkn.					*X2*
Cocke, Henry	Kt. 97	84–86, 93				
Cocke, Joseph	Merc.		24			
Cocke, William	Merc.					*X2*
Cockett, Edward	Kt. 13		18			
Cockram, Joseph	Merc.		18			
Cockram, Richard	Merc.					*X2*
Cockroft, Caleb	Merc.					*R2c*
Coddington, William	Unkn.					*J3*
Codrington, Richard	Unkn.	93				
Codrington, Simon	Unkn.			15		
Coggen, John	Unkn.		11			
Coghan, Richard	Merc.					*S1*
Coghill, Henry	Merc.		22			
Coghill, John	Merc.		99			
Coitmore, Roland	Unkn.			09		
Coke, Edward	Kt. 03	89–93, 21–28				*S1*
Coken, John	Merc.					*X1*
Coker, John	Merc.					*I2*
Cokeson, Anthony	Merc.					*I7*
Colbey, Arthur	Unkn.		28			
Colbey, Edmund	Unkn.			18?		
Colbey, Huntington	Unkn.	14				
Colbey, Thomas	Unkn.			21		
Colbey, Thomas	Unkn.	86				
Colbran, William	Unkn.					*J3*
Coldwell, John	Merc.					*S6*
Coldwell, Richard	Merc.					*S6*
Cole, Anthony	Merc.	97, 04				*GG*
Cole, Edward	Merc.	01–04				
Cole, John	Unkn.	84				

Name & title	Class; date of knight-hood	Parlia-ments (starting dates)	E. Ind. Co.	Va. Co.	Levant Co.	Other companies
Cole, Richard	Merc.	84, 93				
Cole, Roland	Merc.				26	
Cole, Samuel	Unkn.					J3
Cole, Thomas	Unkn.	93–97				
Cole, Thomas	Merc.					X2
Cole, William	M. Kt. 17			09		I4/S1
Cole, William	Merc.					S1
Colebronde, James	Unkn.	97				
Coley, Robert	Merc.					E1
Colfox, Charles	Merc.					S4
Collam, Philip	Merc.			09		
Colledge, Raphe	Merc.					I7
Colles, Edmund	Gent.	97				
Colles, George	Merc.		00			
Colles, John	Unkn.					I9
Collet, John	Gent.			20		
Collet, John	Merc.					E1
Collet, Peter	Merc.					E1/S1
Collet, Stephen	Merc.					E1
Collet, Thomas	Gent.			20		
Collibear, Robert	Merc.					F1
Collier, William	Unkn.					P2
Collimore, Francis	Merc.				19	GG
Collimore, Roger	Merc.					S4
Collins, Edward	Merc.		99		90c	S4
Collins, Francis	Merc.				16	GG
Collins, Henry	Unkn.			09		
Collins, John	Merc.	89–93				
Collins, John	Unkn.					X2
Collins, Peter	Merc.					S6
Collins, Richard	Merc.					BB2c
Collymere, George	Merc.					S6c/X1
Collymere, Henry	Merc.					S6
Colman, Morgan	Unkn.	97				
Colman, Richard	Merc.					S3
Colmer, Abraham	Merc.			18?		S1/X2
Colmer, John	Merc.					S4
Colson, Edward	Merc.				18	
Colston, Christopher	Unkn.					J3c
Colston, Richard	Merc.					X1
Colston, Thomas	Merc.					X2
Colston, William	Merc.					F1/S1/X1
Colthurst, Henry	Merc.				90	B/M/S1/X1
Colthurst, Henry	Merc.			09		
Colthurst, Richard	Merc.			00		
Colthurst, Thomas	Merc.		09	18?		L1/M
Colyer, James	Unkn.	86				
Combe, Ellis	Merc.		24			
Combe, John	Merc.		99c	09		I7c/S1
Combe, Thomas	Merc.			20		X2/GG
Combe, Thomas	Unkn.					X2

Name & title	Class; date of knight- hood	Parlia- ments (starting dates)	E. Ind. Co.	Va. Co.	Levant Co.	Other companies
Combe, William	Gent.	89–97				
Comber, William	Gent.	97				
Comoldon, Roger	Merc.					*S3*
Comock, Thomas	Unkn.			09		
Comps, Edmund	Merc.					*F*1
Compton, Henry	Kt. 03	01–04, 21, 25–28	14			
Compton, Spenser Earl Northampton	Nob.	21				
Compton, William, Lord, Earl Northampton	Nob.		11	09		*Q*
Compton, William	Merc.		07	12		
Conimore, Richard	Merc.					*F*1
Coningsby, Fitzwilliam	Gent.	21				
Coningsby, Humphrey	Gent.	84–97				
Coningsby, Ralph	Kt. 03	14				
Coningsby, Richard	Gent.	93				
Coningsby, Thomas	Kt. 91	93–01		12		
Coningsby, Thomas	Gent.	01–14				
Connock, John	Merc.					*Q*
Connock, Richard	Gent.	93				
*Connock, Richard	Gent.	14		12		*Q*
Conquest, Cornelius	Unkn.					*G8*
Conquest, George	Merc.		24		10	
Conradus, William	Merc.					*I7*
Conranett, Barnard	Merc.					*S6*
Constable, Francis	Merc.					*L1*
Constable, Henry	Kt. 86	84–89, 04				
Constable, John	Kt. 07					*N*
Constable, Robert	Kt. 70	84–86				
Constable, Robert	Gent.	86				
Constable, William	Kt. 99	26–28				
Conway, Edward, Viscount	Nob. 96	04, 21–24		09c		*G7*
Conway, Edward, Viscount	Nob. 18	24, 26		22c		
Conway, Jenkin	Unkn.					*I9*
Conway, Ralph	Unkn.	28				
Conway, Thomas	Kt. 24	24		09		
Conway, Thomas	Kt. 24			12		
Conyers, John	Unkn.	86				
Conyers, William	Unkn.	14–24				
**Cook, Anthony	Gent.	84, 93				*CC2*
Cook, Clement	Gent.	14–21, 26–28				
**Cook, Edward	Merc.		24	12		*J3/X2*
Cook, Francis	Kt. 19					*I4*
Cook, Henry	Gent.	24–26				
Cook, John	Kt. 24	21–28	18	09		
*Cook, John	Merc.	25–26	18			
Cook, John	Gent.	97				
Cook, Richard	Kt. 03	14				*I6c*

Name & title	Class; date of knighthood	Parliaments (starting dates)	E. Ind. Co.	Va. Co.	Levant Co.	Other companies
Cook, Richard	Unkn.	84				
*Cook, Richard	Merc.					X1
Cook, Robert	Kt. 07	24				
Cook, Robert	Gent.	97				
Cook, Robert	Merc.					X2
Cook, William	Kt. 03	97–14		09		
Cook, William	Merc.					X2
Cookworthy, Richard	Unkn.					X2
Coole, William	Merc.					S6
Cooley, Samuel	Merc.		23			
Coolme, Hugh	Gent.					I4
Coop, Isaac	Merc.					S1
Coop, John	Merc.					I7
Cooper, Amynadab	Merc.			09		
Cooper, Benjamin	Merc.	21–24				S4
Cooper, Christopher	Gent.			87		
Cooper, Francis	Merc.		18			
Cooper, John	Merc.		99	09	05c	S4
Cooper, John	Unkn.	84–86				
Cooper, John	Kt. 22	25, 28				
Cooper, Matthew	Unkn.			09		
Cooper, Richard	Kt. 03			12		
Cooper, Richard	Unkn.			09		
Cooper, Robert	Unkn.			09		
Cooper, Thomas	Unkn.					X2
Cooper, Toby	Unkn.			21		
Cooper, William	Merc.		24			
Coote, John	Merc.					E4/F1
Cootes, Mary	Merc.					E3
Cope, Anthony	Kt. 92	86–14		09		I3
Cope, Robert	Merc.				07	
Cope, Theophilus	Unkn.		26			
Cope, Walter	Kt. 03	89, 01–14	?	06c		N/Q/R2/T1/ Z/GG I8
Cope, William	Kt. 03	04–25				
Cope, ?	Unkn.	26–28				I7c
Copinger, Adam	Merc.					
Copinger, Ambrose	Unkn.	86				
Copland, Patrick	Unkn.			21		
Coppin, George	Kt. 03	97		07c		
Coppin, Robert	Gent.?			09		
Coppleston, Christopher	Gent.					X1
Corbett, Andrew	Kt. 17	24–25, 28				
Corbett, Francis	Gent.	01–04‡				
Corbett, Jerome	Gent.	84				R2
Corbett, John	Merc.					F1/X1
Corbett, John	Kt. 23	04, 24–26	09			
Corbett, Miles	Merc.	28				
Corbett, Richard	Gent.	86				
Corbett, Roger	Merc.		29			
Corbett, Thomas	Gent.	93				

Name & title	Class; date of knight-hood	Parlia-ments (starting dates)	E. Ind. Co.	Va. Co.	Levant Co.	Other companies
Cordell, Edward	Gent.					*CC2*
Cordell, John	M. Kt. 41		22c		10c	*I2/S1*
Cordell, Thomas	Merc.		99c	10	90c	*D/I2/S6c/W4/ X1/DD/GG*1
Cordell, William	Kt. 57					*R*1
Cording, James	Merc.			09		
Coren, John	Unkn.					*X2*
Corne, Richard	Merc.					*F*1
Cornelius, Christopher	Merc.					*F*1
Cornelius, John	Merc.		99	09	05	
Cornewall, George	Merc.		27		27	
Cornewall, Gilbert	Unkn.	21				
Cornewall, John	Unkn.	89				
Cornish, Gabriel	Unkn.					*X2*
Cornish, George	Unkn.			21		
Cornish, John	Merc.					*S*1c*/X*1
Cornwallis, Charles	Kt. 03	04				*Q*
Cornwallis, Thomas	Kt. 05					*I2*
Cornwallis, Thomas	Gent.	21				
Cornwallis, William	Kt.†	97, 04				
Cornwallis, William	Kt. 99	14		12		
Corsellis, Luke	Merc.		23			
Corsellis, Nicholas	Merc.		26			
Coryton, William	Gent.	24–28				
Coseworth, Edward	Unkn.	89				
Coseworth, John	Unkn.	28				
Coseworth, Thomas	Unkn.	86				
Costerdyne, Thomas	Merc.					*I7*
Cotteels, Thomas	Unkn.	25				
*Cottells, Thomas	Merc.					*M*
Cotterell, Andreas	Merc.					*S6*
Cotterell, Clement	Kt. 20	21–24				
Cottington, Francis, Lord	Nob. 23	24–25, 28				
Cotton, Allen	M. Kt. 26		09c	10		*Q/T2/X2*
Cotton, Edward	Merc.					*CC*1*/GG*1
Cotton, Edward	Merc.			09		
Cotton, George	Merc.					*S*1
*Cotton, George	Unkn.	14				
Cotton, John	Kt. 99†	93, 01				
Cotton, John	Merc.		22			*GG*1
Cotton, Katherine	Merc.		22			
Cotton, Radulphus	Merc.					*S6*
Cotton, Robert	Kt. 03	01–04, 24–25, 28		20		
Cotton, Roger	Merc.		00			
Cotton, Roland	Kt. 08	26–28		09		
Cotton, Thomas	Unkn.	25, 28				
Cotton, William	Merc.				27	
Cotton, William	Merc.?	93–01	00			
Cotton, William	Merc.		07			*GG*1
Cottonsean, Jacob	Unkn.					*X2*

Name & title	Class; date of knighthood	Parliaments (starting dates)	E. Ind. Co.	Va. Co.	Levant Co.	Other companies
Coucher, John	Unkn.	04–24, 28				
Couchman, John	Merc.				10c	Q/S4
Coulcloughe, Matthew	Merc.					S6
Courte, John	Unkn.	86–89				
Courteen, Peter	M. Kt. 23					GG
Courteen, William	M. Kt. 22					GG
Courteman, William	Unkn.	14				
Courtman, Andrew	Merc.					I7
Courtney, Anthony	Gent.					X1
Courtney, Francis Earl Devon	Nob.	25–26				
Courtney, John	Merc.					F1
Courtney, Thomas	Gent.					X1
Courtney, William Earl Devon	Nob. 76	84, 89, 01				I9
Courtney, William	Kt. 99	01				
Courtney, William	Unkn.			09		
Courtnill, Barnard	Merc.					CC2
Courtnill, Thomas	Merc.					CC2
Coussen, Henry	Unkn.	04				
Coussen, Richard	Unkn.	84–89				
Covell, Francis	Merc.			09		I1c
Covell, Thomas	Merc.		11	18?		Q/T2
Coventry, Thomas, Lord	Nob. 17	21		10c		
Coventry, Thomas, Lord	Nob.	25–28				P2
Covert, John	Gent.	86				
Covert, Richard	Merc.		10			
Covert, Walter	Kt. 91	84–86, 93, 14		12		
Covert, Walter	Kt. 24	26–28				
Cowdray, Michael	Merc.					S1
Cowes, John	Unkn.					X2
Cowley, Francis	Merc.				07	
Cowley, John	Merc.				06	
Cowley, Samuel	Merc.					R2c
Cowley, Thomas	Merc.				00	
Cowley, Walter	Merc.					I7
Cowltres, Henry	Merc.					S6
Cownden, William	Unkn.	04				
Cowper, Barnard	Merc.					F1
Cowper, Edmund	Merc.					E2
*Cowper, John	Unkn.					I9
Cowper, Thomas	Unkn.					N
*Cowper, William	Merc.					I2
Cox, Charles	Pfl/y.		18			
Cox, Edward	Merc.	14				S4
Cox, James	Merc.		28			L1/R2c
Cox, John	Unkn.	84–89				
Cox, John	Merc.		15			L1
Cox, Richard	Merc.		99	09	05	R2/S4
Cox, Robert	Merc.		99c	09	99c	I7/Q/S4
Cox, Samuel	Unkn.	86				

Name & title	Class; date of knight-hood	Parlia-ments (starting dates)	E. Ind. Co.	Va. Co.	Levant Co.	Other companies
Cox, William	Merc.					S6
Cox, William	Merc.		17			L1
*Cox, William	Unkn.	25–28				
Coxsell, George	Merc.					I7
Coyse, William	Gent.			09		
Craddock, Francis	Gent.	84–93				BB3
Craddock, George	Gent.	04				
Craddock, Matthew	Gent.	21–25, 28				
Craddock, Matthew	Merc.		24		27	E3/F2/J2g/ L1/R2c/S2/X2
Craddock, William	Merc.					L1
Crane, Francis	Kt. 17	14–24				
Crane, Martin	Merc.			09		I7
Crane, Robert	Kt. 05	14–28				
Crane, Robert	Merc.					J3
Cranfield, Lionel Earl Middlesex	Nob.13	14–21	18	12c	05	I2/M/T2
Cranfield, Randall	Merc.		18			
Cranley, Richard	Unkn.					X2
Cranmer, William	Merc.			19		L1/M
Cranston, William	Merc.					X1/GG
Crashaw, Ralegh	Unkn.			09		
Crashaw, Richard	Unkn.			25		
Crashaw, William	Unkn.			09		
Cratford, Charles	Gent.			21		
Crathorne, Thomas	Unkn.	25				
Craven, John	Unkn.					X2
Craven, William	M. Kt. 03			10		I7
Crawford, Patrick	Gent.					I8
Crawford, William	Unkn.					X2
Cresheld, Richard	Unkn.	24–25, 28				
Creswell, John	Unkn.	97				
Creswell, Richard	Merc.		15			
Creswell, Robert	Merc.			18?		M
Creswick, Francis	Unkn.					X2
Crew, Anthony	Merc.			09		I2
Crew, Clipsie	Kt. 20	24–26				
Crew, John	Unkn.	25–28				
Crew, Randall	Merc.		24			E3/L1
*Crew, Raphe	Merc.					I2
Crew, Thomas	Kt. 23	04–25				
Crewes, Elizabeth	Merc.		27			
Crewes, Robert	Merc.		09			
Crifte, Robert	Merc.					S4
Crimes, Thomas	Kt. 03	24				
Cripps, Roger	Unkn.					X2
Crispe, Ellis	Merc.		00			M/N/Q
Crispe, ?	Merc.		14			
Crispe, Hester	Merc.		28			
Crispe, Nicholas	Merc.		99c			F1/M/Q
Crispe, Nicholas	Merc.		21c			M/X2/GG

Name & title	Class; date of knight-hood	Parlia-ments (starting dates)	E. Ind. Co.	Va. Co.	Levant Co.	Other companies
Crispe, Samuel	Merc.		21			
Crocker, Hugh	Unkn.					X2
Crocker, Thomas	Merc.					F1/S1
Croft, Anthony	Unkn.	24				
Croft, Barnabas	Unkn.					X2
Croft, Edward	Unkn.	84–86				
Croft, Henry	Kt. 11	24, 26		20		
Croft, Herbert	Kt. 03	89–14		07c		
Croft, James	Unkn.	84–86				
Croft, James	Kt. 47	84–89				S6/W2/CC2
Croft, John	Unkn.	97				
**Croft, William	Kt. 14	14, 26–28				
Crompe, Radulphus	Merc.					S6
Crompton, Barbara	Unkn.		22			
Crompton, Henry	Unkn.	14				
Crompton, Hugh	Unkn.	24				
Crompton, Hugh	Merc.		00			
Crompton, John	Kt. 08	14–21				
Crompton, John	Unkn.		20			
Crompton, Samuel	Merc.					X2
Crompton, Thomas	Kt. 03	97–04				
Crompton, Thomas	Gent.	97–01				
Crompton, Thomas	Gent.	89–93				
Crompton, Thomas	Gent.	89–97				
Crompton, Thomas	Gent.	14–21, 28				
Cromwell, Henry	Gent.	04		09		
Cromwell, Henry	Gent.			10		
Cromwell, Oliver	Kt. 03	89–14, 24–25		07c		
Cromwell, Oliver	Gent.	28				
Cromwell, Richard	Gent.	97–01				
Cromwell, Robert	Gent.	93				
Cromwell, Thomas	Unkn.	84–89				
Croninge, Cornelius	Unkn.					X2
Crony, John	Merc.					F1
Crooke, George	Gent.	97				
Crooke, Henry	Kt. 15	14, 28				
Crooke, John	Kt. 03	84, 97–01, 14				
Crooke, John	Kt. 09	28				
Crooke, John	Merc.					S6c/X1
Crooke, Richard	Unkn.		09			
Crooke, Samuel	Gent.					A
Crooke, Unton	Gent.	26				
Crosby, John	Kt. 28					X2
Crosby, William	Merc.			09		
Croshawe, Edward	Unkn.		09			
Crosley, William	Merc.			09		
Crosse, Edward	Merc.			18		X2
Crosse, George	Merc.					X2
Crosse, Henry	Merc.					F1
Crosse, John	Merc.					S6
Crosse, John	Gent.					X1

Name & title	Class; date of knight- hood	Parlia- ments (starting dates)	E. Ind. Co.	Va. Co.	Levant Co.	Other companies
Crosse, Leonard	Unkn.	97				
Crosse, Robert	Kt. 96	86, 93, 01				X1
Crosse, William	Merc.					I7/X2
Crossen, Hugh	Merc.					S1
Crossing, Francis	Unkn.	26–28				
Crossing, Thomas	Unkn.					X2
Croste, George	Merc.					L1/M
Croste, Robert	Merc.					L1/M
Croston, Henry	Merc.					L1
Croute, Harry	Unkn.					N
Crouther, John	Merc.		14			
Crowe, John	Gent.			10		
Crowe, Sackvill	Kt. 27	25, 28				
Crowe, William	Unkn.			18?		
Crowley, Edward	Merc.					I2
Crowth, John	Merc.					I2
*Crowther, John	Merc.					X2
Crowther, William	Merc.					J1
Cryche, Edmund	Merc.					Q
Cuff, Hugh	Unkn.					I9
Cuff, John	Merc.		24	20		R2/T3
Cuff, Philip	Unkn.					I9
Culemore, Edward	Merc.					S6
Cullimore, James	Merc.		00	18?	05	
Cullimore, Mabel	Unkn.			17		
Culpeper, David	Unkn.			18?		
Culpeper, Edward	Kt. 03			12		
Culpeper, Edward	Gent.			20		
Culpeper, John	Gent.			09		
Culpeper, Thomas	Kt. 03	97–01, 14				
*Culpeper, Thomas	Gent.			09		Q
*Culpeper, Thomas	Kt. 19†	28				
Culpeper, William	Merc.				16	L1/Q
Culverwell, Nicholas	Merc.					AA2
Culverwell, Richard	Merc.					S1
Cumberford, Thomas	Gent.		14			
Cunye, Richard	Unkn.	04				
Cure, Thomas	Merc.	84–86				
Curton, John	Merc.					S6
Curwen, Henry	Kt. 70	21				GG
Curwen, Nicholas	Kt. 03	93				GG
Curwen, Patrick	Kt. 27	25–28				GG
Curzon, John	Unkn.	28				
Cushman, Robert	Unkn.					P2
Cusp, Robert	Merc.					F1
Cust, Samuel	Merc.		26			
Cutler, Benjamin	Merc.					E3
Cutler, Henry	Unkn.		09			
Cutler, John	Merc.					S1
Cutler, Robert	Merc.					E3/S1
Cutler, Roger	Merc.					E3/F1/S1

Name & title	Class; date of knight-hood	Parlia-ments (starting dates)	E. Ind. Co.	Va. Co.	Levant Co.	Other companies
Cutler, Samuel	Merc.					E3/F1/S1
Cutler, Thomas	Merc.		99	09	07	F1/S5
Cutler, William	Merc.					S1
Cutt, Nicholas	Merc.					S6
Cutt, Thomas	Merc.					S6
Cuttance, Henry	Unkn.					X2
Cuttinge, John	Merc.	84				
Cutts, John	Kt. 71	84–86, 01				
Cutts, John	Kt. 03	04–26		10		Q
Cutts, Robert	Merc.					I7
Dabridgecorte, Thomas	Unkn.	93				
Dackombe, Edward	Gent.	04, 26				
Dackombe, John	Gent.	14				
Dackombe, William	Gent.					A
Dacre, Francis	Gent.	89				
Dacres, Henry	Gent.	97				
Dacres, Thomas	Kt. 04	26–28				
Dade, Henry	Unkn.	14				
Dade, John	Merc.		14	09		F1/L1/S4
Dalby, Richard	Merc.					F1/S4
Dalby, Thomas	Merc.					I2/L1c/S1
Dale, Elizabeth	Kt.			21		
Dale, James	Unkn.	89				
Dale, Matthew	Unkn.	01				
Dale, Thomas	Kt. 06		14	10c		
Dale, Valentine	Unkn.	84–89				
Dale, William	Merc.		99			I7c
Dale, ?	Unkn.	84				
Dalkins, Thomas	Merc.				92	
Dallison, Maximilian	Kt. 03	24				
Dallison, Roger	Kt. 03	04–14				
Dallison, Thomas	Kt. 03	04				
Dalmyngton, William	Merc.	86				
Dalrymple, Charles	Merc.					F1
Dalston, George	Kt. 07	21–28				
Dalston, John	Gent.	89				
Dalton, James	Gent.	84–86, 93				
Dalton, George	Pfl/y.					CC2
Dalton, Roger	Unkn.	89–93				I9
Dalton, Thomas	Merc.					H
Damage, Robert	Merc.					F1
Damer, Robert	Merc.					F1
Dames, Galfridus	Merc.					S6
*Damet, J.	Merc.	84				
Damport, ?	Unkn.			22		
Damus, Anthony	Merc.					F1
Danby, Henry	Unkn.			09		
Dancy, George	Merc.					L1
Dancy, Richard	Merc.					L1
Dane, Richard	Merc.					S6/X1
Danford, Richard	Merc.					AA3/BB2

276

Name & title	Class; date of knight-hood	Parlia-ments (starting dates)	E. Ind. Co.	Va. Co.	Levant Co.	Other companies
Danger, Alexander	Merc.					S1
Dangerfield, Thomas	Merc.					L1/M
Daniel, Peter	Gent.	26				
Daniel, Richard	Merc.	24, 28				
*Daniel, Richard	Merc.			09		
Daniel, William	Merc.	01				
Danks, Joan	Unkn.			20		
Dannett, Awdley	Unkn.	89				
Dannett, Thomas	Merc.	84–86, 93, 01–04				
Dansell, William	M. Kt. 53					Mg/R1
Danser, Edmund	Merc.					E2
Danser, William	Merc.					E2
Danvers, Charles	Unkn.	86–89				
Danvers, Charles	Unkn.	14				
Danvers, John	Kt. 09	04–28		10c		G6/T3
Darby, William	Merc.					J1/K5
Darcy, Edward	Unkn.	84				
Darcy, Francis	Kt. 91	01, 21, 28				
Darcy, John	Unkn.	24				
Darcy, Thomas, Lord, Earl Rivers	Nob.					Q
Dare, Ananias	Gent.			87		
Dare, William	Merc.					F1/S1
Darley, Henry	Unkn.	28				
Darling, Edward	Merc.		24			I7
Darling, Richard	Merc.					I7
Darnelly, Daniel	Merc.		24	10		
Darr, Leonard	Merc.	01				
Darrell, Henry	Merc.					L1/M
Darrell, Marmaduke	Kt. 03		18	10		G6/GG
Darrell, Philip	Merc.					X1
Darrell, Sampson	Kt. 19	26				
Darrell, Thomas	Kt. 03	04				
Darrell, Thomas	Unkn.					T3
Darsall, Richard	Merc.				92	DD
Darte, Lewis	Unkn.	86, 01				
Dassell, Anthony	Merc.					B/C/D/X1
Daubney, Clement	Gent.			18?		GG
Daubney, Henry	Gent.			09		
Davenant, Edward	Merc.					S4/GG
Davenant, John	Merc.					R1/S1
Davenport, Humphrey	Unkn.	89				
Davenport, John	Gent.					J3
Davidge, John	Unkn.	93				
Davis, Gilbert	Merc.				10	
Davis, Hugh	Merc.	84–86				
Davis, Hugh	Merc.					X2
Davis, Jeffrey	Merc.					S1
Davis, Jerome	Merc.		01			
Davis, John	Kt.†	04, 21		09		I5c

Name & title	Class; date of knighthood	Parliaments (starting dates)	E. Ind. Co.	Va. Co.	Levant Co.	Other companies
Davis, John	Gent.	97–01				
**Davis, John	Gent.			09		*A*
Davis, John	Merc.					*S4/X2*
Davis, John	Merc.					*Q1/X1/GG*
Davis, John	Merc.					*X1*
Davis, Lancelot	Pfl/y.			09		
Davis, Matthew	Gent.	04–14, 24				
Davis, Nevill	Merc.					*S1*
Davis, Richard	Merc.		11		26	*I7/J1/L1/Q*
Davis, Robert	Merc.					*X1*
Davis, Robert	Merc.					*X2*
Davis, Roger	Unkn.					*X2*
Davis, Thomas	Unkn.					*X2*
Davison, Allen	Unkn.					*X2*
Davison, Christopher	Gent.			21		
Davison, William	Unkn.	86				
Davy, Alexander	Merc.					*F1/R2*
Davy, Henry	Merc.					*I7*
Davy, John	Unkn.	21				
*Davy, John	Merc.					*S1*
Davy, Richard	Unkn.					*X2*
Davy, Thomas	Merc.					*S6*
Davy, William	Merc.					*S1*
Dawbeney, Arthur	Merc.					*B/S6c/W/GG*
Dawborne, Robert	Merc.					*S1*
Dawes, Abraham	Merc.			09		*F1/Q/T2*
Dawkins, Philip	Merc.				00	*S4*
Dawkins, Thomas	Merc.					*DD*
Dawks, Henry	Unkn.			09		
Dawks, John	Merc.					*I7*
Dawks, William	Merc.					*S1*
Dawney, John	Kt. 80	84–93				
Dawsey, Rowley	Unkn.			18?		
Dawson, Matthew	Merc.					*E2*
Dawson, Robert	Merc.			09		
Dawson, Thomas	Merc.					*E2*
Day, Edmund	Unkn.	28				
Day, John	Merc.					*S2*
Day, Samuel	Unkn.					*X2*
Day, William	Merc.			09		
Dean, Edward	Merc.					*I2*
Dean, James	M. Kt. 03		99			
Dean, John	Kt. 03	21				
Dean, Nicholas	Merc.					*F1*
Dean, Richard	M. Kt. 29		00	09	05	*Q/GG*
Deanes, John	Merc.				05	*S6*
Deards, Nathaniel	Merc.		09		10	
Dearing, Anthony	Unkn.	01				
Dearing, Edward	Kt. 19	25				
Debney, Robert	Unkn.	28				
Deconson, Milo	Merc.					*S6*

Name & title	Class; date of knighthood	Parliaments (starting dates)	E. Ind. Co.	Va. Co.	Levant Co.	Other companies
Deconson, Thomas	Merc.					S6
Decrowe, Benjamin	Merc.			12		F1/I2/Q/R2
Decrowe, Valentine	Merc.					R2
Dee, John	Pfl/y.					Q1/W5/CC2/ GG
Deereham, Henry	Merc.		29			
Delaber, John	Unkn.	89				
Delaber, Richard	Unkn.	86, 01–04				
Delasoubye, John	Merc.					F1
Delaun, Gideon	Merc.			18		Q/T2
Delavale, John	Kt. 17	26				GG1
Delbridge, John	Merc.	14–28	11	12c		F1/Q/T2/X2/ GG
Delbridge, Richard	Merc.			21		GG
Delden, Abraham van	Merc.					AA3
Delean, Robert	Merc.		14			
Demaresk, Thomas	Merc.					S6/CC2
Demetrius, Emanuel	Unkn.					AA3
Den, Thomas	Unkn.	24				
Denham, John	Merc.					I2
Denham, John	Kt. 09					I6c
Denley, Elizabeth	Unkn.		27			
Denley, John	Unkn.		11			
Dennis, Edward	Unkn.	84				
Dennis, Edward	Kt. 07	28				
Dennis, James	Merc.					X2
Dennis, John	Merc.			22		X2
Dennis, Thomas	Kt. 86	93	09			
Denny, Edward, Lord, Earl Norwich	Nob. 89	93, 04	12			
Denny, Edward	Kt. 88	84, 97				I9
Denny, Walter	Merc.					X1
Denny, William	Unkn.	21–25				
Dent, Francis	Merc.		00			S4/GG
Dent, John	Merc.					S1
Dent, Thomas	Unkn.		14			
Denton, Adam	Merc.		28			
Denton, Alexander	Kt. 17	25–26				
Denton, Thomas	Kt. 03	04–24, 26–28	10			
Dequester, Matthew	Unkn.		09			
Derefford, ?	Merc.			10		
Derham, John	Merc.		24		07c	F1
Derrickson, Derick	Merc.					X1
Dervall, Hugh	Merc.					CC2
Deslile, John	Merc.					CC2
Deverell, John	Merc.		24		15	
Devereux, Edward	Gent.	89				
Devereux, George	Gent.	89				
Devereux, Robert Earl Essex	Nob.					X1/GG
Devereux, Walter Earl Essex	Nob.					W2

Name & title	Class; date of knight- hood	Parlia- ments (starting dates)	E. Ind. Co.	Va. Co.	Levant Co.	Other companies
Devereux, Walter	Kt. 03	14–28				
*Devereux, Walter	Kt. 17	14, 24				
Dewar, James	Merc.					F1
Dewar, Nicholas	Merc.					F1
Dewars, Walter	Merc.					F1
Dewhurst, ?	Unkn.			09		
Dexter, ?	Unkn.			09		
Dichfield, Richard	Unkn.			19?		
Dickens, John	Merc.					R2
Dickenson, Christopher	Merc.					F1/M
Dickenson, Philip	Merc.					S1
Dickenson, Roger	Merc.					L1
Dickenson, Thomas	Pfl/y.					CC2
Die, Roger	Merc.		00	12		I7/Q
Diego, James	Merc.		18			
Dieper, Anthony	Merc.		24			
Digby, George	Gent.	84				
Digby, George	Unkn.					X2
Digby, John, Lord, Earl Bristol	Nob. 06	04	14	09		Q
Digby, Kenelm	Gent.	84				
Digby, Kenelm	Kt. 23					X2
Digby, Philip	Unkn.	28				
Digby, Robert	Kt. 99	01				
Diggens, William	Merc.					N
Digges, Dudley	Kt. 07	04–28	11c	09c		K4/Qc/R2/ T1/U/Z
Digges, John	Gent.			12		Q
Digges, Richard	Gent.	97–28				
Digges, Thomas	Gent.	84				
Digges, Thomas	Gent.			12		Q
Dighton, Christopher	Merc.	01–04				
Dike, Jeremy	Unkn.		27			
Dike, John	Merc.		15	09	05	F1/R2/T2c/ X2/FFc/GG
Dike, John	Merc.			20		X2
Dike, Richard	Merc.		15		06c	X2
Dike, Thomas	Merc.		09	10		Q
Dike, Thomas	Merc.			20		
Dike, Zachariah	Merc.				17	
Dillin, Anthony	Unkn.	89				
Dillings, Robert	Unkn.	86, 93				
Dillon, John	Gent.					I2
Dimmock, Humphrey	Gent.			89		
Dimscombe, George	Unkn.		26			
Dimster, Roger	Merc.					F1
Dingley, John	Merc.			09		
Dipford, Thomas	Merc.					S1
Dirven, George	Merc.					F1
Ditchfield, Edward	Merc.			09		T2/GG

Name & title	Class; date of knighthood	Parliaments (starting dates)	E. Ind. Co.	Va. Co.	Levant Co.	Other companies
Ditchfield, Henry	Merc.					*I*7
Ditton, John	Merc.					*F*1
Dive, Lewis	Kt. 20	25–28				
Dixon, Robert	Gent.		17			
Dixwell, Basil	Unkn.	26				
Dixye, Wolstan	Kt. 03	25				
Dobb, Robert	Merc.					*S*1c
Dobbins, Daniel	Merc.		29		24	*R*2c
Dobson, Ellis	Gent.					*X*1
Dobson, Robert	Merc.			09		
Dobson, William	Gent.			09		
Dod, Thomas	Merc.					*B*
Dodderidge, John	Merc.					*F*1
Dodderidge, John	M. Kt. 07	89, 04			06c	*N/X*1
Dodderidge, Pentecost	Merc.	14–24				*F*1/*S*1
Dodderidge, Richard	Merc.					*C/S*1/*X*1
Dodderidge, Robert	Merc.					*S*1
Doddington, Herbert	Gent.	26–28				
Doddington, William	Kt. 03	21				
Doddington, William	Kt. 23	24				
Doddington, William	Gent.					*BB*1
Dodrington, Edward	Kt. 16					*I*8
Dodsworth, Edward	Unkn.		17			
Dodsworth, Israell	Merc.					*E*2
Doggett, Edmund	Merc.					*X*1
Doggett, John	Merc.					*L*1/*M*
Doggett, William	Merc.		07			*I*2
Doghill, John	Merc.					*S*5
Dolbery, William	Unkn.					*X*2
D(J)olliffe, Richard	Unkn.					*X*2
Dollin, Jane	Unkn.		28			
Dolman, Richard	Merc.					*I*7
Domelaw, John	Merc.					*I*7
Done, John	Gent.	93				
Donnalt, Gregory	Unkn.	93–01				
Donnatt, Humphrey	Unkn.	93				
Donne, John	Gent.	01, 14		22c		
Donnell, Richard	Merc.					*X*2
Donnington, John	Unkn.	27				
Dorchester, Richard	Merc.					*M/Q*1/*S*6
Doricot, John	Merc.					*C/F*1/*S*1
Doricott, Thomas	Merc.					*C*
Dormer, John	Kt. 03	04–21				
Dormer, Robert	Nob. 91	93				
Dorrell, Thomas	Unkn.	86				
Dorrington, Christopher	Merc.				07	
Dorrington, Francis	Merc.				92c	*I*7/*S*1
Dorrington, George	Merc.		01		00	*S*1
Dorrington, Humphrey	Merc.					*X*1
Dorrington, John	Gent.	84				
Dorrington, John	Merc.				90	*S*1c

Name & title	Class; date of knighthood	Parliaments (starting dates)	E. Ind. Co.	Va. Co.	Levant Co.	Other companies
Dorrington, Richard	Gent.		18			
Doters, William	Unkn.					*I*8
Dottin, Richard	Merc.					*F*1
Dottyn, Walter	Merc.	04				*F*1/*S*1
Doughty, Francis	Merc.					*S*1
**Doughty, John	Unkn.	26–28				*N*
Doughty, Michael	Unkn.	86–93				
Doughty, Thomas	Gent.					*X*1
Doughty, William	Merc.	24, 28				
Dounlee, Edward	Unkn.	84–86				
Dow, Robert	Merc.				90	*R*1/*S*6c
Dowcra, Henry	Kt.†					*I*5c
Dowdall, John	Kt. 94					*I*9
Dowgle, William	Unkn.					*W*5
Downes, Francis	Unkn.	24–25				
Downes, James	Merc.					*S*1
Downes, John	Merc.			12		
Downes, Jonathan	Merc.					*X*2
Downes, Nathaniel	Merc.					*X*2
Downes, Nicholas	Merc.					*S*1
Downes, Roger	Unkn.	01, 21				
Downing, Emanuel	Unkn.					*J*3
Downynge, William	Unkn.	86				
Dowse, Edward	Unkn.	25				
Doyley, Henry	Gent.	01				
Doyley, John	Gent.	04				
Drake, Barnard	Gent.					*X*1/*CC*2
*Drake, Barnard	Unkn.					*X*2
Drake, Francis	Kt. 81	84, 93				*D*/*W*4/*X*1/*GG*
Drake, Francis	Kt. 22	24, 28				
Drake, Francis	Gent.	24–28				
Drake, Henry	Merc.					*X*1
Drake, John	Kt. 16					*X*2
Drake, John	Gent.	14–26		12		*K*4
Drake, Richard	Gent.	84				*X*1
Drake, William	Unkn.					*X*2
Draper, Clement	M. Kt. 66					*R*1
Draper, Clement	Merc.					*S*6
Draper, Jasper	Unkn.			22		
Draper, John	Merc.					*S*6
Draper, Robert	Merc.					*M*
Draper, Sarah	Unkn.			18?		
Draper, Thomas	Gent.			09		
Drausfield, Avery	Merc.		08	09		*Q*
Drayton, William	Unkn.					*X*2
Drew, Edward	Unkn.	84–93				
Drew, John	Unkn.	26				
Drew, Richard	Unkn.	89				
Drew, Richard	Merc.					*F*1
Drew, Robert	Unkn.	97–04, 25				
Drew, William	Merc.		24			

Name & title	Class; date of knighthood	Parliaments (starting dates)	E. Ind. Co.	Va. Co.	Levant Co.	Other companies
Driver, Charles	Merc.					X2
Driver, William	Merc.					X2
Druerdent, Philip	Unkn.		09			
Drury, Andrew	Kt.†		18?			
Drury, Anthony	Kt. 03	25				
Drury, Drew	Kt. 79	84				
Drury, Drew	Kt. 03		09			
Drury, Drew	Gent.	21–24				
Drury, Jeremy	Unkn.	27				
**Drury, Robert	Kt. 03	04–14	11	09c		
Drury, Roger	Gent.	89				
Drury, William	Kt. 70	84				
Dryden, Erasmus	Kt. 19	24				
Dryfield, Thomas	Unkn.	18				
Dubbleday, Edmund	Merc.	14				I7
Duche, Richard	Merc.					M/Q1
Duck, Arthur	Gent.	24				
Duck, Nicholas	Unkn.	24–25				
Duck, William	Merc.					S1
Duckett, Anthony	Merc.					AA1c
Duckett, Jeffrey	Merc.					R1c/W2/AA1
Duckett, John	Unkn.	21–24				
Duckett, John	Merc.	99		23		I2/GG
Duckett, Lionel	M. Kt. 73					M/R1g/S6 W6/AA1g/GG
Duckett, Lionel	Unkn.	01				
Duckett, Stephen	Unkn.	84–86				
Ducy, John	Merc.	22c				
Ducy, Robert	Merc.	01c				L2/M
Dudley, Ambrose Earl Warwick	Nob.					B/W8/BB1/ CC2
Dudley, Anne Countess Warwick	Nob.					W5/BB5
Dudley, Edward	Gent.	84				
Dudley, Edward, Lord	Nob.					GG2
Dudley, John	Gent.					AA1/CC1
Dudley, John	Unkn.	93				
Dudley, John	Gent.	97				
Dudley, John	Unkn.	01				
Dudley, Robert Earl Leicester	Nob.					B/R1/S6/W8/ X1/AA1/BB1/ CC2/GG1
Dudley, Robert	Kt. 96					V/X1/GG1
Dudley, Thomas	Unkn.	84–89				
Dudley, Thomas	Gent.					J3
Dudley, Thomas	Merc.					S6/W2
Dudley, ?	Gent.	97				
Dudson, William	Merc.					X1
*Duke, Richard	Merc.					R2

Name & title	Class; date of knight-hood	Parlia-ments (starting dates)	E. Ind. Co.	Va. Co.	Levant Co.	Other companies
Dull, Walter	Merc.					S6
Dun, Daniel	Kt. 03	01–14		09		F1/N/S1
Dun, William	Unkn.			09		
*Dun, William	Unkn.			09		
Dunch, Edmund	Gent.	24–28				
Dunch, Samuel	Gent.	21				
Dunch, Walter	Unkn.	84, 89				
Dunch, William	Kt. 03	04				
Duncken, James	Merc.		00			
Duncombe, Cicely	Unkn.		22			
Duncombe, Edward	Unkn.	04–14				
Duncombe, George	Merc.		15			A/F1/S4
Duncombe, Giles	Merc.?		99			
Duncombe, John	Unkn.	86				
Duncombe, William	Merc.				05c	S1
Dunton, John	Unkn.					X2
Duport, Henry?	Unkn.	97				
Duppa, James	Merc.			09		X2
Duppa, Jeffrey	Merc.			09		
Durdent, Thomas	Unkn.	04				
*Durette, Philip	Unkn.			09		
Durham, Baldwin	Merc.					S6
Durham, Baldwin	Merc.					S4
Durley, Henry	Gent.					J1
Durninge, John	Unkn.	01				
Dutton, John	Gent.	24–25				
Dutton, Thomas	Kt. 03					A
Dwight, William	Merc.					F1
Dyamant, Walter	Unkn.					X2
Dyer, Edward	Kt. 96	89–93				W5
Dyer, Edward	Gent.			12		
Dyer, James	Unkn.	89				
Dymocke, Charles	Gent.	93				
Dymocke, Edward	Kt. 84	84–93				
Dymocke, John	Merc.					R1
Dynne, Henry	Unkn.	84				
Dynnie, Thomas	Merc.					I7
Dyos, William	Gent.					I1c
Dyott, Anthony	Gent.	01–04		10		
Dyott, Richard	Gent.	21–28				
Each, Thomas	Unkn.			22		
Eaglesfield, John	Merc.		18		18c	
Earle, Christopher	Gent.	21, 26–28		20		
Earle, Martin	Unkn.			19		
Earle, Nicholas	Unkn.		22			
Earle, Walter	Kt. 16	14–28		20c		K5/P2/GG
Earle, Walter	Merc.					S6
Early, Henry	Merc.				27	
Earning, Bartholomew	Unkn.					X2
Earsfield, Anthony	Merc.					X1
Earsfield, Richard	Merc.					X1

Name & title	Class; date of knight- hood	Parlia- ments (starting dates)	E. Ind. Co.	Va. Co.	Levant Co.	Other companies
Earsfield, Thomas	Merc.					*X*1
Earsfield, William	Merc.					*X*1
Earthe, Roger	Unkn.	84				
Eastcourt, Thomas	Merc.					*L*2/*M*
Eastman, Edward	Unkn.					*X*2
Easton, Oliver	Merc.					*I*7
Easton, William	Merc.					*M*/*Q*1
Eaton, Nicholas	Merc.					*X*2
Eaton, Theophilus	Merc.					*E*3/*J*2c
Eaton, Thomas	Merc.		99			*S*4
Eaveres, Sampson	Unkn.	21				
Eawley, Edward	Unkn.			21c		
Eden, Edward	Merc.	84				
Eden, T.	Unkn.	04				
Eden, Thomas	Gent.	26–28				
Eden, Thomas	Unkn.	89				
Edge, Isaac	Merc.		24			
Edge, Thomas	Merc.			09		
Edgecombe, Matthew	Merc.					*F*1
Edgecombe, Peter	Gent.	84–93				*GG*
Edgecombe, Piers	Gent.	28				*AA*2
Edgecombe, Richard	Kt. 03	24, 28				*K*4
Edgecombe, Richard	Gent.	86–93				
Edgecombe, Thomas	Merc.					*F*1
Edmonds, Charles	Gent.		27			
Edmonds, Christopher	Unkn.	84–86				
Edmonds, Clement	Kt. 17	21	15			
Edmonds, Clement	Merc.				05	*R*2
Edmonds, Harry	Pfl/y.					*CC*2
Edmonds, Helen	Unkn.					*CC*2
Edmonds, Henry	Kt. 26	25–26				
Edmonds, Henry	Merc.					*I*7
Edmonds, John	Merc.	86, 04				
Edmonds, Raphe	Merc.					*S*3
Edmonds, Richard	Merc.		99			
*Edmonds, Richard	Merc.					*I*7
Edmonds, Simonde	Merc.		11c		10c	
Edmonds, Thomas	Kt. 03	01–04, 21–28	14			*F*1/*S*1/*CC*1
Edmonds, ?	Kt.†		27			
Edmundson, John	Merc.					*F*1
**Edny, Thomas	Merc.		20			*I*2
Edny, Walter	Gent.					*I*2
Edolph, Robert	Kt. 03			12		
Edred, Thomas	Merc.					*F*1
Edwards, Arthur	Merc.					*R*1
Edwards, Clement	Gent.	04				
Edwards, Evan	Unkn.	28				
Edwards, John	Gent.	89				
*Edwards, John	Gent.	89				
Edwards, John	Merc.					*I*7
Edwards, Richard	Merc.		11	?		*Q*/*T*2c

285

Name & title	Class; date of knight-hood	Parlia-ments (starting dates)	E. Ind. Co.	Va. Co.	Levant Co.	Other companies
Edwards, Robert	Unkn.		18	23		L2/M
**Edwards, Thomas	Merc.	93–97	99		05	I2/X1
Edwards, ?	Unkn.					CC1
Effington, William	Unkn.					X2
Eger, Thomas	Unkn.					X2
Egerton, John, Viscount Brackley, Earl Bridgewater	Nob. 99	01–14				
Egerton, John, Viscount Brackley, Earl Bridgwater	Nob.	97–01				
Egerton, Roland	Kt. 17	24				
Egerton, Stephen	Unkn.		27			
Egerton, Thomas, Lord Ellesmere, Viscount Brackley	Nob. 97	84–89				F1/Q
Egerton, Thomas	Gent.	97				
Egiok, Francis	Kt. 03			12c		
Egiok, George	Unkn.	01				
Egleston, Thomas	Merc.	86				
Elbridge, Giles	Merc.					X2/GG
Elcott, John	Merc.		00			S1
Eldred, John	Merc.		99c	06c	90	F1/Qc/X1/Z/ GG
Eldred, John	Unkn.	84–86				
Eldred, John	Merc.		29		19	
Eldred, Rivet	Merc.				19	
Eldred, Walter	Merc.			09		
Eling, William	Unkn.					CC2
Elkin, John	Merc.			09		
Elkin, Thomas	Merc.					I2
Elkin, William	Merc.					X1/GG
Elkington, Humphrey	Merc.		14			
Elkington, Thomas	Merc.				27	
Ell, John	Merc.					I7
Ellam, Andrew	Merc.		15		05	
Ellawood, James	Merc.				10	
Ellicote, Robert	Merc.					S1
Elliot, Bartholomew	Merc.					X2
Elliot, Francis	Merc.		19			
Elliot, John	Kt. 18	14, 24–28				I4
Elliot, Lawrence	Merc.		19			
Elliot, Paul	Merc.					CC2
Elliots, Samuel	Merc.				27	
Ellis, Edward	Gent.					I4
Ellis, Gabriel	Unkn.					G8
Ellis, Griffyn	Merc.			09		
Ellis, Henry	Merc.					S6
Ellis, John	Merc.			09		X2
Ellis, Philip	Merc.					S1
Ellis, Richard	Merc.					L1

Name & title	Class; date of knight-hood	Parlia-ments (starting dates)	E. Ind. Co.	Va. Co.	Levant Co.	Other companies
Ellis, Thomas	Unkn.	97				
Ellis, Walter	Merc.					S1/X2
Ellis, William	Merc.					S1/X2
Ellis, William	Merc.					S1
Elliwood, Thomas	Merc.	93				
Ellzey, John	Merc.					X2
Elmer, Joshua	Unkn.	89				
Elmeston, Christopher	Merc.	97				
Elner, Richard	Merc.					S6
Elnor, Bartholomew	Merc.			09		
Elsey, John	Merc.					CC2
Eltoft, Edmund	Gent.					CC1
Elton, Thomas	Merc.		23			
Elumer, Henry	Merc.		14			
Elwaies, John	Unkn.		29			
Elwares, Henry	Merc.		18			
Elwes, Jarvis	Merc.					S1
Elwes, Jeffrey	Merc.					I7
Elwes, Jeremy	Merc.					S1
Elwick, James	Merc.					I2
Elwick, William	Merc.					L1/M
Elwyn, Thomas	Merc.			09		
Emerson, Hugh	Merc.				00	
Emerson, Thomas	Gent.					A
Emyn, William	Merc.					I7
Endecott, John	Unkn.					J1
English, John	Merc.					E3/L1c
Ensworth, Henry	Merc.			09		
Ent, Josias	Unkn.		25			
Epps, William	Unkn.					X2
Erderick, Richard	Merc.					H
Erdeswicke, Richard	Gent.	25				
Erick, John	Merc.					S4
Erisie, James	Gent.	84				X1
Errington, Anthony	Gent.		11			GG
Errington, John	Merc.					S6/CC2
Ersant, John	Merc.					F1
Erskine, Thomas, Viscount Fenton, Earl Kelly	Nob.		27			Q
Erundell, Peter	Merc.			12		
Escott, Richard	Unkn.	24–28				
Eslize, John	Merc.					F1
Essex, William	Unkn.	97–01				
Essington, William	Merc.		99	09		
Estcourt, Giles	Kt. 22	28				
Estcourt, Giles	Unkn.	84–86				
Estcourt, Thomas	Kt. 07	97, 24				
Estcourt, William	Gent.	84				
Eston, Jehan Galliers	Unkn.					X2
Etheridge, George	Merc.			09		I7/T2

Name & title	Class; date of knighthood	Parliaments (starting dates)	E. Ind. Co.	Va. Co.	Levant Co.	Other companies
Ethrington, Nathaniel	Unkn.			22		
Eure, Francis	Gent.	04				
Eure, Peter	Unkn.	89				
Eure, Ralph, Lord	Nob.	84		09		
Eurie, William	Gent.	01				
Evans, Adrian	Merc.		24			L1c/S2
Evans, Hugh	Unkn.			09		
Evans, John	Unkn.					X2
Evans, Miles	Merc.					W4
Evans, Raphe	Gent.		09			
Evans, Richard	Merc.		07	09		
Evans, Thomas	Merc.					L1
Evans, William	Merc.		07	09		Q/S3
Evelin, John	Kt. 23	26		12		Q/GG
Evelin, John	Kt. 41	28	24	12		
Evelin, Robert	Merc.			09		GG
Eveling, George	Unkn.					G8
Everard, Anthony	Unkn.	89				
Everard, Michael	Kt. 14			09		
Everden, John	Merc.					I7
**Evers, Peter	Unkn.	89, 01				
Eversfield, Nicholas	Unkn.	24–28				
Eversfield, Thomas	Kt. 03			12		
Every, Henry	Merc.					F1/S1
Every, Thomas	Merc.					F1/S1
Evington, Francis	Merc.		00	09		Q
Ewens, Matthew	Unkn.	84–86				
**Ewens, Ralph	Gent.	97–01		09		
Ewens, William	Merc.			23		X2
Exton, Edward	Merc.					F1
Exton, John	Unkn.			18?		
Exton, Nicholas	Merc.			09		F1/T2
Exton, Thomas	Unkn.					X1
Eyans, Thomas	Merc.		24			L2/M/GG
Eyles, John	Merc.					CC2
**Eyre, Christopher	Merc.		22c			F1/M
Eyre, Eleazar	Merc.					GG1
Eyre, George	Merc.		08			F1
Eyre, John	Merc.					F1
Eyre, John	Kt. 05	26–28				
Eyre, John	Merc.				06	S1
Eyre, Robert	Merc.					I3
Eyre, Thomas	Unkn.	97				
Eyre, Thomas	Merc.				21	T3/GG1
Eyre, William	Kt. 92	97, 04				
Eyton, Edmund	Merc.					S1
Eyton, John	Unkn.	14				
Facet, Edward	Gent.			09		T2
Fairebrother, William	Merc.			09		
Fairfax, Ferdinand	Kt. 08	14–28				
Fairfax, Thomas	Merc.					S4

Name & title	Class; date of knighthood	Parliaments (starting dates)	E. Ind. Co.	Va. Co.	Levant Co.	Other companies
Fairfax, Thomas	Kt. 79	86				
Fairfax, Thomas	Kt. 03	01, 21–26				
*Fairfax, Thomas	Kt. 91	86–89, 01, 25				
Fairfax, William	Kt. 60	97				
Fairweather, Richard	Merc.					R1
Faldow, William	Merc.			12		
Falkner, Edward	Unkn.		09			
Fallett, John	Merc.					S6
Fallowfield, Henry	Merc.					R1
Fane, Francis Earl Westmorland	Nob. 03	01–24				
Fane, George	Kt. 03	01–24, 26–28				
Fane, Henry	Kt. 11	14–28		10		
Fane, Henry	Unkn.	93				
Fane, Mildmay Earl Westmorland	Nob.	21, 25–26				
Fane, Thomas	Unkn.	89–97				
Fanshawe, Henry	Kt. 03	89–97		09c		Q
**Fanshawe, Thomas	Kt. 24	04–28	16?			
Fanshawe, Thomas, Viscount	Nob. 26	24–25, 28				
Fanshawe, Thomas	Unkn.	84–97				
Fanshawe, Thomas	Unkn.	01				
Fanshawe, William	Gent.	14–25	14			Q
Fant, Nicholas	Unkn.	84				
Fantris, John	Unkn.					X2
Farewell, Christopher	Merc.		14			
Farmer, George	Gent.			09		
Farmer, Jerome	Unkn.	89				
Farmer, John	Merc.			09		
Farmer, Robert	Unkn.					X2
Farmor, Thomas	Gent.	86				
Farnefold, Thomas	Kt. 21	24–25, 28				
Farr, Richard	Merc.	84				
Farr, William	Merc.				00	
Farrington, Alice	Merc.		28			
Farrington, Cadwell	Merc.		28		24	
Farrington, Henry	Unkn.				90	B/DD
Farrington, James	Unkn.					X2
Farrington, John	Merc.		18		19	GG
Farrington, Richard	Merc.			09		
Farrington, Thomas	Merc.		99c		92	I7/S1
Favor, John	Merc.					S6/CC2
Fawance, Richard	Merc.					S6
Fawcet, Lawrence	Merc.					I7
Fawcet, Richard	Merc.					I7
Fawether, John	Merc.					S6c
Fawkener, Lancelot	Merc.					Q
Feilding, Basil	Gent.	14				
Felgate, Toby	Merc.			22		X2
Felgate, William	Merc.			09		T2

Name & title	Class; date of knighthood	Parliaments (starting dates)	E. Ind. Co.	Va. Co.	Levant Co.	Other companies
Fell, Richard	Unkn.					X2
Feltham, ?	Merc.					I7
Felton, Anthony	Unkn.	86				
Felton, John	Merc.	93–97				
Fenne, Robert	Merc.		17c			
Fenner, Edward	Merc.					X1
Fenner, George	Merc.					X1
Fenner, John	Merc.			20		X1
Fenner, Thomas	Merc.	84				X1
Fenner, William	Merc.					X1
Fenton, Edward	Gent.					W4
Fenwicke, John	Kt. 05	24–28				GG
Ferdinando, Simon	Gent.?			87		
Fermis, Robert	Unkn.					X2
Ferne, John	Kt. 03	04		18?	05	
Ferne, John	Merc.			18?		L1/M/T2
Ferner, Robert	Merc.					E2
Ferneley, Thomas	Merc.				00	
Ferrar, Erasmus	Unkn.		09			
Ferrar, John	Merc.	21	14	18?c		I2/L1/M/O/T1c/X1
Ferrar, Mary	Merc.		23			
Ferrar, Nicholas	Merc.		99	09		M/S3/T2/X1/GG
Ferrar, Nicholas	Merc.	24	17	19c		
Ferrar, Roger	Merc.					I7
Ferrar, William	Merc.		23	12	26	I2/Q
Ferrers, Edward	Kt. 91	04				
Ferrers, Edward	Merc.					I2
Ferrers, Henry	Unkn.	97				
Ferrers, John	Kt. 03	86, 93, 04				
Ferris, Henry	Unkn.	93				
Ferris, Richard	Merc.					F1/X2
Ferris, Thomas	Merc.					R2/X2
Ferris, William	Merc.		00			
Fetherstone, Francis	Unkn.	21–24				
Fetherstone, Ralph	Unkn.	21				
Fettiplace, Charles	Merc.		19		20	
Fettiplace, Edmund	Kt. 03					I4
Fettiplace, Giles	Unkn.	01				
Fettiplace, John	Gent.	26–28				
Fettiplace, Mary	Unkn.		23			
Fettiplace, Michael	Gent.			09		
Fettiplace, Thomas	Merc.	97–01	10			I7/Q
Fettiplace, William	Gent.			09		
Field, John	Merc.					S4
Field, Joseph	Merc.	04				F1/Mc
Field, Matthew	Merc.					Mc/R1c/W6/AA1/GG
Field, Theophilus	Pfl/y.	18				
Field, William	Merc.			09		I7

Name & title	Class; date of knight-hood	Parlia-ments (starting dates)	E. Ind. Co.	Va. Co.	Levant Co.	Other companies
Fiennes, Charles	Gent.					*J*3
Fiennes, Edward						
Earl Lincoln	Nob.					*W*7/*X*1
Fiennes, Henry						
Earl Lincoln	Nob.		08c			*X*1
Fiennes, James, Lord &						
Viscount Saye & Sele	Nob.	25–28				
Fiennes, Richard						
Viscount Saye & Sele	Nob. 92	84–89, 97‡				*I*2
Fiennes, Thomas, Lord						
Clinton, Earl Lincoln	Nob.	01–04				
Fiennes, William						
Lord Saye & Sele	Nob.					*FF*
Finch, Francis	Unkn.	24–28				*GG*
Finch, Heneage	Kt. 23	04, 21–26	17	22?c		*GG*
Finch, Henry	Gent.	93–97				*GG*
Finch, Henry	Unkn.	14				
Finch, James	Merc.					*I*2
Finch, John, Lord	Nob. 25	21–24, 26–28				*GG*
Finch, Moyle	Kt. 84	93, 01		12		*GG*
Finch, Theophilus	Kt. 99	14				*GG*
Finch, Thomas						
Earl Winchilsea	Nob. 09	21, 28				*G*7/*GG*
Finch, William	Merc.					*L*1/*X*1/*GG*
Fipps, Humphrey	Merc.		09			*F*1c/*S*4
Fipps, Robert	Merc.		09	09		*L*1
Fish, John	Gent.					*I*2
Fish, Thomas	Merc.					*C*
Fish, Walter	Unkn.	84				
Fish, William	Unkn.	89				
Fishbourne, Richard	Merc.		19c	12	10c	*F*1/*I*2/*Nc*/*X*1
Fisher, Alexander	Merc.	84				
Fisher, Andrew	Unkn.	93				
Fisher, Christopher	Merc.		07			
Fisher, Clement	Unkn.	84				
Fisher, Henry	Unkn.		14			
Fisher, Jeremy	Unkn.		16			
Fisher, John	Unkn.	84				
Fisher, John	Unkn.	86				
Fisher, John	Unkn.	25				
Fisher, John	Merc.					*S*1
Fisher, Richard	Unkn.	04				
Fisher, Thomas	Gent.	89				*F*1/*S*1/*X*1
Fisher, Thomas	Merc.					*S*1
**Fisher, William	Merc.		08			*S*4
Fitch, Raphe	Merc.				92c	*I*7
Fitch, Talbot	Merc.				10	
Fitch, Thomas	Merc.					*X*2
Fitch, William	Merc.			09		
Fitton, Alexander	Gent.					*I*9
Fitton, Edward	Kt. 79	89				*I*9

Name & title	Class; date of knight-hood	Parlia-ments (starting dates)	E. Ind. Co.	Va. Co.	Levant Co.	Other companies
Fitton, Edward	Gent.		18			
Fitton, Richard	Gent.					I9
Fitzalan, Henry						
Earl Arundel	Nob.					R1/GG
Fitzherbert, Humphrey	Merc.					S1
Fitzherbert, Thomas	Unkn.	93				
Fitzjames, John	Kt. 15	84, 01		09?		
Fitzjames, Lewston	Unkn.	97				
Fitzwilliam, Walter	Gent.	21		10		
Fitzwilliam, William	Gent.	84–89				
Flat, Katherine	Gent.			22		
Fleet, William	Gent.			10		
*Fleet, William	Merc.					S1
Fleetwood, Edward	Gent.			09		
Fleetwood, George	Kt. 03	86, 04				
Fleetwood, Gerard	Kt. 03	25–26				
Fleetwood, Henry	Gent.	89, 01–04				
Fleetwood, Henry	Merc.			89		
Fleetwood, Miles	Kt. 02	14–28				
Fleetwood, Thomas	Gent.					I9/BB1
Fleetwood, William	Kt. 03	86–89, 04				
Fleetwood, William	Kt. 03	04, 21–24, 28		10		
Fleetwood, William	Gent.	84–89				
Fleming, Giles	Merc.					X1
Fleming, Philip	Gent.	14–28				
Fleming, Robert	Unkn.					X2
Fleming, Thomas	Kt. 03	97–21				S1
Fleming, Thomas	Merc.	84–93, 01				
Fletcher, George	Merc.				27	
Fletcher, Giles	Unkn.	84				
Fletcher, James	Merc.			24		S4
Fletcher, John	Merc.		00	09	?	L1/Q/S6/T2
Fletcher, Richard	Unkn.	89				
Fletcher, Thomas	Unkn.					P2
Fletcher, Walter	Merc.		99			
Fletcher, William	Merc.					X1
*Fletcher, ?	Unkn.		14			
Flete, John	Unkn.	89				
Fletewood, Humphrey	Merc.					L1
Flower, Francis	Unkn.	84–93				
Flower, Ralph	Merc.					M
Flowerden, Thomas	Gent.					I2
F(f)ludd, Egidine	Merc.					S6
Fludd, Roger	Merc.					E1
Fludd, Thomas	Kt. 89	93–01				
Fluith, Benedict	Merc.					F1
Fluith, Nicholas	Merc.					F1
Flycke, Robarte	Merc.					D/X1
Flyer, Francis	Merc.				12c	J3/R2c
Foden, Anthony	Merc.					I7
Fogg, Ralph	Unkn.			20		

292

Name & title	Class; date of knight-hood	Parlia-ments (starting dates)	E. Ind. Co.	Va. Co.	Levant Co.	Other companies
Foljambe, Francis	Kt. 22	26				
Follett, Anthony	Unkn.					X2
Folliott, Henry	Kt. 99					I4
Foorde, Edward	Merc.					J1/L2/M
Foran, James	Merc.					X2
Foran, John	Merc.					X2
Foran, Peter	Merc.					X2
*Forcett, Edward	Unkn.	04				
Ford, Thomas	Merc.					F1
Forest, Anthony	Kt. 04	24–26		09		
Forest, Edmund	Merc.		14			
Forest, James	Merc.					F1
Forest, Thomas	Unkn.			09		
Forman, Thomas	Merc.					S6c
Fornes, Humphrey	Merc.					S1/X1
Forster, Edmund	Merc.					X2/GG
Forster, Humphrey	Kt. 92	93–97				
Forster, Richard	Merc.					S6
Fortescue, Dudley	Gent.	93				
Fortescue, Edmund	Gent.	93				
Fortescue, Francis	Gent.	89–01				
Fortescue, John	Kt. 92	86–04				
Fortescue, John	Unkn.	93				
Fortescue, Thomas	Gent.	93–01				
Fortescue, Thomas	Gent.	93				
Fortescue, William	Kt. 00	93–97, 04				
Forthe, William	Unkn.	97				
Fortune, William	Unkn.	26				
Fotherby, Henry	Unkn.			18		
Fotherby, Thomas	Unkn.	25–28				
Fothergill, James	Unkn.			23		
Foues, Andrew	Merc.				92	S6/X1
Fouke, John	Merc.				17	
Foulkes, Austin	Merc.					R1
Fowkes, John	Merc.		25c		10c	I2/X2
Fowkes, William	Unkn.	97				
Fowle, Adolph	Merc.				24	
Fowle, Alfonsus	Merc.		00			
Fowle, Matthias	Merc.				10	
Fowler, John	Merc.					L1/M
Fowles, Augustine	Merc.					S6
Fowles, John	Gent.					Q
Fownde, Alexander	Merc.					BB2
Fownes, John	Merc.					S1
Fownes, Warwick	Merc.		28			
Fox, Edward	Kt. 03	28				
Fox, John	Merc.	84				
Fox, John	Merc.				24	X2
Fox, Luke	Merc.					X2
Fox, Richard	Merc.				10c	I7c
Fox, Samuel	Unkn.	89–93				

Name & title	Class; date of knighthood	Parliaments (starting dates)	E. Ind. Co.	Va. Co.	Levant Co.	Other companies
Fox, Thomas	Unkn.			09		
Fox, ?	Merc.		14			
Foxall, John	Merc.					E1/R1
Foxall, Thomas	Merc.		10			
Foxcroft, George	Merc.				27	J1c
Foxcroft, James	Merc.					E2
Foxton, Elias	Unkn.			20		
Foxton, Richard	Unkn.	21				
Foyer, Peter	Merc.					F1
Foyll, John	Unkn.	97				
Francis, Albian	Merc.			09		
Francis, Edward	Kt. 03	01–26				
Francis, Giles	Gent.			09		T2
Francis, John	Unkn.	25				
Francis, Richard	Merc.					I7
Francis, Thomas	Merc.			20		
Frank, Arthur	Unkn.			20		
Frank, George	Merc.					E2
Frank, John	Unkn.	97				
Frank, Peter	Gent.			12		
Frank, Richard	Unkn.	93				
Frank, Walter	Merc.					F1
Frank, William	Unkn.			20		
Frankland, William	Unkn.	28				
Franklin, Emanuel	Merc.					F1/S4
Franklin, George	Merc.		18			M
Franklin, James	Merc.		24			F2/L1
Franklin, John	Kt. 14	25–28				
*Franklin, John	Merc.			09		
Franklin, Richard	Merc.			12		
Franklin, Thomas	Merc.		11			F1/I7/M
Frayne, Hugh	Merc.		14			
Freake, Henry	Unkn.			12		
Freake, John	Merc.	14–24				X2
Freake, Thomas	Kt. 03	04, 26		07c		K2c
Freake, Thomas	Gent.	84				
Freake, Thomas	Unkn.			12		
Frechville, John	Gent.	28				
Frechville, Peter	Kt. 03	01, 21		12		
Freeland, William	Unkn.					X2
Freeman, Blase	Merc.					E1
Freeman, John	Merc.				23	I8
Freeman, Martin	Merc.		07	09		I7c/GG
Freeman, Nicholas	Merc.					F1
Freeman, Ralph	Kt. 17	25, 28	14	12		
Freeman, Ralph	Merc.		99c	09	05c	F1/M/Nc/Qc/ R2/X2/GG1
Freeman, Robert	Merc.		18			R2c
Freeman, Thomas	Merc.		11		06c	R2c
Freeman, William	Merc.		99	11	90c	I1c/M/N/S1/ GG

Name & title	Class; date of knighthood	Parliaments (starting dates)	E. Ind. Co.	Va. Co.	Levant Co.	Other companies
Freeze, James	Merc.				20	R2c
French, John	Unkn.		27			
French, Richard	Merc.					I7
French, William	Unkn.					X2
Frere, Thomas	Unkn.	89				
Freshwater, John	Merc.					E3
Fretwell, Thomas	Merc.			09		
Frier, Clement	Merc.					S4
Frier, John	Merc.		99		00	
Frier, Thomas	Merc.					F1/S1
Frier, ?	Unkn.			09		
Frith, Henry	Merc.					I7
Frith, Richard	Gent.			09		
Frith, William	Merc.					I7
Frobisher, Martin	Gent.					W7/X1
Frosland, Andrew	Merc.					X1/GG
Frost, Robert	Unkn.					X1
Frowde, William	Unkn.	21				
Frowike, Henry	Merc.	01				
Fulford, Andrew	Unkn.					X2
Fulford, Francis	Kt. 05	25				
Fulkes, Augustine	Merc.					E1/S1
Fuller, Bostocke	Unkn.	01				
Fuller, Francis	Unkn.					I2c
Fuller, Nicholas	Gent.	93, 04–14	18	18?		
Fullerton, James	Kt.†	25–26				I5c
Fulwood, William	Gent.			87		
Furley, William	Merc.					I7
Furner, Simon	Merc.					S1c/X1
Fursland, Richard	Merc.		18			
Furzman, George	Unkn.			24		
Fusse, Richard	Merc.	07				
Gaines, John	Merc.					X2
Gainsford, Edward	Merc.					S1
Gainsford, Nicholas	Merc.					S6
Gale, George	Gent.					I4
Gale, Peter	Merc.					I7
Gale, Robert	Merc.					I7
Gall, Edward	Unkn.			09		
Gamage, Anthony	Merc.					R1/S6/AA2/BB1c
Gamage, William	Merc.			89		AA3/BB2
Games, Thomas	Gent.	84–86				
Gamull, Thomas	Merc.	01				
Gamull, William	Merc.	04, 26‡				
Gamyng, William	Merc.					S4
Garaway, Arthur	Merc.		17		17	
Garaway, Francis	Merc.				?	Q
Garaway, Henry	M. Kt. 40		11c		00g	R2g
Garaway, John	Merc.		26		00	
Garaway, Nathaniel	Merc.		17		?	

Name & title	Class; date of knight-hood	Parlia-ments (starting dates)	E. Ind. Co.	Va. Co.	Levant Co.	Other companies
Garaway, Thomas	Merc.		99		92c	*M/Q*
Garaway, William	Merc.				20c	*X2*
Garaway, William	M. Kt. 15		99c	10	90c	*D/Q/T2/X1/ DD/GG*
Gardner, Edward	Merc.				06	
Gardner, Henry	Merc.				27	*GG2*
Gardner, John	Merc.		09	09		*I7c*
Gardner, John	Merc.		29			*X2*
Gardner, John	Merc.					*S6*
Gardner, Oliver	Merc.				00	
Gardner, Richard	Unkn.			18?		
Gardner, Robert	Kt. 91	14				
Gardner, Thomas	Merc.		28			
Gardner, Thomas	Unkn.					*X1*
Gardner, William	Unkn.	89–93				
Gargadnell, John	Unkn.					*X2*
Gargrave, Richard	Kt. 03	97, 04				
Garnons, Luke	Merc.	84, 89, 97–01				
Garnons, Nicholas	Unkn.	89				
Garret, William	Merc.				81	
Garsett, Robert	Merc.			12	10	
Garth, George	Unkn.	89				
Garth, Roger	Unkn.					*I4*
Garveighe, Richard	Unkn.	04				
Gaskin, Jewell	Unkn.					*X2*
*Gasset, ?	Merc.	15				
Gate, Daniel	Unkn.					*X2*
Gate, Edward	Gent.	89–93				
Gate, Geoffrey	Unkn.	84–86				
Gate, Henry	Kt. 47	86				
Gate, Peter	Merc.			09		
Gates, Thomas	Kt. 96			06c		*K1*
Gatonbey, Nicholas	Merc.					*X2*
Gaunt, Nicholas	Merc.	89				
Gauntlett, Roger	Unkn.	14–24				
Gawdy, Anthony	Gent.	97–01				
Gawdy, Bassingbourn	Gent.	84				
Gawdy, Bassingbourn	Kt. 97	93, 01–04				
Gawdy, Clipesby	Gent.	97				
Gawdy, Framlingham	Gent.	14–26				
Gawdy, Henry	Gent.	97–01				
Gawdy, Philip	Gent.	89–14				
Gawdy, Robert	Gent.	97				
Gawsell, Gregory	Gent.					*FF*
Gay, Charles	Merc.			09		
Gay, David	Unkn.					*X2*
Gay, George	Merc.					*F1/S1*
Gay, Jeremy	Merc.					*I7*
Gay, Richard	Merc.		29			
Gay, William	Merc.					*F1/S1*

Name & title	Class; date of knight- hood	Parlia- ments (starting dates)	E. Ind. Co.	Va. Co.	Levant Co.	Other companies
Gayer, David	Merc.					X2
Gayer, Humphrey	Merc.					X2
Gayer, Robert	Merc.				23c	X2
Gayer, Roger	Merc.					X1
Gayer, Thomas	Merc.	24				X2
Gaymer, Henry	Merc.	86, 93				
Geare, John	Unkn.		25c		10c	
Geare, Michael	Merc.					X1
Geare, William	Merc.		29			
Gearing, John	Merc.		08	09		I7/Q/T2
Gearing, John	Merc.?		27			
Gee, John	Merc.					S6
Gee, William	Kt. 03	89, 04		12		
Gefferdsonne, Galfridus	Merc.					S6
Geldart, John	Merc.					E2
Gent, John	Merc.					I7
Gent, Thomas	Merc.					I7
Geoffreys, Robert	Merc.		27c	22		F1/L2/M/R2
George, Degorie	Unkn.					X2
George, John	Unkn.	26–28				
George, Richard	Unkn.	01				
George, William	Merc.			89		
Germaine, Thomas	Unkn.	24				
Gerrard, Anthony	Merc.					B/S6c/X1/GG
Gerrard, Benedict	Gent.		29			
Gerrard, Christopher	Gent.	89				
Gerrard, George	Gent.	21–24, 26–28		12		
Gerrard, George	Merc.					S4
Gerrard, Gilbert	Kt. 79	84				GG
Gerrard, Gilbert	Kt. 83	14–26				FF/GG
Gerrard, Gilbert	Gent.	93				
Gerrard, Jacob	Merc.		26			
Gerrard, John	Merc.		26	89		E3/S4
Gerrard, Nicholas	Merc.					L1
Gerrard, Robert	Merc.					E3/F1/L1/S5
Gerrard, Roger	Gent.					I8
Gerrard, Samuel	Merc.		99			I2/S4/GG
Gerrard, Thomas, Lord	Nob.					AA2/GG
Gerrard, Thomas	Kt. 53					W2
Gerrard, Thomas	Kt. 91	84–01, 14–21		09		X1/GG2
Gerrard, Thomas	Kt. 03	97, 24				GG
Gerrard, William	Merc.		24		24	
Gerrard, William	Gent.	84–86, 93				
Gervys, John	Merc.					S6
Gewen, Thomas	Unkn.	24, 26				
Gibbens, James	Unkn.			23		
Gibbens, John	Merc.			23		X2
Gibbens, Sidrake	Merc.					X2
Gibbens, William	Merc.					Q/X2
Gibbens, William	Merc.					S6/GG
Gibbon, Hamon	Merc.				22	

Name & title	Class; date of knighthood	Parliaments (starting dates)	E. Ind. Co.	Va. Co.	Levant Co.	Other companies
Gibbons, Thomas	Merc.					C
Gibbs, Edmund	Unkn.			20		
Gibbs, John	Unkn.					X2
Gibbs, Thomas	Gent.	14	24	18c		T3c/X2
Gibbs, William	Unkn.			09		
Gibson, Anthony	Merc.		00			
Gibson, John	Kt. 05†	21				
Gifford, Emanuel	Unkn.	21, 26				
**Gifford, George	Kt. 96	84, 97–01				
Gifford, John	Merc.					GG
Gifford, Philip	Gent.			20		N
Gifford, Richard	Kt.†	21–28				
Gifford, Richard	Unkn.					X2
Gifford, Roger	Unkn.	84, 89				
Gifford, Roger	Merc.		17			F1
Gifford, Thomas	Merc.			09		I7
Gilbert, Adrian	Gent.	97				Q1/X1/CC1/ GG
Gilbert, Edward	Merc.					R1c
Gilbert, Humphrey	Kt. 70					W3/X1/CC1/ GG3
Gilbert, John	Kt. 96					K2c/X1/CC1/ GG1
Gilbert, John	Merc.		10	09		
Gilbert, Ralegh	Gent.			06		K1/X2
Giles, Edward	Kt. 03	97, 14–25, 28				K4
**Giles, John	Merc.	86				X1
Giles, William	Unkn.					X2
Gill, John	Kt. 13	26				
Gillett, Edward	Merc.					E2
Gilman, Bartholomew	Merc.				21c	X2
Gipps, Robert	Merc.					E3
Gipps, Thomas	Merc.			09		
Gire, William	Unkn.					X2
Girling, William	Merc.					S1
Girton, Thomas	Merc.					I7
Gittins, John	Merc.					S1
Glanvill, Edward	Merc.					X1
Glanvill, Francis	Merc.					X1
Glanvill, Francis	Kt. 21	14–21, 25, 28		12		
Glanvill, John	Gent.	84–86, 93				
Glanvill, John	Gent.	14–28				
Glanvill, Nicholas	Merc.					X1
Glanvill, Richard	Merc.			09		X1
Glascocke, Charles	Merc.		09		00	S5
Glascocke, Edward	Unkn.	01				
Glascocke, Richard	Merc.					S6/DD/GG
Glascreek, William	Merc.					F1
Glasior, Hugh	Merc.	01–04				
Gleane, Peter	M. Kt. 24	28				
Gleane, Thomas	Merc.	89				

Name & title	Class; date of knighthood	Parliaments (starting dates)	E. Ind. Co.	Va. Co.	Levant Co.	Other companies
Gleman, Charles	Unkn.	24				
Glemham, Charles	Gent.	21, 25				
Glemham, Edward	Gent.					X1
Glemham, Henry	Kt. 91	93, 01–21				
Glemham, Thomas	Kt. 17	21, 25–26				
Glover, John	Unkn.					J1
Glover, Richard	Merc.				29	I2
Glover, Roger	Merc.				27	
Glover, Thomas	Kt. 05				10	
Glover, William	Unkn.	24				
Glynn, Thomas	Gent.	24–25				
Glynn, William	Gent.	93				
Gobbyns, Thomas	Merc.					S1
Godbeare, Richard	Merc.					S1/X1
Godbeare, William	Merc.					S1
Goddard, Richard	M. Kt. 03		99c			S6c/X1/GG
Goddard, Richard	Merc.	89				S6/X1/CC2
Goddard, Richard	Unkn.			09		
Goddard, Thomas	Merc.	84				
Goddard, William	Merc.					I7
Godfrey, Cornelius	Unkn.		27			
Godfrey, Richard	Unkn.	04, 24–26				
Godfrey, Thomas	Unkn.	14, 28				
Godolphin, Francis	Kt. 80	89–93				GG
Godolphin, Francis	Kt. 21	24–26				X2/GG
Godolphin, Francis	Gent.	26–28				
Godolphin, Sidney	Gent.	28				
Godolphin, William	Kt. 99	86, 04		09c		GG1
Godsail, Hugh	Merc.					F1
Godsalve, Roger	Unkn.		09			
Godshall, Joas	Unkn.		21			
Godson, John	Unkn.			23		
Godwin, James	Unkn.	93				
Godwin, John	Merc.			09		
Godwin, Richard	Unkn.	93				
Godwin, Thomas	Unkn.	86				
Godwin, Thomas	Unkn.			09		
Goff, John	Merc.		18	09		X2
Goff, Peter	Merc.					X1
Goff, Thomas	Merc.					J2c/P2
Gold, Edward	Merc.					F1/S1
Gold, Henry	Merc.					F1
Gold, Hugh	Merc.					E1
Gold, Isaac	Unkn.			21		
Gold, James	Gent.					I9
Gold, John	Merc.					F1
Gold, Robert	Merc.				90	
Gold, Walter	Merc.					F1
Golding, Henry	Unkn.	89				
Golding, Roger	Merc.					S1
Golding, William	Merc.					S6

Name & title	Class; date of knight-hood	Parlia-ments (starting dates)	E. Ind. Co.	Va. Co.	Levant Co.	Other companies
Goldsburgh, John	Unkn.	26				
Goldsburgh, Thomas	Merc.	93				
Goldsmith, Samuel	Merc.					I2
Goldwell, John	Merc.					E3/L1
Goldwell, John	Unkn.	84–93				
Gollop, George	Merc.	25–28				
Gombleton, Roger	Merc.					S1
Goning, John	Merc.		18c			S1/X2
Goning, John	Merc.					X2
Gooche, Barnabas	Gent.	21–24				K5
Good, John	Unkn.	04				
Good, Sebastian	Unkn.	25				
**Goodere, Henry	Kt. 99	04		10		
Goodere, Thomas	Gent.?		24	22		
Gooderich, John	Merc.					BB1
Goodinge, John	Unkn.					X2
Goodlacke, Christopher	Merc.					Q/S4
Goodlacke, Nathaniel	Unkn.					X2
Goodlad, John	Merc.					X2
Goodman, John	Unkn.	86				
Goodwin, Arthur	Gent.	21–24, 26				
Goodwin, Francis	Kt.†	04–21, 25–26		10		
Goodwin, Francis	Gent.	86–89, 97				
Goodwin, Ralph	Unkn.	24–28				
**Goodwin, Robert	Unkn.	26–28				I1
Goodyear, Andrew	Merc.					I7
Goodyear, John	Merc.					F1
Goodyear, Michael	Merc.					E3/F1
Goodyear, Zachariah	Merc.					I7
Googes, John	Unkn.			09		
Gookin, Daniel	Unkn.			21		G7
Goore, Paul	Kt. 22					I4
Gordon, Robert	Kt. 25					X2/GG1
Gore, Gerard	Merc.					B/M/S6/X1
Gore, Gerard	Merc.		19			B/S1
Gore, John	M. Kt. 26		99	20?		B/E3/F1/I1c/ L1c/M/S1
Gore, Ralph	Merc.		00	19?c		B/F1
Gore, Richard	Merc.	04				F1/I7/Mc/ S1c/GG
Gore, Robert	Merc.		00	12		B/F1/I7/Q/T2
Gore, Thomas	Merc.					B/S6
Gore, William	Merc.		99	20?		B/F1/M/S1
Gorges, Arthur	Kt. 97	84, 89–93, 01				G7
Gorges, Edward, Lord	Nob.					K4g/GG
Gorges, Ferdinand	Kt. 91	93		06c		A/K1/X1/ EE/GG3
Gorges, Nicholas	Unkn.	84				
Gorges, Robert	Kt. 16	25–28				K5
Gorges, Robert	Gent.					GG
Gorges, Thomas	Gent.	86				

Name & title	Class; date of knighthood	Parliaments (starting dates)	E. Ind. Co.	Va. Co.	Levant Co.	Other companies
Gorges, Tristiam	Kt.†					*GG*
Goring, Edward	Kt. 17	26				
**Goring, George, Lord, Earl Norwich	Nob. 08	21–28		18?		
Goring, George	Gent.	93, 01				
Goring, William	Kt. 22	28				
Gorsuch, Daniel	Merc.		11c			*E3/F1/I2/ L1/Q*
Goslen, Thomas	Unkn.					*X2*
Goslyn, John	Unkn.	14				
Gosnold, Anthony	Gent.			09		
Gosnold, Bartholomew	Gent.			09		*X1/Y*
Gosnold, Martin	Merc.					*S6*
Gosnold, Robert	Gent.			21		
Gosnold, Thomas	Merc.					*M*
Gosse, Thomas	Merc.					*L2/M*
Gossen, James	Merc.		26			
Gossen, Richard	Merc.		00			
Gossen, Robert	Merc.		26			
Gouge, Thomas	Gent.			10		
Gough, George	Merc.					*S1*
Gough, Henry	Merc.					*S6*
Gough, Richard	Merc.					*X2*
Goulston, Theodore	Pfl/y.		14	19c		
Gowen, Walter	Unkn.	04–14				
Gower, Nicholas	Gent.					*X1*
Gowerson, William	Merc.				05c	
Grace, Edward	Merc.					*L1*
Grafton, Richard	Unkn.	84, 89				
Grafton, William	Merc.					*X1*
Grame, Richard	Unkn.	26–28				
Grantham, Thomas	Kt. 03	04–28		10		
Granule, Robert	Merc.					*S1*
Graunt, John	Pfl/y.					*FF*
Graves, Bartholomew	Merc.					*S1*
**Graves, John	Merc.	01		18?		
Graves, Robert	Merc.	25				
Graves, Stephen	Merc.				10	
Graves, Thomas	Gent.			09		
Graves, William	Merc.	01				
Gray, Elizabeth	Kt.			12		
Gray, Henry Earl Kent	Nob.					*BB5*
Gray, Henry Lord Groby	Nob. 87	89				
Gray, Henry Lord Groby	Nob. 03	01, 14				*G7*
Gray, James	Unkn.					*X2*
Gray, John	Kt. 96	01–04		10		
Gray, John	Gent.	86				
Gray, John	Unkn.			09		
Gray, Robert	Merc.			09		

Name & title	Class; date of knighthood	Parliaments (starting dates)	E. Ind. Co.	Va. Co.	Levant Co.	Other companies
Gray, Thomas	Kt. 47	86				
Gray, William						
Lord Warke	Nob. 03	21–24				
Greame, George	Kt. 03					I4
Greame, Paul	Gent.					I4
Green, Elizabeth	Merc.					E3
Green, Gabriel	Unkn.					X2
Green, Giles	Unkn.	21, 25–28				
Green, John	Merc.					S4
Green, Lawrence	Merc.		99c	09	05c	F1/Q/R2/S1c
Green, Michael	Merc.					X2
Green, Reynold	Merc.		99c			F1c/Q
Green, Richard	Unkn.	28				
Green, Robert	Merc.					S4
**Green, William	Merc.	97	09	09		F1/L1
**Green, William	Merc.	19	19			P1
Green, ?	Unkn.					I8
Greenige, John	Unkn.			18?		
Greenway, Robert	Merc.					F1
Greenwell, Anne	Merc.		22			
Greenwell, John	Merc.		18			L2/M
Greenwell, Robert	Merc.				15	E4/L1/M
Greenwell, William	Merc.		00c	10c	05c	E4/F1/I7c/L1c /Qc/S4/T2/Z
Greenwood, John	Merc.		00		05	S4
Gregory, Philip	Merc.					S1
Gregory, Robert	Merc.	89				
Gregory, Thomas	Merc.					C/S1
Gregory, William	M. Kt.†	01, 14				
Greni, John	Pfl/y.					CC2
Grenowes, Richard	Merc.					L1/M
Grenville, Barnard	Gent.	97		17		K2c
Grenville, Bevill	Gent.	21–28				
Grenville, George	Kt. 03					X2
Grenville, George	Gent.	84, 93				
Grenville, Richard	Kt. 77	84		84		I9/X1/GG
Grenville, Richard	Kt. 27	28				
Gresham, Thomas	M. Kt. 59					M/R1/S6/ W6/GG
Gresham, Thomas	Kt. 03	04–21, 25				
Gresham, William	Gent.	86				
Gresley, George	Kt. 11	28				
Gresley, Thomas	Gent.	97				
Gresson, Nathaniel	Merc.				10	
Greute, Edward	Merc.					F1/S1
*Greves, William	Merc.					S4
Grevill, Edward	Kt. 03	93, 04				
Grevill, Fulke						
Lord Brooke	Nob. 97	84–01, 21		17		K2c
Grevill, Robert						
Lord Brooke	Nob.	28				FF

302

Name & title	Class; date of knight-hood	Parlia-ments (starting dates)	E. Ind. Co.	Va. Co.	Levant Co.	Other companies
Grice, Nicholas	Unkn.			09		
Grice, William le	Merc.	84–86				
Griffin, Hugh	Merc.					X1
Griffin, William	Merc.					I7
Griffith, Edward	Gent.	84				
Griffith, George	Merc.		24		18	X2/GG2
Griffith, John	Merc.?	04–14				S1
Griffith, John	Gent.	04				
Griffith, John	Gent.	21, 26–28				
Griffith, Nicholas	Gent.	01, 14–21				
Griffith, Robert	Gent.	93				
Griffith, William	Gent.	86, 97				
Grilles, William	Merc.					F1
Grimes, Christopher	Merc.					L1
Grimes, George	Gent.	28				
Grimes, Philip	Merc.				90	
Grimes, Thomas	Kt. 03	01, 14–21				
Grimrood, William	Merc.					F1
Grimsditch, Charles	Gent.					I4
Grimsditch, Thomas	Unkn.	84				
Grimston, Edward	Gent.	89				
Grimston, Edward	Gent.	93				
Grimston, Edward	Gent.	21				
Grimston, Harbottle	Kt. 03	14, 26–28				
Grimston, Harbottle	Gent.	28				
Grimwade, William	Merc.					E3
Grindal, Robert	Merc.					F1
Griston, Thomas	Pfl/y.					CC2
Grobham, Richard	Kt. 03			10c		T2
Grollier, Peter	Unkn.					X2
Grose, Alexander	Merc.					GG
Grose, Charles le	Kt. 16	26–28				
Grose, Lawrence	Merc.					CC2
Grose, Samuel	Merc.					X2
Grose, William	Merc.					CC2
Grosvenor, Humphrey	Unkn.					X2
Grosvenor, Richard	Kt. 17	21, 26–28				
Groves, John	Merc.					S1
Groves, Robert	Merc.					X2
Groves, Thomas	Merc.					X1
Growne, Oliver	Merc.					S6
Gruff, Thomas	Unkn.	93				
Gryme, Robert	Merc.		24			F1
Gryndon, Thomas	Unkn.					X2
Gudburn, Peter	Unkn.					P2
Guilford, Henry	Kt. 91					Q
Guillet, William	Merc.					X2
Gulliford, Ezra	Merc.			26		
Gunnell, William	Merc.			05		
Gunston, Roger	Merc.					S5

Name & title	Class; date of knight-hood	Parliaments (starting dates)	E. Ind. Co.	Va. Co.	Levant Co.	Other companies
Gunter, Philip	Merc.					R1
Gunthrop, Miles	Merc.			09		
Gurdon, Brampton	Unkn.	21				
Gurdon, John	Gent.					FF
Gurgeing, John	Merc.					S5
Gurlinge, Nathaniel	Unkn.	26				
Gurlyn, Thomas	Merc.	25–26				S4/X2
Gurney, John	Merc.				00	
Gurney, Richard	Merc.					E1
Gurney, Thomas	Merc.	04–14				E1
Gurney, William	Merc.					F1
Guy, Anthony	Merc.					X2
Guy, Arthur	Merc.					X2
Guy, Henry	Merc.			07		
Guy, John	Merc.	21–24				N/S1
Guy, Philip	Merc.?					N
Guy, Reynold	Merc.					B
Guy, Richard	Unkn.	26				
Guybon, Gregory	Merc.					S4
Guybon, Thomas	Unkn.	97				
Gwillim, Moore	Merc.	84–86				
Gwin, Owen	Unkn.			10		
Gwym, Hugh	Gent.	89				
Gwyn, Rice	Unkn.	14				
Gylpin, Nicholas	Merc.					M
Gyttyns, William	Merc.					S6c
Hackett, Edmund	Unkn.			20		
Hackett, Richard	Merc.					Q
Hackshaw, Thomas	Unkn.			18?		
Hackwell, John	Merc.					S6
Hackwell, Thomas	Unkn.					X2
Hackwell, William	Gent.	01–24, 28‡		01		
Hadderton, Edward	Merc.					I7
Haddock, Richard	Unkn.					X2
Haddon, Francis	Merc.		07			F2/L1/S2
Hadds, Matthew	Unkn.	04				
Hagget, Bartholomew	Merc.		00		06	
Hagget, Humphrey	Unkn.	25–26				
Hake, Edward	Unkn.	89				
Hake, Thomas	Merc.	86				
Hake, William	Merc.	93				
Hakluyt, Richard	Pfl/y.			89		
Hakluyt, Richard	Pfl/y.		11	06		Q
Hale, Edmund	Merc.					H/M
Hale, John	Merc.		11			M/S4
Hale, Richard	Merc.		00			S6
Hale, William	Merc.		00			
Hales, Edward	Kt. 03	04–14, 25–26				
Hales, John	Kt. 25	28				
Hall, Arthur	Unkn.	84				
Hall, Christopher	Merc.					R1

Name & title	Class; date of knight- hood	Parlia- ments (starting dates)	E. Ind. Co.	Va. Co.	Levant Co.	Other companies
Hall, Daniel	Merc.					F1
Hall, Edward	Merc.					S5
Hall, Henry	Merc.	01				
Hall, Humphrey	Merc.					F1/O/S3
Hall, James	Merc.					U/X2
Hall, John	Merc.		09			F1c/L1?/S6
Hall, John	Merc.					F1/S3/X2
**Hall, Richard	Merc.		29	12		X1
Hall, Richard	Merc.			12		
Hall, Robert	Merc.			21		R2c
Hall, Thomas	Merc.		18			F1/L1
Hall, William	Merc.			12		X1
Hall, William	Merc.					X2
Hallet, John	Unkn.					X2
Halley, James	Unkn.	86				
Halliday, John	Merc.					F1/L2/M
Halliday, Leonard	M. Kt. 03		99c		05	I7/M/X1
Halliday, Leonard	Merc.		19c			X1
Halliday, William	Merc.		99g			F1/I2/M/X1?
Hallsall, Cuthbert	Kt. 99	14				
Hallswell, Michael	Kt.†	04				
Hallswell, Robert	Gent.	14				
Hallwood, Thomas	Merc.					I7/S1
Hallworthy, Richard	Merc.					N/S4
Halsey, Duncombe	Merc.				22	L1/M
Halsey, Grevile	Merc.					X1
Halsey, Henry	Merc.					F1
Halsey, John	Merc.			17		I7/L1
Halsey, Nicholas	Merc.					X1
Halsey, Richard	Merc.					I7
Halsey, William	Merc.					X2
Halton, Robert	Unkn.					W2
Hambyn, Robert	Merc.					S6
Hamer, Ralph	Merc.		99	09		
Hamer, Ralph	Gent.?			09		T2
Hamer, Thomas	Merc.		14	09		
Hamersley, Hugh	Merc.					S4
Hamersley, Hugh	M. Kt. 28		01c	09	00g	F1?/Q?/R2g/ S1/GG
Hamford, William	Merc.					S6
Hamilton, James, Marquis, Earl Cambridge	Nob.			22c		K4/T2
Hamland, James	Merc.					F1
Hammon, Alexander	Merc.					S6
**Hammon, Thomas	Kt.†	97, 04, 21				
Hammond, Cordell	Merc.					I7
Hammond, Humphrey	Merc.			09		
Hammond, John	Merc.	84–86				
Hammond, Matthew	Merc.		99			
Hammond, Richard	Gent.					X1

Name & title	Class; date of knighthood	Parliaments (starting dates)	E. Ind. Co.	Va. Co.	Levant Co.	Other companies
Hammond, Susan	Unkn.			20		
Hammond, Thomas	Gent.					CC1
**Hammond, Thomas	Merc.		18	09		I7/K4
Hammond, William	Gent.					I8
Hampden, Alexander	Gent.	01				
Hampden, Griffith	Gent.	84				
Hampden, John	Gent.	21, 25–28				
Hampden, Richard	Gent.	25				
Hampden, William	Unkn.	93				
Hampson, Robert	M. Kt. 03		99			R2
Hampson, Thomas	Merc.		22			F1/L1/M/S4
Hampson, William	Unkn.			09		
Hampton, John	Merc.					H
Hampton, Thomas	Merc.			12		
Hanbury, John	Merc.			09		
Hanbury, John	Unkn.	28				
Hanbury, Richard	Merc.	93				BB1
Hanbury, Thomas	Unkn.	97				
Hancock, Edward	Unkn.	93–01				
Hancock, William	Merc.			09		S1
Handcorne, William	Merc.		18			
Handford, Hugh	Unkn.		15			
Handford, Humphrey	M. Kt. 22		00c	10		F1/Qc/S4/GG
Handford, John	Merc.			09		
Handford, Richard	Gent.					BB1
Handley, Robert	Merc.					S6
Handsome, Robert	Unkn.		24			
Hangate, William	Merc.					S1
Hanger, George	Merc.			18?		S1c/X1
Hanham, John	Kt. 03	01–04		10		
Hanham, Thomas	Gent.	84–93		06		I9
Hanham, William	Unkn.					N
Hankin, Richard	Merc.					R2
Hankinson, George	Unkn.			09		
Hanmer, John	Kt. 20	24				
Hanmer, Thomas	Gent.	93				
Hansard, Richard	Kt. 04					I4
Hansford, John	Merc.			09		
Hanson, John	Unkn.			22c		
Hanson, Raphe	Merc.		24		10	Q
Harby, Clement	Merc.		18c		16c	F1/M/R2/X2/ GG
Harby, Erasmus	Merc.					X1/GG
Harby, Job	Merc.		18c		16c	F1/R2c/GG
Harby, John	Merc.		99			R1/S6c
Harby, John	Merc.		25			S1
Harby, Thomas	Merc.				25	
Harby, William	Merc.					S1
Harcourt, Michael	Unkn.	84				
Harcourt, Robert	Gent.					G3
Harcourt, Simon	Kt. 27					G7

Name & title	Class; date of knight- hood	Parlia- ments (starting dates)	E. Ind. Co.	Va. Co.	Levant Co.	Other companies
Harcourt, Walter	Kt. 91	89–97				
Harding, Matthias	Unkn.			24		
Harding, Richard	Merc.					S6
Harding, Thomas	Merc.			89		
Harding, ?	Unkn.					T3
Hardware, George	Merc.	14, 24				
Hardy, Richard	Unkn.	86–89				
Hardy, Robert	Merc.					S4
Hare, Andrew	Unkn.					X2
Hare, Hugh	Unkn.	89				
Hare, John	Kt. 18	25–28		10		
Hare, John	Unkn.	84–04				
Hare, John	Merc.		24			
Hare, Mary	Merc.		27			
Hare, Milcah	Unkn.		23			
Hare, Nicholas	Unkn.	84–89				
Hare, Ralph	Unkn.	01				
Hare, Samuel	Merc.		00		05c	F1/M/Q
Hare, Walter	Unkn.		27			
Hare, William	Merc.		28			
Hareborne, Edward	Merc.		14		13	
Hareborne, William	Merc.			09	81	I7/S6c
Hareford, Anthony	Merc.					F1
Harewell, Henry	Merc.	24–26				
Harfleets, Thomas	Kt. 03			10		
Harflett, Walter	Merc.		11			Q
Harker, William	Unkn.					X2
Harley, Robert	Kt. 03	04, 24, 26–28		22?		
Harlowe, Pedahell	Merc.		27			
Harlowe, Peter	Unkn.			09		
Harlowe, Robert	Merc.		09			
Harlowe, Samuel	Merc.		15			
Harman, Robert	Merc.					X2
Harman, William	Merc.					X2
Harp, John	Merc.			09		I7
Harper, John	Merc.		07	09		S6
Harper, John	Kt. 03	97, 04				
Harper, Richard	Merc.			12		
Harrington, James	Kt. 65	86–89				
Harrington, James	Gent.	97, 04‡				
Harrington, John, Lord	Nob. 84	86, 93, 01–04				T1/GG
Harrington, John, Lord	Nob. 05			10c		Q
Harrington, William	Unkn.					W3
Harrington, William	Kt. 15	21, 25–26				
Harris, Andreas	Merc.					S6
Harris, Arthur	Kt. 06	24–25, 28		12		
Harris, Bartholomew	Merc.					F1
Harris, Christopher	Kt. 07	84		12		
Harris, Christopher	Gent.	21–28				
Harris, Edward	Unkn.					X2
Harris, Gabriel	Merc.			89		

307

Name & title	Class; date of knight-hood	Parlia-ments (starting dates)	E. Ind. Co.	Va. Co.	Levant Co.	Other companies
Harris, George	Unkn.					X2
Harris, Gilbert	Merc.					F1
Harris, John	Gent.			10		
*Harris, John	Gent.	04–21, 28				
*Harris, John	Gent.	01				
*Harris, John	Unkn.	28				
Harris, Richard	Merc.				13	F1
Harris, Nicholas	Unkn.					X2
Harris, Robert	Merc.	84–89				
Harris, Roger	Merc.			10		
Harris, Thomas	Gent.	84–01				
Harris, Thomas	Merc.		25			
Harris, Thomas	Gent.	97				
Harris, Thomas	Unkn.	86				
*Harris, Thomas	Gent.			09		
Harris, William	Kt. 03			10		
Harris, William	Merc.					S6
Harris, William	Unkn.					X2
Harrison, Brian	Unkn.					X2
Harrison, Edward	Merc.		00	09		I7
Harrison, George	Gent.			18?		
Harrison, Harman	Gent.			09		
Harrison, James	Gent.			12		
Harrison, John	Merc.					R1c
Harrison, John	Merc.		11	09		L1
*Harrison, John	Gent.			22		
Harrison, Ralph	Merc.		09	09	05	I7
Harrison, Richard	Kt. 21	21–24, 28				
Harrison, Robert	Merc.		14			
Harrison, Samuel	Gent.					I4
Harrison, Thomas	Merc.			09		
Harrison, William	Merc.		99c		05c	F1c/I7c/L1c/ Qc/R2/S4/GG
Harrold, John	Merc.					S1
Hart, Eustace	Kt.†			12		
Hart, Henry	Gent.					I8
Hart, John	Merc.					F1
*Hart, John	Merc.					I7
Hart, John	M. Kt. 91	93–97	99g		81	M/R1g/X1/GG
*Hart, John	Unkn.		21			
Hart, Percival	Kt. 01	97–01	20			
Hart, Richard	Unkn.					X2
Hart, Roger	Merc.					S1
Hart, ?	M. Kt.		27			
Hartford, William	Merc.			09		
Hartley, Robert	Unkn.			18?		
Hartopp, Edward	Kt. 19	28				
Hartwell, Abraham	Unkn.	86, 93				
Harvest, Thomas	Unkn.					I1
Harvey, Amias	Merc.					S1
Harvey, Anne	Unkn.					J3

Name & title	Class; date of knighthood	Parliaments (starting dates)	E. Ind. Co.	Va. Co.	Levant Co.	Other companies
Harvey, Daniel	Merc.		24c		18	GG
Harvey, Dionise	Gent.			87		
Harvey, Eliot	Merc.		28			
Harvey, Francis	Unkn.	84–93				
Harvey, Francis	Unkn.	97				
Harvey, George	Kt. 03	04				
Harvey, John	Merc.		00			
Harvey, Matthew	Merc.		28			
Harvey, Michael	Merc.		28			
Harvey, Robert	Merc.				05c	GG
Harvey, Roger	Merc.		14		10	
Harvey, Sebastian	Merc.					I7
Harvey, Simon	Merc.		07			
Harvey, Stephen	Merc.		00		10c	R2
Harvey, Thomas	Merc.				16	M/GG
Harvey, Walter	Merc.					S1
Harvey, William, Lord	Nob. 96	01–04				
Harvey, William	Kt. 08	24–25, 28	18			G6
Harvey, ?	Unkn.			20		
Harvey, ?	Unkn.	21				
Harwarr, Thomas	Merc.			09		I7
Harwell, Edmund	Kt. 03			22		
Harwell, Francis	Unkn.			21		
Harwell, Thomas	Kt. 03			09		
Harwood, Edward	Kt.†			09c		T3/FF
Harwood, George	Merc.					J1c
Harwood, Leonard	Merc.			09		T2
Haselden, William	Merc.			10		Q
Haselock, John	Unkn.	26–28				
Haselrig, Francis	Gent.			09		
Haselrig, John	Unkn.	89				
Haselrig, Thomas	Kt. 08	14, 24				
Hassall, Percival	Merc.					S6
Hassall, Robert	Merc.				00	
Hassard, John (see Hazard)	Merc.	84–86, 04				S1/X1
Hassard, Robert	Merc.	89–93				S1c/X1
Hassard, Robert	Merc.	21–24				
Hastings, Edward	Kt. 70	97				
Hastings, Ferdinand Earl Huntingdon	Nob.	25, 28				
Hastings, Francis	Kt. 92	84, 89–04				
Hastings, Francis	Gent.	86, 93				
Hastings, George Earl Huntingdon	Nob. 65	84–86				
Hastings, George	Kt. 17†	14–26				
Hastings, Henry Earl Huntingdon	Nob.			12c		GG
Hastings, Henry	Kt. 03	01, 21–24, 26				
Hastings, Henry	Unkn.					X2
Hastlemay, Richard	Merc.				10	

309

Name & title	Class; date of knighthood	Parliaments (starting dates)	E. Ind. Co.	Va. Co.	Levant Co.	Other companies
Hatch, George	Merc.					X2
Hatch, John	Merc.					X2
Hatcher, Thomas	Unkn.	24, 28				
Hatclyff, Thomas	Unkn.	97				
Hatherley, Timothy	Unkn.					P2
Hatton, Christopher	Kt. 77	84–86				I9/W4/X1/ CC2/GG1
Hatton, Christopher	Kt. 03	01–14				
Hatton, Christopher	Gent.	24–25				
Hatton, Robert	Kt. 17	14–25				
Hatton, Thomas	Kt. 16	21–25, 28				
Hatton, William	Kt. 86	86–89				I9
Haveland, Anthony	Merc.					E3/N
Havercampe, Godfrey	Merc.		27			GG
Havers, Gilbert	Merc.				25	
Havers, Thomas	Merc.				05	F1/S1/GG
Haviland, John	Merc.					S1
Haviland, Matthew	Merc.					S1
Haviland, Robert	Merc.					S1
Haward, Leonard	Merc.					S3
Haward, Thomas	Merc.					CC2
Hawes, Andrew	Merc.					I7
Hawes, Humphrey	Merc.		07	09		
Hawes, James	M. Kt. 75					S6c
Hawes, John	Merc.					S6c
Hawes, John	Merc.					S4
Hawes, M.	Unkn.			?		
Hawes, Nathaniel	Merc.		19			
Hawes, Nicholas	Merc.		27			
Hawes, Robert	Merc.					S1c
Hawes, ?	Unkn.	04				
Hawkenson, George	Unkn.			18?		
Hawkes, Dudley	Merc.					X1
Hawkes, Henry	Merc.					S6
Hawkes, John	Merc.					S6
Hawkes, Thomas	Merc.					L1
Hawkins, Charles	Merc.		09	09		I7
Hawkins, Edward	Unkn.		28			
Hawkins, George	Merc.		24			
Hawkins, John	Merc.		00	09		Q
Hawkins, John	M. Kt. 88				92	X1/GG
Hawkins, Margaret	M. Kt.					X1
Hawkins, Mark	Unkn.					X2
Hawkins, Nicholas	Merc.	97				
Hawkins, Richard	M. Kt. 03	04				A/K2/S1c/X1
Hawkins, Thomas	Unkn.			18?		
Hawkins, William	Merc.		07			K2/M/X1
Hawkins, William	Merc.					W4/X1/CC1
Hawkins, William	Merc.		07		06	X1
Hawkridge, Giles	Merc.			12		
Hawkridge, William	Merc.					X2

310

Name & title	Class; date of knight-hood	Parlia-ments (starting dates)	E. Ind. Co.	Va. Co.	Levant Co.	Other companies
Hawley, Edward	Gent.			09		
Hawley, Francis	Unkn.	84–89				
Hawley, Henry	Merc.		23c			M/X2
Hawley, James	Merc.		25			
Hawtrey, Ralph	Unkn.	28				
Hay, James, Lord, Viscount Doncaster, Earl Carlisle	Nob.			12c		G7/K5/X2/GG
Hay, Roger	Unkn.					CC2
Hayden, Jeremy	Merc.			09	10	T1
Hayes, Edward	Merc.					X1/CC1
Hayes, Joseph	Kt. 19		24			
Hayes, Martha	M. Kt.		17			
Hayes, Thomas	M. Kt. 03		01			M/Q
Hayes, Thomas	Merc.		15			E3/F1/L2/M
Hayman, Nicholas	Merc.	86, 93				
Hayman, Peter	Kt.†	21–24, 26–28				
Haynes, John	Merc.	26				X2
Haynes, William	Merc.		10		05	
Hayward, George	Kt. 04			09		Q
Hayward, Henry	Merc.					E3/F1/I7
Hayward, James	Merc.		15	09	07	
Hayward, John	Kt. 09			10		Q/T2
Hayward, John	Kt. 19	21, 26		18?		T2
Hayward, John	Pfl/y.			10		
Hayward, John	Gent.	21–24				
Hayward, John	Merc.					F1
Hayward, Robert	Merc.			09		
Hayward, Roland	M. Kt. 70					M/R1g/W4/ BB1g
Hazard, John (see Hassard)	Merc.					S1
Headland, George	Merc.					X2
Heaman, John	Unkn.					X2
Hearde, Alexander	Unkn.					X2
Hearne, Richard	Merc.		00	12		
Heath, John	Merc.		24			
Heath, Nicholas	Merc.					S4
Heath, Richard	Merc.					I2
Heath, Robert	Kt. 21	21–25		19c		K4
Heath, Thomas	Unkn.					P2
Heath, William	Merc.	97–01				
Heather, John	Merc.		18			L1/M
Heather, John	Merc.					L1
Heather, Matthew	Unkn.					X2
Heather, William	Merc.					L1
Heaton, Francis	Merc.					BB1c
Heaton, George	Merc.					S6/BB4
Heaton, Theophilus	Merc.					L1/M
**Heaton, Thomas	Merc.	93				I2/Mc/R1/S1/ X1

Name & title	Class; date of knight-hood	Parlia-ments (starting dates)	E. Ind. Co.	Va. Co.	Levant Co.	Other companies
Heightley, Peter	Unkn.			18?		
Heiton, Francis	Gent.			12		
Hele, John	Merc.	84, 93–01				
Hele, John	Gent.	01				
Hele, John	Gent.	04				
Hele, Nicholas	Gent.	21–25				
Hele, Robert	Merc.			09		*I*7
Hele, Sampson	Gent.	14, 24				
Hele, Thomas	Kt. 27	26–28				
Hele, Thomas	Merc.					*F*1
Hele, Warwick	Kt. 03	97, 04–21, 25		09		*A/K*4
Helman, William	Merc.					*E*1
Helme, John	Merc.			09		
Helmes, Henry	Kt. 03	04				
Helyn, Peter	Merc.		01			
Helyn, Roland	Merc.					*F*1/*R*2
Heman, Graves	Merc.					*I*1c
Heming, Roger	Merc.		00			*E*3/*I*2/*L*1c
Hender, John	Unkn.	89–93				
Hendon, Edward	Unkn.	14				
Heneage, Michael	Unkn.	89–93				
Heneage, Thomas	Kt. 77	84–93				*W*9
Henley, Andrew	Merc.		?			*F*1
Henley, George	Merc.		18			*X*2
Henley, Robert	Merc.					*C*
Henshaw, Benjamin	Merc.		14			
Henshaw, Robert	Merc.					*X*1
Henshaw, Thomas	Merc.	97–01	99	09		*I*7
Herbert, Arnold	Kt. 17	14, 25				*A*
Herbert, Charles	Gent.					*I*9
Herbert, Christopher	Merc.					*F*1
Herbert, Edward	Gent.	89				
Herbert, Edward Lord Cherbury	Nob. 03	01–04				
Herbert, Edward	Kt. 41	21–28		19c		
Herbert, George	Gent.	24–25				
Herbert, Henry	Gent.	97				
Herbert, Henry	Kt. 23	26				
Herbert, Henry Earl Pembroke	Nob.					*W*7/*AA*1/*BB*1
Herbert, John	Kt.†	86–04				
Herbert, John	Merc.					*F*1
Herbert, Mary Countess Pembroke	Nob.			12		*W*5
Herbert, Matthew	Gent.	86				
Herbert, Nicholas	Gent.	84				
Herbert, Percy	Kt. 22	21–24				
Herbert, Philip Earl Montgomery (Earl Pembroke in 1630)	Nob. 03	04	11	09c		*G*7/*Q*/*X*2/*GG*1
Herbert, Philip	Merc.					*E*2

Name & title	Class; date of knighthood	Parliaments (starting dates)	E. Ind. Co.	Va. Co.	Levant Co.	Other companies
Herbert, Richard	Gent.	84				
Herbert, Richard	Gent.	84				
Herbert, Thomas	Merc.					E2
Herbert, William Earl Pembroke	Nob.		11	09c		A/G7/K4/Q/ T3/AA3/BB2/ GG2
Herbert, William	Kt. 78	84–86, 93				I9
Herbert, William	Gent.	21, 26–28‡				
Herbert, William Lord Powys	Nob. 03	97, 04–28				
Herbert, ?	Unkn.			09		
Herle, William	Unkn.	86				
Herne, John	Gent.	28	24			
Herne, Nicholas	Merc.		24			
Herne, Thomas	Kt. 08	14, 24–26				
Heron, Edward	Kt. 03			10		
*Heron, John	Gent.					I2
Herret, Leonard	Merc.					F1
Herrewinn, Jacob	Unkn.		24			
Herrick, Robert	Merc.	89				
Herrick, William	M. Kt. 05	01–04, 21		12		GG
Herriot, George	Merc.		24			
Herriot, James	Merc.		24			
Herst, Gregory	Unkn.		18?			
Herwick, Abraham van	Merc.					GG
Herwick, Stephen van	Merc.					GG
Hesketh, Robert	Gent.	97				
Hesketh, Thomas	Kt. 03	86–89, 97–04				
Hetley, Thomas	Unkn.	04				
Hetley, ?	Unkn.	21				
Hetherall, George	Merc.			09		I7
Heveningham, John	Kt. 03	28				
Hewett, Henry	Merc.				90	S6
Hewett, John	Merc.		99			
Hewett, Nicholas	Merc.					S6
Hewett, Thomas	M. Kt. 13		00	12		T3
Hewett, Thomas	Merc.	28				
Hewett, William	M. Kt. 59		00			M/S6c
Hewett, William	M. Kt. 06	24–25				
Hewishe, Richard	Unkn.	86–93				
Hewkley, Thomas	Merc.		19			S4/GG
Hewson, Richard	Merc.					S6
Hewson, Thomas	Merc.					J1
Hext, Edward	Kt. 03	97, 04				I9
Hext, Philip	Merc.		19		19	
Hext, Thomas	Merc.				27	
Heyborne, Ferdinand	Kt. 11			10		
Heyborne, Robert	Kt.†					I7c
Heydon, Christopher	Gent.	89				
Heydon, Gideon	Unkn.					X2

Name & title	Class; date of knight-hood	Parliaments (starting dates)	E. Ind. Co.	Va. Co.	Levant Co.	Other companies
Heydon, John	Merc.					S6c
Heydon, Michael	Unkn.	01				
Heyhoe, Robert	Merc.					I7
Heyhoe, Thomas	Merc.			09		
*Heylin, Roland	Merc.					I7
Heywood, Peter	Unkn.	26				
Hibbins, Arthur	Merc.					S1
Hibbons, Anthony	Merc.					L1
Hiccocke, Thomas	Merc.		99			B
Hickes, Baptist Viscount Campden	Nob. 03	21–28	99	09c		I2/T1
Hickes, John	Merc.					I7
Hickes, Michael	Kt. 04	84, 89–04				
Hickes, Nicholas	Merc.					S1
Hickes, Thomas	Merc.		09			F1/R2
Hickes, William	Kt. 19	26–28				
*Hickes, William	Merc.			18?		S1
Hickford, Henry	Unkn.			20		
Hickford, William	Unkn.	14				
Hickman, Eleazar	Merc.				00	
Hickman, Henry	Unkn.	01				
Hickman, Walter	Unkn.	14				
Hickman, William	Merc.					I7
Hickockes, John	Merc.				12	
Hide, William	Merc.					I7
Hider, John	Merc.				13	
Hider, Richard	Unkn.		07			
Higgens, James	Merc.		15	00c		
Higgens, John	Merc.			06		
Higgens, Peter	Unkn.			09		
Higgens, Thomas	Merc.					S1
Higgens, William	Merc.					X1
Higges, William	Merc.					I2
Higginson, Francis	Unkn.					J3
Higham, Clement	Kt. 91	93, 04				
Higham, Edward	Merc.		11			L1/Q
Higham, John	Kt. 79	84–86				
Higham, John	Merc.		17			
Higham, Robert	Unkn.		11			
Highlord, John	Merc.		99c			F1/S1c/GG
Highlord, John	Merc.		09			F1/Q
Highlord, Zachariah	Merc.		24			E3
**Hildyerd, Christopher	Kt. 03	89–04, 21–28				
Hildyerd, William	Gent.	86				
Hill, Barnard	Merc.					S6
Hill, Daniel	Merc.	89				L1c/S4
Hill, Edmund	Merc.					S1
Hill, Edmund	Merc.					S4
Hill, Henry	Merc.					F1
Hill, John	Merc.	28				S1/X2
Hill, Joseph	Merc.					J3

Name & title	Class; date of knighthood	Parliaments (starting dates)	E. Ind. Co.	Va. Co.	Levant Co.	Other companies
Hill, Peter	Merc.					GG
Hill, Richard	Merc.		11			Q
Hill, Robert	Unkn.			09		
Hill, Thomas	Merc.					X2
Hill, Tristiam	Unkn.			09		
Hill, William	Merc.					F1/S4/X2
Hillyard, John	Merc.					S6
Hilsdon, James	Gent.					CC1
Hilson, Robert	Merc.					E1
Hilton, Anthony	Merc.					GG
Hilton, Charles	Merc.					I7
Hilton, George	Gent.					I4
Hinckley, Henry	Unkn.					X2
Hines, Thomas	Merc.		99			
Hinson, John	Merc.					R2
Hinson, Thomas	Unkn.	86–89, 97, 04				
Hinson, Toby	Merc.			09		
Hinton, Anthony	Kt. 20			12		T2/X2
Hinton, Griffith	Unkn.			09		
Hinton, Thomas	Kt. 19	21, 25–26				
Hippisley, John	Kt. 17	21–28				X2
Hippisley, Richard	Gent.					X2
Hippisley, Richard	Gent.					I9
Hitch, John	Unkn.			22		
Hitch, Talbot	Merc.				18	
Hitcham, Robert	Kt. 03	97, 04–26				
Hitchcocke, Thomas	Unkn.	04–14				
Hitchmun, Robert	Unkn.	97				
Hobart, Henry	Kt. 03	89, 97–04	17	09c		Q
Hobart, John	Kt. 03	04, 21–24, 26	27			G7
Hobart, Miles	Kt. 23	28				
Hobart, Miles	Merc.		99			
Hobart, Nathaniel	Unkn.					G8
Hobart, William	Unkn.		23			J3
Hobbes, Thomas	Pfl/y.		18			
Hobby, Edward	Kt. 82	84–14				
Hobby, Posthumus (Thomas)	Kt. 94	89–97, 04–28				
Hobby, Richard	Merc.					N/S4
Hobson, John	Merc.		28		26	L1
Hobson, Thomas	Merc.		14			
Hobson, William	Merc.					I7/P2
Hochstetter, Daniel	Merc.					AA1g
Hochstetter, Daniel	Merc.					AA3
Hochstetter, Emanuel	Merc.					AA3
Hockmore, William	Unkn.	21–24				
Hodder, William	Merc.					X1
**Hoddesdon, Christopher	M. Kt. 03	93				E1/Mg/R1/ S6c/W5/X1/ GG1

315

Name & title	Class; date of knighthood	Parliaments (starting dates)	E. Ind. Co.	Va. Co.	Levant Co.	Other companies
Hodges, Bartholomew	Unkn.					CC2
Hodges, Edward	Unkn.			09		
Hodges, Henry	Merc.					E3
Hodges, John	Merc.		09	10		T2
Hodges, John	Merc.		11		14	
Hodges, Thomas	Merc.			09		
Hodges, William	Gent.			12		
Hodgson, James	Merc.					I7c
Hodgson, John	Merc.		00	09		
Hodgson, Stephen	Merc.		00			F1
Hodsall, John	Merc.			12		
Hodson, Christopher	Unkn.	14				
Hodson, Daniel	Merc.					J1
Hogan, Edmund	Merc.					S6/W6/GG
Hogan, Gresham	Merc.		07	10		R2
Holcomb, Thomas	Merc.					X1
Holcroft, Henry	Kt. 22	24, 28	29			
Holcroft, Jeffrey	Unkn.			09		
Holcroft, Thomas	Kt. 03	93, 01–04		07c		
Holcroft, Thomas	Unkn.			09		
Holder, Butolph	Merc.					S6
Holdich, Philip	Merc.	01				S1c
Holdich, Philip	Merc.	26				
Holdippe, Andrew	Merc.		07		05	
Holland, Bartholomew	Merc.		00		00c	F1/S4
Holland, John	Merc.					L1/M
Holland, Owen	Gent.	84				
Holland, Richard	Merc.	86				
Holland, Robert	Unkn.					P2
Holland, Thomas	Kt. 22	01				
Holland, Thomas	Kt. 08	21–24				
Holland, Thomas	Gent.	93, 04				
Holland, William	Unkn.			20		
Holles, Denzill	Gent.	84–86				I9
Holles, Denzill	Gent.	24, 28				
Holles, John, Lord Houghton, Earl Clare	Nob. 93	04–14		09c		I9/Q
Holles, John Earl Clare	Nob.	21–24				
Holles, ?	Unkn.			09		
Holliland, Samuel	Gent.			12		
Holliland, William	Unkn.			20		
Hollingworth, Reginald	Merc.					S6
Hollinshead, W.	Merc.		24			
Holloway, Humphrey	Merc.		14			
Holloway, John	Merc.		07	20	05	Q
Holman, George	Merc.		99	09	05c	F1/I7/Q/S1/ T2
Holman, George	Merc.		08			I7
Holman, Gregory	Merc.				12	
Holman, Peter	Unkn.					X2

Name & title	Class; date of knight-hood	Parlia-ments (starting dates)	E. Ind. Co.	Va. Co.	Levant Co.	Other companies
Holman, William	Merc.					X1
Holmeade, John	Merc.					I7
Holmeden, Edward	M. Kt. 03		99c		90	B/D/X1/DD
Holmeden, Edward	Merc.		14			
Holmes, Christopher	Merc.					R1
Holmes, George	Merc.					E1/S6c/GG
Holmes, Leonard	Merc.					S4
Holmes, Robert	Merc.					R2c
Holmes, Thomas	Gent.					CC2
Holmes, Thomas	Merc.				09	
Holt, Christopher	Unkn.			09		
Holt, John	Gent.			09		
Holt, William	Unkn.	97				
**Holt, ?	Unkn.	04, 21				
Honnyman, Philip	Merc.					S1
Honnyman, Thomas	Merc.					S4
Honyngs, Edward	Unkn.	89–04				
Honywood, Christopher	Merc.	84, 97				
Honywood, Isaac	Merc.				29	
Hood, Thomas	Merc.			89		
Hooke, Humphrey	Merc.					N/X2
Hooke, Robert	Unkn.		25			
Hooker, George	Gent.			09		
Hooker, John	Merc.	86				
Hooker, Nicholas	Merc.			10		
Hooker, Richard	Unkn.			09		
Hooper, Richard	Unkn.					X2
Hoost, Peter	Merc.		14			
Hoost, William	Merc.		14			
Hoost, William	Merc.		24			
Hootham, John	Gent.	84–86				
Hootham, John	Kt. 17	25–28				
Hope, John	Unkn.	84				
Hope, John	Unkn.			20		
Hopkins, Henry	Pfl/y.					CC2
Hopkins, John	Merc.	01		09		L1/M/S6c/X1
Hopkins, Owen	Kt. 61	84, 89				
Hopkins, Randall	Unkn.		08			
Hopkins, Sampson	Merc.	14–21				
Hopkins, Thomas	Merc.					S1/X1
Hopkins, William	Merc.			09		S1
Hopton, Arthur	Gent.	89				
Hopton, John	Merc.					CC2
Hopton, Philip	Merc.					X1
Hopton, Ralph	Kt. 26	21, 25, 28				
Hopton, Robert	Gent.	04, 21				
Hopton, Thomas	Gent.	26				
Hopton, William	Merc.				27	
Hopwood, Edward	Merc.					I7/X2
Horde, Thomas	Merc.	01				

Name & title	Class; date of knighthood	Parliaments (starting dates)	E. Ind. Co.	Va. Co.	Levant Co.	Other companies
Hore, Christopher	Unkn.			09		
Horne, Lawrence	Unkn.	21				
Horner, Jock	Merc.					F1
Horner, John	Kt. 14	26				
Horner, Maurice	Gent.	84				
Horner, Thomas	Gent.	84–86				
Horner, Thomas	Gent.	26–28				
Horner, Thomas	Merc.					F1
Horner, Thomas	Kt. 03	93–04				
Horsey, Edward	Kt. 77					W9/X1/CC1
Horsey, George	Kt. 19	21–24				
Horsey, George	Unkn.	86				
Horsey, Jerome	Kt. 03	93–21				
Horsey, Ralph	Kt. 91	86, 97				
Horsey, Ralph	Gent.					X2
*Horsley, George	Unkn.	14				
Horsley, Jerome	Merc.					R1
Horth, Thomas	Unkn.					X2
Horton, Jeremy	Unkn.					X2
Horton, Lawrence	Merc.					M
Horton, Thomas	Merc.		00			F1/I2
Horwell, Thomas	Kt. 03			10		
Horwood, ?	Pfl/y.	18				
Hoskins, Charles	Merc.			09		
Hoskins, John	Gent.	04–14, 28		10		
Hoskins, Oswell	Merc.			09		I7
Host, Derick	Unkn.		15			
Hough, Atherton	Gent.					J3
**Hough, John	Merc.	89				E1/S1
Houghton, Ferrais	Merc.					I7
Houghton, Gilbert	Kt. 03	14–21, 26				
Houghton, Nicholas	Merc.					I7
Houghton, Peter	Merc.					X1
Houghton, Richard	Kt. 00	01–04				GG
Houghton, Robert	Unkn.	93				
Houghton, Simon	Merc.					I2
Houlden, John	Merc.					L1/M
Houlden, William	Unkn.			18?		
Howard, Charles, Lord, Earl Nottingham	Nob.		09			C/F1/G1/Q/ S1/W9/X1/Z/ GG1
**Howard, Charles, Lord, Earl Nottingham	Nob. 03	97–14	18			
Howard, Charles	Kt. 12	14–21, 25–28‡				
Howard, Edward	Kt. 03	01, 14, 24–25, 28				
Howard, Francis	Kt. 03	04				
Howard, Henry Earl Northampton	Nob.					F1/I2/N/Q/ S1/Z
Howard, Henry	Gent.	14				

Name & title	Class; date of knighthood	Parliaments (starting dates)	E. Ind. Co.	Va. Co.	Levant Co.	Other companies
Howard, Henry-Frederick, Lord Maltravers, Earl Arundel	Nob.	28				
Howard, John	Merc.			09		S4
Howard, Philip Earl Arundel	Nob.					W4
Howard, Robert	Kt. 16	24–28				
Howard, Theophilus, Lord Walden, Earl Suffolk	Nob.	04	11	09c		Q/X2/Z
Howard, Thomas Earl Arundel	Nob.			20c		G6/K4/Q/GG1
Howard, Thomas Earl Arundel	Nob.			09c		I2/L1/Q/X1/ Z/GG2
Howard, Thomas, Lord Walden, Earl Suffolk	Nob. 05	04–21	18			
Howard, Thomas	Unkn.	14				
Howard, William	Kt. 96	84–93				
Howard, William	Kt. 23	24–26				
Howard, William Lord Effingham	Nob.	97–01				
Howe, Edmund	Merc.		09			Q
Howe, George	Gent.		87			
Howe, John	Merc.					GG
Howe, Robert	Merc.					B/S6
Howe, Roger	Merc.		99c			D/S1c/X1
Howell, James	Unkn.	28				
Howell, John	Merc.	01				X1
Howell, Richard	Unkn.			09		
Howell, Thomas	Merc.					X1
Howell, Valentine	Unkn.	04				
Howgan, Thomas	Kt.†					T2
Howke, Guydo	Merc.					S6
Howland, John	Kt. 17		28			
Howland, Robert	Unkn.	89				
Howling, George	Merc.					S6
Howmer, John	Merc.					F1
Howse, Richard	Merc.		99			I2/S4
Howson, Henry	Merc.			09		
Hoyle, John	Merc.					M/CC2
Hoyle, Thomas	Merc.	28				E2c
Hubberd, Edward	Unkn.	93–97				
Hubbtyn, Robert	Merc.					S6
Huddleston, Ferdinand	Gent.	24				
Huddleston, John	Unkn.					X2
Huddleston, Richard	Unkn.	89				
Huddleston, William	Gent.	01				
Huddye, William	Merc.	89				X1
Hudson, Robert	Merc.		24	18		
Hudson, Thomas	Merc.		24			P2
Huggeford, John	Unkn.	86				

Name & title	Class; date of knighthood	Parliaments (starting dates)	E. Ind. Co.	Va. Co.	Levant Co.	Other companies
Huggeford, John	Unkn.	93				
Hughes, Hugh	Gent.	97				
Hughes, Robert	Merc.			09		
Hughes, Thomas	Unkn.	86				
Hughes, Thomas	Unkn.	21–25				
*Hughes, Thomas	Merc.					X2
Hughesson, Abraham	Merc.					X2
Hughesson, James	Merc.		23			X2
Hull, Henry	Merc.					S1
Hull, Robert	Merc.					X2
Hull, William	Kt. 21					X2
Hull, William	Unkn.					X2
Humble, George	Unkn.		11			
Humble, Harris	Merc.		27			
Humble, Peter	Gent.		11	25		Q
Humble, Richard	Merc.		01	09		I7/L1
Humfrey, John	Merc.		99		05	S4
Humfrey, John	Gent.		27			J1
Humfrey, Michael	Unkn.	26				
Humfrey, Thomas	Unkn.	89				
Humfrey, Thomas	Merc.					I7
Humfrey, William	Merc.					R1/AA1/BB1c
Hun, Edmund	Unkn.			22		
Hungate, Henry	Kt. 19	25–26				
Hungate, Robert	Merc.					I2
Hungate, William	Merc.					S3
Hungerford, Anthony	Gent.	93–04				
Hungerford, Edmund	Gent.	86				
Hungerford, Edward	Kt. 01	01				K2c
Hungerford, Edward	Kt. 26	14–25, 28				
Hungerford, John	Kt. 91	97, 04		10		
Hungerford, John	Gent.	04				
Hungerford, John	Gent.	84–93				
Hungerford, Thomas	Gent.	93				
Huninges, Henry	Gent.					I2
Hunkshief, William	Merc.					E2
Hunniwood, Robert	Gent.					Q
Hunt, Henry	Merc.				22	
Hunt, John	Merc.					S6
Hunt, Michael	Merc.					X2
Hunt, Thomas	Unkn.			09		
Hunter, Henry	Merc.				27	
Hunting, Edward	Merc.					S1
Huntley, George	Kt.†			12		
Huntley, John	Unkn.			09		
Huntley, Thomas	Merc.					M
Hurd, Edward	Unkn.			22		
Hurdman, Walter	Merc.	01–04				
Hurleston, John	Unkn.					X2
Hurleston, Ranulph	Unkn.	86				
Hurte, George	Unkn.					X2

320

Name & title	Class; date of knight- hood	Parlia- ments (starting dates)	E. Ind. Co.	Va. Co.	Levant Co.	Other companies
Husband, Richard	Merc.		09	05		*L*1
Husey, Lawrence	Merc.					*R*1
Husey, Sampson	Gent.	97				
Husey, Thomas	Gent.	93				
Hutchins, Giles	Merc.	93–97				
Hutchins, John	Merc.					*S*6
Hutchins, Richard	Merc.					*X*1
Hutchins, Thomas	Unkn.					*J*1c
Hutchinson, Edward	Unkn.	86				
Hutchinson, James	Merc.					*E*2
Hutchinson, Stephen	Unkn.	26				
Hutchinson, Thomas	Merc.					*I*7
Hutchinson, Thomas	Kt. 17	26				
Hutton, Matthew	Gent.	26				
Hutton, Richard	Kt. 25	21–28				
Hutton, Richard	Merc.	84–97				
Huxlye, George	Merc.					*M*
Hyde, Arthur	Unkn.					*I*9
Hyde, Barnard	Merc.					*Q*
Hyde, George	Gent.	97–01				
Hyde, Henry	Unkn.	89, 01				
Hyde, John	Merc.		07	09		*I*7/*Q*
Hyde, Lawrence	Kt. 14	84–86, 97–04, 21		10c		*O*/*T*2
Hyde, Nicholas	Kt. 27	01–14, 25		10c		*O*/*T*2
*Hyde, Richard	Gent.	25				
Hyde, Robert	Kt. 03	21, 25–26				
Hyde, Robert	Gent.	84–86, 14				
Hyde, Thomas	Merc.					*F*1
Hygges, William	Merc.					*S*6
Hylckes, Nicholas	Merc.					*S*6
Hynde, Francis	Kt. 78	89				
Hynde, William	Merc.		00		05	*M*
*Hynde, William	Gent.	97				
Ianson, William	Unkn.		18?			
Ilcomb, John	Merc.					*X*1
Ince, Thomas	Merc.		14			
Ingleby, John	Gent.					*G*7
Inglethorpe, William	Merc.					*E*3
Ingold, John	Merc.		27			
Ingram, Arthur	M. Kt. 13	04–28	?	10c		*G*5/*M*/*GG*1
*Ingram, Arthur	M. Kt. 21	24				
Ingram, Hugh	Merc.					*S*6
Ingram, John	Merc.					*Q*
Irby, Anthony	Kt. 03†	89–21	10			
Irby, Anthony	Kt. 24	28				
*Irelande, George	Gent.	84				
Irelande, George	Gent.	24				*X*2
Irelande, Thomas	Kt. 17	14–21‡				
Irish, Thomas	Unkn.					*X*2
Ironmonger, William	Unkn.					*I*1

Name & title	Class; date of knighthood	Parliaments (starting dates)	E. Ind. Co.	Va. Co.	Levant Co.	Other companies
Ironside, Edward	Gent.		29			*J3*
Ironsides, Richard	Merc.		00	09		*Q/R2/S1*
Isaack, George	Merc.				24	
Isham, George	Merc.			18?		*I7/Q/R2*
Isham, Henry	Merc.					*E1/S6*
Isham, John	Merc.					*E1*
Isham, Nathaniel	Merc.					*S4*
Isham, Roger	Unkn.					*I9*
Issac, Edge	Unkn.		27			
Issac, Nicholas	Merc.		09	09		
Issackson, Powell	Merc.			12		
Ivatt, Thomas	Merc.		24		00	*S5*
Ivatt, William	Unkn.		29			
Ive, Edward	Merc.					*I7*
Ive, William	Unkn.	24				
Jackman, Edward	Merc.					*M/R1c*
Jackman, Henry	Unkn.	89–01				
Jackson, Anchor	Merc.	97				
Jackson, Arthur	Merc.				92	*M/S1c/X1*
Jackson, Henry	Merc.			09		*I7/M*
Jackson, Isaac	Merc.					*S1*
Jackson, James	Unkn.		25			
Jackson, John	Kt. 19	24–28				
Jackson, John	Unkn.	89				
Jackson, John	Merc.		01			*D/X1*
Jackson, Joseph	Merc.		25			*R2/S1*
Jackson, Matthias	Merc.					*F1*
Jackson, Rachel	Merc.		25			
Jackson, Richard	Pfl/y.					*CC2*
Jackson, Robert	Kt. 17	21–28				
Jackson, Stephen	Merc.					*I7*
Jackson, Thomas	Merc.			20		*I7/GG*
Jackson, William	Unkn.	01–04				
Jacob, Abraham	Merc.		26			*Q*
**Jacob, John	Merc.	24				*F1*
Jacob, Richard	Merc.					*I7/X2*
Jacob, Theodore	Merc.					*R2*
Jacobson, James	Merc.		23	22		
Jacobson, Joseph	Unkn.		24			
Jacobson, Peter	Merc.		09			
Jacobson, Philip	Merc.		24	09		*T2*
Jacques, Gabriel	Unkn.			18?		
Jacques, Roger	Merc.					*E2*
Jadwine, Thomas	Unkn.			10		*T2*
Jakes, Robert	Merc.					*S6*
James, Edward	Merc.		99c	12	10c	*E3/F1/I7/Q/ R2/S1c/*
James, Edward	Merc.		20	09	20	
James, Francis	Unkn.	93–04				
James, Humphrey	Merc.			09		
James, John	Unkn.	84, 93				

Name & title	Class; date of knight- hood	Parlia- ments (starting dates)	E. Ind. Co.	Va. Co.	Levant Co.	Other companies
James, John	Merc.					S1
James, Richard	Merc.	97–04				
James, Richard	Merc.					X2
James, Robert	Merc.		09			
James, Roger	Kt. 13	25				
James, Thomas	Merc.	97, 04–14		06c		S1c/X1/GG
James, Thomas	Merc.					X2
James, Valentine	Unkn.					I1
James, William Bishop Durham	Nob.		12			
Jane, Joseph	Unkn.	26				
*Janson, Brian	Kt. 24					I3/J3
*Janson, William	Merc.					I7
Janurynne, Peter	Merc.					S6
Jay, John	Unkn.	14				
Jay, Thomas	Kt. 25	26–28				
Jeames, Thomas	Pfl/y.	18				
Jeffreys, George	Unkn.	04				
Jeffreys, John	M. Kt. 03	04				F1/X1
Jeffreys, John	Unkn.	14				
Jeffreys, Peter	Merc.					W4
Jeffreys, Rice	Merc.					X2
Jeffreys, Thomas	Unkn.	08				Q
**Jenkins, Henry	Kt. 04	04				
Jenkins, William	Unkn.					X2
Jenkinson, Anthony	Merc.					S6/W6
Jenkinson, Margaret	Merc.	18				
Jenkinson, Richard	Merc.		09			
Jenkinson, Robert	Merc.	11				I7c/Q
Jenkinson, Robert	Merc.	18				
Jenens, Owen	Merc.	28				
Jenner, Robert	Unkn.	28				
*Jennings, Abraham	Merc.					X1
Jennings, Abraham	Merc.					K5/N/X2/GG
Jennings, Ambrose	Merc.					M
Jennings, Henry	Merc.					S4
Jennings, John	Kt. 03†	28				
Jennings, Thomas	Merc.		24	09		X1
Jennings, William	Merc.		00c		10	B/F1/S6
Jennison, William	Merc.	84				
Jennison, William	Merc.	01, 14				
Jenny, Richard	Unkn.					I1
Jenny, Robert	Merc.					F1/S1
Jenvey, Richard	Unkn.	04				
Jephson, John	Kt. 03	21–25, 28				
Jephson, William	Kt. 03	04				
Jermyn, Alexander	Merc.					S1
Jermyn, Henry	Unkn.	25–28				
Jermyn, Philip	Unkn.		20c			
Jermyn, Robert	Kt. 78	84–89				
Jermyn, Robert	Unkn.	21				

Name & title	Class; date of knighthood	Parliaments (starting dates)	E. Ind. Co.	Va. Co.	Levant Co.	Other companies
**Jermyn, Thomas	Kt. 91	89, 04–28		10		
Jermyn, Thomas	Unkn.	25–28				
Jermyn, William	Unkn.					X2
Jervis, Arthur	Merc.					S6
Jervis, Arthur	Unkn.	21				
Jervis, Thomas	Kt. 07	21–28				
Jessop, William	Unkn.					T3
Jewell, James	Unkn.			18?		
Jobson, Francis	Kt. 49					BB1
Jobson, Humphrey	Gent.			12		
Jobson, Walter	Unkn.			18?		
Jobson, William	Unkn.			18?		
Johan, George	Unkn.			09		
John, Henry	Gent.			09		
John, Jacob	Unkn.		29			
Johnson, Brian	Merc.					F1c/S3
Johnson, Edward	Gent.		22?			G7/X2
Johnson, Francis	Merc.	97				
Johnson, George	Merc.			09		
Johnson, Henry	Merc.					S4
Johnson, Hugo	Merc.					S6
Johnson, Hugo	Merc.					S6
Johnson, Humphrey	Merc.			10		
Johnson, Isaac	Unkn.					J1
Johnson, John	Merc.		14	09		I7/L1/X2
Johnson, John	Merc.					S6
Johnson, Richard	Merc.			09		I7
Johnson, Robert	Kt. 03	97–14		09		
Johnson, Robert	Merc.		00c	09c	05	M/Q/S1/T1g/ X1/GG
Johnson, Thomas	Merc.		11	09		I7/M/Q/T2
Johnson, Thomas	Merc.			09		
Johnson, Thomas	Unkn.	84–86				
**Johnson, Thomas	Merc.	26	11			X2
**Johnson, William	Merc.	21		09		I7/L1/M/S1
Jolie, John	Merc.					X1
Joliffe, Henry	Merc.					X1
Jolles, Thomas	Merc.					I7
Jones, Alexander	Merc.	97				S1c/X1
Jones, Arnold	Merc.					H
Jones, Benjamin	Pfl/y.		18			
Jones, Charles	Gent.	24–28				
Jones, Edward	Unkn.	93–04				
Jones, Edward	Unkn.					X2
Jones, Francis	M. Kt. 17			10		Qc/U/Z
Jones, Henry	Kt. 03†			19		
Jones, Henry	Merc.					S1/X1
Jones, Inigo	Unkn.	21				
Jones, Isaac	Merc.					L1/M
Jones, John	Merc.			09	23	L1/M/Q/X2/ GG

Name & title	Class; date of knighthood	Parliaments (starting dates)	E. Ind. Co.	Va. Co.	Levant Co.	Other companies
Jones, John	Merc.		12			
*Jones, John	Unkn.	04				
Jones, Joseph	Gent.					I4
Jones, Nicholas	Gent.					X1
Jones, Philip	Merc.					A/S3
*Jones, Philip	Gent.	89				
Jones, Richard	Merc.					S6/GG
Jones, Richard	Gent.	28				
Jones, Robert	Gent.	26–28				
Jones, Roger	M. Kt. 03					S3
Jones, Thomas	Kt. 84	86, 97				
**Jones, Thomas	Gent.	86, 01				I4
Jones, Thomas	Merc.		17	18		M/Nc/Q/GG
Jones, Thomas	Merc.		28			
Jones, Walter	Unkn.	84–93				
Jones, William	Merc.					I7/L2/M/Nc/ X2/GG
*Jones, William	Merc.					X1
Jones, William	Gent.	97–14				
Jones, William	Gent.	14				
Jones, Zachariah	Gent.			09		
Jope, John	Merc.					X2/GG
Jordan, Edward	Merc.		25			L1/M/R2
Jordan, Edward	Merc.					L2/M
Jordan, Ignatius	Merc.	21, 25–28				M/S1
Jordan, Nicholas	Unkn.	26				
Jordan, Richard	Merc.					M/Q1/CC2
Jordan, Samuel	Unkn.			19?		
Jordan, William	Unkn.	93				
Joshua, John	Gent.			09		
Jowles, John	M. Kt. 06				05	F1/I1c/S1
Joyce, John	Unkn.	84				
Juke, Anthony	Merc.			09		
Jukes, Thomas	Unkn.	84, 97				
Juxon, Arthur	Merc.		28			
Juxon, John	Merc.		24	09		N
Juxon, Thomas	Merc.		99	09		Nc/Q
Juxon, Thomas	Merc.		14			
Kaiston, William	Gent.	04				
Kaly, Christopher	Merc.		24			M
Kay, John	Kt. 07	04				
Kay, Robert	Merc.		24			Q
Kaye, Abraham	Merc.					I7
Kaye, Thomas	Merc.					F1
Kean, Robert	Merc.					J3/P2
Keate, Roger	Unkn.					I9
Keatley, John	Pfl/y.			12		
Kebett, William	Merc.					S6
Kedley, William	Merc.					F1
Keeble, Joseph	Merc.		26	15		
Keeling, John	Unkn.	25–26				

Name & title	Class; date of knight-hood	Parlia-ments (starting dates)	E. Ind. Co.	Va. Co.	Levant Co.	Other companies
**Keeling, William	Merc.		07			S6
Keightley, Christopher	Unkn.	28				
Keightley, Thomas	Merc.	21	22c	09c		L1
Keile, John	Kt.†			12		X1
Kelke, Charles	Kt. 03			09		
Kelke, Richard	Merc.					S6
Kelke, Thomas	Merc.					S6/W2
Kellett, William	Merc.		01		00	GG
Kellond, Christopher	Merc.					F1/S1
Kellond, John	Merc.					F1/S1
Kellond, Richard	Merc.					F1/S1
Kelly, Thomas	Merc.					F1
Kelweye, Francis	Unkn.	86–89				
Kelweye, Simon	Unkn.	89				
Kemp, Bartholomew	Unkn.	84–89				
Kemp, Edward	Unkn.					X2
Kemp, John	Merc.					R1
Kemp, Nicholas	Kt. 17		19			
Kempton, Robert	Unkn.	29				
Kemys, Edward	Gent.	93				
Kemys, Nicholas	Gent.	28				
Kendal, Noah	Merc.					F1
Kendal, Nicholas	Unkn.	25				
Kendrick, John	Merc.					L1c/M
Kenn, Christopher	Unkn.					I9/CC2
Kenneridgburg, Richard	Gent.			09		
Kenninges, Robert	Pfl/y.					CC2
Kent, Henry	Unkn.			18?		
**Kent, John	Unkn.	97, 21–24				
Kent, John	Merc.					R1
Kent, Thomas	Unkn.	28				
Kent, William	Unkn.	14				
Kentish, Martin	Merc.				13	
Kepp, John	Merc.	23				
Kerne, Nicholas	Unkn.					X2
Kerridge, Thomas	Merc.		29	22		
Kerril, Richard	Unkn.			09		
Kervyn, Henry	Merc.	97				
Kete, Gilbert	Unkn.					X2
Kettle, William	Unkn.		11			
Kettleby, John	Gent.			09		
Kettleby, John	Gent.			12		
Kevall, William	Merc.					S1
Key, Anthony	Merc.					S6
Key, Edmund	Merc.		17			
Key, John	Merc.			09		
Keych, Edmund	Unkn.		11			
Keymes, John	Merc.					L1
Keys, Robert	Merc.		00			
Keyson, John	Merc.					I7
Kightley, Philip	Kt. 03	04				

Name & title	Class; date of knight- hood	Parlia- ments (starting dates)	E. Ind. Co.	Va. Co.	Levant Co.	Other companies
Kilborne, Isaac	Merc.					*I2*
Killigrew, John	Gent.	84–86, 97				
Killigrew, Joseph	Kt. 13	14				
Killigrew, Robert	Kt. 03	01–28		07c		*O/X2*
Killigrew, William	Kt. 03	84, 93–97, 04–14				*W2*
Killigrew, William	Kt. 26	28				
Kimball, Thomas	Merc.					*F1*
Kindersley, Anne	Unkn.					*W2*
Kindersley, Henry	Merc.		11	09		*F1/S4*
Kindersley, Matthew	Unkn.					*W6*
Kindersley, Robert	Unkn.					*W5*
Kindlemarsh, Anthony	Unkn.					*X2*
King, Alexander	Unkn.	89–93, 01				
King, George	Merc.					*E3*
King, Henry Bishop Chichester	Nob.					*G7*
King, John Bishop London	Nob.			20c		
King, John	Merc.		11		10	*F1/I7/S1*
King, John	Merc.					*I2*
*King, John	Unkn.			10		
King, Ralph	Merc.		14	09		*I7/T2*
King, Thomas	Unkn.					*X2*
King, Thomas	Unkn.					*X2*
King, William	Unkn.			09		*X1*
King, William	Merc.					*I7*
Kingsmill, George	Gent.	84–86				
**Kingsmill, John	Gent.	84–86				*I4*
Kingsmill, Richard	Gent.	84–86				
Kingston, Felix	Merc.		18			
Kingston, John	Merc.				19	
Kingswell, Edward	Gent.					*I3*
Kingswell, William	Kt. 03	97–04				
Kinnarsley, ?	Unkn.	21				
Kinnaston, Brian	Merc.		09c			*F1/I7*
Kinnaston, Edward	Merc.					*I7*
Kinnaston, Ellis	Merc.					*F1*
Kinnaston, Francis	Kt. 19	21				*G6*
Kipe, John	Merc.				10	
Kippax, Richard	Unkn.	21				
Kirby, Edward	Unkn.			20		
Kirby, Francis	Unkn.					*J3*
Kirby, Jeffrey (George?)	Merc.		00c		00c	*F1/Q/S1*
Kirby, Jeffrey	Merc.		22c			
Kirby, John	Merc.			09		*I7*
Kirk, David	Merc.					*X2*
Kirk, George	Unkn.	26				
Kirk, Gervase	Merc.					*Q/X2/GG*
Kirk, Robert	Merc.					*F1*
Kirk, Thomas	Merc.					*X2*

Name & title	Class; date of knight-hood	Parliaments (starting dates)	E. Ind. Co.	Va. Co.	Levant Co.	Other companies
Kirk, William	Merc.					S6
Kirkham, Edward	Merc.				14	
Kirkham, Robert	Gent.	28	11			N
Kirkham, Walter	Gent.			12		
Kirkley, Michael	Merc.					M
Kirrell, Jo	Unkn.					T2
Kirton, Edward	Unkn.	21–28				
Kirton, James	Gent.	93, 01–14				
Kirton, James	Gent.	01–04				
Kirton, Josias	Unkn.			09		
Kitchin, Abell	Merc.					S1
Kitchin, Robert	Merc.					S6/X1
Knaplock, Robert	Gent.					CC2
Knaplock, William	Gent.					CC2
Knapman, James	Gent.					GG
Knapp, Leonard	Merc.					F1
Knapp, Robert	Merc.					E3
Knapp, Thomas	Merc.					F1
Knatchbull, Norton	Kt. 03	04				
Knevit, Henry	Kt. 74	84–97				W2/CC2
Knevit, Ranulph	Unkn.	93				
Knevit, Thomas	Kt. 03	93, 01				
Knevit, Thomas, Lord Knevit or Knyvett of Escrick	Nob.	84–89, 97–04				CC2
Kneviton, Gilbert	Kt. 05	14				
Knifton, William	Gent.	04				GG
*Knifton, William	Merc.					R1
Knight, Elizabeth	Unkn.					P2
Knight, John	Unkn.					P2
*Knight, John	Merc.	93				CC2
Knight, Simon	Merc.					S6
Knight, Thomas	Merc.					I7
Knight, William	Merc.	01				
*Knight, William	Unkn.					X2
Knightley, Richard	Kt. 65	84–89, 97–01				
Knightley, Richard	Gent.	21–25, 28		18		T3/FF
Knightley, Valentine	Kt. 03	84–86, 93–97, 04		12		Q
Knipton, James	Merc.					I7
Knott, Oliver	Merc.					X1
Knowles, Francis	Kt. 47	84–93				W5/CC2
Knowles, Francis	Kt. 87	84–89, 97, 04‡				
Knowles, Francis	Kt.†	97, 24–28				
Knowles, Francis	Unkn.					X2
Knowles, Henry	Gent.					X1/CC2
Knowles, Miles	Unkn.					P2
Knowles, Richard	Gent.	84–89				
Knowles, Robert	Kt. 03	84–04				
Knowles, Robert	Kt. 13	14–28				
Knowles, Robert	Gent.	14				

Name & title	Class; date of knight- hood	Parliaments (starting dates)	E. Ind. Co.	Va. Co.	Levant Co.	Other companies
Knowles, Samuel	Merc.					BB4
Knowles, Thomas	Unkn.			09		
Knowles, William, Lord, Viscount Wallingford, Earl Banbury	Nob. 86	84, 93–01	12			
Kydman, Robert	Unkn.	01				
Kympton, William	Merc.					S6
Kyrwyn, George	Merc.					S6
Kyttingall, John	Merc.					S1
Lackland, Edward	Merc.					X1
Lacon, Francis	Kt. 99	04				GG
Lacon, Roland	Unkn.	14				
Lacon, William	Unkn.	97				
Lacy, John	Merc.					S1
Lacy, Richard	Merc.					F1/S1
Lacy, Robert	Merc.					I7
Lacy, Thomas	Merc.					S6
Lake, Arthur	Kt. 17	24–26	17			
Lake, Emery	Merc.					S6/CC2
Lake, John	Unkn.					X2
Lake, Richard	Merc.				10	
Lake, Thomas	Kt. 03	93, 01–14, 26	09			F1/Q/S1
Lake, Thomas	Kt. 17	25–28	17			
Lake, Thomas	Merc.	84–86				
Lambe, John	Unkn.			20		
Lambe, Richard	Merc.		14	20	10	L1/M
Lambell, Gilbert	Merc.					S1
Lambell, John	Merc.					S1
Lambert, Charles, Lord	Nob.	26–28				
Lambert, Christopher	Gent.	93				
Lambert, Francis	Merc.					S1
Lambert, Miles	Merc.					M/CC2
Lambert, Oliver, Lord	Nob. 96	97				I6c/X1
Lambert, Thomas	Gent.	86, 01				
Lambert, Thomas	Unkn.	25–26				
Lamberton, Thomas	Unkn.					X2
Lancaster, James	M. Kt. 03		00c			D/Qc/U/X1/ Z/BB2
Lancaster, Richard	Merc.		18			
Lancaster, Thomas	Unkn.	84				
Land, Simon	Merc.					S1
Landman, Christopher	Gent.			18?		F1
Landman, John	Unkn.			18?		
Lane, Augustine	Merc.					B
Lane, Edward	Unkn.	84				
Lane, George	Merc.					S1
Lane, John	Unkn.					X2
Lane, Josias	Merc.					F1
Lane, Ninus	Merc.					S4
Lane, Ralph	Gent.			85		W2/X1
Lane, Richard	Unkn.					X2

Name & title	Class; date of knight-hood	Parlia-ments (starting dates)	E. Ind. Co.	Va. Co.	Levant Co.	Other companies
Lane, Thomas	Unkn.	25, 28				
Lane, William	Merc.			09		
Lane, William	Merc.			09		
Lane, William	Kt. 97	93, 01				
Langborne, ?	Unkn.					X2
Langford, John	Unkn.	01				
Langford, Richard	Merc.					S6
Langford, Richard	Merc.					X2
Langham, George	Merc.					X2/GG1
Langham, John	Merc.		26c		15c	
Langham, Roland	Merc.					X2
Langhorn, George	Merc.					F1
Langhorn, William	Unkn.	89				
Langhorn, William	Merc.				10	R2c/GG
Langhorn, William	Merc.			29		
Langley, John	Merc.		24c	18?	19	
Langley, Peter	Unkn.		19			
Langley, Philip	Merc.					X1
Langley, Ralph	Merc.					X2
Langley, Richard	Merc.					S1
Langton, Anthony	Unkn.	14–21, 25–26				
Langton, John	Merc.			09		E1/N/S1
Langton, Robert	Unkn.	84–93				
Langton, Thomas	Merc.		19	09		I7/N
Langton, Thomas	Unkn.	01				
Lanye, John	Unkn.	86				
Larder, Nathaniel	Merc.					I7
Larkyn, Robert	Merc.		10			
Larte, John	Merc.					S1
Lashbrooke, Lewis	Unkn.	01				
Lasher, James	Unkn.	04–21				
Laskey, Bartholomew	Merc.					F1
Lassells, Brian	Gent.	89				
Lassells, George	Gent.	21				
Lassells, ?	Unkn.	04				
Latham, Thomas	Unkn.		23	23		I1
Latham, William	Merc.					L1
Laughton, Thomas	Unkn.			20		
Law, ?	Unkn.	24				
Lawley, Edward	Kt. 19	14–21		20c		
Lawley, George	Gent.	04				
Lawley, Robert	Gent.	89, 04				
Lawley, Robert	Merc.					I2
Lawley, Thomas	Gent.	84–86				
Lawley, Thomas	Gent.	25–28				
Lawman, Edward	Merc.		09			F1
Lawnce, ?	Pfl/y.			22		
Lawne, Paul de	Merc.?	11				
Lawrence, Edward	Unkn.	26				
Lawrence, John	Unkn.			20		
Lawrence, Paul	Merc.					I7

Name & title	Class; date of knighthood	Parliaments (starting dates)	E. Ind. Co.	Va. Co.	Levant Co.	Other companies
Lawrence, Simon	Merc.		00c			B/M/S1/X1
Lawrence, Simon	Merc.					S3
Lawrence, Thomas	Merc.				90	
Lawrence, William	Merc.			18?		F1
Lawson, Thomas	Gent.			09		
Lawson, Wilfrid	Kt. 03	93, 04–14				
Lawson, William	Kt. 53†	01				
Lawson, William	Merc.			09		
Lawton, Thomas	Merc.	84				
Lawton, Thomas	Unkn.	04				
Layer, Christopher	Merc.	84, 97				
Layer, John	Merc.					F1
Layer, Richard	Merc.					F1
Layer, Thomas	Merc.	86		18?		
Layton, Hugo	Merc.					S6
Leache, Thomas	Merc.					I1c
Leate, Hewett	Merc.				26	GG
Leate, Nicholas	Merc.		99c	10	92c	E3/F1/I7c/M/ Qc/R1/S4/X2/ GG1
Leate, Nicholas	Merc.				24	GG
Leate, Richard	Merc.		24	09	13c	
Leaveinge, Edward	Merc.		00			
Ledgent, William	Unkn.					X2
Lee, Charles	Merc.					G2/X1/GG1
Lee, Edward	Gent.	97				
Lee, Edward	Gent.	84				
Lee, Edward	Pfl/y.	23				
Lee, Francis	Kt. 03	01–21		10		
Lee, Francis, Lord, Earl Chichester	Nob. 13	25				
Lee, Francis	Kt. 18	25–28				
Lee, Francis	Gent.	97				
Lee, Gervase	Unkn.	84				
**Lee, Henry Earl Marlborough	Nob. 17	14–26	19			
Lee, Henry	Merc.					X2
Lee, Henry	Gent.	86				
Lee, Henry	Gent.			09		
Lee, Henry	Merc.		29		16	X2
Lee, Henry	Merc.					X2
Lee, Hugh	Merc.					D/S1/X1
Lee, Humphrey	Merc.					E1
Lee, James Earl Marlborough	Nob. 03	97, 04–21				G7/I5c/GG
Lee, John	Kt. 96	97–04				G2
Lee, John	Merc.			09		F1/Q
**Lee, John	Gent.	14				I3
Lee, John	Gent.	89–97				
Lee, Matthew	Gent.	97–14				
Lee, Matthew	Merc.		15			R2

Name & title	Class; date of knight-hood	Parliaments (starting dates)	E. Ind. Co.	Va. Co.	Levant Co.	Other companies
Lee, Moses	Merc.					*I*7
Lee, Olyffe	Kt. 13					*G*2
Lee, Peter	Kt. 99	86–89, 01				
**Lee, Richard	Kt. 99	93, 04				
Lee, Richard	Unkn.	93				
Lee, Richard	Gent.		18	12		
Lee, Richard	Merc.					*I*7
Lee, Richard	Merc.					*F*1/*L*1/*S*1
Lee, Robert	M. Kt. 03		99	12	05	*S*1c
Lee, Robert	Unkn.	93				
Lee, Robert	Merc.					*I*7
Lee, Roland	Unkn.	84				
Lee, Roland	Merc.					*F*1
Lee, Thomas	Kt. 08	28				
Lee, Thomas	M. Kt. 16					*H*
Lee, Thomas	Unkn.					*X*2
Lee, Thomazine	Kt.		28			
Lee, Walter	Unkn.	84				
Lee, William	Merc.					*R*2c/*X*2
Lee, William	Unkn.					*X*2
Leech, Edward	Kt. 21	21–25, 28				
Leech, Edward	Unkn.	01–14				
Leech, Richard	Unkn.	93				
Leech, ?	Unkn.			22		
*Leechland, Edward	Merc.				92	*DD*
Leechland, Roger	Merc.					*S*1
Leechland, William	Merc.					*S*1/*X*1
*Leechland, William	Merc.					*X*2
Leeds, John	Kt. 11	14–21				
Leeds, Thomas	Kt. 03			10		
Leek, Francis, Lord, Earl Scarsdale	Nob. 04	01				
Leek, Richard	Unkn.	97				
Leek, Simon	Merc.			21		*G*7
Leek, Thomas	Merc.					*S*1
Leek, William	Pfl/y.	24	17			
Leere, Richard	Merc.					*S*1
Legate, John	Gent.			10		
Leicester, George	Unkn.	97				
Leicester, William	Unkn.	89				
Leighton, Thomas	Kt. 79	01				*X*1
Leighton, Thomas	Gent.	97				
Leighton, William	Unkn.	01				
Leman, Robert	Unkn.		22			
Leming, Joseph	Unkn.			21		
Lemon, John	M. Kt. 17		01			*I*1c
Lenthall, William	Unkn.	24				
Leonard, Henry	Kt. 96	97				
Leonard, Sampson	Kt. 03	84–01		10		
Leonard, Sampson	Gent.	14				
*Leonard, Samuel	Gent.	93				

332

Name & title	Class; date of knight-hood	Parlia-ments (starting dates)	E. Ind. Co.	Va. Co.	Levant Co.	Other companies
Leonard, William	Merc.	97				
Leson, Walter	Merc.					*S6*
Lestrange, Hamon	Kt. 03	14–21, 25				*Q*
Lever, Edmund	Merc.		11			*L1/Q*
Lever, Edward	Unkn.		24			
Lever, John	Unkn.	84–89				
Lever, Katherine	Merc.		22			
Lever, Richard	Unkn.		25			
Lever, Thomas	Merc.		10	09		*Q/T2*
Leverett, Christopher	Unkn.					*K5*
Leverett, Thomas	Unkn.					*J3*
Leveson, John	Kt. 89	84, 97–04		10		
Leveson, Richard	Kt. 96	89, 04				*X1*
Leveson, Richard	Kt. 26	24, 26				
Leveson, Thomas	Merc.			21		*X2*
Leveson, Walter	Kt. 87	84–89, 97				*X1*
Leveson, William	Merc.			20		*F1/I2/M/Q/R2*
Levet, Christopher	Merc.					*K5/GG*
Levet, John	Merc.			09		*F1*
Levinge, Timothy	Unkn.	21–25, 28				
Levitt, Arthur	Merc.		18			
Levitt, Percival	Merc.					*E2*
Lewellin, John	Merc.		14		16	*L2/M*
Lewellin, Maurice	Merc.		00	09		
Lewen, Edward	Merc.	86				
Lewen, William	Unkn.	86–93				
Lewer, John	Unkn.					*X2*
Lewis, Edward	Kt. 03†					*Q*
Lewis, Edward	Merc.			09		*S6/X1*
Lewis, Gabriel	Unkn.	89				
Lewis, George	Unkn.	86				
Lewis, Hugh	Gent.	97				
Lewis, James	Gent.	24–28				
Lewis, Jevan	Gent.	89				
Lewis, John	Kt. 03	04				
Lewis, John	Merc.					*R1*
Lewis, Richard	Merc.					*E1*
**Lewis, Robert	Merc.	21–24				*F1/S4*
Lewis, Thomas	Gent.	84–89				
Lewis, Thomas	Merc.					*E3*
**Lewis, William	Unkn.	93				*N*
Lewis, William	Unkn.	84				
Lewis, William	Gent.	01				
Lewis, ?	Unkn.					*T2*
Lewknor, Christopher	Gent.	28				
Lewknor, Edward	Kt. 03	84–97, 04–14				
Lewknor, John	Merc.					*R1*
Lewknor, Lewis	Kt. 03	97, 04				
Lewknor, Richard	Gent.	84–97				
Lewknor, Richard	Gent.	21–28				
Lewknor, Samuel	Gent.	04				

Name & title	Class; date of knight-hood	Parliaments (starting dates)	E. Ind. Co.	Va. Co.	Levant Co.	Other companies
Lewknor, Thomas	Gent.	86				
Lewknor, William	Merc.					R1
Libby, Jeffrey	Merc.					F1
Lichfield, Nicholas	Gent.			12		
Lidall, Thomas	Merc.		00		10	GG
Lidall, ?	Unkn.	21				
Lillo, Henry	M. Kt. 08		08		00	
Lilly, John	Unkn.	89–01				
Lindley, Henry	Unkn.	97				
Lindsey, Edward	Unkn.	26				
Lindsey, George	Merc.					X2
Lindsey, Richard	Unkn.			09		
Ling, John	Unkn.		14		14	P2/X2
Ling, Nicholas	Merc.		99c		10	S1c
Linley, E.	Unkn.	24				
Linley, Henry	Gent.	97				
Linley, Nicholas	Merc.					M
Linsell, Augustine	Unkn.			20		
Linze, Edward	Unkn.					X2
Lion, Robert	Merc.				10	B
Lison, Oliver	Merc.					S6
Lister, Charles	Unkn.	01				
Lister, John	Merc.	01, 21–28				M/S1c
Lister, Martin	Gent.	04				GG
Litherland, Zachariah	Merc.					I7
Little, Francis	Unkn.	97				
Littlefield, Edward	Unkn.			09		
Littlejohn, George	Unkn.					X2
Littleton, Edward	Kt. 03	04				
Littleton, Edward	Kt. 21	24				
Littleton, Edward, Lord	Nob. 35	14, 25–28				
Littleton, George	Gent.	86				
Littleton, John	Gent.	84–86, 97				
Littleton, Thomas	Kt. 18	21–26				
Littleton, Thomas	Merc.					G8/GG
Litton, Roland	Kt. 03	86, 97, 04				
Litton, William	Kt. 24	24, 28		12		
Lloyd, David	Merc.			18?		X1
Lloyd, Edward	Unkn.			09		
Lloyd, Elisha	Gent.	14				
Lloyd, Evan	Gent.	84				
Lloyd, Griffith	Gent.	86				
Lloyd, John	Merc.		24			
Lloyd, Oliver	Gent.	86				
Lloyd, Richard	Unkn.	84				
Lloyd, Richard	Unkn.	28				
Lloyd, Robert	Kt. 16	21				
Lloyd, Robert	Gent.	86, 01				
Loane, Nathaniel	Merc.					I7
Lobbyn, John	Merc.					S1c
Lock, Eleazar	Merc.					W2

Name & title	Class; date of knight- hood	Parlia- ments (starting dates)	E. Ind. Co.	Va. Co.	Levant Co.	Other companies
Lock, Gerson	Merc.					*W2*
Lock, Henry	Merc.					*W2*
Lock, Henry	Unkn.	01				
Lock, John	Merc.					*X2*
Lock, Michael	Merc.				00	*S6/W6*
Lock, Zachariah	Unkn.	93, 01				
Locksmith, Richard	Unkn.	09				
Lockwood, Nicholas	Merc.					*F1/S4*
Lockyer, John	Unkn.					*X2*
Lodge, Francis	Unkn.			18?		
Lodge, Henry	Merc.					*GG*
Lodge, Joyce	Unkn.			21		
Lodge, Luke	Unkn.			09		
Lodge, Peter	Unkn.			18		
Lodge, Thomas	M. Kt. 62					*H/M/R1g*
Lofte, Anthony	Merc.					*I7*
Loftes, Robert	Merc.		17			
Loggyn, Christopher	Merc.					*S6*
Loggyn, John	Merc.					*S6*
Loggyn, Richard	Merc.					*S6*
Lomley, Martin	Merc.					*L1c*
Loner, Johan	Merc.					*AA1c*
Longe, George	Merc.					*E3/L1*
Longe, Gifford	Gent.	25				
Longe, John	Merc.					*F1/S4*
Longe, Richard	Merc.					*X2*
Longe, Robert	Gent.	26–28				
Longe, Thomas	Merc.					*F1*
Longe, Walter	Kt. 89	93				
Longe, Walter	Kt. 25	21, 25–28‡				
Longe, Walter	Gent.	25–28				
Longe, William	Gent.					*X1*
Longston, Francis	Merc.					*L1*
Lonison, John	Merc.					*BB1*
Lonison, Thomas	Merc.					*BB4*
Lore, Peter van	M. Kt. 21			18?		*O*
Lorte, Sampson	Merc.					*S1*
Lougher, John	Unkn.	01				
Love, Thomas	Kt. 25					*A/K5/X2*
Lovelace, Anne	Gent.		28			
Lovelace, Richard, Lord	Nob. 99	01–21	10	12		
Lovelace, Richard	Gent.	21				
Lovelace, William	Kt. 09	14	28	09		
Lovelace, William	Kt. 99			12		
**Lovell, Henry	Unkn.	21, 26				*I1*
Lovell, Samuel	Merc.					*E3*
Lovett, Francis	Kt. 03					*G6*
Lowe, Francis	Merc.				26	
Lowe, George	Unkn.	25–28				
Lowe, George	Merc.					*M/GG*
Lowe, John	Unkn.	97				

Name & title	Class; date of knighthood	Parliaments (starting dates)	E. Ind. Co.	Va. Co.	Levant Co.	Other companies
Lowe, John	Unkn.					X2
Lowe, Richard	Unkn.	97–01, 14				
Lowe, Thomas	M. Kt. 03	04–21			99g	Mg
Lowe, Thomas	Merc.				10	
Lowe, Vincent	Unkn.			09		
Lower, William	Kt. 03	01–04	10			
Lowther, Gerard	Gent.	01				
Lowther, John	Kt. 26	24–28				GG
*Lowther, John	Gent.	28				
Lowther, Richard	Gent.	26–28				
Lowther, Robert	Gent.					X2
Lucas, Thomas	Merc.					F1
Lucatella, Augustine	Unkn.		22			
Lucatella, Jasper	Unkn.		28			
Lucy, Francis	Gent.	24–28				
Lucy, Thomas	Kt. 65	84				
Lucy, Thomas	Kt. 92	14–28				
Ludlow, Edmund	Kt. 01	97, 04–21				
Ludlow, Henry	Kt.†	01–24				
Ludlow, Roger	Unkn.					J3
Luke, John	Kt. 03	04, 24–25				
Luke, Nicholas	Gent.	84				
Luke, Oliver	Kt. 03	97, 14–28				
Lukin, Edward	Gent.			09		T2
Lukin, Edwin	Gent.			09		
Lukin, Robert	Unkn.	25				
Lulls, Arnold	Merc.			09		Q
Lummer, Robert	Merc.					F1
Lupo, Aliano	Unkn.			20		
Luptone, John	Unkn.					X2
Lusher, Nicholas	Kt. 03					I2
Lusher, William	Gent.					I2
Luther, Jeffrey	Merc.				06	
Lutterford, Edward	Merc.		00c			F1/Q
Luttrell, George	Unkn.	84				
Luttrell, John	Unkn.	86–89				
Luttrell, Thomas	Unkn.	25				
Lutwich, John	Unkn.	86–97				
Lycett, Oliver	Merc.					R2
Lydiat, George	Merc.					B/GG
Lyfe, Richard	Merc.	89–04				
Lyfield, Thomas	Unkn.	89				
Lygon, William	Kt. 03	89, 04				
Lymber, Robert	Merc.					E3/S1
Lymbrey, John	Unkn.					X2
Lynch, Edward	Merc.					S4
Lyne, Richard	Gent.		19			
Lyne, William	Unkn.					I1
Lynn, George	Unkn.	84				
Lynn, Humphrey	Kt. 13	26	23			
Lynn, John	Merc.	28				X2

Name & title	Class; date of knighthood	Parliaments (starting dates)	E. Ind. Co.	Va. Co.	Levant Co.	Other companies
Lysley, Joseph	Unkn.					X2
Lyvely, Edward	Unkn.	24, 28				
Lyvermore, John	Merc.					S6
Machell, John	Gent.		17			
Machen, Thomas	Unkn.	14				
Machett, James	Gent.					I2
Mackett, John	Merc.					S4
Macklyn, Robert	Merc.			89		
Mackwilliam, Henry	Gent.	84–86				CC1
Macy, Gabrahell	Merc.					S1
Macy, Richard	Merc.					S1
Maddison, Isaac	Unkn.			21		
Maddock, Thomas	Unkn.		15	18?		
Maile, Thomas	Gent.			09		
Mailerd, Thomas	Merc.	93				
Mainstay, John	Unkn.		11			
Maiott, Robert	Merc.					E1
Malbon, John	Unkn.					J3
Mallet, James	Merc.			09		
Mallet, John	Kt. 03					K2c
Mallet, John	Unkn.	24				
Mallet, Thomas	Unkn.	14–21, 25–26				
Mallory, Andrew	Gent.					CC2
Mallory, John	Kt. 03	01–04		09		GG
Mallory, Richard	Merc.					M/R1
Mallory, William	Gent.	84				
Mallory, William	Gent.	14–25, 28				
Mallowes, Edward	Merc.					I7
Manby, Francis	Gent.					X1
Mandit, Henry	Unkn.					G8
Manesty, Nathaniel	Merc.					J1
Manley, Nicholas	Merc.		00			
Mann, Edward	Merc.	89–93, 04				S4
Mann, Edward	Merc.					F1
Mann, Eustace	Unkn.					X2
Mann, Francis	Merc.					L2/M
Mann, James	Unkn.					X2
Mann, John	Merc.					S1/X2
Mann, Joseph	Unkn.			19		T3
Mann, Nathaniel	Merc.					I7
Mann, Theophilus	Unkn.					X2
Mann, William	Unkn.	21–25				
Mannering, Arthur	Kt. 03	24–26		10		Q
Mannering, Edmund	Unkn.					I9
Mannering, Edward	Unkn.	01, 25				
Mannering, George	Kt. 95					I8
Mannering, Henry	Kt. 18	21–24		20		X2
Mannering, Philip	Unkn.	24–28				
Manners, Francis Earl Rutland	Nob.		17			G6/GG

Name & title	Class; date of knight-hood	Parlia-ments (starting dates)	E. Ind. Co.	Va. Co.	Levant Co.	Other companies
Manners, George						
Earl Rutland	Nob. 99	04–25				GG
Manners, George	Gent.	89–93				
Manners, John						
Earl Rutland	Nob.	26				GG1
Manners, Oliver	Gent.	01				
Manners, Roger	Gent.	01				
Manners, Thomas	Kt. 70	84–86				
Manning, Edmund	Merc.					L1
Manning, Gerson	Merc.					L1/M
Manning, John	Merc.		20			
Manning, Randall	Merc.					S1
Mansell, Peter	Unkn.			09		
Mansell, Robert	Kt. 96	01–14, 24–28	09	07c		A/K3/Qc/R2/ T1/Z/GG2
Mansell, Thomas	Kt. 11	97, 04–14		12		
Mansfield, John	Unkn.	93				
Mansfield, Ralph	Unkn.					I2
Mansfield, Robert	Unkn.		11			
Mansfield, Thomas	Merc.					I7
Manstedg, Thomas	Merc.					S1
Mantell, Richard	Merc.		14		26	E3/L1
Manwood, Peter	Kt. 03	89–21		09c		
Manyngton, Ambrose	Unkn.	21–24				
Mapes, Francis	Unkn.			09		
Maplesden, Edward	Merc.	25				X2
Maplesden, Richard	Merc.		08	09		Q/T2
Marberie, Anthony	Unkn.					X2
Marberie, Robert	Unkn.					X2
Marberie, Thomas	Gent.		10			
Marden, John	Merc.			09		
Margettes, William	Merc.		19			X2
Markes, Edmund	Merc.				27	
Markes, Walter	Unkn.					I1
Markham, John	Merc.				10	
Markham, Nathaniel	Merc.					I7
Markham, Richard	Unkn.			22		
Markham, Robert	Gent.	86–89				
Markham, Valentine	Merc.					F2/L1/S2
Marlen, Walter	Merc.			89		
Marler, Christopher	Merc.					R1
Marlott, William	Unkn.	24–28				
Marlowe, Anthony	Unkn.					W3
Marmeel, William	Merc.					F1
Marmyng, Ranulph	Merc.					S6
Marsh, Daniel	Merc.					I7
Marsh, Gabriel	Unkn.					X2
Marsh, Hugh	Merc.					S6
Marsh, John	Merc.					H/Mg/R1/S6g
Marsh, John	Merc.			09		S6
Marsh, Richard	Merc.					I7
Marsh, Roger	Merc.			09		

Name & title	Class; date of knighthood	Parliaments (starting dates)	E. Ind. Co.	Va. Co.	Levant Co.	Other companies
Marsh, Thomas	Merc.		00			*W2*
Marsh, Thomas	Unkn.					*J3*
Marshall, George	Unkn.	14				
Marshall, John	Unkn.					*X2*
Marshall, Thomas	Unkn.	04				
Marston, William	Merc.			26		
Martin, Christopher	Unkn.			17		
Martin, George	Unkn.	84				
Martin, George	Unkn.					*X2*
Martin, Giles	Merc.		22c	14c		
Martin, Henry	Kt. 16	25–28				
Martin, Henry	Unkn.	04				
*Martin, Henry	Unkn.	86				
Martin, John	Unkn.			09		
Martin, John	Gent.			09		
**Martin, John	Merc.		25			*F1/X2*
Martin, John	Unkn.	25				
Martin, John	Merc.					*BB1*
Martin, Michael	Unkn.	28				
Martin, Nathaniel	Merc.			00		*S1/BB2*
Martin, Nicholas	Merc.	86				*M/CC2*
Martin, Peter	Merc.					*F1*
**Martin, Richard	Gent.	01–04		09c		*I7c/T1*
Martin, Richard	M. Kt. 89				81	*S6/W2/AA2/ BB1*
Martin, Richard	Merc.				92	*F1/R1g/S6/ BB2*
Martin, Robert	Merc.					*W6/X1*
Martin, Simon	Merc.					*F1*
Martin, Susan	Unkn.		25			
Martin, Thomas	Merc.			89		*F1/M/S6/CC2*
Martin, Thomas	Merc.			26		*S1*
Martin, Thomas	Gent.	14		12		
Martin, William	Merc.	97				*F1/S6c/CC1*
Martin, William	Merc.					*G7*
Martin, ?	M. Kt.					*W3*
Martley, Nicholas	Merc.					*S1*
Marvyn, Edmund	Unkn.	84–89				
Marvyn, James	Kt. 74	97				
Mascall, William	Merc.					*S1*
Masham, William	Kt. 21	24–28‡				
Mason, George	Unkn.			18?		
**Mason, John	Gent.			09		*X2/GG2*
Mason, William	Merc.			09		
Massam, Thomas	Merc.				29	*R2c/GG*
Massam, William	Merc.				90c	*S6c*
Massingherd, John	Merc.		24			
Masson, Robert	Unkn.	26–28				
Masson, William	Unkn.	26				
Masters, George	Gent.	86–89				
Masters, Nathaniel	Unkn.		24			

339

Name & title	Class; date of knight- hood	Parlia- ments (starting dates)	E. Ind. Co.	Va. Co.	Levant Co.	Other companies
Masters, Robert	Unkn.	01				
Masters, William	Kt. 22	24				
Masterson, Lawrence	Unkn.			20		
Masterson, Thomas	Unkn.			20		
Mather, Walter	Merc.					*F1*
Mathew, Griffith	Merc.					*I7*
Mathew, Roger	Merc.	21–28				*F1/X2*
Mathew, Thomas	Unkn.					*X1*
Mathew, Toby	Gent.	01–04				
Mathew, Walter	Merc.					*S1*
Mathew, William	Merc.					*E2*
Mathewson, Bartholomew	Merc.					*X1*
Maud, Josiah	Unkn.			09		
Maudley, Roger	Unkn.	97				
Mawdet, John	Merc.			09		
Mawdet, Otho	Merc.			09		
Mawle, John	Gent.					*CC2*
Mawle, Robert	Gent.					*CC2*
Maxwell, Robert	M. Kt.†			11		
May, George	Merc.				05	*S3*
May, Hugh	Gent.					*G7*
May, Humphrey	Kt. 13	04–28		12c		
May, Richard	Merc.				92	*S6/GG*
May, Thomas	Gent.	21				
May, ?	Merc.					*M/R1*
Maycott, Cavaliero	M. Kt. 03			09c		*S1*
Mayde, Thomas	Unkn.					*X2*
Maydo, George	Gent.					*CC1*
Maydwell, Anthony	Merc.					*Q*
Mayhewe, William	Unkn.	04				
*Maynard, Charles	Gent.	24				
Maynard, Christopher	Merc.					*S1*
Maynard, Henry	Gent.	84–01				
Maynard, John	Kt. 26	24–25, 28				
Maynard, William	Kt. 09	04–14		12c		*Q*
Mayne, Henry	Unkn.					*X2*
Maynewright, John	Merc.			09		
Mayney, Anthony	Kt. 88†	04–14				
*Mayney, Anthony	Kt. 93†	14				
*Mayney, Anthony	Kt. 09†	14, 24‡				
Mayor, Henry	Merc.					*X2*
Mayor, John	Merc.	28				
Mayor, Robert	Merc.					*X2*
Mayott, Christopher	Merc.			09		
Mead, Robert	Unkn.					*X1*
Mead, Thomas	Merc.		24			*F1/M*
Meadows, James	Pfl/y.			09		
Meath, Henry	Unkn.					*X2*
Medkerk, Alfonsus van	Unkn.			18?		
Medlycot, James	Merc.					*L1*

Name & title	Class; date of knighthood	Parliaments (starting dates)	E. Ind. Co.	Va. Co.	Levant Co.	Other companies
Megge, William	Merc.		01			*F*1
Megge, William	Merc.		28		18	
Meggs, ?	Unkn.					*I*8
Melhuish, Thomas	Unkn.					*X*2
Melling, Thomas	Merc.		14	20		*T*3
Mellow, Abraham	Unkn.					*J*3
Mellow, John	Merc.					*S*6
Mellyn, Thomas	Merc.					*S*6/*X*1
Mellyn, William	Merc.					*R*2/*S*1
Meoles, Henry	Unkn.			18?		
Mercer, Edward	Unkn.	04				
Mercy, William	Merc.					*F*1
Mere, Henry	Unkn.	01				
Meredith, John	Merc.			09		
Meredith, Richard Bishop Bath & Wells	Nob.			20		
Meredith, Richard	Gent.					*BB*5
**Meredith, William	Gent.	93				*N*
Merman, Richard	Merc.					*F*1
Merrett, Hugh	Unkn.		26			
Merrett, Humphrey	Merc.			12		
Merrick, Gellius	Unkn.	89, 97				
Merrick, Hugh	Unkn.		11			
Merrick, John	M. Kt. 14		00c	09		*Q*/*R*1g/*S*1/ *T*2/*Z*
Merrick, John	Merc.					*S*1
Merrick, Roland	Unkn.	14				
Merrick, William	Merc.					*R*1/*S*6
Merrifield, Ralph	Merc.					*X*2/*GG*
Merring, Robert	Unkn.					*X*2
Merry, Thomas	Kt. 17		17	12		
Mervin, Henry	Kt. 19	14–21				
Mervin, John	Gent.	84–89				
Messenger, Arthur	Unkn.	89–93, 01				
Messenger, Richard	Unkn.	01				
Methwold, William	Merc.		28			
Mettcalf, Christopher	Unkn.					*X*2
Mettcalf, Matthew	Merc.		26			
Meverell, Francis	Unkn.			18		*T*3
Mewe, John	Merc.		15			
Mewes, William	Unkn.	84, 04				
Mewles, John	Merc.					*S*1
Mewtis, Henry	Unkn.	21				
Mewtis, Thomas	Kt. 11			09		
Mewtis, Thomas	Unkn.	21, 25–28				
Michael, John	Merc.					*F*1/*S*1
Michelborne, Arthur	Merc.				10	
Michelborne, Edward	M. Kt. 99	93	00	07c		*GG*
Michelmore, Ely	Merc.					*F*1
Michell, Barnard	Unkn.	04–14, 25–26		09		
Michell, Christopher	Unkn.					*X*2

Name & title	Class; date of knighthood	Parliaments (starting dates)	E. Ind. Co.	Va. Co.	Levant Co.	Other companies
Michell, Edward	Unkn.					X2
Michell, Gilbert	Unkn.	84				
Michell, Henry	Unkn.					X2
Michell, Humphrey	Gent.	93				BB5
Michell, Isaac	Unkn.			09		
Michelson, William	Merc.					X1
Micklewait, Charles	Merc.					E2
Middleton, David	Merc.		07			
Middleton, Francis	Unkn.			18?		
Middleton, Henry	M. Kt. 06		07			
Middleton, Henry	Merc.					O
Middleton, Hugh	M. Kt. 22	04–28				O/X1/GG1
Middleton, Hugh	Merc.					O
Middleton, John	Merc.		00c			
**Middleton, John	Gent.	14–28		12		
Middleton, Peter	Merc.		27		27	
Middleton, Richard	Merc.		24		22	I1/O
Middleton, Richard	Merc.			20		
Middleton, Robert	Merc.	04–14	99c	09	05	F1/I1c/M/Qc/ S5/X1
Middleton, Thomas	M. Kt. 03	97, 24–26	99	09		G1/O/X1/GG2
Middleton, Thomas	M. Kt. 17	24–25				
Middleton, Timothy	Merc.					O
Middleton, William	Merc.		24			O
Middleton, William	Merc.					O
Midwinter, Edmund	Unkn.	84				
Milbere, Edward	Unkn.					X2
Milburne, Peter	Unkn.					J3/X2
Mildmay, Anthony	Gent.	84, 97				
Mildmay, Henry	Kt. 07			?		
Mildmay, Henry	Kt. 05			?		
Mildmay, Henry	Kt. 17	21–25, 28		22c		G7
Mildmay, Humphrey	Gent.	84–86				
Mildmay, Robert	Merc.		00	09		Q
Mildmay, Thomas	Kt. 03	93		10		
Mildmay, Walter	Kt. 47	84–89				BB1/CC2
Mildnall, John	Merc.				00	
Miles, John	Merc.	93				
**Mill, John	Kt. 19†	24–28				
Mill, Richard	Gent.	97				
Mill, William	Unkn.	89				
Mill, William	Gent.	24–26				
Miller, Alexander	Merc.			09		
Miller, John	Merc.			12		
Miller, Richard	Merc.		24			L1
Miller, Robert	Kt. 03	01–04		10		
Miller, William	Merc.		24			
Millet, William	Merc.		00c	12	05	F1/M/Q
Millongton, Thomas	Merc.					S6
Mills, Arthur	Unkn.	86				
**Mills, Francis	Gent.	84–89				S1/W2/CC2

342

Name & title	Class; date of knight-hood	Parlia-ments (starting dates)	E. Ind. Co.	Va. Co.	Levant Co.	Other companies
Mills, John	Unkn.	25				
Mills, Robert	Unkn.					X2
Mills, ?	Unkn.		09			
Millsop, Thomas	Unkn.					P2
Milo, John	Merc.				26	
Milward, Humphrey	Merc.		00		05	
Milward, John	Merc.		11c			I7/L1/Q
Milward, John	Merc.?		11			
Milward, Richard	Merc.				06	
Milward, Thomas	Merc.?		22c			
Ming, John	Merc.	93, 01				
Misselden, Edward	Merc.		14			L2/M
Mitchell, Bartholomew	Kt. 03					K2c
Mitchell, Francis	Unkn.		19			
Mitchell, John	Merc.					X1
Mitford, Henry	Merc.	89–93				
Mitford, Thomas	Merc.		14			
Mitton, Henry	Unkn.	24				
Moham, Barnabas	Unkn.					X2
Moham, William	Gent.					CC1
Mohun, John, Lord	Nob.	24–25				
Mohun, Reginald	Kt. 99	14, 25				
Mohun, Reginald	Gent.	84–86				
Mohun, Reginald	Gent.	26				
Mohun, William	Kt. 83	84–86				
Moises, Stephen	Merc.					I7
Mokett, John	Merc.	97				
Mole, George	Merc.			22		GG
Mole, Philip	Unkn.			18?		
Molesworth, Bevill	Merc.					Q
Mollineux, Edmund	Merc.					I2
Molton, John	Unkn.					X2
Molyneux, John	Gent.	84				
Molyneux, Richard	Kt. 86	84, 93, 04				I9
Molyneux, Richard	Kt. 13	14, 25, 28				
Molyns, Michael	Unkn.	89				
Molyns, Michael	Unkn.	25				
Mompesson, Giles	Kt. 16	14–21				A/K4/GG
Mompesson, Richard	Unkn.	93				
Monck, John	Unkn.					X2
Monck, Levinus	Gent.	01	09c			F1
Monck, Thomas	Kt. 03	26				
Monger, James	Merc.			09		L2
Monnox, Edward	Merc.		23			S5
Monroes, John	Unkn.					I7c
Monson, John	Kt. 26	25–26				G7
Monson, Robert	Kt. 03	26				
Monson, Thomas	Kt. 98	97, 04–14		09		
Monson, William	Kt. 96	01		20		X1
Monson, William	Kt. 23	26				
Montague, Charles	Kt. 03	21–25				

343

Name & title	Class; date of knight- hood	Parlia- ments (starting dates)	E. Ind. Co.	Va. Co.	Levant Co.	Other companies
Montague, Edward, Lord	Nob. 03	84, 01–21				
Montague, Edward, Lord Kimbolton, Viscount Mandeville, Earl Manchester	Nob. 26	24–26				
Montague, Henry Lord Kimbolton, Viscount Mandeville, Earl Manchester	Nob. 03	93–14	17	06c		*I*1c/*O*/*T*3
Montague, James	Gent.	28				
Montague, James Bishop Bath & Wells	Nob.			09c		
Montague, Sidney	Gent.	93, 01, 14				
Montague, Walter	Kt. 03	14				
Montaine, George Archbishop York	Nob.			12		*G*7
Montaine, James	Unkn.			09		
Montford, Thomas	Gent.			09		
Montgomery, George Bishop Derry	Nob.					*I*5c
Montlowe, ?	Unkn.	04				
Monyngton, Richard	Unkn.			12		
Moody, Edward	Merc.			09		
Moody, Henry	Kt. 06	25–28				
Moody, John	Merc.					*X*2
Moone, Anthony	Merc.					*S*1/*X*1
Moone, Churchill	Unkn.			21		
Moone, Morgan	Merc.	84–86				
Moone, Nicholas	Unkn.			18?		
Moore, Adrian	Merc.		11	10	12	*F*1/*I*1c
Moore, Alexander	Unkn.	28				*X*2
Moore, Andrew	Unkn.			09		
Moore, Archibald	Gent.					*I*4
Moore, Brent	Gent.					*I*4
Moore, Edward	Kt. 00	84, 01				
Moore, Edward	Unkn.	25				
Moore, Elias	Unkn.					*T*3
Moore, Francis	Unkn.	89, 97–14				
Moore, George	Kt. 98	84–26		06c		*Q*
Moore, Gerald	Kt. 99					*I*6c
Moore, Henry	Gent.					*CC*2
Moore, Hugh	Merc.					*E*1
Moore, Hugh	Merc.					*I*2
Moore, John	Merc.		99c			*E*3/*S*1/*X*1/*GG*1
Moore, John	Gent.	97–04		09		
Moore, John	Gent.	24–26		09		
Moore, John	Merc.	84–86				
Moore, Poynings	Gent.	24–28				
Moore, Raphe	Merc.					*I*7
Moore, Richard	Merc.			18?		*F*1
Moore, Richard	Unkn.	86–89				

344

Name & title	Class; date of knight-hood	Parlia-ments (starting dates)	E. Ind. Co.	Va. Co.	Levant Co.	Other companies
Moore, Richard	Unkn.	01				
Moore, Robert	Kt. 03	01–25				
Moore, Robert	Merc.					S6/CC2
Moore, Samuel	Gent.	21–24				
Moore, Thomas	Merc.					E4/L1
Moore, William	Kt. 76	84–97				
*Moorer, Richard	Merc.		24	12		T2
Moorewood, Andrew	Merc.		27			
Mootham, James	Unkn.			22		
Mordaunt, Robert	Unkn.	84				
Mordent, Geoffrey	Unkn.			22		
Mordent, George	Merc.			22		
Mordon, Oliver	Unkn.			22		
Morecomb, William	Merc.					X1
Morell, Hugh	Unkn.					I1c
Moretoste, Valentine	Merc.					F1
Morgan, Charles	Kt. 03			09		
Morgan, Edmund	Kt. 59	01				
Morgan, Edmund	Kt.†	21				
Morgan, Edward	Merc.			20		I2/L1/M/X2
Morgan, Edward	Gent.	84–86				
Morgan, Edward	Gent.	97				
Morgan, George	Merc.					L1/M
Morgan, Henry	Gent.	01				
Morgan, John	Merc.					X1
Morgan, Lewis	Unkn.	28				
Morgan, Matthew	Kt. 91	93				
Morgan, Meredith	Gent.	14				A
Morgan, Richard	Unkn.	93				
Morgan, Thomas	Kt. 87	93				
Morgan, Thomas	Kt. 23	04–28				A
Morgan, Thomas	Gent.	89				
Morgan, William	Kt. 74					W2/CC1
Morgan, William	Kt. 03	24–25				
Morgan, William	Unkn.	86				
Morgan, William	Gent.	28				
Morley, Edward	Gent.	14				
Morley, Herbert	Gent.	89–93				
Morley, Jacob	Merc.					S6
Morley, John	Kt. 03	01–21				
Morley, John	Unkn.	84–86				
Morley, John	Merc.					S1
Morley, Robert	Gent.	21–24, 28				
Morley, Thomas	Merc.					F1/L1c/M/Q/ GG
Morley, William	Kt. 25	26				
Mormay, William	Merc.					I7
Morrall, William	Merc.			09		
Morring, Robert	Unkn.					X2
Morris, Edward	Merc.					S1
Morris, Isabrande	Merc.				?	L1

345

Name & title	Class; date of knighthood	Parliaments (starting dates)	E. Ind. Co.	Va. Co.	Levant Co.	Other companies
Morris, James	Unkn.	84–93				
Morris, John	Kt. 03	01–04				
Morris, John	Merc.		99			E4/F1/L1/Q/ S4/X2
Morris, Thomas	Unkn.	28				
Morris, Thomas	Merc.				09	I7
Morris, William	Kt. 03	93, 01–04				
Morrison, Charles	Kt. 03	21–28				
Morrison, Richard	Kt. 99	21				
Morrison, Thomas	Merc.	84–89				
Morse, Thomas	Unkn.			23		
Morse, William	Merc.					F1/S4
Morton, Albert	Kt. 17	25				
Morton, George	Kt. 03	26				
Morton, Ralph	Gent.			09		
Morton, Richard	Unkn.			18?		
Morton, Thomas, Bishop Chester, Lichfield, Durham	Nob.					G7
Morton, Thomas	Pfl/y.					GG
Morton, William	Merc.	84, 89–93				
Morwood, Gilbert	Merc.		24	22		
Moseley, Anthony	Merc.		01			
Moseley, Clement	Merc.		99			
Moseley, Edward	Kt. 14	14–24				
Moseley, Henry	Merc.					L1/M
Moseley, Nicholas	M. Kt. 00		99		92	R1
Moseley, Thomas	Merc.	97				
Moss, Clement	Unkn.					I1
Moss, Francis	Merc.					E2/GG
Mostin, John	Gent.	24				
Mostin, Peter	Gent.					I4
Mostin, Robert	Unkn.			21		
Mostin, Roger	Kt. 06	21				
Mott, Robert	Unkn.					X2
Mott, Thomas	Unkn.					P2
Moulsoe, John	Unkn.			09		
Moulson, Thomas	Merc.	28				F1/M
Moundeford, Edmund	Kt. 29	28				FF
Mounsey, John	Unkn.					GG
Mountney, Richard	Merc.		07			I7/Q
Mouse, Arthur	Merc.			09		L1
Moxey, John	Merc.					S4
Moyer, James	Merc.				10	X2
Moyle, Adam	Merc.	86–89				
Moyle, John	Merc.			27		
Mudford, Richard	Pfl/y.					CC2
Muffet, Peter	Merc.					M/S4
Muffet, Thomas	Unkn.	97				
Mulles, John	Merc.					F1
Munday, Edward	Merc.					S1

346

Name & title	Class; date of knighthood	Parliaments (starting dates)	E. Ind. Co.	Va. Co.	Levant Co.	Other companies
Munday, Henry	Merc.					S1
Munday, Robert	Unkn.					X2
Munden, Edward	Unkn.					X2
Mundes, Jarvis	Merc.			10		
Munger, James	Unkn.		15			
Munks, Lawrence	Merc.			09		
Munn, Thomas	Merc.		15c		00	
Muns, John	Merc.				00c	GG
Murray, David	Kt. 05			10		Q
Murrey, John	Unkn.	21				
Murrey, William	Unkn.	26–28				
Muschamp, William	Unkn.	24				
Musgrave, Edward	Kt. 03	04				
Musgrave, Richard	Kt. 03	04				
Muskott, John	Merc.					I7
Mustard, Thomas	Merc.		18c		17c	
Mustard, Thomas	Merc.				14c	
Mutes, Philip	Unkn.			20		
Mutton, John	Unkn.					X2
Mutton, Peter	Kt. 22	04, 24				
Myers, Edmund	Merc.					L1
Myles, Gabriel	Merc.					M
Mylle, Thomas	Merc.					I7
Myn, George	Merc.	21–24	27			
Mynard, Christopher	Merc.					F1
Myngaye, Francis	Unkn.	01, 24				
Mynnes, John	Merc.					X2
Naldrett, Henry	Merc.				11	
Nanney, Griffith	Gent.	93				
Napper, Gerard	Gent.	28				
Napper, Nathaniel	Kt. 18	25–28				
Napper, Robert	Kt. 11	86, 01–04				
Napper, Robert	M. Kt. 12		99c		92c	F1/Q/S4/Z
Napper, Robert	Kt. 23	26–28				
Narme, ?	Unkn.					K5
Nash, Richard	Merc.	84				
Naunton, Robert	Kt. 15	04–26				G7
Neale, Francis	Unkn.	93–97				
Neall, Peter	Unkn.					X2
Nearne, Alexander	Unkn.		27			
Neason, Robert	Merc.					X2
Neathway, Thomas	Merc.					X1
Necton, William	Unkn.	84–97				
Needham, Arthur	Merc.					S1
Needham, Francis	Merc.					F2/L1/N/S2/ AA3
Needham, George	Merc.					AA1
Needham, Robert	Kt. 94	93, 04				
Needham, Robert	Unkn.	14				
Needler, George	Merc.					I7
Nelson, Francis	Merc.					Q

Name & title	Class; date of knight- hood	Parlia- ments (starting dates)	E. Ind. Co.	Va. Co.	Levant Co.	Other companies
Nelson, Matthew	Merc.			09		
Nelson, Thomas	Merc.		07			
Nelson, William	Merc.		19			
Nethersall, ?	Unkn.					X2
Nethersoll, Francis	Kt. 19	24–25, 28				
Nevey, William	Merc.					S1c
Nevill, Alexander	Unkn.	84, 01				
Nevill, Christopher	Kt. 26	14–24				G7
Nevill, Edmund	Merc.			89		
Nevill, Edward	Gent.	89–93				
**Nevill, Francis	Gent.	04, 28				X2
Nevill, Henry	Gent.	84–97				
Nevill, Henry	Kt. 96	01–04	14	07c		F1
Nevill, Henry	Kt. 09	14–21		10		A/O
Nevill, Henry	Kt. 49	84				
Nevill, Henry Lord Abergavenny	Nob.			12		
Nevill, John	Unkn.		14	22		
Nevill, Peter	Merc.					X1
Nevynson, Thomas	Unkn.					G8
Newbald, Fria.	Unkn.					P2
Newberry, Humphrey	Unkn.	26				
Newberry, John	Merc.				90	
Newbridge, Joseph	Merc.			09		
Newce, George	Gent.			09		
Newce, Henry	Unkn.			09		
Newce, William	Kt. 21			21?c		
Newcomen, Robert	Kt. 05					I8
Newdigate, John	Unkn.	28				
Newdigate, Robert	Unkn.	97				
Newdigate, Robert	Kt. 01	01				
Newe, Randolph	Unkn.					X2
Newgate, Christopher	Merc.			09		
Newhouse, John	Unkn.			09		
*Newland, Robert	Unkn.					X2
Newland, ?	Unkn.			21		
Newman, Gabriel	Merc.					I1c/L2/M/O
Newman, George	Kt. 16	01, 14–21				
Newman, James	Merc.					E1
Newman, John	Merc.		99			F1/L1/M/S6c
Newman, John	Merc.					S3/X2
*Newman, Richard	Merc.					S6
Newman, Richard	Merc.					S4
Newport, Andrew	Gent.	89				
Newport, Christopher	Merc.			09		X1
Newport, Elizabeth	Merc.		25			
Newport, Francis	Gent.	93				
Newport, Richard	Kt. 15	14–25, 28				
Newport, Sampson	Merc.		22		10c	L2/M
Newport, Thomas	Merc.				12	L2/M
*Newport, ?	Unkn.			21		

Name & title	Class; date of knighthood	Parliaments (starting dates)	E. Ind. Co.	Va. Co.	Levant Co.	Other companies
Newton, Adam	Gent.					Q
Newton, Henry	Merc.					S4
Newton, John	Merc.					B/S6c/X1
Newton, John	Merc.					M/S4/GG
Newton, Richard	Merc.					F1
Newton, Thomas	Unkn.			22		
Newtoninnes, John	Merc.					I2
Nicholas, Bartholomew	Unkn.					X2
Nicholas, Edward	Unkn.	21–24, 28				
Nicholas, Reginald	Unkn.	89, 04				
Nicholas, Thomas	Unkn.	21				
Nicholls, Archibald	Unkn.					X2
Nicholls, Christopher	Merc.		01	09	05	
Nicholls, Edward	Unkn.				18	
Nicholls, Francis	Gent.	21–25, 28‡				
Nicholls, Humphrey	Unkn.	28				
Nicholls, John	Gent.			87		
Nicholls, Matthias	Pfl/y.					J3/GG
Nicholls, Oliver	Gent.			12		A
Nicholls, Thomas	Merc.		11	09		W2
Nicholls, William	Merc.			18?		T2
Nicholson, Edmund	Merc.		99			S5
Nicholson, Francis	Merc.				19	
Nicholson, Michael	Merc.		09			
Nicholson, Otho	Gent.					AA3
Nicke, Nicholas	Merc.					I7
Nightingale, Luke	Merc.					R2
Nightingale, William	Merc.				06	
Nixon, Oswald	Unkn.					X2
Noble, William	Merc.	84				
Noell, Andrew	Kt. 86	84–01				
Noell, Edward, Lord, Viscount Campden	Nob. 02	01				
Noell, Henry	Gent.	89–93				CC1
Noell, Increase	Unkn.					J1
Noell, William	Unkn.	28				
Nokes, Bartholomew	Merc.		26			
Noor, Ralph	Merc.					E3
Nordern, Thomas	Merc.				92	
Norgreene, William	Merc.				13	
Norman, Robert	Merc.					S6
Nornicot, Thomas	Merc.			09		T2
Norris, Edward	Kt. 86	84, 89				X1
Norris, Francis, Lord, Viscount Thame, Earl Berkshire	Nob.			12		
Norris, Henry	Kt. 86	89, 97				
Norris, John	Kt. 86	89				
Norris, John	Kt. 01	97–01				
Norris, John	Merc.			86		F1/S1/X1
Norris, Richard	Merc.					F1/S1/X1

Name & title	Class; date of knighthood	Parliaments (starting dates)	E. Ind. Co.	Va. Co.	Levant Co.	Other companies
Norris, Thomas	Kt. 88	86				I9
North, Charles	Kt. 18			21		
North, Dudley, Lord	Nob.			12		G6
North, Dudley, Lord	Nob. 16	28				G7
North, Gilbert	Gent.					G6
North, Henry	Kt. 86	84, 89, 97				
North, John	Kt. 96	84–93				G6
North, Roger, Lord	Nob.					CC1
North, Roger	Kt. 18	21–28				G7
North, Roger	Gent.					G6
North, Thomas	Merc.					L1/M/S5
Norton, Daniel	Kt. 03	21–25, 28				
Norton, Dudley	Unkn.		11			
Norton, Gregory	Kt. 24		29			
Norton, Richard	Kt. 11†	21				
Norton, Samuel	Unkn.					I9
Norton, Thomas	Kt. 07	14				
Norton, Thomas	Unkn.			18?		
Norton, William	Merc.				11	
Norwood, Richard	Unkn.			23		
Norwood, Valentine	Merc.		18			
Noye, William	Unkn.	04, 21–24, 26–28				
Noyes, John	Unkn.	04				
Noyes, Peter	Unkn.	14				
Nutt, John	Unkn.					X2
Nutt, Robert	Unkn.					X2
Nutt, Thomas	Unkn.		18			
Nuttall, Jonathan	Gent.			12		
Nyell, William	Merc.	21–24				
Oakeley, Francis	Merc.		09			
Oakeley, Richard	Unkn.	24, 26–28				
Oakes, Thomas	Unkn.					X2
Ochterlony, James	Kt. 03					G7
Odiorne, Robert	Unkn.					X2
Oeyll, Jacques	Merc.		15			
Offield, John	Merc.				12	
Offield, Joseph	Unkn.					J3
Offield, Richard	Merc.					X2
Offield, Roger	Merc.		99		00	B/X1/GG
Offield, Samuel	Unkn.	24–28	24			
Offield, ?	Unkn.		24			
Offield, Thomas	Merc.					Q
Offield, Walter	Merc.					S1
Offield, William	Merc.					X2
Offley, Hugh	Merc.					E1c/S6
Offley, John	Kt. 15	25–26				
Offley, John	Merc.		18		18	
**Offley, Robert	Merc.		00c	09c	92c	Qc/S5/T1/GG
Offley, Thomas	M. Kt. 57					H/R1c/BB1c
Offley, Thomas	Merc.				00	

Name & title	Class; date of knight-hood	Parlia-ments (starting dates)	E. Ind. Co.	Va. Co.	Levant Co.	Other companies
Offley, William	Merc.		99			
Oglander, John	Kt. 15	25–28				
Ogle, John	Kt.†			09c		
Oglethorpe, Owen	Unkn.	89, 97				
Okewyn, John	Merc.		25			
Old, Robert	Merc.					I7
Oldberry, Thomas	Merc.					I7
Oldesworth, Arnold	Gent.	93				AA3
Oldesworth, Joseph	Unkn.	97				
Oldesworth, Michael	Unkn.	24–28				
Oldesworth, William	Merc.	97–04‡				
Oldham, John	Unkn.					GG
Oleborne, Henry	Unkn.					X2
Oliver, Eustace	Merc.					S6c
Oliver, Francis	Merc.			18?		S1
Oliver, John	Merc.					X1
Oliver, Richard	Unkn.	21–28				
Onley, Richard	Merc.					R2c
Onslowe, Richard	Kt. 24	28				
Onslowe, William	Unkn.	84–86				
Opie, Nicholas	Unkn.					X2
Orenge, James	Unkn.	93–97				
O'Reyly, Brian-McPhilip	Gent.					I4
Organ, Edward	Merc.					I7
Orme, Humphrey	Merc.					I2
Orme, ?	Unkn.		09			
Ormeshaw, John	Merc.				10	
Ormeshaw, William	Unkn.					W5
Ormstedd, Thomas	Merc.				10	
Orwell, Lewis	Unkn.		09			
Osbaldeston, John	Unkn.	01				
Osborne, Andrew	Merc.		09			
Osborne, Christopher	Unkn.	89				
Osborne, Edward	Merc.				00	
Osborne, Edward	M. Kt. 84	86			81g	E1/R2/S6c
Osborne, Edward	Kt. 20	28				
Osborne, Edward	Unkn.	21				
Osborne, John	Gent.	86–93, 01				BB2
Osborne, John	Merc.		15			R2/T2
Osborne, Peter	Kt. 11	24–25				
Osborne, Peter	Gent.	84–89				AA2/BB1c
Oseley, Nicholas	Merc.					S3
Osmotherly, Richard	Merc.		07	09		I7
Otborowe, William	Merc.					S6
Otwaie, Richard	Merc.			09		L1
Otwood, Edward	Merc.					M
Oughtred, John (see Ughtred)	Merc.					F1
Overbury, Nicholas	Unkn.	04				
Overbury, Walter	Unkn.	21, 26				
Overing, Edward	Merc.		24			F1

Name & title	Class; date of knight-hood	Parlia-ments (starting dates)	E. Ind. Co.	Va. Co.	Levant Co.	Other companies
Overton, Andrew	Merc.		09			
Overton, Henry	Merc.			09		
Owen, Edward	Merc.			09		
Owen, Hugh	Unkn.	26–28				
Owen, John	Unkn.	97				
Owen, Nathaniel	Unkn.		14			
Owen, Nathaniel	Unkn.					W2
Owen, Robert	Merc.					S1
Owen, Roger	Kt. 03	97–14				AA3
Owen, Thomas	Merc.					B/F1/S1c/W5
Owen, Thomas	Gent.	84				
Owen, Thomas	Gent.	24–28				
*Owen, Thomas	Unkn.					X2
Owen, William	Kt. 17	25–28				
Owen, ?	Merc.		07			
Owner, Edward	Unkn.	21, 25				
Oxburgh, Thomas	Merc.	86, 97–14				
Oxenbridge, Robert	Kt. 00	04				
*Oxenbridge, Robert	Kt. 16	21–26				
Oxenbridge, William	Gent.			09		
Oxwicke, John	Unkn.		14			
Oxwith, Robert	Merc.				18	
Packer, John	Merc.	28				O
Packington, John	Kt. 87†	24				GG
Packington, Thomas	Merc.					Q
Paddy, William	Kt. 03	04				Q
Page, Edmund	Merc.		24			
Page, Edward	Unkn.		24			
Page, Gilbert	Merc.					F1/X2
Page, Roger	Unkn.					X1
Pagett, William, Lord	Nob.		11	12c		G6/T1/GG
Pagnam, ?	Unkn.			09		
Pain, Ambrose	Merc.					E3
Painter, Thomas	Unkn.					J3
Painter, William	Unkn.					W5
Palavicino, Edward	Pfl/y.			20		G7
Palavicino, Toby	Unkn.			20		
Palfreeman, Thomas	Merc.					H
Pallett, William	Unkn.					X1
Palmer, Abraham	Merc.					J1
Palmer, Andrew	Merc.	89–93				BB1c
Palmer, Anthony	Kt. 03		14			K2c
Palmer, Edward	Merc.		29	22		
Palmer, Henry	Kt. 86					X1
Palmer, Henry	Gent.					BB2
**Palmer, James	Gent.	21, 26	15			
Palmer, John	Merc.		26			
Palmer, Miles	Unkn.			09		
Palmer, Peter	Merc.		09			
Palmer, Robert	Merc.		09			I7/L1c/M
Palmer, Roger	Kt. 26	14, 24–28				

Name & title	Class; date of knight-hood	Parliaments (starting dates)	E. Ind. Co.	Va. Co.	Levant Co.	Other companies
Palmer, Thomas	Kt. 96	86–89				X1
Palmer, Thomas	Gent.	01				
Palmer, William	Merc.		00	09	10	E3/F1c/L1/M/ Q/S4/T2/X2
Palmer, William	Merc.					F1
Palmes, Brian	Unkn.	26				
Palmes, Francis	Unkn.	86				
Palmes, Guy	Kt. 03	14–25, 28		12		
Panton, John	Merc.	97–01				
Panton, John	Unkn.	04				
Panton, Thomas	Kt. 07			09		
Papilion, Peter	Merc.		15			
Papworth, Robert	Merc.					Q
Papworth, Roger	Unkn.	89				
Paramore, Henry	Merc.					S6
Paramour, Thomas	Unkn.	25–28				
Parham, John	Merc.					F1c/I7/Q
Park, John	Merc.				06	
Park, Joseph	Merc.					F1
Park, Nicholas	Merc.					F1
Park, William	Merc.				10c	
Park, Zachariah	Merc.					S4
Parker, Augustine	Merc.					F1
Parker, Calthrop	Gent.	01				
Parker, John	Gent.	89				
Parker, John	Kt. 03	93, 01–04				
Parker, Leonard	Merc.					S1
Parker, Leonard	Merc.					S1
Parker, Nicholas	Kt. 88	97		12		
Parker, Nicholas	Merc.					R1/W4
Parker, William Lord Mounteagle & Morley	Nob.		09	09c		Q
Parker, William	Merc.					K1/X1
*Parker, William	Merc.			09		
Parkhurst, Anthony	Gent.					CC2
Parkhurst, Henry	Merc.		99			
Parkhurst, John	Unkn.			22		X2
Parkhurst, Robert	M. Kt. 35	25–28	23c	09		
Parkhurst, William	Kt. 19	25				
Parkins, ?	Unkn.		20			
Parkins, Aden	Merc.		11	09		Q
Parkins, Christopher	Kt. 03	97–04		09		
Parkins, Edward	Unkn.		09			
Parkins, George	Unkn.	97				
Parkins, John	Merc.	21				F1
Parkins, Richard	Unkn.	84–93				
Parkins, Thomas	Merc.			09		
Parkins, Thomas	Gent.					I4
Parkins, William	Merc.					J3/X2/GG
Parkins, William	Merc.					S1/X1
Parkinson, Christopher	Merc.	04				

Name & title	Class; date of knight-hood	Parliaments (starting dates)	E. Ind. Co.	Va. Co.	Levant Co.	Other companies
Parkinson, Henry	Merc.					I7
Parkinson, James	Gent.					CC2
Parkinson, Stephen	Merc.					I7
Parkinson, Thomas	Merc.	84–86, 97				
Parrett, James	Kt. 03	97, 04–24, 26–28		10		
Parrett, John	Kt. 61	89				X1
Parrett, Thomas	Kt. 79	86, 93				
Parry, Henry Bishop Worcester	Nob.			12		
Parry, Thomas	Kt.†	86, 04–14				F1
Parry, Thomas	Merc.		24			
Parry, William	Gent.	84				CC2
Parslowe, Giles	Merc.		00	09	05	F1/R2/S3c
Parsons, George	Merc.					X1
Parsons, William	Unkn.					I6c
Partridge, Richard	Unkn.			09		
Pashall, Edmund	Merc			09		S4
Paske, Samuel	Merc.			09		
Pate, Richard	Unkn.	86				
Pate, William	Merc.				06	
Patrickes, Richard	Merc.					R1
Patrone, Ellis	Merc.					X2
Patten, William	Pfl/y.					AA1/BB1
Patteson, Matthew	Unkn.	89, 01				
Pattinson, Robert	Merc.					I7
Paule, Daniel	Merc.					E3
Paule, George	Kt. 07	97–01, 25, 28				
Paule, George	Merc.					F1
Paule, William	Merc.		99			
Paulson, Richard	Merc.			18?		T2
Paulson, Samuel	Merc.					E2/X2
Paulsteed, ?	Unkn.			22		
Pavyer, William	Unkn.		09			
Pawling, Andrew	Merc.			09		
Payne, Griffith	Unkn.	04				
Payne, Isaac van	Merc.		21			
**Payne, John	Gent.?	28		18?		F1
Payne, Robert	M. Kt. 05	14–21, 26–28		09		S1
Payne, Thomas	Merc.					X1
Payne, William	Merc.			09		L1/N/Q/S4/T2
Peacock, Robert	Merc.					S6
Peacock, Robert	Merc.					S4
Peake, Edward	Merc.	84–04				
Peake, George	Kt.†					CC2
Peake, Peter	Merc.	26–28				
Peake, Robert	Merc.			12		
Pearce, Abraham	Merc.			18		F1
Pearce, Edmund	Unkn.			09		
Pearce, Francis	Unkn.	21				
Pearce, John	Merc.					GG

354

Name & title	Class; date of knight-hood	Parlia-ments (starting dates)	E. Ind. Co.	Va. Co.	Levant Co.	Other companies
Pearce, Richard	Merc.		00			*E4*
Pearce, Stephen	Unkn.					*X2*
Pearce, Thomas	Unkn.					*X2*
Pearce, William	Unkn.					*X2*
*Pearce, ?	Unkn.			09		
*Pearce, ?	Unkn.					*T3*
Peard, George	Merc.	97, 04				
Peare, William	Unkn.					*X2*
Pearpoint, William	Merc.			11		*Q*
Peate, Peter	Unkn.			09		
Peate, Richard	Merc.					*Q*
Peatley, George	Unkn.			18?		
Peck, Ashburnham	Merc.	93				
Peck, William	Unkn.					*X2*
Peckett, James	Merc.				25	
Peckett, Marmaduke	Merc.					*L2/M*
Peckham, George	Kt. 70					*CC1/GG1*
Pecott, William	Merc.					*F1*
Peere, Lott	Unkn.			16c		
Peirse, John	Unkn.	14				
Peirson, William	Merc.					*E4/L1/M*
Pelham, Edmund	Gent.	97				
Pelham, Henry	Gent.	21–28		21		
Pelham, Herbert	Gent.	84				
*Pelham, Herbert	Gent.	04				
Pelham, Herbert	Gent.					*J3*
**Pelham, Thomas	Kt. 24	21–25		12		*GG*
Pelham, Thomas	Gent.	84–86				*GG*
Pelham, William	Gent.	97				
*Pelham, William	Unkn.					*W5*
Pelke, John	Merc.					*F1*
Pell, Anthony	Kt. 08			22		
Pemberton, Goddard	Kt. 03	01–04				
Pemberton, James	M. Kt. 03					*I8/BB2*
Pemberton, John	Merc.			09		
Pemberton, Robert	Merc.				23	
Pemble, Thomas	Unkn.			22		
Pembridge, Anthony	Unkn.	97, 04				
Pendelton, Francis	Merc.			09		
Penkevell, Benjamin	Merc.					*Q*
Penkevell, Digory	Merc.					*Q*
Penkevell, Nicholas	Merc.					*Q*
Penkevell, Peter	Merc.					*Q*
Penkevell, Richard	Merc.	89				*Q*
Pennell, Robert	Merc.					*I7*
Pennington, Daniel	Merc.		22			
Pennington, Isaac	Merc.		22		23	
Pennington, John	Merc.					*I2/X2*
Pennington, Joseph	Gent.	97				
Pennington, Robert	Merc.		00	09	23	*Q*
Pennington, William	Unkn.					*P2*

Name & title	Class; date of knighthood	Parliaments (starting dates)	E. Ind. Co.	Va. Co.	Levant Co.	Other companies
*Pennington, William	Merc.					I7
Penny, Allen	Unkn.					X2
Pennyfather, William	Merc.					I7/M
Pennystone, Anthony	Merc.					S6
Pennystone, Anthony	Merc.		24		10c	F1/S1/T3
Penrin, William	Unkn.					P2
Penrose, Henry	Merc.					E2
Penruddock, Edward	Unkn.	84–86				
Penruddock, John	Unkn.	84–86				
Penruddock, Robert	Unkn.	89–01				
Penruddock, Thomas	Kt. 03	01, 14				
Pentecost, Constantine	Unkn.					X2
Pentecost, George	Unkn.					X2
Pentigrace, Robert	Merc.					S1
Pepper, Christopher	Unkn.	24				
Pepper, Cuthbert	Unkn.	97–01				
Pepper, John	Unkn.	84, 93				
Pepwell, Michael	Merc.					X1
Pepys, Talbot	Unkn.	25				
Perch, William	Merc.				06	
Percival, Richard	Gent.	04		09		
Percy, Algernon Earl Northumberland	Nob.	24–26				
Percy, Allen	Kt. 05	04				
Percy, Allen	Unkn.			18?		
Percy, George	Gent.			09		
Percy, Henry	Unkn.	28		22		
Percy, Jeremy	Unkn.			09		
Percy, Robert	Merc.		28			
Perholt, Henry Trall	Merc.					X2
Periam, John	Merc.	84–93				M/Q1/S6/CC1
Perient, Thomas	Unkn.	14				
Perkins, Jacob	Merc.				10	
Perrot, Francis	Merc.		20			
Perry, Francis	Merc.					S5
Perry, Hugh	Merc.		27c			L1c/M
Perry, Richard	Merc.					S6
Perry, Richard	Merc.					J1c
Perry, Robert	Merc.					S1
Perry, William	Merc.					S6
Perryman, George	Merc.					S6
Perryn, Robert	Merc.			09		
Persons, Richard	Merc.		00		15	
Perston, John	Unkn.	93				
Pervis, Edward	Merc.				00	
Pervis, Henry	Merc.				92	
Pervis, Henry	Merc.				18	
Pestword, Michael	Merc.					F1
Peter, Edward	Merc.					X2
Peter, Henry	Unkn.	04				
Peter, John	Merc.					S6/X1

Name & title	Class; date of knight-hood	Parlia-ments (starting dates)	E. Ind. Co.	Va. Co.	Levant Co.	Other companies
Peters, Hugh	Pfl/y.					J1
Peters, Richard	Merc.					X2
Peterson, Heinrick	Merc.					X2
Petit, Simon	Merc.					X2
Petit, Stephen	Merc.					X2
Petre, John, Lord	Nob. 76	84–86		09		G6
Petre, Robert	Unkn.	86				
Petre, William, Lord	Nob. 03	97				
Pett, Arthur	Unkn.			09		
Pett, Phineas	Merc.			09		
Pett, Phineas	Unkn.			12		
Pettus, John	Kt. 07	01–04		12		
Pettey, Maximilian	Unkn.	28				
Pewsy, Daniel	Merc.			09		
Peynton, Alexander	Merc.					S6
Peyton, Edward	Kt. 11	21–26				G7
Peyton, Henry	Kt. 06			09		
Peyton, Henry	Merc.					B/I8/M/S4
Peyton, John	Kt. 03	01				X2
Peyton, John	Kt. 96	93, 04				
Peyton, John	Kt. 86	84, 93–01				
Peyton, Samuel	Kt. 08	14				
Philips, Edward	Kt. 03	84–86, 93–04				Q
Philips, Henry	Merc.					I7
Philips, John	Gent.	97–01		12		
Philips, Robert	Kt. 03	04–25, 28		13?c		
Philips, Robert	Unkn.					T2
Philips, Thomas	Kt. 03	25				
Philips, Thomas	Kt. 07					I9
*Philips, Thomas	Unkn.	84–86				
Philips, Thomas	Unkn.			18		
Philipson, Robert	Merc.					S6
Phillipot, John	Unkn.	28				
Philpot, Henry	Merc.			18?		
Pick, Thomas	Merc.				10	
Pickering, Christopher	Gent.	97				
Pickering, Edward	Unkn.					P1
Pickering, John	Kt. 19	26				
Pickering, Mary	Unkn.					X2
Pickesse, Drew	Unkn.	86				
Pickford, Christopher	Unkn.			09		
Pierdie, Nicholas	Merc.		99		90	
Pierepont, Henry	Gent.	28				
Pierepont, Robert	Gent.	01				
Pierson, Edmund	Merc.					I2
Pierson, Nicholas	Merc.					E1
Pierson, Richard	Merc.			09		
Piggot, Christopher	Kt. 04	04				
Piggot, John	Unkn.			09		
*Piggot, John	Unkn.	89–93, 01				
Piggot, Richard	Merc.				10	

357

Name & title	Class; date of knighthood	Parliaments (starting dates)	E. Ind. Co.	Va. Co.	Levant Co.	Other companies
Piggot, Thomas	Gent.	89				
Pike, John	Merc.					X1
Pilkinton, Robert	Unkn.	89				
Pinchon, Christopher	Merc.		18			
Pinchon, John	Merc.					G8
Pinchon, Robert	M. Kt.†		15			L1/M
Pinchon, William	Unkn.					J3
Pinder, John	Merc.	01				
Pinder, Paul	M. Kt. 20				00	GG
Pinder, Ralph	Merc.				19	
Pinder, Thomas	Merc.				10	
Pitt, Christopher	Merc.					X1
Pitt, Edward	Unkn.	24				
Pitt, George	Merc.		07	09		Q/R2
Pitt, Henry	Merc.					X1
Pitt, John	Unkn.	04				
Pitt, John	Merc.					F1/S1
Pitt, Matthew	Merc.	21–24				
Pitt, Richard	Merc.					S1/X1
Pitt, Thomas	Merc.					S1/X1
Pitt, Thomas	Merc.					S1
Pitt, William	Kt. 19	14–25				
Pitt, William	Merc.					S1/X1
*Pitt, William	Unkn.					X2
Platt, James	Gent.			87		
Plea, George	Merc.					S1
Pledall, John	Unkn.	93				
Pleydall, Thomas	Unkn.			09		
**Plomer, Edward	Merc.		24	12		F1
Plomer, Henry	Merc.					F1/S4
Plomer, John	Unkn.	04				
Plomer, Thomas	Merc.		24	09		F1
Plumleigh, William	Merc.	24				X2
Plumton, John	Merc.				23	
Poakenhorne, Roger	Unkn.					X2
Pocock, John	Merc.					J3c/P2
Poe, Leonard	Pfl/y.		07	09		
Pointell, Richard	Merc.		00	09		I7/L1/Q
Pointell, Timothy	Merc.		24			
Pointes, John	Merc.				13	
Pole, Stephen	Kt. 04			09c		
Polhill, Edward	Merc.		12			Q
Polhill, John	Gent.		09			
Polhill, Thomas	Gent.		15			X1
Pollard, George	Merc.			09		
Pollard, Gregory	Merc.					I7
Pollard, William	Unkn.			20		
Pollington, John	Unkn.			23		
Polsteed, Henry	Merc.		99c			F1/I7/Q
Pomeroy, Henry	Unkn.	04				
Pomet, Richard	Unkn.			09		

Name & title	Class; date of knight-hood	Parliaments (starting dates)	E. Ind. Co.	Va. Co.	Levant Co.	Other companies
Pond, Edmund	Merc.			12		
Pontois, John	Merc.				06	
Pontsonne, Richard	Merc.			12		
Poole, Henry	Kt. 87	93				
*Poole, Henry	Kt. 03	04–24, 26				
Poole, Henry	Gent.	24–25				
Poole, John	Unkn.	86				
Poole, John	Kt.†	93				
Poole, John	Gent.	26				
Poole, John	M. Kt. 28					*I2*
Poole, John	Merc.					*R2*c
Poole, Nevill	Kt. 13	14, 24, 26				
Poole, Nicholas	Merc.					*S1*c
Poole, William	Kt. 07	86		12		
Pooley, Edmund	Unkn.	84–86				
Pooley, John	Unkn.	28				
Pooley, Robert	Unkn.	24, 26				
Pooley, Thomas	Unkn.	86				
Polley, William	Kt. 96	21–24, 26–28				
Pope, Lewis	Merc.	21				*S1*
Pope, Richard	Merc.					*L1*
Pope, Robert	Merc.					*C*
Pope, Thomas	Merc.					*C/S1*
Pope, William	Kt. 16	21				
Popham, Alexander	Gent.	89, 97–01				
Popham, Edward	Gent.	84				
Popham, Edward	Gent.	21–26				
Popham, Francis	Kt. 96	97, 04–28		06c		*K1/X1/AA3/ GG1*
Popham, George	Gent.			06		*I9*
Popham, John	Kt. 92					*I9/K1/X1/ AA3/EE/GG1*
Popham, John	Gent.	28				
Popham, John	Gent.					*I9*
Porie, Robert	Merc.					*I2*
Porter, John	Unkn.	86				
Porter, John	Merc.					*X1*
Porter, John	Merc.					*I7*
Porter, Matthew	Merc.		14			
Porter, Walter	Merc.		99			
Portington, Roger	Unkn.	93–97				
Portman, Henry	Kt. 12	21				
Portman, Hugh	Gent.	97				
Portman, Hugh	Kt. 24	25, 28				
Porty, Robert	Unkn.			18?		
Pory, John	Gent.	04		09		
Posthill, John	Merc.				10	
Posthill, William	Merc.				12	
Potter, John	Merc.		99			*F1/S1*
Potter, Nathaniel	Merc.					*I7*
Potton, Thomas	Merc.				26	

Name & title	Class; date of knight-hood	Parlia-ments (starting dates)	E. Ind. Co.	Va. Co.	Levant Co.	Other companies
Potts, John	Unkn.	89				
Potts, Nicholas	Unkn.	84				
Poulton, Giles	Merc.					L1/M
Pountice, John	Unkn.			18		
Pounttes, Richard	Unkn.					X2
Povey, Justinian	Unkn.		17			
Powell, Henry	Gent.	97				
Powell, Henry	Merc.					X2/GG
Powell, Hugh	Merc.					I7
Powell, John	Merc.					S6
Powell, John	Unkn.	04				
Powell, John	Merc.		26			X2/GG
Powell, Lewis	Gent.	21–25				A
Powell, Richard	Merc.					S1/X1
Powell, Stephen	Kt. 04					G3
Powell, Thomas	Gent.	84				
Powell, Thomas	Merc.					S1
Powell, Walter	Merc.				12	
Powell, William	Gent.			09		I2
Power, Henry Viscount Valentia	Nob. 97†					I6c
Power, Leonard	Merc.				90c	
Powey, Robert	Merc.					S6
Powlett, Charles, Lord, Marquis Winchester, Duke Bolton	Nob.					X2
Powlett, George	Unkn.	89				
Powlett, Hampden	Gent.	84, 89				
Powlett, Henry, Lord	Nob.	26				
Powlett, John, Lord, Marquis Winchester	Nob.	21				
**Powlett, John, Lord	Nob.	04–21		12		
Powlett, Richard	Kt. 91	04–14				
Powlett, Thomas	Unkn.	28				X2
Powlett, ?	Merc.		28			
Poyner, Bartholomew	Merc.					S6
Poynton, Daniel	Unkn.					P2
Poynts, Charles	Gent.					I4
Poyntz, John	Kt. 88	93				
Poyntz, Robert	Kt. 26	26–28				
Pratt, Henry	Merc.			09		
Pratt, John	Unkn.			09		
Pratt, Philip	Merc.					I7/M
Pratt, Roger	Gent.			87		
Pratt, Stephen	Unkn.					X2
Pratt, William	Unkn.	89				
Predis, William	Merc.					F1
Preen, John	Unkn.					X2
Preistley, William	Merc.		07	09		Q
Prentice, Thomas	Merc.					I7
Prescott, Alexander	Merc.		15			

360

Name & title	Class; date of knight-hood	Parlia-ments (starting dates)	E. Ind. Co.	Va. Co.	Levant Co.	Other companies
Prescott, Edward	Merc.		14			
Prescott, Jeffrey	Merc.		22	09		*I*7
Presey, Robert	Merc.					*S*6
Preston, Amias	Kt. 96			09c		*X*1
Preston, John	Gent.		17			
Preston, Raphe	Merc.		14			
**Preston, Thomas	Kt. 03	89, 04				
Prestwich, Edmund	Unkn.		25			
Prestwood, Thomas	Merc.	28				*S*1
Prettiford, Edward	Merc.					*F*1
Prettiford, Thomas	Merc.					*F*1
Pretty, George	Gent.			09		
Pretty, Robert	Merc.		15			
Priaulx, Peter	Merc.		23			*F*1
Price, Cadwallader	Gent.	84				
Price, Charles	Gent.	21–28				
Price, Gregory	Merc.	84–97				
Price, Henry	Unkn.			09		
Price, James	Gent.	93–01, 14–26				
**Price, John	Gent.	01, 26				
Price, Richard	Kt. 03	84, 89–93, 01, 14–21				
Price, Richard	Merc.			22		*I*7
Price, Roger	Unkn.					*I*1
Price, Stephen	Gent.	01				
Price, Thomas	Gent.	97				
Price, William	Merc.	93				
Price, William	Gent.	14–26				
Prichard, Edward	Merc.		24		13	*O*
Prickett, Abacuck	Merc.					*Q*
Prickett, Miles	Unkn.			?		
Prideaux, Humphrey	Unkn.	84				
Prideaux, Jonathan	Unkn.	25				
Prideaux, Thomas	Merc.					*F*1/*S*1
Prince, James	Unkn.					*X*2
Prince, Richard	Merc.					*L*1
Prince, William	Unkn.					*X*2
Pring, Martin	Merc.			22		*X*2
Pringle, John	Unkn.	26				
Printis, Robert	Unkn.	97				
Probe, Peter	Unkn.	93–97				
Proctor, Edward	Merc.			24		
Proctor, George	Pfl/y.			09		
Proctor, Jacob	Merc.		16			
Proctor, Jane	Merc.		18			
Proctor, John	Pfl/y.		12			
Proger, William-John	Gent.	89				
Proude, Lewis	Unkn.	14				
Proude, William	Unkn.			09		
Provis, Thomas	Unkn.	04				
Prowde, John	Merc.			09		*I*7

Name & title	Class; date of knighthood	Parliaments (starting dates)	E. Ind. Co.	Va. Co.	Levant Co.	Other companies
Prowse, Conrad	Unkn.	97				
Prowse, John	Unkn.	04–24				
Prowse, Lawrence	Merc.					X1
Prowse, Richard	Unkn.	84				
Prowse, Richard	Merc.					S1
Prowse, Robert	Merc.	84				
Prowse, Roger	Unkn.	24				
Prowse, Thomas	Unkn.					X2
Prusey, Ambrose	Gent.			09		
Pruson, Edward	Unkn.					X2
Prynne, John	Unkn.					X2
Prynne, William	Unkn.					X2
Puckering, John	Kt. 92	84–86				
Puckering, Thomas	Kt. 11	21, 25–28				Q
Puckle, Gabriel	Unkn.					X2
Puddy, John	Merc.					X1
Puddy, Robert	Merc.					X1
Puddy, William	Merc.					X1
Pugh, Roland	Unkn.	89				
Pugh, Roland	Unkn.	24–25				
Puleston, Roger	Kt. 17	84–93, 04		12		
Pulford, Richard	Unkn.					X2
Pulford, Thomas	Merc.					GG
Pulham, John	Merc.					S1
Puliston, Thomas	Merc.					J3
Pullison, Thomas	M. Kt. 85					E1g/S6c/W4/ X1
Pultney, John	Unkn.	01–04				
Purchas, Samuel	Pfl/y.			22		
Purchas, Thomas	Merc.	28				
Purefey, George	Unkn.	86				
Purefey, John	Merc.		18			
Purefey, Michael	Unkn.	84				
Purefey, Michael	Unkn.	21				
Purefey, Nicholas	Kt.†			18?		
Purefey, William	Unkn.	28				
Purefey, William	Merc.				18	
Purfrey, Thomas	Unkn.	89				
Purslowe, Thomas	Merc.		11			I2
Purslowe, Thomas	Gent.		23			
Puxton, John	Merc.	01, 26				
Pye, Edmund	Unkn.		17			
Pye, Robert	Kt. 21	21–28				
Pye, Thomas	Unkn.					X2
Pye, Walter	Kt. 30†	24–28				
**Pye, Walter	Gent.	21, 28				
Pye, Walter	Unkn.	97				
Pyke, Robert	Merc.					I7
Pykes, Walter	Merc.					S6
Pyle, William	Unkn.					X2
Pym, Alexander	Gent.	84				

Name & title	Class; date of knighthood	Parliaments (starting dates)	E. Ind. Co.	Va. Co.	Levant Co.	Other companies
Pym, Arthur	Gent.	24–26				
Pym, Henry	Merc.					*I7*
Pym, Hugh	Gent.	28				
Pym, John	Gent.	21–28				*T4/FF*
Pyne, Jasper	Merc.					*S1*
Pynnar, Nicholas	Gent.					*I4*
Pynner, William	Merc.					*S1*
Pyott, Richard	Merc.		00			
Pyott, Richard	Merc.		18			
Quaile, Richard	Unkn.					*X2*
Quarles, John	Merc.					*Mc/R1c*
Quarles, John	Merc.			09		
Quarles, Robert	Kt. 08	26				
Quarles, William	Merc.		09			*I2/M/P2/Q*
Quick, Michael	Merc.					*S1*
Quick, William	Merc.			09		*T2*
Quirke, James	Merc.	93				
Quirke, Robert	Merc.					*S1*
Radcliffe, Alexander	Kt. 26	28				
Radcliffe, Alexander	Unkn.	89				
Radcliffe, Frances Countess Sussex	Nob.					*W3*
Radcliffe, Edward Earl Sussex	Nob. 94	86–04				
Radcliffe, John	Kt. 99	14–26		09		
Radcliffe, John	Unkn.			09		
Radcliffe, John	Merc.	21, 28				
Radcliffe, Thomas Earl Sussex	Nob.					*W6/CC2*
Radcliffe, Thomas	Gent.	84				
Radford, Lawrence	Gent.					*CC1*
Radford, William	Merc.					*S6*
Rainbridge, John	Unkn.					*X1*
Rainsborowe, Henry	Merc.				10	
Rainsborowe, William	Unkn.					*X2*
Rainsford, Henry	Kt. 03		18c			
Rainsford, Miles	Unkn.	01				
Rainton, Nicholas	M. Kt. 33		18?			
Raleigh, Carew	Kt. 01	84–89, 01–04, 21		84		*I9/X1/CC1*
Raleigh, Carew	Gent.			23		*G7*
Raleigh, Gilbert	Gent.	14				
Raleigh, Walter	Kt. 84	84–86, 93–01		84		*G1/I9/Q1/X1/ CC1/GG2*
Ram, Anthony	Merc.		09			
Ramridge, John	Merc.		99			*S3*
Ramsay, John, Viscount Haddington, Earl Holderness	Nob.					*K4*
Ramsden, John	Kt. 19	28				

Name & title	Class; date of knight-hood	Parlia-ments (starting dates)	E. Ind. Co.	Va. Co.	Levant Co.	Other companies
Ramsden, Millicent	Unkn.			09		
Ramsden, William	Merc.					E2
Rand, John	Merc.		23			E3
Randall, Hugh	Merc.					X1
Randall, John	Merc.	97				X1
Randall, Noah	Merc.					S1/X1
Randall, Thomas	Merc.					X2
Randolph, Barnard	Pfl/y.					R1
Randolph, Thomas	Unkn.					W6
*Randolph, Thomas	Unkn.	84–89				
Rant, William	Pfl/y.		11			
Rashley, John	Merc.	89, 97				
Rashley, Jonathan	Merc.	14–21, 25				
Rashley, Robert	Merc.	28				
Rastell, Thomas	Merc.		28c			X2
Raven, William	Unkn.					I1
Raven, ?	Pfl/y.		23			
Ravenscroft, Robert	Gent.	14				
Ravenscroft, Thomas	Unkn.	21				
Ravenscroft, Thomas	Merc.					I7
Ravenscroft, William	Gent.	04–28		10		
Ravenscroft, William	Gent.	86, 97–01				
Ravenson, John	Unkn.					G4
Rawdon, Robert	Merc.			09		I7
Rawlins, Robert	Merc.					S1
Rawlins, Thomas	Unkn.	97				
Ray, Edward	Unkn.					X2
Ray, John	Gent.					I1
Raymell, Humphrey	Unkn.			18?		
Raymond, George	Merc.					X1
Rayney, John	Merc.			09	05	L1
Read, Clement	Merc.					E4/L1
Read, Edward	Unkn.					I9
Read, Gerard	Merc.		11			E4/L1c/Q
Read, Henry	Unkn.	89				
Read, Joan	Unkn.			22		
Read, John	Merc.					E4
Read, Lawrence	Merc.					E4/L1
Read, Morgan	Merc.					S1
Read, Thomas	Kt. 92	89–93				
Read, Thomas	Unkn.			22		
Read, William	Kt. 86	93				
Reasbrook, Phineas	Unkn.					X2
Redmayne, Marmaduke	Unkn.					I9
Reeves, John	Merc.		28		15	X2
Remchinge, Thomas	Unkn.	04				
Remcott, John	Merc.					F1
Remington, Robert	Kt. 96	04				I2
Reskeimer, James	Merc.					X2
Revell, John	Merc.					J3/P2
Revell, Thomas	Gent.	84–86				

Name & title	Class; date of knight-hood	Parlia-ments (starting dates)	E. Ind. Co.	Va. Co.	Levant Co.	Other companies
Revett, John	Merc.				06	$E3/L1$
Reynardson, Abraham	Unkn.		18			
Reynell, Carew	Kt. 99	93, 01, 14–21				
Reyner, Marmaduke	Unkn.			23		
Reynerson, Thomas	Merc.					$F1$
Reynolds, Augustine	Unkn.					$CC2$
Reynolds, Cuthbert	Unkn.	93				
Reynolds, Edward	Gent.	97–01				
Reynolds, George	Kt. 03	14				
Reynolds, Henry	Gent.			09		
Reynolds, Humphrey	Unkn.			09		
Reynolds, James	Merc.					$F1$
**Reynolds, John	Merc.			12		$F1/X1$
*Reynolds, John	Merc.					$X2$
Reynolds, Luke	Gent.					$X1$
Reynolds, Richard	Merc.					$S6c$
Reynolds, Richard	Merc.			09		$S6$
Reynolds, Richard	Unkn.	93				
Reynolds, Roland	Gent.		11			Q
Reynolds, Stephen	Unkn.					$X2$
Reynolds, Thomas	Kt. 25	24–28				
Reynolds, William	Merc.			09		$S6$
Rice, John	Unkn.	01				
Rice, Thomas	Merc.					$I7$
Rice, Walter	Kt. 03	84, 01–04				
Rich, Edward	Unkn.	24				
Rich, Edwin	Kt. 96		19			
Rich, Frances, Lady, Countess Warwick	Nob.					$J3$
Rich, Henry Earl Holland	Nob. 10	04–14		12		$G7/T3/FFg$
Rich, Nathaniel	Kt. 17	14–28		19c		$K4/T2/FFc$
Rich, Robert, Lord, Earl Warwick	Nob. 03	04–14	28	12c		$A/G6/K4/T2g/$ $X2/FF/GG3$
Rich, Robert, Lord, Earl Warwick	Nob.					A/GG
Rich, Robert, Lord, Earl Warwick	Nob.	28				
Rich, Robert	Unkn.			09		$T3$
Richards, Henry	Merc.					$R1/S6$
Richards, John	Unkn.					$X2$
Richardson, Abraham	Merc.				18	
Richardson, Edward	Merc.					$F1$
Richardson, John	Merc.					$F1$
Richardson, Thomas	Merc.		00			$L1$
Richardson, Thomas	Unkn.	21				
Richardson, William	Gent.		17			
*Richardson, ?	Unkn.	14				
Richaut, Peter	Merc.		19			$X2$
Richeson, ?	Unkn.	04				

Name & title	Class; date of knight- hood	Parlia- ments (starting dates)	E. Ind. Co.	Va. Co.	Levant Co.	Other companies
Riddell, John	Unkn.			12		
Riddell, Peter	Kt. 17	24, 26–28				
Riddell, Thomas	Kt. 16	21, 25, 28				
Riddleson, Stephen	Kt. 03	93		09		X1
Rider, Edward	Unkn.			21		
Ridge, Robert	Unkn.	84				
Ridges, John	Pfl/y.					CC2
Ridgeway, George	Gent.					I2
Ridgeway, John	Unkn.					I4
Ridgeway, Thomas	Gent.	84				
Ridgeway, Thomas Earl Londonderry	Nob. 00	04		09		I2
Ridgeway, ?	Gent.					CC1
Ridley, Robert	Merc.					I7
Ridley, Thomas	Unkn.	86, 01				
Rigdon, Robert	Gent.		17			
Rile, Walter	Merc.			09		I7
Rilston, Thomas	Merc.					I7
**Risely, Thomas	Unkn.	21–24		20		
Ritch, Thomas	Merc.		24			
Rithe, Christopher	Unkn.	84				
Rithe, Miles	Unkn.	84				
Rithe, Robert	Merc.	01				
Riveley, Nicholas	Merc.					F1
Rivers, George	Kt. 05	97–14, 25–28				GG
Rivers, John	M. Kt. 73					Mc/R1/S6
Rivett, Edward	Merc.					F1/S1
Rivett, Nicholas	Unkn.	24				
Rivett, Thomas	Unkn.					W2
Rivett, Thomas	Unkn.	97, 04				
Rivett, Thomas	M. Kt.†					AA1
Rivett, William	Merc.					AA2
Rivett, ?	Unkn.					J3
Roade, Richard	Merc.					F1
Robbins, George	Merc.		11	09		F1/I7/Q/T1
Robbins, Richard	Unkn.			18?		
Roberts, David	Unkn.	93				
Roberts, Edmund	Merc.					R1/BB1/GG
Roberts, Edward	Unkn.	24–26				
Roberts, Elias	Merc.		?	10		T2
Roberts, Elias	Unkn.			22		T3
Roberts, Elizabeth	Unkn.		24			
Roberts, George	Unkn.			10		
Roberts, Henry	Merc.					S6
Roberts, John Earl Radnor	Nob.					FF
Roberts, John	Unkn.	04				
*Roberts, John	Merc.					S1
Roberts, John	Gent.					CC1
Roberts, Lewis	Merc.				25	
Roberts, Tedder	Merc.		09	09		I7

366

Name & title	Class; date of knight-hood	Parlia-ments (starting dates)	E. Ind. Co.	Va. Co.	Levant Co.	Other companies
Roberts, Thomas	Merc.	04				X2
Roberts, William	Gent.					BB1
Robins, Arthur	Unkn.					I9
Robinson, Anthony	Unkn.	21–24				
Robinson, Arthur	Merc.		09	09		I2/Q
Robinson, Christopher	Merc.					F1
Robinson, Edward	Merc.			09		
Robinson, Henry	Unkn.		07			
Robinson, Henry	Merc.		99c	09		M
Robinson, Humphrey	Merc.		00c		00	Q
Robinson, Jehu	Gent.			09		
**Robinson, John	Merc.		99	09		F1/I9
Robinson, John	Gent.			12		
Robinson, Mary	Merc.			18		
Robinson, Robert	Merc.		00	09	13	I2/Q/X2
Robinson, Robert	Merc.		18			
Robinson, Roger	Unkn.					X2
Robinson, Thomas	Merc.					F1/S6
Robinson, William	Merc.	84, 89				
Robinson, William	Gent.		18			
Robinson, William	Merc.		07		11	F1/X2
Robinson, William	Merc.					I2
Robson, George	Merc.			09		
Robson, John	Unkn.	21				
Roch, Jerome	Unkn.					X2
Roch, Nicholas	Merc.					CC2
Roch, Thomas	Gent.					I2
Rochester, John	Unkn.					X2
Rockthorne, Humphrey	Merc.					S6
Rod, Chidiac	Merc.					S5
Rodde, James	Unkn.	21				
*Rodde, Richard	Merc.	21				
Rodde, Thomas	Merc.	24				
Rodford, John	Unkn.					CC1
Rodney, Edward	Kt. 14	21–28				
Rodney, John	Kt. 03	04				
Rodway, Richard	Merc.			09		
Roe, Francis	Kt. 03					I4
Roe, Henry	M. Kt. 03					I2/M
Roe, Henry	Merc.			09		I2
Roe, Jasper	Merc.				00	
Roe, John	Merc.			09		
Roe, Lawrence	Unkn.					J3
Roe, Owen	Merc.					J3
Roe, Thomas	Kt. 05	14–21		07c	21	G3/K3
Roe, Thomas	Merc.					I7
Rogers, Andrew	Gent.	84–89, 97				
Rogers, Daniel	Unkn.	89				
**Rogers, Edward	Gent.	84	?			I9/K2c
Rogers, George	Pfl/y.	19				
Rogers, Henry	Merc.					X1

367

Name & title	Class; date of knighthood	Parliaments (starting dates)	E. Ind. Co.	Va. Co.	Levant Co.	Other companies
Rogers, John	Gent.	84–89				
Rogers, John	Unkn.	01				
Rogers, Richard	Merc.		11	09		Q/T2
Rogers, Roger	Merc.					S1
Rogers, Thomas	Gent.	93				
Rogers, Thomas	Merc.					L1
Rogerson, John	Unkn.	04				
Rolfe, Henry	Unkn.			18?		
Rolfe, William	Merc.		11			
*Rolfe, William	Unkn.	28				
Rolle, Henry	Merc.	21–28				
Rolle, John	Merc.	01				
Rolle, John	Merc.	26–28			24	
Rolle, Samuel	Kt. 19	25				
Rolle, William	Merc.	04–14				
Rolleston, Richard	Unkn.					I2
Romney, Isaac	Merc.					Q
Romney, Rebecca	M. Kt.					Q/Z
Romney, William	M. Kt. 03		99g	06c	07	Mg/R2/S1c/Z
Romney, ?	Unkn.			09		
Ronyhedd, Richard	Merc.					S6c
Rookes, George	Merc.		14			X2
Rookes, George	Merc.					E1
Rookes, Newman	Unkn.					P2
Rookwood, ?	Unkn.			09		
Roope, Nicholas	Merc.					X2
Roos, John	Unkn.	97				
Roots, George	Unkn.					X2
Roper, Lancelot	Merc.	26				F1
Roscarrock, William	Gent.			12		
Rose, Alexander	Merc.		17			
Rose, John	Merc.		15	09		L1
*Rose, John	Merc.	84–86				
Rosewell, Henry	Kt. 19					J1/GG
Rosse, George	Merc.					F1
Rosse, Richard	Merc.	21				
Rosse, Thomas	Merc.					S6
Rossiter, Edward	Gent.					J3
Rotheram, Edward	Merc.			18?		I1c/M/GG
Rotheram, George	Gent.	84–86, 93–97				
Route, Stephen	Unkn.					X2
Rowborrowe, John	Merc.					S1
Rowe, Gregory	Unkn.					X2
Rowe, William	Unkn.					X2
Rowland, Henry	Unkn.			20		
Rowland, Thomas	Merc.					S6
*Rowle, John	Merc.					S6
Rowle, Stephen	Merc.					I7
Rowley, Francis	Merc.					I2/S6
Rowley, John	Gent.					I1
Rowley, Thomas	Unkn.					N

Name & title	Class; date of knight-hood	Parlia-ments (starting dates)	E. Ind. Co.	Va. Co.	Levant Co.	Other companies
Rowley, William	Merc.					*R2*
Rowse, Ambrose	Gent.	04				
Rowse, Anthony	Kt. 03	84, 04				
Rowse, Anthony	Unkn.	28				
Rowse, Dennis	Unkn.					*X1*
Rowse, Francis	Gent.	26–28				
Rowse, John	Kt. 07	26				
Rowse, John	Kt. 05	24–26				
Rowse, Richard	Merc.					*S6*
Rowse, Simon	Unkn.					*G7*
Rowse, William	Gent.	25				
Roy, John	Merc.	14				*S4/X2*
Roydon, Marmaduke	Merc.	28				*F1/O/X2/GG2*
Royell, Roger	Merc.					*S4*
Rudhall, John	Unkn.	25–26				
Rudyard, Benjamin	Kt. 18	21–28				*FF*
Rudyard, James	Merc.		24			
Rugg, Francis	Unkn.	89				
Rumbald, Francis	Merc.					*S4*
Rummo, William	Unkn.					*X2*
Rusham, Jeffrey	Unkn.	86				
Russell, Daniel	Unkn.			22		
Russell, Edward Earl Bedford	Nob.			12		*T2*
Russell, Edward	Unkn.					*I2*
Russell, Francis Earl Bedford	Nob.					*W2*
Russell, Francis	Kt. 07	04				
Russell, Francis Earl Bedford	Nob. 70	84				
Russell, James	Unkn.					*X2*
Russell, James	Unkn.		09			
Russell, John	Kt. 87	84–89				
Russell, John	Merc.		09			
Russell, Lucy Countess Bedford	Nob.			12		*T2*
Russell, Richard	Unkn.					*X2*
Russell, Robert	Merc.					*CC2*
**Russell, Thomas	Merc.					*E1g/I7/L1/S6*
**Russell, Thomas	Gent.	01, 14				
*Russell, Thomas	Merc.					*F1/GG*
Russell, William	M. Kt. 18	26	09c	09	05	*I2/Qc/R2/X1/ Z*
Russell, William	Gent.	25				
Russell, ?	Merc.					*I7*
Russon, John	Gent.					*I4*
Rutlidge, Edward	Gent.					*I4*
Rycarbye, John	Merc.					*S6*
Rymell, Hugh	Merc.		09			
Ryther, James	Unkn.	86				
Ryves, John	Unkn.	14				*I9*

Name & title	Class; date of knighthood	Parliaments (starting dates)	E. Ind. Co.	Va. Co.	Levant Co.	Other companies
Ryves, John	Merc.				28	
Sabin, Richard	Merc.					I2
Sacheverell, Francis	Gent.?					I2
Sacheverell, Henry	Merc.					I7
Sacheverell, John	Unkn.					X2
Sachfield, John	Merc.					S6/X1
Sackford, Henry	M. Kt. 03			09		S6/X1
Sackford, William	Unkn.					W2
Sackville, Anne Countess Dorset	Nob.					G7
Sackville, Edward Earl Dorset	Nob. 16	21		12c		Q/T3g
Sackville, John	Gent.	25–26				
Sackville, Richard Earl Dorset	Nob.			09c		G6
Sackville, Robert Earl Dorset	Nob.	84, 89–04				
Sackville, Thomas, Lord Buckhurst, Earl Dorset	Nob.					S1/GG
Sad, Stephen	Unkn.			18?		
Sadler, Edmund	Gent.					A
Sadler, Edward	Merc.				92	DD
Sadler, Francis	Merc.		11			Q
**Sadler, Henry	Gent.	84–86				I1
Sadler, Nicholas	Merc.		27			
Sadler, Ralph	Kt. 47†	84–86				
Sadler, Robert	Merc.				90	D/W4/X1/ DD/GG
Sadler, Roland	Merc.					I7
St. Amand, John	Unkn.	24–25				
St. Aubyn, John	Gent.	14–21				
St. Aubyn, Thomas	Gent.	01, 14, 26				
St. Barbe, Edward	Unkn.					I9
St. John, Alexander	Kt. 08	14–28				
St. John, Anthony	Kt. 08	24–28				
St. John, Beauchamp	Kt. 19	21, 26–28				
St. John, Henry	Kt. 19	21–25				
St. John, Henry	Unkn.		29		28	
St. John, Henry	Unkn.	89–93				
St. John, John	Kt. 09	24		09		
St. John, Oliver, Lord Tregoz, Viscount Grandison	Nob. 00	93, 04–14				I5c
St. John, Oliver	Gent.			19		A/FF
St. John, Oliver, Lord, Earl Bolingbroke	Nob. 10	01–04				
St. John, Oliver, Lord	Nob.	89–97				
St. John, Oliver, Lord	Nob.	24–28		22		G7
St. John, Roland	Kt. 16	14, 25				
St. John, William	Kt. 07			09c		Ag

Name & title	Class; date of knighthood	Parliaments (starting dates)	E. Ind. Co.	Va. Co.	Levant Co.	Other companies
St. Leger, Anthony	Kt. 93					*I5c*
St. Leger, John	Kt. 49†	84				
St. Leger, Warham	Kt. 65					*I9*
St. Leger, Warham	Kt. 08			12		
St. Poll, George	Kt. 93	89–93, 04				
Saker, William	Unkn.					*G7/X2*
Salbank, Joseph	Merc.		00			
Sales, William	Merc.			09		
Salford, Richard	Merc.					*A*
Salisbury, John	Kt. 97	01				
Salisbury, John	Merc.					*F1/S1*
Salisbury, John	Gent.	26				
Salisbury, John	Merc.					*F1*
Salisbury, Pirseus	Merc.					*S6*
Salisbury, Robert	Gent.	86–89				
Salisbury, William	Gent.	21				
Salkins, William	Merc.					*E1*
Salleneuve, Peter	Merc.					*X2*
Salmon, Christopher	Unkn.			09		
Salter, Edward	Kt. 21	04		12		
Salter, George	Merc.				92	*S5*
Salter, Nicholas	M. Kt. 18		00	09	90c	*Qc*
Salter, Robert	Merc.				19	*X2*
Salter, Thomas	Merc.				16	
**Salter, William	Merc.	89, 04				*S6c*
Salter, William	Merc.				18	
Salter, ?	Unkn.	21				
Saltonstall, Charles	Merc.					*X2*
Saltonstall, Richard	M. Kt. 97	86	99		92	*Mg/R1/S6c/ X1/GG*
Saltonstall, Richard	M. Kt. 17					*J3*
Saltonstall, Samuel	M. Kt. 03†			12		*G7/S1/X1/GG*
Saltren, Richard	Merc.					*S6*
Saltren, William	Merc.					*S6*
Saman, Robert	Merc.		09c			*X2*
Sambach, William	Unkn.			09		
Sambrooke, Jeremy	Merc.		18			
Sameflow, John	Merc.					*I7*
Samford, Robert	Merc.					*S6*
Samford, William	Merc.					*X1*
Sammes, George	Gent.			12		
Sammes, John	Kt. 99	04–14		10c		*Q*
Samon, Edward	Merc.					*F1*
Samon, William	Unkn.					*X2*
Sampson, John	Gent.			87		
Sampson, Thomas	Merc.					*CC2*
Samuell, George	Merc.					*S1*
Samwayes, Henry	Merc.					*S1*
Sandcrofte, John	Merc.		14			
Sandy, John	Merc.					*S6*
Sandys, Edward	Unkn.			12		

Name & title	Class; date of knighthood	Parliaments (starting dates)	E. Ind. Co.	Va. Co.	Levant Co.	Other companies
Sandys, Edwin	Kt. 03	86–93, 04–26	11c	07g		T1
Sandys, Edwin	Kt. 17	14–21	18	12		
**Sandys, Edwin	Kt. 99	14				I9
Sandys, George	Kt. 26	26–28		09		
Sandys, George	Gent.			12c		T3
Sandys, Henry	Gent.			09		
Sandys, Henry	Gent.	25		12		
Sandys, Miles	Kt. 03	14–21, 28				
Sandys, Miles	Kt. 19	25				
Sandys, Miles	Gent.	84–97				
Sandys, Richard	Unkn.	01				
Sandys, Richard	Gent.			09		
Sandys, Samuel	Kt. 03	86, 04–21		09c		T2
Sandys, Thomas	Gent.			09		
Sandys, William	Kt. †	14				
Sanford, Hugh	Unkn.	97–04				
Sanford, John	Merc.					S1
Sanford, John	Merc.					S1
Sanford, Thomas	Unkn.	97				
Santy, Thomas	Merc.			09		
Saris, George	Merc.		11			
Saris, John	Merc.		11			
Saris, Thomas	Merc.					R1
Saule, Thomas	Unkn.					I1c
Saunders, Blase	Merc.					H/R1c/S6c
Saunders, Carew	Merc.		22			M
Saunders, Daniel	Merc.					L1
Saunders, Drew	Merc.					H/R1
Saunders, Edmund	Unkn.	84–86				
**Saunders, John	Merc.	21–28	18			
Saunders, John	Merc.					S6
**Saunders, Nicholas	Kt. 03	89–04, 26				
Saunders, Richard	Unkn.					X2
Saunders, Robert	Merc.			09		
Saunders, Simon	Unkn.					M/Q1
Saunders, Thomas	Merc.	86–01				
Saunderson, John	Merc.				00	GG
Saunderson, Nicholas	Kt. 03	93, 25				
Saunderson, Robert	Unkn.	89				
Saunderson, Robert	Merc.				90	
Saunderson, Robert	Pfl/y.					G8
Saunderson, William	Merc.			84		G1/Q1/X1/CC2
Savage, Edward	Unkn.	84–86, 01				
**Savage, Edward	Unkn.	14, 26–28				
Savage, John	Gent.	86–89				
Savage, John, Viscount, Earl Rivers	Nob. 24	24–25				
Savage, Robert	Merc.					C/S1c
Savage, William	Unkn.	21–24				
Savery, Christopher	Merc.	84, 93				
Savery, Richard	Merc.					S1

Name & title	Class; date of knighthood	Parliaments (starting dates)	E. Ind. Co.	Va. Co.	Levant Co.	Other companies
Savery, Timothy	Merc.					S1
Savile, George	Kt. 87	86, 93				
Savile, George	Kt. 03	01, 14, 24‡				
Savile, Henry	Merc.				15	
**Savile, Henry	Kt. 03	89–93, 04–14, 28				
Savile, John, Lord	Nob. 97†	86, 97, 04–14, 24, 26				
Savile, Thomas, Lord, Viscount, Earl Sussex	Nob. 17	24, 28				GG
Savile, William	Unkn.			22		
Saving, John	Merc.					S4
Sawle, John	Gent.	24				
Sawyer, Edmund	Kt. 25	24–25, 28				
Sawyer, ?	Unkn.					X2
Sayer, Richard	Unkn.	89, 97				
Scales, Richard	Merc.					I7
Scamler, James	Unkn.	84				
Scarpe, John	Unkn.			09		
Scattergood, Anthony	Merc.		19			
Scobell, John	Unkn.					X2
Scoles, Mark	Unkn.					X1
Scorye, Silvanus	Unkn.	97				
**Scott, Edmund	Merc.	01, 14–24	01c	12		L1/M/Q/T2
Scott, Edward	Kt. 26	26–28				
Scott, Edward	Merc.				10	
Scott, Elizabeth	Unkn.			10		
Scott, George	Merc.		09	09c		Q/T1
Scott, John	Kt. 88	04–14		07c		
Scott, Leonard	Merc.					E2
Scott, Reginald	Gent.	89				
Scott, Robert	Merc.		19			F1
Scott, Thomas	Kt. 70	86				
Scott, Thomas	Gent.	86		09		
Scott, Thomas	Merc.					X1
Scott, Thomas	Gent.	24, 28				
Scott, William	Merc.					E2/F1
Scott, William	Unkn.	01				
Scras, Tuppyn	Merc.					X2
Scras, William	Merc.					X2
Scriven, Reginald	Unkn.	86–01				
Scrivener, Matthew	Gent.			09		
Scrope, Henry	Gent.	89–01				
Scrope, Thomas, Lord	Nob. 85	84, 89				GG
Scudamore, Clement	M. Kt. 05					I7
Scudamore, Clement	Unkn.					I1c
Scudamore, James	Kt.†	04–14		10		
Scudamore, John	Kt. 96	84–89, 97				
Scudamore, John	Kt. 20	21–25, 28		?		
Seabright, William	Gent.			09		
Seager, Edward	Merc.		18			

Name & title	Class; date of knighthood	Parliaments (starting dates)	E. Ind. Co.	Va. Co.	Levant Co.	Other companies
Searl, Thomas	Merc.					S6
Seavy, William	Unkn.					X2
Seaward, Isaac	Unkn.			19		
Seaward, Samuel	Unkn.			22		
Seckford, Henry	Unkn.					G7
Sedborough, John	Gent.					I2
Sedgwick, John	Merc.					I7/S6/CC2
Seely, Thomas	Merc.					E3/X2
Selby, George	M. Kt. 03	01–14				
Selby, John	Kt. 05	14–21, 25				
Selby, John	Unkn.					X2
Selby, William	Gent.	89–01				
Selby, William	Kt. 03	01–14				
Selden, John	Pfl/y.	24, 26–28		?		
Sells, Thomas	Merc.					F1
Seluen, Thomas	Unkn.	97				
Semeon, George	Kt. 04†	14–24				
Semper, Nathaniel	Merc.		17			
Semper, Owen	Merc.		08			
Sendall, Thomas	Merc.					S1
Senyor, Robert	Merc.			09		
Seracold, Raphe	Merc.?		14			
Seracold, Thomas	Merc.		11			I2/S3/GG
Seracold, William	Merc.					Q/R2
Serle, John	Unkn.	14				
Servye, John	Merc.					F1
Sewall, Henry	Merc.	21				
Sewall, Thomas	Merc.					X1
Sewster, Edward	Merc.		24			
Sewter, Henry	Merc.					E3/F1
Sexton, George	Unkn.					I6c
Seyer, Thomas	Gent.			09		
Seymour, Edward Earl Hertford	Nob.			20		X1/GG
Seymour, Edward	Kt. 03	01, 14–25	25			K4/X2
Seymour, Edward	Kt. 11	93, 01–04				K2c
Seymour, Francis, Lord	Nob. 13	21–25, 28				
**Seymour, John	Unkn.	89				I9
Seymour, William, Earl & Marquis Hertford, Duke Somerset	Nob. 16	21				
Seymour, ?	Kt.		25			
Shacley, William	Merc.			09		
Shales, William	Unkn.				92	
Shapleigh, Alexander	Unkn.					X2
Shapleigh, John	Unkn.					X2
Shapler, John	Merc.					F1
Shappey, Robert	Merc.					S6
Shapton, Christopher	Merc.					I7
Share, William	Merc.					F1
Sharowe, John	Unkn.					X2

374

Name & title	Class; date of knighthood	Parliaments (starting dates)	E. Ind. Co.	Va. Co.	Levant Co.	Other companies
Sharp, Samuel	Merc.					J3/P2
Sharp, Thomas	Merc.					J3
Sharp, William	Unkn.			09		
Sharpulls, John	Merc.					F1
Shaw, Francis	Merc.					S1
Shaw, George	Merc.					I7
Shaw, John	Merc.			09		
Shaw, Leonard	Merc.					S4
Shaw, Randall	Merc.					W4
Shaw, Robert	Merc.					E3
Shawcroft, William	Merc.					S6
Sheere, Arthur	Merc.		24		11c	X2
Sheere, William	Merc.					S1
Sheering, ?	Unkn.					I8
Sheffield, Edmund	Kt. 03	04				
Sheffield, Edmund, Lord, Earl Mulgrave	Nob. 88			09c		G7/K4/GG1
Sheffield, John	Kt. 05	01–04				
Sheffield, William	Kt. 17	14, 24				
Shelbery, John	Unkn.	93				
Shelley, Henry	Unkn.	86, 04		09		
Shelley, Henry	Unkn.	14				
Shelley, Thomas	Unkn.	14				
Shelley, Walter	Unkn.			18?		
Shelton, Ralph	Kt. 07			12		
Shelton, ?	Unkn.			09		
Shepherd, George	Unkn.					X2
Shepherd, John	Merc.					I7
Shepherd, Stephen	Merc.					I7
*Sheppard, John	Merc.					X1
Sheppard, Matthew	Merc.			09		T2
Sheppard, Richard	Unkn.			09		
**Sheppard, Thomas	Merc.	21	19	19c		L1/M
Sheppard, William	Merc.					M/GG
Sherfielde, Henry	Unkn.	21–28				
Sherland, Christopher	Gent.	24–28				FF
Sherman, Gabriel	Merc.					X2
Sherratt, Henry	Merc.					S1
Sherren, Thomas	Unkn.					X2
Sherrington, John	Merc.		09			F1/S3/X2
Sherrington, William	Merc.					B/M/S1
Sherston, William	Merc.	84–86, 93–04				
Sherwill, Nicholas	Merc.			18		F1/X2
Sherwill, Richard	Merc.					F1
Sherwill, Thomas	Merc.	14–28		18		F1
Sheward, Robert	Merc.					S6
Shilds, Thomas	Merc.			12		
Shilleto, George	Unkn.	21				
Shilton, Richard	Kt. 25	26–28				
Shipley, Hugh	Gent.			09		
Shipton, Thomas	Merc.		00	09		I7

Name & title	Class; date of knight-hood	Parlia-ments (starting dates)	E. Ind. Co.	Va. Co.	Levant Co.	Other companies
Shipton, Thomas	Unkn.		09			
Shirley, Anthony	Kt. 91					X1/GG1
Shirley, James	Merc.		24			P2
Shirley, John	Gent.	84, 89, 04				
**Shirley, John	Kt. 03	93–97, 04, 25				
Shirley, Thomas	Kt. 73	84, 93, 01				
Shirley, Thomas	Kt. 89	84, 93, 01–21	10			X1
Shirley, Thomas	Gent.	97				
Shopley, John	Merc.					S1c
Shore, John	Merc.					S1
Short, John	Merc.					N
Short, Robert	Merc.					S6
Short, William	Merc.		09			
Shorter, Richard	Merc.					S3
Shorter, Solomon	Merc.					S4
Shorter, William	Merc.					S1
Shoter, Thomas	Unkn.	89				
Shurt, George	Merc.					F1
Shute, Richard	Unkn.	93				
Shute, Robert	Unkn.	21				
Shute, William	Merc.					X1
Shuter, John	Unkn.	24–26				
Siddenham, Michael	Unkn.					I9
Sidney, Henry	Kt. 49					R1/BB1/CC2/ GG
Sidney, Philip	Kt. 83	84				W6/X1/CC2/ GG
Sigesmult, John	Merc.					F1
Silvester, Emanuel	Merc.					X1
Simonds, Thomas	Merc.		99		92c	E4/L1c/S6
Simonds, Thomas	Merc.		18		18	X2
Simons, Robert	Unkn.		19			
Simpson, Henry	Merc.					E2
Simpson, Nicholas	Merc.					E1
Simpson, William	Merc.					X2
Singe, Richard	Unkn.	14				
Singleton, Richard	Merc.					F1
Singleton, Robert	Unkn.		09			
Singleton, William	Merc.					F1
Sipthorpe, Edward	Gent.					I8
Skedyngton, William	Merc.					S6
Skeete, John	Merc.				05	
Skeffington, John	Kt. 24	26				
Skeffington, Richard	Kt. 24	25				
Skeffington, Thomas	Gent.	93				
Skegge, Edward	Merc.					S4
Skelton, James	Unkn.		09			
Skelton, William	Merc.					F2/L1/M/S2/ GG1
Skeyre, John	Merc.					I7
Skidmore, William	Merc.					S6

Name & title	Class; date of knight-hood	Parlia-ments (starting dates)	E. Ind. Co.	Va. Co.	Levant Co.	Other companies
Skinner, Anthony	Merc.				06c	
Skinner, Augustine	Unkn.		99			*F*1
Skinner, George	Merc.					*S*1
Skinner, Nicholas	Merc.		08			*S*1
Skinner, Vincent	Kt. 03	84–97, 04				
Skinner, William	Gent.	26				
Skip, Thomas	Merc.					*I*2
Skipwith, Edward	Gent.	01				
Skipwith, Henry	Gent.	84–86				
Skipwith, William	Kt. 03	01–04				
*Skutt, George	Unkn.					*X*2
Skybow, John	Merc.					*S*4
Slack, William	Merc.					*S*1
Slany, Henry	Kt.†					*T*2
Slany, Humphrey	Merc.		19c	20	12	*A*/*M*/*Nc*/*S*4/ *X*2/*GG*2
Slany, Humphrcy	Merc.				18	
Slany, John	Merc.		10			*I*1c/*M*/*Ng*/*R*1/ *X*2/*GG*1
Slany, Moses	Merc.					*X*2
Slany, Richard	Merc.					*X*2
Slater, Francis	Merc.		27			
Slater, William	Merc.					*I*7
Slatter, Thomas	Merc.					*E*1
Slee, George	Merc.					*S*1
Slee, George	Merc.					*S*1
Slee, Richard	Merc.					*S*1
Slegge, Roger	Merc.	84–89				
Sleigh, Richard	Merc.					*I*7
Slighe, Edmund	Merc.	04				
Slingesby, Francis	Gent.	84				
Slingesby, Henry	Kt. 02	01–24				
Slingesby, Henry	Gent.	25				
Slingesby, William	Kt. 03	97–04, 26				*GG*
Slingesby, ?	Unkn.			09		
Slowin, John	Unkn.					*X*2
Sly, John	Merc.					*X*1
Smallman, Francis	Merc.	21, 26		12		
Smarte, John	Unkn.					*X*2
Smarte, William	Unkn.	89				
Smartfote, Thomas	Merc.			09		*I*7
Smethwicke, Thomas	Merc.		24			*R*2
Smith, Anthony	Merc.					*I*7
Smith, Barnabas	Merc.					*I*7
Smith, Barnard	Merc.					*CC*1
Smith, Cleophas	Merc.			09		*T*2
*Smith, Edmund	Merc.					*S*6
Smith, Edmund	Unkn.			09		
Smith, Edward	Merc.			09		
*Smith, Edward	Unkn.	14				
Smith, Elias	Merc.		22			

Name & title	Class; date of knighthood	Parliaments (starting dates)	E. Ind. Co.	Va. Co.	Levant Co.	Other companies
Smith, Ezekiel	Unkn.		09			
Smith, Fabian	Merc.					R2
Smith, George	Merc.					M/S6/CC2
Smith, George	Merc.		27	22	28	I1c/T2
Smith, George	Unkn.	24				
Smith, George	Kt. 03	04				
Smith, Gilbert	Merc.					C/S1
Smith, Henry	Merc.		27		10	
Smith, Hugh	Unkn.					W2
Smith, Humphrey	Merc.		00c	10	05	I7/Q/R2
Smith, Humphrey	Merc.		17c		27	
Smith, James	Gent.	97				
Smith, James	Gent.	97				
Smith, Jeremy	Merc.		17			
Smith, Jessy	Gent.					I9
Smith, John	Kt. 03	84–89, 04		09		AA3
Smith, John	Kt. 14†	25–26				
*Smith, John	Kt. 17	26	19	12c		Q
Smith, John	Pfl/y.			09		J3/X2
Smith, John	Gent.	21	24	12		T3
Smith, John	Unkn.	89				
*Smith, John	Gent.					CC2
Smith, John	Merc.					S6/CC2
Smith, John	Merc.				13c	F1
Smith, Jonathan	Unkn.			18?		
Smith, Leonard	Merc.					I7
Smith, Matthew	Unkn.					W2
Smith, Nicholas	Kt. 03	93–97, 14				
Smith, Nicholas	Merc.			09	06	F1/S3
Smith, Noah	Merc.			09		
Smith, Othowell	Merc.			09		F1/I7
Smith, Philip	Merc.					F1/S1
Smith, Philip	Merc.					S3
Smith, Phineas	Merc.					S6
Smith, Richard	M. Kt. 03	84, 01, 14‡	14	12	12	Q/R2/T2
Smith, Richard	Merc.			09		F1/M
Smith, Richard	Unkn.					X2
Smith, Robert	Merc.		18	09c		I7/M/S1/T2/ X2
Smith, Samuel	Unkn.			09		
Smith, Simon	Merc.		24			E4/L1/S4
Smith, Thomas	M. Kt. 96	04–21	99g	06g	05	F1g/Qg/R1g/ S1c/T1g/U/Z K2c
Smith, Thomas	Kt. 03					
Smith, Thomas	Merc.			89	81g	Q1/R1/S6/W4/ AA1g/BB1/ CC1
Smith, Thomas	Unkn.	97				
Smith, Thomas	Merc.			12	24	F1/L2/M/Q/ S1
Smith, Thomas	Unkn.	89–93				

Name & title	Class; date of knighthood	Parliaments (starting dates)	E. Ind. Co.	Va. Co.	Levant Co.	Other companies
**Smith, Thomas	Merc.	26–28	18			
Smith, Triamore	Merc.					*I7*
Smith, Walter	Merc.					*F1/S1*
Smith, Warren	Unkn.					*T2*
Smith, William	Merc.	86				*S6*
Smith, William	Kt. 03	89, 04‡	00c	12		
*Smith, William	M. Kt. 23†		10		00	*E3/I2*
Smithers, George	Unkn.					*I7c*
Smithers, John	Merc.					*E3*
*Smithes, George	Merc.		00c			*I8*
Snagg, Thomas	Gent.	86–89				
Snagg, Thomas	Gent.	86				
Snawsell, George	Merc.				21	
Snead, Thomas	Merc.		09	09		*F1/I2*
Snelling, Charles	Merc.		29			*R2c*
Snelling, Edward	Gent.					*CC1*
Snelling, Richard	Merc.					*S1*
Snelling, Robert	Merc.	14–26	11			*E3/F1*
Snelling, Walter	Merc.					*F1/S1c*
Snelling, William	Merc.					*I7*
Snigge, George	Kt. 05	89, 97–04				
Snigge, George	Merc.					*S6*
Snode, Giles	Merc.					*S1*
Snott, John	Merc.					*F1*
Snowe, John	Unkn.	93–97				
Snowe, Thomas	Merc.					*S1*
Soame, John	Merc.				15	*L1*
Soame, Stephen	M. Kt. 99	01	99	09	10	*E4/F1/H/I7/ L1/S3*
Soame, Stephen	Merc.				06	*L1*
Soame, Thomas	Merc.		11		11c	*L1/R2c/X2*
Soane, Joseph	Unkn.		09			
Soane, Sidrake	Unkn.		18			
Soda, Anthony	Unkn.					*I7c*
Solda, Richard	Merc.					*S1*
Solden, William	Merc.					*M*
Somaster, Henry	Unkn.	86				
Somell, Henry	Merc.					*C*
Somers, George	Kt. 03	04		06		*T3/X1*
Somers, John	Merc.					*R1c/W3*
Somerset, Edward Earl Worcester	Nob.		09			*I2/Q/GG*
Somerset, Thomas	Kt. 05	01–04				*G6*
Sondes, Michael	Kt. 98	84–89, 97–04		09c		
South, Edward	Merc.					*F1*
South, Nicholas	Merc.					*F1*
South, Robert	Merc.		29			
Southcote, George	Gent.	97				
Southcote, John	Merc.					*R1*
Southcote, Richard	Gent.	93				
Southcote, Thomas	Merc.					*M/Q1*

Name & title	Class; date of knighthood	Parliaments (starting dates)	E. Ind. Co.	Va. Co.	Levant Co.	Other companies
Southcote, Thomas	Gent.					J3
Southerne, William	Unkn.			09		
Southerton, Elias	Merc.			23	12	
Southerton, George	Merc.	93–97	11	09		F1/S6
Southerton, Nowell	Unkn.	89–97				
Southerton, Thomas	Unkn.	97				
Southey, Henry	Unkn.			21		
Southland, William	Merc.	84–89				
Southmead, John	Gent.					GG
Southwell, Francis	Unkn.					I1
Southwell, Robert	Kt. 85	97				
Southwell, William	Unkn.	21–24				
Southwick, George	Merc.					X1
Southwick, John	Unkn.			09		
Southwick, Robert	Merc.					X1
Southwick, Thomas	Merc.		00		05c	F1/Q/R2/S3
Southworth, Henry	Merc.					I2/Q
Southworth, Thomas	Unkn.	14–24				
Sowthehouse, Christopher	Unkn.	84				
Sozar, John	Merc.					S4
Spalding, Augustine	Merc.		14			
Sparchford, Richard	Merc.			09		
**Sparke, John	Unkn.	28				X2
Sparke, John	Merc.					R1c/S6/X1
Sparke, Peter	Merc.			09		
Sparke, Robert	Merc.					S6
Sparke, Thomas	Merc.			09		S6
Sparke, Thomas	Merc.					S6
Sparke, William	Merc.					X1
Sparpoule, John	Unkn.		11			
Sparrow, Stephen	Merc.			09		I7/T3
Sparry, Richard	Unkn.	93				
Sparthe, John	Merc.					F1
Sparthe, William	Merc.					S6
Speccott, Paul	Unkn.	24–28				
Speccott, Peter	Unkn.	24				
Speckart, Abraham	Merc.			12		I2/T2
Speecott, ?	Unkn.	04				
Speight, Marmaduke	Merc.					GG
Speight, William	Merc.					F1c/I7/S1
Speke, George	Unkn.					I9
Spelman, Henry	Kt. 03	93–97, 25				G6/K5
Spence, John	Merc.					S4
Spence, Robert	Merc.				05	
Spencer, Adam	Unkn.		18			
Spencer, Edmund	Merc.		00			
Spencer, Edmund	Gent.					I9
Spencer, Edward	Kt. 25	21–26		?		
Spencer, Humphrey	Merc.					N/S1c
Spencer, John	M. Kt. 95		99		90	M/R1/S6c/GG1

Name & title	Class; date of knight-hood	Parlia-ments (starting dates)	E. Ind. Co.	Va. Co.	Levant Co.	Other companies
Spencer, John	Unkn.			09		
Spencer, John	Unkn.					J3/X2
Spencer, Richard	Kt. 03	84, 89, 04		10		
Spencer, Richard	Gent.	21–28				
Spencer, Richard	Merc.			09		
Spencer, Robert, Lord	Nob.			12		G7
Spencer, Robert, Lord	Nob. 01	97				
Spencer, Robert	Merc.					I7
Spencer, Thomas	Kt. 12	04				
Spencer, Thomas	Merc.					I2
Spencer, Urie	Unkn.			09		
Spencer, William, Lord	Nob. 16	14–28				
Spencer, William	Unkn.	84–86				
Spencer, William	Merc.					I7
Spicer, Christopher	Merc.					S1
Spicer, John	Unkn.	04				
Spicer, Nicholas	Merc.					C/E3/S1c
Spicer, Richard	Merc.					S6
Spicer, Thomas	Merc.					M/S6/CC2
Spicer, William	Merc.	97–04				
Spike, Thomas	Merc.		19		10	
Spiller, Henry	Kt. 18	14–28				
Spiller, Robert	Kt. 22	21–24				
Spillman, Daniel	Merc.					I7
Spillman, John	Gent.	26				
Spinola, Benedict	Merc.					AA1c
Sprake, Richard	Merc.					S1
Spranger, Henry	Unkn.			09		
Spray, Christopher	Unkn.	14				
Spray, Nicholas	Unkn.	04				
Springe, William	Kt. 11	24–25, 28				
Springham, Matthew	Merc.			09		I1c/R2
Springham, Richard	Merc.					M/R1/AA1
Sprinson, Hildebrand	Unkn.			09		T2
Sprint, Gregory	Gent.	86–89		12		
Sprint, William	Unkn.	86				
Sprott, Jeremy	Merc.					L1
Sprott, Roger	Merc.			09		
Sprott, William	Merc.			09		
Spry, Henry	Unkn.			09		
Spurling, John	Unkn.	86–89				
Spurstowe, William	Merc.		23c			I2/J3
Spurwaie, Walter	Merc.					S1?c
Squire, Roland	Merc.		24			
Squire, William	Merc.					S1
Stables, Robert	Unkn.	14				
Stacy, Thomas	Unkn.			17		
Stafford, Edmund	Gent.					CC2
Stafford, Edward	Kt. 83	93–04				
Stafford, John	Kt. 96	84–86, 01				
Stafford, Reade	Unkn.	93–97				

Name & title	Class; date of knighthood	Parliaments (starting dates)	E. Ind. Co.	Va. Co.	Levant Co.	Other companies
Stafford, Richard	Unkn.			09		
Stafford, Thomas	Kt. 11	93, 21–24				
Stale, Edward	Merc.			09		
Stallarge, John	Merc.					*F1*
Stallenge, William	Merc.	97–01		09		
Stamford, William	Merc.					*I7*
Stampe, John	Unkn.	84				
*Stampe, John	Merc.					*L1/M*
Stampe, Thomas	Unkn.	86–89				
Standish, Francis	Merc.					*L1*
Stanfast, Walter	Merc.					*S6*
Stanford, John	Merc.	93				
Stanford, John	Merc.	97				
Stanford, Robert	Kt. 03	04				
Stanhawe, William	Unkn.					*I2*
Stanhope, Edward	Kt.†	01				
Stanhope, Edward	Unkn.	84–86				
Stanhope, Edward	Gent.	01				
Stanhope, Henry	Kt. 26	25–28				
Stanhope, John, Lord	Nob. 96	84–89, 97–01		09c		*C*
Stanhope, John	Kt. 03	04‡				
*Stanhope, John	Kt. 07	24–28				
Stanhope, Michael	Kt. 03	84, 97–04				
Stanhope, Thomas	Kt. 75	86				
Stanlack, Anthony	Merc.					*E1*
Stanlack, William	Merc.					*S1/X1*
Stanley, Elizabeth Countess Derby	Nob.			12		
Stanley, Henry	Unkn.	25				
Stanley, James, Lord Strange, Earl Derby	Nob.	25				
Stanley, Robert	Gent.	26				
Stanley, Thomas	Gent.	25–26				
Stanley, William	Merc.			09		
Stannard, William	Merc.?			09		
Stanton, John	Unkn.					*X1*
Stanton, Robert	Unkn.					*X2*
Stanton, Thomas	Unkn.					*X2*
Staper, Edward	Merc.					*S6*
Staper, Hewett	Merc.		09	10	00c	*F1/Qc/R2/S4/ Z/GG1*
Staper, James	Merc.				92	*S6*
Staper, Richard	Merc.		99c	09	81g	*B/E1/M/R1/ S6c/X1/GG1*
Staplehill, Adrian	Unkn.					*X2*
Staplehill, Gilbert	Merc.					*X1*
Stapleton, Robert	Kt. 70	04				
Stapleton, Robert	Unkn.	28				
Stapleton, Thomas	Merc.			09		
Stapley, Anthony	Unkn.	24–25, 28				
Staresmore, Francis	Gent.	26				

Name & title	Class; date of knight-hood	Parlia-ments (starting dates)	E. Ind. Co.	Va. Co.	Levant Co.	Other companies
Starkey, Philip	Merc.				00	
Starkey, Thomas	Merc.					B/Mc/S6c/ W4/X1
Starkey, William	Merc.		00			
Starr, Richard	Merc.		24			
Staveby, Paul	Merc.					S6
Staveley, William	Merc.					S6c
Steede, William	Kt. 03					Q
Steele, Edward	Merc.					I7
Steele, Michael	Merc.		09			
Steer, William	Unkn.		14			
Stephens, Edward	Unkn.	89				
*Stephens, Edward	Merc.					F1
Stephens, John	Unkn.					X2
Stephens, Nathaniel	Gent.	28	17			
**Stephens, Richard	Merc.	93	99	22		S4
*Stephens, Richard	Unkn.					X2
Stephens, Robert	Unkn.					X2
**Stephens, Thomas	Gent.			87		Q
**Stephens, Thomas	Gent.	93	03	10		Q
*Stephens, Thomas	Merc.					J1
Stephens, Timothy	Merc.		24			L1/M
Stephens, William	Unkn.				18	X2
Stephenson, George	Merc.					F2/L1/S2
Stephenson, Richard	Merc.	86, 93–97				
Stepnethe, Alban	Unkn.	84–89, 04				
Stepney, Thomas	Unkn.					X1
Stercke, Arthur	Merc.					X1
Stervill, Henry	Merc.					R2
Steward, Augustine	Gent.			10		
Steward, Francis	Kt. 10	26–28				
Steward, Mark	Unkn.	89, 97				
Steward, Simian	Kt. 03	14, 24, 28				
Steward, Thomas	Merc.		09			
Steward, Walter	Unkn.	24–25				
Steward, William	Gent.					I4
Steward, ?	Unkn.	04				
Stewart, James Lord Ochiltree	Nob. 30					GG
Stewkley, Thomas	Kt. 03			12		
Stile, Humphrey	Merc.		00	09		M
Stile, Nicholas	Merc.		99			B/M/S1c/X1
Stile, Oliver	Merc.		99c		99	B/M/Q/S1/X1
Stile, Richard	Merc.					GG
Stile, Thomas	Merc.		07c	12	05	E3/F1/L1/S4/ X2
Stileman, Elias	Unkn.					J3
Stingar, George	Merc.		24			
Stockambe, Aldred	Merc.					X1
Stockeman, William	Unkn.	04				
Stocker, Matthew	Merc.		09		07	

Name & title	Class; date of knight-hood	Parlia-ments (starting dates)	E. Ind. Co.	Va. Co.	Levant Co.	Other companies
*Stockes, John	Merc.					D/X1
Stoddard, John	Merc.					S6
Stoddard, Nicholas	Kt. 03			12		
Stoddard, William	Merc.		08			
Stoickden, John	Merc.		09	12		
Stoke, John	Merc.		08	09		X1
Stokeley, John	Merc.		00c	09		F1/Nc/S3
Stokeley, Thomas	Merc.					S4
Stokes, Roland	Merc.					X1
Stokes, Thomas	Unkn.			18?		
Stone, Andrew	Merc.					L1
Stone, Christopher	Unkn.	04				
Stone, George	Unkn.			18?		
Stone, John	Unkn.	04				
*Stone, John	Merc.		29			
**Stone, Robert	Merc.		24			X1
Stone, Simon	Gent.					N
Stone, Thomas	Merc.					F1/L1/Q/S1/ X2
Stone, William	Merc.		99c	89		F1/I1c/M/Qc/ S1
Stonehowse, James	Kt. 03		14			
Stonehowse, John	Kt. 29†	28	14			
Stonell, Nicholas	Unkn.		11			
Stoner, Francis	Unkn.	86				
Stoner, Peter	Merc.					S6
*Stonnard, William	Unkn.			18?		
Storyes, Robert	Merc.					F1
Stoughton, Adrian	Unkn.	93–14				
**Stoughton, Anthony	Merc.	28	14			
Stoughton, George	Gent.	14				
Stoughton, John	Merc.		10			
Stoughton, Lawrence	Gent.	84–86, 93				
Stoughton, Nicholas	Gent.	24				
Stoughton, Richard	Kt.†	04				
Stoughton, William	Unkn.	84				
Stowell, John	Kt. 74					I9
Stowell, John	Gent.	25				
Stowell, Nicholas	Merc.					I7
Strachey, John	Merc.				06	S4
Strachey, William	Gent.			09		
Stradling, John	Kt. 08	24–26		12		
Stradling, John	Merc.					S1
Stradling, Lamarock	Unkn.			12		
Strange, John	Unkn.			19		X2
Strange, Robert	Unkn.	14				
Strangwaies, John	Kt.†	14–28				
Strangways, Nicholas	Merc.					X2
Stratford, Anthony	Merc.		00			
Stratford, Henry	Merc.					E3
Stratford, Richard	Merc.		08			

Name & title	Class; date of knighthood	Parliaments (starting dates)	E. Ind. Co.	Va. Co.	Levant Co.	Other companies
Stratford, Robert	Merc.		00			
Strawe, Nicholas	Merc.					S1
Strayer, Nicholas	Merc.					F1
Streete, Humphrey	Merc.					I7
Strelley, Philip	Kt.†	93				GG
Strete, John	Unkn.			09		
Strete, Robert	Merc.					E1
Strewer, Thomas	Merc.					F1
Strickland, Robert	Gent.	24				
Strickland, Thomas	Kt. 03	01–04				
Strickland, William	Unkn.	84				
Stringer, Edward	Merc.				10	
Stringer, Robert	Merc.	93–97				
Stringer, Thomas	Merc.		15			
Strode, George	Gent.	93				
Strode, George	Gent.		23c		15	R2/X2
Strode, John	Unkn.					I9
Strode, John	Kt. 23	21, 25				
Strode, John	Unkn.					X2
Strode, Richard	Kt. 03	04, 26				
Strode, William	Kt. 98	97–26		12		
Strode, William	Gent.	24–28				
Strong, John	Merc.					X1
Stronginarme, John	Merc.					I7/S3
Stronginarme, Richard	Merc.		07	09		
Strutt, Robert	Merc.			12		
Stuart, King Charles	Nob.		18			O
Stuart, Frances, Duchess Lennox & Richmond	Nob.		25			
Stuart, Prince Henry	Nob.					G3/GG
Stuart, King James	Nob.					O/GG1
Stuart, Ludovic, Duke Lennox & Richmond	Nob.		25			G6/K4/Q/GG1
Stubbins, Thomas	Unkn.			20		
Stubbs, Anthony	Merc.					F1/L1/M
Stubbs, John	Unkn.	89				
Stubbs, Richard	Unkn.	89				
Stubbs, William	Unkn.	84				
Stubbs, ?	Unkn.			20		
Studley, Andrew	Merc.					CC2
Studley, Nathaniel	Gent.		19			
Studley, Robert	Merc.					CC2
Sturdon, Robert	Unkn.			17		
Stutevill, Martin	Kt. 03	01		18?		
Suckling, John	Kt. 16	01, 14, 24–26	19c			
Suckling, Robert	Merc.	86				
Suger, Jerome	Merc.		99			
Sullen, Thomas	Merc.					F1
Sunnibanck, ?	Pfl/y.			22		
Suragold, John	Merc.					S6
Sutcliffe, Matthew	Pfl/y.			09		K2c

Name & title	Class; date of knighthood	Parliaments (starting dates)	E. Ind. Co.	Va. Co.	Levant Co.	Other companies
Sutor, John	Unkn.	21				
Sutton, Isaac	Merc.				10	*I7/L1*
Sutton, Richard	Kt. 19					
Sutton, Richard	Unkn.	86–89				
Sutton, Robert	Gent.	24				
Sutton, Robert	Merc.					*I7*
Sutton, Thomas	Kt.†			09		
Sutton, William	Merc.					*I7*
Suzan, John	Merc.					*B/X1*
Swaddon, William	Unkn.	04				
Swale, Richard	Unkn.	89				
Swann, Libbias	Merc.			09		
Swayne, Arthur	Unkn.			20		
Swayne, Miles	Merc.					*F1*
Swayne, Richard	Merc.	97–01				
Swayne, Thomas	Unkn.			20		*X2*
Swayne, William	Unkn.	89				
*Swayne, William	Unkn.			20		
Sweete, Gilbert	Unkn.					*X2*
Sweeting, ?	Unkn.					*X2*
Swetnam, Lawrence	Merc.					*S1*
Swette, Henry	Merc.					*S1*
Swette, Richard	Merc.					*S6*
Swift, Edward	Kt. 03	04				
Swift, James	Unkn.			09		
Swift, Richard	Merc.		23			*R2c*
Swifter, John	Merc.					*I2*
Swinhoe, George	Merc.		11		10	*Q/T2*
Swinhoe, John	Merc.			09		
Swynnerton, John	M. Kt. 03	01–04	99			*F1g/S1c*
Swynnerton, John	Merc.					*B?/S1*
Swynnerton, Robert	Merc.					*GG*
Sydney, Robert, Lord, Viscount Lisle, Earl Leicester	Nob. 86	84–86, 93–97		09c		*Q/GG*
Sydney, Robert, Lord, Viscount Lisle, Earl Leicester	Nob. 10	14–25				*GG*
Sydney, Sarah Countess Leicester	Nob.		25			
Symcotts, James	Merc.					*S6*
Symcotts, John	Merc.					*S1/GG*
Symes, John	Gent.	24				
Symes, Randall	Merc.					*S6/X1*
Symes, Richard	Merc.					*F1/S4*
Symes, Thomas	Merc.					*S1c*
Symnell, Richard	Merc.	97–01				
Symonds, Jarvis	Merc.					*E1*
Symonds, Richard	Merc.		24		14	
Symons, George	Kt. 04	14				
Taaffe, William	Kt. 03					*I4*

Name & title	Class; date of knighthood	Parliaments (starting dates)	E. Ind. Co.	Va. Co.	Levant Co.	Other companies
Taders, Simon	Merc.					C
Tafter, Peter	Unkn.					$I1$
Tailbie, Richard	Merc.		00		05	$S5$
Talbot, Anne, Lady	Nob.					$W5$
Talbot, Edward	Gent.	84–86				
Talbot, George Earl Shrewsbury	Nob.					$R1/W4/X1/GG6$
Talbot, Gilbert Earl Shrewsbury	Nob.			12		$I2/Q/GG4$
Talbot, Henry	Gent.	84–86				
Talbot, Mary Countess Shrewsbury	Nob.			12		
Talbot, Sharington	Unkn.	97				
Talbot, Thomas	Merc.		00			
Talbot, Thomas	Unkn.		17			
Talbot, Walter	Gent.					$I4$
Tamworth, Henry	Gent.					$AA3/BB2$
Tanfield, Lawrence	Kt. 03	84–04				N
Tanner, George	Unkn.					$X2$
Tanner, John	Merc.			09		$I7$
Tanner, William	Merc.					$I7$
Taper, Oliver	Merc.					$S1$
Tartrey, Thomas	Merc.					$F1$
Tasburgh, John	Gent.	97				
Tasburgh, Thomas	Gent.	84–97				
Tasker, Peter	Merc.					$I1c$
Tate, Francis	Gent.	01–04		10		
Tate, Lewis	Unkn.			09		
*Tate, Lewis	Unkn.			12		
Tate, William	Kt. 06	93, 14				
Tatem, Richard	Unkn.			23		
Taverner, Edmund	Kt.†	26–28				
Taverner, John	Gent.			09		
Taverner, John	Merc.				21	
Taylor, Andrew	Merc.					$F1$
Taylor, Francis	Merc.		00			$F1c/S3$
Taylor, Henry	Unkn.					$X2/GG$
Taylor, James	Merc.					$I7$
Taylor, John	Merc.					$E1$
Taylor, John	Merc.					$E2/X2$
*Taylor, John	Gent.					$I2$
Taylor, Michael	Unkn.					$I7c$
Taylor, Peter	Unkn.					$X2$
Taylor, Richard	Unkn.	21–28				
Taylor, Richard	Merc.					$X2$
Taylor, Robert	Merc.					$I7/S6$
Taylor, Thomas	Merc.					$X1$
Taylor, William	Merc.			09		
Tedcastle, John	Merc.					$B/S4$
Tegg, Richard	Merc.					$S1$

Name & title	Class; date of knighthood	Parliaments (starting dates)	E. Ind. Co.	Va. Co.	Levant Co.	Other companies
Temple, Alexander	Kt. 03	26				G7
Temple, Thomas	Unkn.	89				
Temple, William	Unkn.	97				
Temple, William	Merc.				12	
Tenant, Richard	Merc.			09		I7
Tenycar, Thomas	Merc.					E1
Ter, Edward	Unkn.	04				
Terringham, Edward	Merc.					L1
Tessemond, Thomas	Merc.					S4
Tewsley, John	Merc.				29	
Tey, John	Unkn.	04				
Thatcher, John	Unkn.		15			
Theakston, Richard	Unkn.	93, 01				
Thelieur, John le	Merc.		29			
Thelwall, Bevis	M. Kt. 23					GG1
Thelwall, Eubule	Kt. 19	24, 26–28				
Thelwall, Simon	Gent.	93, 14				
Theobaldes, Stephen	Unkn.	01				
Theopham, Matthew	Merc.					F1
Thibaut, Daniel	Unkn.					X2
Thimbleby, Stephen	Merc.	84				
Thomas, Abell	Unkn.					X2
Thomas, Edward	Unkn.	25–28				
Thomas, Henry	Merc.					I7
Thomas, John	Merc.					S6
Thomas, John	Merc.					S6
Thomas, Robert	Merc.					S6
Thomas, Samuel	Merc.					X1
Thomas, Walter	Merc.					S1
Thomas, William	Gent.	93				
*Thomas, William	Gent.	84				
Thomas, William	Unkn.					X2
Thomas, William	Merc.					S6
Thomas, ?	Unkn.			09		
Thomason, John	Merc.					X1
Thompson, Allen	Merc.					S1
Thompson, David	Pfl/y.					K5/GG
Thompson, Henry	Merc.					E2/F1
Thompson, John	Unkn.	26				
*Thompson, John	Merc.					E2
Thompson, Lawrence	Unkn.	84–89				
*Thompson, Lawrence	Gent.					W2/CC2
Thompson, M.	Kt.†					T3
Thompson, Maurice	Merc.			23		X2/GG
Thompson, Walter	Unkn.		24			
**Thompson, William	Unkn.	25		22		
Thorley, William	Unkn.	86				
Thornborough, Edward	Unkn.	93				
**Thornborough, John	Unkn.	01		20		
Thorne, Nicholas	Merc.					S6
Thorne, Octavian	Unkn.			09		

Name & title	Class; date of knighthood	Parliaments (starting dates)	E. Ind. Co.	Va. Co.	Levant Co.	Other companies
Thornebush, John	Unkn.					X2
Thorned, John	Unkn.					P2
Thornehague, John	Kt. 03	04				
Thornehill, Matthew	Unkn.					P2
Thornehill, Samuel	Unkn.	93				
Thornehill, Thomas	Merc.		18			X2
Thornehill, Timothy	Kt. 14			23		
Thorney, Thomas	Merc.	86–97				
Thornton, Christopher	Merc.					S6
Thornton, Edward	Merc.					S6
Thornton, George	Unkn.					I9
**Thornton, John	Merc.	84				S6c
Thornton, Richard	Pfl/y.					G8
Thornton, Robert	Unkn.			09		
Thornton, William	Merc.					E2
Thorogood, John	Merc.		14			
Thorogood, John	Unkn.	24–28				
Thorold, Edward	Merc.			09		
Thorold, Thomas	Merc.		29		10	F1
Thorold, William	Unkn.	84				
Thorpe, George	Gent.	14		12c		T2
Thorpe, John	Merc.					L1/M
Thorpe, Thomas	Merc.					I7
Thorpe, William	Merc.					X1
Thrale, ?	Merc.					I7
Throgmorton, Arthur	Unkn.	89				
Throgmorton, Clement	Kt.†	24–26				
Throgmorton, Job	Gent.	86				
Throgmorton, John	Gent.	01–04				
Throgmorton, Nicholas	Gent.	01				
Throgmorton, Thomas	Kt. 87	89				
Throgmorton, William	Kt. 11		14	12		
Throughton, Andrew	Merc.			10		
Thurbarne, James	Merc.	97				
Thurbarne, Robert	Merc.	86				
Thurland, Edmund	Gent.					AA1
Thurland, Jarden	Merc.					S6
Thursby, Cuthbert	Merc.					I7
Thurscroste, Luke	Merc.					S6
Thurston, Alexander	Merc.	01				
Thurston, Richard	Merc.					X1
Thurston, William	Merc.					F1/S4
Thwaite, Thomas	Merc.					I2
Thynn, Charles	Unkn.	14, 28				
Thynn, John	Kt. 03	84–04				
Thynn, Thomas	Gent.	93				
Thynn, Thomas	Kt. 04	01–04, 21–28				
Tichborne, Benjamin	Gent.	89–93				
Tichborne, Benjamin	Gent.	26–28				
Tichborne, Henry	Pfl/y.		23			
Tichborne, Richard	Kt. 03	97, 14–28				

Name & title	Class; date of knight-hood	Parliaments (starting dates)	E. Ind. Co.	Va. Co.	Levant Co.	Other companies
Tichborne, Walter	Kt. 03	14, 25				
Tiebbes, Jelmer	Unkn.					*X2*
Tickner, Samuel	Unkn.					*T3*
Tilden, Joseph	Unkn.					*P2*
Tilliard, William	Merc.					*F1*
Timberlake, Henry	Merc.		26	12		*Q/T2*
Tindall, Robert	Merc.			12		*S6*
Tipper, Robert	Merc.					*S1*
Tipper, William	Merc.					*S6*
Tipton, Hugo	Merc.					*S6*
Tirhitt, Timothy	Kt.†	04				
Tirrell, Edward	Kt. 03	04				
Tirrell, Francis	Merc.		99	09		*D/GG*
Tirrell, Richard	Gent.					*I4*
Tirringham, Anthony	Kt. 03	04				
Tiringham, Arthur	Gent.	14				
Tisdall, Richard	Unkn.	21				
Tither, Edward	Unkn.		15			
Tokeley, Robert	Unkn.					*X2*
Tolderby, Christopher	Gent.	97–04				*AA3/BB2*
Tolderby, Philip	Merc.					*F1*
Tollemach, Lionel	Kt. 12	21, 28				
Tomkins, Humphrey	Unkn.			20		
Tomkins, James	Unkn.	24–28				
Tomkins, Nathaniel	Unkn.	14–28				
Tomkins, William	Unkn.	28				
Tomlins, Richard	Gent.	21–28		12c		*T2*
Tomlinson, Gabriel	Merc.					*L1*
Tomlinson, John	Merc.					*X2*
Tomlinson, Thomas	Merc.		24			*L1*
Tooker, Baptist	Merc.					*F1*
Tooker, Giles	Unkn.	01–14				
Tookie, Bartholomew	Unkn.	28				
Toose, Leonard	Merc.					*F1*
Toothby, Richard	Unkn.	14				
Topcliffe, Richard	Unkn.	84–86				
Topfield, Henry	Merc.					*X1/GG*
Topham, Christopher	Merc.					*E2*
Topham, Matthew	Merc.					*E1*
Topley, Stephen	Merc.			09		
Topson, William	Unkn.					*X2*
Touchet, George, Lord Audley, Earl Castlehaven	Nob.					*I2*
Towell, Anthony	Merc.					*I7*
Towerson, Gabriel	Merc.?		15			
Towerson, Nicholas	Merc.					*S1*
Towerson, Parnell	Merc.					*S1*
Towerson, Robert	Merc.		00			*S4*
Towerson, William	Merc				07	*E1/Mc/R1/ S6c/W4/X1/GG*

Name & title	Class; date of knighthood	Parliaments (starting dates)	E. Ind. Co.	Va. Co.	Levant Co.	Other companies
Towerson, William	Merc.	21, 28	19c			F1/I7c/M/Q/ S3c/X2
Towker, John	Merc.					S1
Towler, Charles	Unkn.			09		
Townshend, Henry	Kt. 03	14				
Townshend, Heyward	Unkn.	97–01				
Townshend, John	Kt. 96	93–04				
*Townshend, John	Kt. 03			09		
Townshend, John	Merc.	97–14				
Townshend, Robert	Kt. 03	01–04				
Townshend, Roger	Kt. 88	21, 28				
Townshend, Warren	Unkn.			12		
Townson, Leonard	Unkn.			18?		
Townson, Thomas	Merc.			09		
Towse, Henry	Merc.					F1
Towse, John	Merc.		15			
Towse, William	Unkn.	86				
Towse, William	Unkn.	14–26				
Towsee, Nicholas	Merc.		14			
Tracy, John	Kt. 74	84, 97				
Tracy, Robert	Kt. 16	21, 26				
Tracy, Thomas	Kt. 09	21		12		A
Tracy, William	Unkn.			19		X2
Tradescant, John	Unkn.			17		
Trafford, Edmund	Kt. 03	89–93				
Travell, John	Merc.		15			E3/L1
Travicc, Henry	Merc.					Q
Travis, Edmund	Merc.		11			S4
Travis, James	Merc.		11		27	F1
Travis, Philip	Merc.					I7
Treffrey, John	Unkn.	21				
Treffrey, Thomas	Unkn.	97				
Treffrey, William	Unkn.	84				
Trefusis, John	Unkn.	21				
Trefusis, Nicholas	Unkn.	28				
Trefusis, Richard	Unkn.	84–89				
Tregenna, John	Unkn.	04				
Treherne, John	Unkn.	01				
Trelaron, Robert	Unkn.					X2
Trelawney, Edward	Gent.	86, 97				
Trelawney, Jonathan	Kt. 98	86–97, 04				
Trenchard, George	Kt. 88	84				
Trenchard, George	Gent.	01				
Trenchard, John	Gent.	21–25				
Trenchard, Thomas	Kt. 13	21				
Trenchard, William	Gent.					I9/X1
Trenchfield, Thomas	Unkn.					X2
Trentham, Francis	Gent.	04				
Trentham, Thomas	Gent.	01				
Tresham, Lewis	Kt. 12			12		
Treswell, Robert	Unkn.					I7c

Name & title	Class; date of knighthood	Parliaments (starting dates)	E. Ind. Co.	Va. Co.	Levant Co.	Other companies
Trevanyon, Charles	Gent.	84				
Trevanyon, Charles	Gent.	25				
Trevanyon, Richard	Gent.	86				
Trevegham, Hugh	Unkn.					X2
Trevor, John	Kt. 03	93–21, 25		06c		X1/GG
Trevor, John	Kt. 19	21–25, 28		23		
Trevor, Richard	Kt. 97	97		12		
Trevor, Sackvill	Kt. 03	25				
Trevor, Thomas	Kt. 19	01–24	18			
Trewe, Andrew	Merc.	93				
Trigge, Paul	Merc.					S1
Trilany, John	Merc.					S1c
Trilany, Robert	Merc.					S1
Trist, John	Merc.					F1
Tristram, Thomas	Merc.			09		I7
Trose, John	Merc.					S1
**Trott, John	Merc.	04–14				L1
Trott, Nicholas	Unkn.	97				
Trotter, Thomas	Merc.			08	10	L1/S5/X2
Troughton, Nicholas	Unkn.	01				
Trowte, Thomas	Merc.					DD
Truelove, Roland	Unkn.			21		
Truestone, Robert	Merc.					F1
Trumball, Thomas	Merc.					S1
Trumball, William	Gent.	26	18		18	G7
Truslove, John	Unkn.	89				
Truston, Thomas	Unkn.			09		
Tubman, Samuel	Unkn.			18		
Tuck, Richard	Merc.					I7
Tucker, Daniel	Unkn.			09		T3
Tucker, Francis	Merc.					S6
Tucker, George	Gent.		12	12		Q/T3
Tucker, John	Unkn.			19		
Tucker, Mansfield	Merc.					L1
Tucker, Robert	Merc.					S1
Tucker, Valentine	Merc.					S6
Tucker, William	Gent.			10		X2
Tudor, Queen Elizabeth	Nob.			85	81	D/W5/X1/ BB1/GG1
Tue, Mary	Unkn.			22		
Tuffneale, Richard	Merc.					J1
Tufton, Nicholas, Lord, Earl Thanet	Nob. 03	01, 24		18c		GG
Tufton, Richard	Gent.	14, 28				
Turbridge, John	Unkn.	89				
Turetine, John	Merc.		23			
Turk, George	Merc.					I7
Turner, Arthur	Unkn.	14				
Turner, Christopher	Merc.					I3
Turner, Edward	Merc.			99		
Turner, George	Merc.					S6

Name & title	Class; date of knight-hood	Parlia-ments (starting dates)	E. Ind. Co.	Va. Co.	Levant Co.	Other companies
Turner, James	Merc.		99			
Turner, John	Merc.		29			
Turner, John	Unkn.	01				
Turner, Nicholas	Merc.					C/X1
Turner, Peter	Unkn.	84–86				
*Turner, Peter	Pfl/y.			09		
Turner, Richard	Merc.			09		I7
Turner, Robert	Unkn.	97–01				
Turner, Samuel	Unkn.	26				
Turner, William	Merc.		99		05	I7c/L1/M/Nc
Turner, William	Pfl/y.			18?		
Turpyn, Anthony	Unkn.	01–04				
Turpyn, William	Gent.	89				
Turville, Ambrose	Kt. 03	04	12			
Turvine, William	Unkn.					I2
Turvyle, Jeffrey	Unkn.					W5
Tutt, Alexander	Unkn.	04				
Tweedy, Henry	Gent.		19			Q
Tweedy, Roger	Unkn.					X2
Twisden, Roger	Kt. 20	25–26		23		
Twisden, William	Kt. 03	93, 01–14, 28		10		
Twyne, William	Gent.		19			
Twynehowe, William	Kt.†	04				GG
Tyllet, James	Merc.					F1/S1
Tyndale, Francis	Unkn.	93				
Tynes, Edward	Merc.		24			
Tyringham, Edmund	Unkn.		23			
Tyrwhite, Tristiam	Unkn.	86–89				
Ubanck, Robert	Merc.					I7
Udall, Francis	Merc.		18		18	
**Ughtred, Henry (see Oughtred)	Merc.	84, 89				I9/W9/X1
**Umpton, Edward	Gent.	84–86				I9
Umpton, Henry	Kt. 86	84, 93				
Underhill, Clement	Merc.					F2/L1/S2
Underwood, Jasper	Merc.					I7
Unton, Thomas	Unkn.	04				
Upton, Christopher	Merc.					F1
Upton, George	Unkn.	84, 01–04				
Upton, John	Gent.					CC1
Upton, John	Unkn.	25–28				
Utley, George	Merc.		00			
Uvedall, Edmund	Kt. 88	01				
Uvedall, Edward	Merc.		19		14	
Uvedall, William	Kt. 13	14–28				
Vale, Richard	Merc.					I7
Valentine, Benjamin	Unkn.	28				
Vanderputt, Giles	Merc.		25			
Vassal, John	Merc.			09		
Vassal, Samuel	Merc.		28		20c	J2c/X2
Vassal, William	Merc.					J2c

Name & title	Class; date of knighthood	Parliaments (starting dates)	E. Ind. Co.	Va. Co.	Levant Co.	Other companies
Vasse, Daniel	Unkn.					*X2*
Vaughan, Andrew	Merc.					*F1*
Vaughan, Charles	Kt. 08	14, 25				
**Vaughan, Edward	Gent.	26		09		
Vaughan, George	Merc.					*F1*
Vaughan, Henry	Gent.	21–28				*I4/GG*
Vaughan, Hugh	Unkn.	84–86, 93				
Vaughan, James	Unkn.	28				
Vaughan, John	Unkn.	84–86				
*Vaughan, John	Kt. 99	01				
Vaughan, John	Kt. 17	21		12		*I4/X1*
Vaughan, Richard Earl Carbery	Nob. 26	24–28				
*Vaughan, Richard	Gent.	28				
**Vaughan, Walter	Kt. 03	93, 04		10		
Vaughan, Walter	Merc.	97				
Vaughan, William	Kt. 28					*GG*
**Vavasor, Thomas	Kt. 97	84–89, 04–14				*L1*
Vawer, William	Merc.					*S1*
**Venables, Richard	Merc.	14–21				*S6c/GG*
Venn, Arthur	Gent.			09		
Venn, John	Merc.					*J1c*
Venn, Richard	M. Kt. 38		16c	09	05	*F1/M*
Verdon, Jonas	Unkn.		27			
Verdon, William	Unkn.		27			
Vere, Edward Earl Oxford	Nob.					*Q1/W7*
Vere, Edward	Kt. 07	24				
Vere, Francis	Kt. 86	93				
Vere, Horatio, Lord	Nob. 96			09c		*G7*
Vere, Elizabeth Countess Oxford	Nob.			12		
Verney, Edmund	Kt. 11	24–25, 28				
Verney, Grevile	Kt. 17	14–21				
Verney, Richard	Kt. 03	89, 01–14				
Vernon, George	Unkn.	25–26				
Vernon, John	Merc.					*I7*
Vernon, Richard	Merc.					*M/R2*
Vernon, Richard	Gent.	04				
Vernon, Robert	Kt. 03†	21				
Vernon, William	Unkn.	89				
Vertur, Christopher	Merc.			09		*I7*
Vesy, William	Unkn.			22		
Vickars, Thomas	Merc.					*L1*
Vicker, James	Merc.					*R2c*
Vigars, John	Merc.			09		*N*
Villiers, Edward	Kt. 16	21–25				*GG*
Villiers, George	Kt. 93	04				
Villiers, George, Marquis & Duke Buckingham	Nob.					*G7/K4/GG*

Name & title	Class; date of knight-hood	Parlia-ments (starting dates)	E. Ind. Co.	Va. Co.	Levant Co.	Other companies
Villiers, John						
Viscount Purbeck	Nob. 16		17			
Villiers, William	Merc.					*S6*
Vincent, Christopher	Merc.					*E3/L1*
Vincent, Francis	Kt. 03	26				
Vincent, Henry	Merc.			09		*F1/M/O*
*Vincent, Henry	Unkn.	93				
Vincent, Thomas	Unkn.	84				
Vines, Richard	Unkn.					*GG*
Vinie, John	Unkn.					*X*1
Viollett, Richard	Merc.					*F1*
Vischer, Samuel de	Unkn.		23			
Vischer, William de	Unkn.		23			
Vitters, Sebastian	Merc.			12		
Vivian, Charles	Merc.				22	
Vivian, Christopher	Unkn.			23		
Vivian, Francis	Unkn.	04–14				
Vivian, Hannibal	Unkn.	84–89, 01				
Vivian, Hannibal	Unkn.	28				
Vivian, Michael	Unkn.	97				
Vivian, Roger	Merc.				20	
Vos, Cornelius de	Merc.					*AA*1
Voysey, Andrew	Unkn.					*X*2
Vyner, Thomas	Unkn.			20		
Wadden, James	Unkn.					*X*2
Wadden, John	Merc.					*S1/X*1
Wade, Nathaniel	Merc.		18	09		*R*2
Wade, Samuel	Unkn.					*X*2
Wade, Thomas	Gent.		24			*J*3
Wade, Thomas	Merc.			89		
*Wade, Thomas	Unkn.	84				
Wade, Timothy	Merc.		18		18	
Wade, William	Kt. 03	84, 89, 01–04		06c		*S1/T*1
Wadlow, Francis	Merc.		15			*E3/L1*
Wadlow, Simon	Merc.					*I*7
Wadsworth, John	Merc.					*F1*
Wadsworth, Robert	Merc.					*E*2
Waggstaff, Richard	Unkn.		22			*G*8
Waindeford, John	Merc.				06	
Wainwright, Thomas	Unkn.			22		
Wainwright, ?	Unkn.					*CC*2
Wake, Isaac	Kt. 19	24				
Wakefield, Edward	Merc.	86				
Wakeham, John	Merc.					*S1*
Wakeman, Thomas	Merc.					*S4*
Walcott, Charles	Unkn.	86–89				
Walcott, Gawen	Merc.					*S3*
Walcott, Humphrey	Merc.		00			*F1/I7/M*
Walcott, Richard	Merc.		24			
Waldegrave, Edward	Gent.	84				
Waldegrave, George	Gent.	97				

Name & title	Class; date of knight-hood	Parlia-ments (starting dates)	E. Ind. Co.	Va. Co.	Levant Co.	Other companies
Waldegrave, William	Kt. 95	97				
Walden, Edward	Merc.			89		
Walden, Isaac	Merc.	26–28				
Walden, Robert	Merc.					X1
Waldoe, Alice	Merc.		18			
Waldoe, John	Merc.		14			Q
Waldoe, Lawrence	Merc.		00			
Waldoe, Lawrence	Merc.		19			
Waldoe, Richard	Unkn.			09		
Waldoe, Robert	Merc.		00			Q
Waldron, Richard	Kt. 16					I2
Wale, Humphrey	Unkn.	89				
Wale, Thomas	Merc.			10		I2/T2
Walgrave, Thomas	Gent.					J3
Walkaden, Robert	Merc.					B/M/S6/X1/ GG
Walker, Christopher	Unkn.	89				
Walker, Edward	Merc.		01			
Walker, George	Merc.		09	09		
Walker, John	Gent.					BB5
Walker, Thomas	Gent.			09		
Walker, Thomas	Merc.					M/S1c
Wall, William	Merc.					L1/M
Waller, Edmund	Unkn.	24, 26–28				
Waller, Henry	Merc.	28				
Waller, Henry	Gent.					J3
Waller, John	Gent.			09		
Waller, Thomas	Kt. 97	04				
Waller, Walter	Kt. 72	93				
Waller, William	Unkn.			20		
Walley, John	Unkn.	89				
Wallis, Henry	Merc.					S6
Wallis, John	Unkn.	21–24				
Wallis, Robert	Merc.	97–04				
Wallop, Henry	Kt. 69					I9/W5
Wallop, Henry	Kt. 99	97–01, 14–28				
Wallop, Robert	Gent.	21–28				
Wallop, William	Gent.	86, 97				
Walmsley, John	Gent.	86				
Walmsley, Thomas	Kt. 17†	21–24				
*Walmsley, Thomas	Gent.	89				
Walrond, Henry	Merc.					S1
Walrond, John	Merc.					S1
Walrond, Osmond	Merc.					S1
Walshe, William	Gent.	93				
Walsingham, Francis	Kt. 77	84–89		85		Q1/R1/S6/W8/ X1/AA2g/ CC2/GG2
*Walshingham, Thomas	Kt. 97	97–14				
Walsingham, Thomas	Kt. 13	14–28		10		
Walt, Nicholas	Merc.				07	

Name & title	Class; date of knight-hood	Parliaments (starting dates)	E. Ind. Co.	Va. Co.	Levant Co.	Other companies
Walter, Edward	Merc.		00			
Walter, James	Unkn.	89				
Walter, John	Kt. 19	21–24		12		T2
Walter, John	Merc.					Q1
Walter, Robert	Unkn.	93				
Walter, Thomas	Merc.					S1
Walter, William	Kt. 03	14, 26–28				
Walter, William	Unkn.	28				
Walthall, Anne	Merc.		17			
Walthall, John	Merc.		17			
Walthall, Luke	Merc.					F1
Walthall, Mary	Merc.		18			
Walthall, Richard	Merc.					F1/I2
Walthall, William	Merc.					I2
Waltham, Henry	Merc.	28				X2
Waltham, Richard	Merc.		11			F1/S4
Waltham, Thomns	Merc.					S1/X2
Waltham, William	Merc.					S4/X2
Walton, George	Gent.	86				
Walton, Henry	Merc.					E1
Walton, John	Merc.					X1
Walton, Richard	Merc.					X1
Walton, Robert	Merc.					E1
Walton, Thomas	Merc.					X1
Walton, William	Merc.		00		00	F1/S4/X1
Walwyn, Humphrey	Merc.					S4/GG
Wandesford, Christopher	Unkn.	21–28				
Wandesford, John	Unkn.	24				
Wannerton, Thomas	Pfl/y.					GG1
Waplett, Richard	Unkn.		11			
Warburton, Peter	Unkn.	84–89, 97				
Warburton, Richard	Kt. 03	01–04				
*Warckhope, ?	Gent.					CC1
Warcupp, Ralph	Gent.	01				
Warcupp, Thomas	Gent.	84–89				
Ward, Edward	Gent.					I2
Ward, Gilbert	Merc.					L1
Ward, Henry	Merc.			18		
Ward, John	Merc.					L1/R2c
Ward, Luke	Unkn.					W4
Ward, Richard	Unkn.		15			
Ward, Thomas	Unkn.					P2
Ward, Walter	Merc.			21		
**Ward, William	Merc.		18?			L1/M
Wardall, John	Merc.			10		R2c/X2
Warden, John	Unkn.	04–14				
Warden, Richard	Merc.					S6
Warden, Thomas	Merc.					S1
Warder, William	Merc.					F1
Wardour, Chidiac	Unkn.	89–93				
Wardour, Edward	Kt. 18	21–25	24			

Name & title	Class; date of knighthood	Parliaments (starting dates)	E. Ind. Co.	Va. Co.	Levant Co.	Other companies
Ware, Nicholas	Merc.					S6
Warford, William	Merc.					S6
Waring, Michael	Merc.		27		26	
Warnecombe, John	Unkn.	01				
Warner, Edward	Merc.		11c			F1
Warner, Henry	Gent.	97–01				
Warner, Henry	Merc.		25			
Warner, Richard	Merc.			10		
Warner, Thomas	Kt. 27					GG
**Warr, Roger	Gent.	21–24				I9
Warr, Thomas	Gent.	14		06c		
Warren, Edward	Unkn.	89				
Warren, John	Merc.				00	F1/S1
Warren, Richard	Gent.	93				
Warren, Thomas	Merc.					X1
Warren, William	Gent.					I3
Warren, ?	Unkn.					J3
Wase, John	Merc.					L2/M
Washborne, Herriott	Merc.		29			
Washborne, Richard	Merc.		15			
Washborne, Robert	Merc.					B/M/X1/GG
Washborne, Robert	Merc.		24			
Washer, Richard	Merc.		00			S4
Washert, Michael	Unkn.					X2
Washington, John	Kt. 23					G7
Washington, Lawrence	Unkn.	04				
Wasse, Richard	Merc.					E3
Wastell, William	Merc.		00		00	S3
Watcham, John	Merc.					F1
Waterhouse, David	Unkn.	89, 01		10		
Waterhouse, Edward	Kt. 03			09		
Waterhouse, Edward	Unkn.			21		
Waterhouse, Robert	Unkn.	84				
Waters, Edward	Unkn.			?		
**Waters, John	Unkn.			20		I1/T3
Waterton, Richard	Gent.					CC2
Watkins, Brian	Merc.					I7
Watkins, David	Merc.		14			Q
Watkins, John	Merc.		21		22	A/S1
Watkins, Matthew	Unkn.					X1
Watkins, William	Unkn.	97				
**Watkinson, James	Merc.	28				F1
Watkinson, John	Merc.					X1
Watson, Edward	Gent.	01				
Watson, John	Merc.					S6/GG
Watson, John	Merc.					S1
Watson, Lewis	Kt. 08	21–24				
Watson, Roger	Merc.					E1
Watson, Roland	Unkn.	84–93				
Watson, Thomas	Kt. 17	14		09c		Q
Watson, Thomas	Merc.					I7/S4

Name & title	Class; date of knighthood	Parliaments (starting dates)	E. Ind. Co.	Va. Co.	Levant Co.	Other companies
Watson, William	Merc.					E1
Watson, William	Unkn.			20		
Wattey, William	Unkn.			09		
Watts, Daniel	Merc.					L2/M
Watts, George	Merc.					S1
Watts, Jeffrey	Merc.					S1
Watts, John	M. Kt. 03		00g	09c		D/S6c/T2/X1/GG
Watts, John	M. Kt. 25					S1/X1/X2
Watts, Richard	Merc.					S1
Watts, Thomas	Merc.					S1
Watts, William	Merc.					S1
Way, George	Merc.					J1
Way, Thomas	Merc.	84				
Wayte, ?	Merc.			29		
Weaver, Richard	Unkn.	21–26				
Webb, Christopher	Merc.					S1
Webb, Edward	Unkn.			09		
Webb, Francis	Unkn.					J1
Webb, George	Gent.			09		
Webb, John	Merc.				06	
Webb, Richard	Merc.			09		T2
Webb, Robert	Merc.					E3
Webb, Sands	Gent.			09		
Webb, Thomas	Gent.			09		
Webb, Thomas	Unkn.			09		J3?
Webb, William	M. Kt. 92					R1
Webb, William	Unkn.			22		T3
Webber, John	Unkn.					X2
Webster, William	Merc.		21	09		T2
*Weddell, John	Unkn.					X2
Weddell, Leonard	Merc.					E2
Wednester, Charles	Unkn.	93				
Weeks, Christopher	Merc.	84–89				
Weeks, Thomas	Merc.			09		
Weeks, William	Merc					S6
Weeks, ?	Unkn.					GG
Welby, Richard	Merc.		99		05	F1/I1c
Welby, William	Merc.			09		T2
Welch, Edward	Unkn.			09		
Welcham, Jeffrey	Merc.					S1
Weld, Humphrey	M. Kt. 03			09c		R2
Weld, John	M. Kt. 17†		14	10	15c	Nc/T2/GG
Weld, John	Gent.					Nc
Welden, Richard	Merc.		22			
Welden, William	Merc.					S6
*Welden, William	Unkn.			21		
Wellen, Cornelius	Merc.			09		
Wells, Thomas	Merc.			09		T2
Wenman, Francis	Kt. 18	28		09		
Wenman, Richard	Kt. 96	97, 21, 25				

Name & title	Class; date of knighthood	Parliaments (starting dates)	E. Ind. Co.	Va. Co.	Levant Co.	Other companies
Wenman, Thomas	Kt. 03			09		
*Wenman, Thomas	Kt. 17	21–28				
Wentworth, Henry	Unkn.			22		X2
Wentworth, John	Gent.	97–01				
Wenthworth, John	Kt. 03	28		10		X2
Wentworth, Peter	Gent.	86–93				
Wentworth, Thomas, Viscount, Earl Strafford	Nob. 11	14–25, 28				
Wentworth, Thomas	Gent.	04–28		12		
Wentworth, Walter	Unkn.	01				
Were, Humphrey	Unkn.	14, 24				
West, Cicely Lady De La Warr	Nob.			20		
West, Francis	Merc.		11			Q/T3
*West, Francis	Gent.			09		
West, George	Merc.			09		
West, Henry Lord De La Warr	Nob.			19c		
West, Henry	Unkn.					X2
West, John	Merc.			09		I7/S1/T2
West, Katherine	Merc.			09		
West, Nathaniel	Gent.			17?		
West, Nicholas	Unkn.					J3
West, Richard	Merc.					F1/X2
West, Robert	Unkn.	93				
West, Thomas	Kt. 91	86–93				
West, Thomas Lord De La Warr	Nob.		11	09c		
West, Thomas Lord De La Warr	Nob. 99	97				
West, William	Unkn.			?		
Westby, John	Merc.		19			
Westby, Richard	Merc.		18			
Westby, Titus	Merc.			09		
Westcombe, Justinian	Merc.					F1
Westley, John	Merc.				18	
Westley, Thomas	Merc.					I7
Weston, Edward	Kt.†	24				
Weston, Edward	Merc.					L1
Weston, Garret	Unkn.			18?		
Weston, Henry	Kt. 59	84				
Weston, James	Gent.	84				
Weston, Jerome	Unkn.	28				
Weston, Richard	Gent.	93				
**Weston, Richard Earl Portland	Nob. 03	01–26	17			
Weston, Richard	Gent.	01, 21				
Weston, Simon	Kt. 99	24–26				
Weston, Thomas	Merc.					P1/GG
*Weston, Thomas	Merc.					R2

Name & title	Class; date of knight- hood	Parlia- ments (starting dates)	E. Ind. Co.	Va. Co.	Levant Co.	Other companies
Weston, William	Unkn.	93				
Westrow, John	Merc.		01	09		F1
Westrow, John	Merc.		09			
Westrow, Mary	Merc.		26			
Westrow, Thomas	Merc.		99c			I7/Q
Westwood, Humphrey	Merc.			09		
Wetherall, Lawrence	Merc.		99		05	
Wetherall, Roger	Gent.					AA1c/BB1
Wetherall, Thomas	Merc.			20		L1/S4/X2
Wethered, George	Unkn.	21				
Wethered, John	Unkn.	14				
Wetherfield, Henry	Merc.					I7
Wetherley, Thomas	Unkn.					X2
Wetwood, Randall	Unkn.			09		
Weymouth, George	Unkn.			?		
Weymouth, William	Merc.					CC1
Whalley, Richard	Gent.	97–01				
Whaphlet, Anthony	Merc.					I7
Wharton, Anthony	Merc.					E2
Wharton, George	Kt. 03	01		09		GG
Wharton, Michael	Unkn.	86				GG
Wharton, Philip, Lord	Nob.					W2/GG
Wharton, Thomas	Kt. 11	14–21				GG
Whatman, Thomas	Unkn.	21–24, 26				
Wheat, William	Gent.			21		
Wheatley, Henry	Merc.					X2/GG
Wheatley, Robert	Merc.					GG
Wheatley, Thomas	Merc.		07	09c	10	L1/Q/T2
Wheatstones, George	Gent.					CC1
Wheatstones, Luke	Unkn.					X2
Wheeler, Ambrose	Merc.		00		12	
Wheeler, Edward	Unkn.					I7c
Wheeler, Humphrey	Unkn.	01				
Wheeler, John	Merc.					BB1
**Wheeler, John	Merc.	04	15			L1c/M
Wheeler, Nicholas	Merc.			18?		
Wheeler, Richard	Unkn.	84–97				
Wheeler, Thomas	Merc.		99	09		
Whetcombe, Samuel	Merc.				23	
Whetcombe, Simon	Merc.		24		10	J1c
Whethill, Richard	Merc.					H
*Whichcock, Charles	Merc.				27	
Whichcote, Charles	Gent.					J1
Whistler, Francis	Gent.			09		
Whistler, John	Unkn.	24–28				
Whitaker, Alexander	Pfl/y.			12		
Whitaker, Henry	Unkn.	86				
Whitaker, Henry	Merc.		15			L1/M
Whitaker, Lawrence	Unkn.	24–28				
Whitaker, William	Unkn.	24–28‡				
Whitbourne, Richard	Unkn.			?		GG

Name & title	Class; date of knight-hood	Parlia-ments (starting dates)	E. Ind. Co.	Va. Co.	Levant Co.	Other companies
Whitby, Edward	Unkn.	14–28				
*Whitcombe, ?	Unkn.			20		
White, Adam	Unkn.	04				
White, Edmund	Merc.					J3
White, F.	Pfl/y.			?		
White, Francis	Merc.					S6
White, Francis	Gent.					I1
White, George	Merc.					S1/X2
White, George	Merc.					S1
White, Henry	Unkn.					X1
White, James	Gent.			09		
**White, John	Gent.	89		87		
White, John	Gent.		29	23c		J1/P2/X2
White, John	Gent.					J3
White, John	Merc.					F1/S6
White, Leonard	Gent.		99	09		
White, Peter	Merc.					X2
White, Richard	Kt. 01	14				
White, Richard	Unkn.					J3
White, Robert	Merc.	04				X1
*White, Robert	Merc.					X2
White, Thomas	Merc.		00	09		X1
*White, Thomas	Merc.					X2
White, William	Unkn.	89				
White, William	Merc.		24			
Whitechurch, Marmaduke	Gent.					I4
Whitehead, Christopher	Merc.					H
Whitehead, Henry	Kt. 03	25–28				
Whitehead, Richard	Unkn.	28				
Whitehead, Thomas	Merc.					C/S1
Whiteway, William	Merc.	24–25				F1/S4
Whiteway, William	Merc.	26				
Whitewell, William	Unkn.					I1
Whitfield, John	Merc.					F1
Whitfield, Ralph	Gent.	24				G7
Whitley, Thomas	Merc.					I7
Whitlock, Bulstrode	Unkn.	26				
Whitlock, James	Kt. 20	04–21				
Whitlock, Richard	Merc.					E3/L2/M
Whitmore, George	M. Kt. 32		99	09		F1/S4
Whitmore, William	Kt. 21	21–25				
Whitmore, William	Merc.					S6
Whitner, Francis	Unkn.			19		
Whitney, Robert	Gent.	84				
Whitson, John	Merc.	04–21, 25–26		22		S1c/X1/GG
Whitstones, Barnard	Kt. 03	04				
Whitstones, Michael	Merc.					I7
Whittall, John	Merc.					S6
Whittingham, John	Merc.			09		I7/N
Whittingham, Timothy	Kt. 03	04				

402

Name & title	Class; date of knight-hood	Parlia-ments (starting dates)	E. Ind. Co.	Va. Co.	Levant Co.	Other companies
Whittingham, Thomas	Unkn.			09		
Whittle, Edmund	Merc.					*I*7
Whittle, Thomas	Merc.					*F*1
Whittocke, John	Unkn.					*X*2
Whitton, George	Unkn.	84–86				
Wich, Edward	Merc.		15		25	
Wich, James	Merc.		99			*F*1/*R*2/*S*3
Wich, Jeane	Merc.					*R*2
Wich, Peter	Kt. 26				26	
Wich, Richard	Merc.		99c		05c	*F*1/*Qc*/*R*2/ *S*1c/*X*1
Wich, Richard	Merc.				12	*S*4
Wich, Thomas	Merc.		15		16	
Wickham, William	Merc.		14			
Widdowes, Richard	Unkn.			09		
Widdrington, Henry	Kt. 03	04–21				
Widdrington, Robert	Gent.	89–93				
Widnall, William	Merc.					*S*6c/*GG*
Wiet, Ralph	Merc.	86				
Wiffin, David	Unkn.			18		
Wiffin, Richard	Gent.			09		
Wig, John	Merc.					*F*1
Wig, Thomas	Merc.					*X*1
Wight, Raphe	Merc.					*F*1/*S*1
Wight, Thomas	Merc.	84				
Wightman, John	Merc.		17			
Wightman, Peter	Merc.					*I*7
Wightwick, John	Unkn.	24				
Wigmore, Richard	Kt. 03			09		*CC*1/*GG*1
Wigmore, Thomas	Unkn.	84–86				
Wignall, William	Gent.		15			
Wilborn, Ranulph	Merc.					*S*6
Wilbraham, Roger	Kt. 03	04–14				*I*8
Wilcock, Robert	Unkn.	14				
Wild, George	Unkn.	84, 93, 04				
Wild, George	Unkn.	28				
Wild, Gervase	Merc.				10	
Wild, John	Unkn.	21–28				
*Wild, John	Merc.		24			*X*2
Wild, Thomas	Merc.					*X*2
Wild, William	Merc.					*I*7
Wildicoth, Richard	Merc.					*I*7
Wilford, James	Merc.					*S*1
Wilford, John	Merc.					*R*1
Wilford, Thomas	Kt. 07	25		10		
Wilford, Thomas	Merc.					*E*1/*S*6g
Wilford, William	Merc.					*S*6
Wilkes, Edward	Unkn.			09		
Wilkes, John	Merc.				00	
Wilkes, Thomas	Kt. 91	84–93				
Wilkes, William	Merc.				92	

Name & title	Class; date of knight-hood	Parlia-ments (starting dates)	E. Ind. Co.	Va. Co.	Levant Co.	Other companies
Wilkins, Anthony	Merc.			09		
Wilkins, George	Merc.					S1
Wilkinson, Edward	Merc.					X1
Wilkinson, Richard	Merc.					R1c
Wilkinson, Robert	Unkn.					X2
Wilkinson, ?	Merc.					I2
Willan, Leonard	Merc.	89–97				
Willard, William	Merc.					S1
Willeston, William	Merc.		00	12		F1c/Q
Willett, John	Merc.			10		
Willett, Richard	Merc.					X1
Willett, Thomas	Merc.					F1
Willett, William	Unkn.			18?		
Williams, Abell	Merc.				24	
Williams, Abraham	Gent.					A
Williams, Charles	Gent.	21				
Williams, Daniel	Merc.				24	
Williams, Davey	Merc.				10	
Williams, David	Gent.	84–89, 97				
Williams, Edward	Merc.					L1/M/S1
Williams, Henry	Kt. 03	01–04, 21–24				A
Williams, Henry	Gent.	28				
Williams, John	Merc.		26c		10c	I7/R2c
Williams, Reginald	Gent.	93				
Williams, Richard	Unkn.	84				
*Williams, Richard	Gent.	21				
Williams, Richard	Merc.			09		
Williams, Sidrake	Merc.				22	X2
Williams, Thomas	Kt. 03†					I4
Williams, Thomas	Unkn.	26				
Williams, Walter	Merc.					B
Williams, William	Merc.					BB1
Williams, William	Merc.				19	
Williamson, Lawrence	Unkn.			23		
Williamson, Richard	Kt. 03	14		09c		
Williamson, William	Merc.		08	18?		I7
**Williamwott, Edward	Merc.		24			I2
Willis, Emanuel	Merc.					S6
Willis, John	Merc.					X1
Willis, Richard	Merc.					E1
Willis, Simon	Unkn.	93–01				
Willoughby, Edward	Merc.				11	N
Willoughby, Francis	Gent.					I2
Willoughby, George	Merc.	28				
Willoughby, Percival	Kt. 03	04–14		10		Nc/GG3
Willoughby, Robert	Merc.			09		
Willoughby, Thomas	Unkn.	93				
Willoughby, Thomas	Unkn.					X2
Willoughby, William	Kt. 03	14				
Wills, Matthew	Unkn.		25			
Wills, William	Merc.					S6

Name & title	Class; date of knight-hood	Parlia-ments (starting dates)	E. Ind. Co.	Va. Co.	Levant Co.	Other companies
Wills, William	Unkn.					X2
Wilmer, Andrew	Unkn.		28	09		
Wilmer, Clement	Gent.			09		
Wilmer, George	Gent.		24	09		
Wilmer, Samuel	Unkn.		28			
Wilmot, Charles	Kt. 99	14		09		
Wilson, Anthony	Merc.		21		14c	
Wilson, Anthony	Merc.				21	
Wilson, Edward	Merc.					Q
Wilson, Felix	Unkn.			09		
Wilson, George	Merc.					S6
Wilson, Godfrey	Merc.					E1/S6
Wilson, Henry	Merc.					R2c
Wilson, John	Unkn.	21				
Wilson, Marmaduke	Unkn.					X2
Wilson, Roland	Merc.		17			I7/X2
Wilson, Thomas	Kt. 18			09		
Wilson, Thomas	Unkn.					W5
Wilson, William	Unkn.					I2
Wilson, William	Merc.					S6
*Wilson, William	Unkn.					X2
Wilson, ?	Gent.					W2
Wilston, Hugh	Unkn.			09		
Winch, Daniel	Merc.		29	09		I7/J3
Winch, Humphrey	Kt.†	93–04				I6c
Windham, Edmund	Unkn.	25, 28				
Windham, Hugh	Merc.		14	19		L1
Windle, John	Merc.					I7
Windsor, Frederick	Unkn.					X2
Wingatt, Nicholas	Unkn.		17			
Wingfield, Anthony	Gent.	84–89				
Wingfield, Anthony	Unkn.	93				
Wingfield, Edward	Gent.	93				
Wingfield, Edward	Kt. 86	86–93				
Wingfield, Edward	Merc.	86				
Wingfield, Edward-Maria	Unkn.			06		
Wingfield, Henry	Gent.	84				
Wingfield, Jacques	Unkn.					I9
Wingfield, John	Kt. 86	93				
**Wingfield, John	Gent.	97, 21, 26				
Wingfield, Richard	Kt. 95	86–89				I6c
Wingfield, Richard	Pfl/y.			21c		
Wingfield, Robert	Kt. 03	84–04				
Wingfield, William	Gent.	14–28				
Winne, Edmund	Merc.			09		F1/I7
Winne, Ellis	Unkn.	97				
Winne, George	Merc.		24	09		
Winne, Harry	Gent.	24–25				
Winne, John	Kt. 06	86				GG
Winne, John	Merc.					I2/L2/M/Q

405

Name & title	Class; date of knight-hood	Parlia-ments (starting dates)	E. Ind. Co.	Va. Co.	Levant Co.	Other companies
Winne, Maurice	Merc.		24			
Winne, Peter	Unkn.			09		
Winne, Peter	Unkn.	28				
Winne, Richard	Kt. 16	14–25				
Winne, Robert	Gent.	89				
Winne, Thomas	Unkn.			09		
Winne, William	Unkn.	24				
Winroll, Robert	Merc.					S1
Winslow, Edward	Unkn.					P2
Winston, Thomas	Pfl/y.		24	19c		
Winter, Anthony	Merc.					I7
Winter, Edward	Kt. 95	86–89, 01				AA3
Winter, George	Merc.					W5/X1
Winter, Richard	Merc.					S1
Winter, William	M. Kt. 73	86				S6/W2/X1/ AA2c/CC2
Winter, William	Merc.			09		X1/CC2
Winterton, Francis	Unkn.	28				
Winthrop, John	Gent.					J3
Wintroppe, William	Merc.					S6
Winwood, Ralph	Kt. 07	14		11c		T2
Wipplet, Edmund	Merc.					F1
Wipplet, John	Merc.					F1
Wirrall, Hugh	Kt. 03			09		I2
Wise, Christopher	Merc.					F1/S1
Wise, Eustace	Merc.					F1/S1
Wise, John	Merc.					F1/S1
Wise, Nicholas	Merc.					F1/S1
Wise, Samuel	Merc.					F1/S1
Wise, Thomas	Kt. 03	21				
Wise, Thomas	Gent.	25–28				
Wise, Thomas	Merc.					X2
Wise, William	Merc.					F1/S1
Wiseman, John	Merc.					F1/L1/M
Wiseman, Kenelm	Unkn.					X2
Wiseman, Mary	Merc.		27			
Wiseman, Richard	Merc.		99c	21c	18	T3
Wiseman, Thomas	Merc.		24			
Wiseman, William	Unkn.	84, 97–04				
Withan, George	Merc.					L1
Withers, Anthony	Merc.		19	21		L1/M
Withers, George	Merc.					I7
Withers, John	Gent.			10		
Withers, John	Merc.				18	
Withers, Richard	Unkn.			24		
Withers, Thomas	Merc.				06	I7
Withins, Walter	Merc.					M
Withipole, William	Kt. 17	25				
Woadson, Robert	Unkn.		08			
Wodder, Edmund	Unkn.		17			
Wodder, William	Merc.				05	S3

Name & title	Class; date of knighthood	Parliaments (starting dates)	E. Ind. Co.	Va. Co.	Levant Co.	Other companies
Wodenoth, Arthur	Merc.			?		
Wogan, Devereaux	Merc.		11	10	06	F1
Wogan, John	Gent.	14–21, 25–28				
Wolf, Thomas	Merc.			09		
Wolridge, John	Unkn.	97				
Wolridge, Thomas	Unkn.	21–25				
Wolstenholme, Henry	Merc.			12		Q
Wolstenholme, John	M. Kt. 17	28‡	00c	09c		Qc/T1/U/ X2/Z
Wolstenholme, John	M. Kt. 33	25–26	18	12		Q
Wonder, William	Merc.					F1
Wood, Ambrose	Unkn.			21		
Wood, Edward	Merc.	84–86				
Wood, John	Merc.		24			S1
*Wood, John	Unkn.	14–21				
Wood, Philip	Unkn.			22		
Wood, Simon	Merc.			09		
Wood, Stephen	Merc.		17			
Wood, Thomas	Unkn.			09		
**Wood, Thomas	Merc.			09		M
Wood, Timothy	Merc.	14				
Wood, William	Merc.				10	J3
Woodall, John	Pfl/y.		24	09		T2
Woodall, William	Unkn.					X2
Woodcock, Thomas	Merc.			09		
Woodcot, James	Unkn.			21		
Woodford, John	Unkn.	21–24				
Woodgate, Thomas	Merc.					F1
Woodgate, ?	Unkn.					J3
Woodhouse, David	Gent.			09		
Woodhouse, Henry	Kt. 78	89				
Woodhouse, Henry	Unkn.			09		
Woodhouse, Philip	Gent.	86				
Woodhouse, Roger	Kt. 78	86				
Woodhouse, William	Kt. 91	04–14				
Woodhouse, William	Merc.			21		
Woodliffe, John	Gent.			09		
Woodly, John	Unkn.					X2
Woodrosse, Nicholas	M. Kt. 80	84				
Woodroste, James	Merc.					F1
Woodson, John	Merc.					X2
Woodson, Thomas	Merc.					X2
Woodward, Christopher	Merc.					I7
Woodward, Fulke	Merc.				13	
Woodward, George	Unkn.	86				
Woodward, John	Merc.?		22?			
Woodward, Katherine	Merc.					Q
Woodward, Odiell	Merc.		29			
Woodward, Richard	Merc.		24c			
Woodward, Thomas	Unkn.	14, 24				
*Woodward, Thomas	Unkn.					X2

Name & title	Class; date of knight-hood	Parlia-ments (starting dates)	E. Ind. Co.	Va. Co.	Levant Co.	Other companies
Woodworth, John	Merc.					R1
*Wooleston, William	Merc.				23	GG
Wooller, Edward	Merc.			09		
Wooller, John	Merc.			09		
Woolley, Francis	Kt. 03	01		09		
Woolley, John	Kt. 92	84–93				W2
Woolley, John	Unkn.		11			
Woolley, Randall	Merc.			09		I7
Woolner, John	Unkn.					X2
Woolslake, Thomas	Merc.					F1
Woolverston, John	Merc.			09		
Woolverston, Robert	Unkn.	14				
Wooten, Thomas	Merc.		26			
Worgreen, John	Unkn.					X2
Wormell, Bartholomew	Merc.					S4
Wormell, John	Merc.					S4
Worsky, Othowell	Merc.			09		
Worsley, Richard	Kt. 11	14–21		19?		
Worsley, Robert	Gent.	89				
Worsopp, John	Merc.					F1/S3
Worth, Hugh	Unkn.					I9
Wortley, Edward	Kt. 21	21–24, 26‡				
Wortley, Francis	Kt. 11	24–25	29	10		G7
Wotton, Edward, Lord	Nob. 92	84				
Wotton, Henry	Kt.†	84				
Wotton, Henry	Kt. 03	14, 25		12		
Wotton, Humphrey	Merc.					S4
Wotton, Thomas, Lord	Nob.			?		
Woulton, John	Unkn.	89				
Wrag, John	Merc.		00		00	
Wrag, Richard	Merc.		99		00	
Wray, Christopher	Kt. 23	21–25, 28				
Wray, Edward	Gent.	25				
Wray, George	Unkn.	93				
Wray, John	Kt. 12	14, 25, 28				
Wray, Robert	Gent.					CC1
Wray, William	Kt. 96	84, 01–04‡				
Wray, William	Unkn.	24				
Wrenham, John	Unkn.	21				
Wright, Benjamin	Merc.				29	
Wright, Daniel	Merc.		15			
Wright, Edmund	Merc.		15			
*Wright, Edward	Unkn.					Q
Wright, George	M. Kt. 03	21				I7
Wright, George	Merc.				05	
Wright, John	Merc.		27	09		I2
Wright, Lawrence	Pfl/y.		19			
Wright, Lionel	Gent.		18			
Wright, Michael	Merc.					X2
Wright, Nathaniel	Merc.		29		12	J1c/R2c/X2
Wright, Richard	Merc.		00	89	00	

Name & title	Class; date of knight-hood	Parlia-ments (starting dates)	E. Ind. Co.	Va. Co.	Levant Co.	Other companies
**Wright, Richard	Unkn.	97, 04				I7
*Wright, Richard	Merc.					P2/X2
Wright, Richard	Merc.					I7
Wright, Robert	Merc.					F1/I7
Wright, Robert	Unkn.	89–93				
Wright, Theophilus	Unkn.					X2
Wright, Thomas	Merc.				05	E4/F1/I7/M
Wright, Thomas	Merc.					F1/X2
Wright, William	Merc.		24	09		L2/M
Wrightinton, Edward	Unkn.	21				
Wriothesley, Henry Earl Southampton	Nob.		09	09g		G3/K4/Q/T1g/ X1/Y/Z/EE/ GG2
Wriothesley, James, Lord	Nob.	21–24				
Wrosse, Clement	Merc.					I1c
Wrote, Robert	Unkn.	84–86				
Wrote, Samuel	Gent.			20c		T3
Wroth, John	Gent.			16c		T2
Wroth, John	Unkn.	93				
Wroth, Robert	Kt. 97	84–04				
Wroth, Robert	Kt. 03	01–04		09		
Wroth, Thomas	Kt. 13	28		21?		E4/K4/T3
Wroughton, James	Unkn.	97				
Wyatt, Francis	Kt. 18			20		
Wyatt, Thomas	Unkn.			09		
Wyatt, William	Merc.					X2
Wycliffe, Richard	Unkn.					BB4
Wyles, John	Merc.					M
**Wymarke, Edward	Unkn.	97–14				
*Wymarke, Edward	Unkn.	14				
Wymer, William	Merc.					I7
Wymes, Humphrey	Merc.		99			S1
Wynd, Robert	Kt. 03	14				
Wynniff, Nicholas	Merc.			09		I7
Wyth, James	Merc.					S1
Wyth, Thomas	Merc.					S1
Wyvell, Marmaduke	Unkn.	84, 97				
Wyvell, Thomas	Unkn.	04				
Yardeley, Robert	Unkn.	01				
Yarham, Robert	Merc.	93				
Yaxley, John	Merc.	97–04				
Yaxley, Robert	Kt. 99	14		12		
Yeardley, George	Kt. 18			09c		
Yearwood, Richard	Unkn.	14–28				
Yeates, Edward	Unkn.					X2
Yeene, Richard	Merc.		24			
Yelverton, Christopher	Kt. 03	93–97				
Yelverton, Christopher	Kt. 23	26–28				
Yelverton, Henry	Kt. 13	97, 04–14	17			
Yeomans, Robert	Merc.					L2/M

Name & title	Class; date of knight- hood	Parlia- ments (starting dates)	E. Ind. Co.	Va. Co.	Levant Co.	Other companies
Yeomans, Simon	Merc.			09		
Yevane, Milo	Merc.					*S6*
Yorke, Peter	Unkn.	89				
Young, Augustine	Merc.					*S4*
Young, Gregory	Merc.					*S6*
Young, James	Merc.		20		17	*E3/J3*
Young, John	Kt. 25					*J*1c
Young, John	Merc.					*C/M/Q1/X*1
*Young, John	Unkn.	86–89, 97, 04				
Young, Richard	Kt. 18	21–24	18			
Young, Richard	Merc.					*R1/S6/W7/GG*
Young, Richard	Merc.					*J*1
Young, Robert	Merc.		14		23	
Young, Thomas	Merc.					*C*
Young, William	Merc.			09		*F1/S6/GG*
*Youngs, ?	Unkn.					*T3*
Zouch, Edward	Kt.†					*K4*
Zouch, Edward, Lord	Nob.			09c		*K4*
Zouch, Francis	Unkn.	86–93				
Zouch, John	Kt. 18†			16?		
Zouch, John	Kt. 08†	89				*EE/GG*
Zouch, Richard	Unkn.	84				
*Zouch, Richard	Unkn.	21–24				
Zouch, Thomas	Unkn.	04				

INDEX

Italicized page numbers indicate references to the bibliography.

Abbot, Sir Maurice, 52

Admissions to companies: dates of, 8, 11, 105–106, 166; fluctuations of, 71–92, 119; in the 1620's, 86

Africa, 70, 85, 163, *195, 197, 198, 212;* trade to, 48n. *See also* Barbary; Guinea; Senegal

Africa Company, 25, 30, 46n, 54n, 89, 96, 113, 137, 147; investments in, 59. *See also* Royal Africa Company

Agriculture, 82; profits of, 32, 99–100; studies of profits of, 33n; and continental gentry, 13n

Aldermen, 42n

Alexander, Sir William, 24, 36, 160, 168, *203, 207, 218*

Alum, 163

Amazon, 152–153. *See also* Guiana

Amazon Company, *see* Guiana Company

Ambergris, 69

America, 2, 29, 31, 69, 70, 81, 83, 87, 99, 111, 147, 156, *195, 196, 197, 204, 208, 209, 210, 212. See also* New England; Virginia

Anderson, Sir Henry, 111

Andrews, K. R., 61–62, 80, 137n, 161; quoted, 41n–42n, 148

Arctic Ocean, 29, 169

Aristocracy, *see* Peers

Armada, 41, 148

Artisans, 13

Athens, 41

Aydelotte, W. O., 134n

Aylmer, G. E., 26

Azores, 149n

Bacon, Sir Francis, Viscount St. Albans, 26n, 171, 173; quoted, 39n, 51n, 69n, 118n, 147n

Baffin, William, 31–32, 62, 110, 116, 118, 127, 147, 153–154, 160–161, *196;* investments in voyages of, 63

Bailey, Thomas, 163

Baltic Sea, 1, 52, 99, 150, 169; imports from, 64–65. *See also* Eastland Company

Baltimore, Lord, *see* Calvert

Banking, 1

Banning, Andrew, 111

Banning, Paul, Jr. (Viscount), 137n

Banning, Paul, Sr., 111, 137n

Barbary, 24; pirates from, 148

Barbary Company, 28, 79, 112, 116, 118, 147–148, *192, 212. See also* Pirates

Barnes, Sir George, 82

Barnes family, 52, *218*

Bateman, Robert, 52

Baynam, Thomas, 58n

Bermuda, 59n, 69, 84, 85, 111, *196*

Bermuda Company, 25, 42, 49, 54n, 59, 76, 78, 82, 88, 89, 96, 97, 105, 107, 112, 113, 114, 116n, 121, 125, 129n,